Communications in Computer and Information Science 1087

Commenced Publication in 2007
Founding and Former Series Editors:
Phoebe Chen, Alfredo Cuzzocrea, Xiaoyong Du, Orhun Kara, Ting Liu,
Krishna M. Sivalingam, Dominik Ślęzak, Takashi Washio, Xiaokang Yang,
and Junsong Yuan

More information about this series at http://www.springer.com/series/7899

Juan Luis Crespo-Mariño ·
Esteban Meneses-Rojas (Eds.)

High Performance Computing

6th Latin American Conference, CARLA 2019
Turrialba, Costa Rica, September 25–27, 2019
Revised Selected Papers

 Springer

Editors
Juan Luis Crespo-Mariño (iD)
Costa Rica Institute of Technology
Cartago, Costa Rica

Esteban Meneses-Rojas
Costa Rica Institute of Technology
Cartago, Costa Rica

ISSN 1865-0929   ISSN 1865-0937 (electronic)
Communications in Computer and Information Science
ISBN 978-3-030-41004-9   ISBN 978-3-030-41005-6 (eBook)
https://doi.org/10.1007/978-3-030-41005-6

This Springer imprint is published by the registered company Springer Nature Switzerland AG
The registered company address is: Gewerbestrasse 11, 6330 Cham, Switzerland

Preface

The use and development of high performance computing (HPC) in Latin America is steadily growing. New challenges come from the capabilities provided by clusters, grids, and distributed systems for HPC, promoting research and innovation in many scientific disciplines. Building on the great success of the previous editions, the 6th Latin American Conference on High Performance Computing (CARLA 2019) was held in Turrialba, Costa Rica, during September 25–27, 2019. The main goal of CARLA 2019 was to provide a regional forum to foster the growth of the HPC community in Latin America through the exchange and dissemination of new ideas, techniques, and research projects. This edition also had a new element: the special track on Bioinspired Processing (BIP). It constituted the evidence of the growing crossover between HPC sciences and both theoretical and applied nature-related disciplines. The conference featured invited talks from academia and industry in the form of short- and full-paper sessions, presenting both mature work and new ideas in research and industrial applications.

The list of topics included, among others: Parallel Algorithms-Multicore Architectures and Accelerators, Parallel Programming Techniques-Grid, Cloud and Edge Computing, HPC Education and Outreach, HPC Infrastructure and Datacenters, Large-scale Distributed Systems-Scientific and Industrial Computing, HPC Applications and Tools, Biodiversity Informatics (application of ICT to biodiversity conservation), Ambient Computing, Visual Analytics for Biological Information, Ecoinformatics, Healthcare Informatics, Pattern Recognition for Biological and Related Signals, Bioinformatics, Biocomputing, and Computational Systems Biology.

All submitted papers were carefully examined by at least three reviewers. Out of the 62 submissions received, 32 were accepted to be presented at the conference.

September 2019

Juan Luis Crespo-Mariño
Esteban Meneses-Rojas

Organization

General Co-chairs

Esteban Meneses   Costa Rica National High Technology Center, Costa Rica

Francisco Siles   Pattern Recognition and Intelligent Systems Laboratory (PRIS-Lab), Costa Rica

BIP Track Chair

Erick Mata-Montero   ITCR, Costa Rica

Publicity Co-chairs

Philippe Navaux   UFRGS, Brazil
Esteban Arias-Méndez   TEC Costa Rica, Costa Rica

Sponsor Co-chairs

Carlos Barrios Hernández   Universidad Industrial de Santander, Colombia
Allan Campos   Costa Rica National High Technology Center, Costa Rica

Website Chair

Andrés Segura   Distance State University, Costa Rica

Workshops Chair

Nicolás Wolovick   Universidad Nacional de Córdoba, Argentina

Posters Co-chairs

Andrés Segura   Distance State University, Costa Rica
Harold Castro   Universidad de los Andes, Colombia

Tutorials Co-chairs

Robinson Rivas-Suarez   UCV, Venezuela
Rodrigo Mora   University of Costa Rica, Costa Rica

BIP Program Committee Chair

Juan Luis Crespo-Mariño   Tecnológico de Costa Rica, Costa Rica

Publications Chair

Juan Luis Crespo-Mariño   Tecnológico de Costa Rica, Costa Rica

Transportation Chair

Esteban Arias-Méndez   TEC Costa Rica, Costa Rica

Local Arrangements Chair

Álvaro Mena   University of Costa Rica, Costa Rica

University of Costa Rica Liaison

Marvin Coto-Jimenez   Universidad de Costa Rica, Costa Rica

Costa Rica Institute of Technology Liaison

Erick Mata-Montero   ITCR, Costa Rica

National University of Costa Rica Liaison

Jorge Arroyo   National University of Costa Rica, Costa Rica

Distance State University of Costa Rica Liaison

Andrés Segura   Distance State University, Costa Rica

National Technical University of Costa Rica Liaison

Mauricio Rodriguez   National Technical University of Costa Rica,
Costa Rica

Logistics Staff

Kimberly Sánchez   Costa Rica National High Technology Center,
Costa Rica
Daniel Alvarado   Costa Rica National High Technology Center,
Costa Rica
Maripaz Montero   Costa Rica National High Technology Center,
Costa Rica

Jean Carlo Umaña   Costa Rica National High Technology Center,
                              Costa Rica
Diego Jiménez   Costa Rica National High Technology Center,
                              Costa Rica
Mariana Cubero   Costa Rica National High Technology Center,
                              Costa Rica

Steering Committee

Carlos Barrios Hernández   Universidad Industrial de Santander, Colombia
Harold Castro   Universidad de los Andes, Colombia
Gilberto Díaz   Universidad Industrial de Santander, Colombia
Isidoro Gitler   Center for Research and Advanced Studies
                              of the National Polytechnic Institute, Mexico
Gonzalo Hernandez   Universidad de Santiago de Chile, Chile
Esteban Meneses   Costa Rica National High Technology Center,
                              Costa Rica
Esteban Mocskos   Universidad de Buenos Aires, Argentina
Philippe Navaux   UFRGS, Brazil
Sergio Nesmachnow   Universidad de la República, Uruguay
Luis Alberto Núñez de   Industrial University of Santander, Colombia
  Villavicencio Martínez
Carla Osthoff   National Laboratory for Scientific Computing, Brazil
Mateo Valero   Barcelona Supercomputing Center, Spain
Nicolás Wolovick   Universidad Nacional de Córdoba, Argentina
Alvaro de la Ossa   Universidad de Costa Rica, Costa Rica

Program Committee (HPC Track)

Bilge Acun   IBM Thomas J. Watson Research Center, USA
Carlos Barrios Hernández   Universidad Industrial de Santander, Colombia
Leonardo Bautista Gomez   Barcelona Supercomputing Center, Spain
Xavier Besseron   University of Luxembourg, Luxembourg
Jesus Carretero   University of Carlos III of Madrid, Spain
Oscar Carrillo   University of Lyon, CPE Lyon, INSA Lyon, CITI,
                              France
Luis F. Castillo Ossa   Universidad de Caldas, Colombia
Harold Castro   Universidad de los Andes, Colombia
Marcio Castro   Federal University of Santa Catarina (UFSC), Brazil
Jorge Castro   Centro Nacional de Alta Tecnología, Costa Rica
Dennis Cazar Ramírez   Universidad San Francisco de Quito, Ecuador
Daniel Cordeiro   Universidade de São Paulo, Brazil
Ulises Cortés   UPC, BSC, Spain
Alvaro Coutinho   COPPE, Federal University of Rio de Janeiro, Brazil
Emmanuell D. Carreno   UFPR, Brazil
Matthieu Dreher   Canadian Bank Note, USA

Gilberto Díaz	Universidad Industrial de Santander, Colombia
Pablo Ezzatti	Universidad de la República, Uruguay
Eduardo Fernandez	Facultad de Ingeniería UdelaR, Uruguay
Pablo Guillen-Rondon	University of Houston, USA
Juan Galvez	University of Illinois at Urbana-Champaign, USA
Ivan Girotto	Abdus Salam International Centre for Theoretical Physics, Italy
Isidoro Gitler	Center for Research and Advanced Studies of the National Polytechnic Institute, Mexico
Jose Luis Gordillo	UNAM, Mexico
Oscar Hernandez	ORNL, USA
Benjamin Hernandez	Oak Ridge National Laboratory, USA
Esteban Hernández	PSL Software, Colombia
Nikhil Jain	Nvidia, USA
Terry Jones	ORNL, USA
Filip Krikava	Czech Technical University, Czech Republic
Ignacio Laguna	Lawerence Livermore National Laboratory, USA
Laércio Lima Pilla	LRI, CNRS, Université Paris-Sud, France
Víctor Martínez	Universidade Estadual de Campinas, Brazil
Rafael Mayo-Garcia	CIEMAT, Spain
Lucas Mello Schnorr	UFRGS, Brazil
Esteban Meneses	Costa Rica National High Technology Center, Costa Rica
Harshitha Menon	Lawerence Livermore National Laboratory, USA
Esteban Mocskos	Universidad de Buenos Aires, Argentina
Philippe Navaux	UFRGS, Brazil
Sergio Nesmachnow	Universidad de la República, Uruguay
Xiang Ni	IBM Research, USA
Nick Nystrom	Pittsburgh Supercomputing Center and Carnegie Mellon University, USA
Ulises Orozco	CETYS Universidad, Mexico
Carla Osthoff	National Laboratory for Scientific Computing, Brazil
Maria Pantoja	CalPoly San Luis Obispo, USA
Guilherme Peretti-Pezzi	ETH Zurich, CSCS, Switzerland
Michel Riveill	UNS, I3S, Polytech, France
Cristian Ruiz	INTM, France
Robinson Rivas-Suarez	UCV, Venezuela
Eduardo Rodrigues	IBM Research, Brazil
Elvis Rojas	UNA, Costa Rica
Ricardo Román-Brenes	Universidad de Costa Rica, Costa Rica
Claudia Roncancio	Grenoble INP, France
Thomas Ropars	Université Grenoble Alpes, France
Isaac Rudomin	UNAM, Mexico
John Sanabria	Universidad del Valle, Colombia
Osman Sarood	Mist Systems, USA
Bruno Schulze	National Lab for Scientific Computing (LNCC), Brazil

Francisco Siles   Pattern Recognition and Intelligent Systems Laboratory
                                  (PRIS-Lab), Costa Rica
Roberto Souto   National Laboratory for Scientific Computing (LNCC),
                                  Brazil
Luiz Angelo Steffenel   Université de Reims Champagne-Ardenne, France
Andrei Tchernykh   CICESE Research Center, Mexico
Nicolás Wolovick   Universidad Nacional de Córdoba, Argentina
Alvaro de la Ossa   Universidad de Costa Rica, Costa Rica

Program Committee (BIP Track)

Pablo Alvarado-Moya   Tecnológico de Costa Rica, Costa Rica
Esteban Arias-Méndez   TEC Costa Rica, Costa Rica
Arturo H. Ariño   University of Navarra, Spain
José Antonio Becerra   Universidade da Coruña, Spain
  Permuy
Francisco Bellas   Universidade da Coruña, Spain
Saul Calderon-Ramirez   Instituto Tecnologico de Costa Rica, Costa Rica
Jose Carranza   Rakuten, Japan
Arys Carrasquilla-Batista   Instituto Tecnológico de Costa Rica, Costa Rica
Marvin Coto-Jimenez   Universidad de Costa Rica, Costa Rica
Daniel Eftekhari   University of Toronto, Canada
Juan Esquivel-Rodriguez   Instituto Tecnológico de Costa Rica, Costa Rica
Fabián Fallas-Moya   Universidad de Costa Rica, Costa Rica
Angel Garcia-Pedrero   Universidad de Valladolid, Spain
Renato Garita Figueiredo   Universität Osnabrück, Germany
Hervé Goëau   Cirad, France
Luis Guerrero   Universidad de Costa Rica, Costa Rica
Mauricio Hess Flores   Stratovan Corporation, USA
Mónica Karel Huerta   Universidad Politécnica Salesiana, Ecuador
Ronald Loaiza-Baldares   Instituto Tecnológico de Costa Rica, Costa Rica
César Martínez   UNL, Argentina
Erick Mata-Montero   ITCR, Costa Rica
Esteban Meneses   Costa Rica National High Technology Center,
                                  Costa Rica
Jose Arturo Molina Mora   Universidad de Costa Rica, Costa Rica
Ricardo Monge   Universidad de Costa Rica, Costa Rica
Juan Monroy   Universidade da Coruña, Spain
Gabriela Ortiz-Leon   Instituto Tecnológico de Costa Rica, Costa Rica
Alejandro Paz   University of A Coruna, Spain
Gustavo Ramirez   University of Wuppertal, Germany
Daniel Riccio   Università di Napoli Federico II, Italy
Roberto   Universidad de Costa Rica, Costa Rica
  Rodríguez-Rodríguez
Juan Carlos Saborío   University of Osnabrück, Germany
  Morales

Francisco Siles   Pattern Recognition and Intelligent Systems Laboratory
                               (PRIS-Lab), Costa Rica
Jordina Torrents Barrena   Rovira i Virgili University, Spain
Francisco J. Torres-Rojas   Instituto Tecnológico de Costa Rica, Costa Rica
Marta Eugenia   Tecnológico de Costa Rica, Costa Rica
    Vílchez-Monge

Contents

**Regular Track on High Performance Computing: Architectures
and Infrastructures**

Special Track on Bioinspired Processing (BIP): Neural and Evolutionary Approaches

Special Track on Bioinspired Processing (BIP): Image and Signal Processing

**Special Track on Bioinspired Processing (BIP): Biodiversity
Informatics and Computational Biology**

Regular Track on High Performance Computing: Applications

Optimizing Water Cooling Applications on Shared Memory Systems

Edson Luiz Padoin[1,2(✉)], Andressa Tais Diefenthaler[1], Matheus S. Serpa[2], Pablo José Pavan[2], Emmanuell D. Carreño[3], Philippe O. A. Navaux[2], and Jean-François Mehaut[4]

[1] Department of Exact Sciences and Engineering, Regional University of the Northwest of the State of Rio Grande do Sul – UNIJUI, Ijuí, Brazil
{padoin,andressa.tais}@unijui.edu.br
[2] Informatics Institute, Federal University of Rio Grande do Sul – UFRGS, Porto Alegre, Brazil
{msserpa,pjpavan,navaux}@inf.ufrgs.br
[3] Department of Informatics, Federal University of Paraná – UFPR, Paraná, Brazil
edcarreno@inf.ufpr.br
[4] Laboratoire d'Informatique de Grenoble, University of Grenoble – UGA, Grenoble, France
jean-francois.mehaut@imag.fr

Abstract. The Network Search method is not yet widely used in computational simulations due to its high processing time in the solutions' calculation. In this sense, this paper seeks to analyze the gains achieved with the parallel implementation of the Network Search method algorithm for shared memory systems. The results achieved with the parallel implementation of the algorithm applied in a real water cooling system achieved a reduction of the total execution time by up to 160 times and reduction of energy consumption by up to 60 times. Given the significant reduction of the execution time achieved with the parallelization of the Network Search method, it can be applied in different scientific problems in substitution of other methods that have less accuracy in their results.

Keywords: Network Search method · High performance computing · Water cooling

1 Introduction

Computing has been responsible for significant changes in science. Through computers, problems that until now could not be solved, or that required a long time to be solved, were within reach by the scientific community. The evolution of computer processors, which currently incorporate multiple processing units, allow the execution of tasks in parallel, allowing a reduction in execution time and an increase in the accuracy of the results. Thus, with the significant increases in computational power of computer architectures, the range of problems that can be treated computationally has been broadened.

J. L. Crespo-Mariño and E. Meneses-Rojas (Eds.): CARLA 2019, CCIS 1087, pp. 3–17, 2020.
https://doi.org/10.1007/978-3-030-41005-6_1

These problems include the principles of thermodynamics, an area of physics dedicated to the study of heat movement, which helps explain different real physical phenomena related to temperature variation. In everyday life, it is possible to identify different situations and phenomena related to thermodynamics, such as the conservation of hot water in thermal bottles, which is directly related to the phenomenon of heat transfer, with heat, according to Halliday et al. [11], energy transferred from a system to the environment or vice versa by virtue of a temperature difference [7].

This water cooling process was modeled in an experiment involving four glass ampoules, differentiated by the presence or absence of vacuum and mirroring [6]. In order to obtain the mathematical model that describes the experimental data's behavior, the Inverse Problem's resolution was considered by the numerical method Network Search, which was validated by the Direct Problem's solution by Newton's Cooling Law.

However, the Network Search method is configured as an exhaustive method, which finds the best set of parameters by calculating the data distributions through all the possibilities of combinations of parameters, within the initially defined intervals, which demands a high time computational [25].

In this context, aiming to analyze the use of multicore processors in solving scientific problems, this paper presents a parallelization study of the Network Search method applied in a real application of water cooling in ampoules of thermal bottles. Our main contributions are:

- Parallel implementation of the Network Search method algorithm for shared memory systems;
- Analysis of the power demand, execution time and power consumption of the parallel version with mapping techniques;
- The tradeoff between execution time and energy consumption.

The remainder of the paper is organized as follows. Section 2 discusses related work. Section 4 describes the methodology used in the execution of the tests, the equipment used, the mathematical modeling of the real application through the inverse problem and direct problem. Results are discussed in Sect. 5, followed by conclusions and future work, in Sect. 6.

2   Related Work

Power consumption today is a central issue in the development of the next generations of supercomputers. Research efforts have focused on both performance and energy consumption, with priority being given to reducing power demand. However, there are still gaps for parallelization of scientific applications. Some research has focused on the use of ARM processors and others the use of GPGPU accelerators to increase the energy efficiency of HPC systems.

In the first group, Andreolli et al. [1], the authors focused on acoustic wave propagation equations, choosing the optimization techniques from systematically tuning the algorithm. The usage of collaborative thread blocking, cache blocking, register re-use, vectorization, and loop redistribution resulted in significant performance improvements. Our proposal chooses a largely used seismic imaging simulation based on the acoustic wave propagation and provides a deeper evaluation of the hardware impact of the optimizations applied to the Xeon and Xeon Phi processors. Blake et al. [2] developed a comparison between multicore processors. In this study, aspects such as caching and microarchitecture are analyzed from ARM Cortex-A9, Intel Atom, XMOS XS1-G4, Intel Core i7, and Sun Niagara T2 processors. Dongarra et al. [8] analyze the energy efficiency of equipment with ARM, Intel, AMD, and NVIDIA processors. The results point to the better energy efficiency of ARM processors. However, their energy consumption measurements considered the entire system and not just the processing unit. Similar, in the work of Valero et al. [28] are presented results of Cortex-A9 architecture. In this work, an efficiency of up to 8 GFLOPS is estimated for the Cortex-A15 ARM processors. The use of ARM and Intel processors has been an important topic of research in scientific applications of Padoin et al. [20], highlighting the metrics runtime, power demand, and power consumption. Liu et al. [17] propose an approach based on profiling to determine thread-to-core mapping on the Knights Corner architecture that depends on the location of the distributed tag directory, achieving significant reductions on communication latency. Caballero et al. [4] studied the effect of different optimizations on elastic wave propagation equations, achieving more than an order of magnitude of improvement compared with the basic OpenMP parallel version.

In the second group, several studies have evaluated the performance and power consumption of GPUs. Huang et al. [13], compare performance between CPUs and GPUs using matrix multiplication algorithms. The authors conclude that heterogeneous systems with GPUs achieve performances up to 46 times higher with energy consumption up to 17 times lower. Buck et al. [3] propose four applications to evaluate the performance of heterogeneous architectures. Jiao et al. [16] utilized a subset of these applications to analyze the performance and energy efficiency of CPUs and GPUs when their dynamically changed voltage and clock frequency. Both authors indicate that using GPUs is the right course to achieve green computing. In a similar work, Padoin et al. [21] investigate the energy efficiency of a heterogeneous system (CPU + GPU) using a scientific application. In Luk et al. [18], the authors propose a methodology that automatically performs workload mapping and allocation in heterogeneous systems. Its approach reduces execution time by up to 25% and power consumption by up to 20% when compared to workload allocation statically.

The third group focused on process mapping as an effective way to improve the performance of parallel applications and propose new methods to perform the mapping more efficiently. Tousimojarad and Vanderbauwhede [27] show that the default thread mapping of Linux is inefficient when the number of threads is as large as on a many-core processor and presents a new thread mapping policy that uses the amount of time that each core does useful work to find the best target core for each thread. Liu et al. [17] propose an approach based on profiling to determine thread-to-core mapping on the Knights Corner architecture that depends on the location of the distributed tag directory, achieving significant reductions on communication latency. He, Chen, and Tang [12] introduces NestedMP, an extension to OpenMP that allows the programmer to give information about the structure of the tasks tree to the runtime, which then performs a locality-aware thread mapping. Cruz et al. [5] improve state of the art by performing a very detailed analysis of the impact of thread mapping on communication and load balancing in two many-core systems from Intel, namely Knights Corner and Knights Landing. They observed that the widely used metric of CPU time provides very inaccurate information for load balancing. They also evaluated the usage of thread mapping based on the communication and load information of the applications to improve the performance of many-core systems. Serpa et al. [23] focus on Intel's multi-core Xeon and many-core accelerator Xeon Phi Knights Landing, which can host several hundreds of threads on the same CPU. Execution time was reduced by up to 25.2% and 18.5% on Intel Xeon and Xeon Phi Knights Landing, respectively.

Other works explore the use of ARM processors and GPGPU accelerators to improve runtime and power consumption. This work seeks to explore the use of the various processing units present in the current multicore processors, making it possible to use the network searching method. Thus, this paper discusses the gains of the parallelization of this method based on aspects of a real thermodynamics application.

3   Thermodynamics and Computational Models

Thermodynamics is related to the different phenomena of everyday life that involve temperature variations, which instigate as to its cause or effect. Among these situations, it is worth noting the cooling of the hot water in thermal bottles. The scientific application that refers to the processes of transfer of heat in ampoules of thermal bottles is not recent. The invention of these containers is related to the creation of the Dewar flask in the 19th century by the Scottish physicist-chemist James Dewar (1842–1923). When evidencing that the best thermal insulator is the vacuum, Dewar began to manufacture bottles with double walls, leaving a space between them (vacuum) and coating its interior with a silver film, in order to reflect the radiation [14].

The thermos bottle is a container composed of an external body (jar or bottle made of different materials such as plastic, stainless steel) and an internal part constituted by an ampoule (usually glass). These bottles are widely used in the daily life of individuals to conserve the temperature of drinks, hot or cold, and are also manufactured in different capacities and with different storage systems.

It is to be understood that the ampoules currently manufactured are composed of two glass walls, with or without a vacuum between them, and may or may not be mirrored. According to [19] these constituent materials are determinants for the operation of the containers, which is based on the principle of avoiding the exchange of heat between the contents of its interior and the environment. Seeking to prevent the occurrence of the three forms of heat transfer:

(i) Conduction: the heat exchange occurs by the shock of the particles that make up the system [15]. It is avoided due to the material in which the ampoule is manufactured, the glass, which is considered good thermal insulation; (ii) Convection: occurs in the fluids (gases and liquids), caused by the difference in the density of the system components [11]. In the ampoules, it is avoided due to the vacuum between the double walls of glass and the insulating cover, which prevents the contact between hot water and air; and (iii) Radiation: it occurs from electromagnetic waves, and the mirrored walls cause the infrared rays emitted by the hot water to be reflected, attenuating the heat exchanges. Despite these characteristics, there are no perfect insulating materials, and therefore, there is still heat exchange, which causes the hot water inside the containers to cool down over time.

In conducting heat transfer, the exchange occurs by the shock of the particles. In this way, conduction is avoided due to the material from which it is produced, the glass, which is considered excellent thermal insulation, because it has high thermal resistance (R). A property obtained by the ratio between the thickness L of a plate and the thermal conductivity k of the material in which it is manufactured: $R = \frac{L}{k}$ (the glass is an insulation material, has a low thermal conductivity (k) 1,0 W/mK, which guarantees its higher capacity to conserve heat) [11].

The vacuum region between the ampoules' double walls also serves to prevent heat transfer by conduction and convection. The convection exchange occurs in the fluids (gases and liquids), caused by the system components' density variation [11]. In this way, the vacuum, as well as the presence of an insulating cover (to keep the bottle closed), prevent contact between hot water and air, thereby attenuating this form of heat transfer.

When the ampoules are mirrored, the infrared rays emitted by the hot water are reflected, attenuating the heat exchanges by radiation and aiding in the water temperature's conservation. In this way, due to the ampoules' characteristics, the heat transfer can be reduced - by conduction, convection, and radiation - and conserve the hot water for longer inside the thermal bottles. However, there are no perfect insulating materials, and after a while, the water cools [19].

3.1   Mathematical Modeling

For the data's mathematical modeling, we considered the equation of the natural exponential function decreasing (since the temperature of the water decreases and tends to stabilize over time), that is, $y = A * e^{-Bx} + C$, with three non-linearizable parameters A, B and C. In [6], the characteristic equations of the data sets (nonlinear adjustment of curves) were obtained, from the resolution of the Inverse Problem through the Network Search method, being these validated by means of a comparison with the equations and determination coefficients found by the resolution of the Direct Problem, considering, for this, the Law of Cooling of Newton's bodies.

Diefenthaler et. al [6] model the problem of heat transfer in bottles. For this, a practical experiment related to the principles of thermodynamics was carried out and the four types of glass ampoules efficiency, differentiated by the presence or absence of vacuum and mirroring, from the cooling process the hot water over time was analyzed. The experimental data obtained were modeled, is possible to find the cooling curves' equations in each container from the Inverse Problem's resolution through the Network Search method, which was validated through the comparison with the results provided by the Direct Problem resolution, by Newton's Cooling Law. From the developed one, the method's efficiency was evidenced, because the results were coherent, and high determination coefficients were obtained.

In each ampoule, a volume of 1 L of hot water was added at an initial temperature of 70 °C. Temperature measurements were performed using four Mercury thermometers, ranging from −10 °C to 110 °C. Temperatures were recorded every 20 min (1200 s by SI) in degrees Celsius, for a time of 7 h (25200 s), totaling 22 measurements. To obtain the data, in [6] the temperature of 1 L of water at an initial temperature of 70 °C over 7 h (25200 s) was measured, which were measured every 20 min (1200 s), totalizing a set of 22 data. This article considers only the bulb manufactured in a vacuum and mirrored glass, since it presents better performance in heat conservation, as can be observed in the results shown in Fig. 1.

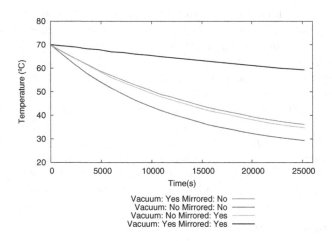

Fig. 1. Data measured in the laboratory in the process of water cooling in ampoules.

3.2   Inverse Problem via Network Search Method

The problem is configured as an Inverse Problem since from the realized experiment we have the phenomenon's effects (the experimental data), but its causes are unknown, as well as the equation (mathematical model) that represents the phenomenon and allows obtaining these data. In this way, the Inverse Problem consists of determining unknown causes from desired or observed effects [9] and [25]. In a resolution by the Direct Problem, the cause and the equation are known - Newton's Cooling Law - from which the effects are determined - the temperature that the water reaches at a given time -. Already in the resolution by the Inverse Problem, we have only the experimental data and, observing its behavior and using numerical methods; it is possible to model the data and obtain an equation that "causes these effects."

Thus, in the case of an inverse problem, the problem presented here is considered an ill-posed problem. According to [10], a well-put problem is one that presents three characteristics: (i) Existence of solution; (ii) Uniqueness (existence of a single solution), and (iii) Stability of the solution (the solution has a continuous dependency *smooth* with the input data).

In order to determine the parameters of the equation $y = A * e^{-Bx} + C$, in [6] it was proposed the resolution through the Network Search method, which consists in the definition of valid intervals for each parameter to be estimated and of several partitions for each interval. This method finds the best set of parameters by exhaustion, calculating the distributions of the data through all possibilities of combinations of parameters, within the defined initial intervals [24]. Thus, according to [26], this method can be considered a method of suboptimal solutions, since there is no convergence criterion and the guarantee that the optimal solution belongs to the predefined intervals.

This method was implemented based on information: number of points (22), Vector X (time vector in seconds), Vector Y (temperature vector in Celsius), previous intervals in which the parameter values (A - 0 to 50, B - -0.01 to 0 and C - 0 to 50) and the number in which each of these intervals (1000 divisions) will be divided. Thus, the following algorithm was used to determine the Z parameters:

Step 1 - It is estimated the intervals (minimum and maximum) of values of each parameter A, B, C, that contain the optimal value of A, B, C;

Step 2 - Construct a partition of n points in which each interval is divided (in this case, we have 1000 possible values for A, 1000 for B and 1000 possibilities for the value of C);

Step 3 - For each set of values ($A1$, $A2$, ..., $A1000$; $B1$, $B2$ ..., $B1000$; $C1$, $C2$, ..., $C1000$), solve the function that represents the Direct Problem;

Step 4 - Calculate the differences between the estimated solutions and the experimental data; and

Step 5 - Identify the smallest difference, which corresponds to the set of parameters A, B and C optimal for the estimated interval.

This method was chosen because of its efficiency and practicality because it is possible to define the previous intervals for each parameter to be estimated in this situation and also because it does not involve the calculation of derivatives; however, is a method that demands long execution time.

There are different methods for solving an Inverse Problem since the choice of the Network Search algorithm is due to its efficiency and practicality since it is possible to predefine intervals for the parameters to be estimated (A, B, and C) and not wrap or derivative calculation. Although the method is exhaustive (combining all possibilities of solution), this problem seeks to determine only three parameters, a number that does not require a large execution time, which allows a solution via the Network Search method in an easy and efficient.

The values' choice of the intervals of A,B, and C and the number of subdivisions were made from the scatter diagram of the collected data. Through it, it was evidenced that the temperature decreases over time, but remains positive until reaching the thermal equilibrium with the medium, which was maintained at a constant temperature of 23 °C, which justifies the choice of intervals from 0 to 50 for parameters A and C. As for parameter B, it was verified that the temperature variation is minimal for a time long interval (in seconds) and will be negative, due to the cooling process (decreasing exponential), so opted by the range of -0.01 to 0, adopting 1000 divisions for all intervals.

4   Methodology

This section describes the methodology used in this study. First, it presents the execution environment for parallel execution. In the sequence is presented the measurement methodology used in the experiments and the real thermodynamics application that was modeled through the inverse problem and validated from the direct problem.

4.1   Execution Environment

The platform used for the experiments is an Altix UV 2000 designed by SGI. The platform is composed of 24 NUMA nodes. Each node has an Intel Xeon processor E5-4640 Sandy Bridge-EP x86-64 processor with eight physical cores of 2.40 GHz. Each core of the Intel Xeon E5-4640 has L1 cache memories of 32 KB for instruction and 32 KB for data and 256 KB of L2 cache. All eight cores share a cache of 20 MB L3. Each node has 32 GB of DDR3 memory, which is shared with other nodes in a cc-NUMA form through SGI's NUMAlink6. In general, this platform has 192 physical cores and 768 GB of DDR3 memory. The platform runs an unmodified SUSE Linux Enterprise Server operating system with kernel 3.0.101-0.29 installed. All applications were compiled with GCC 4.8.2. Table 1 displays the main execution environment's characteristics.

4.2   Measurement Methodology

To analyze the performance, power demand, energy consumption, and define a Tradeoff of performance × energy. The EMonDaemon [22] tool was used to collect and analyze runtime and processor power demand during execution. This tool facilitates the relation of this information since the current systems have different interfaces to collect information about its components. Also, some of the existing tools provide data to be parsed only after execution. Thus, for performing the EMonDaemon tool tests, it has been configured to perform processor power demand measurements every 1 s.

Table 1. Equipment's configuration

Platform	Intel Sandy Bridge-EP
Manufacturer	Intel
Processor model	E5-4640
Clock frequency	2,4 GHz
Number of cores	8
Memory	32 GB
Cache L1	64 KB
Cache L2	256 KB
Cache L3	20 MB
Manufacturing technology	32 nm
Instruction set architecture	AVX
Floating-Point Unit (FPU)	VFPv3
Out-of-order execution	Yes

In order to increase the performance of this application in multicore systems, a parallel version was implemented in language C with *OpenMP* [1], popular programming for shared memory systems. The parallel version of the application distributes the iteration intervals between the available cores. For the mapping of threads, the tool *hw ₗock*[2] was used.

Each of the tests performed in this work was repeated 10 times, to achieve a relative error of less than 5% and 95% of statistical confidence for a Student's t-distribution. Between each of the tests, the system was left in *idle* for at least 20 s, so that the power demand of the system stabilized.

5   Results

This section describes the results measured with the Network Search method's parallel runtime applied in a real water cooling system in ampoules. For the measurements, the platform described in Sect. 4.1 and the EMonDaemon tool. In order to facilitate the analysis, the results were organized in the following order:

- Power demand of processors with or without thread mapping;
- Execution Time versus energy consumption with or without thread mapping; and
- Tradeoff between Execution Time and Energy Consumption of the parallel version.

---

[1] http://www.openmp.org/.
[2] https://www.open-mpi.org/projects/hwloc/.

5.1 Power Demand

Our testbed equipment has 24 processors, each one with 8 cores, totaling 192 cores. Thus, in the first test, each processor power demand was measured when the equipment was idle. This measurement is important to define the power demand in idle and its an increasing during the executions of each test. In the idle state, the average power demand measured of the processors was (20.54 W).

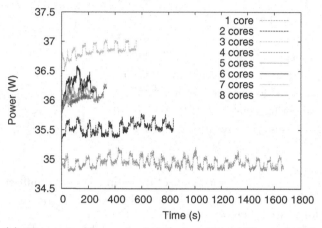

(a) The power demand of the executions *without* threads mapping

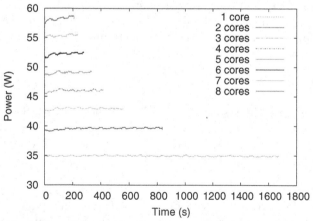

(b) The power demand of the executions *with* threads mapping

Fig. 2. Instantaneous power measured for each processor during executions.

The first test was performed without the thread mapping. 8 threads were created leaving to the operating system the decision to choose which of the 192 cores to run each one of the threads. Thus, the threads were randomly mapped in cores of different processors. For the power analysis, it then measured of each one of the processors used in the execution. In Fig. 2(a) is showed the instantaneous power of the processors used in the tests. Each row represents an execution of the application for several threads. From the analysis of the results, we can see a small difference between the processors' power demands, which had a variation of 8%. In this test, the power varies between 34.77 W and 37.03 W.

A second test was performed using the thread mapping with the tool (*hw_lock*). The main goal this test is to execute all threads on the same processor; each one is mapped to each of the cores. In this test, given the different amount of cores used, there are different power demands for each execution. When only 1 core is used, the average power demand was 34.9 W. On the other hand, the power demand achieves 57.8 W when all 8 cores were used.

However, as the execution time and the power demand determine the total energy spent, the next section will analyze the impact of these variations.

5.2 Execution Time and Energy Consumption with Thread Mapping

The execution time of the sequential version of the application is 1679.2 s for a matrix order equal to 1.000 (Table 2).

With the parallel version's development that uses shared memory, the execution time has been reduced from 1679,2 s to 210,1 s, representing a gain or *speedup* of 7.99 to 8 cores, that is, a speedup practically linear.

Statistical tests indicate that the runtimes' results presented in this section are significantly similar since small variations were observed in the measurements performed between the two sets of tests performed (with or without mapping). Thus, in this section, for the energy consumption analysis and comparison, the average execution time measured in the two tests was taken as the basis.

In the first test (without thread mapping) different processors were used. Thus, to compute the total energy spent was considered the processors' average power that performs threads added to the processors' average power demand that remained in idle state.

In this way, it is noticed that with the parallel implementation is achieved a reduction of 79.98% in total energy consumption when running the application with 8 threads in 8 different processors. The total energy spent was reduced from 300.2 KJ to 60.1 KJ. The runtimes, the power demands, and total energy consumption for different threads numbers are presented in Table 2.

In the second test was used the threads mapping aiming at the execution of the 8 threads in the 8 cores of the same processor. As shown in the previous section, for each threads number, there is a processor power demand, which varies from 34.9 to 57.8 W. On the other hand, processors that have remained idle have an average power demand of 20,546 W. Thus, running 8 threads on 1 single processor was achieved a reduction of up to 85.88% in total energy consumption. It is observed, however, that with the use of thread mapping, it was possible to reduce energy consumption even further, which was 5.9% higher

Table 2. Execution time, power demand and power consumption *without* thread mapping

Processors	1	2	3	4	5	6	7	8
Time (s)	**1679,2**	839,7	561,1	419,5	337,2	281,7	241,3	**210,1**
Power of used processors (W)	34,9	71,0	110,2	143,6	179,3	216,2	250,9	286,0
Power of processors in idle (W)	143,8	123,3	102,7	82,2	61,6	41,1	20,5	0,0
Energy (KJ)	300,2	163,1	119,5	94,7	81,2	72,5	65,5	60,1
Energy save (%)		45,66	60,19	68,44	72,93	75,85	78,18	**79,98**

than the unmapped tests. The tests' results with mapping for different threads number are presented in Table 3.

5.3   Execution Time × Energy Consumption Tradeoff

As the mapping presented a more significant reduction in energy consumption, a third test was carried out aiming to relate the runtime to the total amount of energy consumed when the number of threads is increased until all the system's cores are used. In Fig. 3 shows the execution times and power consumption when varied the number of threads from 1 to 192.

Since the application is highly parallelable and does not have much communication, we realize that, with the parallel implementation, was obtained a total execution time's reduction of 160 times for 192 cores, that is, the time was reduced from 1679.2 s to 10.3 s. The total power consumption was also reduced with the parallel version. In the sequential version, considering the 24 processors octa cores of the system, the energy consumption was 866,5 KJ. With the parallel implementation that uses the 192 available cores, the consumption has been reduced to 14.4 KJ, which represents a reduction of 60.3 times.

Two factors justify the difference between time and consumption gains, 160 times, and 60.3 times, both for 192 cores. The first is linear velocity observed up to approximately 70 threads. From these cores used, the execution time's reduction became smaller tending to stabilize, as shown in Fig. 3. The second is due to the increase in static power demand of approximately 14.9 W each inclusion of a new processor in the parallel application execution.

Table 3. Execution time, power demand and power consumption *with* thread mapping

Processors	1	2	3	4	5	6	7	8
Time (s)	**1679,2**	839,7	561,1	419,5	337,2	281,7	241,3	**210,1**
Power of used processors (W)	34,9	39,5	42,7	45,9	48,8	51,8	54,9	57,8
Energy of used processors (KJ)	58,6	33,1	24,0	19,2	16,4	14,6	13,2	12,2
Total power demand (W)	178,8	183,3	186,6	189,7	192,6	195,6	198,8	201,6
Total energy spent (KJ)	300,2	153,9	104,7	79,6	64,9	55,1	48,0	42,4
Energy save (%)		48,72	65,12	73,49	78,36	81,64	84,02	**85,88**

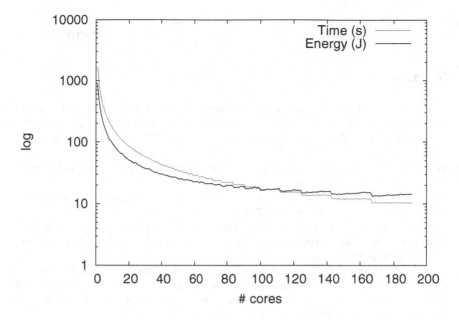

Fig. 3. Execution time and energy consumption for different number of threads.

However, according to the results obtained, it can be concluded that the Network Search method is shown as a practical and accurate and efficient method when used in its parallel version. Thus, the problem related to the high sequential version's execution time could be solved with parallel implementation and execution in multicore environments.

6   Conclusions

In this paper, we discuss our gains of up to 160× in time and up to 60× in energy consumption achieved with parallelization and process mapping in multicore processors of Network Search method applied to an actual water cooling application.

We showed that parallel Network Search Method has good efficiency and accuracy, as well as the influence the computer's configurations and architecture. We also show that Network Search Method can be applied in different scientific problems in substitution of other methods that have less accuracy in their results.

Future work includes working with other methods of parameter determination (Inverse Problem) to see if the simulation time is better than this one.

Acknowledgments. This work has been partially supported by *PETROBRAS* oil and gas company under Ref. 2016/00133-9 and the project GREEN-CLOUD: Computação em Cloud com Computação Sustentavel (Ref. 16/2551-0000 488-9), from FAPERGS and CNPq Brazil, program PRONEX 12/2014 and CNPq-Universal

436339/2018-8. We also thank *RICAP*, partially funded by the Ibero-American Program of Science and Technology for Development (*CYTED*), Ref. 517RT0529.

References

1. Andreolli, C., Thierry, P., Borges, L., Skinner, G., Yount, C.: Characterization and optimization methodology applied to stencil computations. In: Reinders, J., Jeffers, J. (eds.) High Performance Parallelism Pearls, pp. 377–396. Morgan Kaufmann, Boston (2015)
2. Blake, G., Dreslinski, R., Mudge, T.: A survey of multicore processors. IEEE Signal. Proc. Mag. **26**(6), 26–37 (2009)
3. Buck, I., et al.: Brook for GPUs: stream computing on graphics hardware. ACM Trans. Graph. (TOG) **23**(3), 777–786 (2004)
4. Caballero, D., Farrés, A., Duran, A., Hanzich, M., Fernández, S., Martorell, X.: Optimizing fully anisotropic elastic propagation on Intel Xeon Phi coprocessors. In: 2nd EAGE Workshop on HPC for Upstream, pp. 1–6 (2015)
5. Cruz, E.H., Diener, M., Serpa, M.S., Navaux, P.O.A., Pilla, L., Koren, I.: Improving communication and load balancing with thread mapping in manycore systems. In: 26th Euromicro International Conference on Parallel, Distributed and Network-based Processing (PDP), pp. 93–100. IEEE (2018)
6. Diefenthäler, A.T., Avi, P.C.: Determinać cão da curva de resfriamento da água em ampolas de garrafas térmicas. In: Anais do VII MCSUL - Conferência Sul em Modelagem Computacional, Rio Grande/RS (2016)
7. Diefenthäler, A.T., Avi, P.C., Padoin, E.L.: Processamento paralelo na determinać cão da curva de resfriamento da Água pelo método de procura em rede. In: Congresso Nacional de Matemática Aplicada e Computacional (CNMAC), São José dos Campos/SP (2017)
8. Dongarra, J., Luszczck, P.: Anatomy of a globally recursive embedded LINPACK benchmark. In: 16th IEEE High Performance Extreme Computing Conference (HPEC) (2012)
9. Engl, H.W., Hanke, M., Neubauer, A.: Regularization of Inverse Problems. Mathematics and Its Applications. Springer, Dordrecht (1996). 322 p
10. Hadarmard, J.: Lectures on the Cauchy Problem in Linear Partial Differential Equation. Yale University Press, New Haven (1923). 338 p
11. Halliday, D., Resnick, R., Walker, J.: Fundamentos de física, volume 2: gravitação, ondas e termodinâmica, vol. 8. LTC, Rio de Janeiro (2009). 295 p
12. He, J., Chen, W., Tang, Z.: NestedMP: enabling cache-aware thread mapping for nested parallel shared memory applications. Parallel Comput. **51**, 56–66 (2016)
13. Huang, S., Xiao, S., Feng, W.C.: On the energy efficiency of graphics processing units for scientific computing. In: IEEE International Symposium on Parallel & Distributed Processing, IPDPS, pp. 1–8. IEEE (2009)
14. Ibarra, J.R.M.: La materia a muy bajas temperaturas. Revista Ingenierías **11**(38), 7–16 (2008)
15. Incropera, F.P., Dewitt, D.P.: Fundamentos de transferência de calor e de massa, vol. 6. LTC, Rio de Janeiro (2011). 698 p
16. Jiao, Y., Lin, H., Balaji, P., Feng, W.: Power and performance characterization of computational kernels on the GPU. In: IEEE/ACM International Conference on Green Computing and Communications (GreenCom) and International Conference on Cyber, Physical and Social Computing (CPSCom), pp. 221–228. IEEE (2010)

17. Liu, G., Schmidt, T., Dömer, R., Dingankar, A., Kirkpatrick, D.: Optimizing thread-to-core mapping on manycore platforms with distributed tag directories. In: 20th Asia and South Pacific Design Automation Conference (ASP-DAC), pp. 429–434. IEEE (2015)
18. Luk, C., Hong, S., Kim, H.: Qilin: exploiting parallelism on heterogeneous multiprocessors with adaptive mapping. In: Proceedings of the 42nd Annual IEEE/ACM International Symposium on Microarchitecture, pp. 45–55. ACM (2009)
19. Marques, N.R.L., Araujo, I.S.: Física térmica. In: Textos de apoio ao professor de Física, no. 5. vol. 20. UFRGS, Instituto de Física, Porto Alegre/RS (2009). 73 p
20. Padoin, E.L., de Oliveira, D.A.G., Velho, P., Navaux, P.O.A.: Time-to-solution and energy-to-solution: a comparison between ARM and Xeon. In: Third Workshop on Applications for Multi-Core Architectures (WAMCA SBAC-PAD), New York, USA, pp. 48–53 (2012). https://doi.org/10.1109/WAMCA.2012.10
21. Padoin, E.L., Pilla, L.L., Boito, F.Z., Kassick, R.V., Velho, P., Navaux, P.O.A.: Evaluating application performance and energy consumption on hybrid CPU+GPU architecture. Cluster Comput. **16**(3), 511–525 (2013). https://doi.org/10.1007/s10586-012-0219-6
22. Padoin, E.L., Pilla, L.L., Castro, M., Boito, F.Z., Navaux, P.O.A., Mehaut, J.F.: Performance/energy trade-off in scientific computing: the case of ARM big.LITTLE and Intel Sandy Bridge. IET Comput. Digital Tech. **2**(3), 1–14 (2014)
23. Serpa, M.S., Krause, A.M., Cruz, E.H., Navaux, P.O.A., Pasin, M., Felber, P.: Optimizing machine learning algorithms on multi-core and many-core architectures using thread and data mapping. In: 26th Euromicro International Conference on Parallel, Distributed and Network-Based Processing (PDP), pp. 329–333. IEEE (2018)
24. Silva, B.F.: Método da procura em rede melhorado: uma proposta para a estimação dos parâmetros do modelo de rakhmatov e vrudhula. Dissertação de Mestrado do Programa de Pós-Graduação em Modelagem Matemática da Unijuí, Maio 2013. 64 p
25. Silva Neto, A.J.: Técnicas de inteligência computacional inspiradas na natureza: Aplicações em problemas inversos em transferência radiativa. In: Notas em Matemática Aplicada, 2nd ed. vol. 41. SBMAC, São Carlos/SP (2012). 148 p
26. Silva Neto, A.J., Moura Neto, F.D.: Problemas Inversos: Conceitos Fundamentais e Aplicações. UERJ, Rio de Janeiro (2005). 168 p
27. Tousimojarad, A., Vanderbauwhede, W.: An efficient thread mapping strategy for multiprogramming on manycore processors. In: Parallel Computing: Accelerating Computational Science and Engineering (CSE), Advances in Parallel Computing, vol. 25, pp. 63–71 (2014)
28. Valero, M.: Towards ExaFlop supercomputers. In: High Performance Computing Academic Research Network (HPC-net), Rio Patras, Greece, pp. 1–117 (2011)

Collaborative Development and Use of Scientific Applications in Orlando Tools: Integration, Delivery, and Deployment

Alexander Feoktistov[1]([✉]), Sergei Gorsky[1]([✉]), Ivan Sidorov[1],
Igor Bychkov[1], Andrei Tchernykh[2,3,4]([✉]), and Alexei Edelev[5]

[1] Matrosov Institute for System Dynamics and Control Theory of SB RAS,
Irkutsk, Russia
{agf, gorsky, ivan. sidorov, bychkov}@icc. ru
[2] CICESE Research Center, Carretera Ensenada-Tijuana 3918, Post Box 360,
22860 Ensenada, BC, Mexico
chernykh@cicese. mx
[3] Ivannikov Institute for System Programming of RAS, Moscow, Russia
[4] South Ural State University, Chelyabinsk, Russia
[5] Melentiev Energy Systems Institute of SB RAS, Irkutsk, Russia
flower@isem. sei. irk. ru

Abstract. The paper addresses practical challenges related to the development and application of distributed software packages of the Orlando Tools framework to solve real problems. Such packages include a special class of scientific applications characterized by a wide class of problem solvers, modular structure of software, algorithmic knowledge implemented by modules, computations scalability, execution in heterogeneous resources, etc. It is adapted for various categories of users: developers, administrators, and end users. Unlike other tools for developing scientific applications, Orlando Tools provides supports for the intensive evolution of algorithmic knowledge, adaptation of existed and designing new ones. It has the capability to extend the class of solved problems. We implement and automate the non-trivial technological sequence of the collaborative development and use of packages including the continuous integration, delivery, deployment, and execution of package modules in a heterogeneous distributed environment that integrates grid and cloud computing. This approach reduces the complexity of the collaborative development and use of packages, and increases software operation predictability through the preliminary detecting and eliminating errors with significant reduction of the correcting cost.

Keywords: Grid · Cloud · Applied software packages · Continuous integration · Delivery · Deployment · Collaborative computing

© Springer Nature Switzerland AG 2020
J. L. Crespo-Mariño and E. Meneses-Rojas (Eds.): CARLA 2019, CCIS 1087, pp. 18–32, 2020.
https://doi.org/10.1007/978-3-030-41005-6_2

1 Introduction

High-performance computing is nowadays one of the main components in the process of supporting large-scale experiments. Such experiments are related to solving complex scientific and applied problems in various spheres of human activity. Depending on the scale of problems, the computational infrastructure may include personal computers (PCs), servers, clusters, resources of public access computer centers, Grid systems, and cloud platforms. Thus, a heterogeneous distributed computing environment is created to execute applications that are characterized by the following properties:

- Varying degree of computation scalability,
- Different sensitivity to a resource heterogeneity,
- A necessity of environment resource virtualization,
- A demand for integrating subject domains of applications with information about the software and hardware of nodes including administrative policies defined in them.

Applications that are sensitive to resource heterogeneity are usually executed in the homogeneous cluster nodes or in a virtual environment. The need for such virtualization also arises for applications that use software other than that installed in the nodes.

Among the applications being developed for a distributed computing environment, we distinguish a special class of applications that includes distributed applied software packages. Such packages are characterized by the use of a modular approach, a high degree of scalability, and the possibility of their execution on heterogeneous resources.

Usually, collaborative development and use of packages by various categories of users (developers, administrators, and end-users) is implemented. This often leads to the necessity of integrating different packages through the computational models, calculated data, and computations management transferring.

End-users of packages are interested in maximizing the summarized computing performance of the environment. In the models of subject domains in packages, the computational process is represented as a problem-solving scheme. Such scheme closely correlates with the concept of the workflow [1]. Systems for developing and applying workflows can be considered as a special case of distributed applied software packages.

Software, hardware, and information resources of heterogeneous distributed computing environments tend to permanent change. This entails the following problems:

- Reconfiguring the computing environments of packages,
- Module libraries modification and/or development of new software,
- Supporting the interaction correctness of different versions of modules within a problem-solving scheme,
- Accounting the conditions of applying these versions.

To solve the aforementioned problems, the tools for Continuous Integration, Delivery, and Deployment (CIDD) of software can be used to one or the other extent [2].

However, supporting the technological chain that integrates CIDD is still a non-trivial problem for the package development tools, including systems for the workflow applying [3]. These tools are often not ready to fully support the complex CIDD process in packages. The main difficulty arises from the need to support the conceptual modeling traditionally used in such packages. In addition, applying of subject-oriented knowledge extended by specialized information about the software and hardware infrastructure of the environment is required.

In this regard, we propose a new approach to ensuring CIDD for package modules. It is based on the merging of the methodology for creating such packages with modern software development practices based on its CIDD. We assume to use the subject-oriented knowledge where is it possible. In addition, we developed a technological scheme for joint use of our developed tools and external CIDD systems.

The rest of the paper is structured as follows: Sect. 2 provides a brief overview of tools for CIDD. It also discusses some important problems in their integration. Section 3 addresses issues related to the development of distributed applied software packages in Orlando Tools. In Sect. 4, we offer the technological scheme for the CIDD of package modules. The practice results of applying CIDD in Orlando Tools are given in Sect. 5. Finally, Sect. 6 concludes with the main results of our study.

2   Related Work

In the process of developing complex software systems, their developers need to support interaction between the components of such systems. Individual components can be created by different developers using a wide set of programming languages. They also can be oriented to work under the control of various software and hardware platforms. The main CIDD purpose is to identify and eliminate problems of interaction between individual components during the software system operation by automating their assembly, debugging, joint testing, etc. [4].

Over the years, a wide set of tools designed to automate different CIDD processes during the development of complex software systems is developed. Systems CircleCI [5], Jenkins [6], TeamCity [7], Travis [8], GitLab [9], and many other tools [10, 11] are among them. Each system has its own specific features related to the provided capabilities, a sequence of actions taken by users of this system, and its administration. All of them have certain advantages and drawbacks.

For example, CruiseControl.NET [12] and Apache Gump [13] are strongly oriented to the programming language that maximizes their own capabilities in conjunction with specialized tools for managing program libraries. An example of such a specialized tool is the Conan system for C++ [14].

Other tools provide access only as of the cloud service (CircleCI or TeamCity). They do not allow developers placing all the necessary set of CIDD tools on their resources.

Distinct difficulties arise with the integration of some tools (BuildMaster [15] and Travis [16]) with development environments due to the use of different data formats.

Fulfilled comparative analysis of the CIDD tools allows us to conclude that GitLab is one of the most promising systems for our purpose. It provides integration of automated software testing processes and storing its source code using the Git repository [17]. GitLab also supports rich test run capabilities on software build servers. For tests run, we can apply the following means:

- SSH network security access protocol [18],
- Scripts in the Shell programming language [19],
- VirtualBox software package for virtualization of various operating systems (Windows, Linux, FreeBSD, macOS, Solaris/OpenSolaris, ReactOS, etc.) [20],
- Parallels virtualization software products [21],
- Docker [22], Docker Swarm [23], and Kubernetes [24] for automating the deployment and management of applications taking into account all dependencies that need to their run,
- Container registry [25] for storing the Docker images.

Package developers have the ability to install GitLab on their own computational resources. This ability enables the developers to support the necessary level of security and flexibility of the CIDD system overall.

Table 1 provides a comparative analysis of the provision of important capabilities in GitLab and the most popular CIDD tools. The analysis results show the advantage of GitLab in providing the full spectrum of the considered capabilities in comparison with other systems.

Table 1. Results of the comparative analysis

Capability	Travis	TeamCity	Jenkins	CircleCI	GitLab
Installing the system on developer resources	−	+	+	−	+
Software testing support for Linux	+	+	+	+	+
Software testing support for Windows	−	+	+	−	+
Monitoring software	−	−	−	−	+
Program code quality verification	−	−	+	−	+
Supporting the container registry	−	−	−	−	+
Supporting the delivery and deployment of software	+	+	+	+	+

Information elicited from the subject-oriented data, and the problem-solving results obtained in executing packages are often the weakly structured, heterogeneous, and frequently changed. In this regard, CIDD processes require the use of a flexible, knowledge-based model. It has to allow developers to determine the relations between the primary information and the data structures used by such packages. Well-known CIDD tools do not support this feature.

3   Orlando Tools: Development and Use of Distributed Applied Software Packages

We develop distributed applied software packages for solving large-scale scientific and applied problems using the Orlando Tools framework [26]. It provides the created of subject-oriented computing environments in which various infrastructures that support both grid and cloud computing are integrated.

Three conceptually separate layers of knowledge (computational, schematic, and productional) form a computational model of the package that is developed in Orlando Tools. On this model, problems are formulated, and schemes of their solving are constructed.

Modules that represent applied software of the package implement the computational layer. Parameters and operations of the package reflect schematic knowledge. The parameters represent the relevant characteristics and properties of the subject domain. Operations determine the relations of computability between two subsets of subject domain parameters. Such a relation makes it possible to calculate the searched values for the parameters of the first subset when the values for the parameters of the second subset are known.

Package modules are software that implements operations. The specification of each module includes information about the executable program (name, version, input and output parameters, assembly and compilation processes, launch instructions, allowable classes of resources for its execution, etc.).

Conditions of performing operations form the productional layer of knowledge. The current computations progress of the problem-solving scheme execution and state of resources determine the fulfilment of these conditions.

A problem formulation is the formalized description of the problem in terms of parameters and operations. Problem formulations are formed on the computational model of the package. The problem statement determines the following conditions:

- Input parameters (data required to solve the problem),
- Output parameters (results of solving the problem),
- Operations that can or must be performed over the parameter field,
- Constraints that determine the ability to perform operations,
- Quality criteria (time, cost, reliability, etc.) for problem-solving.

The problem-solving scheme is planned based on its formulation. It reflects the information and logical relations between package operations. The problem-solving scheme can be included in a computational model of any package as a new operation.

4   Technological Scheme of CIDD in Orlando Tools

In the paper, we represent a prototype of the new Orlando Tools subsystem that supports CIDD. The Git repository is applied in Orlando Tools for managing module source code versions. GitLab is used to access to the Git repository and manage by the CIDD pipeline process.

The building of modules is carried out automatically when making changes related to the adding or modification of a module source code in Git. The building runs on specialized servers or nodes of the environment using the pre-installed GitLab Runner agent executed in the Docker container.

We plan to support GitLab Runner agents for a different type of programming languages and with different compilers for modules. Each module specification contains a section with requirements for GitLab Runners. Figure 1 shows the general scheme of the interaction of Orlando Tools with the external CIDD systems.

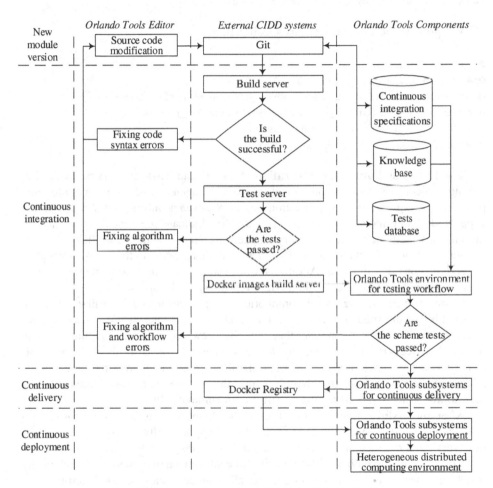

Fig. 1. Scheme of supporting CIDD in Orlando Tools

The syntax of specifications for the main objects of the computational model of a package in Orlando Tools is shown below.

```
Parameter Parameter_name Extension;
Operation Operation_name module | task
Module_name | Task_name (Input_parameters > Output_parameters);
Module Module_name (Input_parameters > Output_parameters)
Repository_name Project_name;
Task t1(Input_parameters > Output_parameters);
```

We provide the examples of this specifications:

```
Parameter z1 xml;
Operation o1 module m1 (z1, z3, z2, z4 > z7, z9);
Module m1 (initial_data,vulnerable_elements multiplicity,
number_of_perturbation_subsets > perturbation_subsets,
statistics_file_name) repo1 R1.master;
Task t1(z1, z2, z3, z4, z5, z6 > z8);
```

The keywords **Parameter**, **Operation**, **Module**, and **Task** correspond to the following objects of the computational model: parameter, operation, module, and problem-solving scheme. Specification items *Repository_name* and *Project_name* support the continuous integration process. They indicate the repository name and module project name in the repository respectively. In the module specification, these elements contain information about the location of this module in the repository and its dependency on other modules. Additional information about the module required for its launch and testing is stored in the module repository in the special files.

In the case of the successful compilation and passing tests of the first stage, the binary files of the module are packed into a Docker-container at the Docker images build server. The Docker-container that contains a new version of the module is sent to the Docker Registry. In addition, the Docker-container is placed in the Orlando Tools test environment. There it is used in each distributed applied software packages for the advanced testing the problem-solving schemes that include operations implemented by the module. The advanced testing is carried out automatically.

After successful completion of all tests, the Orlando Tools subsystem for continuous delivery creates new versions of distributed applied software packages with the new version of the module. Then the Orlando Tools subsystem for continuous delivery interacts with the Orlando Tools subsystem for continuous deployment to automatically install the new version of the module to all required nodes of the heterogeneous distributed computing environment.

Verification of tests status at CIDD stages and transitions between them can be performed automatically or step-by-step in the manual mode.

5 Applying CIDD in Orlando Tools

As an example of applying CIDD, we consider the development of the distributed applied software package for vulnerability analysis of energy systems. Energy systems play a crucial role in the modern world. A failure in such a critical infrastructure leads to great damage to the economy and society as a whole. Thus, ensuring critical infrastructures resilience has great priority on both the national and international levels. Resilience is often understood as the ability of a system to reduce the disturbance probability, mitigate disturbance consequences, and rapidly recover after a failure.

The system vulnerability can be defined as the overall sensitivity of a system to a particular disturbance. It can be measured by the damage magnitude that occurs because of the disturbance.

The system vulnerability conditioned by failures in its elements shows their criticality. The more system sensitive to element failures leads to the more critical of these elements [27].

The vulnerability analysis helps a lot in support of decision making in providing critical infrastructure resilience. A vulnerability analysis related to the determination of the critical elements is extremely difficult when estimating multiple simultaneous failures.

A failure set is defined as a specific combination of failed elements. It is characterized by a set size, which indicates the number of elements that fail simultaneously. Applying the analysis of the critical elements, we process and compare sets of different sizes separately before ranking them. The number of possible failure sets is $\frac{t!}{(t-k)!k!}$, where t is the total number of elements and k is the size of a failure set [27]. Thus, for a system consisting of some hundreds of elements and more, we use distributed computing for processing the failure sets included larger than two elements.

An energy system under consideration is the Russian natural gas supply system. At the initial time moment of the modeling, its network includes 387 nodes (33 producers, 96 consumers, 29 underground storages, and 229 key compressor stations) and 786 pipelines sections as arcs. There are 415 arcs and 291 nodes that can be failed. Thus, $t = 706$. The failure sets size k is changed from 1 to 3.

The computational model of the package for analyzing the critical elements of the energy system includes two problem-solving schemes.

The scheme t_1 generates the failure sets of the specific size and calculates the consequences of simultaneous failures for elements combination. It includes the operations $f_2 - f_6$.

At the first stage of executing the scheme t_1, the operation f_4 calculates a number of records needed to keep the consequences data of every failure set of specific size. Next, two operations are performed. The operation f_6 prepares the distributed database for storing consequences data. The operation f_2 generates failure sets of specific size. Then the operation f_3 estimates the consequences of simultaneous malfunction of elements of the generated set in parallel. Finally, the operations f_5 increases the failure set size by 1. In the computational model, the scheme t_1 is represented by the operation f_7.

The scheme t_2 generates and processes failure sets of different sizes in a loop. It calls the operation f_7 until the modeling with all failure sets sizes of the given interval are carried out.

Figures 2 and 3 show the schemes t_1 and t_2 created in the Orlando Tools graphical editor.

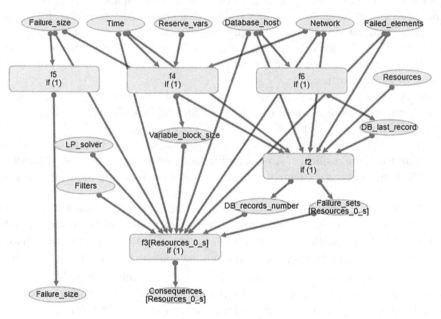

Fig. 2. Problem-solving scheme t_1

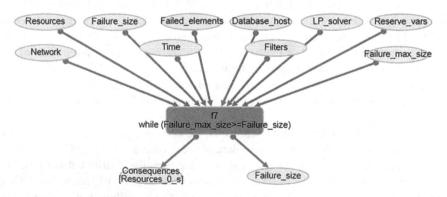

Fig. 3. Problem-solving scheme t_2

Parameters in Figs. 2 and 3 are interpreted as follows:

- *Network* is multi-period data of the energy system network,
- *Failure_size* is the specific size of failure sets,
- *Time* is a time moment at which the energy system network data is retrieved,
- *Failed_elements* is a set of failed network elements,
- *Resources* is the list of computing resources allocated for problem-solving,
- *Database_host* is the host address of a distributed database where failure sets and consequence data are read from and written to,
- *DB_records_number* is a total number of records in the distributed database,
- *DB_last_record* is the last record number in the distributed database,
- *LP_solver* is a name of the linear programming problem solver that is applied to optimize the energy flow over the given energy system network,
- *Filters* is a list of the filters for the decision variables after applying the solver,
- *Reserve_vars* is the extra number of the distributed database records to keep the consequences data of every failure set of the specific size,
- *Failure_sets* is generated failure sets,
- *Variable_block_size* is a variable block size,
- *Consequences* is a failure set consequences,
- *Failure_max_size* is the maximum size of failure sets.

The parameters *DB_records_number*, *DB_last_record*, *Failure_sets*, and *Variable_block_size* are intermediate parameters of the scheme t_1.

In the package, the operations f_2-f_6 are implemented by the cross-platform applied modules m_2-m_6. These modules are built using additional software libraries.

The development of the current package version and the computational experiments took about 30 h. All computations are carried out using 1 personal computer (PC) of the package developers and resources of public access computer center Irkutsk Supercomputer Center of SB RAS (2 pools of HPC-cluster nodes) [28]. The quotas of end-users of the computer center are limited to 10 nodes.

Table 2 shows the time of solving the scheme t_2 on heterogeneous resources in seconds for different values of k. This time was obtained taking into account the wait time of jobs for executing modules in queues of local resource managers.

Table 2. Time of solving the scheme t_2

k	PC (1 core Intel Core i5-650, 3.4 GHz, 8 GB RAM)	Pool 1: 10 nodes with 2 processors AMD Opteron 6276 (16 core, 2.3 GHz, 64 GB RAM)	Pool 2: 10 nodes with 2 processors Intel Xeon CPU X5670 (18 core, 2.1 GHz, 128 GB of RAM)
1	362	179	174
2	190479	475	411
3	>540000	53093	25790

It is obvious that the end-user can rationally select resources for problem-solving, depending on the k. When $k = 1$, the use of resources of the pools 1 and 2 is irrational owing to the large overheads related to starting instances of the module m_3, which implements operation f_3. With an increase k, the use of these resources significantly reduces the problem-solving time.

The computational model of the package allows Orlando Tools automatically selects the necessary computing resources based on the failure sets size k. In the Table 2, we represent the evaluation of the scheme t_2 solving time on PC for $k = 3$.

Figure 4 represents the time spent by the package developer at various stages of their work with CIDD using Orlando Tools (OT) and the estimated time that can be spent by the developer without Orlando Tools (Without OT). The developer makes the following main actions:

- Preparation of data for CIDD (A1),
- Configuring of the CIDD process (A2),
- Development or modification the package modules (A3),
- Module sources commit to the GitLab server (A4),
- Modules build (A5),
- Testing the modules (A6),
- Placing the modules into a binary repository (A7),
- Package modification (A8),
- Testing problem-solving schemes with the package modules (A9),
- Verification of tests results (A10),
- Delivery of the package modules (A11),
- Deployment of the package modules (A12),
- Launch and shutdown of external systems for CIDD (A13).

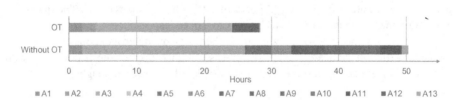

Fig. 4. Continuous integration runtime

These results show a significant decrease in the time spent by the developer in the first case with the Orlando Tools use. The stages of the module build, testing the module, placing the module into a repository, testing schemes with the module, verification of tests results, module delivery, and module deployment are performed in Orlando Tools automatically without the direct participation of the developer. Largely, this is due to the carrying out the configuring of the CIDD process.

The time decrease in the first case is because of the exclusion of the overheads. In the second case, such overheads are associated with the launch and shutdown of external systems for CIDD, and the conversion or transfer of data between them. In the first case, the developer spent time on different stages of developing and using the package.

Results for the second case were obtained on the base of the average time of developer actions evaluated by developers of the similar packages represented in [26, 29]. The developers took into account both the development and integration of these packages. They made about 30–40 module modifications a week.

Based on the experience in modular programming, the developers evaluate the increase of the software operation predictability through the preliminary detecting and eliminating errors about 35–40%. In addition, they highlight decreasing the error correction cost about 50–60%.

In many cases, the average time spent for one module modification significantly exceeds the computation time (Fig. 5). This is a common situation for the subject domain of the package. Thus, reducing the experiment preparation time through CIDD is extremely relevant.

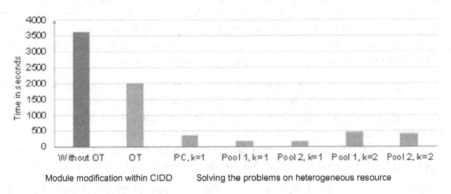

Fig. 5. Average continuous integration runtime for the modification of one module via the problem-solving time for t_2 on the heterogeneous resources

We provide a comparative analysis of the main capabilities of GitLab and the developed prototype the CIDD system of Orlando Tools (Table 3). It shows the opportunity of applying the new additional key possibilities of the proposed prototype in developing distributed applied software packages. These possibilities are especially important when the collaboration is implemented within integrating different packages through the computational models, calculated data, and computations management transferring.

Table 3. Results of the comparative analysis of possibilities

Possibility	GitLab	Orlando Tools
Applying CIDD within the collaborative development of modules	+	+
Automation of modules CIDD	+	+
Manual configuring of modules CIDD for heterogeneous resources	+	+
Automated configuring modules CIDD for heterogeneous resources	−	+
Applying CIDD within the collaborative development of problem-solving schemes in packages	−	+
Automation of CIDD of problem-solving schemes in packages	−	+

6 Conclusions

We propose a new approach to ensuring CIDD for modules of distributed applied software packages that developed and used with the help of Orlando Tools for the special class of scientific applications. We develop a new subject-oriented subsystem that implements CIDD. In contrast to the well-known tools of similar objective, it provides both the traditional functions (software version control, automation of their assembly and testing, etc.) and new automated functions, such as:

- Unifying module assembly processes both on the dedicated servers and on the developer machines through using the specialized virtual machines,
- Synthesizing test problem-solving schemes on conceptual models,
- Testing problem-solving schemes on heterogeneous resources,
- Integration of CIDD processes into the unified technological sequence,
- Applying CIDD within the collaborative development and application.

Application of the developed prototype to solve real problems demonstrates the following advantages:

- Reducing experiment preparation time within the collaborative development and use of packages,
- Increasing the predictability of a software package operation in heterogeneous resources through the preliminary detecting and eliminating errors,
- Decreasing the error correction cost.

The future work is related to the CIDD extension. We plan to implement methods and tools for predicting modules' execution times on heterogeneous resources. We will use new methods and tools to allocate resources more efficiently. We will develop the subject-oriented environment for solving large spectrum problems of decision-making for supporting the energy resilience adapted for developers with different affiliations and locations. Packages for problem-solving will be integrated within a framework of the environment using computational models and data transferring management.

Acknowledgment. The study is supported by the Russian Foundation of Basic Research, projects no. 19-07-00097-a and no. 18-07-01224-a. This work was also supported in part by Basic Research Program of SB RAS, projects no. IV.38.1.1 and no. III.17.5.1.

References

1. Barker, A., van Hemert, J.: Scientific workflow: a survey and research directions. In: Wyrzykowski, R., Dongarra, J., Karczewski, K., Wasniewski, J. (eds.) PPAM 2007. LNCS, vol. 4967, pp. 746–753. Springer, Heidelberg (2008). https://doi.org/10.1007/978-3-540-68111-3_78
2. Duvall, P.M., Matyas, S., Glover, A.: Continuous Integration: Improving Software Quality and Reducing Risk. Addison Wesley Professional, Boston (2007)
3. Deelman, E., et al.: The future of scientific workflows. Int. J. High Perform. Comput. Appl. **32**(1), 159–175 (2018)
4. Krol, M., Rene, S., Ascigil, O., Psaras, I.: ChainSoft: collaborative software development using smart contracts. In: 1st Workshop on Cryptocurrencies and Blockchains for Distributed Systems, pp. 1–6. ACM (2018)
5. Sochat, V.: Containershare: open source registry to build, test, deploy with CircleCI. J. Open Source Softw. **3**(28), 1–3 (2018)
6. Soni, M., Berg, A.M.: Jenkins 2.x Continuous Integration Cookbook. Packt Publishing, Birmingham (2017)
7. Machiraju, S., Gaurav, S.: Deployment via TeamCity and Octopus Deploy. In: Machiraju, S., Gaurav, S. (eds.) DevOps for Azure Applications, pp. 11–38. Apress, New York (2018)
8. Beller, M., Gousios, G., Zaidman, A.: Oops, my tests broke the build: an explorative analysis of travis CIDD with GitHub. In: 14th International Conference on Mining Software Repositories, pp. 356–367. IEEE (2017)
9. Gruver, G.: Start and Scaling Devops in the Enterprise. BookBaby, Pennsauken (2016)
10. Shahin, M., Babar, M.A., Zhu, L.: Continuous integration, delivery and deployment: a systematic review on approaches, tools, challenges and practices. IEEE Access **5**, 3909–3943 (2017)
11. Wolff, E.: A Practical Guide to Continuous Delivery. Addison-Wesley, Boston (2017)
12. CruiseControl.NET. https://sourceforge.net/projects/ccnet. Accessed 7 May 2019
13. Apache Gump. https://gump.apache.org/. Accessed 7 May 2019
14. Conan C/C++ package manager. https://www.conan.io. Accessed 7 May 2019
15. BuildMaster. https://inedo.com/buildmaster. Accessed 7 May 2019
16. Heckel, T.: Meet Travis CI: Open Source Continuous Integration, InfoQ (2013). https://www.infoq.com/news/2013/02/travis-ci. Accessed 7 May 2019
17. Chacon, S., Straub, B.: Pro Git. Apress, New York (2014)
18. Barrett, D., Silverman, R., Byrnes, R.: SSH: The Secure Shell (The Definitive Guide). O'Reilly, Sebastopol (2005)
19. Blum, R.: Linux Command Line and Shell Scripting Bible. Wiley, Hoboken (2017)
20. Colvin, H.: VirtualBox: An Ultimate Guide Book on Virtualization with VirtualBox. CreateSpace Independent Publishing Platform, Scotts Valley (2015)
21. Parallels RAS. https://www.parallels.com/ru/products/ras/remote-application-server/. Accessed 7 May 2019
22. Kane, S., Matthias, K.: Docker: Up and Running: Shipping Reliable Containers in Production. O'Relly Media, Sebastopol (2018)
23. Smith, R.: Docker Orchestration. Packt Publishing, Birmingham (2017)

24. Luksa, M.: Kubernetes in Action. Manning Publications, Shelter Island (2018)
25. Container Registry. https://docs.gitlab.com/ee/user/project/container_registry.html. Accessed 7 May 2019
26. Feoktistov, A., Gorsky, S., Sidorov, I., Kostromin, R., Edelev, A., Massel, L.: Orlando tools: energy research application development through convergence of grid and cloud computing. In: Voevodin, V., Sobolev, S. (eds.) RuSCDays 2018. CCIS, vol. 965, pp. 289–300. Springer, Cham (2019). https://doi.org/10.1007/978-3-030-05807-4_25
27. Jonsson, H., Johansson, J., Johansson, H.: Identifying critical components in technical infrastructure networks. Proc. Inst. Mech. Eng. Part O J. Risk Reliab. **222**(2), 235–243 (2008)
28. Irkutsk Supercomputer center of SB RAS. http://hpc.icc.ru. Accessed 7 May 2019
29. Edelev, A.V., Sidorov, I.A., Feoktistov, A.G.: Heterogeneous distributed computing environment for vulnerability analysis of energy critical infrastructures. In: Massel, L., Makagonova, N., Kopaygorodsky, A., Massel, A. (eds.) 5th International workshop on Critical infrastructures: Contingency management, Intelligent, Agent-based, Cloud computing and Cyber security. Advances in Intelligent Systems Research, vol. 158, pp. 37–42 (2018)

BS-SOLCTRA: Towards a Parallel Magnetic Plasma Confinement Simulation Framework for Modular Stellarator Devices

Diego Jiménez[1(✉)], Luis Campos-Duarte[1,2], Ricardo Solano-Piedra[3],
Luis Alonso Araya-Solano[3], Esteban Meneses[1,2], and Iván Vargas[3]

[1] Advanced Computing Laboratory, Costa Rica National High Technology Center,
San José, Costa Rica
{djimenez,lcampos,emeneses}@cenat.ac.cr
[2] School of Computing, Costa Rica Institute of Technology, Cartago, Costa Rica
[3] Plasma Laboratory for Fusion Energy and Applications,
Costa Rica Institute of Technology, Cartago, Costa Rica
{risolano,luaraya,ivargas}@tec.ac.cr

Abstract. Hand in hand, computer simulations and High Performance Computing are catalyzing advances in experimental and theoretical fusion physics and the design and construction of new confinement devices that are spearheading the quest for alternative energy sources. This paper presents the *Biot-Savart Solver for Computing and Tracing Magnetic Field Lines* (BS-SOLCTRA), a field line tracing code developed during the first Stellarator of Costa Rica (SCR-1) campaign. We present the process towards turning BS-SOLCTRA into a full parallel simulation framework for stellarator devices. Message passing, shared-memory programming, and vectorization form the underlying parallel infrastructure and provide scalable execution. The implemented parallel simulator led to a $1,550X$ speedup when compared to the original sequential version. We also present the new powerful scientific visualization capabilities added to the BS-SOLCTRA framework.

Keywords: Plasma fusion · Simulation · High Performance Computing · Parallelism · Stellarator · Message Passing Interface (MPI) · Open Multi-processing (OpenMP) · Vectorization

1 Introduction

Nuclear fusion has become a very relevant topic in scientific research worldwide. This relevance comes out of the quest for alternative energy sources that is driving many initiatives to find a solution to the emerging energetic crisis, as the world population rapidly increases. Fusion represents an attractive idea for obtaining energy as it exploits the type of phenomenon that fuels the Sun, that is, energy gain through the fusion reaction of hydrogen or hydrogen isotope

J. L. Crespo-Mariño and E. Meneses-Rojas (Eds.): CARLA 2019, CCIS 1087, pp. 33–48, 2020.
https://doi.org/10.1007/978-3-030-41005-6_3

particles, which gives rise to faster particles capable of enabling further fusion. It is easy to see why the idea of fusion became relevant considering the high abundance of hydrogen and hydrogen related isotopes present on this planet.

Despite representing a striking idea, putting fusion to action in a controlled manner is a different story. There are many challenging issues all over the fusion field. These challenges are more related to the engineering part of fusion rather than to the physics involved. To date, the fusion scientific community has opted for the development of two kind of controlled thermo nuclear fusion devices: *tokamaks* and *stellarators* [5]. Simulations are of great importance as these allow analysis of how well a particular magnetic structure (among many other important issues) could enhance fusion parameters safeguarding the cost-benefit ratio of the device operation.

Advances in experimental and phenomenological plasma physics are being catalyzed by computer simulations and the growth of High Performance Computing (HPC). Understanding fusion and plasma physics is one of the major challenges in the search for clean and renewable energy sources. The use of supercomputers in the design, construction, and validation of new confinement devices like stellarators and tokamaks has become ubiquitous thanks to the ability to simulate complex plasma phenomena with increasing detail.

1.1   Plasma Confinement in Stellarator Devices

Plasma confinement in stellarator devices is a result of a helicoidal magnetic field that is composed of toroidal and poloidal magnetic fields. This combination of magnetic fields is used because there are drifts that would lead to a complete loss of charged particles if a pure toroidal magnetic field was used [13]. Helicoidal magnetic fields generate force lines that act as tracks that charged particles follow freely around the device. This force lines are under constant pressure as long as the magnetic field is sustained.

As magnetic force lines are projected into a perpendicular toroidal plane, irrational closed surfaces named magnetic flux surface are created. They are called *irrational* surfaces because each force line does not pass at the same point that it started. In fact, many force lines compose the cross-section of the magnetic flux surface, which is nested to a characteristic line force that converges in the same point at all flux surfaces called magnetic axis.

Being able to determine magnetic flux surfaces and other physical parameters of a plasma confinement device is crucial to verify whether an specific stellarator design would actually confine plasma.

Fig. 1. SCR-1 stellarator

1.2 SCR-1

The Stellarator of Costa Rica 1 (SCR-1) started operations on 2016 and is the first modular stellarator in Latin America [11,12]. The main characteristics of this device, shown in Fig. 1, are: 2 field periods, mayor radius of 247.7 mm and an aspect ratio of 6.2. Its magnetic field is created by twelve modular coils and an input current of 4350 A which produce an average magnetic field strength of 41.33 mT. The SCR-1 is equipped with an electron cyclotron heating system (ECRH) whose maximum input power is 5 kW and heats at the second harmonic with microwaves at 2.45 GHz. The SCR-1 construction lasted for six years and required an investment of $500,000. With this achievement, Costa Rica became part of the fusion research community in stellarators, made up of the United States, Australia, Japan, Germany and Spain. Currently, the SCR-1 stellarator is in an experimental campaign where plasma diagnostics are being implemented to characterize the real conditions of the plasma and to optimize plasma heating to obtain higher electron density and temperature.

The goal of this paper is to present a new plasma confinement simulation code, BS-SOLCTRA, and describe the first steps in the process of turning it into a full-scale, parallel simulation framework for stellarator devices with modular coil systems. BS-SOLCTRA is a field line tracing code that simulates a 3D vacuum magnetic field using Biot-Savart's law and a simplified model of the device coils. It also provides input for scientific visualizations like the magnetic flux surfaces. This simulation code was specially developed for the first stellarator of Costa Rica (SCR-1). The paper is organized as follows:

- The basic computing model used in BS-SOLCTRA and the functionality provided by the code are presented in Sect. 2.
- An analysis of sequential performance and the parallelization process to improve BS-SOLCTRA is shown in Sect. 3.
- An overview of how the results of BS-SOLCTRA are used to generate scientific visualizations is given in Sect. 4.

2   Biot-Savart Solver for Computing and Tracing Magnetic Field Lines

As part of the design and verification process for the SCR-1, the *Biot-Savart Solver for Computing and Tracing Magnetic Field Lines* (BS-SOLCTRA) was created. This C++ code is based on the field line tracing technique and it simulates a 3D vacuum magnetic field using Biot-Savart's Law. Through this simulator, the user is able to determine whether or not plasma particle confinement is being achieved under an specific coil configuration and further plasma phenomena can be inferred from simulation results.

2.1   Simulation and Modeling

BS-SOLCTRA computes particle trajectories based on the influence of the magnetic field created by the modular coils present in the SCR-1 device. For a set of input particle positions, their movement is calculated in simulation steps, using a configurable amount of steps and step size. For each particle, every step is calculated sequentially, until the entirety of the steps have been completed or until a divergence criterion is fulfilled. The simulator finishes when particles complete their step count or all particles diverge.

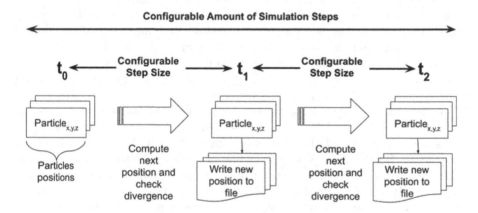

Fig. 2. BS-SOLCTRA simulator

As Fig. 2 shows, in each simulation step the code has the task of updating the position of each particle. This is done by computing the new location based solely on the effects of the magnetic field, created by the set of modular coils, over each particle. Particle interactions and further physical phenomena derived from said behavior is not taken into account in BS-SOLCTRA. With this in mind, each particle and their trajectories are totally independent from each other.

Simulation requires a set of input particle positions which are read from a file as (x, y, z) initial conditions. Next-steps computation is done by using a simplified model of the SCR-1 modular coils to determine the magnetic field they create and the influence they have over each input particle. Calculating the magnetic field produced by known currents in coils is a well-known process in plasma physics. BS-SOLCTRA is based on a technique that approximates each coil as a sequence of straight line segments, each connected end-to-end to form a closed polygon in space [6]. Coil data is loaded into BS-SOLCTRA from files. Each SCR-1 coil is represented as a set of (x, y, z) points.

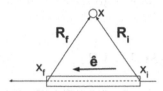

Fig. 3. Filamentary segment contribution to magnetic field

Figure 3 shows a diagram of a single filamentary segment and important measures to model the influence it has on an observation point x. The segment starts at position x_i and finishes at x_f. With this in mind, the length of the segment is defined as $L = |x_f - x_i|$, the unit vector along the segment is $\hat{e} = (x_f - x_i)/L$. $R_{i(f)} = x - x_{i(f)}$ are the vectors from segment end points to the observation point x and $R_{i(f)} = |x - x_{i(f)}|$. The magnetic field is approximated using Eq. 1 [6] and contributions from each segment are then added numerically to obtain the total magnetic field over an observation point.

$$B = \frac{\mu_0 \cdot I}{4\pi} \hat{e} \times R_i \frac{2L(R_i + R_f)}{R_i R_f} \frac{1}{(R_i + R_f)^2 - L^2} \tag{1}$$

A Runge-Kutta fourth order (RK4) algorithm is used to determine the trajectory of each particle under the explained model for the magnetic field. Coil information for the simulation is loaded once during the whole execution. A loop is executed for each particle to get the RK4 calculation like shown in Algorithm 1.

Algorithm 1. Fourth Order Runge-Kutta Algorithm

```
 1: procedure RK4(start_point, num_steps, coils_data)
 2:     P0 ← start_point
 3:     for i ← 0, num_steps do
 4:         K1 ← MAGNETIC_FIELD(P0, coils_data)
 5:         P1 ← K1/2 + P0
 6:         K2 ← MAGNETIC_FIELD(P1, coils_data)
 7:         P2 ← K2/2 + P0
 8:         K3 ← MAGNETIC_FIELD(P2, coils_data)
 9:         P3 ← K3/2 + P0
10:         K4 ← MAGNETIC_FIELD(P3, coils_data)
11:         P0 ← P0 + (K1+2*K2+2*K3+K4)/6
12:         WRITE_TO_FILE(P0)
13:     end for
14: end procedure
```

A divergence criterion is checked every timestep for each particle. Basically, if the new position of the particle is anywhere outside or on the border of the SCR-1 dimensions, the simulation for that particle is finished as the model given in Eq. 1 diverges and behavior is no longer scientifically sound. As a consequence of the Runge-Kutta algorithm, the used magnetic field model, and the number of computations per particle and per timestep that most be solved, BS-SOLCTRA is a CPU-bound application. However, because of the independent nature of the particle trajectories, this code is a great candidate for parallelization on HPC architectures.

3 Accelerating BS-SOLCTRA

The parallelization process and the measurements presented in this section were carried out using Intel's second generation of Xeon Phi processors, the Knights Landing architecture (KNL). Specifically, the KNL model used was the 7210 with 64 cores @ 1.3 GHz and hyper-threading capabilities. Knights Landing is a Many-Integrated Core (MIC) architecture standalone processor in which cores are integrated as couples into structures named tiles. Each tile has a shared 1 MB L2 cache and each core is connected to two vector processing units. This last feature makes vectorization fundamental in exploiting this platform's computational power.

KNL architecture introduced the 512-bit Advanced Vector Extensions (AVX-512). These 512-bit vector instructions provide SIMD support and allow up to eight double-precision multiply-add operations or sixteen single-precision multiply-add operations. Most AVX-512 programming can be done on high-level C/C++ languages through vectorizing compilers and pragmas to guide vectorization. In addition to vectorization support, the traditional hybrid MPI+OpenMP programming is also useful in getting the most out of a KNL cluster.

The following subsections detail the process we followed in order to accelerate BS-SOLCTRA and reduce the time-to-results for the physics team in this plasma fusion project. We used an incremental approach to building a full multinode parallel version of BS-SOLCTRA. All versions of the code were compiled using *gcc 7.2.0*. Different compilation flags were used during the different stages of parallelization. These flags will be specified in every subsection. All experiments have been carried out using a workload of 1024 particles, 500 k simulation steps and a step size of 0.001 m. Each experimental setup was executed 20 times and the arithmetic mean is used to report back results.

3.1 Sequential Profiling

The first step towards transforming BS-SOLCTRA into a parallel simulation framework was locating the main performance bottlenecks in the code. To do so, a profiling study of the code was done using the GNU gprof performance analysis tool, specifically *gprof 2.27-34.base.el7*. GNU gprof is able to measure code that has been instrumented by the compiler. This is done by using the *-pg* flag during the compilation/linking phase.

Sequential execution of BS-SOLCTRA for the input problem size of 1024 particles and 500 k simulation steps took 119.64 h. Profiling results reflected on what was already expected from this code. The amount of time spent in the magnetic field computation from Eq. 1 hoards up the simulation as the number of particles and the simulation steps increases. According to gprof results, the magnetic field computation function represents 99.69% of the execution time in this simulation. All other functions in BS-SOLCTRA are negligible in terms of computing time.

Computing the magnetic field for an observation point using the model explained in Sect. 2.1 is computationally intensive. For a given observation point, the influence of a coil is calculated as the sum of magnetic contributions for each filamentary segment that makes up a coil. For each pair of vectors R_i and R_f that represent the distance from the end-points of a segment of the coil to the observation point, Eq. 1 is used. Furthermore, this needs to be done for all of the twelve coils in the SCR-1. Adding to this, each RK4 iteration calls the magnetic field function four times and RK4 execution depends on the amount of simulation steps. Based on this outlook, the magnetic field function was the first hot spot we needed to address in terms of parallelism.

3.2   Vectorization

Announced as one of KNL's key features, the AVX512 vector operations are crucial to the performance of most of the applications that run on the Knights Landing Architecture [8]. Building on this hardware support, vectorization was the first approach we used to accelerate BS-SOLCTRA. Specifically, we used it to improve the performance of the magnetic field function which is the greatest time consumer in this simulation.

In terms of code, the magnetic field function computes Eq. 1 in phases. As Algorithm 2 shows, for each coil and for all of the x, y, z points that make up a coil (loops in lines 3 and 4), the R_i and R_f vectors for each filamentary segment to the observation point are calculated (loop in line 7). This is done for the three x, y, z components of the vectors. These operations are completely independent so vectorization can be used to compute the vectors simultaneously. Furthermore, computing the actual magnetic field x, y, z components can also be done concurrently as well as the intermediate operations (loop starting in line 12).

Vectorization currently relies on two aspects. First, modern compilers are able to identify loops that can be vectorized. Second, the programmer can explicitly point out vectorizable portions of code by using SIMD language directives. As a first step, we let the compiler figure out what could be vectorized, so a set of compilation flags to enable AVX512 vector and KNL architecture-specific instructions was used (*-ffast-math -march=knl -mavx512f -mavx512pf -mavx512er -mavx512cd*). We added the *-fopt-info-vec-all* flag to determine whether the compiler had automatically managed to vectorize the magnetic field algorithm. Even

---

Algorithm 2. Magnetic Field Function

```
 1: procedure MAGNETIC_FIELD(obs_point, coils_data)                    ▷ Magnetic Field at obs_point
 2:     multiplier ← μ*I/4π
 3:     for i = 0 to TOTAL_OF_COILS do
 4:         for j = 0 to TOTAL_POINTS_COIL do
 5:             final ← End_of_Chunk                          ▷ Total coil points divided into chunks
 6:             #pragma omp simd
 7:             for jj = j to final do
 8:                 Rmi[i].{x,y,z}[jj] ← obs_point.{x,y,z} − coils_data.{x,y,z}[jj]
 9:                 Rmf[i].{x,y,z}[jj] ← obs_point.{x,y,z} − coils_data.{x,y,z}[jj + 1]
10:             end for
11:             #pragma omp simd reduction(Bₓ, Bᵧ, B_z)
12:             for jj = j to final do
13:                 norm_Rmi ← |Rmi|
14:                 norm_Rmf ← |Rmf|
15:                 U.{x,y,z} = multiplier * ê.{x,y,z}                    ▷ Left term of cross product
16:                 C = 2*L*(norm_Rmi+norm_Rmf)/(norm_Rmi*norm_Rmf) * 1/((norm_Rmi+norm_Rmf)²−L²)
17:                 V.{x,y,z} = Rmi[i].{x,y,z}[jj] * C                    ▷ Right term of cross product
18:                 Bₓ = Bₓ + ((U.y * V.z) − (U.z * V.y))                ▷ Cross product component x
19:                 Bᵧ = Bᵧ − ((U.x * V.z) − (U.z * V.x))                ▷ Cross product component y
20:                 B_z = B_z + ((U.x * V.y) − (U.y * V.x))              ▷ Cross product component z
21:             end for
22:         end for
23:     end for
24: end procedure
```

$$multiplier \leftarrow \frac{\mu*I}{4\pi}$$

$$C = \frac{2*L*(norm\_Rmi+norm\_Rmf)}{norm\_Rmi*norm\_Rmf} * \frac{1}{(norm\_Rmi+norm\_Rmf)^2 - L^2}$$

---

though the compiler managed to vectorize some other minor loops in the code, it reported issues due to *unaligned access* on the magnetic field algorithm loops. To solve this, we re-factored the involved memory allocations to use *GNU*'s *aligned_alloc* function. However, for C/C++ arrays, aligning the data is not enough and an __assume_aligned declaration must be used before the loops of interest. In the case of the magnetic field function, this data alignment was applied to the Rmi and Rmf vectors.

As a way to enforce vectorization and ensure the compiler that no further dependencies existed between data in the loops in Algorithm 2, OpenMP SIMD directives were added. SIMD provides data-parallelism so that a single instruction can be applied to multiple data items simultaneously [9]. The OpenMP *SIMD construct* was applied to loops in lines 7 and 12. By performing all of these changes, execution time was reduced from 119.64 h, as reported in the sequential section, to 26,53 h (95,533 s) amounting to a 4.5× gain in performance. *Intel VTune Amplifier 2019* was used to profile this version of the code and a 97% VPU utilization was reported. This proves that vectorization was successfully added to BS-SOLCTRA and that it is a key parallelization technique to exploit the hardware resources of the KNL architecture. The next sections will use the vectorized time result as the performance baseline rather than the pure sequential version.

3.3 Shared-Memory

The next stage in this parellelization effort was taking advantage of the independence of each particle trajectory. As stated in Sect. 2.1, the fourth order

Runge-Kutta algorithm is applied to each of the input particles in the simulation. Each RK4 execution does not depend on the results of other particles so this was a clear candidate for OpenMP parallelization. A simple *for* loop was being executed to iterate over each input particle and within that loop, the RK4 function was called. Algorithm 3 shows the basic execution flow for the simulation. As stated, each iteration of the loop is completely independent so OpenMP threads can be used to concurrently compute various particle trajectories. A simple OpenMP *parallel for* pragma was used to distribute work among shared-memory threads. The *-fopenmp* flag was added to the compiler set of flags, building on the vectorization ones used before. In terms of OpenMP environment variables to control thread behavior, we set the scheduling policy to dynamic (OMP_SCHEDULE=dynamic), we specified that each OpenMP thread should run on a KNL core (OMP_PLACES=cores) and that they should be scattered across all cores(OMP_PROC_BIND=spread). This set up was chosen after trying out different combinations of environment variables and measuring their performance.

Algorithm 3. Run Particles Function

```
 1: procedure RUNPARTICLES(coils_data, particles_data, num_particles, num_steps)
 2:     cartesian A = 0, 0, 0
 3:     #pragma omp parallel for private(A) schedule(runtime)
 4:     for i ← 0, num_particles do
 5:         A.x = particles_data[i]
 6:         A.y = particles_data[i]
 7:         A.z = particles_data[i]
 8:         RK4(A, num_steps, coils_data)
 9:     end for
10: end procedure
```

We performed classic strong scaling experiments to measure the impact of adding threads to the simulation. We measured execution time for the experimental setup explained in the beginning of this section. The number of threads was varied from 1 and up to the maximum number of threads the KNL architecture supports, 256 threads. Figure 4a shows speedup results obtained under this strong scaling single-node scheme. Each point is labeled with the number of threads used for each experiment.

As expected because of the independent nature of the particle trajectories, adding more threads does increase performance. The maximum speedup obtained was 59.8× for 128 threads. However, speedup gains seem to saturate after 64 threads and efficiency diminishes significantly after this point, as Fig. 4b shows. Because of this behavior, using 64 threads per KNL node (1 thread per physical core due to the selected thread affinity) seems to be the best configuration to maximize speedup and resource utilization for this application. This shows that the KNL is able to reach maximum performance with one thread per core [8] in BS-SOLCTRA, thanks to the efficient VPU usage and an appropiate software mapping to the underlying resources.

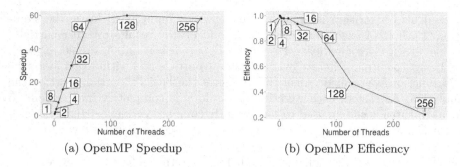

(a) OpenMP Speedup   (b) OpenMP Efficiency

Fig. 4. Strong scaling results for OpenMP BS-SOLCTRA version

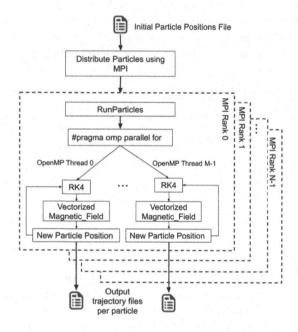

Fig. 5. BS-SOLCTRA parallel implementation and execution flow

3.4   Distributed-Memory

Finally and again building on the independence among particle computations, we added a third level of parallelism through the Message Passing Interface (MPI). In doing so, multiple KNL nodes can be used to accelerate the simulation. We used the *MPICH version 3.2.1* implementation of the MPI standard as it was the one available on the execution platform. Before reaching the loop shown in Algorithm 3, the total amount of particle positions is divided among variable amounts of MPI ranks. We relied on simple MPI_BCAST operations to communicate basic simulation parameters like the number of simulation steps, step sizes and the amount of particles to simulate. The body of particle positions

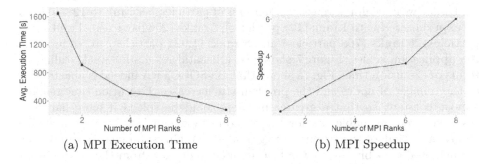

(a) MPI Execution Time   (b) MPI Speedup

Fig. 6. Strong scaling results for MPI+X version

was divided as evenly as possible and distributed through MPI_Scatterv function calls. Each MPI rank is assigned a sub-group of particles to compute and report as Fig. 5 shows.

The final parallel version of BS-SOLCTRA follows the execution flow shown in Fig. 5. Particles are distributed among MPI ranks, each rank then uses a configurable amount of OpenMP threads to concurrently compute the trajectories of its corresponding particles. Each Runge-Kutta step relies on the vectorized magnetic field function shown in Algorithm 2. At the end, each simulated particle produces a trajectory file that can be used to study further physical phenomena.

We performed strong and weak scaling experiments to determine whether this parallel implementation betters simulation performance or not. For strong scaling, we varied the number of MPI ranks from 1 and up to 8. Each rank occupies a whole KNL node and spawns 64 OpenMP threads. This MPI ranks/OpenMP threads ratio configuration was chosen after measuring performance of different scenarios and determining which one provided the best performance-efficiency relation.

Figure 6 shows experimental results for the specified configurations under strong scaling (fixed problem size of 1024 particles). Figure 6a displays how increasing the amount of KNL nodes impacts the execution time of the simulation. Considerable execution time reductions are achieved all the way up to 4 nodes after which performance gains seem to be not as steep as before. This behavior is reflected in Fig. 6b where quasilinear speedup behavior is achieved for the different configurations. This means that adding more KNL nodes does indeed increases performance whilst maintaining a relatively acceptable usage of resources. However, we presume that the observed sub-linear speedup is a result of load imbalance in the simulation. As explained in Sect. 2, certain particles diverge during the simulation before completing all of the simulation steps. This is, some particle trajectories are shorter than others leading to some KNL cores doing much more work than others, thus reducing the total amount of resource utilization. However, at this point, execution time for BS-SOLCTRA and the 1,024 particle problem has been reduced from 119.64 h, for the pure sequential version, to just 4.58 min with the 8 node MPI+X version of the simulator.

Under weak scaling, we set the number of particles per rank to 128. This is, we experimented with 1 rank (128 particles), 2 ranks (256 particles), 4 ranks (512 particles), 6 ranks (768 particles) and 8 ranks (1,024 particles) to see how well the application scales. Figure 7 shows experimental results for weak scaling. In terms of execution time, Fig. 7a shows that BS-SOLCTRA indeed is able to scale as the number of nodes and the problem size increases. Execution time remains almost constant so that a greater problem could be solved if more hardware resources were available. As for the speedup shown in Fig. 7 we see a similar behavior to that of the strong scaling analysis. Again, sub-linear speedup gains are achieved possibly due to the load imbalance derived from the nature of the simulation. This result is rather important because it would be possible to scale the problem greatly and maintain a small execution time if enough hardware resources were available.

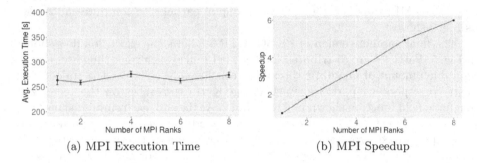

(a) MPI Execution Time   (b) MPI Speedup

Fig. 7. Weak scaling results for MPI+X version

Table 1. Speedup obtained after different parallelization strategies used

Program	Duration (s)	Speedup
C++ Sequential	430,730.00	$1X$
Vectorized version	95,533.30	$4.51X$
OpenMP (64 Threads) + Vectorized	1,671.54	$57.15X$
MPI+X (8 nodes)	274.52	$6.01X$
Total	–	$\approx 1,550\ X$

In summary, through vectorization, threading and distributed processes, execution time for BS-SOLCTRA was reduced by considerable factors. Furthermore, for physicists, the possibility to simulate greater bodies of particles and verify their confinement is now a reality thanks to the parallel nature of the BS-SOLCTRA framework. Table 1 sums up the success of the implemented parallelization strategies used in BS-SOLCTRA. A total speedup of approximately $1,550X$ was achieved through careful vectorization, threading, and load distribution among hardware nodes.

4   Scientific Visualization

Numerical methods allow researchers to test, simulate, and study complex plasma phenomena. As part of the process of turning BS-SOLCTRA into a simulation framework for stellarator devices, scientific visualization capabilities are being added to it. Specifically, as a result of the Runge-Kutta method (RK4) used in this simulator, raw data is obtained which requires some processing so that it can be used as input for the generation of visualizations. These visualizations allow physicists to identify and verify various machine characteristics like coil configurations or magnetic flux surfaces, which are essential to the operation of stellarator devices.

The visualization software selected as the main tool was Paraview 5.6.0 [1] because of its ease of use and the variety of filters that it offers. Additionally, it adapts to the needs of the visualizations required for this research project. Also, the amount of data that needs to be handled for this problem is a manageable volume for the software.

Output data from the BS-SOLCTRA simulation was converted into a Paraview compliant format, usually structured as a table of 500,000 rows with 3 or 4 columns. Three columns are used to represent each point on the x, y, z dimensions and an optional fourth column may represent the magnitude of the magnetic field ($|B|$) that affects a point, as influenced by the coil configuration at execution time. Once the data is entered into the visualization software, filter layers are applied to give a context to the data. In our case, *dataset grouping filters* are applied to unify the different data sources and a final representation of the data as a table is obtained through the *Table to Points* filter.

One of the key aspects that researchers need to understand through simulation is how the magnetic field is shaped throughout the vacuum chamber of an stellarator device. To do so, they normally rely on the visualization of magnetic flux surfaces. These surfaces are produced by the magnetic confinement but they are not visible so diagnostics are added to Stellarators to approximate them. Because of this, a representation called a Poincaré plot can be created with the results of computer simulations to validate and visualize magnetic flux surfaces. Poincaré plots are obtained from planes extracted from a segment of the toroid. They are called poloidal planes, which intersect the confinement chamber of the stellarator in the form of a toroid and are perpendicular to the magnetic axis. A plot consists of several concentric rings, each composed of a finite number of points. To produce these rings, the intersections of a magnetic field line with a poloidal plane are calculated at an arbitrary angle. Figure 8a shows some of the resulting Poincaré plots created through BS-SOLCTRA simulations and the added Paraview tool. Another important aspect for physicists is the creation of animations the enable the analysis of plasma behavior under confinement conditions at a given time. Results of BS-SOLCTRA simulations provide sufficient data to recreate a short time period of the plasma particle trajectories present in the vacuum chamber. For the construction of these particle trajectories animations, collecting a certain amount of particles and their simulation steps is necessary to animate their trajectories. A 8,192 particle simulation is used as

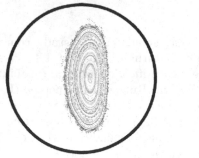 

(a) BS-SOLCTRA Poincaré plot   (b) BS-SOLCTRA animation with 8,192 simulated particles

Fig. 8. Scientific visualizations constructed for BS-SOLCTRA

the basis of the visualization. Each particle trajectory file used is composed by 500,000 simulation steps where each step is an x, y, z position in the space of the simulation.

Subsequently, a data unification procedure, which consists of the union of instants of the simulation, is needed to generate the input data for the visualization software. The process consists of iterating over all particle trajectory files and extracting the points belonging to the same instant of the simulation. For all particle trajectory files, the same line or instant is extracted and written into a new file that represents the instant N, where N is the line number that was taken from the files. As Fig. 8b shows, once all the files were generated they were used as input for the visualization software and the animations of the particles are displayed with their respective confinement trajectory.

5   Related Work

Simulators for plasma fusion physics are not new to the scientific computing community. Several efforts have been carried out to advance research in magnetic confinement devices. A previous attempt to accelerate BS-SOLCTRA was done using Intel's AVX-512 vectorization, threading and MPI [3]. Several optimizations were applied to the core code (AoS to SoA transformations and strip-mining for example). However, because of design choices, parallelism was limited by the number of coils in the SCR-1 which heavily impaired performance gains. Furthermore, Intel's compiler technology was used so the application was also poorly portable.

A similar project to BS-SOLCTRA was developed for the Wendelstein 7-X(W7-X) modular stellarator [2]. A web-service based field line tracer was created for the W7-X that enabled scientists to produce Poincaré plots, construct magnetic coordinates and determine the spectra of error fields. However, this simulator was not optimized for HPC architectures as its focus was on providing the web-service to scientists.

One of the most relevant codes for confinement studies of plasma phenomena is the Variational Moments Equilibrium Code (VMEC)[7]. This code enables scientists to simulate the equilibrium problem found in the physics of magnetic fusion devices through magnetohydrodynamics (MHD). It allows the full 3D nature of stellarators to be studied using a steepest descent method that minimizes the MHD energy functional. VMEC has been parallelized for distributed-shared memory machines using the *Power Fortran Analyzer* and a message passing version obtained through *shmem*[10].

Many other codes have been developed for studying specific phenomena of plasma physics or confinement in Tokamak devices. CORSICA [4], GTS [14], FOCUS [15] are some of the simulation tools in the fusion plasma ecosystem. However, many of these codes are specific to a machine topology or research group and access to these simulators is usually restricted to users of certain clusters or supercomputers.

6   Final Remarks

This paper presented the first steps in turning the BS-SOLCTRA simulator into a full scale parallel simulation framework for stellarator devices. Vectorization through AVX-512, shared-memory threading through OpenMP and distributed-memory parallelism through MPI were the key techniques used to increase simulation performance. All these optimizations were applied using GNU's *gcc* compiler to ensure portability. A final speedup of approximately $1,550X$ was achieved thanks to the parallel implementation. Furthermore, BS-SOLCTRA is capable of scaling successfully and enabling physicists to perform bigger experiments while maintaining a satisfactory execution time. Additionally, new visualization capabilities have been added that help scientists understand and characterize some of the complex phenomena present in magnetic plasma confinement.

Future work for this framework includes increasing software modularity so that different stellarator configurations and topologies can be used as input. Also, new tools are being developed to provide physicists with further understanding of plasma phenomena like the rotational transform, magnetic profiles, magnetic well, and magnetic field error estimation. In terms of visualization, parallel and *in-situ* techniques will be explored to accelerate this process. This work is the cornerstone for a simulation framework that will allow scientists to design, explore, and verify new plasma confinement devices in a high performant computing manner.

Acknowledgments. This research was partially supported by a machine allocation on Kabré supercomputer at the Costa Rica National High Technology Center.

References

1. Ahrens, J., Geveci, B., Law, C.: ParaView: An End-user Tool for Large Data Visualization. Visualization Handbook. Elsevier, Amsterdam (2005)
2. Bozhenkov, S.A., Geiger, J., Grahl, M., Kisslinger, J., Werner, A., Wolf, R.C.: Service oriented architecture for scientific analysis at w7–X. an example of a field line tracer. Fusion Eng. Des. **88**(11), 2997–3006 (2013)
3. Chavarría-Ledezma, L.D.: Parallelization of plasma physics simulations on massively parallel architectures. Unpublished master's thesis, Costa Rica Institute of Technology, School of Computing, Cartago, Costa Rica (2017)
4. Crotinger, J.A., LoDestro, L., Pearlstein, L.D., Tarditi, A., Casper, T., Hooper, E.B.: Corsica: a comprehensive simulation of toroidal magnetic-fusion devices. final report to the LDRD program. Technical report, Lawrence Livermore National Laboratory, CA (United States) (1997)
5. Freidberg, J.P.: Plasma Physics and Fusion Energy. Cambridge University Press, Cambridge (2008)
6. Hanson, J.D., Hirshman, S.P.: Compact expressions for the Biot-Savart fields of a filamentary segment. Phys. Plasmas **9**(10), 4410–4412 (2002)
7. Hirshman, S., Betancourt, O.: Preconditioned descent algorithm for rapid calculations of magnetohydrodynamic equilibria. J. Comput. Phys. **96**(1), 99–109 (1991)
8. Jeffers, J., Reinders, J., Sodani, A.: Intel Xeon Phi Processor High Performance Programming: Knights Landing Edition. Morgan Kaufmann, Burlington (2016)
9. van der Pas, R., Stotzer, E., Terboven, C.: Using OpenMP–The Next Step: Affinity, Accelerators, Tasking, and SIMD. Scientific and Engineering Computation. MIT Press, Cambridge (2017)
10. Romero, L.F., Ortigosa, E.M., Zapata, E.L., Jiménez, J.A.: Parallelization strategies for the VMEC program. In: Kågström, B., Dongarra, J., Elmroth, E., Waśniewski, J. (eds.) PARA 1998. LNCS, vol. 1541, pp. 483–490. Springer, Heidelberg (1998). https://doi.org/10.1007/BFb0095372
11. Solano-Piedra, R., et al.: Overview of the SCR-1 stellarator, March 2017. https://nucleus.iaea.org/sites/fusionportal/SharedDocuments/RUSFD23th/Pres/31.03/Solano-Piedra.pdf
12. Vargas, V., et al.: Implementation of stellarator of Costa Rica 1 SCR-1. In: 2015 IEEE 26th Symposium on Fusion Engineering (SOFE), pp. 1–6. IEEE (2015)
13. Wakatani, M.: Stellarator and Heliotron Devices. Oxford University Press, Oxford (1998)
14. Wang, W., et al.: Gyro-kinetic simulation of global turbulent transport properties in tokamak experiments. Phys. Plasmas **13**(9), 092505 (2006)
15. Zhu, C., Hudson, S.R., Song, Y., Wan, Y.: New method to design stellarator coils without the winding surface. Nucl. Fusion **58**(1), 016008 (2017)

Optimizing Big Data Network Transfers in FPGA SoC Clusters: TECBrain Case Study

Luis G. León-Vega[1(✉)], Kaleb Alfaro-Badilla[1(✉)],
Alfonso Chacón-Rodríguez[1(✉)], and Carlos Salazar-García[2(✉)]

[1] Escuela de Ingeniería Electrónica, Tecnológico de Costa Rica, Cartago, Costa Rica
{lleon95,jaalfaro}@estudiantec.cr, alchacon@tec.ac.cr
[2] Área Académica de Ingeniería Mecatrónica, Tecnológico de Costa Rica,
Cartago, Costa Rica
csalazar@tec.ac.cr

Abstract. Spiking Neural Network (SSN) simulators based on clusters of FPGA-based System-on-Chip (SoC) involve the transmission of large amounts of data (from hundreds of MB to tens of GB per second) from and to a data host, usually a PC or a server. TECBrain is an SNN simulator which currently uses Ethernet for transmitting results from its simulations, which can potentially take hours if the effective connection speed is around 100 Mbps. This paper proposes data transfer techniques that optimize data transmissions by grouping data into packages making the most of the payload size and the use of thread-level parallelism, trying to minimize the impact of multiple clients transmitting at the same time. The proposed method achieves its highest throughput when inserting simulation results directly into a No-SQL database.

Using the proposed optimization techniques over an Ethernet connection, the minimum overhead reached is 2.93% (out of the theoretical 2.47%) for five nodes sending data simultaneously from C++, with speeds up to 95 Mbps on a network at 100 Mbps. Besides, the maximum database insertion speed reached is 32.5 MB/s, using large packages and parallelism, which is 26% of the bandwidth of the connection link at 1 Gbps.

Keywords: High perfomance computing · No-SQL · High-speed networks · Embedded software

1 Introduction

The typical approach to create supercomputers is by clustering servers [18], trying to exploit modern processors in parallel, with Instruction Set Architectures (ISA) that include instructions for complex data manipulation and computation. However, there are alternative techniques for particular niche application-specific supercomputers, which use Field-programmable Gate Arrays (FPGA)

J. L. Crespo-Mariño and E. Meneses-Rojas (Eds.): CARLA 2019, CCIS 1087, pp. 49–62, 2020.
https://doi.org/10.1007/978-3-030-41005-6_4

[3], heterogeneous Systems-on-Chips and Graphics Unit Processors (GPU) [10] as cluster nodes.

Clusters based on GPUs and FPGAs are becoming more popular in High-Performance Computing (HPC) as they are more efficient in terms of computations per unit of power (given in GFLOPs/Watt) than standard server clusters [7] [9]. And in terms of computation performance per unit of power, FPGAs take the lead over GPU-based servers. Recent comparisons point that, for instance, while NVidia Jetson boards have a typical performance of around 50 GFLOPs/watt [14] for a particular application, a Xilinx Kintex-7 FPGA can perform under the same specifications at 70 GFLOPs/watt [9].

The intrinsic parallelism capability and logic flexibility of FGPAs arguably allow for the more efficient tackling of complex problems involving large amounts of data [20]. This would lead to better results against traditional CPU and GPU approaches, when developing application-specific clusters. Furthermore, the reconfigurability of FPGAs offers the possibility of having, for instance, an heterogeneous SoC FPGA based board in which the main processor is coupled with a flexible accelerator residing on the fabric; such accelerator may be reconfigured on-the-fly depending on the specific requirements of the models being executed, adapting it to its optimal conditions.

These considerations are at the base of TECBrain, a biologically accurate neural network hardware accelerated simulator developed by Instituto Tecnologico de Costa Rica (see [2]). Using FPGA based heterogeneous boards as cluster node technology, makes the simulator capable of running multiple models by simply reconfiguring the hardware accelerators that best fits the simulation model running on the SoC cores. And as the simulated network grows in size, it can be partitioned among several similar nodes. One major bottleneck, nonetheless, quickly surfaces as simulation results need to be taken from the cluster and sent for storage and analysis in another platform with visualization capabilities (typically a PC). In the case of TECBrain, an initial approach was storing the simulation results into an SD card; this, of course, severely impacts efficiency as a class 10 SD Card can achieve up to 10 MB/s in transmission speed, with the added limitation in data size handling for larger simulations.

Now, considering that in the case of TECBrain it is possible to simulate up to 8000 eHH neurons in a cluster composed of four Zedboards (see [2,21]), and the voltage values are represented by Floating-Point numbers, each simulation step consumes 31.25 kB according to [21]. For 10000 simulation steps, the entire results file needs 2.98 GB of space. Additionally, the simulator is intended to be available online, which means that the results have to be available to the users through the Internet. Retrieving all results from a master node will take some time and fragmenting the data for their visualization is laborious. After discarding the storing data into an SD Card, TECBrain now uses 1 Gbps Ethernet for communication with the data server, streaming each result as soon as it is ready to be sent. However, the effective transmission speed is currently less than 30% of the channel capacity, leading to high latency and the increase of the total simulation time.

Other SNN simulators have faced the same problem with transmission through Ethernet, reporting bottlenecks when transmitting results. *SpiNNaker*, for instance, a SNN simulator, which utilizes 864 ARM processors as computing units embedded in several customized SoCs [8]. The stimulus data and results are transferred through 100 Mbps Ethernet. The authors highlight that this connection is the primary bottleneck in the system, which they propose solving by using an FPGA-based Gigabit Ethernet bridge. Another case reported in [16] for a radar application with multiple devices sending data simultaneously, uses a 1 Gbps Ethernet link, achieving a maximum transference speed of 500 Mbps by means of an Ethernet controller implemented into an FPGA. They report a two times gain in speed by moving the Ethernet control from the CPU to FPGA.

Another existing bottleneck TECBrain is the insertion time taken when writing results. The storage of results is based on MongoDB, which is a No-SQL database. A Mongo database was initially selected for TECBrain because of emerging popularity of No-SQL databases for remote data logging, due to their reported higher capability for managing larger amounts of data [13]. Specifically, the superiority of No-SQL databases in Create, Read, Update, and Delete (CRUD) operations are reported in [19], where after evaluating SQL against No-SQL databases, results show that in terms of CRUD operations, insertion times for MySQL (SQL) take 14.69 times more than in MongoDB (No-SQL). Nonetheless, using MongoDB results in a restriction in the number of data written per document (16 MB per document according to [15]). Consequently, the current database scheme must be redesigned in order to be suitable for storing a many data.

This paper proposes an optimized method for data transmission to a database server for the storage of simulation data, and its subsequent retrieval for analysis and display via a web server. The method is founded on the evaluation of network transmission speed, the total delivery time of result packages, latency inside the server and communication degradation when the server receives data from multiple master nodes simultaneously, incorporating as well the analysis of database insertion time when there are single or multiple operations on the database, gaining up to 3.24 times in results transmission and 1022.7 times in database insertion time.

This document starts with Sect. 2, describing the current design used in the project and also the considerations for improving it. Then, Sect. 3 describes the two back-end frameworks considered for the project data server, emphasizing on their features and libraries available for connecting to databases. Section 4 shows the results after evaluating each architecture by using different results package sizes and a different number of clients transmitting results to the data server, demonstrating the superiority of C++ over NodeJS for handling data reception and the communication throughput in each experiment case. Section 5 presents a data schema proposal for expanding the storage capability by selecting a proper data representation and using data pagination. Also, it shows the performance of MongoDB while inserting data from a single and multiple threads, leading to a proposal for maximizing the data insertion throughput. Finally,

Sect. 6 summarizes the results obtained after studying the back-end technologies and MongoDB data insertion.

2   Design Considerations

TECBrain currently implements several biologically accurate SNN models on a cluster of Zedboards, with the main portion of the algorithms running on the Zedboard's Zynq Z7020 SoC cores (called the PS in Xilinx's lingo), with a DMA AXI-Stream interface to the SoC FPGA fabric, called the PL, from Programmable Logic, in Xilinx's lingo (see Fig. 1). Data is transferred to the hardware accelerators in the fabric as required, avoiding unneeded extensive memory transfers while the simulation is running (as explained in [1,2]). This strategy reduces communication overhead during execution on the fabric. Each Zedboard is interconnected through a 1 Gbps Ethernet switch using the TCP-IP protocol, with the SoC cores in charge of the protocols for loading and retrieving data from each node, and the whole cluster being managed using MPI. Using such interconnection approach for the simulation process of course comes with the inherent limitations of TCP-IP Ethernet for the final goal of TECBrain: real brain time simulation of a sizable amount of cells (at least 100, implying time steps in the order of 50 µs to 1 ms depending on the use of white box or black box neural cell models [2]), and fast simulations for SNN populations of 1000 and more. This situation, nonetheless, is not the main focus of this paper and is to be handled elsewhere. Anyway, in the case of final results' handling for display and offline analysis, where such timing restrictions are not applicable, TCP-IP Ethernet would still be the best I/O scheme for TECBrain for it flexibility and ease of integration with existing database architectures.

Regarding results' data handling, TECBrain currently uses a back-end framework entirely based on NodeJS. Under this framework, the master node streams each input/output datum as it is produced by the simulator, in order to avoid local storage of data. This, under the current interconnect architecture, interferes to top it all with simulation data exchange among the boards, subtracting from the available bandwidth for the simulation itself. This results in longer simulation and transmission times than those expected, taking up to one minute in a simulation with 1000 eHH neurons and 10000 steps, which involves 40 MB of data. This was observed after finishing the simulation. The application still keeps sending data even when the OLED showed that the simulation was completed. Hence, as already mentioned, an alternative interconnect strategy is currently being designed for the cluster, to improve data sharing bandwidth. But even after this is carried out, the communication of the simulator with the server for final data storage, display and analysis keeps being a challenge requiring a transmission scheme with low latency.

It is also crucial to check the use of CRUD operations by the database in order to avoid possible asynchronous bottlenecks while writing or retrieving results. TECBrain currently writes the results by appending them to a array in a single document in double precision floating-point format. This technique has two major negative consequences: first, more CRUD transactions; and, second,

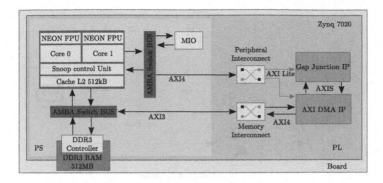

Fig. 1. Current heterogenous SoC architecture to simulate SNN with eHH model. The main portion of the algorithms runs on the Zynq Z7020 ARM-A9 cores, and the SoC FPGA fabric executes the electrical synapses of each neuron.

wasted space because of the use of double precision floating-point representation. Therefore, an exploration aimed at minimizing the number of queries to the database is also pertinent.

Nevertheless, the key issue for effectively joining database and network resides in the server application. It must allow multiple connections with low resources consumption. A potential communication bottleneck is the writing of results, where the database middleware is supposed to introduce minimum overhead to the streaming.

3 Server Back-End Architectures Under Study

There are two possible approaches for selecting the server back-end framework: first, focusing on performance and basing it all on C/C++ language; and, second, considering languages typically used for heavy load traffic, such as NodeJS.

Both C++ and NodeJS have libraries (called middlewares in the case of NodeJS) which provide MongoDB connectivity. In case of C++, MongoDB developers have MongoCXX for C++ [4], while Mongoose exists for NodeJS [17]. In order to measure each architecture's performance and their network throughput, a particular scheme is set up, as outlined in Fig. 2, according to the ultimate purposes of this work (all the measurements are referred to TCP sockets, because of TCP's reliability in error and flow control).

NodeJS is a Web server back-end framework that uses Javascript, with non-blocking instead of thread-based execution, which should perform better at handling network instructions [17]. Now, though Javascript execution is single-threaded, it is also capable of managing events, making thus the most of multi-core platforms. This feature allows for simultaneous file reading, database querying and HTTP requests handling, without the need for explicit use of threading structures in the code. This is possible because NodeJS can use the `libuv` library, that focuses on asynchronous I/O and just-in-time execution [11]. The NodeJS

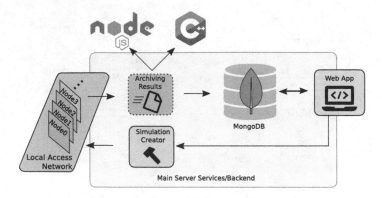

Fig. 2. Current TECBrain architecture for communicating the simulator FPGA-based nodes with the user website. The back-end is in charge of performing the archiving of results and preparing the nodes for the simulation of a determined model. One of the points to evaluate is whether to use NodeJS or C++ for implementing the nearer modules to the nodes.

developers emphasize its enhanced networking capability, which according to them is even better than alternatives such as PHP. However, being NodeJS is interpreted, it is inherently inferior in performance than compiled language such as C++ [6].

For this paper, throughput measurements were carried out based on the back-end architecture presented in Fig. 3a. In the particular case of NodeJS, the architecture has events linked to each client, which local variables that monitor the last time (t_{i-1}) and verify the buffer length (l) in order to calculate the data transfer speed in bytes per nanosecond, avoiding thus the need to load each computational event. Each result is appended to a results list which is then written in a file with all results for offline analysis.

The C++ based server back-end behaves similarly to the NodeJS back-end. The main difference relies on how clients are managed. For this particular case, when a new client connects, a new thread (using the `pthread` library), is created for data reception from the connected node. Inside the thread, there is a `blocking` read function which is timed before and after its execution, using a `chrono` high-resolution timer. Measurement includes the time when the system is ready to read new data up until data is completely read. The Δt taken for reading the incoming data is logged into an array.

All client nodes (running on a Zedboard), on the other hand, are written in C++, single-threaded. Figures 3b shows the flow diagram of package handling by the clients.

4   Network Performance of NodeJS and C++

IEEE 802.3 specifies the standard for defining the Ethernet frame size and its binary assignment [12], illustrated in Fig. 4. The Ethernet frame has different

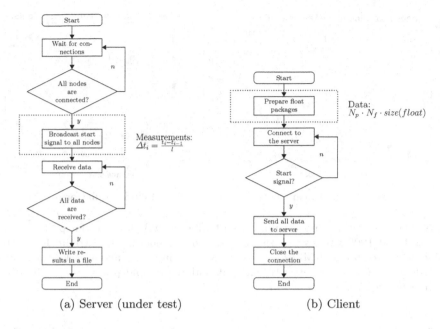

(a) Server (under test)   (b) Client

Fig. 3. Basic scheme used for measuring network throughput. All the clients send data to the server and they are based on C++ because of its compiled nature and performance. The server, instead, is based on either NodeJS and C++, the candidates for the back-end architecture.

control bytes, which makes its size variable depending on the connection maximum speed. Considering the best scenario (a frame of 1538 bytes), the minimum overhead achievable is 2.47%, with 4.15% being the worst case as indicated by [12].

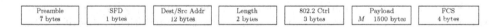

Fig. 4. Ethernet package frame. The control uses between 29-38 bits and the payload uses 1500 for transmitting data. Based on [12].

For measuring the network performance of each basic architecture, five client nodes are run on a small C++ client program, which sends an adjustable number of packages N_p with N_f number of floats each.

For a complete analysis, the C++ clients were made to process packages with sizes between one to 1000 **floats** (four bytes), from three, four and five client nodes, all simultaneously sending data. All the nodes were synchronized by the server program, whether C++ or NodeJS. Servers were run a on personal computer with a Core i7 processor, and with some residual network traffic consumption on a link at 100 Mbps.

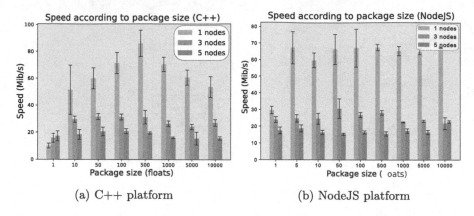

(a) C++ platform   (b) NodeJS platform

Fig. 5. Network speed comparison between both back-end platforms for package sizes between 1 and 1000 `floats`, for three, four and five nodes. The current TECBrain version is able to run at 30 Mbps with NodeJS. Choosing C++ and a package size near the payload size leads to a better throughput, with throughput peaks up to 97.07 Mbps (upper black whisker at 500 floats).

Figure 5a shows that the optimal package size for the current TECBrain Ethernet TCP-IP is around 500 `floats` (2000 bytes). This is naturally close to the optimal payload of the Ethernet protocol [12], 375 floats. After that point, the protocol splits bigger packages and send them separately, leading to expected slower results given that one of the packages has the maximum capacity of the protocol and the other will be smaller than it. In terms of peer-to-peer transmission, the average overhead impact was 13.98%, possibly caused by the package splitting, because at $N_f = 500$, the received/sent package ratio is 1.45, which means that for one package, the server received 1.45 packages (two in average). For three nodes, the minimum overhead reached is 6.70% and for five nodes is 2.93%; both at the same package size point ($N_f = 500$). This means that the C++ architecture is capable of handling at maximum capacity the Ethernet protocol, adding low overhead to the clients, near the theoretical value of 2.47%.

Figure 5b shows the network performance results for NodeJS under the same test. One of the notorious changes is that different N_f values do not affect the performance significantly for $N_f > 5$, as the transfers' throughput keeps on average at 70 Mbps. This means that the event-based data receiver tries to make groups of data. NodeJS is supposed to have a better performance managing data compared to thread-based platforms. Comparing it against a the C++ based server, at $N_f = 500$, NodeJS shows a received/sent package ratio up to 0.9928, which means that data is received in just one transfer.

However, as seen from the evaluation, NodeJS is introducing a higher overhead than C++. At $N_f = 10000$, NodeJS only achieves a maximum transfer speed of 78.59 Mbps, well under the average speed for C++. It results in an overhead 5.16 times greater than C++.

5   MongoDB Performance on NodeJS and C++

MongoDB developers use a special library for communication with C++, called MongoCXX. This library is used to build Binary Javascript Object Notation (BSON) objects and provides the methods to interact with them using C++. On the other hand, NodeJS uses Mongoose, a middleware for communicating with MongoDB. MongoDB is more oriented to NodeJS due to its data handling approach, based on BSON [17]. To measure the dfferences of performance between NodeJS and C++, a test program was used to write floating-point data array into the MongoDB database.

5.1   Proposed Database Scheme

By default, BSON data has a maximum size of 16MB, established by MongoDB's architecture [15]. This limits the maximum storage. In terms of the TECBrain application in particular, only 2,000,000 steps per each neuron can be stored, in double precision floating-point representation This also entails that only 2,285,714 neurons can be simulated, a each neuron ID occupies seven bytes [15].

By default, MongoDB uses 8-byte double precision floating-point representation for representing fractional numbers in BSON, whcrcas TECBrain uses single 4-byte precision floating-point to represent its inputs and outputs. Trying to save TECBrain data directly into the database leads to representing a number in more precision than it comes. Ilence, an enhancement to make the most of the database storage is to save the data keeping the original resolution, using a raw format instead of as numbers.

Still, larger simulations typically require 4,000,000 and more steps to be stored. For example, for $\Delta t = 50\,\mu s$, this represents a simulation of only 200 seconds (3.33 min) To overcome the limitations both in the number of simulation steps and neural cells, TECBrain uses a page indexing strategy, depicted in Fig. 6.

Using this pagination approach, the new limits are now : 2,285,700 × 4,000,000 ≈ 9.143 ×10^{12} simulation steps per each neuron, with 2,285,700 × 2,285,700 ≈ 5.224 ×10^{12} neurons per simulation.

A dedicated server is used for querying data and decoding it from the database, when loading a simulation. Each page requires up to 16 MB of RAM, which means that it is possible to load 64 pages (256M steps per neuron or 146.28M neurons with one step) with 1 GB of RAM. This poses a challenge for the back-end framework with an evident trade-off between storage capability and computation power required for loading and displaying data in the website, as RAM memory usage in a web browser impacts the client speed.

To avoid this, results are compressed before being transmitted, with the real quantity of data sent being adjusted as required by the number of points to be plotted in the webpage.

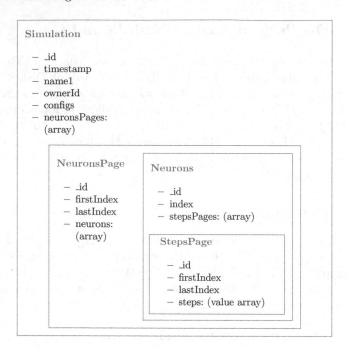

Fig. 6. MongoDB schema proposed by this research

5.2   MongoCXX Performance

Given thus that C++ has shown to more efficient than NodeJS in terms of data reception added overhead, it follows that an evaluation of the impact of inserting data into MongoDB using the C++ MongoCXX library instead of NodeJS is the next step.

Measurements were carried out for the writing of a floating-point array with different lengths. Multiple writing threads were used, in order to check whether there are length related improvements, and how good is the management in writing speed. Both results are presented in Fig. 7.

Figure 7a shows the impact on the writing speed of varying the inserted array size, following two possible techniques: first, inserting directly the array as raw data and, second, inserting each element using a loop with C++ lambdas, as documented in the MongoCXX API [4]. In both cases, it is taken into account the casting and the insertion times from float to either bytes or doubles.

As well as it was seen in the network transmission evaluation, the package size influences the writing speed to the database. When the package is larger, faster is the write speed. It makes possible then to join the network receptor directly to the MongoCXX insertion process without making it granular or decompose data to insert them piece-per-piece. Furthermore, the results illustrate that inserting raw data results in a better throughput compared to using lambda as the MongoCXX documentation suggests. Therefore, it is possible to perform the regis-

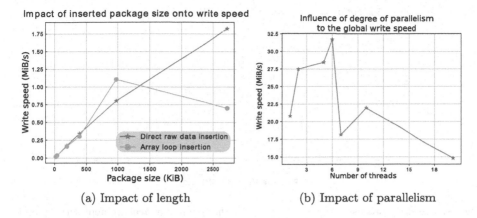

(a) Impact of length   (b) Impact of parallelism

Fig. 7. Impact of length and number of threads on the insertion write speed. By using larger packages and multiple insertion threads lead to better writing speeds compared to performing single-threaded insertions.

tration of the results in two possible ways: first, insert the data as they come, although this technique leads to wasted throughput; second, capture the data into a buffer and register them as soon as it is full, which prepares the data until it has an optimal size to be inserted.

The main reason to evade the iterative insertion using C++ lambdas is due to the loop overhead, whereas inserting the raw data directly avoids loops and makes the most of each write transaction in the server secondary storage. Changing the package size enhances the insertion speed is 82.7 times by using a package size of 3 MB, where the minimum achieved by inserting a 15 kB package is 0.0278 kB/s and the maximum at 3 MB is 2.28 MB/s.

Figure 7b shows the impact of the thread-level parallelism factor on the write speed given a package size of 13.35 MB (near the 16 MB limit). Using multiple threads and large package size for writing results in a speedup of 1022.7 times for insertions. It also is possible to see that there is an optimum number of writing threads, where the global speed (the total data are written per second) is maximum, located near to six threads. After that point, the writing speed decays (57.22% for seven threads). This phenomenon may vary depending on the platform and it must be studied before implementing the desired parallelism.

On the other hand, it is possible to see how the parallelism impacts on each thread. Figure 8 depicts the writing process for 20 threads. The average writing time takes around 5 seconds for every thread, thus improving insertion throughput to the MongoDB server. Notice again however the performance decay when running seven threads, as shown in Fig. 7b. Here, the writing process of the 7th thread has a delay of around 1 s, which suggests the reason for this throughput degradation.

In general, data buffering, and parallelization lead to the highest insertion throughput when using C++ and MongoDB with MongoCXX. It is recommended to consider for future implementations the data loading process, since

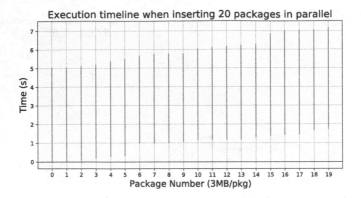

Fig. 8. Insertion processes represented during the time. The measurement script simultaneously sends 20 packages, 3 MB each. Each insertion process has a similar execution time (five seconds), and that boosts the writing speed

at the current version of the database, MongoDB aggregation and filtering capabilities are not used, which can lead to more RAM consumption (see [5]).

6   Conclusions

This study has shown potential optimizations for data transmission and insertion into a database for the TECBrain simulator, making the most of parallelism and the Ethernet protocol. Clearly, data package sizing for Ethernet transmission is a major factor that can maximize the impact of the protocol overhead on the global speed of the transmission.

NodeJS has be shown to be efficient in its treatment of data packages, getting an almost stable reception speed for most of the data package sizes analyzed by this paper. However, NodeJS' interpreted nature limits its maximum speed, degrading the maximum speed by more than 20%, whereas C++ reached more than 95% of the maximum speed achievable, leading to C++ as the best option for the clients' communication side of the back-end, minimizing the overhead impact to 2.93% (from a theoretical 2.47%).

On the other hand, MongoDB performed at a good throughput when the insertion task is split into different threads and package sizes close to the the BSON limit, achieving 32.5 MB/s. This leads to a speed up of 1022.7 times contrasted to 28.42 kB/s achieved by inserting 15 KB of data. Comparing network speeds, it is 2.6 times the transmission speed at 100 Mbps and 26% the transmission speed at 1 Gbps Hence, to make the most of MongoDB, buffering data is highly recommended during data transmission.

This work provides the basis for improving the TECBrain connection system and back-end framework, indicating the way to make the most of the optimal points of the Ethernet protocol and MongoDB server.

At the server client side, the MongoDB thread decay has to be studied in order to determine the optimal number of insertion threads to make the most of the MongoDB service in order to get the highest throughput possible. Besides, the data acquisition side of the back-end has to be studied and analyzed in detail in order to minimize the impact of results' pagination, exploiting alternatives such as caching in both on the web browser and on the server side.

On the other hand, it becomes mandatory to contrast Ethernet against other alternatives, such as PCI-e and custom-made connections, which may have less overhead and better throughput compared to this protocol.

References

1. Alfaro-Badilla, K., et al.: Improving the simulation of biologically accurate neural networks using data flow HLS transformations on heterogeneous SoC-FPGA platforms. In: CARLA 2019 - Latin America High Performance Computing Conference, September 2019
2. Alfaro-Badilla, K., et al.: Prototyping a biologically plausible neuron model on a heterogeneous CPU-FPGA board. In: 2019 IEEE 10th Latin American Symposium on Circuits Systems (LASCAS), pp. 5–8, February 2019. https://doi.org/10.1109/LASCAS.2019.8667538
3. Altera: White paper accelerating high-performance computing with FPGAs. Cluster Computing, pp. 1–8 (2007). https://www.intel.com/content/dam/www/programmable/us/en/pdfs/literature/wp/wp-01029.pdf. Accessed 04 April 2019
4. Arnst, D., Plenk, V., Adrian, W.: Comparative evaluation of database performance in an Internet of Things context comparative evaluation of database performance in an Internet of Things context. In: ICSNC 2018, vol. 13, pp. 45–50, October (2018)
5. Chodorow, K.: MongoDB: The Definitive Guide: Powerful and Scalable Data Storage. O'Reilly Media Inc., Sebastopol (2013)
6. Cramer, T., Friedman, R., Miller, T., Seberger, D., Wilson, R., Wolczko, M.: Compiling Java just in time. IEEE Micro **17**(3), 36–43 (1997). https://doi.org/10.1109/40.591653
7. Dong, T., Dobrev, V., Kolev, T., Rieben, R., Tomov, S., Dongarra, J.: A step towards energy efficient computing: redesigning a hydrodynamic application on CPU-GPU, pp. 972–981, May 2014. https://doi.org/10.1109/IPDPS.2014.103
8. Furber, S.B., Galluppi, F., Temple, S., Plana, L.A.: The spiNNaker project. Proc. IEEE **102**(5), 652–665 (2014). https://doi.org/10.1109/JPROC.2014.2304638
9. Hamada, T., Benkrid, K., Nitadori, K., Taiji, M.: A comparative study on ASIC, FPGAs, GPUs and general purpose processors in the O(N 2) gravitational N-body simulation. In: Proceedings - 2009 NASA/ESA Conference on Adaptive Hardware and Systems (AHS 2009), pp. 447–452 (2009). https://doi.org/10.1109/AHS.2009.55
10. Hsieh, C.W., Chou, C.Y., Tsai, T.C., Cheng, Y.F., Kuo, S.H.: NCHC's Formosa v GPU cluster enters the TOP500 ranking. In: 2012 Proceedings of 4th IEEE International Conference on Cloud Computing Technology and Science (CloudCom 2012), pp. 622–624 (2012). https://doi.org/10.1109/CloudCom.2012.6427507
11. Huang, J., Cai, L.: Research on TCP/IP network communication based on Node.js. In: AIP Conference Proceedings, vol. 1955, issue 1, pp. 040115 (2018). https://doi.org/10.1063/1.5033779. https://aip.scitation.org/doi/abs/10.1063/1.5033779

12. IEEE: IEEE Standard for Ethernet. IEEE Std 802.3-2018, (Revision of IEEE Std 802.3-2015), pp. 1–5600, August 2018. https://doi.org/10.1109/IEEESTD.2018.8457469.
13. Li, C., Yang, W.: The distributed storage strategy research of remote sensing image based on Mongo DB. In: The 3rd International Workshop on Earth Observation and Remote Sensing Applications (EORSA 2014) - (41271390), pp. 101–104 (2014). https://doi.org/10.1109/EORSA.2014.6927858
14. Milluzzi, A., George, A., Lam, H.: Computational and memory analysis of Tegra SoCs. In: 2016 IEEE High Performance Extreme Computing Conference (HPEC 2016), issue (1), pp. 1–7 (2016). https://doi.org/10.1109/HPEC.2016.7761602
15. MongoDB: MongoDB Limits and Thresholds. https://docs.mongodb.com/manual/reference/limits/. Accessed 14 April 2019
16. Rojas, J., Verastegui, J., Milla, M.: Design and implementation of a high speed interface system over Gigabit Ethernet based on FPGA for use on radar acquisition systems. In: Proceedings of the 2017 Electronic Congress (E-CON UNI 2017) (2018). https://doi.org/10.1109/ECON.2017.8247311
17. Satheesh, M., D'mello, B.J., Krol, J.: Web Development with MongoDB and NodeJS. Packt Publishing Ltd., Birmingham (2015)
18. Szebenyi, Z.: Capturing Parallel Performance Dynamics. Forschungszentrum Jülich, Jülich (2012). http://hdl.handle.net/2128/4603
19. Truica, C.O., Radulescu, F., Boicea, A., Bucur, I.: Performance evaluation for CRUD operations in asynchronously replicated document oriented database. In: Proceedings - 2015 20th International Conference on Control Systems and Computer Science (CSCS 2015), pp. 191–196 (2015). https://doi.org/10.1109/CSCS.2015.32
20. Xilinx, Inc.: Xilinx WP375 high performance computing using FPGAs. White Pap. **375**, 1–15 (2010). https://www.xilinx.com/support/documentation/white_papers/wp375_HPC_Using_FPGAs.pdf
21. Zamora-Umaña, D.: Desarrollo y validación de un método para la visualización de resultados en la implementación del algoritmo de simulación de redes neuronales. Bachelor's thesis, Instituto Tecnológico de Costa Rica, Escuela de Ingeniería Electrónica, December 2017

Regular Track on High Performance Computing: Algorithms and Models

A Load Balancing Algorithm for Fog Computing Environments

Eder Pereira[1]($\boxtimes$), Ivânia A. Fischer[1], Roseclea D. Medina[1],
Emmanuell D. Carreno[2], and Edson Luiz Padoin[3]

[1] Federal University of Santa Maria (UFSM), Grupo de Redes e Computação
Aplicada (Greca), Santa Maria, RS, Brazil
{epereira,roseclea}@inf.ufsm.br, ivaniafischer@redes.ufsm.br
[2] Department of Computer Science, Universidade Federal do Paraná (UFPR),
Curitiba, PR, Brazil
ediazc@gmail.com
[3] Department of Exact Sciences and Engineering, Regional University
of the Northwest of the State of Rio Grande do Sul – (UNIJUI), Ijuí, RS, Brazil
padoin@unijui.edu.br

Abstract. Fog Computing is characterized as an intermediate layer
between the Internet of Things layer and the Cloud Computing layer,
which pre-processes information closer to the sensors. However, given
the increasing demand for numerous IoT applications, even when close to
the sensors, Fog nodes tend to be overloaded, compromising the response
times of IoT applications that have latency restrictions, and consequently
compromising users' quality experience too. In this work, we investigated
ways to mitigate this problem in order to keep Fog Computing with a
homogeneous distribution of load, even in heterogeneous environments,
through the distribution of tasks among several computational nodes
that compose Fog Computing, performing a dynamic load balancing in
real time. For this, an algorithm model is presented, which takes into
account the dynamics and heterogeneity of the computational nodes
of Fog Computing, which allocates the tasks to the most appropriate
node according to the policies predefined by the network administrator.
Results show that in the proposed work the homogeneous distribution of
tasks was achieved between the Fog nodes, and there was a decrease in
response times when compared to other proposed solution.

Keywords: Fog Computing · Load balancer · Internet of Things ·
Internet of Everything

1 Introduction

The extensive growth of IoT applications in a wide range of domains has required
a latent demand for solutions that seek to reduce common problems in this environment, such as the massive bandwidth usage and time-consuming response

© Springer Nature Switzerland AG 2020
J. L. Crespo-Mariño and E. Meneses-Rojas (Eds.): CARLA 2019, CCIS 1087, pp. 65–77, 2020.
https://doi.org/10.1007/978-3-030-41005-6_5

times. Fog Computing (FC) is the technology currently designated as the promising technology that provides support for improvements in IoT systems, like response time and network usage performance indexes, that makes a Cloud Computing extension to the edge network [3]. These resources are available in routers, access points and other types of equipment [15], each composing a Fog Node, that provides compute, storage and network services for IoT applications on a virtualized and distributed platform [13]. That is, FC provides distributed resources with greater proximity of users, and consequently, with lower response times, and lower network bandwidth usage, since it is near of the sensors.

Despite this, it is necessary to know that an FC may not be able to meet all the needs of the environment in general, since the number of IoT sensors and applications will reach levels of billions of connected intelligent things, generating and consuming information [1]. Therefore, nothing prevents the FC from overloading, compromising the performance of the system as a whole, thus, the scalability must be a native feature of the Fog Computing [5]. Added to this is the fact to that, some IoT applications can have time-restrict tasks, that needs quick communication, and priority is not the focus of the FC, so, it does not deal with this concerns. Then, the priority-based load balancing technique aims at the best distribution of load between the processors on the systems and aims to improve the performance of such applications [4,10,12].

This article proposes the use of a priority-based load balancer (LB), that is located between the nodes of the FC that employs management methods and creates a holistic view of the infrastructure, which collects detailed information about the computational resources that are available to it. The LB has knowledge of the workload of the FC nodes for any application of balancing policies, as well the priority level of the task coming from the sensors, which was previously defined by the network administrator.

Thus, in this work, a new architecture of IoT environments is proposed and validated, which adopts the proposed algorithm that are priority-based, and therefore, such architecture presents an additional layer defined with LB, whose purpose is to mitigate the load unbalance between the nodes of FC. The LB allocates tasks based on the execution priority and isolates those nodes from the FC that are faulted or overloaded, hiding these issues from the clients on the environment. These factors are achieved by using a load-balancing algorithm where system-ranking policies are created.

The remaining sections of this paper are organized as follows. Section 2 discuss the basic topics that are covered in this work. Section 3 discusses some of the related works on Fog Computing and Load Balancing. The main concepts of our proposed load balancer (SMARTFOGLB), as well as its implementation details, are discussed in Sect. 4. In Sect. 5 we present the evaluation methodology used in the conducted experiments. In Sect. 6 we address the results obtained from the experiments. Finally, the Sect. 7 emphasizes the scientific contribution of the work and notes several challenges that we can address in the future.

2   Theoretical Reference

2.1   Internet of Things

The concept of the Internet of Things refers to sensors and actuators connected, usually through wireless links, where they collect information or interact with the environment in which they are inserted. This interaction may occur by reporting their data to a gateway, making numerous possible applications in the most varied fields of research, among them manufacturing, health care, smart cities, smart campus, smart houses and smart environments in general, security, agriculture, among others [1]. These sensor-based environments capture data and can make decisions based on the discovery of knowledge that occurs through their gateway that processes information, and are also known as the devices that make up the Internet of Everything (IoE) [6]. However, many Internet of Things applications can have time restrictions, like patient monitoring in a hospital, connected vehicles, and others. So, the traditional Internet of Things applications send your data to the cloud, that is far from the sensors/actuators, and then, a high latency, consequently a high response time and high usage of network bandwith may occur.

2.2   Cloud and Fog Computing

In [7], the authors define cloud computing as a convenient structure consisting of hardware and software, with the purpose of providing computing, network, storage services, which can provide rapid provisioning of resources. As large-scale applications are increasingly common, cloud computing makes it easier to deploy, serving a huge number of requests, and providing users with an ever-lower cost, as well as payment for what is consumed. The authors in [12] define that the architecture of Cloud Computing is divided into layers, namely: **(i) Software-as-a-Service (SaaS):** referring to an application service provider model that supports many clients, where they do not care about infrastructure issues, only use the software; **(ii) Platform-as-a-Service (PaaS):** where your target audience is developers, providing systems and environments to deploy the entire lifecycle of your applications; **(iii) Hardware-as-a-Service (HaaS):** In a nutshell, it is the situation where customers buy servers for some period of time, but may not need them, so it only pays for what to use; **(iv) Infrastructure-as-a-Service (IaaS):** that refers to the delivery of all computational infrastructure to the client, being that it manages to his liking, and still, the customer pays only for what to use.

Fog Computing is an extension of Cloud Computing, which is performed closer to the sensors (data source) and actuators (data source and consumer). Thus, this new paradigm is positioned at the edge of the network where IoE applications send their data to be treated in the fog. In the context of Fog Computing surveys have been developed. The authors [3] proposed the concept of Fog Computing, where it extends cloud computing capabilities to the edge of the network, available in routers, access points and other types of equipment [15], each composing a fog-forming node, providing computational resources such as processing, storage, and network to the IoT application sensors on a virtualized and distributed [13] platform. Such a paradigm is located at the edge of the network, or at most a leap away from the sensor, providing low latency, location awareness as well as a geographically distributed platform, which meets the needs of mobile users based on their location. The Fog Computing plays a key role in Internet of Things environments, because the increasing adoption of Internet of Things sensors in several applications, a growing demand for processing and data volume will be generated, justifying the adoption of Fog Computing and consequently, of load balancing between its nodes.

2.3   Load Balancer

Load Balancing has been proposed to achieve the best load distribution between the processors in parallel systems and aim to improve the performance of parallel applications [10]. Load balancing consists of the distribution of tasks between nodes, where these nodes are under the management of a balancer that receives the requests and distributes them between their nodes to be processed, in a fair way among all [14]. In distributed systems such as Cloud Computing, load balancing plays an important role, since in the cloud, systems must meet all client requests in the best possible time, and must be tolerant of network failures, such as delays heterogeneity, processing node failures, and other [2].

Load balancing algorithms are classified as static and dynamic. Stable and homogeneous environments benefit from static algorithms. However, such algorithms are not flexible and do not take into account sudden changes in the environment in question. On the other hand, dynamic algorithms are more flexible, taking into account heterogeneous environments and their different attributes at run time, adapting to the sudden changes that may occur in the environment, however, they have a higher computational cost [2]. The author in [4] highlights that the scheduling problem have three main components: **(i)** consumers, **(ii)** resources and **(iii)** policy. In this work, the consumers are the sensors/actuators, the resources are the Fog nodes, and the policy is subject of this work, that is about the scheduling algorithm.

3   Related Work

In analyzing the literature, some works shown the concern of authors in trying to mitigate the unbalance of the Fog Computing systems. In this sense, among the works found, the authors Oueis *et al.* [9] are concerned with the Quality of Experience (QoE) of the users, so they proposed the establishment of a low complexity computational cluster in 5G networks. That is, an LB is proposed applied in a specific domain, also, it presents an algorithm that does not worry about the separation of priority levels, only knows the time limit of execution.

In the work of the authors Yin *et al.* [16], a proposal is presented to balance the load between the containers in an industrial network, based on the evaluation if it can process the task in question. The request evaluator, that was proposed by the authors, performs an evaluation of the tasks, and decides if such is processed on the fog layer (that is formed by containers) or on the cloud layer. A increase of 5% of accepted tasks was achieved, and a 10% of reduction time of each task too. But this work does not deal with priority of the tasks, that is the main focus of our paper.

A different approach is presented by the authors Ningning *et al.* [8], that is a self-organized topology through the technique of graph repartitioning, where was proposed an algorithm that organizes the Fog Computing nodes in such a way that most of the overloaded ones are not scaled. On the other hand, the priority of the tasks was not discussed in the work.

The author Puthal *et. al.*[11] went beyond load balancing in Edge Data Centers environments, proposing a secure authentication method between them, and later load balancing. However, this work does not classify the priorities of the sensor requests, and the tests conducted were performed with a low number of tasks.

With the consistent focus on Fog the author Verma *et al.*[14] proposed a balancer called Fog Master Server, applied at two priority levels, however, when a real task arrives at the balancer, it performs the actual processing itself, that is, it assumes this task, thus compromising the performance of the main load balancing activity. This work is near of the our paper, but, in our work the load balancer only performs load balancing tasks, that is better for performance issues.

From the exposed works we define open-ended gaps presented that this work intends to fill, for that the allocation of the tasks be on the dedicated load balancer, and also, the proposed scheduling algorithm takes into account the priority level of the tasks. The Table 1 presents the differences between the implementation of the previous papers correlated with this work exposed here, whose objective is to fill this gap.

Unlike these works, our proposed approach uses the fog-shaped gateway and also a load balancer for task allocation based on its priority, and we also present a 2-priority priority classification, where SMARTFOGLB ranks and chooses where to allocate the task based on it in its priority. The one related work that deal with priority, is the work of Verma *et al.* [14], but the referenced work process the high priority tasks on the load balancer, what may cause the high workload, and may compromises the performance of the main function of the LB.

4   Architecture and Load Balancer Proposal

In this section, we will present a general architecture of the proposed load balancer, as well an algorithm to perform the balancing task.

4.1   Internet of Things Architecture

The Internet of Things architecture in this article is organized in 3 layers:

Sensing. This is the first layer of the architecture, and is also known as the ubiquitous computing or IoE layer, that consists of sensors and actuators, whether

Table 1. Comparison between works

Work	Priority level	LB implementation
Oueis *et al.* [9]	0	Clients send computational tasks with a maximum time requirement
Ningning *et al.* [8]	0	Self-organizing topology by the repartitioning of graphs, there is no central element that performs the distribution of tasks
Verma *et al.* [14]	2	Data arrives at the fog server master and are allocated on the nodes, but real-time tasks are allocated in the fog server master itself
Yin *et al.* [16]	0	Allocate the task in the container based on the evaluation of the task
Puthal *et al.* [11]	0	The data arrives in the Edge Data Center, if it is overloaded, the task is sent to another neighboring data center, and so on until finding a node with a low workload
SMARTFOGLB	2	Tasks are allocated according to their priority, where nodes are allocated according to specific policies, but never in the balancer itself

mobile or not. The sensors act by capturing data from the environment, for example, a temperature sensor, offloading requests of mobile devices, smart vehicles, among others. Such devices capture data and send it to Layer 2, i.e., the Fog Computing. Actuators are devices that interact with the environment, such as a relay that drives a lamp or air conditioner, or an electronic door lock. These devices receive instructions that come from layer 2, the Fog Computing.

Fog Computing. It is the layer responsible for processing and making decisions in the environment. A Fog Computing is composed of many nodes with lower computational power than the cloud. However, they are more in number, and they have higher processing power than the sensors from IoT applications. It can be understood as a gateway that aggregates incoming data, processes it and generates information for decision making and also, this layer acts by sending the generated data to persistence in the cloud.

Cloud Computing. It is the layer that receives the processed data from the middle layer for storage. This layer is not the subject of discussion in this work.

Therefore, considering the Internet of Things architecture, we propose the SMARTFOGLB load balancer, that is inside of layer two, but can be managed by Fog Controller in layer three, as shown in the Fig. 1. The Fog Controller have the architecture overview, and it can instantiates more fog nodes if necessary, or

alocate virtual servers on the cloud, if the fog computing resources are overloaded, however, this is not the focus of this work.

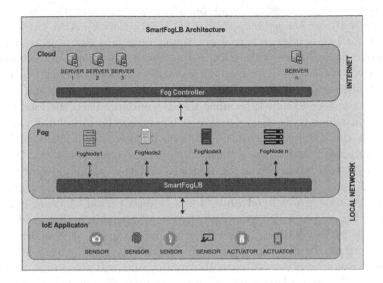

Fig. 1. General Internet of Things architecture

4.2   SmartFogLB

The SMARTFOGLB is implemented in the second level and the Fog Controller
in the third level. SMARTFOGLB logically positions itself between the source of
the data (sensors and actuators) and their destination (nodes that make up the
Fog Computing), which will process them. The goal of the load balancer in the
architecture is to distribute tasks from the first layer (IoT sensors), allocating
them among the nodes that are under its control, as well, isolate the fog nodes
that are unhealthy by any reason.

Some tasks have time constraints, for example, a vehicle network that needs
to know the best way to guide the car between two points in a smart city, or a
patient in a hospital that needs to have your health monitored. If the respective
application gateway fails, the entire application may be compromised, and can
cause serious damages. This tasks needs to be performed as quickly as possible
because the car is in movement, and the embedded GPS that is inside of the car
needs to be updated with the best path; or, the patient is in movement but needs
to take your remedy quickly. In this way, some nodes for the processing of this
and other tasks will be necessary, which makes the figure of the load balancer
vital because it is aware of the current workload of the fog nodes as well as
the computational power (CPU, memory), network (bandwidth, latency), and
priority of the task that arrives at it for processing.

Algorithm. In this subsection, we will deal with the algorithm responsible for load balancing tasks from the Internet of Things sensors that compose the smart city.

When the task reaches the load balancer, it must take into account two priority levels: 0 (*for low priority*) and 1 (*for high priority*). Also, the algorithm responsible for balancing needs to know the number of nodes that are under its management. For each node under its management, the balancer needs to know the number of cpu cores, current load average, available memory(%), network bandwidth utilization(%), network latency between the fog node and balancer, available disk space(%) and time since the last update. Then the load balancer will decide on which node that is under its command the task will be allocated.

To assist the main algorithm on decision making about where to allocate the task, a daemon that runs in the background becomes necessary. It collects necessary information about the fog nodes so that the balancing algorithm uses them in real-time, and also, in the case of a node having its load average greater than or equal to a pre-defined limit, for a defined period of time, it will not receive new tasks, nor will it compose the list of available nodes. Additionally, if a node fails for any reason, it also does not enter the list of available nodes.

The algorithm in question has three distinct phases: the first is the task receiving phase, where it will know its priority and will store in a temporary table the job id, remote host address and its priority. In the second phase, task allocation is performed at a specific node. The third phase refers to the return of the task by the node to the balancer.

After the first phase, the next step will be load balancing. At this point, the algorithm will query the list of available nodes that are under its command, as well as the availability of computational resources of each. This list is populated by the daemon running in the background, and the collected data are kept in the memory, such data are updated in a predefined interval.

The policy to allocate the task to a particular node is as follows: for tasks with high priority (1), we consider that this type of priority must have the fastest processing time, and so, the fog node table will be sorted by lowest load average, lowest latency, the highest number of cores and available memory, in a descending order. Of these, the node with lower load average, higher available memory, lower latency and greater network bandwidth will be selected to process the task. Thus, the task will be executed on the minor possible time. For the tasks with low priority (0), we assume that this type of task does not need to be performed on the minor possible time, and so, the same can wait for processing, or be forwarded to the cloud, that is not subject of this work. For these tasks, the selected node will be the one that has a lower load average, independently of the other attributes. Once the processing node is defined, the load balancer will allocate the task with its id on its node, and so, in turn, receives the task, processes and resends the load balancer.

Just for instance, in the Table 2 we give an hypothetical scenario with three fog nodes. If a high priority task arrives the load balancer, then the fog node one will be selected, because the node satisfies the requirements of the previous algorithm. However, if a low priority task arrives the load balancer, the fog node three will be selected, because only lowest load average it matter.

Table 2. Hypothetical scenario with 3 Fog nodes

Fog node	1	2	3
Current Load Average (%)	40	50	40
CPU Cores	4	8	2
Free Memory (MB)	400	800	200
Latency (ms)	15	15	15
Network Bandwidth (Mbps)	100	100	100

The third balancing moment deals with the result of the task performed by the node on the load balancer, where the balancer receives back the result and the process id, then it can mark the task as completed, and optionally return feedback to the sensor or another sensor/actuator a specific command. This moment is important because if the fog node fails, the task that was allocated to the node is lost, so, the load balancer algorithm waits the response from the node, and, in case of failure, the task is realocated to another node.

5 Experimental Methodology

For validation of the proposal, the entire structure described previously was implemented using the object-oriented Java programming language. The tests were conducted in two moments, the first without load balancer, and the second with using SMARTFOGLB, for a environment with $1,000$, $10,000$ and $100,000$ sensors.

The tests were performed ten times each, totaling thirty tests at each moment. The tests with load balancing were performed with 2 and 5 fog nodes, and were conducted on an Altix UV 2000 platform designed by SGI. Our platform is composed of 24 NUMA nodes, each node has an Intel Xeon E5-4640 Sandy Bridge-EP x86-64 processor with 8 physical cores running at 2.40 GHz. The platform runs an unmodified SUSE Linux Enterprise Server operating system with kernel 3.0.101-0.29 installed. All applications were compiled with Java version 1.8 update 191. The results presented are the average of at least 10 runs. The relative error was less than 5% using a 95% statistical confidence by Student's t-distribution.

For the tests, the policy of task allocation, overhead and response time adopted was the same in both moments of simulation, so that the results are fair. Each sensor sends to his gateway his requests that are packets, and, it has been defined that when the packet arrives at the fog node, it checks whether its current load is below 90% of its capacity. If it is equal or above, the processing time of the package is penalized with 10 ms of execution delay and waits for the node to decrease its processing; still, the execution is stopped in 10 ms in both cases for to simulate the latency of the network. If the node's current load is at 100%, then it has no more capacity to process it, so for this test, the packet that arrived at this node will be discarded (dropped).

Each instantiated sensor stays within a thread and afterward, each one sends the data to its gateway, either the fog node (for the test without balancer) or the balancer. The job on the fog node that receives the packet to be processed is encapsulated inside a method in the developed simulation tool, which in turn is in a java class that represents the object of the fog node. Thus, given the number of threads involved, the fog node receives the data, increases the processor load by 5% for each packet, after the load is checked and if there is no overflow, the packet is processed, reaching the end of the method decreasing 5% load. The method undergoes a delay in its execution, which is the latency of the network, and in case of overloading, it is added to the total execution delay.

The fact of the processes occurs in threads gives dynamicity to the environment, and so, they do not necessarily occur at the same time. A package may suffer a delay, or be rejected because of the fog node is overloaded on the moment it arrives at the fog, or be processed quickly if the fog node load is below 90%. These results, therefore, justify the high rates of packet rejection when there is no load balancer present.

In the process involving the load balancer, that is represented by another java class, the sensors are unaware of the presence and amount of fog nodes that are under the management of the balancer, since they only send their data so that they are processed along with their priority in the same amount of threads and same policies at the moment of the test without balancer. When the packet arrives on the balancer, the algorithm that is responsible for scheduling checks if the packet priority is 0 or 1, and orders its nodes according to the policy.

If the packet has high priority, we understand that the same has to be processed on the minor possible time, what means the high urgency of a service like a patient monitoring in a hospital, or a connected smart vehicular network. Then, the Fog nodes with the lowest load average, lower latency to the balancer, higher number of CPU, higher available memory, higher available free disk space, and higher available network bandwidth will be selected to process the package, what results in a more quickly compute.

On the other hand, if the packet has low priority, we understand that the same has no urgency for quickly processing, and if it is the case, can wait a more significant time to be processed. Then, for this packet, the Fog node that will be selected, will be the node with lower load average.

6   Results

In this section, we will discuss the results that were obtained from the proposed method. First, we defined that when the Fog node reaches the load average equal to or greater than 90%, the packet will be rejected (dropped). With our proposed load balancer, it has been proved that with the adoption of more than one cooperating Fog node, the discarded packet rates have been reduced to zero. This result happens because the balancer is endowed with intelligence to indicate which node is the most appropriate.

The load average rates were reduced inversely proportional to the more significant number of nodes that are processing, so, the more Fog nodes that are processing, the lowest load average of them will be obtained.

It is observed that although having many nodes in the Fog Computing, it is necessary a layer that manages them, whose objective is the distribution of the packets between these Fog nodes, avoiding the workload imbalance. For this work, this layer is the SMARTFOGLB, and Fig. 2 shows the results of the implementation, that is highlighted the response time of the proposed algorithm.

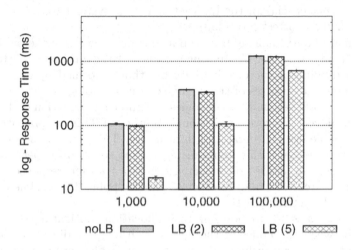

Fig. 2. Response Time measured in tests with SMARTFOGLB- log.

It is noted that an increase in the number of sensors in 10 times, from $1,000$ to $10,000$, the response time increase from 105.7 ms to 360.47 ms, which represent an increase of 3.4 times. Similarly, from $10,000$ to $100,000$ sensors, the response time also increase 3.3 times that was of 360.47 ms to $1,200.76$ ms. So, we can understand that our proposed algorithm can scale and handles a high number of requests, and the response times will be lower as possible.

We also realized that without the SMARTFOGLB, the drop rate increases with the increase in the number of sensors. In the first test, with $1,000$ sensors, the drop rate was 91.16%. Since the fog node is overloaded (CPU load of 100%), so a high amount of packets was discarded. When the number of sensors was increased to from $10,000$ and $100,000$, the drop rate increase to 98.61% and 99.64% respectively. In these tests, almost all packages were discarded.

On the other hand, the discarded packet rate was reduced to 0% from 2 fog nodes regardless of the number of sensors. This happens first because there are more than one Fog node, and also because the balancer can allocate the task in the fog node with a lower load average, distributing the packets that arrive in it somewhat, so that the nodes can hardly reach 100% of their capacity due to this. Already the response times, decreased by 6.06% and 63.95%, using two and five fog nodes on the balancer.

7   Conclusions

Providing adequate infrastructure for Internet of Things environments requires the adoption of many technologies since it needs to perform a series of activities interconnecting many systems. The adoption of IoT has been increasingly adopted, and Fog Computing comes to potentiate it, saving on network bandwidth width and decreasing response times. Thus, workload distribution between its nodes becomes crucial for the Internet of Things systems to operate without breaks and in the shortest possible time.

Performing Load Balancing has been a constant concern in the most diverse sub-areas of computing. Fog Computing will also take advantage of this technique since it is a dynamic structure, in the sense that is formed by heterogeneous nodes, and takes advantages of the virtualization technologies.

With the use of these new technologies, a significant reduction of data transfer can be achieved. However, traditional Internet of Things applications have become a sizeable critical amount of data mover. This concern is now growing when applying together with ubiquitous techniques, so, in this paper, in response to this challenge, we focused on reducing the data transfer, response times and proposed a new architecture to Internet of Things applications and new Fog load balancers called SMARTFOGLB.

Our main idea is to provide fair task allocation, mitigating the workload unbalance between the nodes of the fog, as well as, providing fault tolerance, hiding from the sensor possible faults that may occur. Experimental results presented improvements in response time average and dropped packets rate when our SMARTFOGLB load balancer was used with $1,000$, $10,000$ and $100,000$ sensors. The drop pack rate was reduced to zero, response fell 68%, maintaining the load average below 90%.

For this work, we have defined that when the Fog node reaches the threshold of workload in 100%, the packet will be dropped. In a real scenario, however, this behavior may not be acceptable, then as future work, we plan to implement a queue mechanism, or a cloud environment to receive low priority tasks. This will avoid the high packet drop rates and will be more suitable to implement in a real scenario. Another point is that the proposed load balancer is a point of failure, and this needs our attention in future works, as well, the failure of the Fog nodes. Also, we intend to provide internal improvements in the balancer and to prove its effectiveness by allocating Internet of Things environments with up to 1 million of sensors, as well compare it with one of the related works.

Acknowledgments. This research was supported by MCTIC/CNPq - Universal 28/2018 under grants 436339/2018-8 and CAPES-Brazil under grants 1765322. It was also supported by University of Grenoble, Grenoble – France.

References

1. Al-Fuqaha, A., Guizani, M., Mohammadi, M., Aledhari, M., Ayyash, M.: Internet of things: a survey on enabling technologies, protocols, and applications. IEEE Commun. Surv. Tutor. **17**(4), 2347–2376 (2015)
2. Al Nuaimi, K., Mohamed, N., Al Nuaimi, M., Al-Jaroodi, J.: A survey of load balancing in cloud computing: challenges and algorithms. In: 2012 Second Symposium on Network Cloud Computing and Applications (NCCA), pp. 137–142. IEEE (2012)
3. Bonomi, F., Milito, R., Zhu, J., Addepalli, S.: Fog computing and its role in the internet of things. In: Proceedings of the First Edition of the MCC Workshop on Mobile Cloud Computing, pp. 13–16. ACM (2012)
4. Casavant, T.L., Kuhl, J.G.: A taxonomy of scheduling in general-purpose distributed computing systems. IEEE Trans. Softw. Eng. **14**(2), 141–154 (1988)
5. Consortium, O.: OpenFog reference architecture for fog computing. Architecture Working Group (2017)
6. Dey, S., Saha, J.K., Karmakar, N.C.: Smart sensing: chipless RFID solutions for the Internet of Everything. IEEE Microw. Mag. **16**(10), 26–39 (2015)
7. Jadeja, Y., Modi, K.: Cloud computing-concepts, architecture and challenges. In: 2012 International Conference on Computing, Electronics and Electrical Technologies (ICCEET), pp. 877–880. IEEE (2012)
8. Ningning, S., Chao, G., Xingshuo, A., Qiang, Z.: Fog computing dynamic load balancing mechanism based on graph repartitioning. Chin. Commun. **13**(3), 156–164 (2016)
9. Oueis, J., Strinati, E.C., Barbarossa, S.: The fog balancing: load distribution for small cell cloud computing. In: 2015 IEEE 81st Vehicular Technology Conference (VTC Spring), pp. 1–6. IEEE (2015)
10. Padoin, E.L., Navaux, P.O.A., Méhaut, J.F.: Using power demand and residual load imbalance in the load balancing to save energy of parallel systems. In: International Conference on Computational Science (ICCS), Zurich, Switzerland, pp. 1–8 (2017)
11. Puthal, D., Obaidat, M.S., Nanda, P., Prasad, M., Mohanty, S.P., Zomaya, A.Y.: Secure and sustainable load balancing of edge data centers in fog computing. IEEE Commun. Mag. **56**(5), 60–65 (2018)
12. Subashini, S., Kavitha, V.: A survey on security issues in service delivery models of cloud computing. J. Netw. Comput. Appl. **34**(1), 1–11 (2011)
13. Vaquero, L.M., Rodero-Merino, L.: Finding your way in the fog: towards a comprehensive definition of fog computing. ACM SIGCOMM Comput. Commun. Rev. **44**(5), 27–32 (2014)
14. Verma, M., Bhardwaj, N., Yadav, A.K.: Real time efficient scheduling algorithm for load balancing in fog computing environment. Int. J. Inf. Technol. Comput. Sci. **8**(4), 1–10 (2016)
15. Yi, S., Li, C., Li, Q.: A survey of fog computing: concepts, applications and issues. In: Proceedings of the 2015 Workshop on Mobile Big Data, pp. 37–42. ACM (2015)
16. Yin, L., Luo, J., Luo, H.: Tasks scheduling and resource allocation in fog computing based on containers for smart manufacturing. IEEE Trans. Ind. Inf. **14**(10), 4712–4721 (2018)

Multi-objective Configuration of a Secured Distributed Cloud Data Storage

Luis Enrique García-Hernández[1] , Andrei Tchernykh[1,3,4(✉)] ,
Vanessa Miranda-López[1] , Mikhail Babenko[2] ,
Arutyun Avetisyan[4] , Raul Rivera-Rodriguez[1] ,
Gleb Radchenko[4] , Carlos Jaime Barrios-Hernandez[5] ,
Harold Castro[6] , and Alexander Yu. Drozdov[7]

[1] CICESE Research Center, 22860 Ensenada, BC, Mexico
{lgarcia, vmiranda, rrivera}@cicese.edu.mx,
chenykh@cicese.mx
[2] North-Caucasus Federal University, Stavropol 355009, Russia
mgbabenko@ncfu.ru
[3] Ivannikov Institute for System Programming RAS, Moscow 109004, Russia
[4] South Ural State University, Chelyabinsk 454080, Russia
arut@ispras.ru, gleb.radchenko@susu.ru
[5] Universidad Industrial de Santander, Bucaramanga, Colombia
carlosjaimebh@computer.org
[6] Universidad de los Andes, Bogotá, Colombia
hcastro@uniandes.edu.co
[7] Moscow Institute of Physics and Technology (State University),
Moscow, Russia
alexander.y.drozdov@gmail.com

Abstract. Cloud storage is one of the most popular models of cloud computing. It benefits from a shared set of configurable resources without limitations of local data storage infrastructures. However, it brings several cybersecurity issues. In this work, we address the methods of mitigating risks of confidentiality, integrity, availability, information leakage associated with the information loss/change, technical failures, and denial of access. We rely on a configurable secret sharing scheme and error correction codes based on the Redundant Residue Number System (RRNS). To dynamically configure RRNS parameters to cope with different objective preferences, workloads, and cloud properties, we take into account several conflicting objectives: probability of information loss/change, extraction time, and data redundancy. We propose an approach based on a genetic algorithm that is effective for multi-objective optimization. We implement NSGA-II, SPEA2, and MOCell, using the JMetal 5.6 framework. We provide their experimental analysis using eleven real data cloud storage providers. We show that MOCell algorithm demonstrates best results obtaining a better Pareto optimal front approximation and quality indicators such as inverted generational distance, additive epsilon indicator, and hypervolume. We conclude that multi-objective genetic algorithms could be efficiently used for storage optimization and adaptation in a non-stationary multi-cloud environment.

© Springer Nature Switzerland AG 2020
J. L. Crespo-Mariño and E. Meneses-Rojas (Eds.): CARLA 2019, CCIS 1087, pp. 78–93, 2020.
https://doi.org/10.1007/978-3-030-41005-6_6

Keywords: Cloud storage · Multi-objective optimization · Genetic algorithm

1 Introduction

In cloud storages, data is housed in a virtualized storage space, usually provided by third parties accessible throughout the internet. There are many publicly available data storages like Google Drive, Microsoft OneDrive, Dropbox, Amazon Cloud Drive, Windows Azure Storage, etc. However, reliability, security, and quality of service required for long-term data storage are still emerging problems.

To improve these characteristics, Basescu et al. [1] proposed a multiple clouds model called inter-cloud or cloud-of-clouds. This model uses multiple services from different providers in a transparent manner for users; that is, they are provided as services of a virtually single cloud.

There are numerous studies of cloud storage security. As mentioned by AlZain et al. [2]: "Ensuring the security of computing in the cloud is a factor of great importance because users regularly store important information with their respective suppliers, they tend to distrust these providers." This distrust is one of the issues which does not allow increasing the popularity of multi-cloud environments.

In 1979, Shamir [4] proposed (k, n) threshold Secret Sharing Schemes (SSS). These schemes are of special interest, since, due to their distributed nature, they can be used in the multi-cloud environment.

Ermakova et al. [5] presented real case studies of European hospitals in multi-cloud architecture and evaluated the performance of encryption algorithms.

Tchernykh et al. [3] provided a study of uncertainty on large scale computing systems and cloud computing systems. They address methods for mitigating the risks of confidentiality, integrity, and availability associated with the loss of information, denial of access for a long time, and information leakage.

Miranda-López et al. [6] provided an experimental analysis of a distributed cloud storage with eleven real storage providers. The authors used Asmuth-Bloom and Mignotte (k, n) threshold schemes, and evaluated upload-download and coding-decoding speeds with different (k, n) configurations.

Babenko et al. [7] addressed error correction codes to improve the performance of Berkeley Open Infrastructure for Network Computing under uncertainty of users' behavior. The authors used Redundant Residue Number System (RRNS) moduli set of the special form to correct user unfairness and increase data reliability, decreasing redundancy and network traffic.

Chervyakov et al. [8] proposed a data storage scheme called Approximate Rank RRNS (AR-RRNS), which combines the concept of RRNS and SSS properties to divide and distribute secrets. The authors use numerical approximation strategies to reduce the computational cost of the algorithm. By the theoretical analysis, they show that through the appropriate selection of the RRNS parameters, the system allows configuring security, reliability, as well as data redundancy.

Tchernykh et al. [9] proposed the algorithm called Anti-Collusion RRNS (AC-RRNS) a computational secure and reliable SSS in RRNS. They solve the problem of cloud collusion by the simultaneous use of the ideas behind the Mignotte SSS and asymptotically ideal Asmuth–Bloom SSS.

Tchernykh et al. [10] proposed a multi-cloud storage model called Weighted Access RRNS (WA-RRNS) that combines the weighted access scheme, SSS, and RRNS with multiple failure detection/recovery mechanisms and homomorphic ciphers.

In this work, we provide mechanisms for multi-objective configuration and optimization of the AR-RRNS data storage model.

In the (k, n) RRNS, a file is divided into n chunks in such a way that with k chunks or more, data can be recovered. To select (k, n) parameters of the system and define specific clouds to be used for data storage, three optimization criteria are taken into account: probability of information loss/change, extraction time, and data redundancy.

Multi-objective optimization has practical importance since almost all real-world optimization problems are suited to be modeled using multiple objectives. A Multi-objective Optimization Problem (MOOP) deals with more than one objective function.

Genetic algorithms (GAs) are among the most successful computational intelligence techniques. They are meta-heuristics suitable to solve multi-objective optimization problems. That is why, in this paper, we propose an approach based on genetic algorithms for multi-objective optimization and configuration of AR-RRNS data storage model.

The rest of the paper is organized as follows. In Sect. 2, we present the data storage model and formulate MOOP. In Sect. 3, we present the design of our GA-based approach. In Sect. 4, we provide an experimental study. In Sect. 5, we describe the obtained results. Section 6 concludes the paper and describes future work.

2   AR-RRNS Data Storage Model: Multi-objective Scenario

In this section, we briefly describe the residue number system and AR-RRNS data storage model. We define the configuration of the storage model as a multi-objective optimization problem and specify objective functions and restrictions.

2.1   Residue Number System and Its Properties

RNS represents an integer as a set of its residues according to a moduli set. RRNS is formed by adding redundant moduli into an existing moduli set to extend the legitimate range of the original information moduli [11].

Given a set of k pairwise prime positive integers $m_1, m_2, \ldots, m_k$ called moduli set, a nonnegative integer X uniquely represented by the n-tuples $x_1, x_2, \ldots, x_k$ of their residues modulo $m_i \left(x_i = |X|_{m_i}, i = 1, 2, \ldots, k \right)$ in the range $[0, M)$, where $M = m_1 * m_2 * \ldots * m_k$ [12].

RRNS uses a set of $n = (k + r)$-tuples to represent an integer in the range $[0, M)$. It uses $m_1, m_2, \ldots, m_k, m_{k+1}, \ldots, m_n$ modulis and $x_1, x_2, \ldots, x_k, x_{k+1}, \ldots, x_n$ digits. $m_{k+1}, \ldots, m_n$ and $x_{k+1}, \ldots, x_n$ are called the redundant moduli and redundant digits, respectively.

2.2   AR-RRNS Data Storage Model. Problem Statement

AR-RRNS is based on configurable and reliable RRNS systems in multi-cloud environments to ensure security, robustness, and confidentiality [13]. The operation that consumes more resources in the implementation of RNS is the operation of division while finding RNS residues of dynamic range. To increase the efficiency of the data processing and decrease the energy consumption during the coding and decoding of data, RNS moduli of a special form $2^b \pm \alpha$ are used, which allow finding a division residue with linear complexity. The approximation of the range (AR) allows to substitute operations of finding residue by taking higher bits of a number based on the introduced function of computing the approximate rank of RNS number. Based on the properties of the approximate value and arithmetic properties of RNS, the AR-RRNS method was proposed for error detection, correction, and controlling computational results.

Let us consider a set of N clouds $C = \{c_1, c_2, \ldots, c_N\}$. Each cloud $c_j = \{u_j, d_j, err_j\}$ is characterized by the speed of uploading u_j, speed of downloading d_j and failure probability err_j, for all $j = \{1, \ldots, N\}$.

In RRNS with a (k, n) setting, where data D is divided into n chunks, data can be recovered with k or more chunks. Each chunk $i = \{s_i\}$ has size s_i for each $i = \{1, \ldots, n\}$. Table 1 shows used notations.

To apply AR-RRNS, we have to find the configuration (k, n) and a subset C' of clouds minimizing the probability of information loss $(P_r(k, n))$, redundancy (R), and extraction time (T_{ex}). The problem can be formalized as:

- Minimize $P_r(k, n)$, which is calculated as:

$$P_r(k, n) = \sum\nolimits_{A \in F_{n-k+1}}^{n} \prod_{j \in A} err_j \prod_{j^c \in A^c} (1 - err_{j^c}), \qquad (1)$$

where F_{n-k+1} is the set of all $n - k + 1$ possible subsets of C. Information can be lost only if $n - k + 1$ parts are lost.

- Minimize R, which is the ratio of the size of the stored coded information D_E and original size D:

$$R = \frac{D_E}{D} \qquad (2)$$

- Minimize T_{ex}, which represents how fast it downloads information from each of the clouds and decodes it. It is calculated as the sum of the decode time T_D and download time T_{dow}:

$$T_{ex} = T_D + T_{dow}, \quad T_{dow} = \sum_{i=n-k+1}^{n} \frac{s_{Ei}}{d_i} \qquad (3)$$

We assume that each chunk is sequentially downloaded from the clouds. The process ends when k pieces are downloaded correctly.

Table 1. Notation of the AR-RRNS data storage model.

	Definition		Definition
D	Size of the original data	T_{down}	Encrypted data upload time
D_E	Size of the encrypted data	T_{up}	Encrypted data download time
d_i	Size of the $i - th$ chunk	T_s	$T_E + T_{up}$
v_{down_i}	Download speed of $i - th$ chunk	T_{ex}	$T_{down} + T_D$. Extraction time
v_{up_i}	Upload speed of $i - th$ chunk	R	Redundancy
T_E	Data encryption time	err_i	Probability of the $i - th$ storage failure
T_D	Data decryption time	$P_r(k,n)$	Probability of information loss

The probability of information loss $P_r(k,n)$ conflicts with the other two criteria T_{ex} and R. For $P_r(k,n)$, the configurations that generate the worst solutions are in the form (n,n). While for T_{ex} and R, these configurations generate the best solutions. The strategy that provides the best result for $P_r(k,n)$ is the least suitable for the criteria T_{ex} and R.

Other constraints to guarantee a security threshold are:

(a)   At least 2 clouds must be used for storage chunks of information: $n \geq 2$;
(b)   At least two clouds are needed to reconstruct the original information: $k \geq 2$;
(c)   The number of clouds where the information is stored must be greater than or equal to the number of clouds needed to retrieve the information: $k \leq n$.

2.3   Multiobjective Optimization

Let us consider MOOP (X, f), where X is the solution space, and $f = (f_1, \ldots, f_i, \ldots, f_d)$ is an objective function vector such that f_i is to be minimized for all $i \in \{1, \ldots, d\}$. Let $Z = f(X)$ be the objective space, $Z \subseteq \mathbb{R}^d$. Each solution $x \in X$ is associated with an objective vector $z \in Z$ such that $z = f(x)$.

An objective vector $z \in Z$ is dominated by an objective vector $z' \in Z(z \prec z')$ iff $\forall i \in \{1, \ldots, d\} : z'_i \leq z_i$ and $\exists i \in \{1, \ldots, d\} : z'_i \leq z_i$ such that $z'_i < z_i$. Two objective vectors $z, z' \in Z$ are mutually non-dominated iff $z \nprec z'$ and $z' \nprec z$. An objective vector $z^* \in Z$ is Pareto optimal or non-dominated iff there does not exist a $z \in Z$ such that $z^* \prec z$.

Similar definitions can be formalized for solutions $x \in X$ by using the associated objective vectors $z \in Z$, such as $z = f(x)$. The Pareto front $Z^* \subseteq Z$ is the set of non-dominated objective vectors. The Pareto set $X^* \subseteq X$ is a set of solutions that maps to the Pareto front, i.e. $f(X^*) = Z^*$. One of the most challenging issues in multiobjective optimization is to identify the Pareto set/front, or its good approximation for complex problems [14].

In our multi-objective optimization problem, we define the following objective functions: $f_1 = P_r(k, n)$, $f_2 = R$, and $f_3 = T_{ex}$. Thus, $f = (f_1, f_2, f_3)$ is the objective function vector such that f_i is to be minimized for all $i \in \{1, 2, 3\}$.

3 System Design and Implementation

In this section, we briefly describe the essential concepts of Genetic Algorithms (GAs) and present the design of our GA-based approach.

3.1 Genetic Algorithms

The concept of genetic algorithm was developed in the 1960s and 1970s. GAs are inspired by evolutionary theory: weak and unsuitable species face extinction by natural selection, and stronger ones have more opportunities to pass on their genes to future generations through reproduction. In GA terminology, a solution is called an individual or chromosome. A chromosome corresponds to a unique solution in the solution space. The GA works with a set of chromosomes called population. It uses two operators to generate new solutions from the existing ones: crossing and mutation. They form the basis of evolutionary systems: 1. Variation operators (crossing and mutation) create the necessary diversity within the population; 2. Selection acts as a force increasing the average quality of the solutions in the population. Their combination produces the improvement of the objective function.

Being a population-based approach, GAs are well suited to solve MOOP. The ability of GA to simultaneously search different regions of a solution space provides finding a diverse set of solutions for difficult problems with non-convex, discontinuous, and multi-modal solutions spaces. The crossover operator of GA exploits structures of good solutions with different objectives to create new non-dominated solutions in unexplored parts of the Pareto front.

In a cloud storage system, performance and quality are the most important requirements. Multi-Objective Cellular Genetic Algorithm (MOCell) [15] demonstrates a better performance and quality solutions than the existing algorithms according to some chosen test problems.

Fast Nondominated Sorting Genetic Algorithm (NSGA-II) [16] is a genetic algorithm, which is the standard algorithm in multi-objective optimization.

Improved Strength Pareto Evolutionary Algorithm (SPEA2) [17] shows very good performance in comparison to other multi-objective evolutionary algorithms. It has been a point of reference in various studies.

We include SPEA2, NSGA-II, and MOCell in our experimental study to verify how they can be used for the optimization of the AR-RRNS storage system. Table 2 shows the main characteristics of these algorithms.

There are several programming frameworks for multi-objective optimization with metaheuristics. Among them, JMetal stands out for the following reasons: it is an object-oriented Java-based framework, open source, based on software design patterns, easy to use, with flexibility, extensibility, and portability, parallel execution, support, and improvements.

It is a tool used by many researchers in the area with excellent results. For all these reasons, JMetal is chosen as the framework for the optimization of the AR-RRNS storage system.

Table 2. SPEA2, NSGA-II and MOCell comparisons.

Algorithm	SPEA2	NSGA-II	MOCell
Fitness assignment	Strength of dominators	Ranking based on non-domination sorting	Ranking based on non-domination sorting
Diversity mechanism	Density-based on the k-th nearest neighbor	Crowding distance	Cell-based crowding distance
Elitism	Yes	Yes	Yes
External population	Yes	No	Yes
Advantages	Improved SPEA. Make sure extreme points are preserved	Single parameter (N) Well tested Efficient	Good performance Fast convergence
Disadvantages	Computationally expensive fitness and density calculation	Crowding distance works in objective space only	Not popular

3.2   Chromosome Encoding

We use a representation of the chromosome containing two variables: the first one is a binary vector representing the parameter k, while the second one is a binary vector of length N (amount of clouds). If a position j is set to 1, the cloud c_j is used to store information. The number of non-zero elements determines n of our (k, n) configuration.

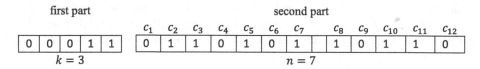

Fig. 1. Example of chromosome representation.

For example, the chromosome in Fig. 1 represents a solution $k = 3, n = 7$, that is $(k, n) = (3, 7)$. It specifies that the information is stored in the clouds $c_2, c_3, c_5, c_7, c_8, c_{10}, c_{11}$.

4   Experimentation

In this section, we present the process of calibrating GA parameters, the input data, genetic operators, configuration of the algorithms, quality indicators to evaluate genetic algorithms and describe the methodology of the experimental evaluation.

4.1 Quality Indicators

A (unary) quality indicator is a function $2^Z \rightarrow \mathbb{R}$ that assigns each approximation set to a (scalar) value reflecting its quality.

We use a subset of conventional quality indicators from the multi-objective literature. Let $A \subseteq Z$ be a set of mutually non-dominated objective vector (i.e. a Pareto front approximation), and $R \subseteq Z$ be a reference set (ideally the exact Pareto front when it is discrete, i.e. $R = Z^*$). Below, we describe three used quality indicators: inverted generational distance, additive epsilon indicator, and hypervolume.

IGD: The inverted generational distance [18] gives the average distance between any point from the reference set R and its closest point from the approximation set A.

$$\text{IGD}(A) = \frac{1}{|R|} \sqrt{\sum_{r \in R} \min_{a \in A} \|a - r\|_2^2} \tag{4}$$

The Euclidean distance (L2-norm) in the objective space is usually used for distance calculation. Obviously, the smaller the IGD value, the closer the approximation set from the reference set. An indicator value of 0 implies $R \subseteq A$.

EP: Additive epsilon indicator [19] gives the minimum factor by which the approximation set has to be translated in the objective space to (weakly) dominate the reference set. It is based on an additive factor.

$$\text{EP}(A) = \max_{r \in R} \min_{a \in A} \max_{i \in \{1,\dots,d\}} (a_i - r_i) \tag{5}$$

The smaller the EP value, the closer the approximation set from the reference set. An indicator value of 0 implies $R \subseteq A$.

HV: Hypervolume [20] gives the multidimensional volume of the portion of the objective space that is weakly dominated by an approximation set.

$$\text{HV}(A) = \int_{z^{min}}^{z^{max}} \alpha_A(z)dz,$$

$$\text{where}: \alpha_A(z) := \begin{cases} 1 \; if \; \exists \, a \, A \, such \, that \, z \prec a \\ 0 \; otherwise \end{cases} \tag{6}$$

In practice, only the upper bound vector $z^{max} \in \mathbb{R}^d$ is required to compute the hypervolume. This parameter is called a reference point. A Pareto front with a higher HV than another one could be due to two factors: some solutions in the former front dominate solutions in the second one, or, solutions in the first front are better distributed than in the second one. Thus, algorithms with larger values of HV are desirable. The main advantage of the hypervolume over many other performance indicators is its Pareto compliance property.

4.2   Calibration of GA Parameters

The method used in the calibration of the parameters for the experimental analysis has the following steps:

(a) test all instances produced with possible combinations of parameters for each algorithm;
(b) obtain the best solution for each instance;
(c) apply the Multifactor Variance Analysis (ANOVA) with a 95% confidence level to find the most influential parameters;
(d) set algorithm parameters based on selected parameters values;
(e) calculate the relative difference of the calibrated algorithm and other adapted algorithms over the best solutions.

In experiments, we use the following software platform: JMetal 5.6 and JDK 11.0.1 (64-bits). The hardware platform is Dell Precision T3610, Intel Xeon CPU E5-1606 @ 2.80 GHz, 16 GB DDR3 RAM with Windows 10 Enterprise 64-bits.

The following parameters are set for the calibration: Crossover operators: "Single Point Crossover" and "HUX Crossover"; Crossover probability (Pc): 0.6, 0.7, 0.8 and 0.9; Mutation probability (Pm): 0.05, 0.1, 0.2 and 0.3.

Hence, 2 * 4 * 4 = 32 different setups are considered to calibrate the algorithms. We also use the common configurations: Mutation operator: "Bit Flip Mutation," Population size: 100, Maximum number of evaluations: 25,000, Selection method: "Binary Tournament Selection." Table 3 shows characteristics of the eleven cloud storage providers used in our study.

The performance measure of the algorithms is calculated as the percentage of the relative distance of the obtained solution from the best one:

$$\frac{Heu_{sol} - Best_{sol}}{Best_{sol}} \times 100, Heu_{sol} = (1 - I_{HV}) + I_{EP} + I_{IGD}, \tag{7}$$

where Heu_{sol} is the sum of the quality indicators (EP: Epsilon, HV: Hypervolume, and IGD: Inverted generational distance) normalized in the range $\{0\ldots 1\}$. $Best_{sol}$ is the best value obtained during the testing of all possible parameter combinations.

To assess the statistical difference among the experimental results and observe how the selection of the parameters impacts on the quality of the solution, the ANOVA technique is applied. The analysis of variance is used to determine factors that have a significant effect and are most important. Parameters of the genetics algorithms are considered as factors and their values as levels. The results are presented as increase over the best solution in percent. The data are expressed in terms of mean and standard deviation (the lowest value is the best). The crossover operator "Single Point Cross-over" ($1.0350 \pm_{1.3e-02}$) is better than "HUX Crossover"($1.0420 \pm_{1.1e-02}$). The crossover probability 0.9 ($1.0440 \pm_{1.4e-02}$) is better than 0.6 ($1.0455 \pm_{1.3e-02}$), 0.7 ($1.0450 \pm_{1.1e-02}$), and 0.8 ($1.0445 \pm_{1.4e-02}$). The mutation probability 0.1 ($1.0425 \pm_{1.1e-02}$) is better than 0.05 ($1.0462 \pm_{1.3e-02}$), 0.2 ($1.0430 \pm_{1.2e-02}$), and 0.3 ($1.0475 \pm_{1.4e-02}$).

4.3 Experimental Setup

All algorithms (SPEA2, NSGAII, and MOCell) are executed with a maximum of 25,000 evaluations.

Our genetic algorithms are tuned up by the following parameters obtained during the calibration step. The population size is 100. The probability of the crossover operator is $P_c = 0.9$, the probability of the mutation operator to $P_N = 1/N$ (where N is the number of clouds. E.g., for $N = 11$, it would be, ≈ 0.1). The crossover method is "Single Point Crossover," The mutation type is "Bit Flip Mutation" and the selection method is "Binary Tournament Selection".

We carried out an experimental study to compare SPEA2, NSGA-II, and MOCell. Four instances of the problem are considered: GAKN1 (8 clouds), GAKN2 (9 clouds), GAKN3 (10 clouds), and GAKN4 (11 clouds).

We performed 50 independent runs of each experiment, and record the mean and standard deviation. As there is no reference Pareto Front for our problem, we calculate the approximate Pareto front, from the combination of the non-dominated points of SPEA2, NSGAII, and MOCell.

We use real data of eleven cloud storage providers from the works [10, 21], where average values of download speed, upload speed, and failure probability are provided (Table 3).

Table 3. Characteristics of the clouds

	Cloud storage provider	Average upload speed (MB/s)	Average download speed (MB/s)	Average probability of failure
c_1	Google Drive	2.98	3.06	0.00109019
c_2	Microsoft OneDrive	1.46	2.18	0.00099030
c_3	Dropbox	2.93	3.25	0.00145548
c_4	Box	2.55	2.62	0.00269549
c_5	Egnyte	1.70	2.30	0.00109874
c_6	Sharefile	0.51	0.75	0.00021404
c_7	Salesforce	0.64	0.71	0.00092609
c_8	Alibaba Cloud	2.73	2.86	0.00109345
c_9	Amazon Cloud Drive	1.28	2.79	0.00058234
c_{10}	Apple iCloud	2.75	2.48	0.00056648
c_{11}	Windows Azure Storage	2.24	2.71	0.00043609

5 Obtained Results and Discussion

The results of the experimental study of SPEA2, NSGA-II, and MOCell algorithms for AR-RRNS storage model are presented below.

Tables 4, 5, and 6 show the quality indicators described in Sect. 4.1. The best value of each quality indicator is marked by shaded background.

Considering Epsilon quality indicator (EP) (Table 4), MOCell achieves the best results (the lowest value with lower standard deviation), followed by SPEA2, then by NSGA-II. It has I_{EP} 77.5% better than NSGA-II and 83.3% better than SPEA2.

Table 5 shows the hypervolume indicator (HV), where the larger value with lower standard deviation is better. The first place is MOCell and NSGA-II, then SPEA2, both achieving a value in I_{HV} 2.0% better than SPEA2.

Table 4. EP quality indicator. Mean and Standard Deviation.

Problem	SPEA2 $\bar{x}_{\sigma_n}$	NSGA-II $\bar{x}_{\sigma_n}$	MOCell $\bar{x}_{\sigma_n}$
GAKN1	$0.00e+00 \pm_{0.0e+00}$	$1.34e-03 \pm_{4.2e-04}$	$0.00e+00 \pm_{0.0e+00}$
GAKN2	$5.20e-03 \pm_{1.3e-03}$	$2.71e-03 \pm_{3.7e-04}$	$5.87e-04 \pm_{0.0e+00}$
GAKN3	$1.42e-02 \pm_{3.2e-03}$	$4.46e-03 \pm_{2.6e-03}$	$2.08e-03 \pm_{4.4e-04}$
GAKN4	$2.53e-03 \pm_{1.0e-03}$	$3.78e-03 \pm_{5.2e-04}$	$8.98e-04 \pm_{1.0e-04}$

Table 5. HV quality indicator. Mean and Standard Deviation.

Problem	SPEA2 $\bar{x}_{\sigma_n}$	NSGA-II $\bar{x}_{\sigma_n}$	MOCell $\bar{x}_{\sigma_n}$
GAKN1	$9.55e-01 \pm_{0.0e+00}$	$9.55e-01 \pm_{1.2e-06}$	$9.55e-01 \pm_{0.0e+00}$
GAKN2	$9.51e-01 \pm_{1.2e-03}$	$9.54e-01 \pm_{2.9e-06}$	$9.54e-01 \pm_{5.7e-08}$
GAKN3	$9.63e-01 \pm_{1.8e-03}$	$9.67e-01 \pm_{9.4e-05}$	$9.67e-01 \pm_{1.0e-06}$
GAKN4	$9.77e-01 \pm_{1.2e-04}$	$9.77e-01 \pm_{9.3e-06}$	$9.77e-01 \pm_{1.5e-07}$

Table 6. IGD quality indicator. Mean and Standard Deviation.

Problem	SPEA2 $\bar{x}_{\sigma_n}$	NSGA-II $\bar{x}_{\sigma_n}$	MOCell $\bar{x}_{\sigma_n}$
GAKN1	$0.00e+00 \pm_{0.0e+00}$	$3.09e-04 \pm_{5.6e-05}$	$0.00e+00 \pm_{0.0e+00}$
GAKN2	$1.21e-04 \pm_{1.6e-05}$	$4.03e-04 \pm_{3.6e-05}$	$5.13e-05 \pm_{9.0e-07}$
GAKN3	$2.83e-04 \pm_{1.9e-04}$	$3.51e-04 \pm_{3.9e-05}$	$1.08e-04 \pm_{2.4e-05}$
GAKN4	$8.28e-04 \pm_{4.7e-04}$	$3.14e-04 \pm_{7.9e-06}$	$1.12e-04 \pm_{1.2e-05}$

Considering IGD indicator (Table 6), where the lowest value with lower standard deviation is better, MOCell outperforms the rest of the algorithms, reaching a value of I_{IGD} 78.0% better than SPEA2 and 80.3% better than NSGA-II.

We can conclude that MOCell is better than SPEA2 and NSGA-II in all test cases, taking into account three quality indicators. It reaches a good balance between convergence and diversity.

Concerning the number of obtained solutions (Table 7) that belong to Pareto optimal, we observe that MOCell has the best results. MOCell is 10.3% better than NSGA-II and 21.9% better than SPEA2. For example, if we focus on the GAKN4 problem, MOCell is in the first place, followed by NSGA-II and SPEA2 (71, 68 and 53 Pareto optimal solutions, respectively). The data in Table 7 represent the mean and standard deviation. The highest value is the best.

Table 7. Results of the number of solutions contained in the best front found.

Problem	SPEA2 $\bar{x}_{\sigma_n}$	NSGA-II $\bar{x}_{\sigma_n}$	MOCell $\bar{x}_{\sigma_n}$
GAKN1	$5.68e+01 \pm_{2.8e+0}$	$4.02e+01 \pm_{2.8e+0}$	$4.90e+01 \pm_{2.8e+0}$
GAKN2	$4.62e+01 \pm_{1.6e+0}$	$6.90e+01 \pm_{3.1e+0}$	$6.80e+01 \pm_{2.5e+0}$
GAKN3	$3.45e+01 \pm_{1.5e+0}$	$4.21e+01 \pm_{2.1e+0}$	$5.63e+01 \pm_{1.3e+0}$
GAKN4	$5.37e+01 \pm_{2.1e+0}$	$6.82e+01 \pm_{4.3e+0}$	$7.14e+01 \pm_{2.8e+0}$

Performing 1000 iterations, the algorithms found excellent approximations to the Pareto front in an acceptable time: NSGA-II ($4.51e+02 \pm_{2.5e+01}$ ms), MOCell ($5.33e+02 \pm_{4.9e+01}$ ms) and SPEA2 ($5.34e+02 \pm_{2.4e+01}$ ms).

Figures 2 and 3 show the results of bi-objective optimization. Figure 2 shows the probability of information loss versus redundancy. Figure 3 shows the probability of information loss versus extraction time.

We can see that MOCell obtains a front that covers a wide range of different solutions, as well as obtains a greater number of solutions that integrate the approximate Pareto front.

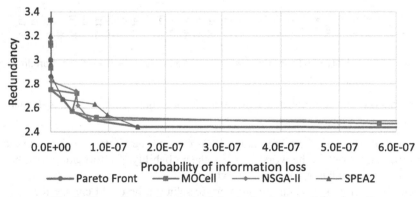

Fig. 2. Examples of the obtained front of solutions. $P_r(k, n)$ vs R

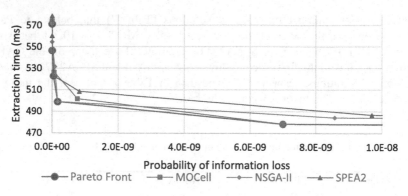

Fig. 3. Examples of the obtained solution fronts. $P_r(k, n)$ vs T_{ex}

In Fig. 4, we plot normalized values obtained by MOCell, when performing multiobjective optimization of $P_r(k, n)$, R, and T_{ex}.

The normalization is done using the min-max method to place all the values within the range [0, 1], where 0 represents the best value and 1 the worst.

We can observe that at the points where the value of k is far from the value of n, for example (2, 10) or (2, 11), we obtain the best values of probability of information loss, but the worst values of redundancy and extraction time.

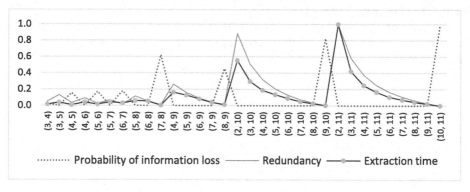

Fig. 4. Points of the approximate Pareto front, plot three objectives vs (k, n) configuration.

While in the points where the value of k is close to the value of n, for example (9, 10) or (10, 11), we obtain the worst value of the probability of information loss, but the best values of redundancy and time of extraction.

If the decision-maker wants a compromise solution, he could choose the configuration (8, 10) or the (9, 11), where the three objectives have lowest values.

Table 8 shows examples of obtained solutions, indicating the clouds that should be used to store the information, configuration (k, n) of the AR-RRNS system, and corresponding values of $P_r(k, n)$, R, and T_{ex}.

Table 8. Examples of solutions. MOCell GA.

Clouds	(k, n)	$P_r(k, n)$	R	T_{ex}
$c_1, \ldots, c_7, c_9, \ldots, c_{11}$	(2, 10)	2.39E−27	10.00	1521.09
$c_1, \ldots, c_7, , c_9, \ldots, c_{11}$	(8, 10)	1.11E−07	2.50	452.73
$c_1, \ldots, c_6, c_8, \ldots, c_{11}$	(9, 10)	4.45E−05	2.22	406.31
$c_1, \ldots, c_{11}$	(2, 11)	2.37E−30	11.00	2421.43
$c_1, \ldots, c_{11}$	(9, 11)	1.52E−07	2.44	443.1
$c_1, \ldots, c_{11}$	(10, 11)	5.38E−05	2.20	399.18

The results show that MOCell is efficient to find a configuration of the secure multi-cloud data storage system in a non-stationarity environment with risks of confidentiality, integrity, and availability violations. It configures parameters to cope with different objective preferences, workloads, and cloud properties. The system selects (k, n) configuration and specific clouds to use. Then, the secret sharing algorithm is applied and the secret is divided into n chunks to be stored in different clouds. When the user requests the data, the system downloads chunks from k clouds that are active to retrieve the original information.

6   Conclusions and Future Work

In this paper, we study the problem of multi-objective optimization of the multi-cloud storage system based on AR-RRNS. We propose mechanisms to configure storage parameters (k, n) for coding/decoding and select specific cloud storages. We consider three optimization criteria: the probability of information loss/change, redundancy, and extraction time. We give a brief description of AR-RRNS data storage model with (k, n) threshold scheme and how this model can be applied to the multi-cloud environment. We design configuration mechanisms based on genetic algorithms specifying the chromosome encoding, fitness evaluation function, and constraints.

We provide an experimental study using real data from eleven cloud storage providers. We compare the performance of three genetic algorithms: MOCell, NSGA-II, and SPEA3 using three quality indicators: Inverted generational distance, additive epsilon, and hypervolume. We show that MOCell outperforms NSGA-II and SPEA2 in all quality indicators. I_{EP} of MOCell is 77.5% better than of NSGA-II and 83.3% better than of SPEA2. The numbers of solutions belonged to the Pareto front approximation of MOCell is 10.3% better than NSGA-II and 21.9% better than SPEA2.

As future work, we will design weighted SSS and study a variety of artificial intelligent and computational intelligent mechanisms to configure distributed cloud storage.

Acknowledgments. The work is partially supported by Russian Federation President Grant MK-341.2019.9.

References

1. Băsescu, C., et al.: Robust data sharing with key-value stores. In: IEEE/IFIP International Conference on Dependable Systems and Networks (DSN 2012), pp. 1–12. IEEE, June 2012
2. AlZain, M.A., Pardede, E., Soh, B., Thom, J.A.: Cloud computing security: from single to multi-clouds. In: 2012 45th Hawaii International Conference on System Sciences, pp. 5490–5499. IEEE, January 2012
3. Tchernykh, A., Schwiegelsohn, U., Talbi, E.G., Babenko, M.: Towards understanding uncertainty in cloud computing with risks of confidentiality, integrity, and availability. J. Comput. Sci. (2016)
4. Shamir, A.: How to share a secret. Commun. ACM **22**(11), 612–613 (1979)
5. Fabian, B., Ermakova, T., Junghanns, P.: Collaborative and secure sharing of healthcare data in multi-clouds. Inf. Syst. **48**, 132–150 (2015)
6. Miranda-López, V., et al.: Experimental analysis of secret sharing schemes for cloud storage based on RNS. In: Mocskos, E., Nesmachnow, S. (eds.) CARLA 2017. CCIS, vol. 796, pp. 370–383. Springer, Cham (2018). https://doi.org/10.1007/978-3-319-73353-1_26
7. Babenko, M., et al.: Unfairness correction in P2P grids based on residue number system of a special form. In: 2017 28th International Workshop on Database and Expert Systems Applications (DEXA), pp. 147–151. IEEE, August 2017
8. Chervyakov, N., Babenko, M., Tchernykh, A., Kucherov, N., Miranda-López, V., Cortés-Mendoza, J.M.: AR-RRNS: configurable reliable distributed data storage systems for Internet of Things to ensure security. Future Gener. Comput. Syst. (2017)
9. Tchernykh, A., et al.: AC-RRNS: anti-collusion secured data sharing scheme for cloud storage. Int. J. Approximate Reasoning **102**, 60–73 (2018)
10. Tchernykh, A., Babenko, M., Miranda-López, V., Drozdov, A.Y., Avetisyan, A.: WA-RRNS: reliable data storage system based on multi-cloud. In: 2018 IEEE International Parallel and Distributed Processing Symposium Workshops (IPDPSW), pp. 666–673, May 2018. IEEE
11. Flores, I.: Residue arithmetic and its application to computer technology (Nicholas S. Szabo and Richard I. Tanaka). SIAM Rev. **11**(1), 103–104 (1969)
12. Barsi, F., Maestrini, P.: Error correcting properties of redundant residue number systems. IEEE Trans. Comput. **100**(3), 307–315 (1973)
13. Tchernykh, A., et al.: Performance evaluation of secret sharing schemes with data recovery in secured and reliable heterogeneous multi-cloud storage. Cluster Comput. **22**, 1–13 (2018)
14. Liefooghe, A., Derbel, B.: A correlation analysis of set quality indicator values in multiobjective optimization. In: Proceedings of the Genetic and Evolutionary Computation Conference 2016, pp. 581–588. ACM, July 2016
15. Nebro, A.J., Durillo, J.J., Luna, F., Dorronsoro, B., Alba, E.: MOCell: a cellular genetic algorithm for multiobjective optimization. Int. J. Intell. Syst. **24**(7), 726–746 (2009)
16. Deb, K., Agrawal, S., Pratap, A., Meyarivan, T.: A fast elitist non-dominated sorting genetic algorithm for multi-objective optimization: NSGA-II. In: Schoenauer, M., et al. (eds.) PPSN 2000. LNCS, vol. 1917, pp. 849–858. Springer, Heidelberg (2000). https://doi.org/10.1007/3-540-45356-3_83
17. Zitzler, E., Laumanns, M., Thiele, L.: SPEA2: Improving the strength Pareto evolutionary algorithm. TIK-report, 103 (2001)
18. Van Veldhuizen, D.A., Lamont, G.B.: Multiobjective evolutionary algorithm research: a history and analysis. Technical report TR-98–03, Department of Electrical and Computer Engineering, Graduate School of Engineering, Air Force Institute of Technology, Wright-Patterson AFB, Ohio (1998)

19. Zitzler, E., Thiele, L., Laumanns, M., Fonseca, C.M., Da Fonseca Grunert, V.: Performance assessment of multiobjective optimizers: An analysis and review. TIK-Report, vol. 139 (2002)
20. Zitzler, E., Thiele, L.: Multiobjective evolutionary algorithms: a comparative case study and the strength Pareto approach. IEEE Trans. Evol. Comput. 3(4), 257–271 (1999)
21. Lopez-Falcon, E.: Adaptive encrypted cloud storage model. In: 2018 IEEE Conference of Russian Young Researchers in Electrical and Electronic Engineering (EIConRus), pp. 329–334, January 2018. IEEE

Bounding Volume Hierarchy Acceleration Through Tightly Coupled Heterogeneous Computing

Ernesto Rivera-Alvarado$^{(\boxtimes)}$ and Francisco J. Torres-Rojas

Computer Science, Costa Rica Institute of Technology, Cartago, Costa Rica
ernestoriv7@yahoo.com, torresrojas@gmail.com

Abstract. Bounding Volume Hierarchy (BVH) is the main acceleration mechanism used for improving ray tracing rendering time. Several
research efforts have been made to optimize the BVH algorithm for GPU
and CPU architectures. Nonetheless, as far as we know, no study has targeted the APU (Accelerated Processing Unit) that have a CPU and an
integrated GPU in the same die. The APU has the advantage of being
able to share workloads within its internal processors (CPU and GPU)
through heterogeneous computing. We crafted a specific implementation
of the ray tracing algorithm with BVH traversal implemented for the
APU architecture and compared the performance of this SoC against
CPU and GPU equivalent implementations. It was found that the performance of the APU surpassed the other architectures.

Keywords: Bounding Volume Hierarchy · Accelerated Processing
Unit · Ray tracing · CPU · GPU · APU · BVH · Heterogeneous
computing

1 Introduction

A ray tracing algorithm spends most of its execution time computing ray/object
intersections [30]. A ray tracer without any acceleration structure has an $O(I\,n)$
complexity, where I is the number of pixels in the image and n is the number
of objects. Scenes with thousands of objects can be unbearable in rendering
time [33]. Several mechanisms have been created to improve performance in
the ray/object intersection, but currently, only two of them are relevant [23]:
Bounding Volume Hierarchy (BVH) which pre-processes the scene to form a tree
of containers that are used to discard big groups of objects [22]; and *Kd-trees*
that uses a recursive adaptive spacial subdivision [8]. Of them, BVH has become
the most popular because of its good performance for static and dynamic scenes,
widely available open implementations, and its use in state of the art tools [8,16].

There have been active efforts to improve the performance of the BVH in
the CPU and GPU architectures [39,42], but as far as we know, no research has
focused on a solution that utilizes the heterogeneous computing capabilities that

© Springer Nature Switzerland AG 2020
J. L. Crespo-Mariño and E. Meneses-Rojas (Eds.): CARLA 2019, CCIS 1087, pp. 94–108, 2020.
https://doi.org/10.1007/978-3-030-41005-6_7

are available in the very available commodity hardware known as the Accelerated Processing Unit (APU). This device is a tightly coupled heterogeneous computer architecture that incorporates a multi-core CPU and a GPU in the same silicon die [15].

We crafted a specific BVH traversal that uses the heterogeneous computing resources of the APU. We found that our implementation delivers better performance than a CPU or GPU from the same price range. The possibility of using the APU architecture for high demanding tasks like the one explored in this work could position this kind of devices as a viable and low-cost solution for computationally expensive workloads [9–11].

Section 2 presents a brief explanation of the BVH mechanism and reviews different efforts aimed at improving its performance. This section also details the heterogeneous computing platform APU. The BVH acceleration method designed for the APU can be found in Sect. 3. Section 4 describes the experiments executed, the hardware used, and the analysis method for the obtained data. The results are presented in Sect. 5 and discussed in Sect. 6. In Sect. 7, we summarize the main conclusions and identify future work.

2 Background

2.1 Bounding Volume Hierarchy

The *Bounding Volume Hierarchy* for accelerating ray/object intersections is based in a subdivision of the objects that are present in the scene. The objects are partitioned in a hierarchy of disjoint sets. As can be seen in Fig. 1 (taken from [30]), elements that are part of the scene are incorporated in containers, forming a binary tree data structure. Objects are stored on the leaves of the tree, and each intermediate node stores a bounding box for the elements in the nodes beneath it [8,33].

When a ray traverses through the BVH tree and does not intersect a bounding box contained in a node, all the subtree for that node can be clipped. This algorithm is a solution to a more general problem called *collision detection*, which is at the core of a broad spectrum of engineering and computer science applications, such as physics-based simulations, robotic motion planning, haptic processing, virtual disassembly, and general computer graphics [12]. The main advantages of the BVH accelerator against other techniques are:

- It is faster to build [38].
- It is numerically more robust and less prone to missed intersections due to rounding errors [30].
- It is used for real-time rendering because of its good performance [8].

The performance gain provided by BVH goes from $O(I\ n)$ to $O(I\ \log n)$. The scene objects will be contained in the leaves of a binary tree of height $log\ n$, so the collision detection for a ray will have to travel in average $log\ n$ nodes (in scenes where the objects are spread) to find if the ray intersects a primitive [12,17,40].

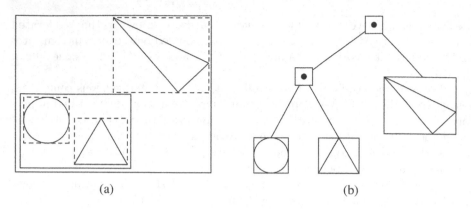

(a)   (b)

Fig. 1. Bounding Volume Hierarchy diagram.

BVH was initially conceived to run in CPUs, and it was later ported to GPUs by [7]. Among other reasons, it is a difficult endeavor to use the GPU as the default platform for ray tracing with BVH because the RAM-VRAM transactions are frequent, and when compared with the CPU, GPU has a small cache, so more bandwidth is needed for memory transactions [16,30]. With that in mind, recent initiatives focus specifically on the acceleration of the ray/object intersection in ray tracing through GPUs [42]. They propose a mechanism to compress the BVH data structures of the pre-processed objects that are sent to the GPU memory, which reduces the required communication bandwidth between RAM and VRAM. A disadvantage of this approach is the additional time for data compressing added to each GPU VRAM transaction. Furthermore, this approach only works well with scenes that require a lot of memory transactions.

Other authors have pointed that BVH traversal does not map well in GPUs [25,36,37]. Naive GPU implementations could result in hardware under-utilization due to inefficient work distribution. This problem leads to modifications of the BVH algorithm to reduce its penalty when running in GPUs [13]. An example of these modifications is the explicit caching of BVH node-pairs to improve its access time the next time that Bounding Volume Test Tree is accessed [13,25,36]. Another method implements private work-stacks to improve memory access costs and reduce inter-thread synchronization [24,25]. Nonetheless, these approaches generate new problems like work-flow divergence and load-imbalances that degrades performance [12].

2.2   PCI-Express

PCI-Express is an I/O standard that implements a switched network with point-to-point serial links [18]. It is widely used in modern computer systems and it is the de facto bus used to interconnect a GPU with a CPU [34]. All traffic form main memory and the CPU to the GPU must go through this communication link. It has the disadvantage that its bandwidth is significantly lower than access to DRAM, so it becomes a serious bottleneck in heterogeneous computing algorithms that are heavily communication-dependent [21].

2.3   Accelerated Processing Unit

An Accelerated Processing Unit (APU) is a tightly coupled heterogeneous computer architecture that in the same integrated circuit has a CPU and a GPU that shares system memory (RAM) and Input/Output resources. Both units have a coherence mechanism between their memories and the ability to share data structures in an efficient manner [15]. This kind of computational unit brings the opportunity of creating specialized algorithms that make use of it specific characteristics to obtain better performance [18,21].

It is mentioned in [21] that there is pending work in evaluating the performance of APUs in tasks where GPU performance is not practical. The APU can provide acceleration in tasks that are impacted by the PCI-Express bus transfer rate, the code is sequential, has a high number of branches, or the inability of efficiently sharing data structures between the CPU and GPU severely degrades performance [20,21].

3   Design

We crafted a novel BVH algorithm for APU that uses all its computing resources to improve the performance of this task. Our mechanism obtains high performance by using the ability to share, in an efficient manner, data structures between the integrated GPU and the CPU as they use the same memory. This advantage avoids the memory transactions that get bottle-necked through the PCI-Express bus [21,42].

We developed the same BVH traversal algorithm for the CPU (using C) and the GPU (using OpenCL). Both processors use the same data structures. None of the implementations provides any optimization that favors any architecture. Our implementation of the BVH traversal is heavily based in [30,32,35]. Also, to obtain acceptable GPU performance we followed the recommendations found in [21]. The APU code of its internal units (CPU and GPU) is exactly the same code as the discrete CPU and the discrete GPU. We used OpenCL in all available GPU architectures as it is the only supported language by the APU GPU. Using CUDA for the discrete GPU adds another factor to the evaluation that could lead to wrong conclusions as the performance across GPUs is being measured for different programming languages.

We used a zero copy mechanism described in [2–4] to share the same data structures between the CPU and the integrated GPU. We verified the behavior of the shared memory data structures between the CPU and the integrated GPU by using the tool CodeXL [1,14]. As expected, none of the data structures were copied (see Fig. 2). This was not the case with the discrete GPU as can be seen in Fig. 3.

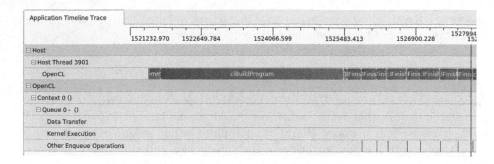

Fig. 2. CodeXL profiling result for the developed APU algorithm with zero data transfer.

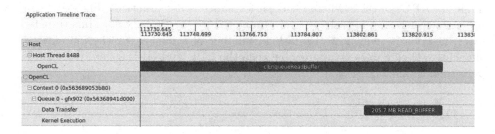

Fig. 3. CodeXL profiling result for the discrete GPU.

Our algorithm is presented in Fig. 4. All CPU and GPU cores works simultaneously to render the image. Both units use the same BVH data structure stored in RAM. The algorithm divides the image into 16×16 pixel workloads. A thread is generated for each available CPU core. Each thread will process a workload and saves its result to memory. If there is no more pending work, the thread will finish. On the GPU side, we follow the recommendations found in [4,21] to maximize the GPU resources utilization. We achieved the desired performance with a workload size of $6 \times N$ units, with N representing the total of computing units in the GPU.

The integrated GPU works in parallel along with the CPU. After processing its work, the GPU checks if there are at least $6 \times N$ workloads available. If the amount is less than that quantity, all remaining work is processed by the CPU cores. When there are no more workloads remaining, the image is generated and the process finishes.

4   Methodology

Factorial Analysis of Variance (ANOVA) methodology was chosen due to its capacity to evaluate the performance of the BVH algorithm across the APU,

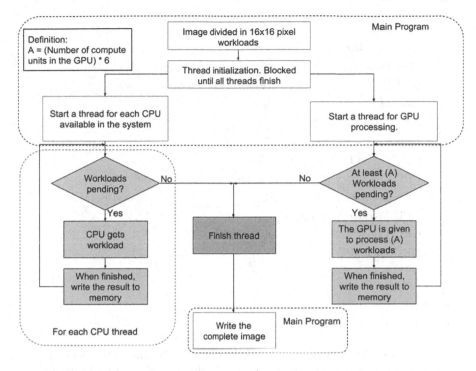

Fig. 4. APU ray tracing algorithm with BVH collision detection.

CPU and GPU architecture in function of the object quantity and resolution factors [26].

The response variable of the experiment is rendering time. A factor is a component that might impact in some way the response variable [26]. Our goal with the ANOVA experiment is to be able to determine if our selected heterogeneous computing platform is statistically different from the other architectures across different object quantities and resolution scenarios.

The factors and its levels that we selected for the experiments are:

- **Architecture:** This factor is crucial to test the ability of our proposed design to accelerate BVH traversal and compare its performance against the CPU and GPU architectures. The levels are:
  - APU.
  - CPU.
  - GPU.
- **Objects:** The number of objects in a scene directly impacts the rendering time as it increases the number of BVH nodes that the ray tracing algorithm needs to traverse [17]. The following amounts for objects were used:
  - 1000.
  - 4000.

Table 1. Hardware description.

Characteristic	CPU	GPU	APU
Manufacturer	AMD	Nvidia	AMD
Model	Ryzen 5 2600	1050Ti	Ryzen 5 2400g
Price ($)	199	199	169
CPU Cores/Threads	6/12	–	4/8
Power Consumption (W)	65	75	65
CPU Cache L2/L3 (MB)	3/16	–	2/4
CPU Frequency (GHz)	3.4–3.9	–	3.6–3.9
GPU Memory (GB)	–	4	Shared RAM
GPU Frequency (GHz)	–	1.29	1.25
GPU Cores	–	768	704
GPU GFLOPS	–	2138	1736

- 16000.
- 65000.
- 260000.

- **Image resolution:** Resolution directly impacts the amount of work that is processed and the number of BVH traversals [19]. The resolutions selected for this experiments are:

  - 1280×720.
  - 1440×900.
  - 1920×1080.

There are $5 \times 3 \times 3 = 45$ combinations of the levels of the factors, since it was decided to have 15 replications, we ended up with $45 \times 15 = 675$ runs of the experiment. Scripts were developed to run the experiments in a random order and recollect data.

This experiment differs from the approach taken in [31], where effects such as transparencies, reflections, and anti-aliasing were contemplated as factors in the ANOVA because their presence impacts rendering time as it loads the processor with mathematical operations. In the specific case of BVH, the 3 factors defined above are sufficient to test the acceleration capabilities induced by the APU.

We used two computers to run the experiments that had the same amount of RAM (8 GB at 2400 MHz single channel) and a 256 GB SSD. One held the CPU and GPU architecture, and the other had the APU. Table 1 shows the details of each system.

For each object quantity scenario, the scene is constituted from randomly placed primitives across the x and y axis of the projection frame and the z axis of the scene. From there the factors of resolution and architecture were adjusted for each experiment run. Following [29], we used rendering time as our response time to evaluate the performance.

Table 2. Obtained metrics for the APU, CPU and GPU architectures (lower is better).

Metric	APU	CPU	GPU
Average Time (s)	67.53	150.18	204.94
Performance/Pixel (μs)	15.75	34.99	47.75

Our acceleration mechanism as well as the obtained data from the experiments can be found in: https://github.com/ernestoriv7/APU-performance-evaluation.

5 Results

The data collected from the experiments needed a square root transformation in order to comply with the ANOVA adequacy requirements [26]. Nonetheless, we present the de-transformed (*i.e.*, elevated to its square) data results in order to simplify reader interpretation.

We used the R software [41] to analyze our experiments. The obtained ANOVA table can be seen in Fig. 5. The average rendering time for each architecture (the crucial factor of this research) is shown in Fig. 6. Finally, Figs. 7 and 8 present the behavior of each architecture in relation to the other factors.

Anova Table (Type II tests)

Response: T_sqrt

	Sum Sq	Df	F value	Pr(>F)	
Architecture	4333	2	3858250.0	< 2.2e-16	***
Objects	34601	4	15403594.9	< 2.2e-16	***
Resolution	699	2	622468.1	< 2.2e-16	***
Architecture:Objects	4437	8	987670.5	< 2.2e-16	***
Architecture:Resolution	32	4	14209.7	< 2.2e-16	***
Objects:Resolution	321	8	71466.4	< 2.2e-16	***
Architecture:Objects:Resolution	30	16	3332.6	< 2.2e-16	***
Residuals	0	630			

Signif. codes: 0 '***' 0.001 '**' 0.01 '*' 0.05 '.' 0.1 ' ' 1

Fig. 5. ANOVA Table.

A summary of the average rendering time and average performance/pixel per architecture (for all the combinations of resolutions and object quantities) is presented in Table 2.

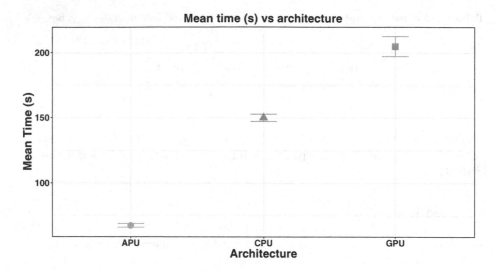

Fig. 6. Average rendering time in function of the architecture.

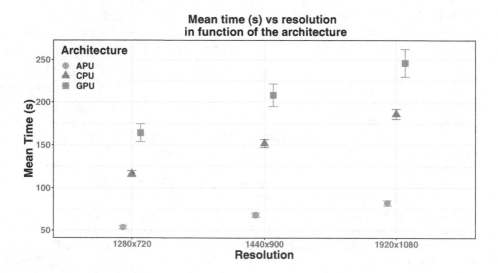

Fig. 7. Resolution and architecture.

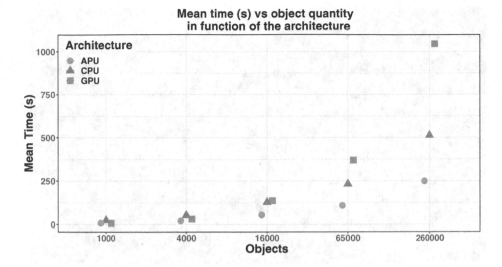

Fig. 8. Object quantity and architecture.

We tested the correctness of our proposed algorithm by verifying that all three architectures render exactly the same image under the same circumstances. Typical images generated through the experiments are shown in Figs. 9 and 10.

Fig. 9. 16000 objects

Fig. 10. 260000 objects

6   Discussion

The ANOVA table presented in Fig. 5 shows that all the main factors defined are statistically significant (p values lower than 0.05 as pointed by the asterisks), which means that all they influence the response variable. A Welch's t pairwise test determined that APU is statistically different from the other two. As Fig. 6 shows, the APU provides the lowest rendering time and the best performance for creating an image with BVH acceleration in the average of all the interactions of object quantities and resolutions.

The metrics obtained in Table 2 are aligned with this result and indicates that the heterogeneous computing capabilities given by the APU and our design delivers the best rendering time per pixel, when compared against the time of the CPU and GPU platforms. Analyzing the performance difference from the same table we can see that the heterogeneous computing capabilities of the APU architecture is able to provide a performance gain of 55.03% against the CPU and a 67.04% gain when compared against the GPU architecture. The impact of resolution, object quantity, and their interactions on rendering time is vastly explained in [8, 19, 30, 32, 35].

Analyzing the graphs of Figs. 5, 7 and 8 through the ANOVA and Welch's t pairwise tests we found that:

– The APU is statistically better in performance to the other two architectures at any level of resolution. The resolution level impacts in the amount of processed work and the number of BVH traversals for each pixel. Processing a pixel implies at least one ray (more because of the anti-aliasing, reflections and transparencies effects in the scene) which in itself triggers intersection

detection through BVH. Hence, Fig. 7 evidences that our acceleration method appears to be less sensitive to the increase of traversals in the BVH data structure.
- The quantity of objects in the scene directly impacts the amount of intersections and nodes that need to be detected through the BVH data structure, which generates more memory accesses and mathematical operations. The Welch's test and the data obtained in Fig. 8 shows that the APU rendering time is statistically different and better than CPU or GPU, for 4000 or more objects. The reason of this behavior is that the internal components of APU architecture have an easy access to RAM where the BVH data tree and objects are stored. This situation is different in a GPU implementation, where as object quantity increases, PCI-Express bus memory transfers also does, which negatively impacts the rendering time. Also, it has been identified that collision detection with GPUs is challenging because of compute units sub-utilization and inefficient memory access patterns due to the unpredictability of which the BVH data structure needs to be accessed [12].

Floating point numbers with 64 bits (FP64) operations are required to calculate correct intersections in the BVH tree for rendering images like the ones illustrated in Figs. 9 and 10. If a lower bit quantity operation is used (FP32) the rendered image shows incorrect artifacts.

Finally, we see that the correct outputs and the metrics obtained from the analysis performed provides evidence that the proposed heterogeneous computing BVH traversal acceleration mechanism crafted specifically for the APU, is a viable option for improving the performance of this task.

7   Conclusions and Future Work

We presented a novel mechanism for accelerating BVH traversal through a tightly coupled heterogeneous architecture known as the APU. Our design utilizes all available computing resources in the APU (integrated GPU and CPU) to render a ray traced image with BVH for collision detection. Our approach takes advantage of the particular characteristics of the APU architecture, for instance, its ability to share data structures from RAM and the ability to efficiently coordinate work within its internal processors.

From our experiments we were able to demonstrate the potential of the selected heterogeneous computing architecture as a viable platform for improving the performance of BVH traversal. Data shows that through our specialized algorithm the APU performance advantage becomes more significant as the memory access, mathematical operations and BVH nodes increases.

The correctness of the generated image is dependent on the floating point operations resolution of the architecture. In our case, FP64 was required for obtaining correct results so it is implemented in our design. This could lead to that other computing platforms with optimized FP64 operations could benefit from our mechanism. On the other hand, several techniques to minimize the FP32 rounding error [30] can also be used.

For future work, we plan to evaluate additional ray tracing features and acceleration methods in our design. We also plan to test new heterogeneous computing platforms as they could change the results of this research. We want to study other workloads besides BVH to measure whether the approach taken in this research effort keeps its performance advantage in those tasks. Also, a more in-depth evaluation that measures the performance in function of the enabled cores in all architectures could provide valuable information. The effect of enabling or disabling hyperthreading and governors in the CPUs to evaluate its impact on performance it's another pending evaluation. Since the APU uses the same code as their CPU and GPU counterparts, it would be interesting to explore the effects of vast optimization of the rendering code in the three architectures with different programming languages and commercial/vendor specific solutions like Nvidia OptiX [27,28], Intel Embree [6], Radeon Rays [5] and PowerVR [40].

References

1. Advanced Micro Devices: Getting Started with CodeXL. AMD, September 2012
2. Advanced Micro Devices: AMD Accelerated Parallel Processing. OpenCL Programming Guide, AMD, November 2013
3. Advanced Micro Devices: AMD APP SDK. OpenCL User Guide, AMD, August 2015
4. Advanced Micro Devices: OpenCL Optimization Guide. AMD, August 2015
5. Advanced Micro Devices: Introducing the Radeon Rays SDK. AMD, August 2016
6. Áfra, A.T., Wald, I., Benthin, C., Woop, S.: Embree ray tracing kernels: overview and new features. In: ACM SIGGRAPH 2016 Talks, SIGGRAPH 2016, pp. 52:1–52:2. ACM, New York (2016)
7. Aila, T., Laine, S.: Understanding the efficiency of ray traversal on GPUs. In: Proceedings of the Conference on High Performance Graphics 2009, HPG 2009, pp. 145–149. ACM, New York (2009)
8. Akenine-Möller, T., Haines, E., Hoffman, N.: Real-Time Rendering, 4th edn. A K Peters/CRC Press, Natick (2018)
9. Angel, E., Shreiner, D.: Interactive Computer Graphics: A Top-Down Approach with WebGL, 7th edn. Pearson, London (2014)
10. Bikker, J.: Ray Tracing in Real-Time Games. Ph.D. thesis, NHTV University of Applied Sciences, Reduitlaan 41, 4814DC, Breda, The Netherlands (2012)
11. Bikker, J., van Schijndel, J.: The brigade renderer: a path tracer for real-time games. Int. J. Comput. Games Technol. **2013**, 1–14 (2013)
12. Chitalu, F.M., Dubach, C., Komura, T.: Bulk-synchronous parallel simultaneous BVH traversal for collision detection on GPUs. In: Proceedings of the ACM SIGGRAPH Symposium on Interactive 3D Graphics and Games, I3D 2018, pp. 4:1–4:9. ACM, New York (2018)
13. Du, P., Liu, E.S., Suzumura, T.: Parallel continuous collision detection for high-performance GPU cluster. In: Proceedings of the 21st ACM SIGGRAPH Symposium on Interactive 3D Graphics and Games, I3D 2017, pp. 4:1–4:7. ACM, New York (2017)
14. Fare, C.: Enabling profiling for SYCL applications. In: Proceedings of the International Workshop on OpenCL, IWOCL 2018, pp. 12:1–12:1. ACM, New York (2018)

15. Gaster, B., Howes, L., Kaeli, D.R., Mistry, P., Schaa, D.: Heterogeneous Computing with OpenCL: Revised OpenCL 1, 2nd edn. Morgan Kaufmann, San Francisco (2012)
16. Haines, E., Akenine-Möller, T.: Ray Tracing Gems: High-Quality and Real-Time Rendering with DXR and Other APIs. Apress, Berkeley (2019)
17. Haines, E., Hanrahan, P., Cook, R.L., Arvo, J., Kirk, D., Heckbert, P.S.: An Introduction to Ray Tracing (The Morgan Kaufmann Series in Computer Graphics). Academic Press, London (1989)
18. Hennessy, J.: Computer Architecture: A Quantitative Approach. Morgan Kaufmann Publishers, an imprint of Elsevier, Cambridge (2018)
19. Hughes, J.F., et al.: Computer Graphics: Principles and Practice, 3rd edn. Addison-Wesley Professional, Boston (2013)
20. Intel Corporation: OpenCL™ Developer Guide for Intel® Processor Graphics. Intel Corporation, February 2015
21. Kaeli, D.R., Mistry, P., Schaa, D., Zhang, D.P.: Heterogeneous Computing with OpenCL 2.0. Morgan Kaufmann, San Francisco (2015)
22. Kay, T.L., Kajiya, J.T.: Ray tracing complex scenes. In: Proceedings of the 13th Annual Conference on Computer Graphics and Interactive Techniques, SIGGRAPH 1986, pp. 269–278. ACM, New York (1986)
23. Laine, S.: Restart trail for stackless BVH traversal. In: Proceedings of the Conference on High Performance Graphics, HPG 2010, pp. 107–111. Eurographics Association, Aire-la-Ville, Switzerland (2010)
24. Lauterbach, C., Garland, M., Sengupta, S., Luebke, D., Manocha, D.: Fast BVH construction on GPUs. Comput. Graph. Forum **28**, 375–384 (2009)
25. Lauterbach, C., Mo, Q., Manocha, D.: gProximity: hierarchical GPU-based operations for collision and distance queries. Comput. Graph. Forum **29**, 419–428 (2010)
26. Montgomery, D.C.: Design and Analysis of Experiments. Wiley, New York (2012)
27. Parker, S.G., et al.: OptiX: a general purpose ray tracing engine. ACM Trans. Graph. **29**(4), 66:1–66:13 (2010)
28. Parker, S.G., et al.: OptiX: a general purpose ray tracing engine. In: ACM SIGGRAPH 2010 Papers, SIGGRAPH 2010, pp. 66:1–66:13. ACM, New York (2010)
29. Patterson, D.: Computer Organization and Design: The Hardware/Software Interface. Morgan Kaufmann, Waltham (2014)
30. Pharr, M., Jakob, W., Humphreys, G.: Physically Based Rendering: From Theory to Implementation, 3rd edn. Morgan Kaufmann, Burlington (2016)
31. Rivera-Alvarado, E., Torres-Rojas, F.: APU performance evaluation for accelerating computationally expensive workloads. In: Conferencia Latinoamericana de Informática, April 2019
32. Shirley, P.: Ray Tracing in One Weekend, 1st edn. Amazon Digital Services LLC, Seattle (2016)
33. Shirley, P., Morley, R.K.: Realistic Ray Tracing, 2nd edn. A. K. Peters, Ltd., Natick (2003)
34. Stallings, W.: Computer Organization and Architecture, 10th edn. Pearson, Hoboken (2015)
35. Suffern, K.: Ray Tracing from the Ground Up. A K Peters/CRC Press, Natick (2007)
36. Tang, M., Manocha, D., Tong, R.: Multi-core collision detection between deformable models. In: SIAM/ACM Joint Conference on Geometric and Physical Modeling, SPM 2009, pp. 355–360. ACM, New York (2009)

37. Tang, M., Wang, H., Tang, L., Tong, R., Manocha, D.: CAMA: contact-aware matrix assembly with unified collision handling for GPU-based cloth simulation. Comput. Graph. Forum **35**, 511–521 (2016)
38. Vinkler, M., Havran, V., Bittner, J.: Bounding volume hierarchies versus Kd-trees on contemporary many-core architectures. In: Proceedings of the 30th Spring Conference on Computer Graphics, SCCG 2014, pp. 29–36. ACM, New York (2014)
39. Wald, I.: On fast construction of SAH-based bounding volume hierarchies. In: Proceedings of the 2007 IEEE Symposium on Interactive Ray Tracing, RT 2007, pp. 33–40. IEEE Computer Society, Washington, DC(2007)
40. Wang, Y., Liu, C., Deng, Y.: A feasibility study of ray tracing on mobile GPUs. In: SIGGRAPH Asia 2014 Mobile Graphics and Interactive Applications, SA 2014, pp. 31–35. ACM, New York (2014)
41. Wickham, H., Grolemund, G.: R for Data Science: Import, Tidy, Transform, Visualize, and Model Data. O'Reilly Media, Sebastopol (2017)
42. Ylitie, H., Karras, T., Laine, S.: Efficient incoherent ray traversal on GPUs through compressed wide BVHs. In: Proceedings of High Performance Graphics, HPG 2017, pp. 4:1–4:13. ACM, New York (2017)

Towards a Lightweight Method to Predict the Performance of Sparse Triangular Solvers on Heterogeneous Hardware Platforms

Raúl Marichal, Ernesto Dufrechou[⊠], and Pablo Ezzatti

Instituto de Computación, Universidad de la República, 11.300 Montevideo, Uruguay
{rmarichal,edufrechou,pezzatti}@fing.edu.uy

Abstract. The solution of sparse triangular linear systems (SpTrSV) is a fundamental building block for many numerical methods. The important presence in different fields and the considerable computational cost of this operation have motivated several efforts to accelerate it on different hardware platforms and, in particular, on those equipped with massively-parallel processors. Until recently, the dominant approach to parallelize this operation on this sort of hardware was the level-set method, which relies on a costly preprocessing phase. For this reason, much of the research on the subject is focused on the case where several triangular linear systems have to be solved for the same matrix. However, the latest efforts have proposed efficient one-phase routines that can be advantageous even when only one SpTrSV needs to be applied for each matrix. In these cases, the decision of which solver to employ strongly depends of the degree of parallelism offered by the linear system. In this work we provide an inexpensive algorithm to estimate the degree of parallelism of a triangular matrix, and explore some heuristics to select between the SpTrSV routine provided by the Intel MKL library and our one-phase GPU solver. The experimental evaluation performed shows that our proposal achieves generally accurate predictions with runtimes two orders lower than the state of the art method to compute the DAG levels.

Keywords: Multi-core · GPU · Sparse triangular linear systems · Parallelism estimation

1 Introduction

Several scientific problems require the solution of sparse triangular linear systems (SpTrSV). Some examples are found in the context of Krylov subspace methods to solve general sparse linear systems, where usually preconditioners have to be applied in each iteration of the solver. A popular family of preconditioners are those based on approximate factorizations, and their application involves the solution of two triangular linear systems [12]. On the context of direct methods,

© Springer Nature Switzerland AG 2020
J. L. Crespo-Mariño and E. Meneses-Rojas (Eds.): CARLA 2019, CCIS 1087, pp. 109–121, 2020.
https://doi.org/10.1007/978-3-030-41005-6_8

this operation is also required to solve the linear systems arising from the sparse LU factorization [2].

Parallel algorithms for the SpTrSV face several performance issues due to the nature of the operation. Specifically, in the general case, the elimination of one unknown in an equation depends on the previous elimination of others, which constrains the parallel scheduling of the algorithm. These dependencies are determined by the sparsity pattern of the sparse matrix, which can be interpreted as a Directed Acyclic Graph (DAG) where each node is an equation or unknown and the edges represent the dependencies between equations. Additionally, the triangular structure of the matrix usually generates load imbalance between tasks.

The importance of this kernel for the construction of numerical algorithms, together with its considerable computational cost, has motivated several efforts to accelerate this operation on different hardware architectures [1,13] and, in particular, on massively-parallel platforms such as GPUs [5,9,11,14]. Much of the research on the subject is focused on the case where several triangular linear systems have to be solved for the same matrix. In this sort of scenarios, the dominant approach to parallelize this operation on this kind of hardware is the level-set method [1]. This method relies on analyzing the dependencies between rows of the sparse matrix to determine an ordered group of level-sets that contain rows that are independent and can be solved in parallel. The cost of this operation is proportional to the number of nonzero entries of the sparse matrix and, in general, is superior to the cost of solving one triangular system. The advantage of this method is that using the analysis information can reduce the runtime of the solution phase significantly. However, recent efforts [3,4] have proposed efficient one-phase routines that can be advantageous even when only one SpTrSV needs to be applied. These are based on a different paradigm where each task is assigned with a row to solve and starts its processing as soon as the dependencies of that row have been solved.

The performance of parallel algorithms for the SpTrSV varies greatly according to the sparsity pattern of the matrix. In these sense, it is useful to determine beforehand which kind of solver is likely to perform better for a specific matrix. Our previous research on the subject [5] suggests that the number of level-sets of a sparse matrix is an important factor to take into account for the prediction of the performance of this kernel on GPUs. In general, it is strongly linked to the degree of parallelism offered by the structure of the sparse matrix. This parallelism can be exploited (or not) by a given SpTrSV implementation. However, the computational effort required to obtain the total number of level-sets is similar to that of solving a triangular linear system with the corresponding matrix, which makes this metric impractical when attempting to predict the performance of a triangular solver.

In this work we propose an algorithm to estimate the total number of level-sets of a triangular sparse matrix that is, in general, several orders of magnitude faster than the proper algorithm to compute the level-sets. Then we show how this estimator can be used to predict whether or not our GPU triangular solver will perform better than the one of the Intel MKL [7] for a given matrix. The experimental evaluation performed showed that our proposal is able to classify the triangular matrices with remarkable accuracy, with an almost negligible computational effort.

The rest of the article is structured as follows. Section 2 summarizes the main aspects related with the solution of sparse triangular linear systems. Later, in Sect. 3, we describe our proposal to estimate the degree of parallelism offered by the sparse triangular linear systems. After that, the experimental evaluation performed is summarized in Sect. 4. Finally, in Sect. 5, the main conclusions arrived in this work and the future lines of work are exposed.

2 Solution of Sparse Triangular Linear Systems

If $L \in \mathbb{R}^{n \times n}$ is a lower sparse triangular matrix, $b \in \mathbb{R}^n$ is the RHS (right hand side) vector, and $x \in \mathbb{R}^n$ is the sought-after solution, the linear system

$$Lx = b \tag{1}$$

can be solved by simple *forward-substitution*. The procedure consists on replacing the value of the solved unknowns on the following equations. To obtain unknown x_i, it is necessary to multiply each nonzero coefficient l_{ij} by x_j, subtract the obtained value from b_i, and finally divide the result by the diagonal element or row i. It can be noticed that the solution of x_i requires that the x_j that correspond to the column indexes of the nonzero entries of row i have been solved previously. This clearly implies some degree of serialization, since row i cannot be computed in parallel with those rows.

Algorithm 1 represents the serial version of the lower SpTRSV, where the matrix L is stored in CSR sparse storage format. The most straightforward procedure to parallelize this algorithm consists on a pool of concurrent tasks, each one responsible of solving one or more equations, that wait until their data dependencies have been resolved to start their execution. We refer to this idea as the *self-scheduled* approach.

A more advanced strategy for the parallelization of this algorithm, called *level-set* scheduling, is based on interpreting the sparse matrix as a Directed Acyclic Graph (DAG) that represents the dependencies of each unknown. A nonzero element in l_{ij} means that the equation i depends on the value of unknown j, so there is an edge in the DAG from node j to node i. By means of renumbering the nodes of this DAG, they can be organized into an ordered list of *levels*, in which the nodes in one level depend only on the nodes of the previous levels; see Fig. 1. This means that all nodes (equations) in one level can be solved in parallel provided that the previous levels have already been computed.

2.1 The *Self-scheduled* strategy in GPU

In 2016, Liu et al. [8,9] presented a synchronization-free SpTRSV method for matrices stored in CSC (Compressed Sparse Columns) format [6,12], that takes

Algorithm 1. Serial solution of sparse lower triangular systems for matrices stored in the CSR format. The vector *val* stores the nonzero values of L by row, while row_ptr stores the indexes that correspond to the beginning of each row in vector *val*, and col_idx stores the column index of each element in the original matrix. The nonzero elements of each row are ordered by column index.

```
1 Input: row_ptr, col_idx, val, b
2 Output: x
    x = b
    for i = 0 to n − 1 do
        for j = row_ptr[i] to row_ptr[i + 1] − 2 do
            x[i] = x[i] − val[j] × x[col_idx[j]]
        end for
        x[i] = x[i]/val[row_ptr[i + 1] − 1]
    end for
```

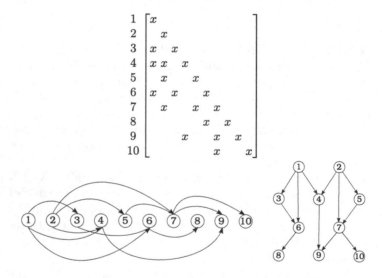

Fig. 1. Nonzero pattern of lower triangular sparse matrix (top), its DAG (bottom-left), and its level-set reordering (bottom-right).

advantage of the computational power offered by modern GPUs. The procedure assigns a *warp* to each column and performs a *busy-wait* until all its dependencies have been fulfilled. This information is obtained through a "vector of dependencies" that needs to be initialized by a fast preprocessing stage. Once the warp has no dependencies it computes the solution element associated with that column and the contribution of each nonzero of the column to the rest of the unknowns, updating the corresponding positions in the vector of dependencies.

In [4], the authors proposed a variant of this strategy for the CSR storage format that does not perform any preprocessing of the sparse matrix but the initialization of one (**ready**) vector, and avoids the use of the slow atomic operations. The experimental results showed that this version outperforms the CSC counterpart in all cases.

Later, in [3] the same authors proposed three other variants of the algorithm, which take advantage of some particularities of the different linear systems and the GPU execution model. In particular an improved version of the one-stage solver that avoids representing the state of each row with an integer in the **ready** vector is presented. Rather, the solution vector is initialized with an invalid value (NaN), and instead of querying the **ready** vector until a nonzero value is obtained, each thread will fetch the corresponding value of the solution vector and consider it the final value if the most significant half of the floating point value is different from NaN.

A simplified version of our GPU kernel is presented in Algorithm 2. The input parameters are the three vectors representing the sparse matrix stored in CSR format, the right hand side, the dimension of the system, and a pointer to the memory reserved for the **ready** vector. As an output parameter, the function receives a pointer to the vector of unknowns.

Algorithm 2. Simplified pseudo-code of our solution kernel.

---

1 **Input:** row_ptr, col_idx, val, b
2 **Output:** x
    $wrp \leftarrow$ global warp identifier
    $lne \leftarrow$ lane identifier
    $row\_start \leftarrow row\_ptr[wrp]$
    $left\_sum \leftarrow 0$
    while not $ready[col\_idx[row + lne]]$ **do**
       ...
    end while
    $left\_sum \leftarrow left\_sum + val[row\_start + lne] \times x[col\_idx[row\_start + lne]]$
    Reduce $left\_sum$ inside the warp
    if $lne = 0$ **then**
       $x[wrp] \leftarrow b[wrp] - left\_sum/val[row\_ptr[wrp + 1] - 1]$
       $ready[wrp] \leftarrow 1$
    end if

2.2 Solution of One Sparse Triangular Linear System

In a previous work [10], we studied the benefits offered by the different SpTRSV methods in the context the resolution of only one linear system.

This study shows that the two best methods to solve sparse triangular linear systems in this context are the routine offered by the MKL library to run in CPU and our method on the GPU. Additionally, the performance advantage of one method or the other is strongly conditioned by the parallel level offered by each the linear system. Specifically, the authors compute the ratio between the number of the levels in the DAG and the dimension of the matrix. However, the computational effort required to obtain the total number of level-sets is similar to that of solving a triangular linear system with the corresponding matrix, which makes this metric impractical when attempting to predict the performance of a triangular solver.

3   Proposal

The number of level-sets of a triangular sparse matrix is equal to the length of the longest-shortest path starting from a root node to any of the nodes (a node with no incoming edges) in the associated DAG.

To obtain the number of level-sets of a lower-triangular sparse matrix L, it is necessary to compute the maximum between the *depth* of all the nodes, which is defined recursively as

$$depth(i) = \begin{cases} 1 & \text{if } l_{ij} = 0 \; \forall j < i \\ \max_{j<i}\{1 + depth(j) : l_{ij} \neq 0\} & \text{otherwise} \end{cases}$$

The computation of the *depth* of all nodes requires $\mathcal{O}(nnz)$ operations. Thus, the computational cost of the operation is similar to that of solving the linear system, which makes impractical the use of the number of level sets to estimate the performance of a following linear system solution. However, a sufficiently accurate estimation of the number of level-sets and, in general, of the available parallelism of the sparse triangular system, can be computed with a much lower computational effort.

Our proposal is based on computing the maximum between the length of a set of paths that are constructed following certain rules. In general, the more paths are constructed the more accurate, but also the expensive the estimator will be.

The paths are constructed departing from a node v in the DAG that has at least one incoming edge. The next node in the path will be the higher numbered node v', with at least one incoming edge, such that there is a directed edge from v' to v. The (lower-)triangular structure of the sparse matrix enforces that all the incoming edges of a given node depart from nodes with lower number. We select the higher numbered node hoping that this will make the number of the following nodes in the path decrease more slowly, and thus result in a longer path. Although this is not necessarily true, it is a reasonable assumption in practice.

The procedure is then repeated replacing v with v' until all the nodes that have outgoing edges ending in v' have no incoming edges.

Considering the sparse matrix, the procedure moves upwards, setting the next row to visit as the column index of the rightmost nonzero entry before the diagonal such that the corresponding row has more than one nonzero. To maximize the probability of finding the longest path with this procedure, it is desirable to select the starting rows such that the rightmost nonzero has a high column index. However, finding the row that maximizes this property can be expensive and does not guarantee the resulting estimation to be more accurate. As a compromise solution, we select the starting rows from the bottom of the sparse matrix.

A pseudocode that describes the procedure that operates on the sparse matrix is presented in Algorithm 3.

Algorithm 3. Pseudo-code for the procedure that computes the estimated number of level-sets of a lower triangular sparse matrix stored in CSR format. The procedure receives the arrays that determine the nonzero structure of the sparse matrix, and the number of paths to construct as parameters. The number of paths is related to the accuracy and to the cost of computing the estimation.

```
1 Input: row_ptr, col_idx, n_paths, n
2 Output: est_levels
    for i = 0 to n_paths − 1 do
      path_length = 0
      current_row = n − i
      while current_row has only one nonzero do
        current_row = current_row − n_paths
      end while
      while current_row has more than one nonzero do
        off = 2
        next_row = col_idx[row_ptr[current_row] + nnz_row − off]
        while next_row has only one nonzero and off < nnz_row + 1 do
          off = off + 1
          next_row = col_idx[row_ptr[current_row] + nnz_row − off]
        end while
        path_length = path_length + 1
        current_row = next_row
      end while
      est_levels = max(est_levels, path_length)
    end for
```

Although the procedure presented is serial, it could be easily parallelized since the construction of the paths is completely independent. After the length of all paths is recorded, the maximum can be taken in logarithmic time by a reduction procedure. As the main purpose of this work is to present and validate the usefulness of the estimation procedure, the parallel implementation is left for future work.

In the worst cases, as the case of a bidiagonal matrix composed by the diagonal and the first subdiagonal, or the case where the bottom row is full and all the other rows have no nonzeros other than the diagonal pivot, the procedure to construct one path requires $\mathcal{O}(n)$ operations. However, on both cases the estimation is equal to the exact number of level-sets. On the average case, the cost of the estimation is expected to be significantly inferior to the cost of the level-set analysis, if a moderate number of paths is constructed.

4   Experimental Evaluation

In this section we present the experimental evaluation performed with the aim of validating our proposal. Next, we describe the hardware platform and test cases employed, to later discuss the experimental results.

4.1   Hardware Platform

The hardware platform employed is a server equipped with a Intel Xeon Gold 6138 CPU of 20 cores at 2.00 GHz and 128 GB of RAM connected to a NVIDIA P100 GPU with 12 GB of RAM. The operation system used is the CentOS Linux 7 (Core) and the CUDA Toolkit for the GPU is version 9.2.

4.2   Test Cases

To perform the experimental evaluation we used a set of real matrices, of medium and large dimension, extracted from the SuiteSparse Matrix Collection[1] (formerly known as the University of Florida Matrix Collection –UFMC–). In particular, we considered the lower triangular part of all the matrices in this collection with real coefficients and of dimension larger than 10,000, obtaining 585 sparse matrices. The execution of the double precision solver failed for 5 of these matrices. This relates to the larger memory requirements of this variant compared with the single precision counterpart. For this reason, the evaluation of the estimator routine is performed on the remaining 580 matrices.

Figure 2 summarizes the distribution of the test cases considering the dimension and the number of nonzero coefficients. It can be observed that, although most matrices do not surpass the 120,000 rows, the test set is sufficiently varied regarding the matrix size. A similar observation can be made regarding the number of nonzeros. Especially considering that the distribution of the number of nonzeros does not correspond with the distribution of the matrix dimension.

All the runtimes presented next are the average of 100 independent executions. Additionally, we employ the IEEE floating point representation, in single or double precision, for all the experiments.

4.3   Experimental Results

The experimental evaluation of our proposal has to be performed considering two different aspects. First, we shall evaluate the accuracy of the estimation of

---

[1]   http://faculty.cse.tamu.edu/davis/suitesparse.html.

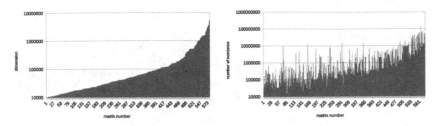

Fig. 2. Dimension (left) and number of nonzero coefficients (right) of the test matrices ordered by dimension. The y axis is in logarithmic scale.

the number of level sets obtained by our proposal. In particular, it is important to evaluate if the obtained estimation is sufficient to distinguish the matrices for which our GPU solver will perform better than the CPU solver. Second, we need to evaluate our proposal from the point of view of its execution time, because the estimation will be useful only if its computation is much faster than computing the actual level-sets.

Figure 3 shows the runtime difference between the GPU solver and the MKL solver relative to the runtime of the slower solver for each matrix, which is calculated as

$$\Delta_T = \frac{t_{MKL} - t_{GPU}}{max(t_{MKL}, t_{GPU})}. \tag{2}$$

We adopt this metric to visualize more clearly the cases for which one solver is better than the other, and so that taking the average for all matrices makes sense. The runtimes in the figure are ordered according to the number of level-sets delivered by each of the evaluated routines.

The first thing that can be observed from the figure is that the shape of the first three graphs is more or less similar, while the fourth graph differs from the others. A breaking point can be clearly spotted between the 300th and the 350th matrix of each of the first three graphs, which is equivalent to approximately 400 level-sets or an estimation of 260 level-sets (note that, by construction, the proposal tends to under-estimate the actual number of level-sets). The matrices that appear before this breaking point are suitable, in general, to be solved by our GPU routine, while the matrices past the breaking point are best suited for the CPU solver. This suggests that both the actual number of level-sets and the estimation, using 500 and 50 paths, are by themselves a good indicator to select one solver or the other.

To evaluate if the proposal is useful in terms of its computation time, we again compute the difference between the runtimes of the routine to compute the depths of all the nodes in the GPU and our proposal (executed with 500, 50, and 5 paths) relative to the runtime of the slower routine. In Table 1 we display the minimum, maximum and average of this metric obtained for each of the estimations. It is important to consider, that this comparison is not fair with our proposal, because the routine that computes the depth of the nodes is parallel and runs on a GPU, while the proposal implementation is serial and

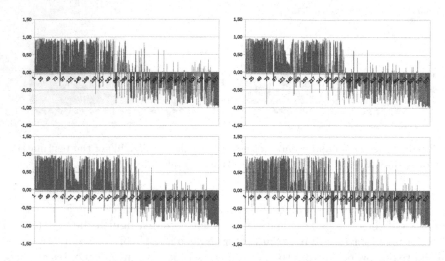

Fig. 3. Runtime difference between the GPU solver and the MKL solver relative to the runtime of the slower solver (Δ_T). The results are presented in four different orders: ordered by ascending actual number of level-sets (top left), ordered by ascending number of level-sets estimated with 500 paths (top right), ordered by ascending number of level-sets estimated with 50 paths (bottom left), ordered by ascending number of level-sets estimated with 5 paths (bottom right). Positive values mean the GPU solver is faster.

runs on a CPU. Furthermore, the GPU routine computes the depth of each node but does not include a reduction of these values to compute the total number of level-sets. However, the results show that even in this conditions, the proposal executed with 500 paths is, on average, 81% faster than computing the actual level-sets, while with 50 paths is at least 72% faster, with an average of 98%. With 5 paths, the proposal has a negligible cost, but the accuracy of the previous classification deteriorates significantly.

Table 1. Runtime difference between the routine to compute the depths of all the nodes in the GPU and our proposal (executed with 500, 50, and 5 paths) relative to the runtime of the slower routine. Positive values mean our proposal is faster.

	Number of paths		
	500	50	5
Min	−0,55	0,72	0,95
Max	1,00	1,00	1,00
Avg	0,81	0,98	0,99

Finally, we evaluate how this estimation of the number of level-sets can be combined with other matrix features to obtain more accurate predictions. In particular, we are interested in evaluating the interaction with the dimension n, the number of nonzero elements nnz and the average number of nonzero elements per row, because this metrics can be obtained in $\mathcal{O}(1)$.

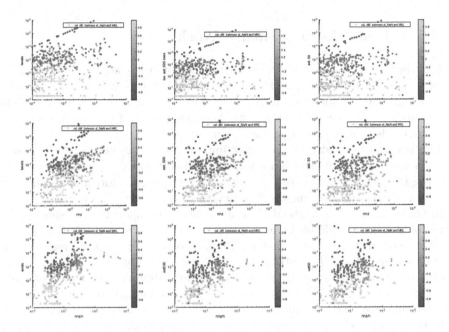

Fig. 4. Relation between Δ_T (color), the actual number of level-sets (left), the estimated number of level-sets with 500 paths (middle), with 50 paths (right), and n (top), nnz (middle), and nnz/n (bottom). The points in yellow correspond to matrices for which our GPU solver shows significantly better performance, while the blue points correspond to those matrices for which the MKL solver is better. (Color figure online)

Figure 4 plots Δ_T according to the actual and estimated number of level-sets and the other three matrix features mentioned above. The points in yellow correspond to matrices for which our GPU solver shows significantly better performance, while the blue points correspond to those matrices for which the MKL solver is better.

In the plots that link the number of level-sets and the dimension, the distribution of the points is similar to the one previously obtained for the number of level-sets alone. Combining the number of level-sets with the dimension does not improve significantly the clustering of the points.

On the other side, in the clustering of the points in the graphs that link the number of level-sets with the number of nonzeros of the matrix, it can be observed that for matrices with large nnz the GPU performance is competitive with that of MKL even when the number of level-sets is large. For the average number of nonzeros per row, this clustering is even clearer.

Given these results, the application of a machine learning algorithm that considers n, nnz and the estimated number of level-sets, as well as an analytical model that links the three metrics, can be useful to achieve a more accurate classification of the matrices.

5   Final Remarks and Future Work

In this work we have advanced in our study towards the characterization of the performance of sparse triangular solvers in HPC hardware platforms. Specifically, we have analyzed the operation in the context of the solution of one linear system per matrix pattern, where one stage methods are preferred in general over two-phase methods that require a preprocessing stage.

The results obtained previous work indicated that the number of level-sets of a triangular sparse matrix is an important factor to take into account when selecting between a parallel GPU solver and a CPU one. Unfortunately, the cost of computing this number makes it impractical to use with this purpose.

In this work we address the design of a lightweight algorithm to estimate the degree of parallelism offered by each linear system. This strategy is a good tool to select between the two prominent HPC methods in this context, namely, our GPU solver and the CPU routine offered by the MKL library.

Our proposal is based on a fast heuristic that estimates the number of level-sets of the sparse matrix. The experimental evaluation of our tool was performed over 580 different sparse triangular linear systems from the SuiteSparse Matrix Collection. Although our method is not computationally optimized, it largely outperforms the runtimes offered by the state of the art (GPU) method. Additionally, the classification of the linear systems obtained with the estimator, according to which is the best performing solver in each case, is remarkably similar than that obtained using the actual number of level-sets.

Some parts of our effort can be extended in order to improve several aspects.

- First of all, it is mandatory to develop a parallel version of our method, possibly including a GPU variant. This will allow to obtain more accurate estimations at a lower computational cost.
- Considering the last part of our experimental evaluation, it seems reasonable to study an estimator that considers also the dimension and number of nonzeros of the system by means of machine learning techniques.
- Finally, another interesting line of work is the study the usage of recent GPU innovations, such as Tensor Core processors and cooperative groups, for both the acceleration of the SpTrSV GPU solver as well as our heuristic.

Acknowledgments. The researchers from *UdelaR* were supported by Universidad de la República and the PEDECIBA.

References

1. Anderson, E., Saad, Y.: Solving sparse triangular linear systems on parallel computers. Int. J. High Speed Comput. **1**(01), 73–95 (1989)
2. Davis, T.: Direct Methods for Sparse Linear Systems. Society for Industrial and Applied Mathematics, Philadelphia (2006)
3. Dufrechou, E., Ezzatti, P.: Using analysis information in the synchronization-free GPU solution of sparse triangular systems. Concurr. Comput.: Pract. Exp., e5499. https://doi.org/10.1002/cpe.5499
4. Dufrechou, E., Ezzatti, P.: Solving sparse triangular linear systems in modern GPUs: a synchronization-free algorithm. In: 26th Euromicro International Conference on Parallel, Distributed and Network-based Processing (PDP), pp. 196–203, March 2018
5. Erguiz, D., Dufrechou, E., Ezzatti, P.: Assessing sparse triangular linear system solvers on GPUs. In: International Symposium on Computer Architecture and High Performance Computing Workshops (SBAC-PADW), pp. 37–42, October 2017
6. Golub, G.H., Van Loan, C.F.: Matrix Computations. Johns Hopkins University Press, Baltimore (2013)
7. Intel. Math Kernel Library (2012). http://developer.intel.com/software/products/mkl/
8. Liu, W., Li, A., Hogg, J., Duff, I.S., Vinter, B.: A synchronization-free algorithm for parallel sparse triangular solves. In: Dutot, P.-F., Trystram, D. (eds.) Euro-Par 2016. LNCS, vol. 9833, pp. 617–630. Springer, Cham (2016). https://doi.org/10.1007/978-3-319-43659-3_45
9. Liu, W., Li, A., Hogg, J.D., Duff, I.S., Vinter, B.: Fast synchronization-free algorithms for parallel sparse triangular solves with multiple right-hand sides. Concurr. Comput. Prac. Exp. **29**(21), e4244 (2017)
10. Marichal, R., Dufrechou, E., Ezzatti, P.: Assessing the solution of one sparse triangular linear system on multi-many core platforms. CLEI (2019). Under Review
11. Naumov, M.: Parallel solution of sparse triangular linear systems in the preconditioned iterative methods on the GPU. NVIDIA Corp., Westford, MA, USA, Technical report, NVR-2011, 1 (2011)
12. Saad, Y.: Iterative Methods for Sparse Linear Systems, 2nd edn. Society for Industrial and Applied Mathematics, Philadelphia (2003)
13. Saltz, J.H., Screduliog Alyc, Becucticy cf Syacercnizatxoi, National Aeronautics, Saltz, J.E.: Automated problem scheduling and reduction of synchronization delay effects. Technical report (1987)
14. Wang, X., Liu, W., Xue, W., Li, W.: swSpTRSV: a fast sparse triangular solve with sparse level tile layout on sunway architectures. SIGPLAN Not. **53**(1), 338–353 (2018)

Accelerating the Calculation of Friedman Test Tables on Many-Core Processors

Diego Irigaray[1], Ernesto Dufrechou[1], Martín Pedemonte[1(✉)], Pablo Ezzatti[1], and Carlos López-Vázquez[2]

[1] Instituto de Computación, Universidad de la República,
11300 Montevideo, Uruguay
{diego.irigaray,edufrechou,mpedemon,pezzatti}@fing.edu.uy
[2] Laboratorio LatinGEO IGM+ORT, Universidad ORT Uruguay,
11100 Montevideo, Uruguay
carloslopez@uni.ort.edu.uy

Abstract. The Friedman Test has been proposed in 1937 to analyze tables of ranks, like those arising from a wine contest. If we have N judges and k wines, the standard problem is to analyze a table of N rows and k columns holding the opinion of the judges. The Friedman's Test is used to accept/reject the null hypothesis that all the wines are equivalent. Friedman offered an asymptotically valid approximation as well as exact tables for low k and N. The accuracy of the asymptotic approximation for moderate k and N was low, and extended tables were required. The published ones were mostly computed using Monte Carlo techniques. The effort required to compute the extended tables for the case without ties was significant (over 100 years of CPU time) and an alternative using many-core processors is described here for the general case with ties. The solution can be used also for other similar tests which yet lack for large enough tables.

Keywords: Friedman Test with ties · Critical values calculation · High Performance Computing · HPC · Graphics Processing Units · GPUs

1 Introduction

The Friedman Test [8] was proposed to analyze a table of ranks. The standard problem can be illustrated with a wine contest, where N judges analyze independently the properties of k wines, producing each a rank among wines without ties. The key problem is to discern if the resulting answers find any difference between the wines or not. If they found it, there exist other test with lower statistical power which will compare the wines pairwise to decide if one is significantly better than the other.

The answers of the judges are organized in a table of integer entries, of N rows and k columns. The original Friedman statistic was designed for the case without ties. Each row has exactly the same set of elements (integers from 1 to k) and

© Springer Nature Switzerland AG 2020
J. L. Crespo-Mariño and E. Meneses-Rojas (Eds.): CARLA 2019, CCIS 1087, pp. 122–135, 2020.
https://doi.org/10.1007/978-3-030-41005-6_9

just differ in the permutation. However, there exist other variants which deal with the general case, and will be presented in Sect. 2. In a particular problem, with k and N given, the statistic is computed and then it should be compared against critical values. In its original paper, Friedman offered exact tables for the critical values of the statistics for low k and N. They were obtained by brute force through enumeration. Later, other researchers expanded somewhat the set of tables using either brute force, symbolic computation and/or Monte Carlo simulation, thus covering low and moderate (k, N) values. For higher values of k and N asymptotic estimates are offered based upon the chi-square and normal distribution.

In practical situations, k and N are given, so practitioners face two situations: if they are lucky enough, there exist a table for such k and N to use. Otherwise, they should use the asymptotic estimate without any clue about the error assumed. Recently López-Vázquez and Hochsztain [13] have presented extended tables for this problem as well as a review of the literature, finding some cases where the use of the asymptotic estimate led to the wrong conclusion because of the lack of a better estimation. They computed such extended tables using an embarrassingly parallel approach, requiring more than a year of wall-clock time using 100 processors for the case without ties.

Since the analytical case is intractable, the procedure to estimate the probability density function (PDF) was based upon Monte Carlo simulation. The PDF of the Friedman's statistic is discrete, a fact which is more evident for low k an N. The authors reported that a significantly large number of events (of the order of 10^8) were required to attain convergence for each pair (k, N). Associated wall time per event varied due to a number of reasons, including the (k, N) values themselves, the sequential CPU processing speed, etc. but has a log-normal distribution.

In recent years, the development of hardware platforms was restrained by the physical limits of materials that compose computer processors. In order to mitigate this deceleration, the most spread strategy is the use of several processor units concurrently. In this line, Graphics Processing Units (GPUs) appeared as new resource on the High Performance Computing (HPC) hardware landscape [11]. GPUs include a large number of processor units, typically hundred or thousands of CUDA cores, reaching impressive performance rates. Another remarkable characteristic of this kind of platforms is that they are largely cheaper than other HPC options (e.g. clusters). Thus, GPUs in the present are widely used in several scientific environments [1,6].

The high execution time involved in the calculation of the Friedman Test tables, caused by both the large number of events (up to 10^8) required for making an accurate estimation, and the elevated number of pairs (k, N) (up to 10390 pair of values [13]), motivates the design of more efficient implementations. Monte Carlo simulations have represented an inspiring problem for the design of GPU implementations, since these type of simulations are highly parallel and well suited for such devices [5].

In this work, we explore the use of GPUs for accelerating the computation of the Friedman's test table. Since the critical values of the statistics have already been calculated for the original Friedman test without ties, we focus in the general case that includes ties. To the best of our knowledge this is the first effort to implement this kind of computation with the massive parallel paradigm. Our goal in this paper is to study how the procedure for estimating the critical values using a Monte Carlo simulation can be ported efficiently to the GPU platform, but not to make the complete estimation of the whole PDF for all the (k, N) pairs. The main idea of our proposal is to group calculations of several events in a single kernel grid, thus generating a large number of thread blocks with a high degree of parallelism.

The experimental evaluation performed over three different test cases in a GeForce GTX 980 Ti GPU obtained runtime reductions that range between $9.97\times$ and $18.90\times$. This reduction means conservatively that for this problem a single GPU is equivalent to the workforce of ten processors. From these results, and since there are no Friedman Test tables in the general case (with ties) at the moment, this effort could be used in the future for making the complete estimation of the PDFs of the statistic.

Additionally, the one by Friedman is not the only statistic proposed for analyzing the table of ranks. Quade [19] designed another statistic that also has an asymptotic chi-square approximation for large N. Iman and Davenport [10] derived an alternative statistic using the one by Friedman as starting point, and proved that asymptotically fits the F-distribution. In a parametric setting, Fawcet and Salter [7] suggested another statistic which also fits asymptotically the F-distribution. This is not an exhaustive list; other less popular proposals exist. In all cases there is no mention about the accuracy of the asymptotic approximation for the case of low and moderate values of k and N. Our proposal in this paper can be easily extended to such statistics.

The rest of the article is structured as follow. Section 2 summarizes the main aspects of the Friedman test, specifically the case that includes rank ties, as well as the procedure for calculating the Friedman Test tables. Later, in Sect. 3, our proposal is described. After that, the experimental evaluation for validating our approach is showed in Sect. 4. Finally, the principal conclusions arrived in our effort and the future lines of work are summarized in Sect. 5.

2   Friedman's Test

The Friedman's test is a non-parametric statistical test developed by Friedman in 1937 [8,9,22]. It is used to detect if an ordinal factor (dependent variable) has any statistical difference between several groups. The test is also used when considering continuos data that is not distributed following a normal distribution (what excludes the use of other tests like one-way ANOVA with repeated measures [22]). For instance, it is frequently employed for checking if the differences in the quality of the numerical results of different stochastic algorithms are statistically significant among a set of problems [2,4,18].

In this section, first we explain the idea of the Friedman's test considering rank ties, and then we address some aspects related to the procedure for calculating the critical values of the statistics for this test.

2.1   Friedman's Test with Rank Ties

To explain the idea of the Friedman's test with ties, we return to the wine contest example. Now, each judge assigns a rank to each wine between 1 (the best ranking) and k (the worst ranking) but ties in the ranking are allowed. The null hypothesis is that there are no significant differences in the quality of the wines, i.e., they taste similarly for the judges involved in the contest.

Since we are dealing with the Friedman's test with rank ties, if there are any ties in the results, the final ranks of the wines are computed as the average rank of the tied wines. For example, if the results are:

$$[2, 3, 5, 3, 1], \tag{1}$$

the final ranks of the wines are:

$$[2, 3.5, 5, 3.5, 1]. \tag{2}$$

After the update of the ranks of the ties, the ranks obtained by each wine for each judge are averaged in order to calculate the final rank (R_j for algorithm j). If all the wines taste similarly for the judges involved in the contest, then their ranks R_j should be similar. The Friedman statistic with ties F_r is computed as [3]:

$$F_r = \frac{N(k-1)\left[\sum_{j=1}^{k}\frac{R_j^2}{N} - C_F\right]}{\sum r_{ij}^2 - C_F} \tag{3}$$

where C_F is the ties correction $(1/4)Nk(k+1)^2$ and r_{ij} is the rank corresponding to the problem j in column i. If the null hypothesis holds, and N and k are big enough, then F_r is distributed according to a chi-square (χ^2) distribution with $k-1$ degrees of freedom.

2.2   Algorithm for Computing the Friedman's Test Table Values

The goal is to produce an implementation that allows to compute a large number of events[1] for each of the required pair (k, N)[2]. For this reason, the implementation has to be efficient in order to complete the Monte Carlo simulations in a reasonable time.

---

[1] Estimated in the order of 10^8.
[2] Set of 10390 pairs $(k; N)$ whose asymptotic estimates differ more than a percentage w.r.t. the Monte Carlo ones.

The set of (k, N) pairs that needs to be estimated was determined in [13]. The region of interest is:

$$\begin{cases} 2 \le k \le 400 \\ 2 \le N \le 3 + \frac{250}{\sqrt{k}} \end{cases} \tag{4}$$

For each pair (k, N), the procedure for computing the Friedman's test table value involves the construction of a histogram that approximates the probability density function. The data for the histogram is generated using Monte Carlo simulations, and therefore a large number of events has to be calculated in order to make an accurate approximation. The steps required for calculating a single event are the following (these steps have to be calculated 10390×10^8 times for completely estimating the Friedman's test table values):

1. Generate a N-by-k matrix of natural numbers between 1 and k following a uniform distribution.
2. Sort each of the rows in ascending order, storing only the index of each element of the sorted row. If there are any ties in the values, the indexes are calculated as the average rank.
3. Compute $\sum_{j=1}^{k} R_j^2$:

    (a) Sum the elements of each column of the matrix obtained in the previous step. The result is a vector of k elements.
    (b) Compute the final result of the experiment as the sum of the squares of the elements of the vector obtained in Step 3a.
4. Compute $\sum r_{ij}^2$:

    (a) Calculate the square of each element of the matrix.
    (b) Sum all the resulting values from in Step 4a.

Thus, the relevant operations to implement efficiently the calculations associated with a single event are:

– the process of generation of random numbers
– the sorting of each row of the matrix
– the computation of the sum of the elements in each column of the matrix
– the sum of the elements of the vector
– the sum of the squares of the elements of the matrix

Random number generation is a rather common problem due to its use in different areas such as statistics and cryptography. In this context, Pseudo Random Number Generators (PRNGs) are used. A PRNG is an algorithm that uses mathematical formulas and an initial value (or seed) to produce a deterministic sequence of numbers with similar properties to random numbers.

CUDA CURAND Library [16] is used for the random number generation on the GPU. Among several generators available in the library, we have selected Philox_4x32_10 [20] since it has pass both the BigCrush test [16] and the Ising test [14]. BigCrush is the most demanding battery in TestU01 [12,17] (a library that provides tools for the statistical testing of random number generators) and it is widely accepted for testing the quality of random numbers. It includes a total of 106 tests and uses close to 2^{38} random numbers.

The Philox_4x32_10 generator is able to produce 2^{64} subsequences of pseudo random numbers with period 2^{128}, which is larger than the maximum amount of numbers required for the experiments ($15 \times 400 \times 10^8$). To generate the random numbers of the algorithm in the CPU, we use the Random123 library [20,21] since it provides a CPU implementation of the Philox_4x32_10 generator.

Next, we briefly comment on the CPU implementation of the other three relevant operations for computing the Friedman's test table values. For sorting each row of the matrix, and since the CPU implementation is coded in C++, we use the sort function available in the C++ Standard Template Library (STL) [23]. The sort function is used on the random number values for computing the index of the ordered values. Finally, for the sum of the columns and of the resulting vector, the implementation on CPU is straightforward and each independent element is processed iteratively.

3   GPU Calculation of the Friedman's Test Table Values

The implementation proposed in this paper offloads the calculation of the events for a given pair (k, N) to the GPU. The algorithm computes the $\sum R_j^2$ and $\sum r_{ij}^2$ on the GPU for each of the events, and transfers the whole results to the CPU. After the results are received by the CPU, in a post-processing stage, that we are not detailing in this paper, the values are adjusted (taking into account the constants involved in Eq. 3) to obtain the numerator and the denominator of Eq. 3. Finally, these values are used for constructing the histogram of the pair (k, N). From now on, when we refer to the algorithm, we are not considering the post-processing stage as a part of the algorithm.

The main concept in our proposal is that the algorithm developed computes several events for a given pair (k, N) in parallel using a single grid of thread blocks. Since the number of events is in the order of 10^8, this idea enables to benefit from the massively parallel paradigm that is the basis of the architecture of GPUs.

Algorithm 1 presents the pseudocode of our proposal for the host side. Initially, the seed for the random number generation is transferred from the CPU to the global memory of the GPU. Then, the states of the random number generator is initialized on the GPU (Step 2). At each iteration, e events are calculated. This calculation involves three different steps, the generation and sorting of the random numbers (Step 5), the sum of the squares of the elements of the matrix and the sum by columns of the matrix (Step 6), and the sum of the resulting vectors (Step 7). Finally, when the algorithm reaches the stop condition, the results are transferred from the GPU to the CPU.

Now, we detail the organization of the data on the GPU memory. The kernel operation is explained next.

```
 1  transfer seed for random numbers to GPU
 2  call initCurandState kernel
 3  events = 0
 4  while events < maxEvents do
 5  |   call generateAndOrderNumbers kernel
 6  |   call sumColumns kernel
 7  |   call sumVectors kernel
 8  |   events = events + e
 9  end
10  transfer results from GPU to CPU
```

Algorithm 1: Host Side Pseudocode.

3.1   Data Organization

Our proposal employs several data structures that are stored in the different memory spaces of the GPU. These data structures are briefly described next:

- *State matrix*: This matrix is used to store the state of each random number generators. The dimension of this matrix is equal to the size of the matrix required for storing random numbers, i.e. $N \times k$. The matrix is stored in the global memory of the GPU.
- *Random numbers vector*: For computing the table values, the random numbers of each row only need to be temporarily stored since the real important data is the ranking. For this reason, a k elements vector for storing the random numbers is allocated in shared memory of the GPU. This structure is used specially for accelerating the ranking computation in the Step 5 of the algorithm.
- *Main matrix*: This matrix is used for storing e times the resulting indexes from the ordering of the rows (e is the number of events that are processed by the grid of thread blocks). The matrix has $N_2 \times e$ rows and k_2 columns, where N_2 and k_2 are the first numbers that are power of 2 and larger than or equal to N and k, respectively. These dimension were chosen in order to make the computation of the reduction more efficient.
- *Partial sum vector*: This vector is used for storing the partial results of the sum by columns of the matrix. It is a vector of k elements of double precision floating point numbers that is stored in shared memory of the GPU. It is employed to accelerate the memory access when computing the sum of squares.
- *Final results vector for* $\sum R_j^2$: This vector is used to store the final result of the sum of squares for each event. This vector has e elements of double precision floating point numbers, i.e., the number of independent events that are concurrently performed.
- *Results vector for* $\sum r_{ij}^2$: This vector is used to store the result of the sum of squares of all the elements of the matrix. This vector also has e elements of double precision floating point numbers.

3.2   Kernel Operation

The `initCurandState` kernel (Step 2 of Algorithm 1) initializes the states of the random number generators. The kernel is launched with N blocks, i.e., one block for each row, and with k threads per block, i.e., one thread for each column. Each thread independently initializes one state using the seed of the experiment and one monotonously increasing number, which is computed using the block id and thread id [16]. As a consequence, each of the matrix elements is initialized with a different value, and thus determines $N \times k$ different random sub-sequences.

The `generateAndOrderNumbers` kernel (Step 5 of Algorithm 1) generates the random number for each row, and then it sorts them. The kernel is also launched with N blocks and with k threads per block. Each block computes a different row. Initially, each thread reads their state from the state matrix, and then repeats e times the following tasks:

1. Generate one random number between 1 and k, and store it in the corresponding position of the random numbers vector.
2. Calculate the ranking associated to the random number. Instead of using an auxiliary structure for the indexes and directly sorting the values, we used a different strategy that is better suited for the GPU. We use two auxiliary counter variables per thread, one for storing the index (initialized in one) and one for the number of ties (initialized in zero). In our strategy, the random number of each thread is compared with the rest of the elements of the vector, adding one to the index variable for each element that is lower than the number associated with the thread, and adding one to the ties variable for each element that is equal to the number associated with the thread. The ranking is thus calculated as the sum of the index variable and half of the ties variable.
3. Store the ranking values in the main matrix in the global memory. The position in the matrix is determined by the number of repetition (that determines which of the e submatrices is involved), the block id (that determines the row) and the thread id (that determines the column). Since the main matrix is stored by rows, all writes are coalesced.

Finally, the states of the generator are stored in the state matrix in order to be used in the next invocation of the kernel.

The `sumColumns` kernel (Step 6 of Algorithm 1) performs the sum by columns of the rankings stored in the main matrix. It involves the application of the well-known reduction pattern [15] and several invocations of the kernel. In each invocation of the kernel, and with the goal of keeping the access coalesced to the global memory, each block reads all the elements of two rows, and sum the values of the same column.

The kernel is invoked $\log_2(N_2/2)$ times (N_2 is chosen as a power of 2), the first time is launched with $e \times N_2/2$ blocks of k threads each, and reducing the number of blocks by half in each invocation. Thus, the final invocation is launched with e blocks, and the resulting sum by columns of each of the e independent events that are being calculated are stored on the first row of each of the e submatrices stored in the main matrix. It should be noted that the input matrix may have more rows than the N required. For this reason, the remaining rows have to completed with zeros to properly compute the reduction without affecting the final result of the sum.

In the first invocation of `sumColumns` kernel, and since all the elements of the matrix are read, the kernel also calculates the sum of squares of all the elements of the matrix. This computation also involves the use of the reduction pattern along the columns, as well as the use of `atomicAdd` operations to sum the values calculated by different blocks without incurring in race conditions. The results is stored in the corresponding position of the results vector for $\sum r_{ij}^2$ in global memory.

The `sumVectors` kernel (Step 7 of Algorithm 1) computes the squares of the elements of the vectors produced by the previous kernel, and then sum the resulting values. The kernel is launched with e blocks (one for each row) of k_2 threads each. First, the kernel copies the values of the row from the global memory to the shared memory and computes the square of the numbers. Then, the sum of squares is computed using the reduction pattern, performing $\log_2(k_2)$ iterations in which pairs of numbers are added together. At last, the final result is copied from shared memory to the corresponding position of the final results vector for $\sum R_j^2$ in global memory.

4   Experimental Evaluation

This section reports on the results of the experiments performed to evaluate the algorithm implemented on the GPU. First, we present the experimental setup. Then, we detail the experimental results and discussion.

4.1   Experimental Settings

We have implemented the algorithm described in Sect. 2.2 (without the histogram calculation) both in CPU and GPU. The CPU implementation was coded in C++, while the GPU implementation was coded in CUDA using the CUDA Toolkit release 9.2.

The execution platform for the CPU implementation was a PC with a Quad Core Intel i7-6700 at 3.40 GHz with 64 GB RAM using the CentOS Linux 7.0 operating system. The CPU implementation was executed as a single-threaded application. The GPU implementation was run in an Nvidia's GeForce GTX 980 Ti (2816 CUDA cores at 1000 MHz, Maxwell architecture) connected to the PC used for the CPU executions.

As we previously explained, the goal of this work is to study how the process of estimating the PDF of the Friedman's statistic with ties can be accelerated, but not to actually estimate it. For this reason, we have selected three different scenarios for the experimental evaluation: $N = 48$ and $k = 30$ (the associated matrix has 1440 elements), $N = 20$ and $k = 200$ (4000 elements), and $N = 15$ and $k = 400$ (6000 elements). It should be noted that even though the scenarios with a larger k have more elements in their matrices, larger values of N involve a greater number of thread blocks in the GPU implementation, which helps to take advantage of the inherent parallelism of the GPU.

4.2   Experimental Results

Before analyzing the performance, we have evaluated the numerical performance of the GPU implementation. With this goal, we have made executions using toy examples that can be calculated analytically. In such cases, the numerical results of the GPU implementation match the results of the analysis. In addition to this, we have also compared the numerical results of the CPU and GPU implementations, corroborating that there are no significant differences.

The first experiment is focused on the study of the effect of the number of events (e) that are computed by a single grid of thread blocks of the GPU. Table 1 presents the runtime in milliseconds in the three previously presented escenarios for an overall of $2^{10} \times 10^2$ (roughly 10^5 events), considering e from 1 and doubling the number of events computed concurrently until 1024.

Table 1. Runtime in milliseconds of the GPU version for $2^{10} \times 10^2$ events.

N	k	Number of events in parallel										
		1	2	4	8	16	32	64	128	256	512	1024
48	30	3971	2387	1596	1213	968	890	845	833	822	815	**810**
20	200	5597	3890	2760	2446	2301	2213	2169	2158	2155	2155	**2150**
15	400	7194	5541	4491	4169	4014	3944	3903	3903	3886	3885	**3879**

The best results are in bold

The results summarized in Table 1 show a similar behaviour for the three scenarios considered. More in detail the computation of less than 64 events by the kernel grid produces an important overhead in the runtime of the algorithm. This is aligned with the theory, since in the sumColumns kernel the last invocation to the reduction procedure is launched with only e blocks. On the other hand, when we consider the configurations with 64 or more events, the differences in runtime are almost negligible in all the cases. In particular, it should be noted that in such configurations the largest difference is less than 4%. Additionally, the best performance for the three cases is obtained when 1024 events are computed by the grid. For this reason, we adopt this configuration that will be used in the rest of the experiments.

Let us now analyze the comparative performance among CPU and GPU implementations. Table 2 presents the runtime in seconds of both implementations and the *Speedup* obtained using the GPU version for three scenarios considered. Both implementations were evaluated considering different number of events, ranging from approximately 10^3 (2^{10}) to more than 10^8 ($2^{10} \times 10^5$).

Table 2. Runtime in seconds and *Speedup* for different number of events.

		Number of events					
		2^{10}	$2^{10} \times 10$	$2^{10} \times 10^2$	$2^{10} \times 10^3$	$2^{10} \times 10^4$	$2^{10} \times 10^5$
$N = 48$	CPU	**0.05**	0.55	5.54	55.50	555.60	5571.81
$k = 30$	GPU	0.50	**0.53**	**0.81**	**3.44**	**29.75**	**294.83**
	Speedup	0.10	1.04	6.84	16.15	18.67	18.90
$N = 20$	CPU	**0.20**	2.05	20.56	206.13	2056.08	20579.09
$k = 200$	GPU	0.52	**0.68**	**2.15**	**16.97**	**166.05**	**1641.77**
	Speedup	0.39	3.01	9.56	12.15	12.38	12.53
$N = 15$	CPU	**0.33**	3.46	33.86	339.11	3372.38	33794.63
$k = 400$	GPU	0.54	**0.86**	**3.88**	**34.40**	**339.31**	**3388.09**
	Speedup	0.62	4.02	8.73	9.86	9.94	9.97

The best results are in bold

The number of events required to make an accurate estimation for each pair (k, N) coincides with the largest case considered in this experiment.

The comparison between the runtime of the CPU and GPU implementations yields predictable results. In other words, when the number of events calculated is small and the massive parallelism of the GPU can not be leveraged, the CPU implementation outperforms the GPU counterpart. Specifically, when only 2^{10} events are calculated, the CPU version has a shorter runtime for the three test cases considered. However, when a medium or large number of events is considered, the GPU variant show its potential and offers an impressive calculation capacity.

Figure 1 shows graphically (using a logarithmic scale on the x axis) the *Speedup* reached by the GPU version according to the number of addressed events. As it can be appreciated both in the table and in the figure, the values of *Speedup* attained with the GPU versions grow strongly with the number of events. Although this improvement stalls (in the first scenario the inflection point is in $2^{10} \times 10^4$, while in the other two cases is around $2^{10} \times 10^3$) when the GPU is completely harnessed, the reached *Speedup* values are at least of 10×. In particular, the *Speedup* values for the number of events involved in the estimation of the PDF are 9.97×, 12.53× and 18.90× for the largest, the medium and the smallest scenarios, respectively. This behaviour, at a first glance, can be considered strange for the typical GPU computations since the better *Speedup* values are obtained for the smaller test case. However, as we explained in Sect. 3, the number of thread blocks of several kernels is determined by e and N, and for this reason, the test cases with a larger value of N show a larger improvement in the performance. Thus, as a future work, we need to consider alternative computation strategies that would allow to increase the number of thread blocks for the different combinations of N and k, e.g., partitioning into several thread blocks the computation of a single row.

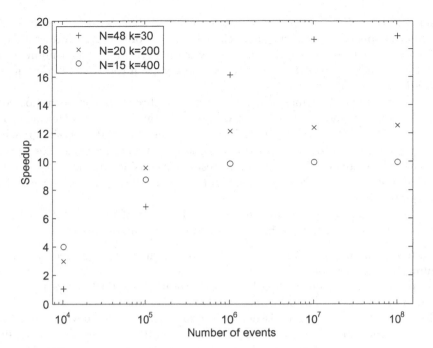

Fig. 1. Evolution of reached speedups according the number of addressed events.

It should be highlighted that the hardware platform used in this work is not a cutting edge GPU. We employed a Geforce GTX 980 Ti, which was launched to the market in 2015. This GPU has a theoretical peak performance in single precision floating point of 4.6 TFLOPS. This performance is low in comparison with current GPUs, such as the Geforce GTX 2080 Ti, which has a peak performance of more than 11 TFLOPS.

From the analysis performed, and even using a not cutting edge GPU, it can be concluded that the runtime reduction of the GPU implementation over the CPU implementation is at least of 10× when considering the number of events needed in the PDF estimation. That is to say that this reduction means conservatively that a single GPU is equivalent to the workforce of ten processors. This is specially remarkable considering the important effort of 100 years of CPU time (equivalent to a year of wall-clock time using 100 processors) that was involved in the Friedman Test without ties table calculation. Thus, our effort opens a real alternative to perform this kind of computations in a reasonable time using a cluster with several modern GPUs.

5   Final Remarks and Future Work

In this work, we have studied the acceleration of the Friedman Test table calculation by leveraging the computational power offered in massive parallel hardware platforms, such as GPUs. In particular, we designed and developed a GPU implementation able to compute several events in a single grid of thread blocks and that is specially parallelized in the dimension of the N parameter. The implementation uses the CURAND library for generating random numbers in the GPUs, which assures that the period is larger than the amount of numbers required for the experiments.

The experimental evaluation carried out over three different scenarios confirms that our proposal is able to obtain an important runtime reductions with respect to the CPU counterpart. More in details, the GPU version reaches *Speedup* values of up to 19×, and when the larger number of events are considered, the values are of at least 10× in all test cases considered. This corroborates that our proposal has a great potential for helping to compute this problem in a reasonable time.

With the experience acquired in the development of the present effort, we have identified several lines of future work. The most highlighted are:

- Evaluate our proposal in a more modern GPU, analyzing the effect in performance of the new technologies.
- Design and implement a distributed extension of our GPU proposal, i.e., a version able to compute in several GPUs at the same time.
- Related with the previous issue, it is also interesting to develop a hybrid version that can exploit both the CPU and the GPU concurrently, offloading the computation of the most time consuming (k, N) pairs to the GPU and computing the smallest scenarios in the CPU.
- Additionally, it is interesting to evaluate other parallelization strategies to exploit the GPU in different contexts, e.g., when the N parameter is not large enough.

Finally, it is interesting to advance in making our source codes available in order to enhance the interaction with the statistics community.

Acknowledgments. The researchers acknowledges partial support from Programa de Desarrollo de las Ciencias Básicas (PEDECIBA), Sistema Nacional de Investigadores (SNI) and Agencia Nacional de Investigación e Innovación (ANII).

References

1. Anzt, H., Dongarra, J.J., Flegar, G., Higham, N.J., Quintana-Ortí, E.S.: Adaptive precision in block-Jacobi preconditioning for iterative sparse linear system solvers. Concurrency Comput.: Practice Experience **31**(6), e4460 (2019)
2. Carballo, P., Perera, P., Rama, S., Pedemonte, M.: A biased random-key genetic algorithm for regression test case prioritization. In: IEEE Latin American Conference on Computational Intelligence, LA-CCI 2018, 7–9 November 2018, Gudalajara, Mexico, pp. 1–6. IEEE (2018)
3. Corder, G.W., Foreman, D.I.: Nonparametric Statistics for Non-Statisticians: A Step-by-Step Approach. Wiley, Hoboken (2009)
4. Derrac, J., García, S., Molina, D., Herrera, F.: A practical tutorial on the use of nonparametric statistical tests as a methodology for comparing evolutionary and swarm intelligence algorithms. Swarm Evol. Comput. **1**(1), 3–18 (2011)

5. Dufrechu, E., Favre, F., Pedemonte, M., Curto, P., Ezzatti, P.: Accelerating radiative heat transfer calculations on modern hardware. In: 2012 XXXVIII Conferencia Latinoamericana En Informatica (CLEI), 1–5 October 2012, Medellin, Colombia, pp. 1–9. IEEE (2012)
6. Abadi, M., et al.: TensorFlow: Large-scale machine learning on heterogeneous systems (2015). Software available from tensorflow.org
7. Fawcett, R.F., Salter, K.C.: A Monte Carlo study of the f test and three tests based on ranks of treatment effects in randomized block designs. Commun. Stat. - Simul. Comput. **13**, 213–225 (1984)
8. Friedman, M.: The use of ranks to avoid the assumption of normality implicit in the analysis of variance. J. Am. Stat. Assoc. **32**(200), 675–701 (1937)
9. Friedman, M.: A comparison of alternative tests of significance for the problem of m rankings. Ann. Math. Stat. **11**(1), 86–92 (1940)
10. Iman, R., Davenport, J.: Approximations of the critical region of the Friedman statistic. Commun. Stat.-Theory Methods **9**, 571–595 (1980)
11. Kirk, D.B., Hwu, W.-M.W.: Programming Massively Parallel Processors: A Hands-on Approach, 3rd edn. Morgan Kaufmann, Burlington (2016)
12. L'Ecuyer, P., Simard, R.: Testu01: A C library for empirical testing of random number generators. ACM Trans. Math. Softw. **33**(4), 22:1–22:40 (2007)
13. López-Vázquez, C., Hochsztain, E.: Extended and updated tables for the Friedman rank test. Commun. Stat. - Theory Methods **48**(2), 268–281 (2019)
14. Manssen, M., Weigel, M., Hartmann, A.K.: Random number generators for massively parallel simulations on GPU. Eur. Phys. J. Spec. Top. **210**(1), 53–71 (2012)
15. McCool, M., Reinders, J., Robison, A.: Structured Parallel Programming: Patterns for Efficient Computation, 1st edn. Morgan Kaufmann Publishers Inc., San Francisco (2012)
16. Nvidia Corporation. CUDA Toolkit 10.0 CURAND Library Programming Guide. Nvidia Corporation, September 2018
17. L'Ecuyer, P., Simard, R.: TestU01 Website (2007). http://simul.iro.umontreal.ca/testu01/tu01.html. Accessed June 2019
18. Pedemonte, M., Luna, F., Alba, E.: A systolic genetic search for reducing the execution cost of regression testing. Appl. Soft Comput. **49**, 1145–1161 (2016)
19. Quade, D.: Using weighted rankings in the analysis of complete blocks with additive block effects. J. Am. Stat. Assoc. **74**(367), 680–683 (1979)
20. Salmon, J.K., Moraes, M.A., Dror, R.O., Shaw, D.E.: Parallel random numbers: as easy as 1, 2, 3. In: Proceedings of 2011 International Conference for High Performance Computing, Networking, Storage and Analysis, p. 16. ACM (2011)
21. Salmon, J.K., Moraes, M.A., Dror, R.O., Shaw, D.E.: Random123 Website (2011). http://www.thesalmons.org/john/random123/. Accessed June 2019
22. Sheskin, D.J.: Handbook of Parametric and Nonparametric Statistical Procedures, Fifth edn. Chapman and Hall, London (2011)
23. Stepanov, A., Lee, M.: The Standard Template Library. Hewlett Packard Laboratories (1995)

Modelling Road Saturation Dynamics on a Complex Transportation Network Based on GPS Navigation Software Data

Mariana Cubero-Corella[1](✉), Esteban Durán-Monge[2], Warner Díaz[1,2],
Esteban Meneses[1,3], and Steffan Gómez-Campos[2]

[1] Advanced Computing Laboratory,
Costa Rica National High Technology Center (CeNAT), San José, Costa Rica
{mcubero,emeneses}@cenat.ac.cr, warnerdiaz@estudiantec.cr
[2] State of the Nation Program, San José, Costa Rica
{eduran,sgomez}@estadonacion.or.cr
[3] School of Computing, Costa Rica Institute of Technology, Cartago, Costa Rica
http://cluster.cenat.ac.cr/, https://www.estadonacion.or.cr/,
https://tec.ac.cr/

Abstract. High traffic concentration during weekdays in the Great Metropolitan Area of Costa Rica causes severe traffic congestion and high costs for the population. It is crucial to deeply understand the dynamics of traffic congestion to design and implement long term solutions. Given the lack of official data to study traffic congestion, we model it using a transportation network based on data captured throughout the year 2018 by a GPS navigation software application (Waze), provided by the Ministry of Public Works and Transportation (MOPT in Spanish). In this paper, we focus on the data transformation procedure to create the transportation network and propose a traffic congestion classification with the available data. We developed a practical methodology which consists of four main stages: data preparation, road network modelling, road saturation estimation, and saturation dynamics analysis. The results show it is possible to model road saturation level using the proposed methodology. We were able to classify road segments in five categories that effectively represent the levels of road saturation. This classification gives us a clear overview of the real-world conditions faced by road network users.

Keywords: Delay · Traffic jam · Transportation network · Urban mobility · Waze

1 Introduction

A total of 1,346,344 vehicles [9] and 47,905 km of roads and highways [15] were reported in Costa Rica in 2015. In that same year, Costa Rica was the second country with more vehicles in Central America following Guatemala [18] and one of the Latin American countries with most vehicles per thousand inhabitants.

© Springer Nature Switzerland AG 2020
J. L. Crespo-Mariño and E. Meneses-Rojas (Eds.): CARLA 2019, CCIS 1087, pp. 136–149, 2020.
https://doi.org/10.1007/978-3-030-41005-6_10

It is only surpassed by Argentina and Mexico [15]. But Costa Rica is a smaller country with a very dense road network where the population struggle to move over a million vehicles with the available road infrastructure. As a result, traffic congestion has become a problem that only becomes more complicated due to the growth of the vehicle fleet. Since most of the traffic congestion is located in the Great Metropolitan Area Road Network [16], these routes make a good place to study traffic congestion effects on mobility.

The Highway Capacity Manual (HCM) allows to perform calculations and predictions of indicators such as the saturation flow rates in roads and highways for optimal infrastructure design [7]. This manual includes accurate methods to predict saturation rates, but to do so it uses many parameters such as base saturation flow rate, adjustment factor for lane width, adjustment factor for heavy vehicles in traffic stream and so on [19]. In Costa Rica most of these parameters can not be measured easily or simply do not exist for the majority of highways and roads. Certainly, finding historical data about traffic dynamics with enough detail is not an easy task.

Since there are no sensors on the field or updated official information available, we use traffic jams data obtained from Waze application data base in 2018 to access information about the behavior of jams throughout the year and study its effects on transportation dynamics on the main roads and highways in the Great Metropolitan Area. Particularly, we consider that this data provides information to estimate road network saturation accurately. This could be a very important information to the decision-makers to prioritize infrastructure projects of the government or a better use of resources. However, the structure of the data is not intended to make this type of estimations. Waze application uses this data in real time to provide navigation information to its users about the best routes available at each moment. We want to take advantage of the annual stored data to calculate road saturation levels and thus understand its effects on vital routes for mobility. Important data transformations are required to allow this analysis.

We developed a methodology to re-build main roads in the Great Metropolitan Area based on Waze application data. Here we present Route 39 transportation network. This road serves as a road ring around the capital city and has an vital role for mobility and reduction of traffic flows entering the city downtown area. Using reported traffic congestion data we estimate delays and their variations for each 100-meter segment of the road to comprehend the geographical distribution of the saturation. This study is the first step to understand and predict saturation rates with the limited data available in Costa Rica. The rest of the paper is organized as follows. Subsection 1.1 refers to related work to this paper. Section 2 presents the data analysis methodology where we explain the process to clean and prepare the data to be analyzed. Section 3 explains how we estimate the road saturation and Sect. 4 shows the results of the analysis. Finally, we present our conclusions and future work related to this research in Sect. 5.

1.1 Related Work

Previous studies on this data pointed out the top ten traffic traps in the country [3,16]. They do a similar analysis as ours, but they focus on the behavior of jams in areas of a city within a diameter of 1 km. In our case we focus on the behavior in the segments of a particular road. Also, using cluster analysis techniques, the State of the Nation Program found that jams reports in 2017 can be grouped in three clusters in the Great Metropolitan Area. These clusters are the roads that connect the center with periphery of the cities, the population centers and the economic centers [3,16]. But Waze data was not the optimal structure to reach the desired level of detail we wanted. In a similar study, but with simulated data Huang et al. [8] propose a hierarchical road model for shortest path discovery in vehicular networks. They use the driving time as the metric for the shortest path calculation. This inspired us to create a weighted road network with the average delay obtained through Waze application data. They also use a hierarchical graph with different types of roads, for instance, urban roads, bypass routes, and express highways. This oriented us to select only the National Road Network in order to consider the fact that not all the roads have the same behavior. Instead of using simulated data, we seek to prove that it is possible to build a road network using Waze data as main input. This a first step to create more complex networks considering the hierarchy proposed by Huang et al. [8].

Also Gebetsroither-Geringer et al. [4] present three cases where web-based applications are useful to support urban decision making and study urban dynamics and traffic congestion. First, to inform, create awareness and increase transparency. Secondly to report or identify current problems. And finally to support mid and long term planning processes. In our case, the lack of official information is one of the main reasons to use navigation software application data as input to identify current problems in congestion. However, the motivation behind this study is closely related to the mentioned use cases. As for the methodology, a similar concept is used by Moore et al. [12] to create a weighted and two way directed graph. In their work they estimate road capacity in a road network as a function of speed.

2 Data Analysis Methodology

To process the data, we followed the workflow shown in Fig. 1. It follows three main steps: (*i*) data preparation of both data sources, (*ii*) exploratory data analysis of the Waze data, (*iii*) road network modelling, where we execute most of the main transformations to the data.

2.1 Data Sources

Waze Dataset. Jams data is provided by the Ministry of Public Works and Transport (MOPT). Downloads take place every 5 min directly through Waze

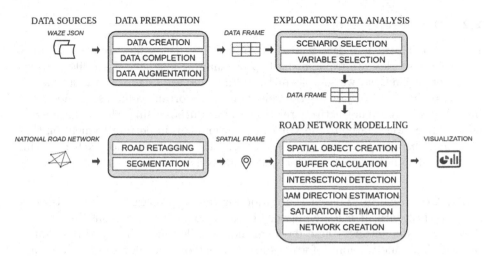

Fig. 1. Data analysis methodology.

Application Programming Interface. In the downloaded data a jam is a combination of jam reports made by several users. The application integrates the set of reports and estimates the indicators, such as delay, by jam. Each report contains a list of coordinates that detail the jam length and exact location. Data is originally stored in JSON (Javascript Object Notation) format and each file is named with the information about its date (year, month, day) and time (hour, minutes, seconds) at the moment of download. This is very important, since date and time data is not registered in the data frame that contains the reports of the traffic jams. The full 2018 data set contains 52,422,040 jams reported throughout the year. During weekdays there are 39,955,000 reports, where Thursdays and Fridays represent 20.7% and 23% of reports, respectively. We use three variables to create the road network:

- *Delay*: the delay in seconds based on the average speed of the segment.
- *Line*: is the list of coordinates (latitude and longitude) of each jam.
- *ID*: the id of each jam.

Other variables in the data set are the city, jam length, road type, speed and street name.

National Road Network. The spatial lines frame object of the National Road Network (NRN) is an essential input for the transportation network construction as it is. This will be the reference to aggregate all the jam information and build the network. This data was provided by the Ministry of Public Works and Transportation as a shape-file. It includes around 7,700 km of roads and gathers the location of more than 300 routes in the country. It comprises the busiest routes in the entire network.

2.2   Data Preparation

Data Creation. Jam data is stored in JSON files. Those files are read and integrated in a single data frame using R programming language. Each file contains a subset of jams, so we join them by column names. One of the first changes made to the table of jams is the selection of important columns. Some of the initial variables are not entirely relevant to our purpose, since these contain specific information related to the Waze application. It is important to mention that although the new frame includes the geographic coordinates for each jam, this format still is not appropriate for spatial analysis.

Data Completion. One of the major hurdles in preparing the data is dealing with lost data. It usually happens because connection problems during data download. Now, clearly these days can not be filled in with any kind of information, let alone random information. We created a strategy to fill in the gaps that does not substantially affect the variance of one day with respect to another. When we find a hole, it is filled with the average of data from the other days that belong to the same day of the week in the same month. For instance, assuming we do not have data for Tuesday January 1, this day will be filled in with the average of information on days January 8, 15, 22 and 29 (the remaining Tuesdays in January). The average of those days is used to add the missing day.

Data Augmentation. There are specifically 5 columns added. These are related to the date, and they are extracted from the name of the files. The 5 columns are: year, month, day of the year, hour, and day of the week that which is obtained from the first three.

National Road Network Retagging and Segmentation. After exploring the spatial data, some corrections are made due to road classification errors and unclassified routes. Jam length may vary a lot according to the moment, place, and severity of each traffic report. So we proceed with the spatial lines segmentation and divide the routes in equal length segments of 100 m. Working with short segments will allow us to explore jams data with great detail in very specific areas. As a result, the National Road Network is divided in 76,884 segments.

2.3   Road Network Modelling

Exploratory Data Analysis. It led us to select the scenarios of interest for this paper. During week days, the hours with more reported jams where from 5 to 7 in the mornings and from 4 to 6 in the evenings. This matches with the hours where most people goes to and from work. The analysis focuses on this time range and includes two scenarios: *mornings* and *evenings*. Considering that the Great Metropolitan Area (GMA) is highly relevant to the economic development of the country, it has a high concentration of population and traffic jams [16]. We first decide to focus on modelling the highly complicated road network in this area as a first step to eventually escalate this work to the whole country.

In order to build the GMA road network we use two main data sources: National Road Network spatial object and traffic jams data obtained from Waze application in 2018. As we mention before, this data is not meant to be used as a formal estimation of saturation rates. We want to build a network to summarize in a easy visual way how users are affected by traffic jams and compare between scenarios. That is why we prepare the data in 5 stages to create the transportation network.

Transforming Jams to a Spatial Object. Waze data is stored as a data frame that contains a list of coordinates for every reported traffic jam. We need to transform this table in order to have a spatial georeferenced format to match the National Road Network spatial object. It is important to note that data frame contains over 4 million reports in the mornings and over 12 million in the evenings. It is necessary to transform each list of coordinates to a spatial line. Then, we aggregate all the lines in one shape and finally assign the corresponding attributes such as the delay, the id of the jam, and the route. To compute this, we used the R [17] function *SpatialLines* of the library *SP 1.3-1* [1,14].

Buffer Creation around the Segmented NRN. A navigation system such as Waze has inaccuracies related to GPS precision. To account for these inaccuracies we transform the segmented National Road Network using buffers. To do so, we build a buffer with the R function *buffer* from the *raster* package [6] of 10 m around the base road network. For the main roundabouts and intersections we used 50 m buffers to capture traffic congestion that affects these areas. The transformed segmented NRN is used as a reference to be compared with the Waze data.

Intersection of both Data Sources. After the data is ready, it is necessary to intersect both spatial objects to identify which jams match each NRN segment in the Great Metropolitan Area. Due to the large volume of data, this phase is divided in a few steps prior to the intersection. The first step is transforming each spatial object to a *simple features* (sf) object in R [13]. This R package transforms the base road network and the jams to a simpler structure that is processed using parallel computing. The second step consists in parallel computing the intersection of both data sources with eight threads using the R packages *foreach* and *doParallel* [2,11]. Once the intersection is done, we transform the data back to an spatial object. The result of this stage is a spatial object with 100 meter long jams that match with the segments of the NRN buffers.

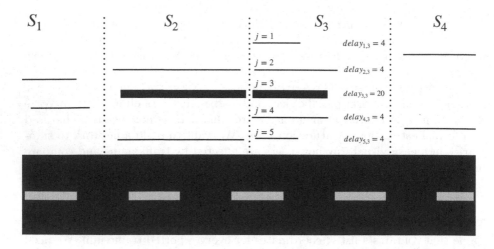

Fig. 2. Road saturation data example and notation.

Jams Direction Classification. Finally, to build the new road network we need to classify every jam according to its direction. The original data does not provide any explicit information about the origin or the destination of the user, or the jam direction, so we use coordinates from both data sources to estimate directions. To do this we take the first and last coordinates of every jam segment and every NRN segment. We compute the bearing [5] between the starting and ending point of each jam segment. Then, for the NRN segments we do the same estimation but in both directions. That is, direction A (from the start to the end point), and secondly direction B (from the end to the start point). Note that the bearing estimates the direction between the two points following the shortest path on an ellipsoid (geodetic) and it changes continuously while going along the path [5]. Then we compare every road segment's bearing to all the matching jams segment's bearings in both directions. If the jam has the same sign, either positive or negative, than that specific direction, it is classified in that direction. If the jams segment's bearing is different from the reference is classified as a jam going in the opposite direction. Once the data is classified, we build the network based on the methodology proposed by Lu et al. using the R package *shp2graph*, which provides tools to convert a spatial objects into an *igraph* graph of the *igraphR* package [10].

3   Road Saturation Estimation

In order to estimate the road saturation with the available data, we use the result of the intersection of the jams segments and the NRN segments. Considering the number of jams that took place in every segment and the registered delay for each jam, we calculate the weighted average delay per segment. We consider only those jams that had a delay greater than 0. We calculate the weight of each jam using the following equation:

$$W_{js} = \frac{delay_j}{\Sigma_{j=1}^{n_s} delay_{js}},\qquad(1)$$

where:

n_s = number of jams in segment s.

j = jam in segment s.

s = segment of network.

The weight W_{js} of each jam helps to summarize the impact of every jam on a particular segment. For example, in Fig. 2 where we have 5 jams in one segment: 4 of them with a delay of 4 min and 1 jam with a delay of 20 min, the length of each line represents the length of each jam. The simple average is 7.2 min of delay and may not show the impact of severe jams. Instead, we use the weighted average $Delay^W$ as shown in Eq. (2). The weighted average of this example is 12.8 min in that segment. This gives a greater impact to the severe jams. To aggregate this information we calculate the weighted average delay per segment as shown below:

$$Delay_s^W = \sum_{j=1}^{n_s} W_{js} \cdot delay_{js}.\qquad(2)$$

Now, with this measure we can easily identify the segments with greater delays and the hot spots in traffic chaos.

But these metrics are simply not enough to understand how traffic behaves. Going back to the example of the 5 jams, we want to identify where it is more likely to be a hot spot in each scenario using Eq. (3).

$$D_s = \frac{n_s}{N},\qquad(3)$$

where:

D_s = density per segment.

N = total number of jams in each road.

Additionally, we want to be able to differentiate segments where the traffic is constantly problematic from sporadic events that may affect the average delay. This is why we also calculate the standard deviation σ_s of the average delay $Delay_s^W$ and the actual observed delay as in Eq. (4).

$$\sigma_s = \sqrt{\sum_{j=1}^{n_s} W_{js}^2 * \sum_{j=1}^{n_s} \left((delay_{js}) - Delay_s^W \right)^2}.\qquad(4)$$

To get the whole picture, we also calculate the density of reports, that is, how many reports we have per segment. Now it is possible to find which are the segments with more reports for each scenario. The idea is to analyze average delay, standard deviation of the average delay, and density. This is an efficient and simple way to find rare events, which is the constant behavior in the studied area.

4   Results

Using the proposed methodology, we build the transportation network. To show the results we present and analyze Route 39 network. Road saturation estimations consider the complete Route 39. This includes some small roads that represent connections to other routes and highways. Visualizations presented here for the road network do not show these connections for aesthetic reasons.

Table 1 shows the estimated performance measures for the Route 39 network modelling procedure. Execution time is presented by stage. As it is shown, phases 1 and 3 have the highest values. These results give the first clues about the need to implement techniques to obtain a better performance, especially if we want to scale up the analysis to the whole country road network.

Table 1. Time required for Route 39 network modelling by stage.

Stage	Duration (s)
Spatial object creation	10,440.9
Buffer calculation	11.9
Intersection detection	4,481
Jam direction estimation	480.3
Saturation estimation	22.8
Network creation	2.9
Total execution time	15,439.8

To show the results obtained through the proposed methodology, first we analyze the network and its behavior in the mornings. To do this, the three estimated saturation measurements are presented and analyzed, these are: average delay, delay standard deviation and jams density. The latter indicates the proportion of traffic jams reported in a segment in relation to the amount of traffic jams reported throughout the whole network for the selected scenario. As we can see in Fig. 3 the relationship between the average delay and its standard deviation is moderately linear in both directions. Segments with greater delay show greater variability. But also, it is important to note that the average delay in most segments is between 5 and 10 min. In the west-to-east direction, two atypical segments with high delay and variability are identified. However, these segments have very low density. These segments show a rare behavior, with intense jams that do not happen often.

Figure 4 shows Route 39 networks in both directions. The edge width represents the average delay estimation and edge color shows the density. Here, it is possible to visualize the results spatially. The observed pattern allows to understand that there are different types of traffic jams. With the estimated indicators we can classify the segments in five categories:

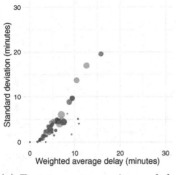

(a) East-to-west morning rush hour

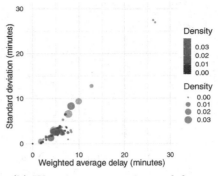

(b) West-to-east morning rush hour

Fig. 3. Comparison of relationship between the average weighted delay and its standard deviation in opposite directions during mornings (based on data from 2018 Waze jam reports in Route 39). The density indicates the proportion of traffic jams reported in a segment in relation to the amount of traffic jams reported throughout the whole network for the selected scenario.

1. *Type 1* includes segments with extreme affectation that have short jams located in few segments, very high delays and constant congestion during most of the week.
2. *Type 2* considers segments with a very high affectation due to cumulative effect that occur in many consecutive segments, with high-intermediate delay levels and steadily during the week.
3. *Type 3* segments have intermediate affectation with short jams, long delays and occur with less consistency on certain days of the week.
4. *Type 4* shows low affectation with jams concentration in few segments and lower delay levels that occur steadily during the week.
5. *Type 5* includes the least problematic segments with better traffic flow.

In Fig. 4 in the east-to-west direction we can see that some segments that are constantly with a medium high delay are the segments located near *Hatillo*. This area represents the 16 percent of the jams in the complete route. Some remarkable hotspots in the west-to-east direction are near the *General Cañas* Highway intersection, the entrance to *Hatillo*, *Zapote*, and *San Pedro* as we can see in Fig. 4.

If we analyze the networks in each direction following the sequence of segments, it is possible to see the location of the above categories. In Fig. 4, starting from *Uruca*, it is easy to note that in east-to-west direction the major problematic area is the *General Cañas* Highway intersection, these few segments with a critical situation are classified as type 1. Right after this area we can observe type 2 segments, where congestion affects many consecutive segments until *Hatillos*. Then there is a sequence of type 3 segments from *Hatillo* to *Parque de la Paz*. Once passed this point the segments becomes of type 5, with a better traffic flow until *San Pedro*. Afterwards type 3 segments appear again. Finally near

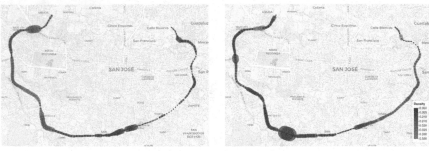

(a) East-to-west morning rush hour   (b) West-to-east morning rush hour

Fig. 4. Comparison between the opposite directions of the weighted road networks during mornings (based on data from 2018 Waze jam reports in Route 39).

Mercedes and *Calle Blancos* we observe type 2 segments until the end of the route.

Also in Fig. 4, in the west-to-east direction starting from *Calle Blancos*, Route 39 begins with a small group of type 5 segments. However, two segments with intermediate delay and constant congestion over the week are observed near Guadalupe. After a few segments with better traffic flow, type 2 segments start in the area near *San Pedro*. Here the effect of congestion accumulates over many segments. This behaviour extends until *Parque de la Paz*. Then the section of the route from *San Sebastián* to *Hatillos* shows type 3 segments, with high-intermediate delays that occur less frequently during the week. From this area and until Highway 27 intersection, type 2 segments take over again. In this direction, the intersection with the highway General Cañas is also a critical point with intermediate delay levels but constant jams during the week. Note that in this direction we observe shorter type 5 jams. It's also important to mention that in this scenario the most common type of jam is the type 2, the impact of this type is higher when we consider it's cumulative.

Now we analyze Route 39 evening network. Figure 5 shows that the linear relationship between the delay and its standard deviation is maintained. However the levels of both indicators are higher in both directions when compared with the morning results. This behavior is stronger in the east-to-west direction where the average delay is almost 9 min. Outlier segments are present in both directions, but now these show a very high density. These atypical segments represent critical spots, with very high delay values and constant congestion during the week.

If we analyze Fig. 6 we find some of the five types of segments listed before, but in this case the volume of reports is almost three times the amount of jams we had in the mornings. Please note that the scales from the figures of the morning scenario is not directly comparable with the figures of the evenings, due to the big difference in the volume of reported jams in both scenarios.

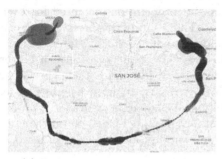
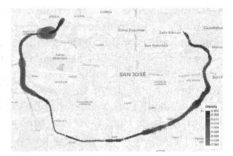

(a) East-to-west evening rush hour   (b) West-to-east evening rush hour

Fig. 5. Comparison of relationship between the average weighted delay and its standard deviation in opposite directions during evenings (based on data from 2018 Waze jam reports in Route 39).The density indicates the proportion of traffic jams reported in a segment in relation to the amount of traffic jams reported throughout the whole network for the selected scenario.

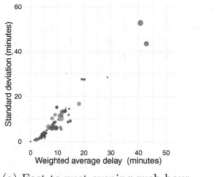
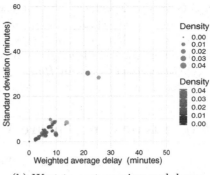

(a) East-to-west evening rush hour   (b) West-to-east evening rush hour

Fig. 6. Comparison between the opposite directions of the weighted road networks during evenings (based on data from 2018 Waze jam reports in Route 39).

As it is shown in Fig. 6, the east-to-west direction network has several segments with high delays at different locations. The *General Cañas* Highway intersection stands out for having the highest values. Once again this sector gathers type 1 segments. Just after this area of high congestion, it starts a long series of segments with high-intermediate delay values, that is, type 2 segments. This behaviour extends until *Hatillos*. Starting from this point, a long chain of type 3 segments begins. We observe a few segments with a good traffic flow near *Parque de la Paz*. Then, in the sectors of *Zapote* and *San Pedro*, another section of high affectation stars due to the accumulated effect of many segments with high values. Then near *Guadalupe* we observe a few type 3 segments almost at the end of the of the network.

Rout 39 network in west-to-east direction (Fig. 6) shows moderate values when compared with the opposite direction. However most of the route suffer the effects of type 2 segments. So the users of the network experience a constant medium - high delay through most of the network. From *San Pedro* and until *Parque de la Paz* there are many consecutive segments with important values in both delay and density. Although there is a section of segments of low affectation in *San Sebastián* sector, from *Hatillo* and until the end of the route there is a clear predominance of type 2 segments.

5   Conclusions and Future Work

One of the most important results of this work is the fact that our methodology to re-built a road network with data not meant for that purpose works. Road saturation estimations are actually helpful to understand the traffic flow dynamics. The data used for this work can be used as a great input in the analysis of traffic dynamics and how the users of the roads and highways are affected by traffic jams. Also we have a very detailed network that helped to identify specifically the problematic spots.

These findings represent an advance in the diagnosis of traffic congestion in the country. Now, it is possible to think of interventions required for each particular case and to prioritize interventions. The result of this investigation can be a useful tool to optimize the resources and create more effective interventions.

This methodology can be escalated to the whole country to give a better understanding of the traffic saturation dynamics inside and outside the Great Metropolitan Area. But in order to do so, it is necessary to improve performance, implement parallel processing and face the typical challenges associated with big data. Considering this, tools like Spark and GraphX might be good options to optimize the use of our computational resources and properly escalate our work.

References

1. Bivand, R.S., Pebesma, E., Gomez-Rubio, V.: Applied Spatial Data Analysis with R, Second edn. Springer, Heidelberg (2013). https://doi.org/10.1007/978-1-4614-7618-4, http://www.asdar-book.org/
2. Corporation, M., Weston, S.: doParallel: Foreach Parallel Adaptor for the 'parallel' Package (2018). https://CRAN.R-project.org/package=doParallel, r package version 1.0.14
3. Duran, E., Leon, J.: Technical report (2018)
4. Gebetsroither-Geringer, E., Stollnberger, R., Peters-Anders, J.: Interactive spatial web-applications as new means of support for urban decision-making processes. ISPRS Ann. Photogram. Remote Sens. Spatial Inf. Sci. **IV-4/W7**, 59–66 (2018). https://doi.org/10.5194/isprs-annals-iv-4-w7-59-2018
5. Hijmans, R.J.: geosphere: Spherical Trigonometry (2019). https://CRAN.R-project.org/package=geosphere, r package version 1.5-10
6. Hijmans, R.J.: raster: Geographic Data Analysis and Modeling (2019). https://CRAN.R-project.org/package=raster, r package version 2.9-5
7. Hong, J.H., Chiew, Y.M., Cheng, N.S.: Scour Caused by a Propeller Jet, vol. 139 (2013)

8. Huang, Y.F., Lin, J.Y., Hsu, C.H., Boonyos, S., Wen, J.H.. In: Lecture Notes in Computer Science (including subseries Lecture Notes in Artificial Intelligence and Lecture Notes in Bioinformatics)

9. José, S., Rica, C.: Compendio de datos del país (2014)

10. Lu, B., Sun, H., Harris, P., Xu, M., Charlton, M.: Shp2graph: tools to convert a spatial network into an igraph graph in R. ISPRS Int. J. Geo-Inf. **7**(8), 293 (2018). https://doi.org/10.3390/ijgi7080293

11. Microsoft, Weston, S.: foreach: Provides Foreach Looping Construct for R (2017). https://CRAN.R-project.org/package=foreach, r package version 1.4.4

12. Moore, E.J., Kichainukon, W., Phalavonk, U.: Maximum flow in road networks with speed-dependent capacities-application to Bangkok traffic. Songklanakarin J. Sci. Technol. **35**(4), 489–499 (2013)

13. Pebesma, E.: Simple features for R: standardized support for spatial vector data. R J. **10**(1), 439–446 (2018). https://doi.org/10.32614/RJ-2018-009

14. Pebesma, E.J., Bivand, R.S.: Classes and methods for spatial data in R. R News **5**(2), 9–13 (2005). https://CRAN.R-project.org/doc/Rnews/

15. PEN-CONARE: Informe estado de la nación 2018. Programa Estado de la Nación, i edn. (1383)

16. Programa Estado de la Nación: Debates para el desarrollo. Technical report

17. R Core Team: R: A Language and Environment for Statistical Computing. R Foundation for Statistical Computing, Vienna, Austria (2019). https://www.R-project.org/

18. Relatório, O.D.O.: ÍNDICE Pág (2005). https://www.mopt.go.cr/wps/wcm/connect/33f1f8e8-f7b8-41ab-883c-4d7bac2b4ba5/Carretera.pdf?MOD=AJPERES

19. Zhang, G., Chen, J.: Study on saturation flow rates for signalized intersections. In: 2009 International Conference on Measuring Technology and Mechatronics Automation, ICMTMA 2009, vol. 3, pp. 598–601 (2009). https://doi.org/10.1109/ICMTMA.2009.451

Regular Track on High Performance Computing: Architectures and Infrastructures

ExaMPI: A Modern Design and Implementation to Accelerate Message Passing Interface Innovation

Anthony Skjellum[1]([✉])[iD], Martin Rüfenacht[1,3], Nawrin Sultana[2][iD],
Derek Schafer[4][iD], Ignacio Laguna[5][iD], and Kathryn Mohror[5][iD]

[1] University of Tennessee at Chattanooga, Chattanooga, USA
{tony-skjellum,martin-ruefenacht}@utc.edu
[2] Auburn University, Auburn, USA
nzs0034@auburn.edu
[3] EPCC, University of Edinburgh, Edinburgh, Scotland, UK
[4] Tennessee Tech University, Cookeville, USA
djschafer42@students.tntech.edu
[5] Lawrence Livermore National Laboratory, Livermore, USA
{lagunaperalt1,kmohror}@llnl.gov

Abstract. The difficulty of deep experimentation with Message Passing Interface (MPI) implementations—which are quite large and complex—substantially raises the cost and complexity of proof-of-concept activities and limits the community of potential contributors to new and better MPI features and implementations alike. Our goal is to enable researchers to experiment rapidly and easily with new concepts, algorithms, and internal protocols for MPI, we introduce ExaMPI, a modern MPI-3.x subset with a robust MPI-4.x roadmap. We discuss design, early implementation, and ongoing utilization in parallel programming research, plus specific research activities enabled by ExaMPI.

Architecturally, ExaMPI is a C++17-based library designed for modularity, extensibility, and understandability. The code base supports both native C++ threading with thread-safe data structures and a modular progress engine. In addition, the transport abstraction implements UDP, TCP, OFED verbs, and LibFabrics for high-performance networks.

By enabling researchers with ExaMPI, we seek to accelerate innovations and increase the number of new experiments and experimenters, all while expanding MPI's applicability.

This work was performed under the auspices of the U.S. Department of Energy by Lawrence Livermore National Laboratory under contract DE-AC52-07NA27344. Lawrence Livermore National Security, LLC (LLNL-CONF-775497) and partial support from the National Science Foundation under Grants Nos. CCF-1562659, CCF-1562306, CCF-1617690, CCF-1822191, CCF-1821431. Any opinions, findings, and conclusions or recommendations expressed in this material are those of the authors and do not necessarily reflect the views of the National Science Foundation or Lawrence Livermore National Laboratory.

J. L. Crespo-Mariño and E. Meneses-Rojas (Eds.): CARLA 2019, CCIS 1087, pp. 153–169, 2020.
https://doi.org/10.1007/978-3-030-41005-6_11

Keywords: MPI · Middleware architecture · Parallel programming models · Performance portability · Cost of portability

1 Introduction

The complexity of leading open source implementations of MPI is daunting when it comes to experimentation and modification with new and different concepts for MPI-4 or other research experiments. Production open source MPIs have successfully focused on completeness of coverage, correctness, compliance, and, of course, middleware portability and performance. But, they typically leveraged software architectures rooted in legacy implementations of MPI-1 or earlier message passing systems, where assumptions were made based on then-extant architectures, processor resources, assumptions of intra-node concurrency, and performance levels. Production open source MPIs possess complex internal architectures, layers, and global state, and cross-cutting issues can arise when trying to experiment. Such issues make it difficult and expensive to achieve new changes, while also limiting certain kinds of experiments like overlapping of communication and computation.

To enhance and simplify researchers' ability to explore new and diverse functionality with MPI with quality performance potential, the authors have devised ExaMPI, a new, BSD-licensed open source implementation. A few factors enhance both the validity and necessity of building up a modular, research MPI at this time. First, over the past few years, a number of robust data movers such as Libfabric, Portals, and even InfiniBand verbs have decreased the importance of complex "channel devices" and other transport abstractions within MPI itself. These transports often include internal progress (independent of user calls to MPI) for sufficiently smart NICs and will soon include collective communication offload for some networks. Second, and as important, most MPI applications don't use a huge fraction of the MPI standard, which means that the complexity associated with full API support isn't needed for many kinds of applications and, hence, application experiments.

The remainder of this paper is organized as follows: Sect. 2 discusses selected prior MPI implementations. Section 3 offers motivations for ExaMPI. Section 4 discusses requirements. Section 5 explores the design of the internal library, and Sect. 6 discusses various implementation topics. Section 7 illustrates the utility of ExaMPI. Lastly, Sect. 8 summarizes the efforts toward the ExaMPI library and mentions future work.

2 Background

MPI implementations have existed since 1993, commencing with MPICH [14] (of which the first author of this paper was one of the original authors). Over the past 26 years, MPICH, Open MPI [12], and other open source MPIs have grown in size, complexity, support, and usership. Commercial MPI products based on proprietary code and/or open source derivatives were also created, and some of them are still in use today.

During this time, there has been consistent and even growing interest in experimenting with MPI in terms of additions, changes, and enhancements to implementations and functionality. Commercial and free derivative products of these open implementations have also been successful, such as Cray MPI [1], Intel MPI [5], IBM Spectrum MPI [2], and MVAPICH [25].

However, the complexity of effecting significant improvements, modifications, and/or changes in design to these large-scale MPIs is a daunting task, with over 1M lines of code present in both middleware products. This large scale makes deep experimentation with or changes to MPI prohibitive, except in device drivers and incremental APIs. For instance, changing the modes of progress or the modes of completion of MPI implementations is a tall order, as is managing their ability to cope with internal concurrency or state.

Furthermore, constrained environments, such as embedded devices and FPGAs, may also prefer to execute MPI functionality without coping with the entirety of large middleware implementations.

In certain of our research projects, we sought to explore different methodologies for implementing MPI, including new modes of strong progress, fault tolerant concepts, and extensions to the standard that require highly effective progress. Such efforts have been thwarted to varying degrees by the legacy assumptions of Open MPI, MPICH, and MVAPICH[1].

The recognition that many MPI applications require only a small to moderate subset of functionality also motivated our design of a new research MPI implementation. By supporting a sound design and allowing functionality to be added systematically over time, we provide incremental ability to run practical codes while reducing the total amount of MPI middleware by orders of magnitude. Furthermore, with a sound, first-principles design, this new MPI would have little dead code, or the technical debt associated with assumptions about node concurrency or progress made in the 1990s.

Furthermore, the availability of high-performance, converged APIs for many networks is a relatively recent development. This growth has enabled ExaMPI's design to focus on Libfabric as the key production networking interface for ExaMPI in addition to fundamental UDP/IP and TCP/IP network drivers. Our decision to focus on Libfabric was pragmatic yet performance-oriented. Libfabric has providers for many fast networks; while Portals is of interest as well, many ideas in Portals have been migrated to Libfabric. UCX was specifically considered but rejected because it is InfiniBand-only, and is immature. However, nothing in our development efforts prevents us or third parties from adding support for Portals and UCX in the future.

---

[1] In fact, a raft of papers (e.g., [7–10, 15, 16, 18, 24, 27, 29]) in the literature show workarounds to polling progress involving sporadically and haphazardly strewing one's code with MPI_Test. Also, the OSU benchmark for overlap explicitly depends on the use of MPI_Test [4, 22].

3 Motivation

The authors' main motivation for MPI is *not* to replace key blocks of function-ality or policy in existing production MPI implementations such as MPICH and Open MPI, or in commercial derivatives thereof. Rather, the following motiva-tions have driven the design, implementation, and future roadmap for ExaMPI. The authors intended to

- Enable rapid prototyping of
  - New algorithms for existing MPI operations,
  - New approaches to progress engines and resource allocation in large mul-ticore nodes, and
  - New MPI operations and APIs well before potential standardization;
- Identify and elucidate opportunities to improve MPI at-large, such as
  - Identifying situations where production MPIs could improve performance,
  - Enabling a community of "MPI makers" who can mix and match pieces to build MPI experimental systems and usable middleware in existing and new applications, and
  - Providing enhanced insights into the use of modern programming tech-niques for "lean middleware" that does not add extra layers or abstraction barriers while being highly maintainable over time;
- Support experimentation, such as
  - Exploration of unified resource management of cores, threads, and mem-ory that unify policies between MPI and OpenMP runtimes and
  - Specialization of entire MPI stacks for large-scale MPI applications that use relatively little of the total source base but want to "aspect" or oth-erwise tune the MPI specifically for their purposes;
- Support the research interests of the authors, including topics such as
  - Designing, prototyping, and eventually standardizing first-class language interfaces for C++, Python, etc., as opposed to purely transliterations of the current MPI C bindings,
  - Exploration of new fault-tolerant MPI approaches (e.g., MPI Stages [28]),
  - Integration of multiple fault-tolerant MPI models insofar as possible,
  - Provision of first-rate support for persistent collective operations using a an RDMA implementation strategy internally,
  - Creation of a platform for experimentation with MPI Sessions,
  - Demonstration of the value of progress and notification options in an open implementation of MPI (including tunability per application or commu-nicator), formerly only in MPI/Pro [3],
  - Study and prototyping of point-to-point and collective partitioned com-munication (finepoints) syntax, semantics, and performance, thereby accelerating its path to standardization by the MPI Forum, and
  - Enablement of experiments with MPI in FPGA softcores and in next-generation programmable NICs, such as Mellanox BlueField.

The overall goal is markedly to reduce time from conception to best practices to adoption of new and better MPI through a free, well-designed middleware research platform.

4   Requirements

In developing ExaMPI, we built on specific functional and non-functional requirements. In certain cases, there are quasi-functional requirements related to the modularity and extensibility of the software itself for use in specific applications. The following non-functional requirements were identified at the outset of the project:

1. Use C++ in a modern development style[2]
2. Create understandable code that is maintainable
3. Enable strong progress[3]
4. Enable choice of polling and blocking notification
5. Employ an extensible software architecture that supports extensibility
6. At least support UDP, TCP, and Libfabric transports
7. Enable experimentation with new fault-tolerance models for MPI
8. Focus on persistent and non-blocking operations as fundamental, rather than blocking (point-to-point and collective)
9. Enable a community of contributors of compatible extensions that are BSD-license compatible
10. Enable efficient overlapping of communication and computation when working with high-performance networks

These functional requirements were identified:

1. Support a useful subset of the MPI 3.1 standard[4]
2. Achieve point-to-point throughput that is initially competitive with production free MPI's
3. Achieve latency that is appropriate for a strong progress implementation
4. Specifically, enable the MPI Stages model of MPI fault tolerance [28].

5   Design

In this section, we provide an overview of ExaMPI's design, then discuss progress-engine design, and conclude with ExaMPI's transport design (data movers).

---

[2] to avoid code cloning, enable use of compiler-supported threads, employ metaprogramming and polymorphism where appropriate, and enable enhanced modularity over C.

[3] independent progress of messages through the network, independently of how often an application calls MPI functions, see also Sect. 5.2.

[4] based on the long experience of the first author and review of many applications' use of MPI as supported by a recent study by some of us and others [23].

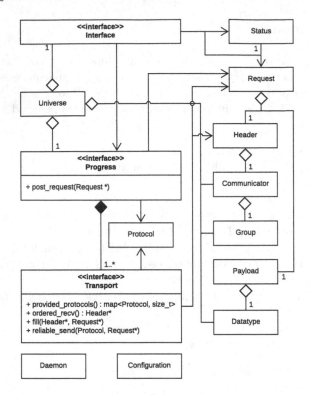

Fig. 1. General overview of the ExaMPI structure

5.1 Overview

The first step in designing ExaMPI was to do a design extraction from the MPI Standard, extending ideas presented in [26]. From this effort thus far, we derived Fig. 1, which provides a Unified Modeling Language (UML) class diagram that also expresses certain choices for practical implementation. This diagram contemplates both the top-down view of the standard APIs and data structures and the bottom-up view of data movers implementing transports for MPI.

Here are some specific facets of the design implied by Fig. 1:

- Different interfaces can be supported for different standard levels (releases) of MPI.
- One can drop in any progress engine rather than having this choice be fixed in the design.
- Transports are also pluggable, akin to other major MPI implementations.
- The Universe is a special class to avoid global state.

Furthermore, the nomenclature and thinking of this MPI's design is required to be compatible with the nomenclature and approach of [6].

Figure 2 reflects the design for the progress engine. First of all, the entire progress engine is pluggable so that other researchers can experiment with alter-

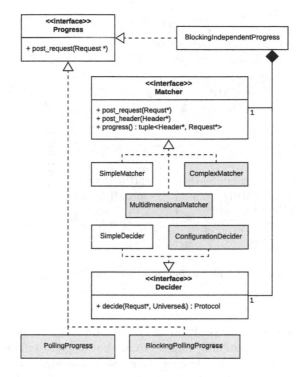

Fig. 2. Structure of the progress layer of ExaMPI

natives to this approach. With reference to Dimitrov's diagram [11] as shown in Fig. 3, we enable all these possible combinations of message progress and notification. This feature is important because prior work has shown that overlapping of communication and computation is severely hampered by polling behavior in progress and/or notification.

5.2 Progress Engine Design

The progress engine abstraction is designed to allow any progress engine to be implemented inside the ExaMPI library. We restrict all progress to be made through the progress engine by requiring all operations to construct a request object. The request object is posted to the progress engine, which then will progress the request objects and the underlying transport implementations.

Figure 3 shows the four classes of MPI progress engines that are possible to be constructed. Currently, ExaMPI implements a strong progress engine. By "strong" we mean that the progress is independent with separate progress threads from the user threads and the notification of completion is blocking. When a user thread waits on a request, the user thread is unscheduled until the request is complete. Further progress engines are being developed to implement the weak and saturated progress classes.

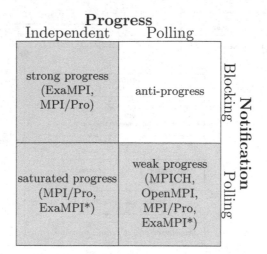

Fig. 3. Dimitrov's progress and notification classification diagram; * Forthcoming modes in ExaMPI

Figure 2 shows the decomposition of the functionality within the Progress class. We separate the matching engine from the progress engine through an interface that allows us to implement many separate algorithms to perform matching. Currently the SimpleMatcher implements a unmatched message queue and posted received queue with a complexity of $O(N^2)$.

In addition, we decompose further the mechanism for decision about which protocol and algorithm is to be used for any MPI operation. The SimpleDecider object implements the expected behaviour of the point-to-point functionality. By implementing a custom decider class, developers can map any MPI operation to any underlying algorithm.

5.3   Transport Design

The transport layer present within ExaMPI is intended to allow abstraction of all available network APIs. Figure 4 shows the hierarchy and required functions any Transport class currently is required to have implemented. Further development on this aspect of the library will enable offloading collectives and one-sided remote memory operations.

The current implementations present are the UDP and TCP transports, which allow for global usage but are not as performant as a high-performance network. Each transport implementation is entirely responsible for handling the memory associated with the network. As such, TCP and UDP use the kernel IP stack as a form of network buffer, but buffer payloads separately once received. Future implementations with more complex communications fabrics will require handling of receive queues.

6   Implementation

In this section, we describe the interface layers (language bindings) and our comprehensive usage of C++17 [21] for performance, flexibility, and code quality.

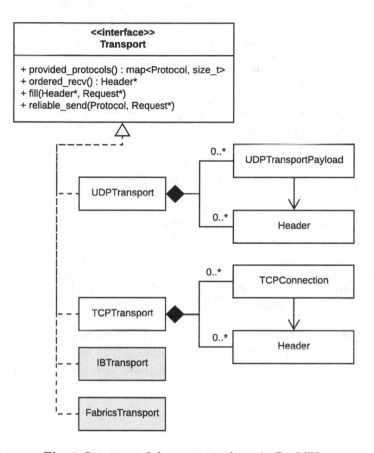

Fig. 4. Structure of the transport layer in ExaMPI

6.1   Interface Layers

The MPI Standard defines bindings for both C and Fortran, which must be available from any compliant MPI implementation. Currently ExaMPI only provides the C language interface, but building the Fortran interface is trivial above the current implementation, similar to other MPI implementations that build their Fortran bindings to simply call the C bindings.

In Fig. 5, the current interface structure of ExaMPI is presented. The C symbol names for both the MPI layer and PMPI layer are defined in the *mpi.h* header file. The MPI symbols are defined to be weak linked to facilitate the

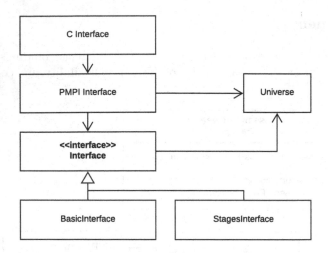

Fig. 5. UML describing interface layers

overloading of their functionality by MPI-compatible tools. The default MPI functions directly call the equivalent PMPI function.

The PMPI layer then uses the root universe to find the interface to the underlying C++ interface. The Interface class declares and defines the same interface as the C bindings of MPI but within a C++ class structure. This structure allows the abstraction of various interfaces for further work such as MPI Stages or FA-MPI.

In addition to extendability, the BasicInterface class allows us to encapsulate all top-level MPI behavior into a single location, which includes error checking and subsetting of blocking and non-blocking paths into persistent path, which is implemented by the underlying library.

6.2 Utilization of C++17

The ExaMPI implementation is written using C++17, which enables many productivity and language features that are not present in earlier C++ or C specifications. In addition, C++ allows for object-oriented programming, which allows the MPI implementation to directly deal with objects instead of the handles to objects. Using objects allows us to develop expressive source code without the clutter required with a C implementation.

We intend for ExaMPI to support full thread safety—with as much internal concurrency as reasonably possible—through the entire library. This arrangement is currently achieved with locks provided by the C++11 specification. By utilizing the built-in threading facilities, we reduce our dependence on external libraries. In the future, we will develop thread-safe, lockless data structures that will allow for the overhead of locking to be removed. They are also supported with built-in atomic operations.

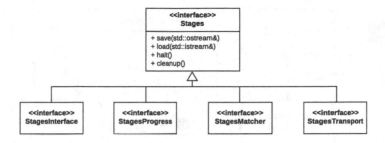

Fig. 6. UML description of stages

The C++ language also provides many capabilities that are tedious to use in C. One of these capabilities is string objects, which provide simpler handling of textual data. Another is exception handling. In C, the error code mechanism requires branches through the code base and forces design decisions. Within C++, exceptions are provided and allow for much cleaner internal working with errors. We utilize exceptions throughout the internal MPI library but provide error codes to the top-level MPI layer.

7 Early Applications of ExaMPI

In this section, we describe practical applications of ExaMPI. Two distinct fault-tolerant MPI models have been integrated into ExaMPI. The prospect of supporting multiple fault-tolerant MPI models at once is also discussed.

7.1 MPI Stages

MPI Stages [28] is a global-restart model that supports fault tolerance in bulk synchronous MPI applications. In this model, a checkpoint of the MPI state is saved along with the application checkpoint: this MPI state can contain a state that is visible to the user (e.g., MPI communicators) and an MPI state that is only visible to the MPI library (such as network connectivity). Each stage is a period between synchronous checkpoints and provides a temporal containment of faults. Upon failure, the runtime system transparently replaces the failed process by restoring both the MPI and application states, respectively, from their last synchronous checkpoints and continue without restarting the overall MPI job. Live processes roll back only a few iterations within the main loop instead of rolling back to the beginning of the program, while a replacement of a failed process restarts and reintegrates, thereby achieving faster failure recovery.

We introduced failure recovery support using MPI Stages in ExaMPI. The ExaMPI library isolates the new API extensions (StagesBasicInterface) added by MPI Stages from the standard MPI API as shown in Fig. 5. We can enable the MPI Stages feature in ExaMPI library using the command line parameter −*enable_mpi_stages* with mpiexec. The two main design aspects of MPI Stages are

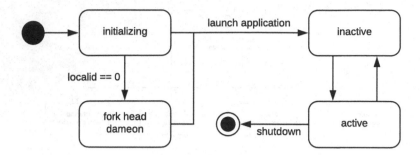

Fig. 7. State diagram of fault dæmon

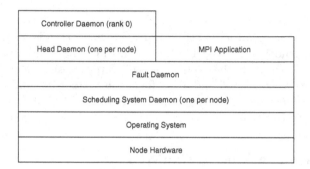

Fig. 8. Runtime system dæmon layers

(1) managing and capturing internal MPI state and (2) transparent replacement of a failed process by the MPI runtime system.

MPI Stages requires the user to save and load the internal state of MPI. To support state checkpointing, the ExaMPI library provides a `Stages` interface as shown in Fig. 6. Different modules of the ExaMPI library (e.g., Progress, Transport) could save/load their MPI state in a checkpoint by implementing this interface. The interface also provides a halt and cleanup method to handle process failure for live processes.

The ExaMPI runtime system supports the transparent replacement of a failed process as required by MPI Stages. The runtime system of ExaMPI supports both local execution and the Slurm job scheduling system. The runtime is designed using a double-dæmon method for compatibility with many job scheduling systems. The job scheduling system has the management daemon on the node that executes the second layer dæmon, the fault dæmon. The fault dæmon then in turn launches the MPI application as a sub-process. This design allows us to intercept any failure of the MPI application and prevents the job scheduling system from terminating the job prematurely. The fault dæmon also prepares the final application environment variables. The fault dæmon waits for the process to terminate and thereby avoids using any processing power from the node.

```
1   int main()
2   {
3       /*MPI Initialization and variable setup*/
4       while(operations_left)
5       {   /*Start the FA-MPI Transaction*/
6           MPI_TryBlock_start(comm, MPI_TRYBLOCK_GLOBAL, &try_request);
7           /*Do normal MPI Operations*/
8           MPI_Operation();
9           /*Finish the FA-MPI Transaction*/
10          return_code = MPI_TryBlock_finish(try_request);
11          /*Check for errors in the transaction*/
12          if(MPI_SUCCESS != return_Code)
13          { /*Perform recovery*/ }
14      }
15      /*MPI Finalize and other cleanup*/
16  }
```

Fig. 9. A simple example of an FA-MPI TryBlock

This feature is useful because there is a one-to-one application and fault dæmon relationship. Figure 7 shows the state diagram of the fault dæmon.

Potentially, two more dæmons are launched. First the fault dæmon, which both executes the local root rank and executes the head dæmon on each node. The head dæmon launches the final dæmon, the controller dæmon, if it is rank 0. With this structure, there are two dæmons (head dæmon and controller dæmon) awake on the root node of the job allocation and one dæmon (head dæmon) on every other node. This arrangement enables hierarchical scaling for side-channel communication—that is, data not directly related to the MPI application via socket-based TCP/IP. Figure 8 shows the sub-process relationships.

7.2 FA-MPI

Fault-Aware MPI (FA-MPI) is a lightweight, transaction-based fault tolerance model for MPI [17]. With this transaction-based model, an application can choose to use FA-MPI to achieve a fine-grain fault tolerance model by encapsulating every MPI operation in a single transaction. Or, should the application want to balance performance with fault tolerance, the application can choose to instead put many MPI operations into a single transaction. As FA-MPI is designed to be an extension of the MPI API, the application can use the fault awareness provided by FA-MPI to determine the level of fault tolerance it wants. While FA-MPI does provide the means to do failure recovery, it is also flexible and lets the application decide what its failure recovery method should be. As stated in the original documentation, "Applications using FA-MPI will run to completion with higher probability than with a non-fault aware MPI" [17].

These nestable transactions allow a series of operations to be committed if they were successful or to be retried if a fault was detected by one or more processes. To create these transactions, FA-MPI uses non-blocking collective functions and encapsulates a transaction with special TryBlock functions. TryBlock transactions can be local in scope—where only the local process must decide what to do—or global in scope—where all failures are synchronized among all processes. FA-MPI incorporates timeouts into its fault detection methods to prevent the possibility of deadlock introduced when dealing with fault tolerance. These timeouts can be user defined. FA-MPI also allows users to raise their own errors, should users want to test their fault tolerance model or have a fault that MPI can't detect. Once a TryBlock has finished, all alive processes will have the same view of the current status of the program. Processes then query FA-MPI for information about the fault, which can then be used to form a consensus on how to proceed. Figure 9 provides a brief example of how the TryBlocks might be used. To help with the recovery process, FA-MPI provides functionality to repair or rebuild communicators that were potentially broken during the fault.

FA-MPI is in the process of being integrated into ExaMPI. This integration will provide several benefits to both ExaMPI and FA-MPI. The first noticeable benefit for FA-MPI is ExaMPI's fundamental focus on non-blocking operations, something FA-MPI makes heavy use of and requires from MPI for its implementation [17]. Additionally, ExaMPI allows for further exploration of the FA-MPI fault tolerance model and how the model performs in the presence of faults. Since FA-MPI has already been implemented and tested in OpenMPI, we have a base level to compare how well FA-MPI performs in ExaMPI. Lastly, ExaMPI will also help quantify the necessary functionality required from MPI implementations to support its fault tolerance model, which will help enable ExaMPI (and perhaps other MPIs) to support fault tolerance models more successfully.

7.3   Multi-FT Library

The authors are designing approaches to compose multiple fault-tolerant models into ExaMPI. Apart from single models such as Reinit or ULFM and checkpoint-restart, we are not aware of successful integration of multiple models. Both the syntax and semantics of such combined models are of interest, but implications for MPI middleware architecture are also of tremendous consequence. We are exploring how to manage the complementary, at-times conflicting, and otherwise independent impacts on an MPI implementation arising from multiple models, including how to manage conflict resolutions between multiple models.

8   Conclusions and Future Work

In this paper, we described ExaMPI, a new, experimental implementation of the MPI Standard. ExaMPI solves the problem that full-scale open source MPIs are legacy middleware projects of large-scale and long-running development by many contributors; they are difficult to learn, modify, and use for middleware research, except in limited ways. Where they are usable, they are adequate, but many experiments are either intractable or require students and professors to spend inordinate amounts of time "modifying around the edges" of such middleware.

Thus far, ExaMPI has proven to be a useful research vehicle for a small number of people. As we move to a community of developers, researchers, and users, we look to increasing that utilization dramatically and expect the modularity of design to allow for many interesting hybridizations of our baseline code and concepts with others' ideas, prototypes, and additions.

A set of robust additions and experiments with ExaMPI are planned for the near future and include support for MPI-4 persistent collective communication [20], support for finepoints [13], and support for MPI-4 Sessions [19]. Also, revisiting unrolling of collective operations and experiments for communication and computation overlap are planned. These projects and others are keyed to the research interests of the authors and their immediate collaborators. We expect further research undertaken by others once the fall 2019 release of ExaMPI occurs contemporaneously with the publication of this paper.

References

1. Cray MPI. https://pubs.cray.com/content/S-2529/17.05/xctm-series-programming -environment-user-guide-1705-s-2529/mpt
2. IBM Spectrum MPI. https://tinyurl.com/yy9cwm4p
3. MPI/Pro. https://www.runtimecomputing.com/products/mpipro/
4. Osu micro-benchmarks 5.6.2. http://mvapich.cse.ohio-state.edu/benchmarks/
5. Intel MPI library, August 2018. https://software.intel.com/en-us/mpi-library
6. Bangalore, P., Rabenseifner, R., Holmes, D., Jaeger, J., Mercier, G., Blaas-Schenner, C., Skjellum, A.: Exposition, clarification, and expansion of MPI semantic terms and conventions (2019). Under review
7. Barigou, Y., Venkatesan, V., Gabriel, E.: Auto-tuning non-blocking collective communication operations. In: 2015 IEEE International Parallel and Distributed Processing Symposium Workshop, pp. 1204–1213, May 2015. https://doi.org/10.1109/IPDPSW.2015.15
8. Castillo, E., et al.: Optimizing computation-communication overlap in asynchronous task-based programs: poster. In: Proceedings of the 24th Symposium on Principles and Practice of Parallel Programming, PPoPP 2019, pp. 415–416. ACM, New York (2019). https://doi.org/10.1145/3293883.3295720
9. Denis, A., Trahay, F.: MPI overlap: benchmark and analysis. In: 2016 45th International Conference on Parallel Processing (ICPP), pp. 258–267, August 2016. https://doi.org/10.1109/ICPP.2016.37
10. Didelot, S., Carribault, P., Pérache, M., Jalby, W.: Improving MPI communication overlap with collaborative polling. In: Träff, J.L., Benkner, S., Dongarra, J.J. (eds.) EuroMPI 2012. LNCS, vol. 7490, pp. 37–46. Springer, Heidelberg (2012). https://doi.org/10.1007/978-3-642-33518-1_9
11. Dimitrov, R.P.: Overlapping of communication and computation and early binding: fundamental mechanisms for improving parallel performance on clusters of workstations. Ph.D. thesis, Mississippi State, MS, USA (2001)
12. Graham, R.L., Shipman, G.M., Barrett, B.W., Castain, R.H., Bosilca, G., Lumsdaine, A.: Open MPI: a high-performance, heterogeneous MPI. In: Cluster 2006, pp. 1–9, September 2006

13. Grant, R.E., Dosanjh, M.G.F., Levenhagen, M.J., Brightwell, R., Skjellum, A.: Finepoints: partitioned multithreaded MPI communication. In: Weiland, M., Juckeland, G., Trinitis, C., Sadayappan, P. (eds.) ISC High Performance 2019. LNCS, vol. 11501, pp. 330–350. Springer, Cham (2019). https://doi.org/10.1007/978-3-030-20656-7_17

14. Gropp, W.: MPICH2: a new start for MPI implementations. In: Kranzlmüller, D., Volkert, J., Kacsuk, P., Dongarra, J. (eds.) EuroPVM/MPI 2002. LNCS, vol. 2474, pp. 7–7. Springer, Heidelberg (2002). https://doi.org/10.1007/3-540-45825-5_5

15. Guo, J., Yi, Q., Meng, J., Zhang, J., Balaji, P.: Compiler-assisted overlapping of communication and computation in MPI applications. In: 2016 IEEE International Conference on Cluster Computing (CLUSTER), pp. 60–69, September 2016. https://doi.org/10.1109/CLUSTER.2016.62

16. Hager, G., Schubert, G., Wellein, G.: Prospects for truly asynchronous communication with pure MPI and hybrid MPI/OpenMP on current supercomputing platforms (2011)

17. Hassani, A.: Toward a scalable, transactional, fault-tolerant message passing interface for petascale and exascale machines. Ph.D. thesis, UAB (2016)

18. Hoefler, T., Lumsdaine, A.: Message progression in parallel computing - to thread or not to thread? In: 2008 IEEE International Conference on Cluster Computing, pp. 213–222, September 2008. https://doi.org/10.1109/CLUSTR.2008.4663774

19. Holmes, D., et al.: MPI sessions: leveraging runtime infrastructure to increase scalability of applications at exascale. In: EuroMPI 2016, pp. 121–129. ACM, New York (2016)

20. Holmes, D.J., Morgan, B., Skjellum, A., Bangalore, P.V., Sridharan, S.: Planning for performance: Enhancing achievable performance for MPI through persistent collective operations. PARCOMP **81**, 32–57 (2019)

21. ISO: ISO/IEC 14882:2017 Information technology – Programming languages – C++. Fifth edn., December 2017. https://tinyurl.com/yct5hxcs

22. Liu, J., et al.: Performance comparison of MPI implementations over Infiniband, Myrinet and Quadrics. In: Proceedings of the 2003 ACM/IEEE Conference on Supercomputing, SC 2003, pp. 58–58, November 2003. https://doi.org/10.1109/SC.2003.10007

23. Laguna, I., Mohror, K., Sultana, N., Rüfenacht, M., Marshall, R., Skjellum, A.: A large-scale study of MPI usage in open-source HPC applications. In: Proceedings of the SC 2019, November 2019 (2019, in press). https://github.com/LLNL/MPI-Usage

24. Lu, H., Seo, S., Balaji, P.: MPI+ULT: overlapping communication and computation with user-level threads. In: 2015 IEEE 17th International Conference on High Performance Computing and Communications, 2015 IEEE 7th International Symposium on Cyberspace Safety and Security, and 2015 IEEE 12th International Conference on Embedded Software and Systems, pp. 444–454, August 2015. https://doi.org/10.1109/HPCC-CSS-ICESS.2015.82

25. Panda, D.K., Tomko, K., Schulz, K., Majumdar, A.: The MVAPICH project: evolution and sustainability of an open source production quality MPI library for HPC. In: WSPPE (2013)

26. Skjellum, A., et al.: Object-oriented analysis and design of the message passing interface. Concurrency Comput.: Practice Exp. **13**(4), 245–292 (2001). https://doi.org/10.1002/cpe.556

27. Sridharan, S., Dinan, J., Kalamkar, D.D.: Enabling efficient multithreaded MPI communication through a library-based implementation of MPI endpoints. In: Proceedings of the International Conference for High Performance Computing, Networking, Storage and Analysis, SC 2014, pp. 487–498. IEEE Press, Piscataway (2014). https://doi.org/10.1109/SC.2014.45
28. Sultana, N., Rüfenacht, M., Skjellum, A., Laguna, I., Mohror, K.: Failure recovery for bulk synchronous applications with MPI stages. PARCOMP **84**, 1–14 (2019)
29. Wittmann, M., Hager, G., Zeiser, T., Wellein, G.: Asynchronous MPI for the masses. arXiv preprint arXiv:1302.4280 (2013)

Assessing Kokkos Performance
on Selected Architectures

Chang Phuong(✉) ⓘ, Noman Saied ⓘ, and Craig Tanis ⓘ

University of Tennessee, Chattanooga, TN 37403, USA
{chang-phuong,noman-saied,craig-tanis}@utc.edu

Abstract. Performance Portability frameworks allow developers to write code for familiar High-Performance Computing (HPC) architecture and minimize development effort over time to port it to other HPC architectures with little to no loss of performance. In our research, we conducted experiments with the same codebase on a Serial, OpenMP, and CUDA execution and memory space and compared it to the Kokkos Performance Portability framework. We assessed how well these approaches meet the goals of Performance Portability by solving a thermal conduction model on a 2D plate on multiple architectures (NVIDIA (K20, P100, V100, XAVIER), Intel Xeon, IBM Power 9, ARM64) and collected execution times (wall-clock) and performance counters with perf and nvprof for analysis. We used the Serial model to determine a baseline and to confirm that the model converges on both the native and Kokkos code. The OpenMP and CUDA models were used to analyze the parallelization strategy as compared to the Kokkos framework for the same execution and memory spaces.

Keywords: Performance Portability · OpenMP · CUDA · Kokkos · High-Performance Computing · HPC · Parallel programming

1 Introduction

The objective of a *performance portability* framework is to allow application developers to focus on science outcomes without concerning themselves with system details [13]. Parallelization and code optimization become the responsibility of the framework. In theory, if a framework is optimized for multiple architectures, the applications based on this framework will be automatically optimized as well [9].

Several such frameworks are under development, such as RAJA, BOAST, and Kokkos [5,10,12,13]. Each framework provides a different approach to separating application details from the architectural details, but a common feature is that

---

This material is based upon work supported by the National Science Foundation under Major Research Instrumentation (MRI) Grant No. 1229213. Any opinions, findings, and conclusions or recommendations expressed in this material are those of the authors and do not necessarily reflect the views of the National Science Foundation.

J. L. Crespo-Mariño and E. Meneses-Rojas (Eds.): CARLA 2019, CCIS 1087, pp. 170–184, 2020.
https://doi.org/10.1007/978-3-030-41005-6_12

the specific parallel programming model for the architecture is not evident in the application code. For example, a framework might use OpenMP directives or CUDA kernels, but this detail is not present in the application code. This lack of detail leaves decisions on how best to parallelize to the framework, which is crucial for high performance.

Pragma-based parallel programming techniques such as OpenMP, OpenCl, and OpenACC hide some details from the programmer, but gaining high performance when using these approaches requires low-level understanding of the target system [5,6].

In our research, we assess how well Kokkos meets the goals of Performance Portability by writing a stencil-based numeric kernel in C++ to solve a thermal conduction model on a 2D plate. These results will enable developers to make a conscious decision and evaluate the trade-offs between portability versus loss/-gains of performance. This code was executed on three programming platforms to capture execution time and performance counters to get performance metrics. The same codebase was transformed with the Kokkos portability framework, and the same metrics were captured for comparison. These tests were performed on several available systems with different architectures to assess how well Kokkos is able to port the code and assess its performance. We intend for our findings to help developers make an informed decision and understand what factors to consider for Performance Portability.

The goals of Performance Portability, Kokkos approach as a Performance Portability framework, and our interest in assessing this process are described in Sect. 2. Section 3 covers related research in HPC and Performance Portability frameworks. Details of the stencil-based numeric problem, the approach we used for our experiments, the data collection process, and the architectures used are included in Sect. 4. The results of our experiments are presented in Sect. 5, and we discuss the execution times and performance counters collected.

2   Performance Portability, Kokkos Framework, and Parallel Programming Models

The goal for Performance Portability is for developers to code a solution for a specific problem on a familiar multi-core architecture and port it to a different architecture with little or no loss of performance [13]. This is the theoretical goal, and it is not easy to achieve [6]. In our research, we assess how well current approaches meet the goals of Performance Portability. To do so, we selected a portability framework and a representative stencil-based numeric kernel to test a computational problem on an HPC system and then port it to other HPC systems. We chose Kokkos as our portability framework for our experiments.

The development of Kokkos is built on key concepts of User Accessibility and Performance Portability [3]. Minimizing the need for users to have specific knowledge of an architecture and limiting usage of parallel directives throughout the code are fundamental to user accessibility [3]. Achieving the same or nearly the same performance is their goal for performance portability [3]. This programming framework provides abstraction layers for data allocation and computation that allows for code written for scientific and engineering applications to be ported to different computing platforms [3,13] and makes it possible to isolate developers from the nuances and complexities associated with these specific architectures.

Kokkos uses template libraries that abstracts and treats execution space and memory space differently where it defines the parallelization strategy and includes details of the physical location of memory respectively [13]. The parallel execution and multidimensional array abstraction layer allows multi-core systems to access architecture-bound memory structure through the Kokkos API and selects the best memory storage ordering (Array of Structures (AoS) or Structure of Arrays (SoA)) without modification of the kernel [3].

Kokkos and programming models like OpenMP hide the architecture from the developer. OpenMP use processor directives to implement multithreading parallelization through a master thread that spawns multiple threads that execute independently within their code sections in each core. All threads use the main memory and respective core caches [8]. CUDA, another programming model, also differs in the way it uses memory and code execution. CUDA uses a master program that runs sequentially on the CPU and invokes compute-intensive code to be executed on the GPU to run on thousands of cores in parallel. The data is managed by the master program in main memory and copies it to and from the GPU's memory when it is needed for execution [7].

3   Related Work

Research and development in the area of Performance Portability has been deemed a priority by the Department of Energy (DOE) [4]. The focus on this research has provided the opportunity to study how these new frameworks behave in comparison to the architecture-specific counterparts. Some of these studies utilize a tool called TeaLeaf [4–6] that contains a collection of physics applications for the purpose of researching performance portability, scalability, and optimization [5], while others use known algorithms such as Jacobi and Dense Linear Algebra [4] that can be adjusted to different computational intensities for the purpose of testing performance.

One of these studies identifies the IBM Power systems and Intel Xeon Phi nodes as the two main architectures in their research [4]. This is a similar approach we utilized in our research. Their main objectives are to understand if it is possible to select a single programming model for developing on multi-core systems and the potential trade-offs in performance and productivity [4]. Their research does not focus on a framework like Kokkos but rather on the new features included in OpenMP 4.5 and OpenACC implementations that allow for execution on homogeneous shared memory systems and offload capabilities to heterogeneous accelerators [4].

BOAST (Bringing Optimization through Automatic Source-to-Source Transformation) is a metaprogramming framework and another option for Performance Portability that is currently on v1.0 as of October 2018. Its aim is to simplify optimization of HPC application computing kernels [12]. The benefits of their framework include portability, increased productivity, good code performance, and non-regression testing [12]. This is achieved by writing the application with BOAST DSL (Domain Specific Language), selecting a target language, and selecting the performance metrics and compiler to use. BOAST currently supports C, C with Vector Library, OpenCL, FORTRAN, and CUDA [12].

Another study explores the portability of OpenCL, OpenMP 4.0, Kokkos, RAJA, and OpenACC [6]. This study uses TeaLeaf as the baseline application to provide standardization of computational problems for testing each of these frameworks and programming models. Similar to our research, they use TeaLeaf to solve a 2-dimensional heat equation and compares them in the categories of Portability, Complexity, Productivity, Tuneability, and Performance [6]. Their findings show a range of scores under each category and provide readers a comparison chart to help make an informed decision on which framework or model to choose.

RAJA is being developed by Lawrence Livermore National Laboratories (LLNL) and uses a C++ abstraction layer that allows for integration of existing code and a development model to be used for new code [10]. This ability to support both existing and new code is advantageous because it saves productivity time and gives the developers the ability to port their existing code rather than having to start a new design from the ground up. The core to RAJA's abstraction is the separation of the inner loop from iteration patterns [10]. It also boasts enhanced readability and maintenance compared to other programming models due to its simplified layout [10].

We have previously analyzed the performance of a Kokkos-enabled finite-element application on a single architecture [11].

4   Methodology and Benchmark

Selecting a computational problem for our experiment is trivial but fundamental to our research. To test the Performance Portability of Kokkos, we had several options to consider such as using TeaLeaf, a scientific application containing physics algorithms [5], or developing our own program based on known algorithms. For the purpose of our research, we wrote a stencil-based numeric kernel to test a computational problem in C++ code to solve the thermal conduction model on a 2D plate with the Poisson equation. We used a single code base configured to compile on their respective testing architecture. The process we used to solve the thermal conduction model with the Poisson equation is described in Algorithm 1.

4.1   Poisson Equation

Poisson is a partial 2D differential equation [1]. Since we have Dirichlet boundary condition (the outer boundaries of the region), we are solving for the interior values. Figure 1 illustrates an example. Given known values from the applied heat source shown by the outer boundary dots, we will use the 2D Poisson Equation to estimate the inner values indicated by the red dots. See Fig. 1.

Algorithm 1. Iterative method for Poisson equation

---

1 Set Tolerance = 1e−10;
2 Set $maxDiff = 0$;
3 initialization: boundaries, inside points;
4 **do**
5 | Save current Grid values (old);
6 | Calculate new Grid values (new);
7 | $diff =\mid new - old \mid$;
8 | **if** $diff \leq maxDiff$ **then**
9 | | $maxDiff = diff$;
10 | **end**
11 **while** $maxDiff \leq tolerance$;

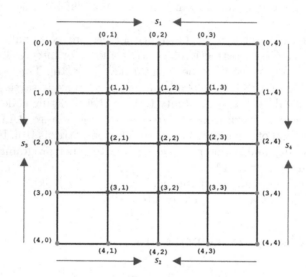

Fig. 1. Thermal conduction model

The Poisson Equation is given as follows.

$$\nabla^2 T = S(x, y) \tag{1}$$

Algorithm Development: (1) can be written as follows.

$$\nabla^2 T = \frac{\partial^2 T}{\partial x^2} + \frac{\partial^2 T}{\partial y^2} = S(x, y) \tag{2}$$

where

$$\frac{\partial^2 T}{\partial x^2} = \frac{T_{i+1,j} - 2T_{i,j} + T_{i-1,j}}{h^2} + \epsilon_1 \tag{3}$$

$$\frac{\partial^2 T}{\partial y^2} = \frac{T_{i,j+1} - 2T_{i,j} + T_{i,j-1}}{k^2} + \epsilon_2 \tag{4}$$

$$h = \triangle x \quad and \quad k = \triangle y \tag{5}$$

Like many numerical iterative methods, the idea is to discretize the solution domain into a grid (structured in this case), using constant spacing (steps) in x-axis and y-axis respectively, and approximate the value of T at a given grid point. The point (i, j) is given by $T_{i,j}$. For a grid with N and M grid points, if $N = M$ i.e $h = k$ the grid is said to be a uniform grid.

For administrative and verification purposes, we will use the following information: $0 \le x \le 2$ and $0 \le y \le 1$, Subject to the following boundary conditions $T(0, y) = 0$, $T(2, y) = 2e^y$, $T(x, 0) = x$, and $T(x, 1) = ex$, and with the following source term $T(x, y) = 2e^y$. Note that the exact solution to the PDE is $T = xe^y$.

Listing 1.1. Serial stencil kernel

```
for (int i=1; i < n-1; i++) {
  for (int j=1; j < m-1; j++) {
    double diff = T(i,j);
    T2(i,j) = (mainCoff*(T(i-1,j)
              + lambda*T(i,j-1)+T(i+1,j)
              + lambda*T(i,j+1)-(H*F(i,j)))));
    diff = fabs(diff - T2(i,j));
    if (diff > maxDiff) {
      maxDiff = diff;
    }
  }
}
```

Listing 1.1 illustrates the main loop that evaluates the 5-point stencil. This loop is parallelized in different ways throughout this project.

4.2   Execution Spaces

We selected three programming platforms to solve this thermal conduction model and refer to these as the native platforms: Serial, OpenMP, and CUDA. These platforms were selected because they allowed us to make a one-to-one comparison with the Kokkos execution space model and assess the approach and performance of the portability code generated by Kokkos. These comparisons were grouped into the Serial, OpenMP (Multi-Core), and CUDA (GPU) Execution Spaces respectively. Compilation of these programs utilized compiler optimization flags uniformly and whenever possible to attain the highest performance allowed. Each program was executed individually to minimize resource sharing and contention on the selected architecture to obtain the best execution time estimation. All versions of the program used the same kernel. Kokkos was built with the default execution space set to Serial, OpenMP, and CUDA versions of Kokkos.

The Serial Execution Space provides us a baseline measurement between a native Serial code and the Serial code generated by Kokkos. The OpenMP Execution Space compares native OpenMP and Kokkos' OpenMP generated code.

The Serial and OpenMP Execution Spaces gave us a view into the performance difference when the code is executed on single-core and multi-core architectures respectively. The CUDA Execution Space allowed us to compare between native CUDA and Kokkos CUDA, as well as between multi-core architecture and GPU on both the native and their counterparts generated by Kokkos.

To experiment with these different execution spaces, we've taken the serial kernel from Listing 1.1 and modified it to parallelize the outer loop in different ways depending on the target architecture. For the native OpenMP version, we simply use a `#pragma omp parallel for` on the outer loop. For Kokkos, we wrap the inner loop in a C++ lambda expression and pass this to a `Kokkos::parallel_for` which parallelizes the outer loop. For native CUDA, we wrote a tiling-based kernel, for comparison. The data accesses using parentheses in the kernel (e.g., `T(i,j)`) are C macros in the native versions, which are replaced by traditional 2D array accesses. In the Kokkos version, this parenthesized syntax is the expected way to access Kokkos `View` data structures.

4.3   Data Collection

The comparisons of these programs were performed through the collection of execution time measurements on a large grid dimension that would provide a high level of density of points for the calculations. Our decision to capture the execution time is to remain true to the concept of Performance Portability [3] and to set a standard metric to benchmark performance. This entails allowing Kokkos to transform the code and to manage the memory space and execution space for parallelization based on the underlying architecture [11,13] so that we can understand the fundamental performance differences based on a native execution time measurement.

Solving a thermal conduction model on a 2D plate is trivial for the HPC domain; however, increasing the plate grid dimension creates a problem that is more interesting and that meets the basic characteristics of a problem that requires Data Parallelism. In our experiment, we used a $1,000 \times 1,000$ grid size for the Serial and OpenMP programs. For CUDA, we used a $10,000 \times 25$ grid size to match the loop structure to the underlying hardware of the multi-cores and memory bandwidth. These programs were executed multiple times for each category to ensure consistency of the execution time.

On the Serial and OpenMP Execution Spaces, perf [2] is used to collect hardware performance counters for analysis. The following selected counters were available and reported on all architectures used in our experiments: cycles, cache-references, cache-misses, total number of instruction, L1-dcache-loads, L1-dcache-load-misses, and time elapsed. These metrics allow us to assess how the code is being executed in each architecture and compare the performance relative to the native and ported code. The collection of perf data was performed on a $1,000 \times 1,000$ grid size over 1, 10, and 100 iterations. For the CUDA Execution Space, nvprof was used to collect GPU performance counter data. This data, in conjunction with execution times, gives a rough measure of how well CUDA kernels are able to take advantage of the GPU hardware.

4.4   Architectures

This experiment was conducted on four architectures for comparison of performance consistency over the three programming models and the selected grid dimensions. Kokkos was compiled on each of the architectures for code optimization. The experiment for the OpenMP Execution Space was conducted on these architectures without hyperthreading to avoid oversubscribing the cores. These architectures are included in Table 1.

Table 1. Architectures

Architecture	XEON K20
Cores	16
CPU	Intel Xeon ES-2650v2 2.60 GHz
RAM	256 GB
GPU	Tesla K20m 2496 Cores 706 MHz
GPU Memory	4 GB 2600 Mhz, 208 GB/s
CUDA Version	9.2
Architecture	XEON P100
Cores	28
CPU	Intel Xeon E5-2680v4 2.40 GHz
RAM	132 GB
GPU	P100 3584 Cores 1329 MHz
GPU Memory	16 GB 715 Mhz, 732 GB/s
CUDA Version	8.0
Architecture	POWER9 V100
Cores	40
CPU	IBM Power9, altivec supported
RAM	256 GB
GPU	V100 5120 Cores 1530 MHz
GPU Memory	16 GB 877 Mhz, 900 GB/s
CUDA Version	9.2
Architecture	XAVIER
Cores	4
CPU	ARMv8 Processor v81 2.26 GHz
RAM	16 GB
GPU	Xavier 512 Cores 1500 MHz
GPU Memory	16 GB 1500 Mhz, 137 GB/s
CUDA Version	10.0

5   Results

5.1   Serial

To confirm that our C++ code works properly and to get a baseline metric on each of the selected platforms, we compiled and executed the code in each of the architectures for native serial and Kokkos serial execution space and allowed the program to run to completion. A grid size of 400 × 400 was used for this experiment, and the number of iterations it took the program to solve the Poisson equation was recorded at 588,921 iterations for all versions of the program to converge.

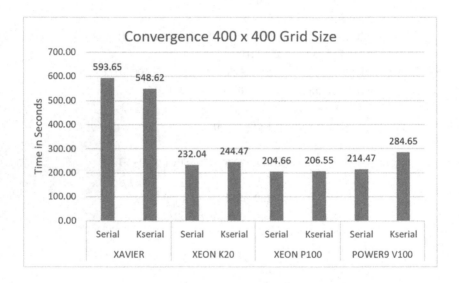

Fig. 2. Serial code execution time in seconds

Native Serial. The execution time for the two XEON and POWER9 architectures performed comparably to each other and were up to 190% faster than the XAVIER architecture. We did not expect to see XEON P100 outperform POWER9 V100 by 5% because the POWER9 V100 is a newer HPC system and has faster cores. See Fig. 2.

Kokkos Serial. The Kokkos version did not perform as well as the Native Serial. When comparing between the Kokkos serial in XEON, POWER9, and XAVIER architectures, the XEON and POWER9 were up to 166% faster than the XAVIER. All architectures performed better in their native serial than Kokkos and stayed within the 10% margin [3]. The exception was on the POWER9 V100 architecture where the Native Serial performed 33% better than Kokkos Serial.

5.2   OpenMP

The first part of our Performance Portability parallel test is performed with the OpenMP execution space. We conducted a series of Strong Scaling tests on each of the architectures with a grid size of $1,000 \times 1,000$ and stopped the execution at 5,000 iterations. Our scaling factor was 1, 2, 3, 4, 8, 16, 28, and 40 cores (Fig. 3). This design allowed us to make a base comparison between each of the architectures along comparable scaling, up to the maximum number of cores (Fig. 4). Hyperthreading was turned off to prevent oversubscribing the cores.

Cores	XAVIER		XEON K20		XEON P100		POWER9 V100	
	OpenMP	KOpenMP	OpenMP	KOpenMP	OpenMP	KOpenMP	OpenMP	KOpenMP
1	29.45	34.58	16.39	21.99	14.01	17.59	11.11	27.75
2	16.13	17.50	8.21	11.34	7.03	9.09	5.66	13.89
3	10.53	12.19	5.62	7.65	4.71	5.96	3.80	10.20
4	8.09	9.60	4.23	5.87	3.54	4.58	2.89	8.46
8	-	-	2.32	3.10	1.97	2.51	1.43	3.53
16	-	-	1.26	1.66	1.07	1.33	0.85	2.70
28	-	-	-	-	0.71	0.84	0.71	1.32
40	-	-	-	-	-	-	0.61	0.98

Fig. 3. Strong scaling execution time in seconds

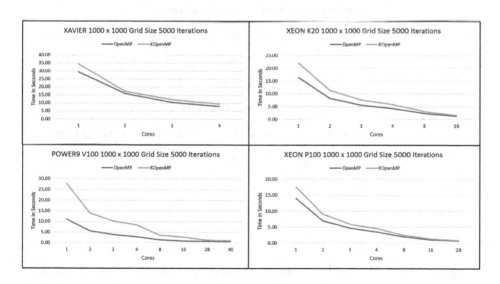

Fig. 4. Line chart - strong scaling execution time in seconds

Native OpenMP. The execution time consistently dropped by half for each of the architectures as the scaling of the cores doubled. This behavior confirms that Strong Scaling is occurring for both Native OpenMP and Kokkos OpenMP execution spaces.

Kokkos OpenMP. We saw a consistent 17%–35% faster performance of the Native OpenMP over the Kokkos version. This result is not consistent with those obtained by other research [3]. POWER9 V100 native OpenMP experienced an average of 170% to as much as 218% faster performance over the Kokkos version. This behavior may be due to the way Kokkos handles memory layout and views for the IBM Power 9 and merits further research with Kokkos developers to determine if our code requires additional optimization flags for the IBM Power 9 versus Intel Xeon.

We ran our kernel with 1, 10, and 100 iterations and collected perf hardware counters. As we increased the number of iterations, the counter stats also increased. We used the perf data to better understand the execution time results. On XAVIER, Kokkos outperformed native OpenMP. The Kokkos version executed 4.06 Instructions per Cycle (IPC) versus 1.95 IPC on native OpenMP. On the XEON architectures, both Kokkos and native versions performed comparably. On POWER9 V100, the results were opposite to XAVIER. Native OpenMP executed 7.53 IPC versus Kokkos 0.77 IPC with a higher percentage of Cache-Misses to Instructions at 1.33% versus 7.56%.

Native OpenMP 1000X1000 100 Iteration				
Performance instructions per cycles (IPC)	XAVIER	XEON K20	XEON P100	POWER9 V100
	1.95	2.07	2.17	7.53
cache-misses to instructions	4.69%	0.02%	0.05%	1.33%
Kokkos OpenMP 1000X1000 100 Iteration				
Performance instructions per cycles (IPC)	XAVIER	XEON K20	XEON P100	POWER9 V100
	4.06	2.12	2.03	0.77
cache-misses to instructions	3.28%	0.01%	0.05%	7.56%

Fig. 5. Native vs Kokkos OpenMP perf stats

Figure 5 estimates the IPC based on the perf data collected. The higher IPC, the more efficiently the processor is executing instruction on the system. The ratio of cache-misses to instructions will give an indication of how well the cache is working.

5.3   CUDA

The second part of our Performance Portability parallel test is performed in the CUDA execution and memory space. In our CUDA experiments, we set Kokkos to use Unified Virtual Memory (UVM) to simplify the process of using a single codebase for all tests. We used two grid sizes, a $10,000 \times 25$ and a $25 \times 10,000$, to make sure the data fits into memory to minimize unnecessary paging and to maximize core parallelization. We captured the execution times at 1,000, 10,000, and 100,000 iterations (Figs. 6 and 7) and nvprof was used to capture the GPU stats.

Iterations	Grid Size	XAVIER	XEON K20	XEON P100	POWER9 V100
1,000	10,000x25	2.64	0.21	0.07	0.10
10,000	10,000x25	10.92	2.07	0.76	0.80
100,000	10,000x25	81.95	19.46	6.56	7.43
1,000	25x10,000	0.69	0.12	0.06	0.06
10,000	25x10,000	6.51	1.17	0.54	0.59
100,000	25x10,000	55.13	11.63	5.32	6.02

Fig. 6. CUDA execution time in seconds

Iterations	Grid Size	XAVIER	XEON K20	XEON P100	POWER9 V100
1,000	10,000x25	0.89	0.18	0.08	0.08
10,000	10,000x25	12.08	1.79	0.64	0.75
100,000	10,000x25	88.22	17.90	6.54	7.34
1,000	25x10,000	15.31	12.09	4.87	2.45
10,000	25x10,000	150.81	120.87	48.70	24.20
100,000	25x10,000	1524.39	1205.73	487.12	242.33

Fig. 7. Kokkos CUDA execution time in seconds

Native CUDA. Execution time increased linearly as the number of iterations increased by powers of 10. This behavior was consistent across all architectures for Native CUDA for both grid sizes of $10,000 \times 25$ and $25 \times 10,000$. The time in seconds is larger for XAVIER but proportionally similar in percentage to the rest of the architectures. The ARM architecture has 512 GPU cores compared to 2496, 3584, and 5120 cores for XEON K20, XEON P100, and POWER9 V100 respectively. XAVIER also has a maximum of 137 GB/s memory bandwidth compared to 208, 732, and 900 GB/s for XEON K20, XEON P100, and POWER9 V100 respectively. These technical specs directly impact the timed results. A notable data point in this experiment is between XEON P100 and POWER9

V100. The XEON P100 GPU runs at 200 Mhz slower than the POWER9 V100 GPU with nearly 1,500 fewer cores and with memory speeds 150 Mhz slower. Even with a slower hardware configuration, the XEON P100 was on average 14% faster than the POWER9 V100. We are anecdotally aware of criticisms surrounding CUDA kernel launch latency on Power9, and will be exploring this in future work.

Kokkos CUDA. As in the OpenMP case, we used a naive Kokkos implementation to replace the outer nested loop with a C++ lambda expression passed to `Kokkos::parallel_for()`. At runtime, each row is handled entirely by a single CUDA thread, which has dramatic influence on execution runtimes.

Execution time increased linearly as the number of iterations increased by powers of 10. This same behavior was consistent across all architectures for Kokkos CUDA for both grid sizes of $10,000 \times 25$ and $25 \times 10,000$. These same results were observed for Native CUDA as well. For the grid size $10,000 \times 25$, Kokkos CUDA overall performance was within expected parameters [13]; however, on the grid size of $25 \times 10,000$, Kokkos CUDA overall performance was much worse by an average of 2,400% on XAVIER, 10,250% On XEON K20, 8,760% on XEON P100, and 4,070% on POWER9 V100.

The poor performance of Kokkos when using the $25 \times 10,000$ grid size is due to a naive approach to parallelism that is somewhat hidden by the Kokkos abstractions. What appeared to be adequately performant on other architectures suffers greatly on GPU hardware, leading to an observation about Kokkos: performance depends on having a clear understanding of how template choices map to architectural details. With this Kokkos::Cuda implementation, each row of the grid is processed by a single CUDA thread, and there is not enough work to take advantage of all the CUDA cores. The Native CUDA implementation does not suffer from this problem because the CUDA kernel uses a 2-dimensional partitioning, producing good performance in any grid configuration.

Iterations	Grid Size	Native	Naïve	MDRange
1,000	10,000x25	0.07	0.08	0.06
10,000	10,000x25	0.76	0.64	0.58
100,000	10,000x25	6.56	6.54	5.73
1,000	25x10,000	0.06	4.87	0.06
10,000	25x10,000	0.54	48.70	0.57
100,000	25x10,000	5.32	487.12	5.69

Fig. 8. XEON P100 Kokkos CUDA MDRange execution time in seconds

Kokkos developers have introduced an experimental MDRangePolicy that reproduces the same 2-dimensional partition configuration utilized in the Native CUDA implementation. MDRangePolicy allows for loop partitioning in multiple dimensions and nested parallization. When we applied this MDRangePolicy in our experiment on the XEON P100, the Kokkos CUDA version achieved performance similar to the Native CUDA version. Figure 8 shows that MDRangePolicy drastically improved the performance over the Naive execution on the XEON P100. Notable differences in the results can be seen between the Native and MDRangePolicy for both $10,000 \times 25$ and $25 \times 10,000$ grid sizes. In the $10,000 \times 25$ grid size, the MDRangePolicy performed better than the Native code. We expect that Kokkos outperforms ours in this instance because its implementation of parallel reduction is more mature than our native version. When the grid size is flipped, the Native code performed better than Kokkos MDRangePolicy; however, the MDRangePolicy performance is within the expected parameters [3].

6   Conclusions

Researchers are developing new programming models and frameworks that enable Performance Portability. Each has distinct features and varying levels of complexity to learn and implement. As shown by previous research [4,6,12,13] and our own here, we have to consider the various factors such as Productivity, Portability, Performance, etc. [6] when making a decision on which portability framework to use and consider the trade-offs. Even after considering these factors, the portability process is not trivial. There are limitations to each of these frameworks associated with their level of support of current HPC architectures that will continue to evolve and make it more difficult to future-proof [6].

Solving a thermal conduction model on a 2D plate is trivial for the HPC domain; however, we believe it is appropriate for the types of experiments we conducted to collect basic performance metrics and to understand the behavior and capabilities of the Kokkos libraries on fundamental transformation operations in contrast to a more complex implementation where additional factors would hinder the analysis. Our research has shown that the effort of writing code to solve a computational problem for parallel programming models such as OpenMP and CUDA is relatively trivial compared to fully achieving Performance Portability [9]. The Kokkos framework provided abstraction layers to shield us from the details of the underlying architecture [13]. The compiled code is supposed to be optimized to the architecture; however, our experiments show that optimization for performance was not always achieved for the specified architecture when we approach the problem with a naive implementation.

Achieving Performance Portability is not without a cost. The developer must make conscious decisions for trade-off on ease of portability versus loss of performance. It is not easy to know the performance gain or loss of code until baseline tests are executed on all HPC systems involved. The developer should also consider the optimization strategy, the architecture limitations, and abstractions supported by the portability framework in the hopes that it will continue to maintain performance on future architectural platforms. If the goal is to achieve portability, then current frameworks will provide the means to do so; however, if the goal is to maintain performance, then the developer should not approach the problem with a naive implementation. In our case, when we approached the problem naively, we did not achieve optimal performance with Kokkos; however, by using multiple levels of parallelism, we were able to achieve the same or nearly the same level of performance [3].

Our future work beyond this research involves exploring how Kokkos optimizes code for the architectures used in these experiments, nested parallelization options used in Performance Portability frameworks, and the effects of hyper-threading on Performance Portability.

References

1. Buchanan, J.L., Turner, P.R.: Numerical Methods and Analysis. McGraw-Hill, New York (1992)
2. De Melo, A.C.: The new Linux 'perf' tools. In: Slides from Linux Kongress, vol. 18 (2010)
3. Edwards, H.C., Trott, C.R.: Kokkos: enabling performance portability across manycore architectures. In: 2013 Extreme Scaling Workshop (XSW), pp. 18–24. IEEE (2013)
4. Lopez, M.G., et al.: Towards achieving performance portability using directives for accelerators. In: 2016 Third Workshop on Accelerator Programming Using Directives (WACCPD), pp. 13–24. IEEE (2016)
5. Martineau, M., McIntosh-Smith, S., Boulton, M., Gaudin, W., Beckingsale, D.: A performance evaluation of Kokkos & Raja using the TeaLeaf mini-app. In: The International Conference for High Performance Computing, Networking, Storage and Analysis, SC 2015 (2015)
6. Martineau, M., McIntosh-Smith, S., Gaudin, W.: Assessing the performance portability of modern parallel programming models using TeaLeaf. Concurrency Comput.: Practice Exp. **29**(15), e4117 (2017)
7. NVIDIA developer (2019). https://developer.nvidia.com/. Accessed 16 Jan 2019
8. OpenMP (2019). https://www.openmp.org/. Accessed 12 Jan 2019
9. Portability across DOE office of science HPC facilities (2019). http://performanceportability.org/. Accessed 14 Jan 2019
10. RAJA: Managing application portability for next-generation platforms, January 2019. https://computation.llnl.gov/projects/raja-managing-application-portability-next-generation-platforms
11. Tanis, C., Sreenivas, K., Newman, J.C., Webster, R.: Performance portability of a multiphysics finite element code. In: 2018 Aviation Technology, Integration, and Operations Conference, p. 2890 (2018)
12. Videau, B., et al.: BOAST: a metaprogramming framework to produce portable and efficient computing kernels for HPC applications. Int. J. High Perform. Comput. Appl. **32**(1), 28–44 (2018)
13. Wiki, K.: Kokkos: The C++ performance portability programming model (2019). https://github.com/kokkos/kokkos/wiki/. Accessed 14 Jan 2019

Improving the Simulation of Biologically Accurate Neural Networks Using Data Flow HLS Transformations on Heterogeneous SoC-FPGA Platforms

Kaleb Alfaro-Badilla[1]([✉]), Andrés Arroyo-Romero[1]([✉]),
Carlos Salazar-García[2]([✉]), Luis G. León-Vega[1]([✉]),
Javier Espinoza-González[3]([✉]), Franklin Hernández-Castro[4]([✉]),
Alfonso Chacón-Rodríguez[1]([✉]), Georgios Smaragdos[5]([✉]),
and Christos Strydis[5]([✉])

[1] Escuela de Ingeniería Electrónica, Tecnológico de Costa Rica, Cartago, Costa Rica
{jaalfaro,aarroyo,lleon95}@estudiantec.cr, alchacon@tec.ac.cr
[2] Área Académica de Ingeniería Mecatrónica, Tecnológico de Costa Rica,
Cartago, Costa Rica
csalazar@tec.ac.cr
[3] Área Académica de Ingeniería en Computadores, Tecnólogico de Costa Rica,
Cartago, Costa Rica
jaespinoza@estudiantec.cr
[4] Escuela de Ingeniería en Diseño Industrial, Tecnológico de Costa Rica,
Cartago, Costa Rica
franhernandez@itcr.ac.cr
[5] Department of Neuroscience, Erasmus Medical Center,
Rotterdam, The Netherlands
{g.smaragdos,c.strydis}@erasmusmc.nl

Abstract. This work proposes a hardware performance-oriented design methodology aimed at generating efficient high-level synthesis (HLS) coded data multiprocessing on a heterogeneous platform. The methodology is tested on typical neuroscientific complex application: the biologically accurate modeling of a brain region known as the inferior olivary nucleus (ION). The ION cells are described using a multi-compartmental model based on the extended Hodgkin-Huxley membrane model (eHH), which requires the solution of a set of coupled differential equations. The proposed methodology is tested against alternative HPC implementations (multi-core CPU i7-7820HQ, and a Virtex7 FPGA) of the same ION model for different neural network sizes. Results show that the solution runs 10 to 4 times faster than our previous implementation using the same board and closes the gap between the performance against a Virtex7 implementation without using at full-capacity the AXI-HP channels.

Supported by Instituto Tecnologico de Costa Rica.

J. L. Crespo-Mariño and E. Meneses-Rojas (Eds.): CARLA 2019, CCIS 1087, pp. 185–199, 2020.
https://doi.org/10.1007/978-3-030-41005-6_13

Keywords: Spiking neural networks · FPGA · HLS · Dataflow ·
HPC · Inferior olivary nucleus

1   Introduction

There has been a growing effort in the field of neuroscience to produce, on the
one hand, accurate-enough neural models that help avoid the use of invasive
in-vivo techniques for the precise characterization of neural tissue responses to
determinate stimuli and, on the other hand, having flexible, tractable models
that allow for the analysis of neural networks of representative sizes in order to
study particular regions of the nervous system [11]. These models are generally
referred to as spiking neural networks (SNNs), because of their ability to imitate
the natural spiking behaviour of real neural cells. The creation of models for this
sort of cells requires, first, the need for integrate numeric modelling techniques
that accurately represent the behavior of nervous cells from a chemical, biological
and physical perspective, while, secondly, optimizing those same models in order
to make them portable to existing computer hardware and software [20]. This
has meant, usually, moving from the theoretical analysis of low level abstraction
models—typically rich in detail—to higher abstraction models, easier to scale
and simulate for more practical situations [20], depending of the final application. But recently, the effort has moved in the direction of tying the low-level
analysis models with large-scale observable experiments, particularly because of
the increasing computing power and computational techniques of the last decade
that, some day, may help improving the comprehension of the brain information
processing, the origin of the consciousness [4], and the understanding of the
mechanics in mental illness such as Parkinson syndrome [9].

A platform which is gaining adoption as a potentially efficient vehicle for
accelerating SNN simulations is the Field Programmable Gate Array (FPGA),
due to its inherent ability to carry out parallel power-efficient numerical computing (see for instance [22] for a completely custom hardware approach of porting
a eHH based SNN to a multi-FPGA platform). Yet, porting software algorithms
to FPGAs is not straightforward for those not versed in synchronous, concurrent
digital design: the dataflow nature of digital hardware, and the timing aspects
related to floor-planning and routing, though somewhat simplified by standard
practices in hardware description languages (HDL) and synthesis tools, escape
software designers, ending in non-optimal designs. It is a common misconcep-
tion, even among junior digital designers, to see HDLs as programming languages
instead of what they really are: a way of structurally describing logical circuits,
that certain tools may correctly (or not) interpret in order to generate the said
circuit. This, of course, complicates the exploration of SNN variants, as custom
hardware design as the one reported in [22] is time consuming, and ends in
systems not amenable to quick modifications.

As a way of bridging this gap between algorithm design and its hardware
implementation, a new batch of high level synthesis (HLS) tools have appeared
in the past decade, aimed at accelerating the deployment time on FPGAs [5].

These tools allow for quick explorations of hardware implementations such as the one reported in [18] (one of the authors in [18] is Smaragdos who is also an author in this work). But such direct translations into hardware from high level language constructs are not as efficient in terms of processing when compared with direct custom implementations in applications specific integrated circuits (ASICs), or even to software running on standard Von Neumann and vectorial processors (particularly because of the 65–70% speed penalty imposed by the programmable FPGA fabric, among other handicaps vis-á-vis integrated circuits clearly explained in [3, 12]), and require extra effort if one intends providing them with standard interfaces that allow for scalability and communication with other computational systems. A way of overcoming this is resorting to heterogeneous platforms such as Xilinx Zynq SoCs, that incorporate both standard processing cores and FPGAs. In this way, those coding structures more amenable to a standard sequential programming model may be implemented directly on the SoC cores (with the added advantage of having access to arithmetic, interfaces and even memory running at full core or bus speed), while a parallel accelerator running on the FPGA takes care of those operations that can run faster in high level described customized hardware.

Our previous implementation of a SoC-FPGA heterogeneous solution for the eHH ION model has already been presented in [1], where the main approach used was a divide and conquer strategy, with the programmable logic (PL) of the device being used for the solution of the expensive $O(n^2)$ GJ operations, while the SoC core (PS) was used both for handling the linear scaling computations of the ION dentrite, soma and axon compartments, and the required data scheduling for the complete simulation of the model. The current work shows how the results obtained in the latter can be improved in at least an order of magnitude, by using particular C++ code transformations within an HLS guided hardware design methodology, applied to the hardware accelerator unit executing the gap-junctions interactions of the network population.

This paper is structured as follows: Sect. 2 gives a theoretical background on SNNs and the complexities associated with accelerating their simulation, and summarizes related work around proposed solutions for the simulation biologically accurate SNN models, centred mainly on recent FPGA-based implementations of the eHH ION model, and their performance against typical HPC multi-core and GPU-based solutions. Section 3 describes in detail the structure of an heterogeneous approach towards SNN simulation acceleration, while Sect. 4 presents the design methodology hereby proposed in order to speed up the latter. Section 5 discusses the results obtained and potential improvements in the system, compared with previous implementations of the ION model, and the authors' previous results given in [1]. This section also discusses how to carry out modifications required in order to simulate alternative SNN models. Section 6 provides with conclusions and recommendations for future work.

2 Spiking Neural Networks Modelling and Simulation Acceleration

Biological neural networks are also referred to as spiking neural networks (SNNs) because of their spiking nature, in order to differentiate them from artificial neural networks (ANNs). Now, depending on the goal of a researcher, a single neuron may be modeled as a simple sum operation or as a multi-compartment system with rich biological detail, with a whole range of multiple levels of model complexity in between [11], where SNNs are typically based on the most complex models and ANNs on the simplest. Almog *et al.* [2] explain that a realistic model is characterized by how effectively does it reproduce the behavior of a biological neuron, but not the other way around. A more complex model requires more fitting parameters and, as such, it becomes easily constrained by the classical multidimensional problem. For practical reasons, a simpler model is always preferred if it recreates the experiments with satisfactory results.

Historically, the first widely accepted low level abstraction model of a neural cell was proposed by Hodgkin and Huxley: a basic Resistance-Capacitance electric model that was able to emulate the behavior of neurons in the analog computers of the 1950s [8]. Other models, such as the Iz model, proposed by Izhikevich, and the Integrate and Fire model (IaF), are also widely used, but their limitations in biologically accuracy sometimes prevent their use in particular cases (see [11] for a good guide on how and when to use each).

Now, the trait that enables neurons to communicate among themselves are the synapses, which are highly specialized structures [7]. There are two main types of synapses: electrical and chemical synapses. The electrical synapses are the simplest form, and consist of inter-cellular channels which allow ions and small molecules to pass from one cell to the next. These synapses are also known as gap-junctions (GJ), and they do not distinguish between pre and post-synaptic interconnects [7]. Chemical synapses, on the other hand, consist of a sequence of interactions, where the pre-synaptic signals are transmitted via the release of neurotransmitters that bind to receptors at the post-synaptic neurons [7].

2.1 The Inferior Olivary Nucleus Model

The inferior olivary nucleus (ION) forms an intricate part of the olivocerebellar system which is believed to be related to the timing of motor commands and learning [6]. The main feature of this cell is that it forms part of the densest brain region where its activity only gets triggered when multiple neurons are synchronized (and subsequently transmitting a short burst of spikes [6]). To effectively emulate this behaviour, De Gruijl *et al.* [6] developed a model based on a three-compartmental cell (dendrite, soma and axon) with GJ interactions between each neuron's dendrite-compartments (see Fig. 1). The model is also called the extended Hodgkin-Huxley model (eHH). The operations are performed with single-precision floating-point (SPFP) representation; a summary of the required SPFP operations and data transfer needed for the different sections of the model are given in Table 1.

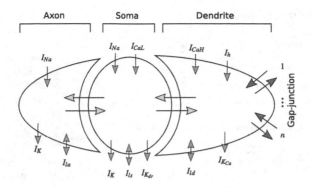

Fig. 1. Schematic representation of the three-compartmental cell model proposed in [6]. Each arrow indicates an ion channel or electrical current direction. Figure based on [6].

Table 1. Single-Precision Floating-Point (SPFP) operations and transfers per simulation step, per neuron [15,16]. Here, N means the total neuron population.

Operational compartment	No. of SPFP operations
Gap junction unit	$12 \times N$
Cell compartment (Axon, soma, dendrite)	859
I/O and storage	No. of SPFP transfers
Neuron state (R/W)	19
Evoked input (R)	1
Connectivity vector (R)	$1 \times N$
Neuron conductances (R)	20
Axon output (W)	1 (axon voltage)

As discussed in [1,16,17], the eHH ION model has a computational complexity that is mainly determined by the GJ interactions, particularly when the network is densely interconnected, being the worst case an all-to-all connection, when the complexity becomes $O_{gj}(n^2)$, with n the number of dendritic connections for each cell. As an aside, since a required property of a biologically accurate cell model is that the neural network must be synchronized in order to guarantee the correct calculation of the dendritic phenomena, event-driven simulations are discarded [19], and the differential equations are usually solved via the Euler method [6].

2.2 FPGA Approaches at Simulating Biologically Accurate SNN Models

Plenty of work has been carried out in porting SNN models to FPGAs, as the already mentioned cases of [18,22]. But there are also simpler based SNN implementations, as that of [13,21], and some have also already used heterogeneous

GJU-IP Overall system architecture

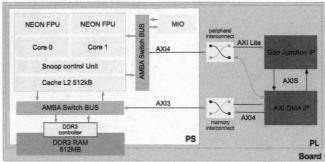

Fig. 2. Overall system architecture. The GJU-IP is managed by one thread of the ARM A9, via AXI4, while the other thread handles the axon, soma and dendritic compartmental models, and takes care of the system's I/O.

platforms as the one used in this work (see [14]), proposing a cluster of 32 boards in order evaluate the communication performance of a sparse graph-oriented application using MPI (in this case a sparsely distributed Iz based SNN). These simple, sparse SNN models are, nonetheless, not able to support the ION model easily, which is one of the main objectives that motivated this work. As already discussed, a key aspect of the ION system is the dense interconnection among the cell population. Researchers in [18] and [22] center their strategy around multiple instances of execution units of neural cells called physical cells (PC). Each cell-state is associated with one PC, then each PC executes a set of cell-states each simulation step. In both cases, their approaches are fast enough to achieve locked-step simulation at a $50\,\mu s$ time step (necessary for the model's convergence, in order to have simulation timings equivalent to the brain's own real time response), but circumscribed to a small cell population in a all-to-all dendritic connection. This sizing restriction is mainly due to the inner gap-junction interactions within the dendrite compartment. These operations are modelled as a pair of nested `for` loops (see Listing 1.1), that scale in a $O(n^2)$ fashion as the number of dendritic connections, n, increases. One could easily try to port to hardware via an HLS loop-unrolling directive that distributes into parallel hardware the arithmetic operations. But this direct approach, unfortunately, does not scale effectively because of hardware resources sharing among the rest of the PC's compartments, which in the case of [18], limit the total number of real-time simulated cells to 96. The work of [22], claims bringing up the total number of real-time running cells up to 768 for a single Zedboard (in what seems to an 8-way connection scheme among neurons, with no specific experimental timing results given for their proposed Multi-FPGA platform), at the cost of a customized structure, not readily ported to a different SNN model. Both [18,22] claim the capacity of accommodating larger SNNs if this real-time constraint is removed, nonetheless.

3   An Heterogeneous Approach to SNN Simulation Accelerators

This work aims at providing an efficient accelerated implementation of the eHH ION model, that is also flexible enough in case of requiring extensive modifications of the model used, without losing efficiency. The overall high level architecture used is shown in Fig. 2, using Avnet's Zynq-7020 SoC ZedBoard with 512 MB DDR3 RAM. The processing region of the Zynq (called PS) includes a dual-core ARM A9 CPU, with NEON SIMD capabilities, plus several I/O controllers such as an Ethernet interface. The integrated Artyx-7 FPGA fabric (called the PL region) is interconnected via several AXI4 bus channels to the PS. The simulation task is partitioned between the PS and PL regions: the soma, the axon, and the dendrite compartments described by the eHH equations (see [1] for details) are executed on the ARM cores. The gap-junction interactions are processed in the PL region. Note that the latter has limited local on-chip memory (technically called BRAM by Xilinx), making difficult for the whole conductance matrix to reside locally next to the gap-junction processing unit (here called GJU), if the said so matrix is over a few thousands elements. This entails a continues transfer of such matrix between the DDR3 RAM and the GJU, in each computation step (a handicap that may easily be overcome on FPGAs with bigger BRAMs).

Listing 1.1. Gap-junction pseudocode

```
float  Vdend[N];  float  Iout[N];
float  Conn[N][C];
for(indxNeu=0; indxNeu<N; indxNeu++){
    float  facc=0;  float  vacc=0;
    for(indxCon=0;indxCon<C;indxCon++){
        v=Vdend[indxNeu] Vdend[indxCon],
        f=v*expf(-v*v*0.01);
        facc+=Conn[indxNeu][indxCon]*f;
        vacc+=Conn[indxNeu][indxCon]*v;
    }Iout[indxNeu]=0.8*facc+0.2*vacc;
}
```

Listing 1.2. Gap-junction strip-mined optimization pseudocode (one strip)

```
VRow[STRIP_SIZE];VCol[STRIP_SIZE];
popFirstV(input,VRow,VCol);
Facc[STRIP_SIZE];Vacc[STRIP_SIZE];
while(count<ColBlockProc){
    for(row=0;row<STRIP_SIZE;row++){
        cond[STRIP_SIZE];
        popCond(input,cond);
        popV(input,VCol);
        for(col=0;col<STRIP_SIZE;col++){
            #pragma HLS UNROLL
            V = VRow[row] - VCol[col];
            F = V * expf(V * V * hundred);
            Facc[row] += F * cond[col];
            Vacc[row] += V * cond[col];
        }
    }count+=STRIP_SIZE
}
I[STRIP_SIZE];
for(row=0;row<STRIP_SIZE;row++){
    I[row]=0.8*Facc[row]+0.2*Vacc[row];
}pushI(output,1);
```

An initial version of the GJU was designed using C++ and compiled to RTL using Vivado HLS. To optimize the parallelism of operation in the programmable fabric, a strip-mined loop transformation was used [5]. Results are reported in [1]. Differences between the optimized code and a naive direct approach (simply porting the original C++ code) describing the GJU as reported in [18] may be gleaned from code Listings 1.1 and 1.2. Note that in Listing 1.2, the **input** and **output**interfaces match to the AXI-Stream interfaces of the GJU. The Xilinx's AXI-DMA IP feeds the voltage from the dendrite and the interconnect conductance values to the interface, then writes back to the RAM the generated current values. As a drawback, the data packets fed to the stream have to be previously sorted in software, imposing an extra processing load on the CPU.

4   Applying Hardware Architecture Design Patterns for Improving the GJ Accelerator in HLS

In order to improve the previous GJU, two specific modifications were first carried out: increasing the GJU input bus-width from 32 to 64 bit in the initial design, and allocating the dendrite's voltage vector on BRAM while executing the GJ interactions (eliminating the cost of DRAM fetching and packets sorting that was required in the implementation reported in [1]). But, most importantly, a structured methodology of design was followed in order to produce the C++ description of the algorithm, such that the HLS would produce the optimal hardware, according to the guidelines for vectorization and pipelining given in [5]. This methodology is general enough to be applied on other instances of high level hardware design, and requires, as an initial step, a block diagram of the intended hardware, that makes explicit the desired data-path procedure.

4.1   Architectural Design and Coding Methodology

As [5] indicates, two different but equivalent C++ portions of code producing the same results, will not necessarily be ported to the same hardware processing structure, let alone the most efficient. The inherent dataflow/parallellism nature of hardware must somehow be made explicit to the HLS, which means that a detailed block diagram of the intended architecture must be constructed in order to facilitate the best resulting code in terms of the final generated hardware. This is a mandatory practice in Register Transfer Level hardware design, which requires at least high level architectural knowledge on behalf of the designer. Even though modern HLS tools ease the translation between the description of functional data processing algorithms and their hardware implementation, the timed, concurrent nature of hardware is still difficult to circumscribe using general programming constructs, which means that synthesis tools are still not capable of generating optimal solutions without guidance.

Therefore, an iterative study of the required GJU operations was first carried out, in order to discover all data dependencies and thus create an efficient datapath. The final block design, shown in Fig. 3, is the result of such iterative process. It is composed of five software-programmable and independent modules. Each module shares configurable parameters which allow for partial or full execution of the GJ interactions, given a maximum defined number of rows in the conductance matrix and a maximum fixed cell population (which in this case was limited to 10000 cells in an all-to-all connection, due to system requirements constraint at this value, nonetheless on the board could fit more cells). Each module is synchronized by FIFO interfaces. The `blockControl` module receives the data from the AXI-DMA stream. Meanwhile, data is packaged in 128-bit words and written through the `V_read` and `acc` FIFO interfaces. The `V_read` module manages the storage of the updated dendrite's voltages in the local BRAM and fetches the voltages according to the access pattern required (based on the conductance matrix row-column indexes). The `calc` module computes the values of v and f (the same name variables as those from Listing 1.1)

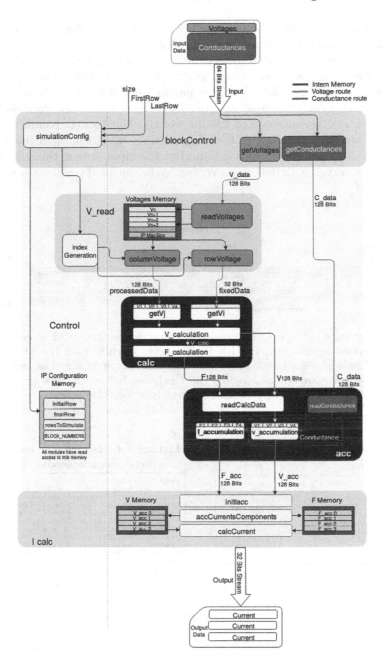

Fig. 3. Overall system architecture. The GJU-IP is managed by one thread of the ARM A9, via AXI4, while the other thread resolves software calculations and I/O outside of the ZedBoard.

in data words of four V_j; therefore, the `acc` module accumulates each word and sends each block component to `I_calc` module.

The data parsing model is shown in Fig. 4; here, the conductance matrix is swept row-wise, each row being divided into sub-matrices (this particular matrix accommodation allows for later partitioning of the network among several boards). Pipelining is used in order to traverse local rows from each sub-matrix (each row is composed of 128-bit words). The `I_calc` module writes to the output-stream in a burst of four I_{out} vectors, when the main row is completed. The design's performance is bound by the input-stream throughput (the time it takes to read each dendrite's voltage and associated conductances matrix from DRAM).

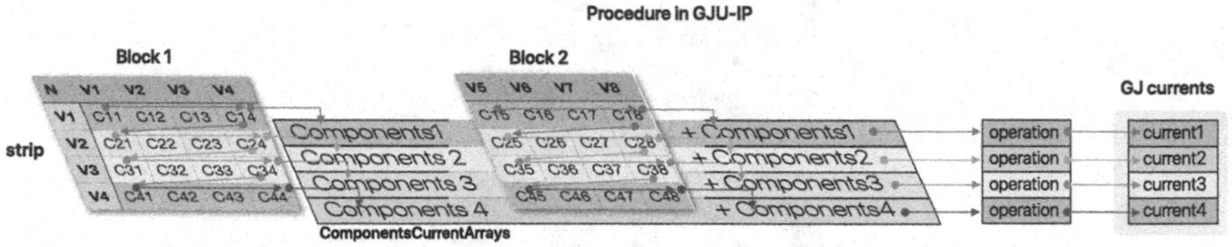

Fig. 4. Representation of the execution procedure in the GJU-IP. The conductance matrix is divided in sub-matrices with 16 conductances each. Each row in the blocks is traversed in a pipelined fashion by the `calc` and `acc` modules. The results after processing each row are accumulated by the `I_calc` module which, after processing all data blocks in the sub-matrix, produces the results of four GJ currents.

Listing 1.3. Gap-junction unit wrapper pseudocode

```
void GapJunctionIP(
in64Bits &input, Stream &output,
int size, int FirstRow, int LastRow){
#pragma HLS INTERFACE axis port=input
#pragma HLS INTERFACE axis port=output
  Config simConfig;
  simulationConfig<Config>
    (simConfig, FirstRow, LastRow, size);
  execute(input, output, simConfig, size);
}
```

Listing 1.4. Gap-junction unit execution processes pseudocode

```
void execute(
in64Bits &input, Stream &output,
Config &simConfig, int size){
static 128bitStream Vdata("Vdata");
static 128bitStream Cdata("Cdata");
static 128bitStream pData("pData");
static Stream fData("fData");
static 128bitStream F("F");
static 128bitStream V("V");
static 128bitStream Facc("Facc");
static 128bitStream Vacc("Vacc");
#pragma HLS DATAFLOW
  blockControl(
    input, Vdata, Cdata, simConfig, size);
  V_read(
    Vdata, pData, fData, simConfig, size);
  calc(
    pData, fData, F, V, simConfig);
  acc(
    F, V, Cdata, Facc, Vacc, simConfig);
  I_calc(
    output, Facc, Vacc, simConfig, size);
}
```

In order to translate into hardware the design in Fig. 3, the C++ code must be now be written using the guidelines given in [5], by identification the appropriate constructs that would described the intended hardware structure. The architecture is functionally translated by dividing each module as a task in which each communicator matches to a FIFO interface during the synthesis process.

Dividing the project in multiple independent modules allows for individual module optimization tuning and testing, and makes therefore for a more maintainable base code. Later performance inspection provides important feedback in order to balance the each module's optimization tweaking, such that there is no module faster in latency than the others (which could complicate general synchronization). A wrapper function is used to contain each modules: code Listings 1.3 and 1.4 show the integration of each module in order to form the GJU-IP main interfaces. Note that the specific **DATAFLOW** directive in Listing 1.4 indicates to the HLS that processes are expected to execute concurrently.

5 Final Results

Xilinx Vivado HLS is used for the implementation on a Zynq XZ7020 of the synthesized design. The GJU-IP, with all the required AXI4 interfaces runs at 120 MHz on the FPGA. The complete system performance is measured at this clock speed. The resources utilization is given in Table 2 an a comparison in Table 3, between the authors' previous work [1] and the current's. Note that the current design needs about 41% less arithmetic primitives (multiply and accumulate units, DSPs in Xilinx lingo) and 43% less look-up tables (LUTs). Nonetheless, due the temporal storage of the dendritic voltages and the FIFO interfaces among the modules, about 14% more programmable LUTRAM and 600% more BRAM are needed. This is not so serious, any way, as total LUTRAM required is under 5% and BRAM at 30% of the XZ7020-1 resources count for each. Table 4 shows a comparison between the effective utilization of the FPGA resources required to solve SPFP operations for same ION model (although not the same connectivity scheme). The current work exhibits better FLOPS throughput per DSPs and LUTs.

Table 2. FPGA resource utilization summary based on the ZedBoard development platform. Note that room is still available if one were to fit another instance of the GJU-IP in order to parallelize simulations further, taking advantage of the four 64-bit AXI4-HP Bus channels available in the XZ7020-1.

Resources	This work	XZ7020-1	Total (%)
LUT	15 266	53 200	28.70
LUTRAM	846	17 400	4.86
FF	21 616	106 400	20.32
BRAM	42	140	30.00
DSP	91	220	41.36

The board software stack is built on a embedded Linux OS (more details at [1]). An open-source memory map driver manages memory coherency between the software applications and the hardware in charge of the DMA transfers. The

Table 3. Comparison between prior authors' work [1] and this one, in terms of FPGA resources utilization for the GJU. The use of LUTRAM and BRAM primitives increase because of the local storage of the dendritic voltages for the GJ execution. Still, major savings are noticeable.

Resources	Prior work	This work	Diff. (%)
LUT	26 877	15 266	↓43.20
LUTRAM	739	846	↑14.48
FF	27 468	21 616	↓21.30
BRAM	6	42	↑600.00
DSP	156	91	↓41.67

Table 4. Utilization of FPGA resources and performance capacity of SPFP operations executed on the FPGA fabric, compared against a all-to-all ION network [18] implementation, and a 8-way connectivity reported in [22]. The t_{step} column represent the execution time during one simulation step and the SimC column means the total of neuron population simulated. This work displays a more efficient performance density (ratio of FLOPS and FPGA resources) for the given DSPs and LUTs units.

Source	FPGA	f_{clk}	DSP	LUT	SimC	t_{step} (ms)	MFP opts	MFLOPS	MFLOPS/ DSP	MFLOPS/ LUT	FLOPS/ (DSP $\cdot f_{clk}$)
This work	Zynq-7000	120 MHz	91	15k	1056	4.8	13.38	2788	30.64	0.183	0.2532
					1188	6.03	16.94	2809	30.86	0.184	0.2551
Smaragdos [18]	Virtex7	100 MHz	1600	251k	1056	1.1	14.29	12990	8.119	0.052	0.0812
Zjajo [22]	Virtex7	100 MHz	1008	190k	1188	0.05	1.135	22690	22.51	0.012	0.2251

execution of the eHH model is distributed on the ARM's two threads. One thread executes the soma and axon compartmental models, while the second manages the GJU-IP in order to carry out the dendrite compartment computations.

A comparison of performance against the authors' previous work and a baseline model performance extrapolated from results from [18] is shown in Fig. 5a (logarithmic scale on both axes). Average resolution time for a computational step is improved here 4× against results in [1] for ION cell populations of 1000 cells and more, while reaching to 10× and more for ION cell populations under 1000 cells (in an all-to-all connection scheme). The system is now only an order of magnitude slower that the results given by [18] for a 100 cells ION simulation, on a much bigger FPGA. The simulation timing step, nonetheless, is still an order of magnitude over the required 50 μs for converging to real brain timing. For reference, a comparison of a simulation output is shown in Fig. 5b. Note here how the error extracted from this simulation case is bounded at 0.00001 for the worst case. The time required to generate three seconds of brain activity in this implementation takes about 9 min (PS@666 MHz, PL@120 MHz), while a multi-threaded PC implementation completes in 2:40 min (i7-7820HQ@3.9 GHz). That's only a third of the speed for a much slower, cheaper alternative, both in cost and in power needs, the latter implied in the total power consumption reported by Vivado for this design: two Watts, against the 45 W reported for a i7-7820HQ@3.9 GHz at full resources utilization (as reported in [10]).

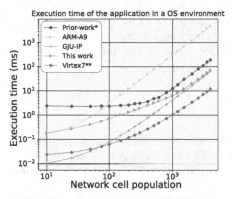

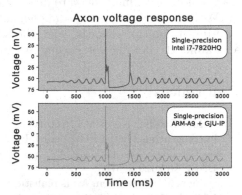

(a) Performance comparison between the implementations of the eHH model for different populations sizes. The GJU-IP curve points out the execution time latency of only the FPGA.

(b) Single neuron time response comparison against C++ golden reference software model for a 1000 ION eHH network, connected all-to-all.

Fig. 5. Results from evaluating the ION eHH model, with the GJU-IP running on a ZedBoard's Zynq XZ7020-1. The soma, axon and dendrite compartments are executed on the Zynq PS, under Linux. The PL runs at a 120 MHz clock frequency. Average computation performance is given in sub-figure 5a for a single step. Sub-figure 5b shows that error ϵ is under 0.00001.

6   Conclusions

This paper has reported the application of a hardware-oriented methodology based on HLS dataflow transformations, in order to improve FPGA-based HLS designs both in time performance and resources saved. As a study case, results on the acceleration of the simulation of a biologically accurate neural network on a heterogeneous SoC-FPGA platform have been presented. The final design consumes fewer resources and runs 10 to 4 times faster than a previous implementation of the same algorithm on the same board: a ION eHH based model. The IP generated for the dendritic gap junction model runs as a hardware accelerator in parallel with the model's implementation on the XZ7020-1 SoC cores, reaching processing speeds only 66% slower than those of an 8 core, Intel based, 64-bit processor at 3.9 GHz processor, and consuming an order of magnitude less power than the latter. For smaller cell populations (<1000), a faster CPU would improve the execution time (for instance using a Ultra96 FPGA board with a 4 core ARM-A53@1 GHz), whereas, for larger cases (>1000), a replication of instances of the GJU-IP would take advantage of the AXI-HP 64-bit channels bandwidth, not used at full capacity in this work. One thing to keep in mind here is that, being this a C++ based design, it is readily portable to faster FPGAs, and may be re-configured to more restrictive FPGAs as well. Additionally, the GJU-IP may be easily reused in other neural models different to the eHH without requiring a re-synthesis of the IP. This because the GJU-IP communicates via an standard Linux software driver to the main model algorithm.

Work in progress seeks to implementing multiple instances of the GJU-IPs running in multiple boards, with the software parts of the model parallelized also along the boards' cores using an openMPI API.

References

1. Alfaro-Badilla, K., et al.: Prototyping a biologically plausible neuron model on a heterogeneous CPU-FPGA board. In: 2019 IEEE 10th Latin American Symposium on Circuits Systems (LASCAS), pp. 5–8, February 2019. https://doi.org/10.1109/LASCAS.2019.8667538
2. Almog, M., Korngreen, A.: Is realistic neuronal modeling realistic? J. Neurophysiol. **116**(5), 2180–2209 (2016). https://doi.org/10.1152/jn.00360.2016
3. Boutros, A., Yazdanshenas, S., Betz, V.: You cannot improve what you do not measure: FPGA vs. ASIC efficiency gaps for convolutional neural network inference. ACM Trans. Reconfigurable Technol. Syst. **11**(3), 20:1–20:23 (2018). https://doi.org/10.1145/3242898, http://ezproxy.itcr.ac.cr:2674/10.1145/3242898
4. Farisco, M., Kotaleski, J.H., Evers, K.: Large-scale brain simulation and disorders of consciousness. Mapping technical and conceptual issues. Front. Psychol. (2018). https://doi.org/10.3389/fpsyg.2018.00585
5. de Fine Licht, J., Meierhans, S., Hoefler, T.: Transformations of high-level synthesis codes for high-performance computing. CoRR abs/1805.08288 (2018). http://arxiv.org/abs/1805.08288
6. de Gruijl, J.R., Bazzigaluppi, P., de Jeu, M.T., de Zeeuw, C.I.: Climbing fiber burst size and olivary sub-threshold oscillations in a network setting. PLoS Comput. Biol. **8**(12) (2012). https://doi.org/10.1371/journal.pcbi.1002814
7. Hennig, M.: Modelling Synaptic Transmission. Modelling Synaptic Transmission, pp. 1–18 (2005). https://doi.org/10.1088/1478-3975/4/1/001, http://homepages.inf.ed.ac.uk/mhennig/synaptic_transmission.pdf
8. Hodgkin, A.L., Huxley, A.F.: A quantitative description of membrane current and its application to conduction and excitation in nerve. J. Physiol. **1**(117), 500–544 (1952). https://doi.org/10.1080/00062278.1939.10600645
9. Humphries, M.D., Obeso, J.A., Dreyer, J.K.: Insights into Parkinson's disease from computational models of the basal ganglia. J. Neurol. Neurosurg. Psychiatry 1181–1188 (2018). https://doi.org/10.1136/jnnp-2017-315922
10. Intel: Intel® Core™ i7-7820HQ Processor (2019). https://ark.intel.com/content/www/us/en/ark/products/97496/intel-core-i7-7820hq-processor-8m-cache-up-to-3-90-ghz.html. Accessed 24 May 2019
11. Izhikevich, E.: Dynamical Systems in Neuroscience, p. 111. MIT Press, Cambridge (2007)
12. Kuon, I., Rose, J.: Measuring the gap between FPGAs and ASICs. In: Proceedings of the 2006 ACM/SIGDA 14th International Symposium on Field Programmable Gate Arrays, FPGA 2006, pp. 21–30. ACM, New York (2006). https://doi.org/10.1145/1117201.1117205, http://ezproxy.itcr.ac.cr:2674/10.1145/1117201.1117205

13. Moore, S.W., Fox, P.J., Marsh, S.J., Markettos, A.T., Mujumdar, A.: Bluehive - a field-programable custom computing machine for extreme-scale real-time neural network simulation. In: Proceedings of the 2012 IEEE 20th International Symposium on Field-Programmable Custom Computing Machines, FCCM 2012, pp. 133–140 (2012). https://doi.org/10.1109/FCCM.2012.32

14. Moorthy, P., Kapre, N.: Zedwulf: power-performance tradeoffs of a 32-node Zynq SoC cluster. In: 2015 IEEE 23rd Annual International Symposium on Field-Programmable Custom Computing Machines, pp. 68–75, May 2015. https://doi.org/10.1109/FCCM.2015.37

15. Smaragdos, G., et al.: Performance analysis of accelerated biophysically-meaningful neuron simulations. In: 2016 IEEE International Symposium on Performance Analysis of Systems and Software (ISPASS), pp. 1–11, April 2016. https://doi.org/10.1109/ISPASS.2016.7482069

16. Smaragdos, G., et al.: Brainframe: a node-level heterogeneous accelerator platform for neuron simulations. IOP abs/1612.01501 (2016)

17. Smaragdos, G., et al.: Performance analysis of accelerated biophysically-meaningful neuron simulations. In: International Symposium on Performance Analysis of Systems and Software, ISPASS 2016, pp. 1–11 (2016). https://doi.org/10.1109/ISPASS.2016.7482069

18. Smaragdos, G., Isaza, S., van Eijk, M.F., Sourdis, I., Strydis, C.: FPGA-based biophysically-meaningful modeling of olivocerebellar neurons. In: FPGA, pp. 89–98 (2014). https://doi.org/10.1145/2554688.2554790

19. Soudris, D., et al.: BrainFrame: a node-level heterogeneous accelerator platform for neuron simulations. J. Neural Eng. 14(6), 066008 (2017). https://doi.org/10.1088/1741-2552/aa7fc5

20. Sprekeler, H., Deco, G., Gerstner, W.: Theory and simulation in neuroscience. Science 338(6103), 60–65 (2012). https://doi.org/10.1126/science.1227356, http://www.ncbi.nlm.nih.gov/pubmed/23042882

21. Sripad, A., et al.: SNAVA-A real-time multi-FPGA multi-model spiking neural network simulation architecture. Neural Netw. 97, 28–45 (2018). https://doi.org/10.1016/j.neunet.2017.09.011

22. Zjajo, A., et al.: A real-time reconfigurable multichip architecture for large-scale biophysically accurate neuron simulation. IEEE Trans. Biomed. Circ. Syst. 12(2), 326–337 (2018). https://doi.org/10.1109/TBCAS.2017.2780287

Delivering Scalable Deep Learning to Research with Bridges-AI

Paola A. Buitrago[1]($\boxtimes$), Nicholas A. Nystrom[1], Rajarsi Gupta[2],
and Joel Saltz[2]

[1] Pittsburgh Supercomputing Center, Carnegie Mellon University,
Pittsburgh, PA 15213, USA
paola@psc.edu
[2] Stony Brook University, Stony Brook, NY 11794, USA

Abstract. Artificial intelligence (AI), particularly deep learning, is enabling tremendous advances and is itself of great research interest. To address these research requirements, the Pittsburgh Supercomputing Center (PSC) expanded its Bridges supercomputer with Bridges-AI, providing the world's most powerful AI servers to the U.S. national research community and their international collaborators. We describe the motivation and architecture of Bridges-AI and its integration with Bridges, which adds to Bridges' capabilities for scalable, converged high-performance computing (HPC), AI, and Big Data. We then describe the software environment of Bridges-AI, particularly the introduction of containers for deep learning frameworks, machine learning, and graph analytics, and PSC's approach to container deployment. We close with a discussion of the range of research challenges that Bridges-AI is enabling breakthroughs, highlighting development of AI-driven methods to identify immune responses with automated tumor detection in breast cancer.

Keywords: Artificial intelligence · Deep learning · Machine learning · GPU · Containers · Singularity · Digital pathology · Cancer

1 Introduction

Artificial intelligence (AI), particularly deep learning, has emerged as a powerful tool for extracting insight from large-scale scientific and societal data, augmenting scientists' abilities and improving the results of simulation and modeling. While AI's progress has been rapid and impressive, it is still in its infancy. Research on AI algorithms and applications is vigorous and increasing with each year [1, 2]. Deep learning is enabling advances such as helping radiologists improve the accuracy of diagnoses, driving the discovery of new materials to produce energy more efficiently, analyzing pedestrian and vehicular traffic patterns to improve urban spaces, and selecting optimal crops to boost agricultural production. Intense interest in AI spurred development of specialized computer processors, initially through incremental advances in graphics processing units (GPUs) and, more recently, through functional units designed specifically to accelerate the tensor operations that are central to deep learning. The new functional units are more than an order of magnitude more powerful, and they are

© Springer Nature Switzerland AG 2020
J. L. Crespo-Mariño and E. Meneses-Rojas (Eds.): CARLA 2019, CCIS 1087, pp. 200–214, 2020.
https://doi.org/10.1007/978-3-030-41005-6_14

pivotal to vital breakthroughs in AI and AI-driven applications. These factors create an urgent need for state-of-the-art cyberinfrastructure to support fundamental AI research, AI applications, and AI-enabled simulation.

Since January 2016, the Pittsburgh Supercomputing Center (PSC) has operated Bridges [3–5], a national supercomputing resource that pioneered the convergence of high-performance computing (HPC), AI, and Big Data. Supported by the National Science Foundation (NSF), Bridges is allocated at no charge for open research and education through the XSEDE (Extreme Science and Engineering Discovery Environment) program. Bridges was designed to bring HPC to communities and applications that traditionally had not made use of HPC. One such community was computer science, and the AI community was, and is, very active on Bridges because of the GPUs (NVIDIA Tesla K80 and P100) that Bridges provides. However, requests for GPU resources on Bridges consistently and greatly exceeded available capacity. Also, emergence of new functional units to accelerate deep learning provided opportunity to introduce to the research community extremely powerful new GPU resources that would accelerate AI research and applications and free the existing GPUs in Bridges for simulation applications, including AI-enabled simulation.

To address the need for new AI technology, in October 2018 PSC introduced Bridges-AI, an expansion of Bridges that supports the most complex deep-learning models with the highest accuracy and incorporating the largest data sets. Bridges-AI balances maximum capability and capacity and is fully integrated with Bridges. PSC conducted an Early User Program in November and December 2018, after which Bridges-AI entered production operation on January 1, 2019.

The remainder of this paper is organized as follows. Section 2 describes the architecture of Bridges-AI. Section 3 addresses the software environment for Bridges-AI including the introduction of containerized frameworks to improve the software environment for users and simplify system administration. Section 4 presents results of some well-known benchmarks to illustrate performance. Section 5 surveys research being done on Bridges-AI, addressing both the Early User Period and current production operations. We conclude with a summary and ideas for next steps.

2 Bridges-AI Architecture

The goal of Bridges-AI is to provide to the research community a resource for scalable AI that integrates with complementary research involving big data and HPC to transform research. Maximum performance, reliability, and reproducibility are essential. Therefore, Bridges-AI targets scaling to large numbers of datacenter class GPUs.

Bridges-AI consists of two kinds of two kinds of nodes: an NVIDIA DGX-2 enterprise AI research system ("AI-V16"), and nine Hewlett Packard Enterprise (HPE) Apollo Gen10 servers ("AI-V32").

The NVIDIA DGX-2 enterprise AI research system provides maximum scalability with 16 NVIDIA Tesla V100 (Volta architecture) GPUs interconnected by the NVSwitch. The DGX-2 serves the applications that need the highest possible number of GPUs, the largest possible aggregate GPU memory, the maximum bisection bandwidth between GPUs, and the highest bandwidth to training data. It also serves large-scale graph analytics requiring large memory and maximum bisection bandwidth.

Nine Hewlett Packard Enterprise (HPE) Apollo 6500 Gen10 servers, each with eight V100 GPUs fully interconnected by NVLink 2, balance great AI capability and capacity. The Apollo 6500 servers are an invaluable complement to the DGX-2, addressing the many AI and ML applications that need performance much greater than that found in campus resource but not at the extreme scale addressed by the DGX-2.

2.1   Bridges: An Architecture and an Ecosystem

AI nodes (servers) alone are not sufficient. An AI platform for research needs an *ecosystem*, consisting also of general-purpose nodes for data preparation, traditional machine learning, and simulation, and a large-capacity, high-performance filesystem. Beyond hardware, the ecosystem must support *collaboration*, including access by researchers across the United States and their collaborators worldwide, community datasets, data sharing with (where necessary) provisions for data use agreements, and interoperation with other computing infrastructure, scientific instruments, and clouds.

Bridges provides the ecosystem into which Bridges-AI is integrated. Bridges was designed to be extensible, and new data infrastructure for the Brain Image Library [6], the Human BioMolecular Atlas Program [7], and other projects has already been integrated. With each addition, the whole become again greater than the sum of its parts.

Figure 1 illustrates Bridges-AI integrated into Bridges. As described in [4], Bridges implements a custom topology designed by PSC for its Omni-Path interconnect, designed to optimally serve moderate-scale HPC, high performance data analytics, and data-intensive workflows and to provide multiple, resilient paths to persistent data. An important characteristic of that configuration is that not all ports of the radix-48 Omni-Path edge switches in the 6-member "core" subnetwork are used, allowing for expansion. Bridges includes the following types of processing nodes: 752 nodes with 2 CPUs with 128 GB of RAM (red cubes); 42 nodes with 4 CPUs (64–80 cores) and 3 TB (purple cubes); 4 nodes with 16 CPUs (288–352 cores) and 12 TB (orange); 32 nodes with 2 CPUs (28 cores), 128 GB, and 2 K80 GPU cards (4 GPUs) (green, third row from front right); and 16 nodes with 2 CPUs (32 cores), 128 GB, and 2 P100 GPUs (green, second row from front right). Bridges-AI (green, front right) adds an NVIDIA DGX-2 containing 16 V100 GPUs, 512 GB of HBM2 memory, 2 CPUs, and 1.5 TB of CPU RAM; and 9 HPE Apollo 6500 GPU servers, each containing 8 V100 GPUs, 128 GB of HBM2 memory, 2 CPUs, and 384 GB of CPU RAM. A custom deployment of the Intel Omni-Path Architecture interconnect (core switches: orange spheres; leaf switches: yellow spheres; links: orange, green, and blue lines, of different colors solely for clarity in the figure) provides high-performance communications between *Bridges'* compute nodes and shared parallel filesystem (gray). An additional leaf switch connects *Bridges-AI* nodes at full bandwidth (12.5 GB/s/direction).

Sections 2.2, 2.3 and 2.4 describe the Volta GPU, DGX-2, and HPE Apollo servers that comprise Bridges-AI. Table 1 details the hardware configuration of Bridges and Bridges-AI.

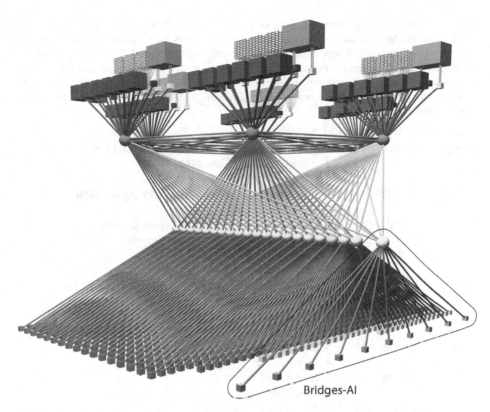

Fig. 1. The Pittsburgh Supercomputing Center's *Bridges* supercomputer couples different types of processor nodes, each optimized for different tasks, using a unique interconnect topology. Its architecture is designed to support the confluence of HPC, AI, and Big Data, including high performance data analytics and data-intensive workflows. Section 2.1 summarizes the full system. *Bridges-AI* (green, front right) adds an NVIDIA DGX-2 and 9 HPE Apollo 6500 GPU servers, totaling 88 NVIDIA Tesla V100 GPUs, fully integrated into Bridges. (Color figure online)

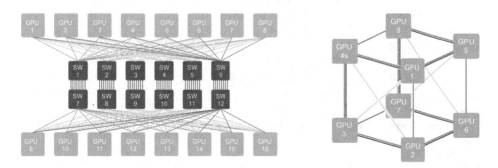

Fig. 2. Internal topology of Bridges-AI NVIDIA DGX-2 (left) and HPE Apollo 6500 (right) nodes. Each is fully connected by NVLink 2.0, with the DGX-2 using 12 NVSwitch chips to realize bisection bandwidth of 2.4 TB/s.

Table 1. Detailed configuration of Bridges compute nodes. New nodes (AI-V32, AI-V16) introduce in Bridges-AI are highlighted in bold. Node types ESM, LSM, and RSM denote Extreme shared Memory, Large Shared Memory, and Regular Shared Memory, respectively. RAM refers to CPU memory. For each CPU type, core counts and base and maximum turbo frequencies are given in parentheses. Bridges also includes a 10 PB (usable) parallel filesystem, served by the 20 Storage nodes below, and 7.3 PB of node-local storage distributed across compute nodes.

Node type	RAM	#	CPU/GPU/SSD	Server type
AI-V32	**1.5 TB^d**	**1**	**16 × NVIDIA V100 32 GB SXM2 + 2 × Intel Xeon Platinum 8168 + 8 × 3.84 TB NVMe SSDs**	**NVIDIA DGX-2**
AI-V16	**192 GB^d**	**9**	**2 × Intel Xeon Gold 6148 + 4 × 2 TB NVMe SSDs**	**HPE Apollo 6500**
ESM	12 TB^b	2	16 × Intel Xeon E7-8880 v3 (18c, 2.3/3.1 GHz)	HPE Integrity Superdome X
	12 TB^c	2	16 × Intel Xeon E7-8880 v4 (22c, 2.2/3.3 GHz)	
LSM	3 TB^b	8	4 × Intel Xeon E7-8860 v3 (16c, 2.2/3.2 GHz)	HPE ProLiant DL580
	3 TB^c	34	4 × Intel Xeon E7-8870 v4 (20c, 2.1/3.0 GHz)	
RSM	128 GB^b	752	2 × Intel Xeon E5-2695 v3 (14c, 2.3/3.3 GHz)	HPE Apollo 2000
RSM-GPU	128 GB^b	16	2 × Intel Xeon E5-2695 v3 + 2 × NVIDIA Tesla K80	
	128 GB^c	32	2 × Intel Xeon E5-2683 v4 (16c, 2.1/3.0 GHz) + 2 × NVIDIA Tesla P100	
DB-s	128 GB^b	6	2 × Intel Xeon E5-2695 v3 + SSD	HPE ProLiant DL360
DB-h	128 GB^b	6	2 × Intel Xeon E5-2695 v3 + HDD	HPE ProLiant DL380
Web	128 GB^b	6	2 × Intel Xeon E5-2695 v3	HPE ProLiant DL360
Other^a	128 GB^b	16	2 × Intel Xeon E5-2695 v3	HPE ProLiant DL360, DL380
Gateway	64 GB^b	4	2 × Intel Xeon E5-2683 v3 (14c, 2.0/3.0 GHz)	HPE ProLiant DL380
	64 GB^c	4	2 × Intel Xeon E5-2683 v3	
	96 GB^d	2	2 × Intel Xeon	
Storage	128 GB^b	5	2 × Intel Xeon E5-2680 v3 (12c, 2.5/3.3 GHz)	Supermicro X10DRi
	256 GB^c	15	2 × Intel Xeon E5-2680 v4 (14c, 2.4/3.3 GHz)	
Total	*286.5 TB*	*920*		

a Other nodes consist of front end (2), management/log (8), boot (4), and metadata server (4).
b DDR4-2133
c DDR4-2400
d DDR4-2666

2.2 Volta: A GPU for Deep Learning

Bridges-AI nodes are accelerated by NVIDIA Tesla V100 GPUs, which introduce NVIDIA's Volta architecture. Volta delivers powerful new capabilities focused on deep learning training, plus improvements across all aspects of performance. The following new features of V100 GPUs accelerate Bridges-AI:

1. A new *Streaming Multiprocessor (SM)* architecture introduces Tensor Cores, independent thread scheduling, combined L1 data cache and shared memory unit, and 50% higher energy efficiency over the previous architecture.
2. *Tensor Cores* accelerate deep learning training and inference, providing up to 12 × and 6 × higher peak flops, respectively, over the P100 GPUs previously available in XSEDE-allocated resources.
3. The *NVLink 2.0* interconnect between GPUs increases link speed to 25 GB/s per direction, delivering 300 GB/s total bandwidth over six links per V100. This is nearly a two-fold increase over Pascal (the previous-generation), which had aggregate bandwidth of 160 GB/s over four NVLink 1.0 links, and it is a 19× improvement over the PCIe 3.0 ×16 interface of the P100 GPUs currently available in XSEDE.
4. *Larger, faster HBM2 memory* doubles maximum GPU memory capacity to 32 GB, enabling larger models, and increases bandwidth to 900 GB/s (from 732 GB/s on Pascal). In addition to the increase in theoretical memory bandwidth, Jia et al. report that ratio of actual to theoretical memory bandwidth is also improved, from 69.6% in GP100 to 83.3% in GV100 [8].
5. Other improvements in Volta include a Multi-Process Service (MPS), enhanced Unified Memory and Address Translation Services, Maximum Performance and Maximum Efficiency Modes, Cooperative Groups and new Cooperative Launch APIs, and Volta-optimized software (see Sect. 3).

2.3 NVIDIA DGX-2

The NVIDIA DGX-2 enterprise AI research system tightly integrates 16 NVIDIA Tesla V100 SXM2 (i.e., NVLink 2.0-connected) GPUs, totaling 81,920 CUDA cores and 10,240 tensor cores, to provide 2 petaflop/s (Pf/s) of mixed-precision tensor performance, 251 teraflop/s (Tf/s) 32-bit performance, and 125 Tf/s 64-bit performance. Each of the DGX-2's 16 Volta GPUs has 32 GB of HBM2 GPU memory, aggregate 512 GB with 14.4 TB/s aggregate memory bandwidth. This is the maximum number of GPUs and GPU memory that currently can be tightly coupled, thereby providing excellent support for large models. The node is supported by two Intel Xeon Platinum 8168 CPUs ("Skylake" microarchitecture, with 24 cores, 2.7 GHz and 3.7 GHz base and boost frequency, 33 MB L3 cache, and 3 UPI links) and 1.5 TB of DDR4-2666 RAM. Twelve NVSwitch chips (described below), each with 900 GB/s aggregate bandwidth, are configured to provide 2.4 TB/s bisection bandwidth. Two 960 GB NVM Express (NVMe) SSDs host the Ubuntu Linux operating system, and eight 3.84 TB (aggregate ∼30 TB) NVMe SSDs provide on-node, high-performance working storage for user data. Eight Mellanox ConnectX adapters support both EDR InfiniBand and 100 Gb/s Ethernet connectivity. Together, the innovations in Bridges-AI's DGX-2 create high system balance and enable models $8\times$ larger and peak performance $20\times$ greater than the 4-way, 16 GB P100 resources previously available through XSEDE.

NVSwitch

The NVSwitch [9] is an 18×18-port, fully connected crossbar. Internally to the DGX-2, 12 NVSwitch chips connect the 16 Volta GPUs with 2.4 TB/s aggregate bandwidth (Fig. 2, left). NVSwitch bandwidth is 25 GB/s/direction per port, 50 GB/s per port bidirectional, totaling 900 GB/s aggregate switch bandwidth. Data integrity is ensured is ensured by link-level cyclical redundancy coding (CRC) checks to detect errors and retry when necessary. Data paths, routing, and state structures are protected with error-correcting codes (ECC). Final hop-address fidelity checks, buffer overflow, and buffer underflow checks are also supported. Data security is supported by indexing and control of routing tables by the NVIDIA fabric manager, which limits applications' access to specific ranges.

2.4   HPE Apollo 6500 Servers

The Hewlett Packard Enterprise (HPE) Apollo 6500 Gen10 servers each integrate eight NVIDIA Tesla V100 SXM2 GPUs to accelerate deep learning (and potentially HPC) workloads. In Bridges-AI, these serve challenging and routine AI applications not needing the leadership-class scalability of the DGX-2, thereby addressing the full spectrum of users' requirements.

Each Apollo 6500 Gen10 server also includes two Intel Skylake Gold 6148 CPUs ("Skylake" microarchitecture, 20 cores, 2.4 GHz and 3.7 GHz base and boost frequency, 27.5 MB L3 cache, and 3 UPI links), 192 GB DDR4-2666 memory, four 2 TB NVMe SSDs, and one 100 Gb/s Intel Omni-Path host channel adapter (HCA).

The eight Volta GPUs and two Xeon CPUs are connected in a hybrid cube-mesh topology (Fig. 2, right), using NVLink 2.0 between the GPUs and PCIe3 to the CPUs, optimized for high performance on deep learning and AI applications.

3   Software Environment

Bridges-AI both supports end-user application of deep learning frameworks and algorithm development that requires access to full-featured software stacks.

Bridges runs the CentOS operating system, currently CentOS 7.4. This is maintained for the AI-V16 nodes. The DGX-2 (AI-V32 node), however, initially supported only Ubuntu, which is also the version of Linux for which various deep learning frameworks are distributed. We retained Ubuntu for the DGX-2 and adapted other aspects of the Bridges user environment to work with Ubuntu, thereby maintaining reasonable consistency across all Bridges and Bridges-AI compute nodes.

Bridges supports an extremely flexible user environment, allowing interoperation of HPC, Spark, Hadoop, and single-node (even single-core) applications and letting users transparently scale Python, Jupyter, R, MATLAB, and Java applications by up to three orders of magnitude by using large memory or advanced GPU resources. Web browser-based access to Jupyter notebooks, R, and MATLAB is provided through an Open

OnDemand interface. Bridges-AI, like Bridges, supports Anaconda as an effective way of managing package installation and the complex dependencies that are typical of today's deep learning frameworks.

Bridges-AI and Bridges also support the *module* utility [10, 11] through which users can selectively load (and unload) specific versions of software such as compilers, libraries, and applications, even including different versions of Anaconda. For example, "module load anaconda3" loads the default version of Anaconda for Python 3 (currently Anaconda 5.2.0, for Python 3.7) into the user environment, and "module load Anaconda2/5.1.0" loads Anaconda 5.1.0 for Python 2.7. Bridges currently supports 545 modules, many of which also apply to Bridges-AI, so rather than bringing software in a virtual machine as users must do for clouds that offer only Infrastructure-as-a-Service (IaaS), in most cases the software that users need is already pre-installed on Bridges. The *module* utility is highly effective for a large number of scenarios, except for managing complex Python dependencies, for which Anaconda and containers are superior.

3.1 Containers

Packages that have complex dependencies, including dependencies on a particular operating system (typically Ubuntu) require an approach that better supports correctly built, well-optimized software. The need is exacerbated by the very rapid evolution of deep learning frameworks, for which new distributions are sometimes released faster than monthly. Building them is laborious and error-prone, especially on non-Ubuntu hosts. This creates a situation that is frustrating for users, who want current, fully-configured versions (and, occasionally, older versions as well, for compatibility with models they have developed), and excessively time-consuming for system administrators, who do not have time to repeatedly rebuild a large suite of frameworks. Underlying these challenges are the complex dependencies in the software stacks on which deep learning frameworks are built, requiring an intricate combination of versions of Python, Python packages, other libraries, and operating systems.

A productive approach to managing that complexity is to distribute applications and frameworks in *application containers*, which are lightweight virtual environments. Application containers are complete environments, including all necessary dependencies and abstracting operating system functions to support the environments of different operating system variants atop a host operating system. Because containers share the kernel of the host operating system, they incur very little performance overhead, at least for applications that run within a node.

Bridges has supported application containers since 2017. Certain science gateways run in vetted Docker containers, such as a Galaxy portal for bioinformatics. However, securing Docker is typically done by running in a virtual environment and avoiding shared infrastructure such as direct access to large parallel filesystems. Therefore, for Bridges, PSC encourages use Singularity [12] containers, which can be run securely in user space. The *singularity build* utility makes it very easy to convert Docker containers to Singularity images.

With Bridges-AI, PSC began to encourage the use of containerized frameworks provided by NVIDIA in NVIDIA GPU Cloud (NGC). NGC now supports containers for HPC, deep learning, machine learning and graph analytics, inference, visualization, and several domains such as smart cities and medical imaging.

NGC containers are distributed as Docker images. These can easily be pulled and converted to Singularity images. On Bridges, Singularity versions are managed by the *modules* utility. An NGC container is converted to Singularity with the following sequence:

```
% The following are typically placed in the user's shell .rc file:
source /etc/profile.d/modules.sh
module load singularity
export SINGULARITY_DOCKER_USERNAME='$oauthtoken'
export SINGULARITY_DOCKER_PASSWORD=your-key-string
export SINGULARITY_CACHEDIR=$SCRATCH/.singularity

% Then the following pulls the NGC Docker container for the 2019 May
% build of TensorFlow and builds a Singularity image:
singularity build tensorflow-19.05.simg \
                  nvcr.io/nvidia/tensorflow:19.05-py2
```

To maximize convenience for Bridges users, each month PSC staff pull the most commonly-used NGC Docker container images, convert them to Singularity images, and maintain those Singularity images in a local repository on Bridges with tags that parallel those in NGC. The local repo has an added benefit of caching a single copy of each NGC container, rather than having potentially hundreds to thousands of replicas of multi-gigabyte containers residing in individual users' directories.

4 Performance

Baseline benchmarks were run using the NGC TensorFlow 1.10 container (tensorflow:18.10-py3). Synthetic image classification data was used to isolate GPU performance from data bandwidth dependencies, which will be addressed in a subsequent paper. The models run were AlexNet [13], Inception V3 [14], VGG16 [15], ResNet-50 [16], and ResNet-152 [16].

Figure 2 illustrates performance of Bridges-AI nodes relative to the previous-generation P100 GPUs (Pascal architecture). The upper, middle, and lower figures show performance for Bridges-AI-V32, Bridges-AI-V16, and Bridges P100 nodes, respectively. For each model, training rates with 1, 2, 4, 8, and 16 GPUs, as applicable to each node type, are shown from left to right. Results for AlexNet are not shown because their much higher training rates (e.g., 43716 images/second for ResNet-50 on AI-V32) would compress the scale, obscuring the salient performance differences between GPU types. Results for K80 GPUs were not obtained because optimized NGC containers are available only for Pascal and Volta architecture GPUs. Standard deviations are generally low, i.e. 0.1–6.4%, with the exception of VGG16 models run on AI-V16 nodes, for which standard deviations were 8.5–35.9%. (The cause for this is being examined.)

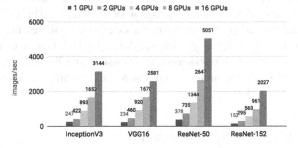

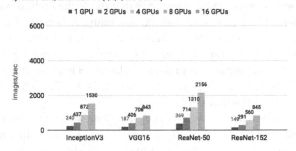

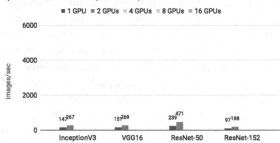

Fig. 3. Performance of Bridges-AI nodes relative to prior Bridges GPU nodes for training InceptionV3, VGG16, ResNet-50, and ResNet-152 using TensorFlow 1.10 for Python 3 (NGC container tensorflow:18.10-py3) and batch size 64 on synthetic data.**Upper:** AI-V32 nodes (NVIDIA DGX-2: 16 V100 SXM2 GPUs, 32 GB HBM2 per GPU).**Middle:** AI-V16 nodes (HPE Apollo 6500: 8 V100 SXM2 GPUs, 16 GB HBM2 per GPU).**Lower:** RSM-GPU nodes (2 P100 GPUs, 16 GB HBM2 each).

Training rates on going from Pascal (P100) to Volta (V100) improve by factors of 1.52–1.69 for Inception V3, ResNet-50, and ResNet-152 for 1 and 2 GPUs. Results for VGG16 are less consistent, showing speedups of 1.24–1.71. The difference between these speedups and the ratios of peak performance can be attributed to a combination of TensorFlow 1.10 not yet optimally using the V100 GPUs' Tensor Cores, data movement exclusive of core tensor operations, and possibly the limited size of the training task imposed by the synthetic image classification benchmark. Additional performance analysis is available in [17].

5 Research Enabled by Bridges-AI

The purpose of Bridges-AI is to enable research. With each new supercomputer, PSC performs an advance evaluation of users' requirements, then follows up with *Early User Programs* prior to production operations to provide the earliest possible access to users and work with them to ensure that the environment is ready for production.

Bridges-AI is now serving 109 production allocations of size ranging from 71 to 58,000 V100-hours and with project-specific storage allocations ranging from 100 GB to 88 TB. Some of those projects also draw on large-scale community data hosted on Bridges, such as The Cancer Genome Atlas, which is 1.2 PB. The 109 projects represent 46 self-reported principal fields of study.

Section 5.1 describes the Early User Program, which served to prepare Bridges-AI for production use, and Sect. 5.2 briefly describes how digital pathology is benefiting from Bridges-AI for analysis of multi-gigapixel whole slide images.

5.1 Bridges-AI Early User Program

The Bridges-AI Early User Program, conducted November through December 2018, provided an opportunity for users to gain experience with Bridges-AI and for PSC to get their feedback on the new resource and its user environment. Groups were provided with new or supplemental XSEDE allocations to streamline their transition to production operation, which began in January 2019. During the Early User Program, usage was not "charged" to users' allocations. ("Charging" is in terms of "service units", which are provided free of cost for open research and education based on peer review of proposals for allocations.) The Principal Investigators (PIs) from each group agreed to provide feedback to PSC by means of a survey following the Early User Program. 59 users from 28 research groups actively participated in the Bridges-AI Early User Program. Of the early users, 20 responded to the survey. Results, on a score of 1 ("poor") to 5 ("excellent") are as follows (Table 2):

The researchers used a wide variety of frameworks including TensorFlow (which was used by most researchers, in addition to other frameworks), PyTorch, Keras, Theano, Kaldi nnet3, and Chainer. Their models were also diverse, including convolutional neural networks (CNNs), three-dimensional CNNs, recurrent neural networks (RNNs), long short-term memories (LSTMs), generative adversarial networks (GANs), and fully-connected networks.

Table 2. Bridges-AI Early User Program survey responses.

Question	Responses	Mean	Std. Dev.
"How would you rate your overall experience with Bridges-AI?"	20	4.50	0.67
"How would you rate the Bridges-AI documentation?"	15	4.40	0.88
"Based on your individual needs, how would you rate the Bridges-AI environment and tools?"	20	4.35	0.65

5.2 AI-Driven Methods to Identify the Immune Response with Automated Tumor Detection in Breast Cancer

Pathology is the central hub of oncology since it informs cancer diagnosis and ultimately therapy decisions, and the precise characterization of tumor tissue is critical for impactful translational cancer science. Tools and methodologies that augment or enable precise characterization of tissue samples for patients with cancer can have a tangible impact in translational cancer research and improve the practice of pathology for precision oncology. The term Pathomics refers to the automated quantification of a image-based phenotypic features from whole-slide images (WSIs) in tissue samples of cancer. We have generated pathomics biomarkers from WSIs in large patient cohorts for discovery studies that include The Cancer Genome Atlas (TCGA), Clinical Proteomic Tumor Analysis Consortium (CPTAC), and cancer surveillance projects such as SEER (Surveillance, Epidemiology, and End-Results).

Quantitative characterization of tumor infiltrating lymphocytes (TILs) to generate spatial maps of different populations of tumor and immune cells is a particularly important and timely problem [18]. These maps provide a snapshot of the interaction between a tumor and the patient's immune system. High densities of TILs correlate with favorable clinical outcomes including longer disease-free survival or improved overall survival in multiple cancer types. The spatial context and the nature of cellular heterogeneity are important in cancer prognosis. TILs are particularly important in predicting response to cancer immune therapics. Since pathology laboratory studies are routinely performed for virtually every cancer patient, it is feasible to obtain large quantities of correlative clinical data to gain an understanding of the significance of TIL maps and their ability to predict patient outcomes and response to cancer treatments.

Figure 3 depicts AI-driven analyses of multi-gigapixel WSIs of breast cancer obtained from the Cancer Genome Atlas (TCGA) collection that is publicly available.

The Saltz group has developed methods capable of (1) resolving TIL infiltrated tissue to a resolution of 50 microns, (2) mapping out the relationship between lymphocytes and tumor cells, (3) identifying and labeling different categories of cells found within a tumor and (4) methods for carrying out high resolution in-stance segmentation of all cells in a tissue specimen. They are working closely with numerous cancer research groups as well as the National Cancer Institute Surveillance, Epidemiology, and End Results Program (SEER; https://seer.cancer.gov/), the International Immuno-Oncology Biomarker Working Group on Breast Cancer (https://www.tilsinbreastcancer.org/),

A. Breast, TCGA-A2-A0D0-01Z, Brisk-Diffuse

B. Breast, TCGA-3C-AALI-01Z, Brisk-Band-like

C. Breast, TCGA-A2-A1G1-01Z, Non-brisk-Multifocal

D. Breast, TCGA-A2-A0YG-01Z, Non-brisk-Focal

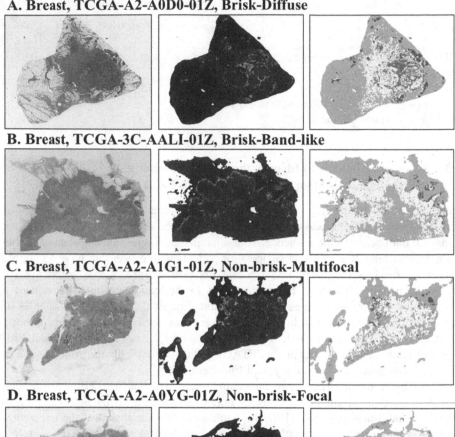

Fig. 4. Rows A-D depict the hematoxylin and eosin (H&E) stained WSIs of tissue sections in the left column, followed by the probability of TILs mapped to the tissue in the middle column, culminating in a combined tumor-TIL map in the right column (tumor detection and probability map by AI-model not shown). (A) depicts an example that is diffusely infiltrated by TILs; (B) shows TILs that are primarily outside and adjacent to the tumor at the invasive leading edge but unable to infiltrate the tumor; (C) shows limited scattered TILs in the tumor; and (D) shows scant TILs in a focal area of the tumor (see [19] for TIL classification scheme).

the NCI Division of Cancer Epidemiology and Genetics (https://dceg.cancer.gov/), and the Food and Drug Administration (Fig. 4).

The work carried out on Bridges-AI has been transformative in allowing the group to develop a new generation of TIL prediction methods. These methods both substantially improve ability to classify TILs for multiple tumor types and also now make it possible to create high resolution characterization of interrelationship between tumor and TIL regions.

6 Conclusions

Bridges-AI introduces transformational new technologies – namely Tensor Cores, NVSwitch, and scalability to 8 and 16 NVIDIA Volta GPUs – to the NSF XSEDE program. Following a successful Early User Program through which advance users helped to ensure a highly usable environment and indicated high satisfaction with the system and its performance, production operations began on schedule in January 2019. An important new element for Bridges-AI is the introduction of containers, specifically a local repository of Singularity images for deep learning frameworks, which has delivered substantial benefit to both users and system administrators. Bridges-AI and Bridges are available at no charge for open research and education to U.S.-based PIs and their (potentially international) collaborators.

Acknowledgments. This work used the Bridges system, which is supported by NSF award number OAC-1445606, at the Pittsburgh Supercomputing Center (PSC). Thanks to PSC's Facilities Technology Group for their contributions to configuring Bridges-AI.

References

1. Shoham, Y., Perrault, R., Brynjolfsson, E., Clark, J.: AI Index 2017 Annual Report. Stanford University (2017)
2. Shoham, Y., et al.: AI Index 2018 Annual Report (2018)
3. Nystrom, N.A., Levine, M.J., Roskies, R.Z., Scott, J.R.: Bridges: a uniquely flexible HPC resource for new communities and data analytics. In: Proceedings of the 2015 XSEDE Conference: Scientific Advancements Enabled by Enhanced Cyberinfrastructure, pp. 1–8. ACM, St. Louis (2015). https://doi.org/10.1145/2792745.2792775
4. Nystrom, N.A., Buitrago, P.A., Blood, P.D.: Bridges: converging HPC, AI, and big data for enabling discovery. In: Vetter, J.S. (ed.) Contemporary High Performance Computing: From Petascale toward Exascale, vol. 3. CRC Press, Boca Raton (2019)
5. Underwood, R.: Building bridges: the system administration tools and techniques used to deploy bridges (2017). https://doi.org/10.1145/3093338.3093339
6. Ropelewski, A.J.: The Brain Image Library (2018). https://www.psc.edu/research/braindata
7. Phillips, J.C., et al.: Scalable molecular dynamics with NAMD. J. Comput. Chem. **26**, 1781–1802 (2005). https://doi.org/10.1002/jcc.20289
8. Jia, Z., Maggioni, M., Staiger, B., Scarpazza, D.P.: Dissecting the NVIDIA Volta GPU Architecture via Microbenchmarking. arXiv:1804.06826 (2018)
9. NVIDIA Corporation: NVIDIA NVSwitch: The World's Highest-Bandwidth On-Node Switch (2018)
10. Environment Modules. http://modules.sourceforge.net/
11. Furlani, J.L.: Modules: providing a flexible user environment. In: Proceedings of the Fifth Large Installation Systems Administration Conference (LISA V), San Diego, Califorinia, pp. 141–152 (1991)

12. Kurtzer, G.M.: Singularity 2.1.2 - Linux Application and Environment Containers for Science (2016). https://doi.org/10.5281/zenodo.60736
13. Krizhevsky, A., Sutskever, I., Hinton, G.E.: ImageNet classification with deep convolutional neural networks. In: Pereira, F., Burges, C.J.C., Bottou, L., Weinberger, K.Q. (eds.) Advances in Neural Information Processing Systems, vol. 25, pp. 1097–1105. Curran Associates, Inc. (2012)
14. Szegedy, C., Vanhoucke, V., Ioffe, S., Shlens, J., Wojna, Z.: Rethinking the inception architecture for computer vision. In: 2016 IEEE Conference on Computer Vision and Pattern Recognition (CVPR), pp. 2818–2826 (2016). https://doi.org/10.1109/CVPR.2016.308
15. Liu, S., Deng, W.: Very deep convolutional neural network based image classification using small training sample size. In: 2015 3rd IAPR Asian Conference on Pattern Recognition (ACPR), pp. 730–734 (2015). https://doi.org/10.1109/ACPR.2015.7486599
16. He, K., Zhang, X., Ren, S., Sun, J.: Deep residual learning for image recognition. In: 2016 IEEE Conference on Computer Vision and Pattern Recognition (CVPR), pp. 770–778 (2016). https://doi.org/10.1109/CVPR.2016.90
17. Buitrago, P.A., Nystrom, N.A.: Open compass: accelerating the adoption of AI in open research. In: Practice & Experience in Advanced Research Computing (PEARC) 2019. ACM, Chicago (2019, to appear)
18. Le, H., et al.: Utilizing Automated Breast Cancer Detection to Identify Spatial Distributions of Tumor Infiltrating Lymphocytes in Invasive Breast Cancer (2019). http://arxiv.org/abs/1905.10841
19. Saltz, J., et al.: Spatial organization and molecular correlation of tumor-infiltrating lymphocytes using deep learning on pathology images. Cell Rep. 23, 181–193.e7 (2018). https://doi.org/10.1016/j.celrep.2018.03.086

Towards a Platform to Evaluate the Impact of Resource Information Distribution in IoT Environments

Paula Verghelet[1] and Esteban Mocskos[1,2]

[1] Departamento de Computación, Facultad de Ciencias Exactas y Naturales, Universidad de Buenos Aires, C1428EGA Buenos Aires, Argentina
{pverghelet,emocskos}@dc.uba.ar
[2] Centro de Simulación Computacional p/Aplic. Tecnológicas/CSC-CONICET, Godoy Cruz 2390, C1425FQD Buenos Aires, Argentina

Abstract. Internet of Things (IoT) is a paradigm in which every object has the capacity of communicating through the Internet. Cloud Computing is designed to provide computational resources to costumers geographically distributed following an elastic payment strategy. Fog/Edge Computing aims to decrease bandwidth usage keeping the computation near the source of data and avoiding the collapse of network infrastructure when moving all the data from the edge to the cloud data centers. Fog and Cloud environments define a large scale distributed system composed of heterogeneous resources, which has huge theoretical computing power. But using these computational resources poses challenges to distributed applications and scheduling policies. In this work, we show the initial steps to develop a tool to support evaluate the impact of resource information quality to guide scheduling policies. This tool combines simulation and validation and simplifies the deployment of experiments on both sides. The evaluation of this initial proof of concept consists of the deployment of experiments with a different number of devices in a single site and in three different sites across France. Our results show that both simulation and validation platforms present good agreement.

Keywords: Resource information · Internet of Things · Validation

1 Introduction

The current trend is continuing with the increment of devices connected to the Internet. Internet of Things (IoT) emerges as the paradigm which is characterized by the massive amount of mobile phones, different types of sensors and even smart clothes that can communicate or collaborate in different computational tasks [1]. The devices involved in IoT have a wide range of characteristics from the computational power to the battery capacity and interconnection technology.

Cloud Computing is designed to provide computational resources to costumers all over the world despite their geographical location and based on an

© Springer Nature Switzerland AG 2020
J. L. Crespo-Mariño and E. Meneses-Rojas (Eds.): CARLA 2019, CCIS 1087, pp. 215–229, 2020.
https://doi.org/10.1007/978-3-030-41005-6_15

elastic payment strategy. The customer can increase the number of resources used according to an increment in their computational needs and can decrease it when they are no longer needed. Resource state information is a fundamental component of any Cloud Service or Federation [9,10].

The expected growth of interconnected devices and the data generated by them pose a challenge to the infrastructure provided by Cloud Computing data centers. This situation could lead to a collapse of this ecosystem, not only for the increasing computational needs but mainly for the network infrastructure that needs to be greatly improved to support the data movement.

Fog Computing was recently proposed [4] to increase the computation being performed near the network edge using smart devices. Fog/Edge Computing aims to decrease bandwidth usage keeping the computation near the source of data and avoiding the movement of information to the cloud data centers. The combination of Fog and Cloud Computing defines a large scale distributed system interconnected by a wide range of network technologies with different computer resources, storage, and latency. Although this system possesses a huge theoretical computing power, there are still challenges to tackle key components to take advantage of it. Scheduling policies, resource discovery and interchange of status information [8] are some of the software actors that have to be modified in this new scenario.

One aspect that is especially important in Fog/Cloud Computing is using the state information and computational characteristics to select the most adequate devices to send tasks to be solved. This scheduling component needs to take into consideration the computational resources available in the device but also its battery capacity and previous history, but in an IoT scenario, it cannot be assumed to have control over the devices. More than one scheduler could be sending tasks to be solved in the edge. This poses additional challenges to the quality of the information used by the schedulers to guide the selection of the resources to be used when trying to solve a computational task. The component responsible for gathering the state information of the resources is known as the *indexer* and the way it is configured to obtain these data is known as the *resource information distribution policy*. Verghelet and Mocskos [16] propose improvements to the resource information distribution policies based on a super-peer overlay. The same authors analyze a learning-based strategy and propose optimizations that lead to a better policy performance [17], but the validation experiments in the scale analyzed in those two papers are almost impossible to perform.

In this work, we show the first steps creating a platform to explore the impact of information quality in the design and development of scheduling policies in Fog/Edge environments combining simulation and validation. The ultimate objective is providing a platform to allow the exploration of new ideas, testing using different conditions and scenarios, and deployment of experiments in a controlled tested to validate their limits and working conditions.

The study of heuristics to obtain better scheduling policies in distributed systems has a long and rich history but also new proposals can be easily found and are being developed by the community. For example, Luo et. al [12] and Anglano et. al [3] propose new scheduling policies in Fog/Edge/Cloud environments in both works the experimentation and validation are not based on an integrated platform and the resource information is not considered as one of the aspects to simulate or evaluate, they suppose that the schedulers have all the information they need. Moreover, the number of available devices to be used in the experiments is small, which also decrease the range of scenarios that can be analyzed. Another approach is shown by Chen and Zang [7] which proposes to handle the need for additional resources using a Device-to-Device (D2D) technique to offload tasks. They use a simulation tool which is not specified and consider different working parameters and no validation is mentioned.

The rest of this paper is organized as follows: Sect. 2 introduces the facility used to deploy the validation experiments while in Sect. 3 we present some details of the simulation engine. The layer of software designed to link both platforms is shown in Sect. 4 and the methodology to evaluate the quality of the information stored in a system is presented in Sect. 5. Finally, in Sect. 6 we detail the experiments performed and Sect. 7 includes the conclusions.

2   Experimental Platform: FIT/IoT-LAB

When considering new scheduling policies in Fog/Edge environments, creation, management, and deployment of a distributed infrastructure to validate new ideas could become extremely difficult or even impossible. In spite of this, the use of hardware similar to the devices that could be installed in the projected scenario could provide insight and a different perspective than only relaying in simulation tools.

FIT IoT-LAB is an open and free to use testbed offering access to a multi-user scientific tool supporting the design, development, tuning, and experimentation related to IoT [2]. FIT IoT-LAB is a facility with thousands of wireless nodes focused on the evaluation and experimentation of very large scale wireless IoT technologies. FIT IoT-LAB testbeds are located at six different sites across France.

To experiment using the FIT IoT-LAB's resources, it is necessary to plan their usage and reserve them using a web-based tool. A reservation is called a *slice* in terms of FIT IoT-LAB's terminology. A slice can be configured to access the resources immediately or for a specific time and date in the future.

The available infrastructure provided by FIT IoT-LAB includes a wide range of sensors, robots and computing resources distributed in different sites. An experiment could use resources from only one site (i.e. local resources) which are connected by a local switch or can be composed of distributed resources among two or more sites. The connectivity between the sites is provided by RENATER which also supports the access of researchers worldwide through the different advanced networks in each country. Experiments can be monitored using usual networks tools and to deploy data or applications to the nodes, each site has a shared file system mounted on each device. As the file system is only shared by

Verghelet, Mocskos

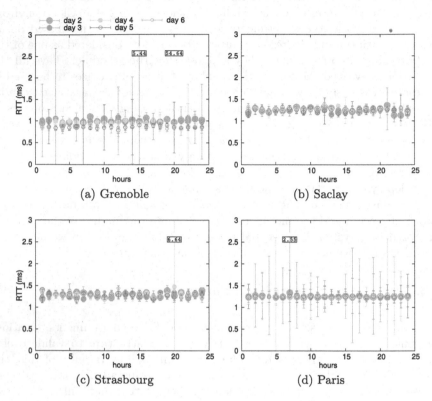

Fig. 1. Verification of the network infrastructure behavior for some of the FIT IoT-LAB's sites. Pings between devices is recorded during five consecutive days during November 2018. Average Round Trip Time (RTT) of near 14000 observations of intrasite connectivity (expressed in ms)

the nodes internally in each site, the user has to manually transfer data between different sites.

When combining validation and simulation, network parameters must be clearly defined. We need to evaluate the behavior of local network infrastructure and intersite links to confirm the values to be used in the simulation tool. We set up an experiment to monitor the state and response time (i.e. RTT) of the connections between four sites and their internal behavior monitoring the RTT during the first 10 min of each hour for five consecutive days.

Figures 1 present the results of monitoring measurements for internal traffic (i.e. intrasite) during November 2018. Saclay, Strasbourg, and Paris present a similar average RTT near 1.2 ms while Grenoble has considerable lower RTT around 1.0 ms. In terms of stability, Saclay and Strasbourg have a more regular behavior with a small deviation. Grenoble and Paris have larger deviations, being Paris the most irregular site. Similarly, intersite latency was also observed (results not show) obtaining, as expected, that the latency depends on the distance (in terms of network hops) between sites. The analysis of intrasite and intersite traffic patterns can help the user to select which site fits better the requirements for each experiment. This analysis also guides the configuration of the network properties in the simulation tool. In this sense, Strasbourg presents more stable traffic intrasite patterns, but using Strasbourg for intersite experiments increments the noise and effective latency.

3 Simulation Platform: Simgrid

The simulation tool needs to capture the main characteristics of a Fog/Edge environment. Some options that can be adopted are: CloudSim [5], Simgrid [6], iFogSim [11], and pysimgrid [15]. But to select the application, some important characteristics should be considered:

- *Computing power*: in a Fog/Edge environment, the devices can have a wide range of type processors and configurations. The simulation tool needs to support executing jobs considering the difference in the resources involved especially in a highly heterogeneous scenario.
- *Connectivity*: to collaborate in a computational task, messages have to be interchanged among the nodes. Data, applications, and synchronization directives have to be distributed in a heterogeneous environment. The simulation tool has to consider the latency and bandwidth of the link to incorporate the effects of generated by, for example, congestion. Moreover, the devices in the edge usually use wireless technology with variable capacity, can be moving or have eventual connectivity.
- *Energy consumption*: the battery capacity is extremely important in devices not connected directly to the power grid. In some cases, these devices can have access to solar panels or local generators which provides energy intermittently. These factors should be considered when distributing computational tasks in a Fog/Edge environment.

Cloudsim and iFogSim are event-based simulators focused on orchestration of virtualization-based systems and analysis of applications to be used in Cloud and Fog scenarios respectively. These tools use very simplified models for communication and computing with no support for wireless communication and mobile devices. As these tools are implemented in Java, adding new modules or models imposes using this technology.

Another event-based tool is Simgrid which has sophisticated and versatile communication and computing models. Similarly to the two previous tools, Simgrid cannot model moving devices. This tool is natively programmed in C/C++ which gives a good performance but can be used also with other languages (like Java and Python). pysimgrid is a Python-based framework to interact with SimGrid.

We select SimGrid and pysimgrid to support the simulation. This selection is based on the versatility of the tool, an active user community and our previous experience using it. In our design, we consider including an abstraction layer to allow using different simulation engines but in this prototype, we tested only Simgrid.

The simulation tool needs to support realistic models for heterogeneous devices and the communication network. Simgrid allows configuring the network topology using an input file in which the topology, bandwidth, and latency for each link are defined. The computing power of all the resources is also specified in this configuration file. SimGrid has several communication models implemented that need to be selected by the user. Each model is focused on different conditions of the network technology and state, then it computes the time required for a message to reach its destination taking into consideration latency, bandwidth, and message size.

4   Linking Simulation with Validation: Watsapi

In spite of having a simulation engine (Simgrid) and a validation platform (FIT IoT-LAB), one more component is still needed. This component has to combine them to ease the configuration, deployment, monitoring, and analysis of results. Additionally, it should implement the indexer to distribute and gather resource information.

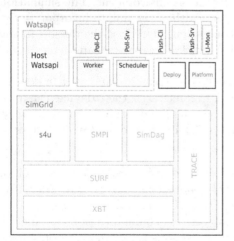
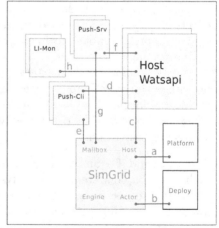

(a) Software modules used and developed.   (b) Interactions between entities.

Fig. 2. Software modules involved in the design of Watsapi, a tool to combine simulation and validation focused on the evaluation of the role of resource information quality in Fog/Edge environments

Watsapi is the software component acting as the glue between simulation and validation. Watsapi uses Simgrid to support network traffic and task execution and prepares the information to deploy the experiments in FIT IoT-LAB. The communication support is provided by `Simgrid'` `s4u` API, which is a replacement for the deprecated `MSG` interface.

Figure 2a presents the current software modules involved in the evaluation of resource information distribution including those present in `Simgrid`. Figure 2b shows how the modules in `Watsapi` and `Simgrid` interact to perform a simulation. The `HostWatsapi` represents the base software entity which can be specialized to become a scheduler or a worker. In this work, we focus on the distribution of resource information between nodes in a P2P way. Every node has also support for indexing resources and querying neighbors for information. In terms of `SimGrid`, each of these entities is an `Actor` executing a process on a Host called `HostWatsapi`. The registration mechanism provided by `SimGrid` allows assigning functions to execute in each entity. These functions are specified in the input configuration file.

The interactions marked in Fig. 2b are described next:

(a) `Simgrid` reads the `platform` file to configure the network topology, link bandwidth and latency, and type and amount of nodes.
(b) The specification of the functions (i.e. processes) to execute in each node is declared in another configuration file which is called `deploy`. This file also specifies the variables to monitor during the simulation. Each host in this file is instantiated as an object of the class `s4u::Actor`.
(c) `Simgrid`'s host class is specialized to support to become the `HostWatsapi` class. This new class supports specific logging functions and the management of the resources owned by neighbors in the system. As in a Fog/Edge environment, on-the-fly clustering is one possible strategy to deal with complex tasks, the knowledge of near resources could be necessary for centralized schedulers, but also for other workers in the edge.
(d) and e) `Push-Cli` class is a specialization of `Actor` class. To be able to communicate with other entities, this class has to define a `Simgrid` communication port (i.e. mailbox in `Simgrid` terminology).
(f) The `Push-Srv` usually have to wait for a message from an instance of `Push-Cli` class. To receive one resource information message, a `Push-Srv` uses the communication infrastructure provided by `Simgrid`. It starts waiting until a message is received in its mailbox.
(g) A `Push-Srv` uses the `Simgrid` communication layer to receive the information from an object of `Push-Cli`, then it updates the resource information dictionary.
(h) The module `LI-Mon` (Local Information Monitor) is included in each instance of `HostWatsapi` class. It computes and stores periodically the quality of the resource information in each host (see LIR definition in Sect. 5).

The standard scenario for our experiments can be described as follows: each node owns some amount of resources which could be used for computing some task, it also has a dictionary of known hosts, resources, and expiration time. Initially, all the nodes only know information about itself. At a predefined period, it uses a resource information distribution policy to select one node to contact and shares its stored information. The distribution policies use periodic cycles to share information between nodes. When a node receives information from another one, the new data can be merged with its dictionary.

5   Methodology

As a simplification, normally the impact of information age is discarded in the evaluation of scheduling strategies in distributed systems, oversimplifying the dynamical nature of this kind of systems. Mocskos et al. [14] propose two metrics to evaluate and analyze the information obtained by the nodes about the resources in the system: Local Information Rate (LIR), which is local to each node and Global Information Rate (GIR) which can be used as a global measure of the information quality distributed in the system:

- **LIR:** captures the amount of information that a particular host has from all the entire system in a single moment. For the host k, LIR_k is:

$$LIR_k = \frac{\sum_{h=1}^{N} f(age_h, expiration_h) \cdot resourceCount_h}{totalResourceCount} \tag{1}$$

where N is number of hosts in the system, $expiration_h$ is the expiration time of the resources of host h in host k, age_h is the time passed since the information was obtained from that host, $resourceCount_h$ is the number of resources in host h, $totalResourceCount$ is the total amount of resources in the whole system, and f is the information decay function which can be selected capture how frequently this information changes.
- **GIR:** captures the amount of information that the whole system knows of itself, calculated as the mean value of every node's LIR.

The resource information can include available processors and their characteristics, free memory, type of network connectivity, network protocols supported among others. There are two main types of information: almost constant and fastly changing. The first could be stored when the resource is discovered initially and only needs to be updated when a major upgrade is performed. The fastly-changing data depend on the task being executed, state of the network and even can depend on the position of the resource. In this work, we focus on this type of information. To inform the state and availability of resources, two strategies can be used: `push` (proactive strategy), `poll` (reactive strategy) [13], or a combination of both. When using the proactive strategy, each node selects another one to send its information about the known resources. On the other case, the nodes chose one node to ask the information it knows.

To be able to coordinate simulation and validation, the network topology used in the simulation tool should follow the real topology of FIT IoT-LAB. This information is extracted from the experiments presented in Sect. 2. On the other hand, the information distributed policy should also be specified in the configuration of both tools (simulation and validation).

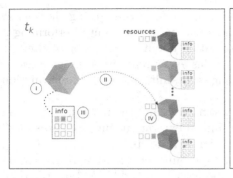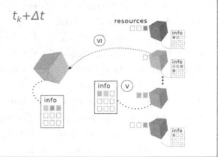

(a) Simulation: Simgrid-based tool

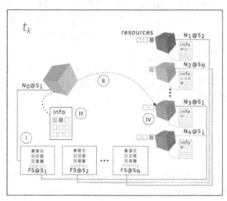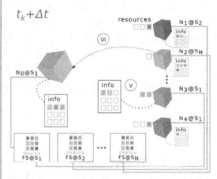

(b) Validation: real hardware execution in distributed sites

Fig. 3. Resource information distribution in simulation and validation platforms. In both cases, one of the nodes sends its information about resources to another one and then it receives the information from another node. The validation platform uses RENATER infrastructure and a distributed filesystem to support the experiments

The relationship between simulation and validation stages is introduced in Fig. 3. The top two figures correspond to two consecutive time steps in the dynamics of the involved entities during the simulation step, while the other two represent the validation step deployed in FIT IoT-LAB.

In these figures, some of the events are marked in both stages to show how they are linked:

(I) In both platforms, the deployment of the experiment includes specifying the resources owned by each node. Watsapi provides tools to automatize the submission of the configuration to the validation platform. For the moment, some manual adjustments are still needed, but work is in progress to improve this support. When the experiment is deployed in FIT IoT-LAB, all the nodes access the file with the deploy information using the shared file system.

(II) Part of the definition of the experiment includes configuring the *refresh period*, which is the amount of time every node waits until performing a query to a neighbor asking for information about resources or sending its own resource information to a peer. This event represents the moment in which the central node sends a message containing its resource information to one of its neighbors.

(III) Every node keeps a record of the known hosts and their resources. Jointly with this information, a timestamp and an expiration time are also stored. When the information is no longer valid, it is deleted.

(IV) A node receives a message asking for its resource information. In simulation and validation, the node has two resources and no additional information. The answer carries this information to the source node.

 (V) After some time (Δt), the node receives the message containing resource information. These data are merged enlarging the knowledge about the resources in the system. In the case of receiving a previously known resource information, the node keeps the newest.

(VI) This last event represents the moment in which another node starts sending a message containing resource information. In this case, this node selects the central one as the message destination.

6   Results

The experiments are focused on testing if the proposed prototype could be used to simulate a Fog/Edge scenario and then validate it in a real hardware platform. When dealing with systems with less than 40 nodes, almost any resource distribution policies shows similar behavior [16,17]. We use a random-based distribution policy to simplify the development and debugging of this proof of concept. Every node randomly selects another one to send a message containing its information about the system. This operation is performed based on the refresh rate selected for each scenario (is one of the parameters of the experiments). The expiration time of the information is fixed at 60 s which is a reasonable time to capture the dynamics of this kind of systems.

In all the experiments, each node uses the deploy file to identify the rest of the nodes in the system, we do not focus on resource discovery. The nodes in both platform (simulation and validation) only execute the indexer components to distribute and store the resource information. The resource information is stored every 5 s by the LI-Mon component in a local file. The experiments last for approximately 1200 s in all cases.

3-nodes Intrasite (Strasbourg). The first experiment corresponds to the deployment of three nodes in the same site, in this case Strasbourg is selected due to the stability of its internal network (recall Fig. 1). One node has two generic computing resource, one three and the last five, totalizing ten resources. This simplifies the comparison between expected and obtained values for LIR and GIR metrics. As with the same of the experiments included in this work, each node sends its information to a randomly selected peer at a predefined period of time. The refresh period is configured to 10 s, 30 s and 60 s.

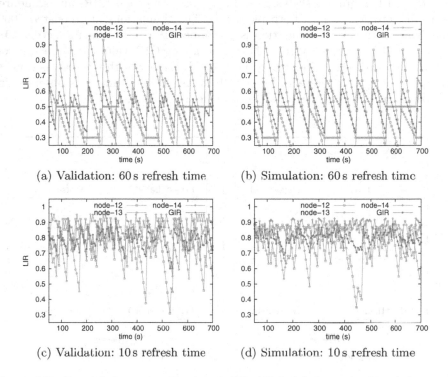

(a) Validation: 60 s refresh time   (b) Simulation: 60 s refresh time

(c) Validation: 10 s refresh time   (d) Simulation: 10 s refresh time

Fig. 4. LIR (Local Information Rate) and GIR (Global Information Rate) for a scenario with three nodes deployed in the same site. Random Policy is used as resource information distribution policy, the expiration time is 60 s, and the refresh interval are 10 s and 60 s

Figure 4 presents the Local Information Rate (LIR) in both platforms jointly with Global Information Rate (GIR) of the system. As was introduced in Sect. 5, LIR and GIR go from 0 (bad) to 1 (ideal). The first column shows the results obtained in the validation platform while the second one includes the obtained values with the simulation tool. In spite of showing a complex behavior based on the stochastic nature of the distribution policy, for all the considered refresh times, both simulation and validation present good agreement.

The peaks in LIR correspond to the arrival of new data while the decay after them are based on the aging of the information. As the nodes to send the information are selected randomly, it may happen that some node is not chosen for one or more cycles. This can be seen in Fig. 4: constant LIR values are observed during some time, in all cases, these values do not decrease further due to the information about their own resources.

As the refresh rate is decreased, the nodes in the system send more messages in the same time period, improving the quality and amount of information they have from the rest of the system. This can be observed by comparing the figures from top to bottom, clearly, the values for more frequent refresh close to the ideal limit of 1. Figure 5a shows, in a single figure, the mean GIRs and standard deviations for each case in both platforms. The simulations are repeated 1000 times while each case of validation is performed 48 times. When selecting 10 s as the refresh rate, the system shows the larger GIR values (at the cost of sending more messages and using more bandwidth). As the refresh period is increased, the system presents lower GIR values. This behavior is observed in both platform, showing a good agreement between them.

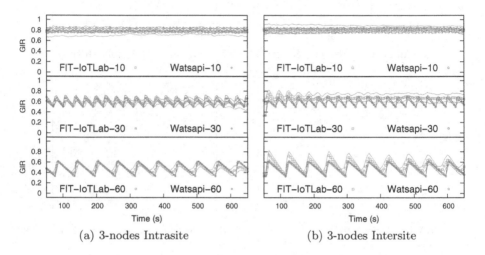

(a) 3-nodes Intrasite   (b) 3-nodes Intersite

Fig. 5. Same cases presented in Fig. 4 but for both 3-nodes Intrasite (5a) and 3-nodes Intersite (5b), showing three refresh times and a random policy. Expiration time is 60 s and the nodes are deployed in Strasbourg (Intrasite) and in Grenoble, Saclay and Strasbourg (Intersite). Average and deviation of 1000 simulations with Watsapi and 48 times on FIT-IoTLab

3-nodes Intersite (Grenoble-Saclay-Strasbourg). In this experiment, we use a similar configuration as in the previous one but the devices are deployed in different sites: Grenoble, Saclay, and Strasbourg. The device in Grenoble has two resources, the one in Saclay three, and in Strasbourg the node has five. As in the previous experiment, every node sends its resource information to a randomly selected node at a predefined refresh time.

Figure 5b compares the obtained GIRs for the scenarios under consideration. The results are similar to the included in Fig. 5a: 10 s of refresh time produces higher GIR using more messages then the rest of the cases. These dynamics are observed in both platforms showing similar behavior. In this system, no impact of the additional latency can be traced in the results.

20-nodes Intrasite (Grenoble). Here, we move towards a larger system. We use 20 nodes in Grenoble, which is selected based on the availability of resources. Every node has one computational resource and sends its resource information to a randomly selected neighbor.

This experiment records a situation that could happen in this kind of facilities: 20 nodes are reserved and granted, but only 17 can be used. The remainder nodes cannot be accessed due to hardware problems or configuration issues that need to be solved by local administrators. To solve this kind of situation, we start a new line of development to add the management of this kind of events to `Watsapi`, which is another work in progress.

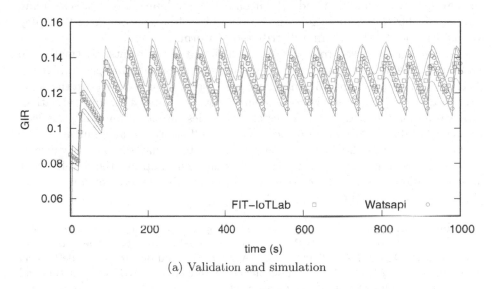

(a) Validation and simulation

Fig. 6. Mean GIR and standard deviation (96 repetitions for validation and 1000 for simulation) in a scenario using 20 nodes deployed in the same site (Grenoble). Random Policy is used as resource information distribution policy, the expiration time is 240 s, and the refresh interval is 60 s

Figure 6 shows mean GIR (points) and standard deviation (limiting lines using the same color as mean values) for both platforms. The two platforms have similar behavior: the peaks corresponds to the moment of new information arrival. During the period between each peak, the information gets older and the mean GIR decreases. As is known from the literature [16,17], the random policy loses performance as the system size increases. In these cases, GIR values are very low, which means that the system has old resource information. This highlights the importance of having up-to-date resource information, if a scheduling policy is based on old information, it could select unavailable nodes or do not manage the system load balancing accordingly.

7   Conclusions

The expected growth of interconnected devices and the data generated by them pose a challenge to the infrastructure provided by Cloud Computing data centers. Fog Computing proposes to increase the use of devices in the network edge, aiming to decrease bandwidth usage by keeping the computation near the source of data and avoiding the movement of information to the cloud data centers. The combination of Fog and Cloud Computing possesses a huge theoretical computing power, but there are still challenges to scheduling policies, resource discovery and interchange of status information.

In this work, we show the initial development of a computation tool to mind the gap between simulation and validation in the development of new scheduling strategies. Our tool combines a simulation tool with a software layer to deploy and control actual devices in a distributed platform.

To test our proposed tool, we present different experiments: (i) small-scale system deployed in the same site, (ii) small-scale system using geographically distributed resources, and (iii) medium-scale system using resources in the same site. In all cases, there is a good agreement between simulation and validation. GIR values for the medium-scale system (20 nodes) are low remarking the need to use up-to-date information to not incur in inefficient task assignment.

Our proposal is the first step in creating a tool that fills a gap which is not covered by any known application and that could improve the development and evaluation of scheduling policies in complex distributed systems such as Fog/Cloud environments.

Acknowledgments. This work is partially supported by Universidad de Buenos Aires (UBACyT 20020170100765BA), Consejo Nacional de Investigaciones Científicas y Técnicas (PIO133201501000020CO), and Agencia Nacional de Promoción de Ciencia y Técnica (PICT-2015-2761). We thank the access to FIT IoT-LAB infrastructure and their support while performing the experiments.

References

1. Aazam, M., Huh, E.N.: Fog computing: the cloud-IoT/IoE middleware paradigm. IEEE Potentials **35**(3), 40–44 (2016)
2. Adjih, C., et al.: FIT IoT-LAB: a large scale open experimental IoT testbed. In: Proceedings of IEEE 2nd World Forum on Internet of Things (WF-IoT), pp. 459–464. IEEE, December 2015
3. Anglano, C., Canonico, M., Guazzone, M.: WQR-UD: an online scheduling algorithm for FemtoClouds. In: Proceedings of the 12th EAI International Conference on Performance Evaluation Methodologies and Tools, pp. 179–182. ACM, New York(2019)
4. Bonomi, F., Milito, R., Zhu, J., Addepalli, S.: Fog computing and its role in the Internet of Things. In: Proceedings of the First Edition of the MCC Workshop on Mobile Cloud Computing. MCC 2012, pp. 13–16. ACM, New York (2012)
5. Calheiros, R.N., Ranjan, R., Beloglazov, A., De Rose, C.A., Buyya, R.: CloudSim: a toolkit for modeling and simulation of cloud computing environments and evaluation of resource provisioning algorithms. Softw. Pract. Exp. **41**(1), 23–50 (2011)

6. Casanova, H.: Simgrid: a toolkit for the simulation of application scheduling. In: Proceedings of the 1st International Symposium on Cluster Computing and the Grid, pp. 430–437. IEEE, Piscataway, May 2001

7. Chen, X., Junshan, Z.: When D2D meets cloud: hybrid mobile task offloadings in fog computing. In: Proceedings of the IEEE International Conference on Communications (ICC), pp. 1–6. IEEE, Piscataway, May 2017

8. Chen, Y.C., Chang, Y.C., Chen, C.H., Lin, Y.S., Chen, J.L., Chang, Y.Y.: Cloud-fog computing for information-centric Internet-of-Things applications. In: Proceedings of the International Conference on Applied System Innovation (ICASI), pp. 637–640. IEEE, Piscataway, May 2017

9. Clayman, S., Toffetti, G., Galis, A., Chapman, C.: Monitoring services in a federated cloud: the reservoir experience. In: Achieving Federated and Self-manageable Cloud Infrastructures: Theory and Practice, pp. 242–265. IGI Global, May 2012

10. Ergu, D., Kou, G., Peng, Y., Shi, Y., Shi, Y.: The analytic hierarchy process: task scheduling and resource allocation in cloud computing environment. J. Supercomput. **64**(3), 835–848 (2013)

11. Gupta, H., Vahid Dastjerdi, A., Ghosh, S.K., Buyya, R.: iFogSim: a toolkit for modeling and simulation of resource management techniques in the Internet of Things, edge and fog computing environments. Softw. Pract. Exp. **47**(9), 1275–1296 (2017)

12. Luo, J., et al.: Container-based fog computing architecture and energy-balancing scheduling algorithm for energy IoT. Future Gener. Comput. Syst. **97**, 50–60 (2019)

13. Meshkova, E., Riihijärvi, J., Petrova, M., Mähönen, P.: A survey on resource discovery mechanisms, peer-to-peer and service discovery frameworks. Comput. Netw. **52**(11), 2097–2128 (2008)

14. Mocskos, E.E., Yabo, P., Turjanski, P.G., Fernandez Slezak, D.: Grid matrix: a grid simulation tool to focus on the propagation of resource and monitoring information. Simul. Trans. Soc. Model. Simul. Int. **88**(10), 1233–1246 (2012)

15. Sukhoroslov, O., Nazarenko, A., Aleksandrov, R.: An experimental study of scheduling algorithms for many-task applications. J. Supercomput. **75**(12), 7857–7871 (2019). https://doi.org/10.1007/s11227-018-2553-9

16. Verghelet, P., Mocskos, E.: Improvements to super-peer policy communication mechanisms. In: Osthoff, C., Navaux, P.O.A., Barrios Hernandez, C.J., Silva Dias, P.L. (eds.) CARLA 2015. CCIS, vol. 565, pp. 73–86. Springer, Cham (2015). https://doi.org/10.1007/978-3-319-26928-3_6

17. Verghelet, P., Mocskos, E.: Efficient P2P inspired policy to distribute resource information in large distributed systems. In: Barrios Hernández, C.J., Gitler, I., Klapp, J. (eds.) CARLA 2016. CCIS, vol. 697, pp. 3–17. Springer, Cham (2017). https://doi.org/10.1007/978-3-319-57972-6_1

GPU Support for Automatic Generation of Finite-Differences Stencil Kernels

Vitor Hugo Mickus Rodrigues[1]([⊠]), Lucas Cavalcante[1], Maelso Bruno Pereira[1], Fabio Luporini[2], István Reguly[3], Gerard Gorman[2], and Samuel Xavier de Souza[1]

[1] Universidade Federal do Rio Grande do Norte, Natal, RN, Brazil
vmickus@ufrn.edu.br
[2] Imperial College London, London, UK
[3] Pazmany Peter Catholic University, Budapest, Hungary

Abstract. The growth of data to be processed in the Oil & Gas industry matches the requirements imposed by evolving algorithms based on stencil computations, such as Full Waveform Inversion and Reverse Time Migration. Graphical processing units (GPUs) are an attractive architectural target for stencil computations because of its high degree of data parallelism. However, the rapid architectural and technological progression makes it difficult for even the most proficient programmers to remain up-to-date with the technological advances at a micro-architectural level. In this work, we present an extension for an open source compiler designed to produce highly optimized finite difference kernels for use in inversion methods named Devito[©]. We embed it with the Oxford Parallel Domain Specific Language (OP-DSL) in order to enable automatic code generation for GPU architectures from a high-level representation. We aim to enable users coding in a symbolic representation level to effortlessly get their implementations leveraged by the processing capacities of GPU architectures. The implemented backend is evaluated on a NVIDIA[®] GTX Titan Z, and on a NVIDIA[®] Tesla V100 in terms of operational intensity through the roof-line model for varying space-order discretization levels of 3D acoustic isotropic wave propagation stencil kernels with and without symbolic optimizations. It achieves approximately 63% of V100's peak performance and 24% of Titan Z's peak performance for stencil kernels over grids with 256^3 points. Our study reveals that improving memory usage should be the most efficient strategy for leveraging the performance of the implemented solution on the evaluated architectures.

Keywords: GPU · Domain Specific Languages · Finite-differences · Stencil kernels · Parallel architectures · Devito · OPS

V. H. M. Rodrigues—The author gratefully acknowledge support from Shell Brasil through the "Novos Métodos de Exploração Sísmica por Inversão Completa das Formas de Onda" project at the Universidade Federal do Rio Grande do Norte, and the strategic importance of the support given by ANP through the R&D levy regulation. This research was supported by the High Performance Computing Center at UFRN (NPAD/UFRN).

© Springer Nature Switzerland AG 2020
J. L. Crespo-Mariño and E. Meneses-Rojas (Eds.): CARLA 2019, CCIS 1087, pp. 230–244, 2020.
https://doi.org/10.1007/978-3-030-41005-6_16

1   Introduction

A wide variety of physical phenomena can be formalized in terms of partial differential equations (PDE) such as sound, heat, diffusion, electrostatics, electrodynamics, fluid dynamics, elasticity, and quantum mechanics. The development of computationally efficient methods for obtaining numerical solutions of PDEs through stencil kernels has been mentioned as a key computational science and engineering challenge to be addressed as one of the "seven dwarfs of computation" for at least the next decade, in 2009 [13]. In fact, large-scale PDE inversion algorithms that can be solved by finite-difference (FD) schemes used in exploration seismology such as full waveform inversion (FWI) and reverse time migration (RTM) constitute some of the current most computationally demanding problems in industrial and academic research.

In general, a stencil on structured grids is defined as a function that updates a point based on the values of its neighbors. The stencil structure remains constant as it moves from one point in space to the next. In the context of a wave-equation solver, the stencil is described by the support (grid-locations) and the coefficients of FD schemes. Using parallel designs such as graphics processing units (GPU) has relatively recently become the preferred choice to improve existing code for the current commercial and scientific community that performs stencil computations.

However, a significant barrier that has become increasingly more notable is the difficulty in programming these systems. As the hardware architectures grow in complexity, exploiting the potential of these devices requires higher know-how on parallel programming. The issue has further been compounded by a rapidly changing hardware design space, with a wide range of parallel architectures. For example, some designs offer many simple processors vs. fewer complex processors, some depend on multi-threading, and some even replace caches with explicitly addressed local stores. As no conventional wisdom has yet emerged, it is unsustainable for domain scientists to re-write their applications for each new type of architecture regarded that developing and validating a PDE solver usually takes decades of effort.

To address the problem of algorithm sustainability, taking into account the uncertainty in future architectures, one solution involves decoupling the work of a domain scientist and a computer scientist. In this approach, Domain Specific Languages (DSL) are developed by high-performance computing (HPC) specialists, and the specifics of the problem and the numerical solution method are specified in the DSL by the domain scientist. Using source-to-source translation, the numerical solver can be targeted towards different hardware backends. This ensures that only the backend that interfaces with the new architectures need to be written and supported by the translator. The underlying implementation of the solver remains the same, thereby introducing a separation of concerns that results in a direct payoff in productivity.

Interest in building generic DSLs for solving PDEs is not new with early attempts dating back as far as 1970 [1–3]. More recently, two prominent finite element software packages, FEniCS [6] and Firedrake [11], have demonstrated the power of symbolic computation using the DSL paradigm. The optimization of regular grid and stencil computations has also produced a vast range of libraries and DSLs that aim to ease the efficient automated creation of high-performance codes [4,5,9,16].

In this work, we present an implementation for automatic GPU code-generation to Devito. This objective can be translated into extending Devito's backend in such a way that the generated stencils are compatible with this target architecture. Currently, two backends exist in Devito: the default backend to run it on standard CPU architectures; and an alternative backend using the YASK stencil compiler to generate optimized C++ code for Intel® Xeon® and Intel® Xeon Phi™ architectures [8]. Our strategy is to utilize one of the Oxford Parallel Domain Specific Languages (OP-DSL), called OPS, to build a third backend for Devito. OPS is a programming abstraction embedded in C/C++ for writing multi-block structured mesh algorithms, and it is composed by the corresponding software library (an Application Programming Interface – API) and code translation tools (compilers) to enable automatic parallelization of the intermediary-level code produced (here, by Devito) using different parallel programming approaches.

As a result, it is expected that executable artifacts wrote in CUDA, OpenACC, OpenCL, OpenMP, and MPI get automatically and transparently composed for a diverse range of hardware from high-level symbolic descriptions of PDEs. It has been shown that OPS generated code is capable of matching or outperforming hand-coded and tuned implementations [12], which implies considerable confidence in such an approach being capable of delivering high performance, code maintainability and future proofing.

It is possible to speculate that it would take much longer not only to compose complex FD problems but also to produce their various hand-coded parallel implementations, each of which would have to be then debugged and validated. The authors claim that the time savings on combining code generation with automatic parallel implementation for state-of-the-art hardware will have a significant impact on the efforts for modeling seismic inversion algorithms.

The remaining of this paper is organized as follows. In Sect. 2 we present both the Devito and the OPS compiler, altogether with the model for isotropic wave propagation considered in our study. Section 2.3 describes how the code generated by Devito should be modified in order to match the syntax of the OPS compiler, and also the roof-line model for evaluating the performance of the generated kernels on the GPU devices considered in this work. In Sect. 4 we show and comment on the the results. Section 5 encloses this paper with concluding remarks.

2   Background

2.1   Devito

Devito is a tool to solve partial differential equations (PDEs) which is a mathematical tool to describe numerous problems that are heavily constrained by physical laws. Some areas in which it has uses are: geophysics, earth and climate science, material science, chemical and mechanical engineering, medical imaging and physics, even in economics. It uses a domain specific language (DSL) as method to simplify development process for the user, and also solve it using finite difference method that is a numerical method.

Devito automatically generates C/C++ code with different levels of optimization for finite-difference schemes from a symbolic Python representation of partial differential equations, with a performance that is competitive with, and often better than, hand-optimized implementations. To illustrate this, consider the Eq. 1 that is a wave propagation with a source injection and its initial conditions.

$$
\begin{cases}
m(x,y,z)\dfrac{d^2u(x,y,z,t)}{dt^2} - \nabla^2 u(x,y,z,t) = q_s, \\
\qquad\qquad\qquad u(x,y,z,0) = 0, \\
\qquad\qquad\qquad \dfrac{du(x,t)}{dt}\Big|_{t=0} = 0,
\end{cases}
\tag{1}
$$

where:

- $m(x,y,z) = \frac{1}{c(x,y,z)^2}$, represents the square slowness model as a function of the three space coordinates (x,y,z);
- $u(t,x,y,z)$, is the spatially varying acoustic wave field in each time step;
- q_s, is the source term representing the source injection;

As Devito uses Sympy library for an easier symbolic representation, writing this equation is as simple as shown in Algorithm 1.1 , which represents a small part of the solution.

```
from sympy import Eq, solve                                        1
from devito import Function, TimeFunction, Grid                    2
                                                                   3
grid = Grid(shape=(size, size))                                    4
u = TimeFunction(name='u', grid=grid, space_order=6,               5
     time_order=2)
m = Function(name='m', grid=grid)                                  6
                                                                   7
#Symbolic representation                                           8
eqn = Eq(m * u.dt2 - u.laplace)                                    9
                                                                   10
stencil = solve(eqn, u.forward)[0]                                 11
```

Algorithm 1.1. Example of Devito declaring an acoustic wave propagation

Devito performs just-in-time compilation and execution, so the domain expert can focus on the mathematical formulations, instead of writing low-level code. Following the example, the C code automatically generated from Devito using Python can be seen in Algorithm 1.2 .

```
for (int x = x_m; x <= x_M; x += 1)                                    1
{                                                                      2
    #pragma omp simd aligned (damp,m,u:32)                            3
    for (int y = y_m; y <= y_M; y += 1)                               4
    {                                                                 5
        float  r0 = 1.0F*dt*m[x+2][y+2][z+2] +                        6
                    5.0e-1F*(dt*dt)*damp[x+1][y+1][z+1];              7
                                                                      8
    u[t1][x+2][y+2][z+2] =                                            9
        1.0F*(-dt*m[x+2][y+2][z+2]*u[t2][x+2][y+2][z+2]/r0 +         10
            (dt*dt*dt)*u[t0][x + 1][y + 2][z + 2]/r0 +                11
            (dt*dt*dt)*u[t0][x + 2][y + 1][z + 2]/r0 +                12
            (dt*dt*dt)*u[t0][x + 2][y + 2][z + 1]/r0 +                13
            (dt*dt*dt)*u[t0][x + 2][y + 2][z + 3]/r0 +                14
            (dt*dt*dt)*u[t0][x + 2][y + 3][z + 2]/r0 +                15
            (dt*dt*dt)*u[t0][x + 3][y + 2][z + 2]/r0) +               16
        2.0F*dt*m[x+2][y+2][z+2]*u[t0][x+2][y+2][z+2]/r0 +           17
        5.0e-1F*(dt*dt)*damp[x+1][y+1][z+1]*u[t2][x+2][y+2][z+2]/r0 - 18
        6.0F*dt*dt*dt*u[t0][x + 2][y + 2][z + 2]/r0;                  19
    }                                                                20
}                                                                    21
```

Algorithm 1.2. Devito auto generated C code using core backend. Represents the propagation update for stencil of space order 2.

The user doesn't even need to see this code, it will all be handled by Devito's compiler and the result from its execution will be available for the developer. Programming the Algorithm 1.1 is much simpler and maintainable than Algorithm 1.2 and it enables the code execution in different architectures using the same python code.

In this work, we leveraged Devito to support the OPS library (described in Subsect. 2.2) for computing stencil kernels in a GPU environment using the CUDA parallel computing platform.

2.2   OPS

OPS provides high-level code abstraction aimed at multi-block structured grid computations. It can be embedded in C/C++ and its API provides a basic structure for grid computations such as: blocks, datasets defined on these blocks representing constants and state variables, and parallel loops across a block, accessing data defined on the grid points. Which are used to deliver code for different parallel architectures: MPI, OpenMP, OpenACC, CUDA and OpenCL.

The diagram in Fig. 1 shows the traditional work flow of OPS programs: starting from the desired structured mesh application then programming the C/C++ algorithm using OPS API, compiling and linking it with OPS libraries and executing the desired platform.

OPS and Devito integration enables automatic code generation for GPU architectures from a high level representation.

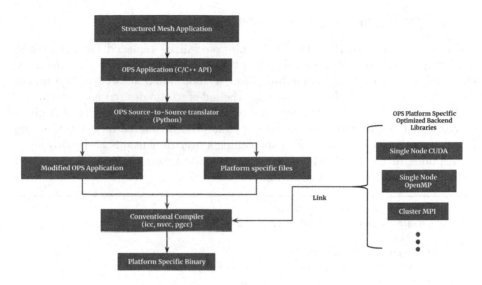

Fig. 1. OPS traditional work flow

2.3   Devito-OPS Integration

To accomplish Devito and OPS integration we need to understand the process Devito uses to generate C/C++ code. Devito generates an intermediate representation to perform a sequence of operations to the expressions and iterations, this includes:

- Equations lowering;
- Local analysis;
- Clustering;
- Symbolic optimization;
- Iteration/expression tree (IET) construction;
- Synthesis;
- Operator specialization through backends;

the last step is where Devito will specialize data types aiming an interested API, which is OPS in this research. Devito with OPS backend share all the compilation pipeline until the specialization.

In this section, we stress seven (i–vii) essential building blocks required to accomplish our prototype solution.

The integration starts with generating *OPS Expression*'s (i), which are expressions translated into OPS syntax. An expression that initially is represented in C/C++ language as

```
u[t+1][x][y] = u[t][x][y] + 1
```

has an OPS representation syntax given by:

```
ut10[OPS_ACC0(0,0)] = ut00[OPS_ACC1(0,0)] + 1
```

The array access u in the first representation will be replaced for ut10 when indicating a one position forward in the time dimension, and replaced for ut00 when accessing the current time dimension. The term OPS_ACC#(0,0) is a macro that OPS syntax uses when translating the index to the desired architecture.

Producing this transformation in Devito requires that the parts of a given expression are separated into nodes. For example, an *Indexed* object containing the indices that corresponds to displacements over dimensions at Devito level, corresponds to C-arrays. The Algorithm 1.3 illustrates the recursive method used to transform Devito expressions.

```
def make_ops_ast(expr, nfops):                                    1
    if expr.is_Symbol or expr.is_Number:                          2
        return expr                                               3
    elif expr.is_Indexed:                                         4
        return nfops.new_ops_arg(expr)                            5
    else:                                                         6
        return expr.func(*[make_ops_ast(i, nfops) for i in       7
    expr.args])
```

Algorithm 1.3. Method to evaluate the given expression and translate to OPS syntax

We are interested in transforming expressions from offloadable loops. These expressions can be parallelized into a device code that will efficiently get executed by GPU architectures. Parallelizable expressions of the same nest can be grouped inside an outlined function that we call *OPS User Kernel* (ii), called by *ops_par_loop* (iii) in the OPS API syntax. The *iteration range* defines the range in which a *OPS User Kernel* will operate over the mesh. It is described as an integer array that defines the boundaries in each spatial dimension. The mesh that will be written into or read from throughout the kernel operation is the dataset that is represented by *ops_dat* (iv) in the OPS API syntax.

Others API calls needed to generate a compilable OPS code ultimately are:

(v) *ops_init* and *ops_end* are calls that will mark the beginning and ending of OPS syntax usage. All OPS declarations must be located between these two calls.
(vi) *ops_block* is used to group datasets together.
(vii) *ops_partition* triggers a multi-block partitioning across a distributed memory set of processes.

The diagram in Fig. 2 represents an overview of the Devito and OPS integration.

The main contribution of this work is a prototype solution that will automatically generate kernel code for a GPU environment. This code can be coupled in a manually generated C code, that is capable of calling this generated kernels. In Sect. 5 we discuss in future works how to fully generate the host code.

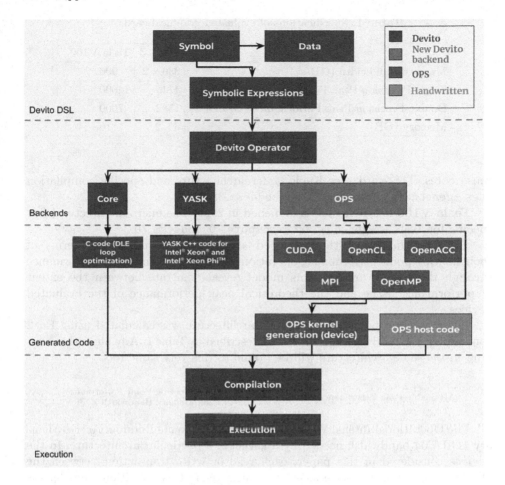

Fig. 2. Diagram of Devito and OPS integration

3 Experiment

3.1 Acoustic Wave Propagation

The current investigation involved generating isotropic 3D wave propagation stencil kernels in an automatic fashion for two NVIDIA architectures and analyzing the performance of the generated algorithms by the roofline model [13]. Kepler and Volta were selected as target GPU architectures, with specifications summarized in Table 1. They use CUDA cores, which is compatible with the syntax supported by the OPS programming interface. Executable artifacts were produced by *NVCC* compiler with flags -Xcompiler=''-std=c99'' -O3, altogether with specific micro architectural flag depending on the specific architecture.

GTX Titan Z is a graphics card launched in 2014. It combines two graphics processors for increased performance, although here we only consider one of

Table 1. Specifications of evaluated graphical cards.

	Titan Z	Tesla V100
Memory Bandwidth (GB/s)	336×2	900
Single Precision Peak Performance (GFLOPS)	4746	14000
Double Precision Peak Performance (GFLOPS)	1582	7000
Memory (GB)	6×2	16

those cores. This card uses Kepler microarchitecture and specific compilation flags `-gencode arch=compute_35, code=sm_35`.

Tesla V100 is a PCIe 16GB launched in 2017. The micro architectural flag specific for Tesla is `-gencode arch=compute_70,code=sm_70`.

The performance of the produced solutions was analyzed in terms of their floating-point performance, operational intensity and memory performance through the roofline model. This model reveals the rate between the extent of performance usage and the theoretical peak performance of the evaluated devices.

The maximum performance of each architecture was calculated using Eq. 2 considering the hardware specifications described in Table 1. Any algorithm running in the same architecture will be bound to this very same roof.

$$\text{Attainable Peak Performance[GFLOP/s]} = \min \begin{cases} \text{Peak Floating-Point Performance} \\ \text{Peak Memory Bandwidth x OI} \end{cases} \quad (2)$$

The Operational Intensity (OI) measures the Dynamic Random Access Memory (DRAM) bandwidth needed by a kernel in a particular architecture. In the devices considered in this paper, each read or write transaction between the DRAM and the caches have a 32 bytes size. Using this definition, the Eq. 3 is used to determine the OI.

$$\text{OI}[FLOP/Byte] = \frac{\#\text{Single Precision Floating-Point Operations}}{(\#\text{Memory Transactions}) * 32} \quad (3)$$

A kernel performance measures the number of floating-point operations per second. Performance can be directly calculated using Eq. 4.

$$\text{Performance}[FLOP/s] = \frac{\#\text{Single Precision Floating-Point Operations}}{\text{Kernel Execution Time}} \quad (4)$$

4   Results

Data obtained in previous studies indicated that Devito is able to efficiently utilise Intel architectures[1] with a high degree of efficiency, while maintaining the ability to increase accuracy by switching to higher order stencil discretization

---

[1] Intel® Xeon® E5-2690v2 with 10 physical cores, and Intel® Xeon® Phi™ accelerator card.

dynamically [8]. Luporini et al. show that remarkable speed-ups from 3x up to 4x can be attainable for those architectures on scenarios with what they call "aggressive" optimizations to avoid redundant computation over 3D grids with space order discretization levels varying from 4 to 16. In our study, we measure the performance of a new backend for Devito on the NVIDIA® architectures GTX Titan Z™ and Tesla V100™ considering scenarios with no symbolic optimizations (basic DSE), and with an aggressive symbolic optimization implemented by Devito (aggressive DSE). An isotropic acoustic wave propagation model with absorbing boundaries as described by Eq. 1 is utilized.

In this study, we measured the rate between attainable performance and the peak machine performance according to specifications, for both the considered devices. We take into account the roofline model described in Sect. 3 to evaluate how efficiently the generated algorithms utilize the GPU for varying space order levels of the generated propagation stencil kernels. For each of the considered space orders we profiled the propagation kernel using *nvprof*[2] in order to obtain: (a) the number of single precision floating-point operations, (b) the number of memory transactions, and (c) the kernel execution time.

For each space order, the produced stencil kernel ran five times for 30.000 time steps. Table 2 shows the values collected for GTX Titan Z and Table 3 shows the values collected for V100, for basic and aggressive symbolic optimization levels, and space orders levels of 8, 12, 16 and 24. The values for OI are obtained according to Eq. 3 whereas the values for performance are obtained according to Eq. 4.

Figures 3 and 4 display the OI (FLOP/Byte) versus performance (GFLOP/s) from the values found in Tables 2 and 3, respectively. Each of the points in those plots are characterized by two values: (i) the space order, and (ii) the percentage from the device peak performance. The performance bounds were obtained from vendor peak performance specifications in Table 1.

Table 2. Data collected from profiling propagation kernel in GTX Titan Z using *nvprof*.

Space order	FP 32 count	Memory operations	Execution time (s)	OI (Flop/Byte)	Performance (GFlop/s)
Basic optimization					
8	1,450,112,268	22,722,746	553.92	1.99	78.54
12	2,013,392,118	28,068,109	854.39	2.24	70.70
16	2,375,372,938	29,871,728	907.72	2.48	78.51
24	2,898,342,158	33,348,001	1,150.01	2.71	75.61
Aggressive optimization					
8	641,887,345	22,637,047	135,73	0.89	141.88
12	760,134,906	27,737,029	179.15	0.86	127.29
16	842,931,505	29,704,549	180,55	0.89	140.06
24	929,761,776	32,926,331	219,76	0.88	126.92

---

[2] The *nvprof* profiling tool enables you to collect and view profiling data from the command-line, and is present in the NVIDIA® CUDA® Toolkit.

Table 3. Data collected from profiling propagation kernel in V100 using *nvprof*.

Space order	FP 32 count	Memory operations	Execution time (s)	OI (Flop/Byte)	Performance (GFlop/s)
Basic optimization					
8	1,450,996,129	9,245,436	553.92	**4.90**	**693.77**
12	2,013,446,796	9,112,947	854.39	**6.90**	**740.48**
16	2,375,384,531	7,722,032	907.72	**9.61**	**816.86**
24	2,898,311,328	11,862,338	1,150.01	**7.64**	**719.60**
Aggressive optimization					
8	641,882,304	9,256,098	15.31	**2.18**	**1258.16**
12	760,133,342	9,289,727	20.37	**2.56**	**1119.42**
16	842,930,745	8,026,245	20.21	**3.28**	**1251.51**
24	929,760,267	11,670,483	18.48	**2.49**	**1509.60**

Considering the results for GTX Titan Z in Fig. 3, we can see that the operation intensity increases with higher space order levels for basic optimization, whereas the operation intensity are nearly the same for an aggressive optimization.

Considering the results for GTX Titan Z in Fig. 3, we can see that for the basic optimization, the operation intensity increase with higher the space orders, while using the aggressive optimization they almost did not differ. One can also see that aggressive optimization produces code with better performance than with basic optimization in all scenarios, enabling approximately 24% of peak performance to be achieved versus 6% for the basic scenario.

Executing the experiment in the V100 graphic card, we achieve better performance, as illustrated in Fig. 4. Performance gains using aggressive optimization

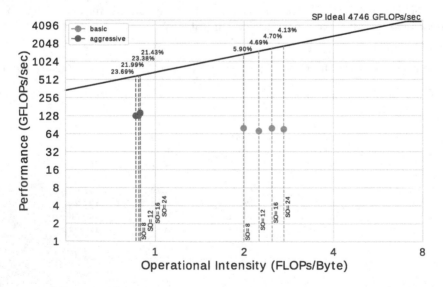

Fig. 3. Roofline chart for GTX Titan Z GPU. Propagation field with 256^3 points and space order values of 8, 12, 16 and 24 using Devito optimizations aggressive and basic.

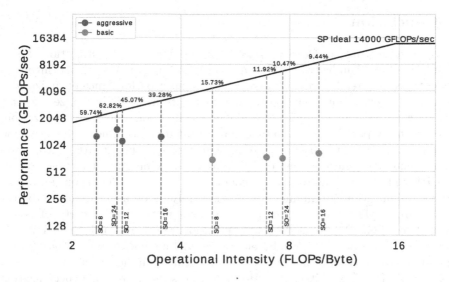

Fig. 4. Roofline chart for V100 GPU. Propagation field with 256^3 points and space order values of 8, 12, 16 and 24 using Devito optimizations aggressive and basic.

goes from approximately 16% to 63%. It is worth noting that there is a decrease in OI for so 24, this result was not expected as there are more operations in higher so. Looking at the data from Table 3 we can verify that the amount of data transferred in so 24 is 45% higher than the so 16, while the difference in data transfer in the other scenarios was at most 15%. We can thus conclude that the amount of data needed for so 24 is much larger than expected, which indicates that memory accesses in GPU are not coalesced for this case.

In both GTX Titan Z and V100 tests, the aggressive optimization led to three times higher peak performance than the basic optimization. The results from the aggressive optimization corroborate results presented in a related experiment, Luporini et al. [8] that enabled Devito to generate code for the YASK framework and obtained peak performances going from 53% to 63% for Intel® Xeon® and Intel® Xeon® Phi™ architectures.

Another analysis possible due to the Roofline model is for future optimizations. All the points are located before the ridge point at both the roofline plots in Figs. 3 and 4, which indicates that all the tested cases are memory bounded instead of compute bounded. This means that the produced codes should get greater benefits from optimizations targeted to perform memory exchanges more efficiently than from optimizations focused on increasing throughput. Therefore, enabling FLOPs reduction and data locality such as common sub-expression elimination, factorization, and code motion should be considered as a priority for future works.

5   Conclusion

The open-source project Devito® [7,8] has been attracting the attention of academic [10,14] and industrial [15] community. As a DSL for seismic inversion applications, it already provides a set of automated performance optimizations during code generation that allow user applications to fully utilize the target hardware without changing the model specification, such as vectorization, shared-memory parallelism, loop blocking, auto-tuning, common sub-expression elimination (CSE), cross-iteration redundancy elimination (CIRE), expression hoisting and factorization. Devito also supports distributed-memory parallelism via MPI, and several halo-exchange schemes are available. Classic optimizations such as computation-communication overlap (relying on asynchronous progress engine) are implemented. It can be integrated with a wide variety of methods (e.g. L-BFGS-B[3]) for solving minimization problems, such as in FWI. It can perform FWI on distributed memory parallel computers with Dask. It also implements support for standard CPU architectures, and for Intel® Xeon® and Intel® Xeon Phi™ architectures. However, the support to code specialization for GPU architectures is yet a work in progress.

In this study, we created an extension of Devito to enable code generation for the OPS syntax. We also evaluated the new backend in terms of processor performance concerning off-chip memory traffic for varying space order discretization levels on the NVIDIA® devices GTX Titan Z™ and Tesla V100™. We found that the implemented backend achieves up to 62.82% of the peak performance on V100, which is consistent with results from work using Devito to generate YASK framework code [8]. We also observed that isotropic 3D wave propagation stencil kernels generated with aggressive symbolic optimizations have three times higher peak performance than with no symbolic optimizations. This study, therefore, indicates that it is possible to use the available power of GPU architectures in Devito for solving seismic inversion algorithms.

This work is the first study to our knowledge that investigates a seamless coupling between Devito and OPS compilers. However, some limitations are worth noting as the capability of the implemented solution still only covers source injection and forward propagation. The forward model is the basis for further implementations of inversion processes using Devito operators. Yet, in order to enable a seamless source-to-source translation of FWI algorithms, future work should provide support for receiver interpolation and backward propagation as well. Moreover, the automatic generation of host code, responsible for calling the device code that will execute in GPU, is currently in implementation. Finally, to complete Devito integration, it is necessary to automatically translate, compile, and execute the GPU code through the Devito pipeline and return the result from the execution to the Devito workflow.

---

[3] Large-scale Bound-constrained Optimization.

References

1. Cárdenas, A.F., Karplus, W.J.: PDEL-a language for partial differential equations. Commun. ACM **13**(3), 184–191 (1970). https://doi.org/10.1145/362052.362059
2. Cook Jr., G.O.: ALPAL: a tool for the development of large-scale simulation codes, Lawrence Livermore National Lab., C.U. (1988)
3. van Engelen, R., Wolters, L., Cats, G.: CTADEL: a generator of multi-platform high performance codes for PDE-based scientific applications. In: Proceedings of the 10th International Conference on Supercomputing - ICS 1996, pp. 86–93. ACM Press, New York (2003). https://doi.org/10.1145/237578.237589
4. Hawick, K., Playne, D.P.: Simulation software generation using a domain-specific language for partial differential field equations. In: Proceedings of the International Conference on Software Engineering Research and Practice (SERP). The Steering Committee of The World Congress in Computer Science, Computer Engineering and Applied Computing (WorldComp), p. 7(2013). ProQuest document ID: 1491419516
5. Henretty, T., Veras, R., Franchetti, F., Pouchet, L.N., Ramanujam, J., Sadayappan, P.: A stencil compiler for short-vector SIMD architectures. In: Proceedings of the 27th International ACM Conference on International Conference on Supercomputing - ICS 2013. p. 13. ACM Press, New York (2013). https://doi.org/10.1145/2464996.2467268
6. Logg, A., Olgaard, K.B., Rognes, M.E., Wells, G.N.: FFC: the FEniCS Form Compiler. In: Logg, A., Mardal, K.A., Wells, G.N. (eds.) Automated Solution of Differential Equations by the Finite Element Method, Lecture Notes in Computational Science and Engineering, Vol. 84, Chap. 11. Springer (2012). https://doi.org/10.1007/978-3-642-23099-8_11
7. Louboutin, M., et al.: Devito (v3.1.0): an embedded domain-specific language for finite differences and geophysical exploration. Geosci. Model Dev. **12**(3), 1165–1187 (2019). https://doi.org/10.5194/gmd-12-1165-2019
8. Luporini, F.,et al.: Architecture and performance of Devito, a system for automated stencil computation, July 2018
9. Membarth, R., Hannig, F., Teich, J., Kostler, H.: Towards domain-specific computing for stencil codes in HPC. In: Proceedings - 2012 SC Companion: High Performance Computing, Networking Storage and Analysis, SCC 2012, pp. 1133–1138. IEEE, November 2012. https://doi.org/10.1109/SC.Companion.2012.136
10. Mojica, O.F., Kukreja, N.: Towards automatically building starting models for full-waveform inversion using global optimization methods: a PSO approach via DEAP + Devito, May 2019
11. Rathgeber, F., et al.: Firedrake: automating the finite element method by composing abstractions, January 2015. https://doi.org/10.1145/2998441
12. Reguly, I.Z., Mudalige, G.R., Giles, M.B., Curran, D., McIntosh-Smith, S.: The OPS domain specific abstraction for multi-block structured grid computations. In: Proceedings of WOLFHPC 2014: 4th International Workshop on Domain-Specific Languages and High-Level Frameworks for High Performance Computing - Held in Conjunction with SC 2014: The International Conference for High Performance Computing, Networking, Storage, pp. 58–67 (2014). https://doi.org/10.1109/WOLFHPC.2014.7
13. Williams, S., Waterman, A., Patterson, D.: Roofline. Commun. ACM **52**(4), 65 (2009). https://doi.org/10.1145/1498765.1498785

14. Witte, P.A., et al.: A large-scale framework for symbolic implementations of seismic inversion algorithms in Julia. Geophysics **84**(3), F57–F71 (2019). https://doi.org/10.1190/geo2018-0174.1
15. Yount, C., Tobin, J., Breuer, A., Duran, A.: YASK - yet another stencil kernel: a framework for HPC stencil code-generation and tuning. In: 2016 Sixth International Workshop on Domain-Specific Languages and High-Level Frameworks for High Performance Computing (WOLFHPC), pp. 30–39. IEEE, November 2017. https://doi.org/10.1109/WOLFHPC.2016.08
16. Zhang, Y., Mueller, F.: Auto-generation and auto-tuning of 3D stencil codes on GPU clusters. In: Proceedings of the Tenth International Symposium on Code Generation and Optimization - CHO 2012, p. 155. ACM Press, New York (2012). https://doi.org/10.1145/2259016.2259037

Special Track on Bioinspired Processing (BIP): Neural and Evolutionary Approaches

Adding Probabilistic Certainty to Improve Performance of Convolutional Neural Networks

Maria Pantoja[1]([⊠]) [iD], Robert Kleinhenz[2], and Drazen Fabris[2]

[1] California Polytechnic State University, San Luis Obispo, USA
mpanto01@calpoly.edu
[2] Santa Clara University, Santa Clara, USA
{rkleinhenz,dfabris}@scu.edu

Abstract. Convolutional Neural Networks (CNN) are successfully being used for different computer vision tasks, from labeling cancerous cells in medical images to identify traffic signals in self-driving cars. Supervised CNN classify raw input data according to the patterns learned from an input training set. This set is typically obtained by manually labeling the image which can lead to uncertainties in the data. The level of expertise of the professionals labeling the training set sometimes varies widely or some of the images used may not be clear and are difficult to label. This leads to data sets with pictures labeled differently by different experts or uncertainty in the experts opinions.

These kind of errors on the training set do happen more frequently when the CNN task is to classify numerous labels with similar characteristics. For example, when labeling damages on civil infrastructures after an earthquake, there are more than two hundred different labels with some of them similar to each other and the experts labeling the sets frequently disagree on which one to use. In this paper, we use probabilistic analysis to evaluate both the likelihood of the labels in the training set (produced by the CNN) and the likelihood's uncertainty. The uncertainty in the likelihood is represented by a probability density and represents a spreading (as it were) of the CNN's likelihood estimate over a range of values dictated by the uncertainty in the truth set.

Keywords: Neural Networks · Belief network · Density function

1 Introduction

CNN have been hugely successful in many classification tasks [14]. Still CNN can easily be fooled [4] giving high confidence predictions for unrecognizable images. Traditional CNN are trained to produce specific outcomes by optimizing a set of tunable parameters, the optimization is typically carried out using some form of gradient descent. For example a CNN can be trained with labeled images of dogs and spiders. During the inference (deployment after training) the CNN

© Springer Nature Switzerland AG 2020
J. L. Crespo-Mariño and E. Meneses-Rojas (Eds.): CARLA 2019, CCIS 1087, pp. 247–261, 2020.
https://doi.org/10.1007/978-3-030-41005-6_17

will be able to automatically label new images of dogs and spiders. But what happen if during inference we feed the network the image of a cow? It will classify the image as a dog with high probability, since a CNN output predictive probability is just the probability with respect to the other labels, and a dog label is more probable then a spider. The CNN output predictive probabilities are often erroneously interpreted as model confidence. A CNN can be uncertain in its prediction even with a high softmax output. This type of problem will happen when the assumption of having distinct classes is not met for example when out of distribution test data (like the dog, spider example), incomplete data (dog is partially hidden), trying to learn from small amounts of data, and other cases. This uncertainty is very important and in some cases it can cost lives. For example, the Tesla incident [3] where a CNN classified a white truck in front of the self-driving car with a very clear path to advance and crushed the car killing the pilot. Some CNN have also been tricked about what kind of road sign they are seeing [4].

In this paper, we propose a method to evaluate the uncertainty for each of the labels the experts tags and use this uncertainty estimation on the CNN as an output. This way if a model returns a result with high uncertainty we can decide to pass the input to a human for classification, instead of returning a completely wrong and potentially dangerous label. In Fig. 1 we show a real example of two different experts labeling the same image, it can be seen that there are clear differences.

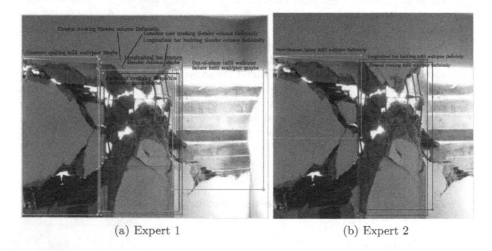

(a) Expert 1   (b) Expert 2

Fig. 1. Two experts labeling same image

1.1   Previous Work

There are several recent papers on how to capture the model uncertainty a posteriori by using Bayesian Neural Networks. *Sun et al.* [4] uses Bayesian learning to quantify posterior uncertainty on deep neural networks (DNN) models parameters; considering the matrix variate Gaussian to develop a scalable Bayesian outline inference algorithm by adopting a probabilistic backpropagation framework and stochastic gradient Markov Chain Monte Carlo (MCMC) on synthetic data. *Kendall and Gal* [5] analyzes the different kinds of uncertainty in the model and focus its work on the importance of adding aleatoric uncertainty (cant be explained away given enough data) to the model; proposes the use of Bayesian Neural Network for computer vision tasks improving 1–3% the model performance. *Gal and Ghahramani* [6] analyzes Neural Networks (NN) model certainty; in the paper they prove that the dropout layer can be used as a Bayesian approximation of a well known probabilistic model, the Gaussian process. The paper uses these outputs to determine the model uncertainty and propose to pass the input to a human for classification if the output has high uncertainty. *Deceus* [7] proposes the use of belief functions to represent imprecise and or uncertain knowledge of class labels (soft labels) and proposed changes to common clustering algorithms to adapt to these types of labels, presenting result on synthetic data. *Kendall et al.* [15] presents a version of the segmentation algorithm SegNet that also outputs the uncertainty of the segmentation regions is presented, and is used on segmentation of street scenes. The authors provide as an output the uncertainty on each frame for the segmentation enabling users to decide on actions if the uncertainty is high. In general Bayesian Neural Networks (BNN) do not have fixed weights for the neurons but a distribution, quantifying the uncertainty in a NN which allows to find images for which the net is unsure of their prediction, but several experiments with BNN [16] show that they also provide a high level of certainty even for out of distribution test data, and they do require long training times, concluding that a Bayesian neural network with Monte Carlo dropout is too crude of an approximation to accurately capture the uncertainty information when dealing with image data. In our paper we approach the problem in a different way than a BNN and instead of adding a probability distribution to the weights of the neurons we will ask the individual expert for their certainty in labeling the images. Then through statistical and probabilistic analysis using belief networks [9–11] we spread the CNN's predicti ve output over a range of values reflecting the expert's own self-certainty.

1.2   Structure of Paper

The remainder of this paper is organized as follows. Section 2 explains how to create a probability density function representing the certitude of an expert's assessment of a (label, image) pair. It may occur that many experts provide an evaluation of the same (label, image) pair. Section 3 explains how these multiple evaluations may be combined into a single (label, image) pair. This combination represents a consensus opinion of the (label, image) certitude by averaging, as it were, the evaluations of all expert opinions. These preparations are made in support of using a belief network model (described in Sect. 4) to get a final quality assessment of both the CNN conclusions and the quality of the expert. Finally, Sects. 5 and 6 presents the simulations results, the conclusions, and future work, respectively.

2   Creating a Probability Distribution Function for Each Expert

Each of the N photographs is assessed by an expert. During this assessment, experts will assign some number of labels to a photograph i. For example, these labels indicate the severity, type, and location of damage exhibited by the structure in the photograph.

2.1   Basic Assignment

Begin by defining the random variable V to be the conditional probability that expert E assigns label L to a given photograph Φ.

$$V = V_{L|E,\Phi} = P[\text{label } L \text{ is assigned by } E \text{ to photograph } \Phi].$$

The variable V is taken to be a continuous random variable whose value is affected by the intrinsic quality of the expert, the focus of the expert at the time of the assessment, the clarity of the photograph, and so on. A conditional probability density function for V is constructed based on two metrics:

1. the expert's self assessment of the likelihood of the assignment of a particular label to the given photograph (call this V^*), and
2. the expert's success percentage compared to the truth source (call this $\tilde{p}$).

Symbolically, the conditional density function is denoted by

$$f_{L|E,\Phi}(x) \qquad 0 \le x \le 1$$

and represents a measure of the certainty (x) attached to each (label, expert, image) association. That is, the probability that the expert's assessment of label likelihood (for a given photograph) falls below x may be measured by

$$P[L \le x \mid E, \Phi] = \int_0^x f_{L|E,\Phi}(y)\,dy \qquad 0 \le x \le 1.$$

A common tactic [9–11] is to adopt a triangularly shaped function as a measure of this density (as shown in Fig. 2). We explain how to obtain these density distributions next.

2.2   Weighted Self-Assessment: V^* Component

As part of the assessment process, each reviewer is required to supply a self-assessment of their certitude (denoted by V^*). According to [9], a self-assessment using familiar qualifiers provides a good mechanism for self-evaluation. Since we want a probabilistic schema we assign values in the range $[0, 1]$ to each qualitative descriptors as follows:

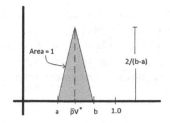

Fig. 2. Density function shape

Definitely: 0.92±   Almost Certain: 0.64±   Probably: 0.36±   Maybe: 0.08±

The descriptors were chosen as a qualitative mechanism through which the experts express their own belief about the certainty in their evaluations. The probabilities attached to each descriptor are the values assigned to V^* – chosen to have a uniform spacing (with some margin on each end) over the interval $[0, 1]$.

To gather this data the GUI shown in Fig. 3 is used. As can be seen the expert who is labeling the data selects the location, damage and the certainty concerting the label assignment.

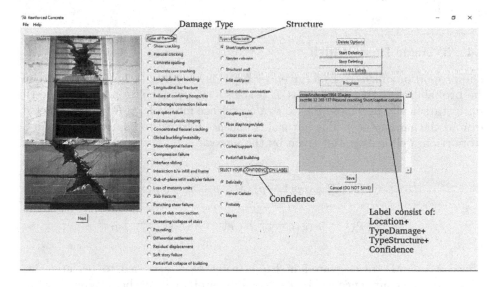

Fig. 3. GUI for gathering expert certainty per label-image

2.3 Weighted Self Assessment: $\tilde{p}$ Component

The expert E labels a group of images and creates for each image a set of (label, image) pairs; note that each image may have one or more labels attached to it.

For each image (call it Φ), let e_Φ, t_Φ, c_Φ represent, respectively, the total number of labels identified by the expert, the total number of labels identified by the truth set, and the total number of labels common to both the expert and the truth set. The quality rating for that expert vis-a-vis a single image Φ is given by the ratio (r) of agreements to the total number of identifications (agreements plus disagreements):

$$r = \frac{c_\Phi}{c_\Phi + (e_\Phi - c_\Phi) + (t_\Phi - c_\Phi)} = \frac{c_\Phi}{e_\Phi + t_\Phi - c_\Phi}.$$

For the complete collection of photos evaluated by expert E, the success percentage is computed by forming the ratio of the total number of agreements found over all photographs examined by the expert to the total number of identifications (agreements, omissions, and additions) made by the expert. This ratio is the success proportion, $\tilde{p}$, and is given by

$$\tilde{p} = \frac{S}{M} = \frac{\sum_\Phi c_\Phi}{\sum_\Phi (e_\Phi + t_\Phi - c_\Phi)}, \tag{1}$$

where $S = \sum_\Phi c_\Phi$ is the total number of agreements between E and the truth set and $M = \sum_\Phi (e_\Phi + t_\Phi - c_\Phi)$ is the total number of identifications made by E and the truth set (the sums are taken over all images examined by the expert E).

2.4   Triangle Base Width

The proportion of successes $\tilde{p}$ (given by Eq. 1) is known to be a good estimate of the probability, p, that the expert E assigns a correct label to a photo. To estimate statistically how close $\tilde{p}$ is to p, a confidence interval, $[L, R]$, is constructed around the parameter p. The natural confidence interval to be used is that for a proportion: well-known and given by the interval

$$[L, R] = [\, \tilde{p} - z_{\alpha/2}\sqrt{\tilde{p}(1 - \tilde{p})/M} \, , \, \tilde{p} + z_{\alpha/2}\sqrt{\tilde{p}(1 - \tilde{p})/M} \,]$$
$$= [\, \tilde{p}(1 - z_{\alpha/2}\sqrt{\frac{1 - \tilde{p}}{\tilde{p}M}}) \, , \, \tilde{p}(1 + z_{\alpha/2}\sqrt{\frac{1 - \tilde{p}}{\tilde{p}M}}) \,],$$

where $\tilde{p}$ and M are as stated in Eq. 1 (note: M is assumed to be large, i.e. $M \geq 30$). The confidence level, $(1 - \alpha)$, is the probability to be assigned (in this analysis) to the truth of the statement: $L \leq p \leq R$.

The base of the triangular distribution function for V is found by scaling the interval $[L, R]$ by V^* (the expert's self-assessment). That is the endpoints of the base of the triangle are given by $a = V^*L$ and $b = V^*R$. It is also desired to keep

$0 < V^*L < V^*R < 1$. Therefore, set $a = 0$ if $V^*L < 0$, set $b = 1$ if $1 < V^*R$. In summary:

$$a = \max \; (0, V^*\tilde{p}(1 - z_{\alpha/2}\sqrt{\frac{1-\tilde{p}}{\tilde{p}M}}))$$

$$b = \min \; (1, V^*\tilde{p}(1 + z_{\alpha/2}\sqrt{\frac{1-\tilde{p}}{\tilde{p}M}})) \; .$$

2.5   Triangle Height

To make this triangular function into a density function, the area under this triangle must equal one. Therefore, the height of the triangle must be $2/(b-a)$. Outside of this triangle the density function is zero.

2.6   Example

Table 1 presents a brief example of how to evaluate the quality of two expert's assignment of labels to two photos. The label name indicates a damage/structure type and its location, for example: "shear flexture Short column 4 100 190 300". This indicates that different damages names with same locations will be consider different labels. The table represents a case in which two experts have evaluated two photographs and attached up to three labels (called A, B, and C) to each image. A corresponding ground truth is also given for these two images.

Table 1. Representative classification

Expert 1	Expert 2	Ground Truth
Photo 1	Photo 1	Photo 1
label A Maybe: 0.08	label A Definitely: 0.92	label A Definitely: 0.92
label B Certain: 0.64	label B Certain: 0.64	label B Definitely: 0.92
label C Maybe: 0.08		
$e_\Phi = 3$ $c_\Phi = 2$	$e_\Phi = 2$ $c_\Phi = 2$	$t_\Phi = 2$
$M_{1,1} = e_\Phi + t_\Phi - c_\Phi = 3$	$M_{2,1} = e_\Phi + t_\Phi - c_\Phi = 2$	
Photo 2	Photo 2	Photo 2
label D Certain:0.64	label D Definitely:0.92	label D Definitely:0.92
$e_\Phi = 1$ $c_\Phi = 1$	$e_\Phi = 1$ $c_\Phi = 1$	$t_\Phi = 1$
$M_{1,2} = 1$	$M_{2,2} = 1$	
$\tilde{p}_1 = 3/4$	$\tilde{p}_2 = 1$	

Out of these values it is now possible to determine the shape of each of the triangular certainty functions, a summary of the calculation can be found in

Table 2. In Sect. 3.1 the certainty functions are denoted by $f_{L|E,\Phi}(l)$. To ease the notation here this form will be abbreviated to $f_{l,e,\phi}$ corresponding to identifiers l:label, ϕ:photograph, and e:expert. Note that for these intervals, a confidence level of 0.05 was assumed.

Table 2. Distribution parameters

(l, e, ϕ)	a = **Left**	$V^*\tilde{p}$ = **Center**	b = **Right**
$(A, 1, 1)$	0.026	0.08	0.094
$(B, 1, 1)$	0.208	0.64	0.751
$(C, 1, 1)$	0.026	0.08	0.094
$(D, 1, 2)$	0.208	0.64	0.751
$(A, 2, 1)$	0.92	0.92	0.92
$(B, 2, 1)$	0.64	0.64	0.64
$(D, 2, 2)$	0.92	0.92	0.92

The certainty functions $f_{l,e,1}$ obtained from the values for photo 1 (stated in Table 2) are represented in Fig. 4. It can be seen that the certainty functions associated with expert 1 are triangular and wider while the certainty functions associated with expert 2 are impulsive. This is due to the fact that expert 1 made several mistakes in assigning labels (compared to the truth set) while expert 2 is not only certain about the labels but has also made correct assignments[1].

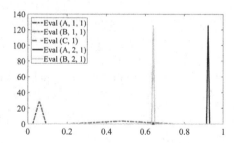

Fig. 4. Experts density function shapes (for Photo 1):$f_{l,e,1}$

3   Combining Multiple (label, image) Expert Evaluations

To model a collection of photos and labels as a belief network, each (label, image) pair is treated as an edge in a directed graph (see Sect. 4). To simplify these

---

[1] At this stage of development, a triangular density function with a very narrow base has been used instead of an impulse.

directed graphs, multiple evaluations of same (label, image) pair by different experts are combined into a single composite evaluation; Fig. 5 shows a graph of this process. Assume that image number s in the truth set (call it Φ_s) has been evaluated independently by K experts each of whom have assigned label L_j to the Φ_s. Assume further that the assignment of images to experts has been done in an unbiased fashion. That is, for example, an expert on structural damage near windows is just as likely to receive a window image as a non-expert.

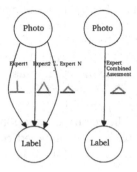

Fig. 5. Combine experts evaluations into one edge

These assumptions yield the following relationship

$$V_{L|\Phi} = P[L_j \,|\, \Phi_s] = \frac{1}{K} \sum_i P[L_j \,|\, E_i, \Phi_s] = \frac{1}{K} \sum_i V_{l_i | F_i, \Phi}.$$

That is, the certitude function for $V_{L|\Phi}$ is the certitude function for the arithmetic average of the variables $V_{L|E_i,\Phi}$. Since the variables $V_{L|E_i,\Phi}$ are assumed to be independent, elementary probability theory provides a way to computing the certitude function for $V_{L|\Phi}$ using two basic equations:

$$f_{aX}(x) = \frac{1}{a} f_X\left(\frac{x}{a}\right)$$
$$f_Y(y) = \left(f_{X_1} \star f_{X_2} \star \ldots \star f_{X_K}\right)(y),$$

where a is a constant, $Y = \sum_i X_i$ is the sum of K independent random variables, and $\star$ represents the convolution operation

$$(f \star g)(x) = \int_{-\infty}^{\infty} f(t)g(x - t)\, dt.$$

In this application, $a = 1/K$ and $X_i = aV_{L|E_i,\Phi}$.

3.1   Example

Continuing with the example in Sect. 2.6, the expert's evaluations yield (label, image) pairs with the following values[2]:

```
(L,E,Φ): label,image(L,Φ), Expert, triangle base: a; V*p̃;    b

(A,1,1): label,image (A,1), Exp1, tri. base: 0.026; 0.06; 0.094
(A,2,1): label,image (A,1), Exp2, tri. base: 0.920; 0.92; 0.920
(B,1,1): label,image (B,1), Exp1, tri. base: 0.208; 0.48; 0.752
(B,2,1): label,image (B,1), Exp2, tri. base: 0.640; 0.64; 0.640
(C,1,1): label,image (C,1), Exp1, tri. base: 0.026; 0.06; 0.094
(D,1,2): label,image (D,2), Exp1, tri. base: 0.208; 0.48; 0.752
(D,2,2): label,image (D,2), Exp2, tri. base: 0.920; 0.92; 0.920
```

Notice that (label, image) pairs $(A, 1)$, $(B, 1)$, and $(D, 2)$ have each been evaluated by experts 1 and 2. The certitude functions for the two evaluations of $(A, 1)$ are convolved together to form a combined certitude function. Note that each expert's certitude function for this (label, image) pair is weighted equally in the convolution.

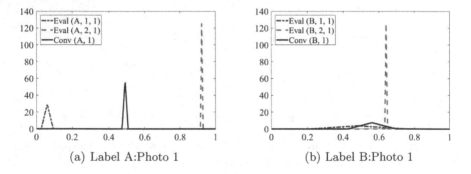

(a) Label A:Photo 1   (b) Label B:Photo 1

Fig. 6. Combined experts 1 and 2 for labels A and B

Figure 6a shows the combined certitude function result for pair $(A, 1)$ as well as the two input certitude functions $(A, 1, 1)$ and $(A, 2, 1)$. The input certitude functions are shown with dashed lines with the combined certitude output represented by a solid line. The Fig. 6b shows the same action applied to combine the two evaluations for (label, image) pair $(B, 1)$. On Fig. 6a, the combined certitude is representative of an average of the two input certitudes – both the expert's evaluations, (as represented by the center location of the triangle base) and quality of the expert (represented by the width of the triangle base) appear to have been averaged. In Fig. 6b, expert 1 has an asymmetric certitude function

---

[2] This is a restatement of Table 2 ordered by photo id.

with a peak over 0.64 while expert 2 is asserting certainty about the evaluation 0.64. Note in this case that the combined certitude still averages the peak values of its inputs (as in Fig. 6a) but has lost the sharpness of expert 2's evaluation while improving the dullness of expert 1's evaluation.

4   Belief Network for Assessing the Uncertainty of the Label

A Belief Network (BN) is a directed graph where each node represents an event, an object, or some similar static item and the directed edges indicate the presence of causality or dependence (see [10]). Consider the belief network shown in Fig. 7. The nodes L_j represent a list of three labels, the nodes Φ_i represent three photographs in the image collection, and Φ represents a new (unseen by any of the experts) image. The directed arrows travelling from the image collection, $\{\Phi_i\}$, to the set of labels, $\{L_j\}$, represent the evaluations done by the experts and the directed arrows going from the given, new image, Φ, to the image collection describe the amount of similarity between the new image and the images in the image collection. Note that the photos Φ_1, Φ_2, Φ_3 are the same images that have been used during the training of the NN.

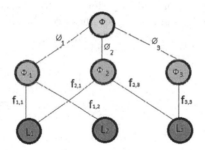

Fig. 7. Example of belief network

A BN (such as the one depicted in Fig. 7) provides a simple way of assigning probabilities and certainty distributions to each of the labels. For a single label, L_j, this equation holds:

$$P[L_j] = \sum_{\Phi_i} P[L_j \mid \Phi_i]\phi_i P[\Phi].$$

Single probabilistic values for the labels L_1, L_2, and L_3 are the outputs from a CNN softmax layer. That is, for example, if the NN output gives $P[L_1] = 0.7, P[L_2] = 0.26$, and $P[L_3] = 0.04$ then it means that the CNN did recognize the existence of label L_1 in the image Φ. The relationships between the values $\phi_i = P[\Phi_i](i = 1, 2, \ldots, I)$ and $l_j = P[L_j](j = 1, 2, \ldots, J)$ are linear:

$$\mathbf{L} = \begin{bmatrix} l_1 \\ l_2 \\ \vdots \\ l_J \end{bmatrix} = \begin{bmatrix} f_{11} & f_{11} & \cdots & f_{1I} \\ f_{21} & f_{21} & \cdots & f_{2I} \\ \vdots & \vdots & \vdots & \vdots \\ f_{J1} & f_{J1} & \cdots & f_{JI} \end{bmatrix} \begin{bmatrix} \phi_1 \\ \phi_2 \\ \vdots \\ \phi_I \end{bmatrix} = \mathbf{F}\mathbf{\Phi}, \qquad (2)$$

where $f_{ij} = P[L_j \,|\, \Phi_i]$. The matrix $\mathbf{F} = [f_{ij}]_{J \times I}$ of conditional probabilities have known conditional distribution functions and from this, the distributions of the quantities in the $\mathbf{L}$ vector may be determined provided that the vector $\mathbf{\Phi} = [P[\Phi_i]]_{I \times 1}$ is known.

In the example at hand (Fig. 7) assume that the links from photo Φ_i to labels L_j have the certitude functions described in Fig. 6 and its accompanying table. These assignments are summarized below:

$$\begin{aligned} \Phi_1 \to L_1 \quad &\Leftrightarrow \quad (A, 1) \\ \Phi_1 \to L_2 \quad &\Leftrightarrow \quad (B, 1) \\ \Phi_2 \to L_1 \quad &\Leftrightarrow \quad (D, 2, 2) \\ \Phi_2 \to L_3 \quad &\Leftrightarrow \quad (C, 1) \\ \Phi_3 \to L_3 \quad &\Leftrightarrow \quad (D, 1, 2) \end{aligned}$$

$$\phi_1 = 6/15 \quad \phi_2 = 6/15 \quad \phi_3 = 3/15$$

With these assignments, probability densities for the components of the vector $\mathbf{L}$ may be determined by simulation. These results are shown in Fig. 8.

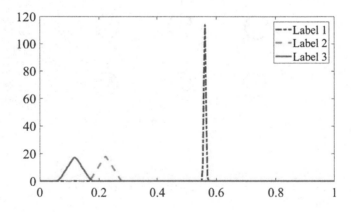

Fig. 8. BN generated certitude functions (from image probabilities)

The incorporation of the NN's estimation of the label probabilities into the generation of certitude functions is accomplished by inverting the linear system described above to produce candidate values for ϕ_i to be used in the *a priori* computations. By using the BN in this manner, we are assigning a certainty function to each value produced by the NN (see Fig. 9).

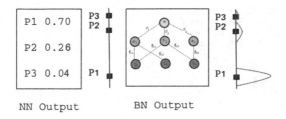

NN Output   BN Output

Fig. 9. Example of Output of a Neural Network with the uncertainty added from Belief Network. The red lines represent the uncertainty distribution for the label

The simplex method should be able (1) to show that a solution to this linear program exists, and (2) to produce a particular solution to the problem, see [13].

5 Results

We did perform several tests to show that the methods described in Sect. 2 through 4 can be used to evaluate the quality of the experts and to assign a certainty range to the labels with which different experts tag the images. To shorten the length of the paper we used synthetic data throughout to show that the proposed method works well without having to add all the details of a real NN configuration. These results are shown in Sect. 2.3 and in Figs. 4, and 6.

The BN described by Fig. 7 has been simulated[3] using the *a posteriori* evaluation described at the end of Sect. 4. The table of (image, label) certitude functions defined by Fig. 7 is summarized below: The values $P1$, $P2$, and $P3$ shown in Fig. 7 are the outputs from the softmax layer in the NN that indicate that the NN recognizes labels $L1$, $L2$, and $L3$ as possibly present in the new input image—$L1$ being the most likely. These NN outputs are used to define the vector $\mathbf{L} = [0.70, 0.26, 0.04]^T$. The matrix equation $\mathbf{L} = \mathbf{F\Phi}$ (Sect. 4 Eq. (2)) is solved to produce candidate solutions $\mathbf{\Phi}$. These solutions are in turn fed back through this same equation (via a simulation) to produce certitude functions for each coordinate of $\mathbf{L}$ (Table 3).

Table 3. Belief network input data (95% confidence)

V*	p~	epsilon	a	V*~p	b	(L, E, Phi) Designation	Individual Mean	(L, Phi) Convolved	Convolved Mean
0.08	0.75	0.565792867	0.026052428	0.06	0.093947572	A11	0.06	A1=A11*A21	0.49
0.64	0.75	0.565792867	0.208419424	0.48	0.751580576	B11	0.48	B1=B11*B21	0.56
0.08	0.75	0.565792867	0.026052428	0.06	0.093947572	C11	0.06		
0.64	0.75	0.565792867	0.208419424	0.48	0.751580576	D12	0.48		
0.92	1	0	0.92	0.92	0.92	A21	0.92		
0 64	1	0	0.64	0.64	0.64	B21	0.64		
0.92	1	0	0.92	0.92	0.92	D22	0.92		

---

[3] The output of the NN are simulated, we guess the output values of a NN based on our previous paper [1] where we used a Single Shot MultiBox Detector (SSD) [18].

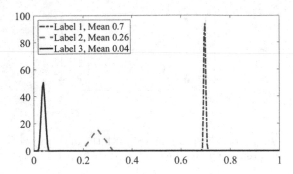

Fig. 10. BN generated certitude functions (from label probabilities)

Figure 10 shows the results of these computations—three certitude functions corresponding to the three softmax layer evaluations by the NN. With respect to label $L1$, the narrow width of the base of the triangular function indicates that the softmax layer value of 0.70 is supported by the expert's opinions. The base of this triangle is the interval [0.688, 0.711] with the peak over the certitude value 0.699 (all values are approximate). In probabilistic terms the probability that an expert would assign label $L1$ to the new image lies between 0.688 and 0.711 (relative error of about ±1.6%). For labels $L2$ and $L3$ the base intervals are [0.195, 0.342] and [0.018, 0.059 with peaks over 0.258 and 0.039 respectively. Similar probabilistic statements apply to labels $L2$ and $L3$ (relative errors of ±28.5% and ±52.6% respectively).

If the reader is interested in replicating the experiments and calculating the BN, you can find all code use here in the github [19].

6   Conclusion and Future Work

In this project we developed a method to evaluate the uncertainty of pictures used for training CNN. We provide a methodology based in probability analysis to combine different experts tagging same images to obtain a more accurate set of training images that can later be used in training a CNN. The assessed quality of the experts evaluated can also be used to spread the output of the Neural Network over a range of values increasing the robustness of the classifier.

The method proposed in this paper can be used in any training set where the labels contain uncertainty and were provided by different experts, for future work we are going to use it on civil engineering damage labeling since we already have the data set labeled by different experts and we already have results showing increase of accuracy of around 3%, for brevity the detailed description to this CNN will be presented in a different paper.

References

1. Patterson, B., Leone, G., Pantoja, M., Behrouzi, A.: Deep learning for automated image classification of seismic damage to built infrastructure. In: Proceedings of the 11th National Conference in Earthquake Engineering (2018)
2. Pantoja, M., Fabris, D., Behrouzi, A.: Deep learning basic overview concrete international magazine, September 2018
3. Tesla Crash Preliminary Report US department of transportation NHTSA PE 16–007
4. Sun, S., Chen, C., Carin, L.: Learning structured weight uncertainty in Bayesian neural networks. In: Proceedings of the 20th International Conference on Artificial Intelligence and Statistics (AISTATS) 2017, JMLR: W&CP, vol. 54, Fort Lauderdale (2017)
5. Kendall, A., Gal, Y.: What uncertainties do we need in Bayesian deep learning for computer vision NIPS (2017). https://arxiv.org/abs/1703.04977
6. Gal, Y., Ghahramani, Z.: Dropout as a Bayesian approximation: representing model uncertainty in deep learning. In: Proceedings of the 33rd International Conference on Machine Learning PMLR, vol. 48, pp. 1050–1059 (2016)
7. Deceus, T.: Handling imprecise and uncertain class labels in classification and clustering. Bayesian Deep Learning COST Action IC 0702 Working group C, Mallorca, 16 March 2009
8. Gal, Y.: What my Deep Learning model Doesnt know, 3 July 2015
9. David, H.: The Certainty-Factor Model, Encyclopedia of Artificial Intelligence. 2nd edn. pp. 131–138, Wiley, New York
10. Pearl, J.: Probabilistic Reasoning in Intelligent Systems: Networks of Plausible Inference. Morgan Kaufmann, San Mateo
11. Zadeh, L.A., Klir, G.J., Yuan, B. (eds.): Fuzzy Sets, Fuzzy Logic, and Fuzzy Systems Selected Papers. Advances in Fuzzy Systems Applications and Theory, vol 6. World Scientific
12. Knuth, D.E.: The Art of Computer Programming, vol. 2, Section 4.3.3, pp. 290 295
13. Press, W.H.: Numerical Recipes in C. Section 8.10, pp. 329–343 (1986)
14. Google Research Research Blog: AlphaGo: mastering the ancient game of Go with Machine Learning, 27 January 2016
15. Kendall, A., Badrinarayanan, V., Cipolla, R.: Bayesian SegNet: model uncertainty in deep convolutional encoder-decoder architectures for scene understanding, CoRR (2015). http://arxiv.org/abs/1511.02680
16. Weideman, H.: Quantifying uncertainty in neural networks. https://hjweide.github.io/quantifying-uncertainty-in-neural-networks
17. Avis, D., Fukuda, K.: A pivoting algorithm for convex hulls and vertex enumeration of arrangements and polyhedra. Discrete Comput. Geom. 8(3), 295–313 (1992)
18. Liu, W., et al.: SSD: single shot multibox detector. In: Leibe, B., Matas, J., Sebe, N., Welling, M. (eds.) ECCV 2016. LNCS, vol. 9905, pp. 21–37. Springer, Cham (2016). https://doi.org/10.1007/978-3-319-46448-0_2
19. Github. https://github.com/mpantoja314/ImageTagVER

Assessing the Impact of a Preprocessing Stage on Deep Learning Architectures for Breast Tumor Multi-class Classification with Histopathological Images

Iván Calvo[1]([⊠]), Saul Calderon[1], Jordina Torrents-Barrena[2], Erick Muñoz[1], and Domenec Puig[2]

[1] Escuela de Computación, Tecnológico de Costa Rica, San Jose, Costa Rica
ivanfelipecp@gmail.com, sacalderon@itcr.ac.cr, erickm968@gmail.com
[2] Dep. d'Enginyeria Informàtica i Matemàtiques, Universitat Rovira i Virgili, Tarragona, Spain
{jordina.torrents,domenec.puig}@urv.cat

Abstract. In this work, we assess the impact of the adaptive unsharp mask filter as a preprocessing stage for breast tumour multi-class classification with histopathological images, evaluating two state-of-the-art architectures, not tested so far for this problem to our knowledge: DenseNet, SqueezeNet and a 5-layer baseline deep learning architecture. SqueezeNet is an efficient architecture, which can be useful in environments with restrictive computational resources. According to the results, the filter improved the accuracy from 2% to 4% in the 5-layer baseline architecture, on the other hand, DenseNet and SqueezeNet show a negative impact, losing from 2% to 6% accuracy. Hence, simpler deep learning architectures can take more advantage of filters than complex architectures, which are able to learn the preprocessing filter implemented. Squeeze net yielded the highest per parameter accuracy, while DenseNet achieved a 96% accuracy, defeating previous state of the art architectures by 1% to 5%, making DenseNet a considerably more efficient architecture for breast tumour classification.

Keywords: Breast cancer · Histopathological images · Deep learning · Multi-class tumour classification

1 Introduction

Cancer is a major public health problem [3], it affects millions of people and every year, new cases and deaths are recorded globally. Breast cancer is the second most diagnosed cancer world-wide. Last year $2,088,849$ new cases of breast cancer were discovered and $626,679$ deaths registered [3].

© Springer Nature Switzerland AG 2020
J. L. Crespo-Mariño and E. Meneses-Rojas (Eds.): CARLA 2019, CCIS 1087, pp. 262–275, 2020.
https://doi.org/10.1007/978-3-030-41005-6_18

Detecting and treating a tumour in early stages increases recovery and survival rates for patients. A method for estimating the stage and type of breast cancer is a histopathological image analysis, in which a pathologist examines a histology to diagnose an existing malign or benign tumour. Histopathological analysis is carried out after suspicious masses are found in a previous diagnostic mammogram. Subjects with mammograms categorized by level 4 or 5 according the *Breast Imaging Reporting and Data System* (BI-RADS) standard, are usually advised to perform further histopathological analysis.

Based on the deep learning and architectures based on convolutional neural networks success for image analysis applications, the development of accurate *Computer Aided Diagnosis* (CAD) systems for medical purposes is becoming increasingly popular, however often limited by data availability from clinics and hospitals. Few initiatives for creating open data repositories can be found in the medical community. An example of these initiatives is the breast cancer histopathological database known as BreakHis [24]. This dataset is composed of breast tumor tissues images labeled as benign or malign.

Automated histopathological analysis systems can be implemented on a medic device or embedded system to support pathologist every day sample analysis, improving tumor detection accuracy, and allowing the pathologist to focus in most urgent cases. Moreover, efficient deep convolutional architectures are of interest for the usage in mobile phones and embedded computers. For small clinics in underdeveloped areas with poor internet access, implementing efficient deep learning architectures can be useful.

Frequently, data samples present noise or signal degradations, decreasing the signal to noise ratio. Therefore a preprocessing stage becomes necessary, with input images transformed, normalized, enhanced, denoised or filtered depending on the problem to solve. In [4,5,17,20], different techniques are proposed for contrast enhancement and edge sharpening preprocessing.

In this work, we assessed the impact of an adaptive unsharp mask filter [17] as preprocessing stage for three different convolutional network architectures based approach for breast tumour multi classification, evaluating the breast cancer histopathological database (BreakHis) as training and testing data.

As contributions, we evaluated the intensity and edge based adaptive unsharp masking filter for color image enhancement as a preprocessing stage for breast tumour classification.

In order to evaluate the impact of a filter in complex and simpler architectures, we chose DenseNet and Squeezenet: two novel state-of-the-art architectures. On the other hand, we also contribute to the state of the art on breast tumour classification, since to our knowledge, there is not a lot of related work with these two architectures on breast cancer multi-class classification problems.

2   State of the Art

Deep learning has been a successful approach for the development of computer-aided systems for medical purposes, since its techniques, methods and architectures applied to medical images have yielded successful and accurate results so far [15,19,21,22]. However, a challenge faced by the scientific community is the lack of open datasets to be able to develop and test these systems since most of the medical information is private. Recently, [24] authors and collaborators released a dataset of breast cancer histopathological images [24] for research and benchmarking purposes, therefore, we focus our literature exploration in works presenting image analysis solutions tested with the BreakHis dataset. Binary classification is a common problem in computer vision and machine learning, in which the data is classified in two classes as BreakHis, that is divided in two mainly classes: benign and malign tumours.

In [2], authors present a study of the state of the art, as they compared their deep learning methods, the baseline model architecture (InceptionV3) and results with [23–25] for binary classification. In [24] authors used classical machine learning classification methods, meanwhile [25] used a standard convolutional neural network architecture and [23] an AlexNet model baseline [8]. [25] obtained the best results on patient level accuracy: 96.7%, 93.2%, 89.8%, 92.3% and 96.1%, 89.9%, 87.2%, 85.2% on image level accuracy in $40\times$, $100\times$, $200\times$ and $400\times$ magnifications respectively, on the other hand, [2] obtained the best results on F1 score: 93%, 88.9%, 89.4% and 86.4% in the respective magnifications.

Binary breast tumour classification is studied on [18], in this work, authors assess the impact of transfer learning on three pre-trained models: VGG16, VGG19, and ResNet50. All the models posses a logistic regression classifier as a top model. The fined-tuned pretrained VGG16 with logistic regression classifier yielded obtained the best performance with 92.60% accuracy.

Recent DenseNet architecture [13], based on the idea of implementing several skip connections to overcome the vanishing gradient problem, has been evaluated in [11] for breast tumour binary classification using the BreakHis dataset as training and testing data. Xgboost [6] was used for feature extraction and principal component analysis for dimensionality reduction. They achieved $94.71 \pm .88$, 95.9 ± 4.2, 96.76 ± 1.09 and 89.11 ± 0.12 in patient level accuracy on $40\times$, $100\times$, $200\times$ and $400\times$ magnifying factors respectively.

The two mainly classes of BreakHis: benign and malign are divided in four subtypes each, allowing to perform a multi-class classification to determinate the type of tumour presented in a histology. Binary classification has been thoroughly investigated, [25] reports a maximum accuracy of 96%, therefore, we consider that binary classification on BreakHis is a solved and well-known problem through deep learning techniques, demonstrating a better performance and efficiency since feature extraction is learned through the training iterations by deep convolutional neural networks instead of handcrafted methods as [24], which employs traditional machine learning and feature extraction techniques to solve the binary classification, performing an accuracy of 73% to 85%. On the other hand, breast tumour multi-class classification is not solved and most of the authors in current literature address and face the multi-class breast tumour classification problem using deep convolutional networks, as is shown in [1], a deep learning convolutional neural network was evaluated and results of 91.54% accuracy have been reported on the BreakHis dataset.

Another approach is proposed in [12], which suggest an end-to-end recognition method by a novel deep learning based architecture to multi-class classification. A frequent problem in breast histopathological images is class imbalance, since samples for certain types of tumours are less common. To handle imbalanced datasets as BreakHis, author used a data augmentation based approach and obtained an average of 93.2% accuracy.

Authors in [9] reported a 95.15% accuracy with a deep residual network based framework. The base model used is ResNet, which classifies between benign or malign, followed by a top meta decision tree that classifies the ResNet output between one of the different eight subtypes of tumours of the BreakHis dataset.

Preprocessing is an important stage on every deep learning baseline, in this step, data can be denoised or filtered depending on the problem to solve, in [4] authors analyze the impact of denoising, contrast and edge enhancement using the deceived non local means filter in a convolutional neural network based approach for age estimation using digital X-ray images from hands, this filter has two remarkable features: noise removing and border highlighting. Since the filter has two parameters, combinations were tested and reported the results for each. As conclusion, authors asserted the significance on how changing the parameters of the filter affects the learning process of the model. They proved that for some combinations, the filter improved the learning process and the accuracy of the deep learning model. This leads us to explore preprocessing impact in a deep learning classification model.

3   Proposed Method

BreakHis dataset presents a wide variety of cases for the adaptive unsharp mask filter to be tested on, four magnification values, four types of benign and malign breast tumours. Since we aim to test the effect of the filter as a preprocessing stage, this assortment of scenarios allows us to test the behaviour of the AUM with images presenting different levels of detail and contrast. As seen in [4,5] a filter can have a significant impact on the learning process and accuracy of a deep learning model.

The tested architectures deep learning DenseNet [13] and SqueezeNet [14]. We compare DenseNet since remarkable results have been reported in [10] on binary breast tumour classification.

We seek to assess the impact of the preprocessing stage has on a lightweight network a heavyweight one, this is why SqueezeNet and DenseNet are used. We know SqueezeNet is a lightweight network with a good number of parameters - accuracy ratio [14], and we aim to measure the impact of the proposed AUM preprocessing step, as also compare its accuracy and resource consumption with the more complex DenseNet architecture. DenseNet implemenents a lot of parameters, and is a huge network in comparison to SqueezeNet, thus we also test its multi classification accuracy. We want to measure the impact AUM has on of both big and small networks alike. All the architectures have a softmax function as a final activation for the eight prediction output, therefore, cross entropy was used as loss function.

3.1   Dataset

We evaluated the Breast Cancer Histopathological Database [24] known as BreakHis, composed of 7,909 microscopic images of breast tumor tissue collected from 82 patients using different magnifying factors (40×, 100×, 200×, and 400×, the × stands for times.) as seen in Fig. 1. The database is basically divided in two major classes: benign and malign. These two classes are then subdivided into four subtypes each: *Adenosis* (A), *Fibroadenoma* (F), *Phyllodes Tumour* (PT) and *Tubular Adenona* (TA) as benign subtypes and *Carcinoma* (DC), *Lobular Carcinoma* (LC), *Mucinous Carcinoma* (MC) and *Papillary Carcinoma* (PC) as malignant subtypes.

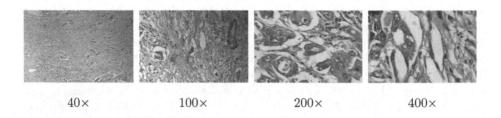

| 40× | 100× | 200× | 400× |

Fig. 1. Samples of the four magnifying factors presented in BreakHis dataset

3.2   Preprocessing: Adaptive Unsharp Mask

Previous work [4, 7] reported a significant performance impact of preprocessing on *Convolutional Neural Networks* (CNNs). Therefore, we used the intensity and edge based *Adaptive Unsharping Mask Filter* (AUM) filter [17] as a preprocessing stage. The main difference in comparison with USM, is the iterative process in which the variable that controls the amount of image enhancement: gain factor is updated. Let G be the enhanced image described by Eq. 1:

$$G = U + \lambda_A B \tag{1}$$

U is defined as the original image, then difference of Gaussians algorithm is applied to U in order to calculate B and λ_A is the adaptive gain factor which can be decomposed as a product of three factors; general gain(λ_G), color enhancement(λ_C) and edge sharpening(λ_E). An example of result G is shown in Fig. 2.

Once AUM is applied, images are normalized from 0 to 1, and resized from 700×460 to ($n \times n$) using bilinear interpolation to keep the image ratio, where n is the input size of the respective model.

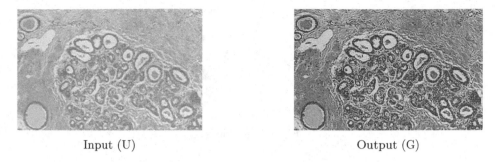

Input (U)   Output (G)

Fig. 2. Example of AUM applied to a BreakHis sample

3.3 DenseNet

The concept of a deep dense convolutional network known as DenseNet was proposed in [13]. The main goal of this architecture is to improve information and gradient flow between layers using dense connectivity blocks as is shown in Fig. 3. We evaluated the DenseNet 161-layer architecture who has 26,474,209 trainable parameters.

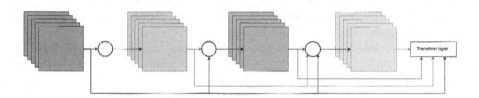

Fig. 3. Densed connectivity block

3.4 SqueezeNet

An important drawback of complex deep convolutional networks is usually the huge amount of parameters, which increases computational time and resources.

To solve the aforementioned problem [14], the well-known SqueezeNet was proposed. It is an AlexNet-based architecture with 50x less parameters, lower size filters, downsampling and channel reduction.

The main feature of this architecture is the fire module. It is combined with convolution layers, another fire modules and max-pooling operations to create the SqueezeNet. A fire module relies on a compressing and expanding layer, the compressing layer has 1×1 convolutional filters, which are then passed to the expanding layer composed of both 1×1 and 3×3 convolutional filters as is shown in Fig. 4. This model has 723,809 trainable parameters.

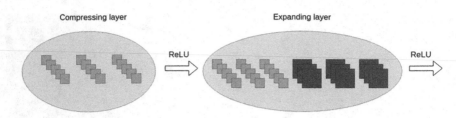

Fig. 4. Fire block

4   Experiments and Results

We used a 5-fold cross-validation for training and testing. To divide the data we accounted for the number of images of each tumour sub type, in order to avoid class bias; the information of each patient was not taken into consideration. To face class unbalance, the loss function was weighted and balanced according to the number of samples of each tumour class, forcing the model to punish more errors in classes with less samples.

Each model was trained with 100 epochs; using Adam [16] optimizer with learning rate of 0.0001. The batch size used for training and testing was 28 and 18 for SqueezeNet and DenseNet, respectively, to avoid memory overflow.

To evaluate the performance of the models, we calculated the patient level accuracy, image level accuracy and F1-score.

The patient level accuracy metric is defined as follows. For each patient, let N_t be the total number of images and N_c the number of images correctly classified, then patient score S can be defined as:

$$S = \frac{N_c}{N_t} \tag{2}$$

Therefore, the patient level accuracy can be calculated as

$$\text{Patient level accuracy} = \frac{\sum_{i=1}^{T} S_i}{T} \tag{3}$$

Where T is the total number of patients.

The image level accuracy measures the rate of correctly classified images to the total number of images in the dataset. Let N be the total number of images in testing data and C the number of correctly classified images.

$$\text{Image level Accuracy} = \frac{C}{N} \tag{4}$$

DenseNet and SqueezeNet have obtained outstanding results [13,14]. Therefore, we also evaluated a 5-layer deep CNN architecture, in order to evaluate the impact of preprocessing on a traditional deep convolutional baseline. The architecture is described in Table 1, where b is the batch size.

Table 1. 5-layer CNN architecture

Layer	Input size	Output size	Kernel size
Conv 1 + ReLU	$(b,3,229,229)$	$(b,32,227,227)$	3
Conv 2 + ReLU	$(b,32,227,227)$	$(b,64,225,225)$	3
Max pooling	$(b,64,225,225)$	$(b,64,112,112)$	2
BatchNorm	$(b,64,112,112)$	$(b,64,112,112)$	-
Conv 3 + ReLU	$(b,64,112,112)$	$(b,128,110,110)$	3
Conv 4 + ReLU	$(b,128,110,110)$	$(b,256,108,108)$	3
Max pooling	$(b,256,108,108)$	$(b,256,54,54)$	2
BatchNorm	$(b,256,54,54)$	$(b,256,54,54)$	–
Flat operation	$(b,256,54,54)$	$(b,256*54*54)$	–
FC + Softmax	$(b,256*54*54)$	$(b,8)$	–

Table 2. F1-score mean $\pm$ std

	Architecture	Preprocessing	
		AUM	No AUM
40×	DenseNet	$0.94 \pm .022$	$0.96 \pm .035$
	SqueezeNet	$0.90 \pm .051$	$0.94 \pm .024$
	5-layer CNN	$0.61 \pm .147$	$0.30 \pm .143$
100×	DenseNet	$0.90 \pm .034$	$0.93 \pm .021$
	SqueezeNet	$0.87 \pm .049$	$0.91 \pm .037$
	5-layer CNN	$0.30 \pm .110$	$0.27 \pm .168$
200×	DenseNet	$0.89 \pm .038$	$0.91 \pm .042$
	SqueezeNet	$0.86 \pm .053$	$0.88 \pm .04$
	5-layer CNN	0.37 ± 104	$0.32 \pm .067$
400×	DenseNet	$0.07 \pm .001$	$0.90 \pm .039$
	SqueezeNet	$0.78 \pm .061$	$0.83 \pm .057$
	5-layer CNN	$0.33 \pm .118$	$0.32 \pm .088$

Table 3. Patient level accuracy mean $\pm$ std

	Architecture	Preprocessing	
		AUM	No AUM
40×	DenseNet	$0.94 \pm .022$	$0.96 \pm .013$
	SqueezeNet	$0.89 \pm .027$	$0.95 \pm .014$
	5-layer CNN	$0.45 \pm .043$	$0.41 \pm .057$
100×	DenseNet	$0.93 \pm .018$	$0.93 \pm .023$
	SqueezeNet	$0.89 \pm .025$	$0.92 \pm .021$
	5-layer CNN	$0.39 \pm .026$	$0.38 \pm .018$
200×	DenseNet	$0.91 \pm .017$	$0.92 \pm .016$
	SqueezeNet	$0.89 \pm .012$	$0.88 \pm .05$
	5-layer CNN	$0.48 \pm .034$	$0.44 \pm .023$
400×	DenseNet	$0.88 \pm .025$	$0.9 \pm .015$
	SqueezeNet	$0.79 \pm .034$	$0.83 \pm .069$
	5-layer CNN	$0.40 \pm .039$	$0.39 \pm .021$

Table 4. Image level accuracy mean ± std

	Architecture	Preprocessing	
		AUM	No AUM
40×	DenseNet	0.95 ± .006	0.96 ± .012
	SqueezeNet	0.90 ± .015	0.94 ± .012
	5-layer CNN	0.53 ± .048	0.48 ± .038
100×	DenseNet	0.92 ± .013	0.94 ± .011
	SqueezeNet	0.88 ± .008	0.91 ± .013
	5-layer CNN	0.45 ± .015	0.45 ± .037
200×	DenseNet	0.90 ± .010	0.92 ± .015
	SqueezeNet	0.87 ± .009	0.89 ± .014
	5-layer CNN	0.51 ± .034	0.50 ± .016
400×	DenseNet	0.89 ± .013	0.91 ± .006
	SqueezeNet	0.80 ± .013	0.84 ± .019
	5-layer CNN	0.50 ± .017	0.46 ± .033

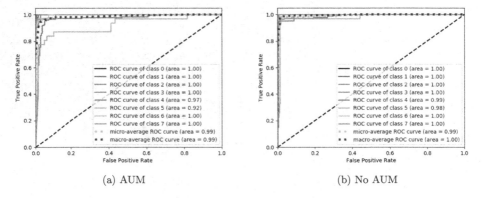

(a) AUM   (b) No AUM

Fig. 5. ROC curve of DenseNet on x40 magnifying factor

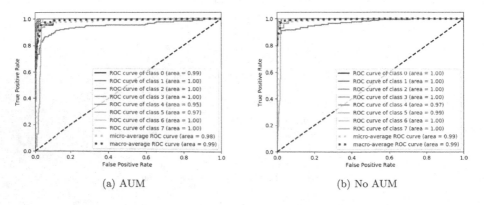

(a) AUM   (b) No AUM

Fig. 6. ROC curve of SqueezeNet on x40 magnifying factor

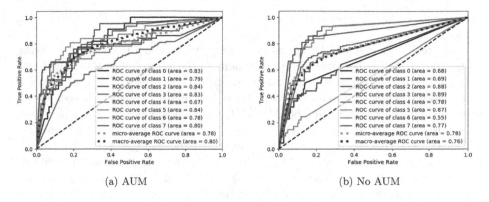

(a) AUM   (b) No AUM

Fig. 7. ROC curve of 5-layer CNN on x40 magnifying factor

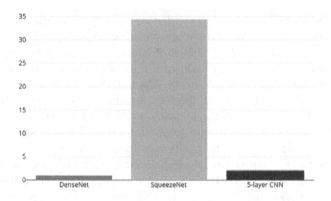

Fig. 8. Accuracy per parameter table scaled 0–100

Table 5. Comparation of 40× magnifying factor results with other works, NR stands by non reported

Work	Patient level accuracy	Image level accuracy	F1-Score	Classification
[2]: Inception v3 + DeCAF	91.5	90.2	93	Binary
[9]: ResNet-152 + Stain norm	NR	95.6	NR	Multi
[12]: CSDCNN	94.1	92.8	NR	Multi
[11]: DenseNet-169 + XGboost	NR	94.7	NR	Binary
[23]: AlexNet + DeCAF	84.0	84.6	88	Binary
[25]: AlexNet	90.0	85.6	92.9	Binary
DenseNet-161 with AUM	94.2	95.6	94.7	Multi
DenseNet-161 without AUM	**96.2**	**96.1**	**96.1**	Multi
SqueezeNet with AUM	89.2	90.1	90.5	Multi
SqueezeNet without AUM	95.1	94.1	94.2	Multi
5-layer with AUM	45.5	53.4	47.3	Multi
5-layer without AUM	41.5	48.3	31.0	Multi

Looking at the F1-score in Table 2 its clear that the preprocessing stage contributes in a negative manner, most of the cases for SqueezeNet and DenseNet, but in case of the 5-layer implementation it seems to improve the accuracy in some cases.

As previously discussed, the use of a adaptive unsharp mask preprocessing stage was proposed because an improvement in the accuracy of the model was expected, but results proved this supposition to be wrong. In Tables 3 and 4 a considerable negative impact on patient and image level accuracy is seen on all implementations when using the AUM. DenseNet achieved 2% lower accuracy when using the AUM filter in it worse case, this can be due to it high amount of parameters that allow it to become numb to the changes made by the filter. On the other hand, the AUM had a larger negative impact on SqueezeNet, where the accuracy loss varies between 1% and 6% using 200x and 40x magnification respectively, it can be argued that this is because of network having less parameters and therefore less flexibility to adjust the change produced by the filter.

As for the 5-layer CNN tested, it yielded an important accuracy increase when using the AUM as a preprocessing stage, yielding an accuracy boost of around 5%, as seen in Tables 3 and 4. The lack of generalization can be appreciated in Fig. 7, which shows the positive ratio of 5-layer CNN model trained with and without AUM. The *Receiver Operating Characteristics* (ROC) curve shows a better positive ratio by the AUM model, showing a better percentage of true positives in comparison to the model without AUM that focus on classes 2 (F), 3 (PT) and 4 (TA). Contrary case is observed in DenseNet and SqueezeNet ROC curves on Figs. 5 and 6, where the positive ratio with and without AUM is alike.

When using the F1 score to measure the accuracy for each class in the dataset, a clear pattern can be seen in Table 5, that is the negative effect the AUM has on elaborate networks like DenseNet and SqueezeNet. It seems like the use of the filter might even removing information useful in the classification process, this effect was not present when the 5-layer CNN was tested, instead an significant improvement of almost 30% was achieved in some cases and in others a downgrade was also reported.

According to the results obtained, DenseNet achieved the highest (96%) F1-score, patient and image level accuracy. Both architectures DenseNet and SqueezeNet demonstrated an important decrease in precision. On the contrary, simpler models (e.g., 5-layer CNN) provided a significant performance gain with AUM images. Therefore, very basic CNNs can take more advantage of preprocessing than complex state-of-the-art architectures. Note that similar results and conclusions were previously obtained in [5].

The top performance of each model is obtained in 40× magnifying factor since the images posses global information that is removed when the magnifying factor increases, affecting the learning of the models. Thus, Table 5 reports the results with other works on this specific magnifying factor, showing that DenseNet obtained a better performance than other works. It can be noted that as the input image has a higher magnifiers factor, the accuracy decreases, this happens not only on DenseNet but all tested architectures. This could be due the fact that as the magnification increases the amount of local information captured in each image is less, and it ends up being a very localized picture, therefore losing important information of the surrounding area.

Moreover, SqueezeNet ranked second using less than 25 million parameters compared to DenseNet. Although it is fast, there is room for improvement regarding accuracy rates. SqueezeNet is also a lightweight network that offers a remarkable efficiency per parameter. This feature could be useful in a embedded environment as a first line of detection in a histology, and become, to our knowledge, the first neural network to be used in a embedded system for breast tumour detection. The considerable resource consumption/accuracy higher ratio of SqueezeNet can be seen in Fig. 8.

5   Conclusions

We analyzed the impact of the preprocessing AUM filter on three different deep learning architectures to classify breast tumours in histopathological images and determined that the usage of this preprocessing stage for DenseNet and SqueezeNet decreases the accuracy of both networks in every single test case, with variable magnification and multiple classes. It can be said that the filter removes key characteristics from the images and this does not help with the learning process of this networks, as also more complex networks are likely to become numb to noisy or degraded samples. On the other hand, the 5-layer CNN architecture improved its results and showed that simple convolutional architectures can be enhanced by the use if this kind of preprocessing stage for histopathological images, as it is less likely to learn the filter behavior by itself.

The results obtained by DenseNet and SqueezeNet shows the negative impact of the filter on complex architectures in comparison with the 5-layer CNN, whose results improved significantly with the filter, meaning that small and simpler convolutional neural networks can take more advantage and benefits of filters than complex architectures.

SqueezeNet yielded an outstanding accuracy per parameter, demonstrating that huge amount of parameters are not necessary to achieve a satisfactory accuracy. Is also a suitable architecture to be used in medical devices or embedded system as an extra help to help detect cases higher risk of developing cancer, being specially useful in places were there are many cases to check but very few people to do the job. SqueezeNet proved to be a potentially viable network to be used in embedded systems due to its low parameter but high accuracy relation, it showed it's capable of being toe to toe with a network as huge as DenseNet.

References

1. Adeshina, S.A., Adedigba, A.P., Adeniyi, A.A., Aibinu, A.M.: Breast cancer histopathology image classification with deep convolutional neural networks. In: 2018 14th International Conference on Electronics Computer and Computation (ICECCO), pp. 206–212. IEEE (2018)
2. Benhammou, Y., Tabik, S., Achchab, B., Herrera, F.: A first study exploring the performance of the state-of-the art CNN model in the problem of breast cancer. In: Proceedings of the International Conference on Learning and Optimization Algorithms: Theory and Applications, p. 47. ACM (2018)
3. Bray, F., Ferlay, J., Soerjomataram, I., Siegel, R.L., Torre, L.A., Jemal, A.: Global cancer statistics 2018: GLOBOCAN estimates of incidence and mortality worldwide for 36 cancers in 185 countries. CA: Cancer J. Clin. **68**(6), 394–424 (2018)
4. Calderon, S., et al.: Assessing the impact of the deceived non local means filter as a preprocessing stage in a convolutional neural network based approach for age estimation using digital hand x-ray images. In: 2018 25th IEEE International Conference on Image Processing (ICIP), pp. 1752–1756. IEEE (2018)
5. Carranza-Rojas, J., Calderon-Ramirez, S., Mora-Fallas, A., Granados-Menani, M.: Unsharp masking layer: injecting prior knowledge in convolutional networks for image classification (in press)
6. Chen, T., Guestrin, C.: XGBoost: a scalable tree boosting system. In: Proceedings of the 22nd ACM SIGKDD International Conference on Knowledge Discovery and Data Mining, pp. 785–794. ACM (2016)
7. Dodge, S., Karam, L.: Understanding how image quality affects deep neural networks. In: 2016 Eighth International Conference on Quality of Multimedia Experience (QoMEX), pp. 1–6. IEEE (2016)
8. Donahue, J., et al.: DeCAF: a deep convolutional activation feature for generic visual recognition. In: International Conference on Machine Learning, pp. 647–655 (2014)
9. Gandomkar, Z., Brennan, P.C., Mello-Thoms, C.: MuDeRn: multi-category classification of breast histopathological image using deep residual networks. Artif. Intell. Med. **88**, 14–24 (2018)
10. Gu, Y., Jie, Y.: Densely-connected multi-magnification hashing for histopathological image retrieval. IEEE J. Biomed. Health Inform. **23**, 1683–1691 (2018)
11. Gupta, V., Bhavsar, A.: Sequential modeling of deep features for breast cancer histopathological image classification. In: Proceedings of the IEEE Conference on Computer Vision and Pattern Recognition Workshops, pp. 2254–2261 (2018)
12. Han, Z., Wei, B., Zheng, Y., Yin, Y., Li, K., Li, S.: Breast cancer multi-classification from histopathological images with structured deep learning model. Sci. Rep. **7**(1), 4172 (2017)
13. Huang, G., Liu, Z., Van Der Maaten, L., Weinberger, K.Q.: Densely connected convolutional networks. In: Proceedings of the IEEE Conference on Computer Vision and Pattern Recognition, pp. 4700–4708 (2017)
14. Iandola, F.N., Han, S., Moskewicz, M.W., Ashraf, K., Dally, W.J., Keutzer, K.: SqueezeNet: AlexNet-level accuracy with 50x fewer parameters and <0.5 mb model size. arXiv preprint arXiv:1602.07360 (2016)
15. Khosravan, N., Celik, H., Turkbey, B., Jones, E.C., Wood, B., Bagci, U.: A collaborative computer aided diagnosis (C-CAD) system with eye-tracking, sparse attentional model, and deep learning. Med. Image Anal. **51**, 101–115 (2019)

16. Kingma, D.P., Ba, J.: Adam: a method for stochastic optimization. arXiv preprint arXiv:1412.6980 (2014)
17. Lin, S., et al.: Intensity and edge based adaptive unsharp masking filter for color image enhancement. Optik **127**(1), 407–414 (2016)
18. Mehra, R., et al.: Breast cancer histology images classification: training from scratch or transfer learning? ICT Express **4**(4), 247–254 (2018)
19. Pertuz, S., Julia, C., Puig, D.: A novel mammography image representation framework with application to image registration. In: 2014 22nd International Conference on Pattern Recognition, pp. 3292–3297. IEEE (2014)
20. Polesel, A., Ramponi, G., Mathews, V.J.: Image enhancement via adaptive unsharp masking. IEEE Trans. Image Process. **9**(3), 505–510 (2000)
21. Shin, H.C., et al.: Deep convolutional neural networks for computer-aided detection: CNN architectures, dataset characteristics and transfer learning. IEEE Trans. Med. Imaging **35**(5), 1285–1298 (2016)
22. Singh, V.K., et al.: Conditional generative adversarial and convolutional networks for X-ray breast mass segmentation and shape classification. In: Frangi, A.F., Schnabel, J.A., Davatzikos, C., Alberola-López, C., Fichtinger, G. (eds.) MICCAI 2018. LNCS, vol. 11071, pp. 833–840. Springer, Cham (2018). https://doi.org/10.1007/978-3-030-00934-2_92
23. Spanhol, F.A., Oliveira, L.S., Cavalin, P.R., Petitjean, C., Heutte, L.: Deep features for breast cancer histopathological image classification. In: 2017 IEEE International Conference on Systems, Man, and Cybernetics (SMC), pp. 1868–1873. IEEE (2017)
24. Spanhol, F.A., Oliveira, L.S., Petitjean, C., Heutte, L.: A dataset for breast cancer histopathological image classification. IEEE Trans. Biomed. Eng. **63**(7), 1455–1462 (2016)
25. Spanhol, F.A., Oliveira, L.S., Petitjean, C., Heutte, L.: Breast cancer histopathological image classification using convolutional neural networks. In: 2016 International Joint Conference on Neural Networks (IJCNN), pp. 2560–2567. IEEE (2016)

Assessing the Robustness of Recurrent Neural Networks to Enhance the Spectrum of Reverberated Speech

Carolina Paniagua-Peñaranda(ID), Marisol Zeledón-Córdoba(ID),
and Marvin Coto-Jiménez(✉)(ID)

PRIS-Lab, Escuela de Ingeniería Eléctrica, Universidad de Costa Rica,
San Pedro, Costa Rica
{carolina.paniaguapenaranda,marisol.zeledon,marvin.coto}@ucr.ac.cr

Abstract. Implementing voice recognition systems and voice analysis in real-life contexts present important challenges, especially when signal recording/registering conditions are adverse. One of the conditions that produce signal degradation, which has also been studied in recent years is reverberation. Reverberation is produced by the sound wave reflections that travel through the microphone from multiple directions.

Several Deep Learning-based methods have been proposed to improve speech signals that have been degraded with reverberation and are proven to be effective. Recently, recurrent neural networks, especially those with short and long term memory (LSTM), have presented surprising results in those tasks.

In this work, a proposal to evaluate the robustness of these neural networks to learn different reverberation conditions without any previous information is presented. The results show the necessity to train fewer sets of LSTM networks to improve speech signals, since a single network can learn several conditions simultaneously, in contrast with the current method of training a network for every single condition or noise level.

The evaluation has been made based on quality measurements of the signal's spectrum (distance and perceptual quality), in comparison with the reverberated version. Results help to affirm the fact that LSTM networks are able to enhance the signal in any of five conditions, where all of them were trained simultaneously, with equivalent results as if to train a network for every single condition of reverberation.

Keywords: Speech enhancement · Reverberation · Deep learning · LSTM

1 Introduction

Speech signals are often affected by additive noise, reverberation and other distortions in real-world environments due to background elements that produce

Supported by the University of Costa Rica.

J. L. Crespo-Mariño and E. Meneses-Rojas (Eds.): CARLA 2019, CCIS 1087, pp. 276–290, 2020.
https://doi.org/10.1007/978-3-030-41005-6_19

sounds or represent obstacles,thus modifying to the signals. Communication devices and applications of speech technologies may be affected in their performance [2, 26, 33, 34] with such noise added to the speech information.

Over the past decades, speech enhancement algorithms have been presented to suppress or reduce such distortions, as well as preserving or enhancing the perceived signal quality [17]. Several recent algorithms for the task of enhancing speech signals are based on deep neural networks (DNN) [7, 8, 16, 25]. The most common approach is that of learning mapping features from noisy speech into the features of the corresponding clean speech, using autoencoders based on perceptrons or recurrent neural networks (RNNs).

Among the new types of RNNs, the LSTM network successfully mapped features derived from the spectrum, usually Mel-Frequency Cepstrum Coefficients (MFCC) [4]. These features have been used widely in speech-related tasks because automatic speech recognition systems are frequently based on them.

The benefits of using RNNs are the better modeling of the dependent nature in speech signals. Among its drawbacks are the high computational cost of their training procedures.

In this work, we extend on the previous experiences of speech enhancement with LSTM by measuring its robustness, considering more than one level of noise with a single network. Benefits from this type of speech enhancement can be applied to more realistic tasks in mobile phones, Voice over Internet Protocol, speech recognition, and devices for hearing-impaired listeners [18].

The idea of enhancing speech signals with DNN has been a hot topic in research during the past few years. Typically, the implementation relies on the enhancement of spectral features, such as MFCC [1, 21, 29].

The deep learning approaches have been successful in outperforming classical methods based on signal processing when the speech signals have been degraded with different types of noise at several Signal-to-Noise Ratio (SNR) [3, 19, 23, 31], or reverberant speech [11, 22, 37]. Also, the advantage in reducing the musical artifact commonly present in speech enhancement using classical algorithms has been observed [35].

The principal method for enhancing the signals using deep learning is to apply the networks as mapping models, adjusting an unknown function from the noise parameters of the speech into the corresponding clean parameters [24, 33]. To provide robust enhancement of reverberated speech, in [34], a combination with signal-processing based algorithms were also proposed. The usage of deep autoencoders has been analyzed in these references also with several parametrizations of the speech signal.

LSTM networks for speech enhancement have been presented previously in [6, 34], using MFCC as features, for the case of applying one LSTM network for enhancement of each noise type and SNR level, or a specific condition. Even though the LSTM outperforms other deep networks in this task, the training process for its successful implementation requires single specific conditions (i.e. a noise level or specific reverberation), and prior knowledge of the noise type, level or reverberation during the test procedure.

In the present paper, we consider a more realistic scenario for speech enhancement under different conditions of reverberation, where the networks are trained with more than one of these conditions. We pretend to measure the capacity of the LSTM networks to enhance speech signals without apriori information of the condition of the signals.

Several objective measures are used to test the results, which show the capacity of the LSTM in robust speech enhancement under reverberation conditions. The rest of this paper is organized as follows: Sect. 2 gives the background and context of the problem of enhancing reverberating speech and the LSTM, Sect. 3 describes the experimental setup, Sect. 4 presents the results with a discussion, and finally, in Sect. 5, we present the conclusions.

2   Background

2.1   Problem Statement of Robust Speech Enhancement

In real contexts where speech signals are being recorded with microphones, it is common the occurrence of reverberations, which are produced by reflections of the signal on its way to the microphone.

In these cases, it can be assumed that the reverberated signal x is a degraded version of a clean signal s. The relationship between both signals can be expressed by [27]

$$x(n) = \mathbf{h}^T(n)\mathbf{s}(n), \tag{1}$$

where $h = [h_1, h_2, \ldots, h_L]^T$ is the impulse response of the acoustic channel from the source to the microphone.

Degraded speech with reverberation can be described as distant, with an echo perception. These effects usually increase as the speaker's distance to the microphone increases.

Since this effect is unwanted for adequate recognition and analysis of the voice, new algorithms have been proposed to minimize it. Algorithms based on machine learning are the ones that have stood out in recent years.

In machine learning-based approaches, $s(n)$ can be estimated using an approximated function $f(\cdot)$ between the reverberated and the clean data of the form:

$$\hat{s}(t) = f\left(x(t)\right). \tag{2}$$

The quality of the approximation $f(\cdot)$ usually depends on the amount of data and the algorithm selected, typically deep neural networks. Previous attempts have estimated $f(\cdot)$ for each condition of reverberation, i.e. for each impulse response associated with a particular space. It means that for N conditions, there is a set of N neural networks, applied separately to estimate the set $f_{R_1}(\cdot), f_{R_2}(\cdot), \cdots, f_{R_N}(\cdot)$, where R_i is the condition for each of the impulse response.

A robust application of enhancing reverberated speech can provide a single network capable of enhance several conditions. It means there is no need to have prior knowledge of the impulse response presented at the input of the network. With this robust network, it is expected to have

$$f_{R_1}(\cdot) \approx f_R(\cdot) \tag{3}$$

$$f_{R_2}(\cdot) \approx f_R(\cdot)$$
$$\vdots \quad \vdots$$
$$f_{R_n}(\cdot) \approx f_R(\cdot),$$

and for any signal at the input, the approximation should be similar to those of the network trained with the specific condition.

2.2 Long Short-Term Memory Neural Networks

Over the last few decades, a variety of neural networks have been tested for classification and regression purposes. Recent kinds of networks, such as DNN, which are organized in many layers, achieved good results when tested for problem-solving of diverse applications.

Since the arrival of RNNs, there have been new alternatives for modeling the dependent nature of sequential information. This kind of neural networks are able to store information by feedback connections between neurons in their hidden layers or another network that is in the same layer [10,36].

With the objective of expanding the abilities of RNNs by storing information in the short-term and long-term, LSTM networks shown in [20] introduced a set of gates within memory cells that are able to control the access, storing and propagation of values over the network. The results obtained by the LSTM networks in areas that depend on previous states of the information, such as speech recognition, music composition, and handwriting synthesis, were encouraging [13,14,20].

To maintain values in the short-term and the long-term, the LSTM has four gates that control the operations of input, output, and erasing the memory. Further details on the training procedure and the mathematical modeling of the LSTM can be found in [12].

Training neural networks in speech enhancement and noise reduction became a solid idea with its first application in binary input patterns. Some years later, this idea was used in the modelling of acoustic coefficients, these were modelled with a single layer. Working with large sets of data or introducing hidden layers was impossible due to limiting computer capabilities and undeveloped algorithms for the purpose [19].

Moreover, with the goal of having the output as close to the uncorrupted signal as possible, training data is used by the network's parameters to perform noise reduction and regression-based tasks [32].

A denoising autoencoder is a recent neural network architecture that has had success in several speech-related tasks [5]. It consists of an encoder that transforms an input vector s into a representation h in hidden layers through a mapping f. It also has a decoder, which takes the hidden representation and transforms it back into a vector in the input space.

The training stage is conducted by using the noise distorted features as inputs of the denoising autoencoders, its clean features are presented as outputs. Further, for the network to learn the complex relationships between these sets of features, the training algorithm adjusts the network's parameters. Today, computers and algorithms have the capacity to accomodate large data sets, as well as networks with lots of hidden layers.

3   Experimental Setup

In order to test the robustness of LSTM networks for enhancing reverberated speech, the experimental setup can be summarized in the following steps:

1. Selection of conditions: Due to the high amount of impulse responses contemplated on the database, we randomly chose five conditions of reverberated speech. Each one of the conditions has the correspondent clean version on the database.
2. Feature extraction and input-output correspondence: A set of parameters was extracted from the reverberated and the clean audio files. Those from the reverberated files were used as inputs to the networks, while the corresponding clean features were the outputs.
3. Training: During training, the weights of the networks were adjusted as the reverberated and the clean utterances were presented to the network. As usual, on recurrent neural networks, the updating is performed using backpropagation through time algorithm. A total of 210 utterances for each condition (about 70% of the total database) were used for training each case. Details and equations of the algorithm followed can be found in [15].
4. Validation: After each training step, the sum of squared errors were computed within the validation set of about 20% of utterances, and the weights of the network updated in each improvement.
5. Test: A subset of 50 randomly selected utterances (about 10% of the total amount of utterances of the database) was chosen for the test set, for each condition. These utterances were not part of the training process, to provide independence between the training and testing.

In the following subsections, further details of the main experimental setup are given.

3.1   Database

In our work, we use the Reverberant speech database [30]. The database was created at the University of Edinburg and was designed to train and test speech dereverberation methods. Reverberated speech was made by convolving clean speech of 56 native English speakers with several room impulse responses. For the purpose of this work, we randomly chose the following conditions: ACE Building Lobby 1, Artificial Room 1, Mardy Room 2, ACE Lecture Room 1 and ACE Meeting Room 2.

3.2 Feature Extraction

The audio files of the reverberated and the clean speech were downsampled to 16 kHz, 16 bits, to extract parameters using the Ahocoder system [9]. A frame size of 160 samples and frame shift of 80 samples were used to extract 39 MFCC, f_0 and energy of each sentence.

For this work, neural networks were applied only to improve the 39 MFCC coefficients, while the rest of the parameters remained invariant.

3.3 Evaluation

To evaluate the results given from our experiments, we use the following well-known speech spectrum measures:

- Euclidean Distance: This measure is computed between each of the MFCC vectors (dimension 39) of clean and enhanced speech in the test set. For a vector s of MFCC, and the corresponding enhanced $\hat{s}$, the distance is computed as:

$$Eu(\mathbf{s_j}, \mathbf{\hat{s}_j}) = \left(\sum_{i=1}^{n} (s_{j_i} - \hat{s_{j_i}})^2 \right)^{\frac{1}{2}}, \tag{4}$$

  where n is the number of frames in the test sentences, and $j \in \{1, \ldots, 39\}$ the index of the MFCC.
- Mean Absolute Distance (MAD): This measure is computed as

$$MAD(\mathbf{x_j}, \mathbf{\hat{x}_j}) = \frac{1}{39} \sum_{j=1}^{39} \frac{1}{n} \sum_{i=1}^{n} |x_{j_i} - \hat{x_{j_i}}| \tag{5}$$

  We use MAD as a measure for each MFCC, but reported the first five measures due to the similar behaviour presented in all of them.
- PESQ (Perceptual Evaluation of Speech Quality): This measure uses a model to predict the subjective quality of speech, as defined in the ITU-T recommendation P.862.ITU. Results are given in the interval $[0.5, 4.5]$, where 4.5 corresponds to a perfect signal enhancing. PESQ is computed as [28]:

$$PESQ = a_0 + a_1 D_{ind} + a_2 A_{ind} \tag{6}$$

  where D_{ind} is the average disturbance and A_{ind} the asymmetrical disturbance. The a_k are chosen to optimize PESQ in measuring the speech overall quality.

Additionally, we show contours of MFCC coefficients to illustrate and compare the results.

3.4 Experiments

For the purpose of testing the robustness of LSTM networks in enhancing reverberated conditions, we train several sets of networks to directly map the reverberating features to the clean features. The experiments are described following the nomenclature:

- LSTM-5: The LSTM network were trained using sentences containing all the conditions at the input and the corresponding clean sentences at the output.
- LSTM-3: The LSTM network were trained using sentences containing MFCC from three conditions at the input. This case required different networks for the experimentation, to consider a target condition and two other conditions randomly chosen.
- LSTM-1 (base system): One network for each condition was trained. This is the case analyzed in previous references, and we consider the base results for comparison.
- Reverb: The evaluation measures were applied to the reverberated speech.

The LSTM architecture for the networks was defined by trial and error. Initially, we considered a single hidden layer with 50 units and then increased the size with steps of 50 units, up to three hidden layers with 300 units in each layer. The final selection consisted of a network with three layers containing 100, 100 and 100 units in each one.

This network gave the best results in the trial experiments, and also had a manageable training time. The training procedure was accelerated by a NVIDIA GPU system, taking about six hours to train each LSTM.

4 Results and Discussion

The results are presented in a comparative way for different conditions: Reverb, LSTM-1, LSTM-3, and LSTM-5. On Table 1, the results of the PESQ measure are shown. The ability of the LSTM-1 neural network to improve the spectrum of Reverb can be observed. However, the values obtained with LSTM-3 and LSTM-5 do not differ significantly from this base result.

Table 1. Mean PESQ Results for the test sets. Higher values represent better results. * is the best result.

Condition	Condition			
	Reverb.	LSTM-1	LSTM-3	LSTM-5
Building Lobby	1.68	2.22	2.26	2.27*
Artificial Room	1.96	3.12	3.14 *	3.07
Mardy Room	1.59	2.09*	2.00	2.02
Lecture Room	1.58	1.94	2.00*	1.97
Meeting Room	1.44	2.00	2.04*	2.01

For the Building Lobby case, LSTM-5 even presented the best result. On the other hand, for the Artificial Room, Lecture Room, and Meeting Room cases, the best results were obtained with LSTM-3. These PESQ results indicate that the LSTM networks obtain similar results regardless of whether they are trained with only one or several conditions.

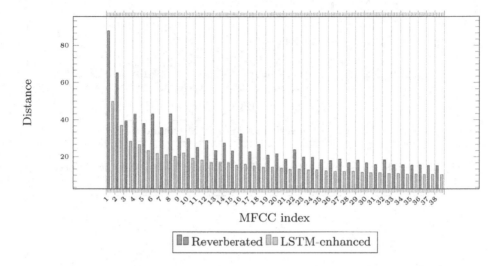

Fig. 1. Euclidean distance between MFCC (Building Lobby) and Clean Speech

Similar results can be observed for the Mardy Room (Fig. 2), Artificial Room (Fig. 3), Meeting Room (Fig. 4) and Lecture Room (Fig. 5). The most outstanding case can be observed in Fig. 3, where reverberation affected the MFCCs of high index considerably and the LSTM networks accomplished significant improvements.

Figure 1 shows the Euclidean distance between each one of the 39 MFCC of the Building Lobby and clean speech condition. It can be observed that a smaller distance, equivalent to improvement, is obtained in each one of the coefficients with the LSTM autoencoders.

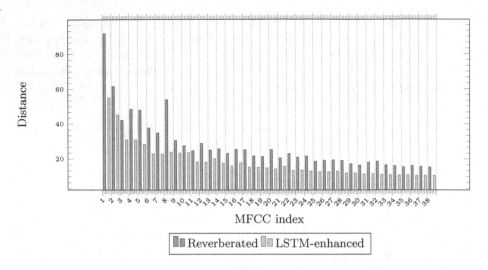

Fig. 2. Euclidean distance between MFCC (Mardy Room) and Clean Speech

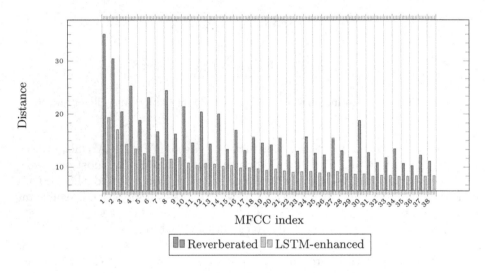

Fig. 3. Euclidean distance between MFCC (Artificial Room) and Clean Speech

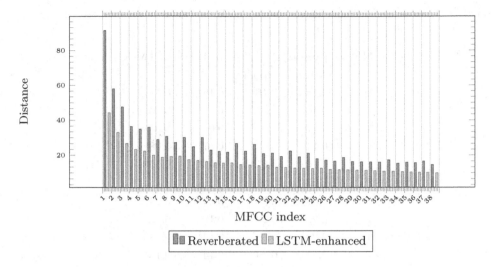

Fig. 4. Euclidean distance between MFCC (Meeting Room) and Clean Speech

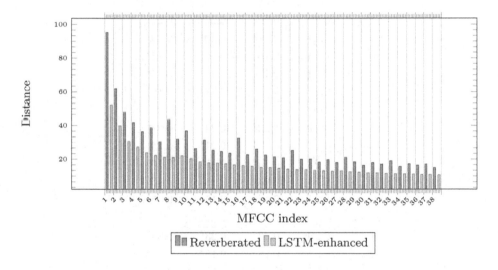

Fig. 5. Euclidean distance between MFCC (Lecture Room) and Clean Speech

The previous results were obtained with LSTM-5, but as it can be verified with the other measures, there is an equivalent between this condition, LSTM-3, and the base case LSTM-1.

Table 2 shows the MAD measure results in each one of the tests performed. These results prove that the LSTM networks are equivalent when trained for one, three, or five conditions simultaneously. In all cases, differences with the Reverb case are notorious.

Table 2. Mean absolute distance results. The lower values represent better results. *
is the best result

MFCC	Reverb.	LSTM-1	LSTM-3	LSTM-5
	Artificial Room			
1	0.18	0.10*	0.10*	0.11
2	0.16	0.09*	0.09*	0.10
3	0.11	0.07*	0.08	0.08
4	0.14	0.07*	0.07*	0.08
5	0.10	0.07*	0.07*	0.07*
	Building Lobby			
1	0.47	0.25	0.24*	0.24*
2	0.33	0.20	0.19	0.18*
3	0.20	0.15	0.14*	0.14*
4	0.22	0.14	0.14	0.13*
5	0.20	0.12*	0.12*	0.12*
	Lecture Room			
1	0.52	0.26	0.26	0.25*
2	0.32	0.20*	0.20*	0.20*
3	0.25	0.16	0.16	0.15*
4	0.22	0.15	0.14*	0.14*
5	0.19	0.13	.012*	0.12*
	Mardy Room			
1	0.47	0.22*	0.24	0.27
2	0.32	0.1*9	0.21	0.24
3	0.22	0.14*	0.15	0.16
4	0.25	0.13*	0.15	0.16
5	0.27	0.13*	0.15	0.15
	Meeting Room			
1	0.50	0.23*	0.23*	0.23*
2	0.32	0.18*	0.18*	0.18*
3	0.27	0.14*	0.15	0.14*
4	0.20	0.13*	0.13*	0.13*
5	0.20	0.13	0.12*	0.12*

The previous results show that LSTM networks are able to generalize dereverberation of the MFCC coefficients. This has significant advantages for its
application in real contexts. For example, it's possible to make improvements of
signals with a small set of neural networks, instead of using a specific one for
each condition.

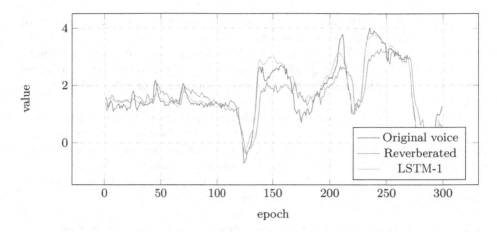

Fig. 6. Trajectory of the first MFCC for the MARDY condition

Finally, Fig. 6 shows the evolution of the first MFCC coefficient during 300 frames, which shows how the improvement with the LSTM network provides a better approximation of the values over time. The way in which reverberation affects this parameter both with values above and below the clean voice is also evident. The LSTM networks managed to improve the parameter in both cases.

In these results, the simultaneous training of several conditions produce results that are comparable or even better than the base case in almost every condition. It has to be taken into consideration that the LSTM-3 has three times the amount of training and validation data than the LSTM-1. In the case of LSTM-5, the amount of data is five times those of the base system.

This larger data-sets provide the network with better information to properly update the amount of internal weights in the network. A detailed study on the influence of the amount of data should be performed to verify the capacity of generalization under lower data.

5   Conclusions

In this work, we assessed the capability of LSTM recurrent neural networks to generalize the enhancement of reverberated speech signal's spectrum. Previous references have analyzed the case of improving speech signals with a specific single neural network for each condition or noise type and level.

The results present in this study show that LSTM networks can learn the approximation function, which achieves the enhancement of the signals, where training with several conditions simultaneously. This new information about the capacity of the LSTM networks is a significant contribution to the comprehension of the capability of recurrent neural networks to solve problems in a real-life context, where there is no previous knowledge of the condition of the signal that needs to be improved.

The capability of the networks to generalize can come from the large sets of data when there is training with several conditions at the same time, instead of a single group of data for a specific case. The methodology to assess this generalization capability can be extended to other types of neural networks and wider noise or reverberation conditions, to test the robustness of other architectures and contexts.

As future work, experimentation with the whole set of reverberation conditions from the database used, as well as the combination of reverberation with natural and artificial noise is proposed, to measure the networks' generalization capability under multiple conditions. Implementing various conditions simultaneously can require considerable quantities of computer capacity and memory, this also represents a challenge for future work.

Acknowledgements. This work was supported by the University of Costa Rica (UCR), Project No. 322-B9-105.

References

1. Abdel-Hamid, O., Mohamed, A.R., Jiang, H., Penn, G.: Applying convolutional neural networks concepts to hybrid NN-HMM model for speech recognition. In: 2012 IEEE International Conference on Acoustics, Speech and Signal Processing (ICASSP), pp. 4277–4280. IEEE (2012)
2. Bagchi, D., Mandel, M.I., Wang, Z., He, Y., Plummer, A., Fosler-Lussier, E.: Combining spectral feature mapping and multi-channel model-based source separation for noise-robust automatic speech recognition. In: 2015 IEEE Workshop on Automatic Speech Recognition and Understanding (ASRU), pp. 496–503. IEEE (2015)
3. Coto-Jiménez, M.: Robustness of LSTM neural networks for the enhancement of spectral parameters in noisy speech signals. In: Batyrshin, I., Martínez-Villaseñor, M.L., Ponce Espinosa, H.E. (eds.) MICAI 2018. LNCS (LNAI), vol. 11289, pp. 227–238. Springer, Cham (2018). https://doi.org/10.1007/978-3-030-04497-8_19
4. Coto-Jiménez, M., Goddard-Close, J.: Lstm deep neural networks postfiltering for enhancing synthetic voices. Int. J. Pattern Recognit. Artif. Intell. **32**(01), 1860008 (2018)
5. Coto-Jimenez, M., Goddard-Close, J., Di Persia, L., Rufiner, H.L.: Hybrid speech enhancement with wiener filters and deep LSTM denoising autoencoders. In: 2018 IEEE International Work Conference on Bioinspired Intelligence (IWOBI), pp. 1–8. IEEE (2018)
6. Coto-Jiménez, M., Goddard-Close, J., Martínez-Licona, F.: Improving automatic speech recognition containing additive noise using deep denoising autoencoders of LSTM networks. In: Ronzhin, A., Potapova, R., Németh, G. (eds.) SPECOM 2016. LNCS (LNAI), vol. 9811, pp. 354–361. Springer, Cham (2016). https://doi.org/10.1007/978-3-319-43958-7_42
7. Deng, L., et al.: Recent advances in deep learning for speech research at microsoft. In: ICASSP, vol. 26, p. 64 (2013)
8. Du, J., Wang, Q., Gao, T., Xu, Y., Dai, L.R., Lee, C.H.: Robust speech recognition with speech enhanced deep neural networks. In: Fifteenth Annual Conference of the International Speech Communication Association (2014)

9. Erro, D., Sainz, I., Navas, E., Hernáez, I.: Improved HNM-based vocoder for statistical synthesizers. In: Twelfth Annual Conference of the International Speech Communication Association (2011)
10. Fan, Y., Qian, Y., Xie, F.L., Soong, F.K.: TTS synthesis with bidirectional LSTM based recurrent neural networks. In: Fifteenth Annual Conference of the International Speech Communication Association (2014)
11. Feng, X., Zhang, Y., Glass, J.: Speech feature denoising and dereverberation via deep autoencoders for noisy reverberant speech recognition. In: 2014 IEEE International Conference on Acoustics, Speech and Signal Processing (ICASSP), pp. 1759–1763. IEEE (2014)
12. Gers, F.A., Schraudolph, N.N., Schmidhuber, J.: Learning precise timing with LSTM recurrent networks. J. Mach. Learn. Res. 3(Aug), 115–143 (2002)
13. Graves, A., Fernández, S., Schmidhuber, J.: Bidirectional LSTM networks for improved phoneme classification and recognition. In: Duch, W., Kacprzyk, J., Oja, E., Zadrożny, S. (eds.) ICANN 2005. LNCS, vol. 3697, pp. 799–804. Springer, Heidelberg (2005). https://doi.org/10.1007/11550907_126
14. Graves, A., Jaitly, N., Mohamed, A.R.: Hybrid speech recognition with deep bidirectional LSTM. In: 2013 IEEE Workshop on Automatic Speech Recognition and Understanding (ASRU), pp. 273–278. IEEE (2013)
15. Greff, K., Srivastava, R.K., Koutník, J., Steunebrink, B.R., Schmidhuber, J.: LSTM: a search space odyssey. IEEE Trans. Neural Netw. Learn. Syst. 28(10), 2222–2232 (2017)
16. Han, K., He, Y., Bagchi, D., Fosler-Lussier, E., Wang, D.: Deep neural network based spectral feature mapping for robust speech recognition. In: Sixteenth Annual Conference of the International Speech Communication Association (2015)
17. Hansen, J.H., Pellom, B.L.: An effective quality evaluation protocol for speech enhancement algorithms. In: Fifth International Conference on Spoken Language Processing (1998)
18. Healy, E.W., Yoho, S.E., Wang, Y., Wang, D.: An algorithm to improve speech recognition in noise for hearing-impaired listeners. J. Acoust. Soc. Am. 134(4), 3029–3038 (2013)
19. Hinton, G., et al.: Deep neural networks for acoustic modeling in speech recognition: the shared views of four research groups. IEEE Sig. Process. Mag. 29(6), 82–97 (2012)
20. Hochreiter, S., Schmidhuber, J.: Long short-term memory. Neural Comput. 9(8), 1735–1780 (1997)
21. Huang, J., Kingsbury, B.: Audio-visual deep learning for noise robust speech recognition. In: 2013 IEEE International Conference on Acoustics, Speech and Signal Processing (ICASSP), pp. 7596–7599. IEEE (2013)
22. Ishii, T., Komiyama, H., Shinozaki, T., Horiuchi, Y., Kuroiwa, S.: Reverberant speech recognition based on denoising autoencoder. In: Interspeech, pp. 3512–3516 (2013)
23. Kumar, A., Florencio, D.: Speech enhancement in multiple-noise conditions using deep neural networks. arXiv preprint arXiv:1605.02427 (2016)
24. Lee, W.J., Wang, S.S., Chen, F., Lu, X., Chien, S.Y., Tsao, Y.: Speech dereverberation based on integrated deep and ensemble learning algorithm. In: 2018 IEEE International Conference on Acoustics, Speech and Signal Processing (ICASSP), pp. 5454–5458. IEEE (2018)
25. Maas, A.L., Le, Q.V., O'Neil, T.M., Vinyals, O., Nguyen, P., Ng, A.Y.: Recurrent neural networks for noise reduction in robust ASR. In: Thirteenth Annual Conference of the International Speech Communication Association (2012)

26. Narayanan, A., Wang, D.: Ideal ratio mask estimation using deep neural networks for robust speech recognition. In: 2013 IEEE International Conference on Acoustics, Speech and Signal Processing (ICASSP), pp. 7092–7096. IEEE (2013)

27. Naylor, P.A., Gaubitch, N.D.: Speech Dereverberation. Springer, London (2010). https://doi.org/10.1007/978-1-84996-056-4

28. Rix, A.W., Hollier, M.P., Hekstra, A.P., Beerends, J.G.: Perceptual evaluation of speech quality (PESQ) the new itu standard for end-to-end speech quality assessment part i-time-delay compensation. J. Audio Eng. Soc. 50(10), 755–764 (2002)

29. Seltzer, M.L., Yu, D., Wang, Y.: An investigation of deep neural networks for noise robust speech recognition. In: 2013 IEEE International Conference on Acoustics, Speech and Signal Processing (ICASSP), pp. 7398–7402. IEEE (2013)

30. Valentini-Botinhao, C.: Reverberant speech database for training speech dereverberation algorithms and TTS models (2016). https://doi.org/10.7488/ds/1425

31. Vincent, E., Watanabe, S., Nugraha, A.A., Barker, J., Marxer, R.: An analysis of environment, microphone and data simulation mismatches in robust speech recognition. Comput. Speech Lang. 46, 535–557 (2017)

32. Vincent, P., Larochelle, H., Lajoie, I., Bengio, Y., Manzagol, P.A.: Stacked denoising autoencoders: learning useful representations in a deep network with a local denoising criterion. J. Mach. Learn. Res. 11(Dec), 3371–3408 (2010)

33. Weninger, F., Geiger, J., Wöllmer, M., Schuller, B., Rigoll, G.: Feature enhancement by deep LSTM networks for asr in reverberant multisource environments. Comput. Speech Lang. 28(4), 888–902 (2014)

34. Weninger, F., Watanabe, S., Tachioka, Y., Schuller, B.: Deep recurrent de-noising auto-encoder and blind de-reverberation for reverberated speech recognition. In: 2014 IEEE International Conference on Acoustics, Speech and Signal Processing (ICASSP), pp. 4623–4627. IEEE (2014)

35. Xu, Y., Du, J., Dai, L.R., Lee, C.H.: An experimental study on speech enhancement based on deep neural networks. IEEE Signal Process. Lett. 21(1), 65–68 (2014)

36. Zen, H., Sak, H.: Unidirectional long short-term memory recurrent neural network with recurrent output layer for low-latency speech synthesis. In: 2015 IEEE International Conference on Acoustics, Speech and Signal Processing (ICASSP), pp. 4470–4474. IEEE (2015)

37. Zhao, Y., Wang, Z.Q., Wang, D.: Two-stage deep learning for noisy-reverberant speech enhancement. IEEE/ACM Trans. Audio Speech Lang. Process. 27(1), 53–62 (2019)

A Performance Evaluation of Several Artificial Neural Networks for Mapping Speech Spectrum Parameters

Víctor Yeom-Song[ID], Marisol Zeledón-Córdoba[ID],
and Marvin Coto-Jiménez[✉][ID]

PRIS-Lab, Escuela de Ingeniería Eléctrica, Universidad de Costa Rica,
San Pedro, Costa Rica
{victor.yeom,marisol.zeledon,marvin.coto}@ucr.ac.cr

Abstract. In this work, we compare different neural network architectures, for the task of mapping spectral coefficients of noisy speech signals with those corresponding to natural speech. In previous works on the subject, fully-connected multilayer perception (MLP) networks and recurrent neural networks (LSTM & BLSTM) have been used. Several references report some initial trial and error processes to determine which architecture to use. Finding the best network type and size is of great importance due to the considerable training time required by some models of recurrent networks. In our work, we conducted extensive tests training more than five hundred networks, with several architectures to determine which cases present significant differences. The results show that for this application of neural networks, the architectures with more layers or the greater number of neurons are not the most convenient, both for the time required in their training and for the adjustment achieved. These results depend on the complexity of the task (the signal-to-noise ratio or SNR) and the amount of data available. This exploration can guide the most efficient use of these types of neural networks in future mapping applications, and can help to optimize resources in future studies by reducing computational time and complexity.

Keywords: Deep learning · LSTM · Noise · Speech enhancement

1 Introduction

Deep learning-based techniques have been prevalent in the denoising speech field for the past few years. Moreover, they often surpass the results of traditional signal processing and statistically-based algorithms. Thus, many different types of Deep Neural Networks (DNN) structures have been considered for this purpose, such as the classic Multilayer Perception (MLP) and recurrent neural networks (RNN). However, little work has been done in systematic comparisons and evaluations of different DNN structures for the task of speech enhancement under

Supported by the University of Costa Rica.

J. L. Crespo-Mariño and E. Meneses-Rojas (Eds.): CARLA 2019, CCIS 1087, pp. 291–306, 2020.
https://doi.org/10.1007/978-3-030-41005-6_20

noisy conditions. To address this limitation, we implement a variety of DNN-based speech enhancing networks with different structures, to map noisy speech spectrum to the corresponding clear speech.

1.1   Related Work

The idea of enhancing speech signals, degraded with noise or reverberation, using DNN has been an important topic in research during the past decade. Generally, the most frequent implementation relies on the enhancement of spectral features, such as MFCC [1,14,23], often used as parameters for classification of these signals.

Several references have reported the DNN approaches as being successful in enhancing speech, outperforming classical methods based on signal processing. [3,13,17,24], or reverberated speech [8,15,29]. The capacity of a neural network to approximate functions (such as mapping between noise and clean speech) have defined its expressive power [19].

The important universal approximation theorem states that depth-2 networks which have suitable activation function can approximate any continuous function on a compact domain to any desired accuracy [2,9]. However, there is no information available regarding the size of each layer for neural networks to perform a particular tasks.

Besides the more traditional MLP, some kinds of RNN, such as Long Short-term Memory (LSTM) and Bidirectional Long Short-term Memory (BLSTM networks) have been previously presented in [4,6,27], for the task of enhancing speech. Although the LSTM outperforms other deep networks in this task, systematic comparisons about training conditions, such as the number of units or layers in the network, is not commonly reported in the references.

A known limitation for the experimentation with a larger amount of units or layers in this RNN is the high computational costs [5,6]. From our own experiences, this is the main reason that limits extender experimentation for this task in previous references.

The search for the better architectures, in terms of a number of units and hidden layers, which have been addressed with bio-inspired algorithms, such as genetic algorithms [21]. Considering the computational cost of recent models or RNN, is not yet possible to implement such algorithms in the search for proper architectures of networks, due that any change in each recurrent network should require several hours to assess the result.

In the present paper, we consider the application of three kinds of artificial neural networks (MLP, LSTM and BLSTM) for the task of speech enhancement. Our main motivation is to contribute to the knowledge of neural networks for this task. Moreover we aim to guide future research through objective knowledge about the neural network architecture that is more convenient concerning capacity and efficiency.

The rest of this paper is organized: Sect. 2 gives the background and context of the problem of selecting an architecture of networks for enhancing noisy speech. Section 3 describes the experimental setup, Sect. 4 presents the results with a discussion, and finally, in Sect. 5, we present the conclusions.

2   Background

2.1   Problem Statement

Given a feedforward neural network θ, which comprises layers of computational units, there is a unique function $f_\theta : \mathbb{R}^d \to \mathbb{R}$, which depends on the particular architecture and configuration of θ. If L denotes the number of internal (hidden) layers of the network, and N the number of units in each layer (assuming a constant number in each layer), the goal of finding a particular θ that satisfies a particular task can be stated as [18]:

$$\min_{\tilde{f} \in \mathcal{F}(N,L)} ||f - \tilde{f}|| \le \epsilon \tag{1}$$

Specifically, it is of interest to find a proper N as a lower bound, for a given fixed value of L. On the other hand, it is also relevant to find a value of L as a lower bound.

In this work, we explore several values of N for different cases of L, in three types of feedforward and recurrent neural networks. The pursuit of a good approximation of f for a denoising tasks, with efficient and manageable time, is the desired application to such a finding.

2.2   Enhancing Speech with Artificial Neural Networks

Training artificial neural networks in speech enhancement became a solid idea with its first application; the modeling of acoustic coefficients with single layer networks. Working with large sets of data or introducing hidden layers was not possible until the last decade, due to limiting computer capabilities and undeveloped algorithms for the purpose [13].

Within the network, an input vector **s** (with information of noisy speech) is transformed into a representation h in hidden layers through a mapping function f. The hidden representation is transformed back into a vector in input space, at the output of the network.

With the goal of having the output of the models being as close to the uncorrupted signal as possible, training data is used by the network's parameters to perform noise reduction and regression-based tasks [25]. The training stage is done by using the noise distorted features as inputs of the networks, and its clean features as the outputs. In order for the network to learn the complex relationships between these sets of features, a training algorithm, such as backpropagation or backpropagation through time, adjusts the network's parameters.

2.3 LSTM and BLSTM Networks

Over the last few decades, a variety of neural networks have been tested for classification and regression purposes, extending the capacities of the MLP.

Since the arrival of RNNs, there have been new alternatives for modeling the dependent nature of sequential information [7, 28].

With the objective of expanding the abilities of RNNs by storing information in the short-term and long-term, LSTM networks shown in [20] introduced a set of four gates within memory cells that are able to control the access, storage and propagation of values over the network.

Instead of direct feed-forward propagation of values, there is a set of equation that models the behaviour of the four gates: i is the input gate (controls whether or not the value enters the unit), f the forget gate (whether or not the internal value is erased), o the output gate (whether or not the unit outputs the value or its memory), and c the internal value of the memory. $\mathbf{W}_{mn}$ are the weight matrices from each cell to gate vector. h is the output at the unit for the LSTM network. The corresponding equations are [10]:

$$i_t = \sigma\left(\mathbf{W}_{xi}x_t + \mathbf{W}_{hi}h_{t-1} + \mathbf{W}_{ci}c_{t-1} + b_i\right) \tag{2}$$

$$f_t = \sigma\left(\mathbf{W}_{xf}x_t + \mathbf{W}_{hf}h_{t-1} + \mathbf{W}_{cf}c_{t-1} + b_f\right) \tag{3}$$

$$c_t = f_t c_{t-1} + i_t \tanh\left(\mathbf{W}_{xc}x_t + \mathbf{W}_{hc}h_{t-1} + b_c\right) \tag{4}$$

$$o_t = \sigma\left(\mathbf{W}_{xo}x_t + \mathbf{W}_{ho}h_{t-1} + \mathbf{W}_{co}c_t + b_o\right) \tag{5}$$

$$h_t = o_t \tanh\left(c_t\right) \tag{6}$$

To train these complex relationships, the backpropagation through time algorithm is applied.

The BLSTM is a more recent model of recurrent neural networks. The idea is to use not only previous information, but also future context with respect to current position in the speech frames. To create a BLSTM network, connections between layers should be made such that the output of each hidden layer will propagate to both the forward and backward LSTM layer forming the successive hidden layer [22].

In our implementation we use the Current system [26, 27]. The forward and backward process represent a higher computational cost during the training of BLSTM.

The results obtained by the LSTM and BLSTM networks in areas that depend on previous states of the information, such as speech recognition, music composition, and handwriting synthesis, were encouraging [11, 12, 20]. Further details on the training procedure and the mathematical modeling of these networks can be found in [10].

3 Experiments

To evaluate the performance of the neural networks proposed in this paper, a procedure was established in the following steps:

3.1   Database and Setup

We used the CMU Arctic databases, constructed at the Language Technologies Institute at Carnegie Mellon University [16]. The databases were designed for research speech synthesis, and consist of around 1150 utterances for each speaker selected from out-of-copyright texts from Project Gutenberg. A detailed report on the structure and content of the database, as well as the recording conditions is available in the Language Technologies Institute Tech Report CMU-LTI-03-177 18. We chose the first female voice of the database (SLT) to add the white noise with five SNR levels.

With this data, the next steps were followed:

1. Selection of conditions: In previous references for the improvement of signals degraded with noise, different levels of natural and artificial noise have been contemplated to affect the signal with slight to high distortion. In our experiments we used white noise and added it to the speech signal with five different SRN levels: SNR-10, SNR-5, SNR0, SNR5, SNR10.
2. Pre-processing and feature extraction: We extracted 39 MFCC for each 10 ms window in each utterance of the database. Each utterance is encoded in 16-kHz, 16-bit WAV format.
3. Training: During training, the pairs (clean speech, speech with noise) are presented to the input and output of each type of neural network considered in this work. The internal weights are adjusted to improve the approximation that the network can make for the mapping between both. Figure 1 illustrates the procedure.
4. Validation: After each training step, the sum of squared errors were computed within the validation set of about 30% of utterances, and the weights of the network updated in each improvement.

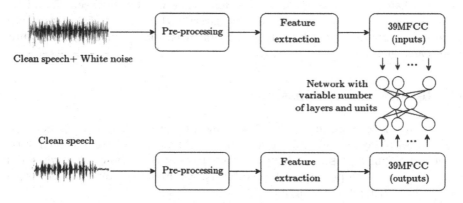

Fig. 1. Procedure followed for data preparation and training strategy

The stop criteria for the networks was 25 epochs since the last best result, or a maximum of 2000 epochs.

3.2   Evaluation

To evaluate the results given by our experiments, we use the following well-known measures for the training efficiency of the networks:

- Number of epochs: Each epoch consists of a feedforward and backforward step to adjust the weights of the connections, when the result in the validation set is improved. The time taken to train a neural network is directly associated with the amount of epochs in training.
- LVE: This is a common measure for lowest validation error during training. LVE is defined as:

$$LVE(\theta) = \sum_{n=1}^{T} (\mathbf{c_x} - \hat{\mathbf{c_x}})^2 \tag{7}$$

$$= \sum_{n=1}^{T} (\mathbf{c_x} - f(\mathbf{c_x}))^2 \tag{8}$$

where $\mathbf{c_x}$ is the desired output of the network, $\hat{\mathbf{c_x}}$ is the obtained output, T the number of frames, and f the mapping function the networks perform between its inputs and its outputs. A lower value of LVE means that the network is producing MFCC coefficients that are more closely related to the those of the natural voice at the output.
- EF: It is the number of the epoch in which the best set of internal weights of the network was found. A lower value of EF means that the training process was more efficient.

Given the high training times required by the LSTM and BLSTM networks, this work only considers networks with one, two and three hidden layers. On the other hand, according to previous references, a number between 25 and 100 neurons were considered in each hidden layer, with steps of 25 between each experiment. There were 180 different neural networks trained in total, three times each one.

4   Results and Discussion

The results are organized in SNR levels and present all the types of networks and number of layers and units. For each type of neural network and each of the five levels of white noise, the networks were trained three times. The repetition of experiments were performed to establish a valid comparison, independent to the random initial set of weights.

We use the following notation to present the results:

- LVE: Lowest Validation Error
- EF: Epoch in which the LVE was found.
- TE: Time per Epoch, in seconds.

Table 1 shows the total number of connections for each type of network contemplated in the present work. It can be seen that the recurrent networks have an average of connections about ten times the number of connections of the MLPs. Thus, the complexity and training time are higher.

Table 1. Number of internal connections (weights) for each type and size of networks

Hidden layers	Units	Network	Number of weights
3	100	MLP	28139
		LSTM & BLSTM	221639
	75	MLP	17364
		LSTM & BLSTM	128739
	50	MLP	9089
		LSTM & BLSTM	60839
	25	MLP	3314
		LSTM & BLSTM	17939
2	100	MLP	18039
		LSTM & BLSTM	140939
	75	MLP	11664
		LSTM & BLSTM	83214
	50	MLP	6539
		LSTM & BLSTM	40489
	25	MLP	2664
		LSTM & BLSTM	12764
1	100	MLP	7939
		LSTM & BLSTM	60239
	75	MLP	5974
		LSTM & BLSTM	37689
	50	MLP	3989
		LSTM & BLSTM	20139
	25	MLP	2014
		LSTM & BLSTM	7589

Table 2 shows the results of the different measures obtained with the SNR-10 noise level in each type of network.

It is observed that BLSTM presents better results than LSTM and MLP in all cases, although with a tendency to a greater number of epochs required and more time in each one. In this SNR, the higher one considered in our experiments, MLP networks do not present any benefit. The results indicate poor capacity to map the noisy spectral coefficients to those of clean speech.

The results for SNR-5 are shown in Table 3. For this noise level, both LSTM and BLSTM greatly exceed what was obtained with MLP. On the other hand, BLSTM tends to obtain better LVE values than LSTM, although the number of epochs required to reach that value tends to be higher. In the same way, time per

Table 2. Results for all type and size of networks for the spectral mapping of speech signals with SNR −10 dB. * is the best result.

Hidden layers	Units	Type	LVE	EF	TE (s)
3	100	MLP	835.48	12	1.3
		LSTM	547.25	152	35.9
		BLSTM	459.85	165	40.5
	75	MLP	836.61	23	1.6
		LSTM	555.56	83	26.2
		BLSTM	456.05	164	31.9
	50	MLP	644.04	2000	1.0
		LSTM	538.06	206	18.4
		BLSTM	448.47	187	25.0
	25	MLP	674.75	2000	0.5
		LSTM	541.03	204	12.3
		BLSTM	455.63	212	18.2
2	100	MLP	683.76	2000	1.5
		LSTM	544.96	277	20.6
		BLSTM	457.77	264	25.7
	75	MLP	682.98	2000	1.1
		LSTM	540.40	159	14.3
		BLSTM	455.15	246	18.1
	50	MLP	681.94	2000	0.7
		LSTM	536.21	182	8.9
		BLSTM	445.97*	326	9.5
	25	MLP	706.17	2000	0.4
		LSTM	539.08	256	4.2
		BLSTM	471.89	179	5.5
1	100	MLP	730.08	2000	0.7
		LSTM	528.63	356	10.5
		BLSTM	476.83	278	12.0
	75	MLP	732.91	2000	0.6
		LSTM	536.88	285	8.0
		BLSTM	473.08	550	10.1
	50	MLP	741.02	2000	0.5
		LSTM	535.70	275	6.0
		BLSTM	498.43	163	8.4
	25	MLP	749.09	2000	0.3
		LSTM	554.98	187	2.9
		BLSTM	489.55	558	4.3

epoch is also greater. For example, for the case of three layers with 100 neurons in each one, the best value obtained with BLSTM required 29% more of the total time, of around 1.5 h.

Table 3. Results for all type and size of networks for the spectral mapping of speech signals with SNR −5 dB. * is the best result.

Hidden layers	Units	Type	LVE	EF	TE (s)
3	100	MLP	554.95	2000	1.3
		LSTM	455.06	150	35.7
		BLSTM	388.76	170	40.6
	75	MLP	556.32	2000	1.6
		LSTM	451.85	167	26.0
		BLSTM	388.87	152	32.0
	50	MLP	560.34	2000	1.0
		LSTM	448.47	219	18.4
		BLSTM	380.53	269	25.0
	25	MLP	568.46	2000	0.5
		LSTM	450.64	300	12.3
		BLSTM	392.44	220	18.2
2	100	MLP	573.80	2000	1.5
		LSTM	251.92	238	20.6
		BLSTM	380.18*	285	25.7
	75	MLP	572.72	2000	1.1
		LSTM	452.96	218	18.1
		BLSTM	381.19	273	14.3
	50	MLP	574.69	2000	0.7
		LSTM	447.65	314	8.9
		BLSTM	388.89	233	9.5
	25	MLP	584.18	2000	0.4
		LSTM	444.56	551	4.2
		BLSTM	383.39	665	5.5
1	100	MLP	591.60	2000	0.7
		LSTM	452.18	279	10.5
		BLSTM	399.95	402	12.0
	75	MLP	596.25	2000	0.6
		LSTM	452.91	333	8.0
		BLSTM	399.14	479	10.0
	50	MLP	596.17	2000	0.5
		LSTM	448.12	373	6.1
		BLSTM	403.96	532	8.4
	25	MLP	605.67	2000	0.3
		LSTM	454.66	469	2.9
		BLSTM	407.31	876	4.3

The results for the SNR0 are shown in Table 4. The difference between BLSTM and LSTM are lower than the two previous cases, although the BLSTM shows tendency to show better values. It is important to note that the best values

Table 4. Results for all type and size of networks for the spectral mapping of speech signals with SNR 0 dB. * is the best result

Hidden layers	Units	Type	LVE	EF	TE (s)
3	100	MLP	477.47	2000	1.3
		LSTM	386.15	203	38.4
		BLSTM	334.80	160	40.8
	75	MLP	474.25	2000	1.2
		LSTM	384.86	228	25.7
		BLSTM	323.97*	305	31.9
	50	MLP	476.13	2000	1.0
		LSTM	283.37	337	18.4
		BLSTM	326.90	248	25.0
	25	MLP	483.80	2000	0.5
		LSTM	392.71	170	12.3
		BLSTM	363.60	99	18.4
2	100	MLP	486.04	2000	1.5
		LSTM	386.55	225	20.6
		BLSTM	350.03	134	25.7
	75	MLP	485.79	2000	1.1
		LSTM	385.87	252	14.3
		BLSTM	326.96	390	18.1
	50	MLP	482.65	2000	0.7
		LSTM	385.47	307	8.9
		BLSTM	329.79	412	9.5
	25	MLP	491.37	2000	0.4
		LSTM	379.47	648	4.2
		BLSTM	329.21	628	5.5
1	100	MLP	491.12	2000	0.7
		LSTM	381.91	504	10.5
		BLSTM	343.70	370	12.0
	75	MLP	491.15	2000	0.6
		LSTM	383.14	402	8.0
		BLSTM	334.61	755	10.0
	50	MLP	493.63	2000	0.5
		LSTM	383.85	385	6.2
		BLSTM	339.30	914	8.4
	25	MLP	499.35	2000	0.3
		LSTM	384.38	656	2.9
		BLSTM	365.16	319	4.4

are not obtained with the network of the largest number of layers and neurons. For example, the two-layer BLSTM, with 75 units in each layer, obtains better LVE values than the three-layer BLSTM of 100 units each. This was even done

Table 5. Results for all type and size of networks for the spectral mapping of speech signals with SNR 5 dB. * is the best result.

Hidden layers	Units	Type	LVE	EF	TE (s)
3	100	MLP	404.18	2000	1.3
		LSTM	330.51	197	35.5
		BLSTM	286.67	244	40.4
	75	MLP	404.32	2000	1.6
		LSTM	335.71	145	25.7
		BLSTM	282.41	343	31.9
	50	MLP	406.14	2000	1.0
		LSTM	330.46	266	18.4
		BLSTM	281.26	474	25.0
	25	MLP	413.36	2000	0.5
		LSTM	334.65	274	12.3
		BLSTM	285.59	772	18.4
2	100	MLP	410.61	2000	1.5
		LSTM	332.71	238	20.6
		BLSTM	279.47	487	25.7
	75	MLP	409.44	2000	1.1
		LSTM	328.29	298	18.1
		BLSTM	282.90	475	14.3
	50	MLP	412.05	2000	0.7
		LSTM	327.0	486	8.9
		BLSTM	277.30*	885	9.5
	25	MLP	416.74	2000	0.4
		LSTM	322.0	1011	4.2
		BLSTM	283.76	1465	5.5
1	100	MLP	413.91	2000	0.7
		LSTM	322.93	722	10.5
		BLSTM	289.62	1060	12.0
	75	MLP	414.30	2000	0.6
		LSTM	326.25	444	8.0
		BLSTM	288.07	1310	10.0
	50	MLP	417.97	2000	0.5
		LSTM	319.57	980	6.0
		BLSTM	292.41	1559	8.4
	25	MLP	422.04	2000	0.3
		LSTM	326.50	1376	4.3
		BLSTM	321.52	329	5.2

with a 15% lower processing time, which means that it is a better option in all aspects with this level of white noise.

The results for the lowest noise levels, SNR5 and SNR10, are shown in Tables 5 and 6 respectively. Again in both cases, the BLSTM networks are the

Table 6. Results for all type and size of networks for the spectral mapping of speech signals with SNR 10 dB. * is the best result.

Hidden layers	Units	Type	LVE	EF	TE (s)
3	100	MLP	341.99	2000	1.3
		LSTM	289.51	182	36.31
		BLSTM	249.93	266	40.5
	75	MLP	367.53	853	1.6
		LSTM	274.87	574	25.6
		BLSTM	242.81*	648	32.0
	50	MLP	345.67	2000	1.0
		LSTM	283.37	337	18.4
		BLSTM	261.12	210	25.0
	25	MLP	351.52	2000	0.5
		LSTM	273.25	1417	12.3
		BLSTM	251.44	927	18.2
2	100	MLP	348.28	2000	1.5
		LSTM	278.06	402	20.6
		BLSTM	243.23	603	25.7
	75	MLP	348.10	2000	1.1
		LSTM	277.13	500	18.1
		BLSTM	250.46	422	14.3
	50	MLP	349.66	2000	0.7
		LSTM	271.63	898	8.9
		BLSTM	243.9	998	9.5
	25	MLP	352.57	2000	0.4
		LSTM	279.0	1070	4.2
		BLSTM	252.69	1491	5.5
1	100	MLP	349.20	2000	0.7
		LSTM	269.27	1111	10.5
		BLSTM	249.60	1247	12.0
	75	MLP	349.95	2000	0.6
		LSTM	275.19	1199	8.0
		BLSTM	249.80	19.44	10.0
	50	MLP	352.54	2000	0.5
		LSTM	275.46	1315	8.4
		BLSTM	254.12	1997	12.1
	25	MLP	358.77	2000	0.3
		LSTM	282.3	1955	2.9
		BLSTM	268.54	2000	4.3

ones that show the best results, however, the number of epochs tends to be considerably higher than with the LSTM.

In the case of SNR5, the best result obtained is with the 2-layer, 50 units per layer architecture. In the case of three-layer networks, the results tend to be more similar to each other than in previous cases. They are similar even considering three and two layers, with small differences in favor of the use of two layers, where the training times also tend to be smaller given the greater simplicity of the network.

For both SNR5 and SNR10, MLPs do not present competitive results with recurrent networks with memory. The results of SNR10 have the greater similarity between LSTM and BSTLM, however, the number of epochs required for BLSTM is considerably higher. For example, for the case of the largest size considered (three hidden layers with 100 units per layer), the difference between BLST (249.93) and LSTM (289.51) is lower than in previous cases, but the total training time increases by 63%.

These results, in which more than five hundred neural network training processes were carried out, show that there is a dependence between the best architecture that can be used and the difficulty in the mapping sought. For example, the more the signal gets degraded by noise, the more convenient it is to use medium-size BLSTM networks, within the range studied.

On the other hand, when the signals have a small noise component, the BLSTM have fewer advantages than the LSTM, and a considerably longer training time. Both BLSTM and LSTM exceed in all cases similar size MLPs, which is an example of the advantages of the recurrent connections and the internal storage capacity of these networks. This is for the considered application, the mapping between coefficients of noisy and clean signals, for the improvement of speech signals.

It is possible that this may be reflected in other cases where neural networks are required to map data sets that present dependent behaviour, as in speech or varied conditions. The dependent behaviour is clearly an indicator of the use of networks with memory. The complexity of the task, namely the difference between one set of values and another, can help make the choice between LSTM and BLSTM in terms of efficiency.

5   Conclusions

In this work we explore several neural network architectures applied to the problem of mapping the spectrum of noisy speech signals to those of clean speech signals. More than five hundred networks were trained, to establish comparisons between different types of neurons and different sizes of layers.

The results have shown that it is not necessarily convenient to apply large or deep networks in this application. Instead, good results can be obtained with architectures of fewer units, which are more efficient to train.

The lower the SNR level of the noisy signal, that is, the greater the difficulty in mapping the spectrum of this signal to clean speech, the BLSTM networks have shown better results. This is in exchange of a longer training time per epoch in all cases, given its greater number of connections.

The amount of data available in the database may depend on the convenience of the size of the neural network applied. When the database is not very large, networks with proportional characteristics may offer better performance and results. Therefore, taking this information into account can guide future extensive experimentation with these types of neural networks in similar applications, where computing time remains an important limitation.

As future work, more experimentation of network architectures, new noise or reverberation conditions, and the study of the dependence of the size of the database with the results are planned. Also, algorithms to explore and find the best architectures automatically can be applied with larger computing capacities.

Acknowledgements. This work was supported by the University of Costa Rica (UCR), Project No. 322-B9-105.

References

1. Abdel-Hamid, O., Mohamed, A.R., Jiang, H., Penn, G.: Applying convolutional neural networks concepts to hybrid NN-HMM model for speech recognition. In: 2012 IEEE International Conference on Acoustics, Speech and Signal Processing (ICASSP), pp. 4277–4280. IEEE (2012)
2. Barron, A.R.: Approximation and estimation bounds for artificial neural networks. Mach. Learn. **14**(1), 115–133 (1994)
3. Coto-Jiménez, M.: Robustness of LSTM neural networks for the enhancement of spectral parameters in noisy speech signals. In: Batyrshin, I., Martínez-Villaseñor, M.L., Ponce Espinosa, H.E. (eds.) MICAI 2018. LNCS (LNAI), vol. 11289, pp. 227–238. Springer, Cham (2018). https://doi.org/10.1007/978-3-030-04497-8_19
4. Coto-Jiménez, M.: Improving post-filtering of artificial speech using pre-trained LSTM neural networks. Biomimetics **4**(2), 39 (2019)
5. Coto-Jiménez, M., Goddard-Close, J.: LSTM deep neural networks postfiltering for improving the quality of synthetic voices. In: Martínez-Trinidad, J.F., Carrasco-Ochoa, J.A., Ayala-Ramírez, V., Olvera-López, J.A., Jiang, X. (eds.) MCPR 2016. LNCS, vol. 9703, pp. 280–289. Springer, Cham (2016). https://doi.org/10.1007/978-3-319-39393-3_28
6. Coto-Jiménez, M., Goddard-Close, J., Martínez-Licona, F.: Improving automatic speech recognition containing additive noise using deep denoising autoencoders of LSTM networks. In: Ronzhin, A., Potapova, R., Németh, G. (eds.) SPECOM 2016. LNCS (LNAI), vol. 9811, pp. 354–361. Springer, Cham (2016). https://doi.org/10.1007/978-3-319-43958-7_42
7. Fan, Y., Qian, Y., Xie, F.L., Soong, F.K.: TTS synthesis with bidirectional LSTM based recurrent neural networks. In: Fifteenth Annual Conference of the International Speech Communication Association (2014)
8. Feng, X., Zhang, Y., Glass, J.: Speech feature denoising and dereverberation via deep autoencoders for noisy reverberant speech recognition. In: 2014 IEEE International Conference on Acoustics, Speech and Signal Processing (ICASSP), pp. 1759–1763. IEEE (2014)
9. Funahashi, K.I.: On the approximate realization of continuous mappings by neural networks. Neural Netw. **2**(3), 183–192 (1989)
10. Gers, F.A., Schraudolph, N.N., Schmidhuber, J.: Learning precise timing with LSTM recurrent networks. J. Mach. Learn. Res. **3**(Aug), 115–143 (2002)

11. Graves, A., Fernández, S., Schmidhuber, J.: Bidirectional LSTM networks for improved phoneme classification and recognition. In: Duch, W., Kacprzyk, J., Oja, E., Zadrożny, S. (eds.) ICANN 2005. LNCS, vol. 3697, pp. 799–804. Springer, Heidelberg (2005). https://doi.org/10.1007/11550907_126
12. Graves, A., Jaitly, N., Mohamed, A.R.: Hybrid speech recognition with deep bidirectional LSTM. In: 2013 IEEE Workshop on Automatic Speech Recognition and Understanding (ASRU), pp. 273–278. IEEE (2013)
13. Hinton, G., et al.: Deep neural networks for acoustic modeling in speech recognition: the shared views of four research groups. IEEE Signal Process. Mag. **29**(6), 82–97 (2012)
14. Huang, J., Kingsbury, B.: Audio-visual deep learning for noise robust speech recognition. In: 2013 IEEE International Conference on Acoustics, Speech and Signal Processing (ICASSP), pp. 7596–7599. IEEE (2013)
15. Ishii, T., Komiyama, H., Shinozaki, T., Horiuchi, Y., Kuroiwa, S.: Reverberant speech recognition based on denoising autoencoder. In: Interspeech, pp. 3512–3516 (2013)
16. Kominek, J., Black, A.W.: The CMU arctic speech databases. In: Fifth ISCA Workshop on Speech Synthesis (2004)
17. Kumar, A., Florencio, D.: Speech enhancement in multiple-noise conditions using deep neural networks. arXiv preprint arXiv:1605.02427 (2016)
18. Liang, S., Srikant, R.: Why deep neural networks for function approximation? arXiv preprint arXiv:1610.04161 (2016)
19. Lu, Z., Pu, H., Wang, F., Hu, Z., Wang, L.: The expressive power of neural networks: a view from the width. In: Advances in Neural Information Processing Systems, pp. 6231–6239 (2017)
20. Ma, X., Zhang, J., Du, B., Ding, C., Sun, L.: Parallel architecture ofconvolutional bi-directional LSTM neural networks for network-wide metroridership prediction. IEEE Trans. Intell. Transp. Syst. **20**, 2278–2288 (2018)
21. Miller, G.F., Todd, P.M., Hegde, S.U.: Designing neural networks using genetic algorithms. In: ICGA, vol. 89, pp. 379–384 (1989)
22. Ray, A., Rajeswar, S., Chaudhury, S.: Text recognition using deep BLSTM networks. In: 2015 Eighth International Conference on Advances in Pattern Recognition (ICAPR), pp. 1–6. IEEE (2015)
23. Seltzer, M.L., Yu, D., Wang, Y.: An investigation of deep neural networks for noise robust speech recognition. In: 2013 IEEE International Conference on Acoustics, Speech and Signal Processing (ICASSP), pp. 7398–7402. IEEE (2013)
24. Vincent, E., Watanabe, S., Nugraha, A.A., Barker, J., Marxer, R.: An analysis of environment, microphone and data simulation mismatches in robust speech recognition. Comput. Speech Lang. **46**, 535–557 (2017)
25. Vincent, P., Larochelle, H., Lajoie, I., Bengio, Y., Manzagol, P.A.: Stacked denoising autoencoders: learning useful representations in a deep network with a local denoising criterion. J. Mach. Learn. Res. **11**(Dec), 3371–3408 (2010)
26. Weninger, F., Geiger, J., Wöllmer, M., Schuller, B., Rigoll, G.: Feature enhancement by deep LSTM networks for ASR in reverberant multisource environments. Comput. Speech Lang. **28**(4), 888–902 (2014)
27. Weninger, F., Watanabe, S., Tachioka, Y., Schuller, B.: Deep recurrent de-noising auto-encoder and blind de-reverberation for reverberated speech recognition. In: 2014 IEEE International Conference on Acoustics, Speech and Signal Processing (ICASSP), pp. 4623–4627. IEEE (2014)

28. Zen, H., Sak, H.: Unidirectional long short-term memory recurrent neural network with recurrent output layer for low-latency speech synthesis. In: 2015 IEEE International Conference on Acoustics, Speech and Signal Processing (ICASSP), pp. 4470–4474. IEEE (2015)
29. Zhao, Y., Wang, Z.Q., Wang, D.: Two-stage deep learning for noisy-reverberant speech enhancement. IEEE/ACM Trans. Audio Speech Lang. Process. **27**(1), 53–62 (2019)

Using Cluster Analysis to Assess the Impact of Dataset Heterogeneity on Deep Convolutional Network Accuracy: A First Glance

Mauro Mendez[1(✉)], Saul Calderon[1], and Pascal N. Tyrrell[2]

[1] School of Computing, Costa Rica Institute of Technology, Cartago, Costa Rica
`mamendez@ic-itcr.ac.cr`, `sacalderon@itcr.ac.cr`
[2] Departments of Medical Imaging and Statistical Sciences, University of Toronto, Toronto, Canada
`pascal.tyrrell@utoronto.ca`

Abstract. In this paper we performed cluster analysis using Fuzzy K-means over the image-based features of two models, to assess how dataset heterogeneity impacts model accuracy. A highly heterogeneous dataset is linked with sparse data samples, which usually impacts the overall model generalization and accuracy with test samples. We propose to measure the Coefficient of Variation (CV) in the resulting clusters, to estimate data heterogeneity as a metric for predicting model generalization and test accuracy. We show that highly heterogeneous datasets are common when the number of samples are not enough, thus yielding a high CV. In our experiments with two different models and datasets, higher CV values decreased model test accuracy considerably. We tested ResNet 18, to solve binary classification of x-ray teeth scans, and VGG16, to solve age regression from hand x-ray scans. Results obtained suggest that cluster analysis can be used to identify heterogeneity influence on CNN model testing accuracy. According to our experiments, we consider that a CV < 5% is recommended to yield a satisfactory model test accuracy.

Keywords: Cluster analysis · Heterogeneity · Transfer learning · Small dataset · Convolutional Neural Network

1 Introduction

The latest advances in medicine and computer science have resulted in the Precision Medicine (PM) field, where several problems in medicine, involving images, patients and medical data are solved by state-of-the-art computer science techniques and can be adequate to individual cases [9]. For instance, physicians and oncologists from all over the world deal with cancer patients every day using imaging techniques due to its non-invasive nature, low risk and cost [9]. X-ray Computed Tomography (CT) is a regularly used imaging technique that measures tissue density at high resolution and exhibition of strong contrasts among

© Springer Nature Switzerland AG 2020
J. L. Crespo-Mariño and E. Meneses-Rojas (Eds.): CARLA 2019, CCIS 1087, pp. 307–319, 2020.
https://doi.org/10.1007/978-3-030-41005-6_21

different tissue types [34]. In the past few years different initiatives in PM have been solved by making use of Convolutional Neural Networks (CNN). Sampaio et al. talks about how segmentation and feature extraction of mammograms are done by a CNN architecture in order to identify tumorous masses [36]. Liang et al. works on a CNN used to automatically classify single cells in thin blood smears on standard microscope slides as either malaria infected or uninfected [30]. Whereas in some cases CNNs can perform in astounding ways, these models have several issues that are far from resolved: hyper-parameter optimization, spatial information loss, cost effective and high data dependency in both quality and quantity [2,37,43].

Due to its high data dependency, CNN models are at risk of being overfit or underfit to the training dataset and therefore usually require the process of tweaking hyper-parameters in order to obtain the best fit. However, when a small dataset is used for training, most of Artificial Intelligence (AI)-models have a hard time to overcome a space with limited samples, which translates in to a highly heterogeneous dataset. This usually results in an unsatisfactory testing accuracy [19]. Literature recommends enlarging the dataset, which can be as simple as collecting more samples, involving costs on experts to label the data; or using artificial data augmentation approaches. Han and Le Guennec et al. show several techniques such as: spatial and morphological transformations, slicing, zooming, noising and filtering, in order to augment the dataset and improve model accuracy [21,29]. Recently, new approaches have been applied to generate new samples using generative adversarial networks [4,16]. These models aim to learn the data distribution and are able to create new samples that were never used on training. However, when we are using a medical imaging dataset it is often not possible to obtain more data given the availability of specific patient types, accurate labeling and high data generation cost. Nevertheless, if it is possible to enlarge the dataset, variation (i.e. heterogeneity) of data points is often ignored at model training. Handling an homogeneous dataset could yield a model that performs poorly on new very atipic data points, whereas having a too heterogeneous but small dataset could limit the learning of the model resulting in a poor testing accuracy for outlier points [20,32].

This paper assess CNN model test accuracy with small datasets using cluster analysis metrics such as the Coefficient of Variation (CV), of image-based features. By evaluating patient clusters that differed in accuracy, dataset-oriented decisions can be done to improve model test accuracy by, for example, adding more layers to the CNN model and tweaking hyper-parameters for reducing overfitting on small heterogeneous sample data sets. Subsect. 1.1 refers to the implications that entails using a small dataset to train a CNN model and Subsect. 1.2 details how cluster analysis can help to identify the problem. Later, on Sect. 2 the proposed method is explained and is tested on Sect. 3 of experiments and results, where the correlation between the proposed CV data heterogeneity metric and model test accuracy is done. Finally, main conclusions and future work is addressed in Sect. 4.

1.1   Importance of Data

Researchers on AI and Data Science often face dataset related short-comings. A common issue is small dataset size, leading to overfitting models and non-optimal solutions. Medical imaging datasets often require complex labels, making labeling a time-consuming and expensive task, which often prevents yielding not enough training samples for the AI model [43]. Several Machine Learning (ML) architectures have been successfully applied on small datasets, where it is shown that supervised fine-tuning with a relatively small dataset on a network pre-trained with a large image dataset of generic objects (e.g., ResNet [22], VGG16 [38]) can lead to significant improvement in performance; an approach known as transfer learning [8,12,18,33,44]. However, using transfer learning does not guarantee a model that performs well for every sample, due to sample size, the observed data points and outliers, which can be linked to dataset heterogeneity.

Data heterogeneity is often analyzed in medical studies from three perspectives: the clinical perspective, referring to data variation from observed subjects. When data heterogeneity is generated from study procedures, it is referred as methodological heterogeneity. Finally, statistical heterogeneity refers to variation on study measurements [14]. In this paper we focus in two applications with clinical and statistical heterogeneity.

Medical heterogeneous datasets have been investigated extensively [5,39]. For instance, Altman et al. assesses heterogeneity on epidemiological clinical trials, aiming to identify different subgroups of patients, to find whether the observed relationship between an exposure and disease is different among these subgroups [3].

For an AI model, a relatively large heterogeneous dataset is desired to train a model, as it can learn from a lot of samples that introduce variation, making the model to adjust better for the problem to estimate, i.e. improving model generalization, as it is better trained for samples that were not used on the training stage. A relatively small heterogeneous dataset forces the model to adjust for the observed sample set, yielding poor accuracy for samples not used in the training stage, i.e. yielding a reduced generalization. Thus, in order to mitigate the effect of heterogeneity from small sample sizes, statistical approaches are used by Frantziskonis and Wardenaar et al. where methods such as: latent class analysis, parametric functions, factor analyses and mixture growth analyses, attempt to change or remove heterogeneous samples to build a more homogeneous dataset [15,40].

1.2   Cluster Analysis of Features as a Mean to Assess the Impact of Heterogeneity

Cluster analysis is the formal study of methods and algorithms for grouping or clustering objects, according to measured or perceived intrinsic characteristics or similarity [25]. There are several techniques to apply clustering analysis on a dataset, used to identify low-heterogeneous subgroups of data with common features [26]. In the medical field, cluster analysis is often used as a way to understand clusters of patients and improve medical diagnosis [23,41]. For instance, Fitzpatrick et al. uses ward hierarchical clustering to identify asthma phenotypes, applied to school-age children with persistent asthma across a wide range of severities, giving as outcome 5 significant clusters [13].

Whereas literature have focused lately on CNN models and cluster analysis, the powerful mixture between both has not yet been fully addressed in literature, specially in medical imaging analysis. Xu et al. addresses sparseness of text representation with a CNN architecture used to extract features from word embeddings to later cluster them with K-means. The model yields a short text classification pipeline capable of outperform related works [42]. Donahue et al. works on semantic clustering on trained CNN's features in order to create a framework for semi-supervised learning [12]. Moreover, no work could be found using both methods and the study of heterogeneity on medical imaging data. Although, similar work has been addressed on the statistical calibration of models as the Hosmer-Lemeshow test [24], where subgroups from a numerical dataset are identified to assess the goodness of fit for logistic regression on small sample sizes.

Sample dimensionality is an issue when clustering is performed [31]. High dimensional samples impairs clustering algorithms performance due to the decreasing significance of the clusters yielded in high dimensional spaces, linked to the curse of dimensionality. In this work the clustered samples are features extracted from a CNN. Moreover, image-based features are often of high dimensionality, making the use of a dimensionality reduction method necessary, like Principal Component Analysis (PCA).

2   Proposed Method

In this work, we aim to evaluate how well a CNN model deals with heterogeneity on small and large datasets using clustering analysis as a tool to measure its impact, using a cluster quantitative measure as the CV. Common CNN-transfer learning based model can be divided in two sections: back model and top model. The back model contains all the convolutional calculation and feature extraction filters, whereas the top model implements data transformations to yield the intended predictions, based on the features from previous stage [19].

This research proposes to perform cluster analysis on the principal components of the back model outputs. Thus, we propose to reduce the original feature space created by the convolutional layers using PCA. We performed PCA assuming that medical data is often generated from normal distributions [27], creating a new feature space with the highest dataset covariance dimensions.

We propose to evaluate model accuracy in the clustered data, using the predictions of the top model. Both the back and top model need to be trained before applying the proposed method.

For the cluster analysis, an exploration on the number of clusters and the algorithm that perform the best for the extracted data was made. If every cluster performs similarly as if the whole dataset was evaluated, we can infer that the back model was able to generalize well, i.e. the heterogeneity in the dataset did not affect model test accuracy. However, differences between the clusters accuracies and the whole dataset are found, suggesting a back model unable to generalize the distribution for every sample given, i.e. data heterogeneity affected the model performance. We propose to use CV [1] as a quantitative normalized measure that takes into account the accuracy for each cluster. CV measures the dispersion on data points, in our case, our data points correspond to cluster's accuracy; if dispersion is relatively high, it means that there is a significant difference in model performance. On the other hand, a relatively low dispersion is a sign of well-generalized training.

We aim to measure and find an appropriate CV interval, which can ensure enough data homogeneity and subsequent model generalization. We tested two models with different datasets and objectives, predicting classification and regression. VGG16 and Resnet18 are popular architectures, the models were selected for their transfer-learning affine structure, the ability to extract image-based features, training simplicity and dataset availability. Tested datasets belong to the medical imaging domain, a domain where the lack of data is usual, yielding into more small and possible heterogeneous datasets. The models are detailed in Sects. 2.1 and 2.2.

(a) PSP plate image

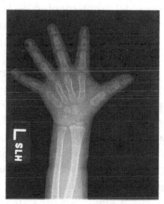
(b) Bone Age Image

Fig. 1. Image from PSP plates dataset (a). Image from Bone Age dataset (b).

2.1 PSP Plates with Resnet18

This model solves the binary classification of each sample between discard the plate (yes) or keep it (no). Due to the number of samples, high resolution images and prediction complexity this model converged easily, making it a good model to try with different sample sizes. A simple metric as the accuracy, number of right decisions over total amount of decisions, will be used.

The first test model was ResNet 18 [22] back model and a fully connected layer as top model. ResNet introduces skip connections in order to avoid the vanishing gradient problem. The features used on this model were the outputs of the last layer of the back model giving 512 image-features to work with.

The dataset for this model is composed by the superimposition of two images, a Physical Photostimulable Phosphor (PSP) plate and a CMOS teeth scan. The dataset was built at the Faculty of Dentistry at the University of Toronto (Toronto, Canada) using a Carestream CS 7600 for the former, MiPACS and Carestream RVG 6200 for the latter. A selection of 25 PSP plates were mixed with 100 cases of CMOS scans giving a total of 2928 samples. The 25 PSP plates consists of 10 severe damage plates, 10 with intermediate damage, 4 new plates, and one blank mask. As well, 25 dentists with at least 1 year of experience labeled the scans in two categories: keep the plate or discard it. The dataset is composed by teeth x-ray scans of 1152×869, as reference see Fig. 1.

2.2 Bone Age with VGG16

This model predicts the bone age for each subject, solving a regression problem. The metric used for this model was the 1-Normalized Root Mean Squared Error (1-NRMSE).

The model implemented is based in a VGG16 [38] back model, and a 4-layers fully connected model as top model [6]. VGG16 uses the smallest filter size capable of encoding directional information, i.e. 3×3 filters. The filters are used along the whole network allowing to learn the same information as the larger filters used on other networks. This feature allows VGG16 to train with significantly fewer parameters. As the previous model, 512 image-features are extracted.

The dataset used in this model consists of radiographs from left hands of both male and female subjects with different races and ages ranging from 1 month to 228 months (19 years) for a total of 12600 samples. The Radiological Society of North America made the dataset publicly available, and was acquired from Stanford Children's Hospital and Colorado Children's Hospital [17], as reference see Fig. 1. For the following experiments because of the computation complexity on training with thousands of images and the number of tests that we had to run, just the female radiographs were used giving a total of 5674 images to work with.

3   Experiments and Results

Four sample sizes on each model were selected to show the increase of accuracy and the expected decrease of heterogeneity; for model Sect. 2.1 the sample sizes were 100, 300, half (1464) and the whole dataset (2928), as well, for model Sect. 2.2, 300, 700, half (2837) and the whole dataset (5674).

The models were trained using 4-fold validation for every sample size, to minimize data split randomness and keep computational requirements reasonable.

For every fold the image-based features (back model outputs) were extracted as well as the model prediction (top model outputs). Cluster analysis was performed on every fold and the metrics were averaged to give an overall representation for the sample size. The metrics were calculated using the model prediction and were performed separately for every cluster.

The extracted image-based features were reduced from their original amount to 10 principal components using PCA. Later, clustering was performed on principal component based space. Dimensionality reduction was performed to attenuate the curse of dimensionality and minimization of correlated features. For cluster analysis, we picked a clustering algorithm and the number of clusters. The latter was unknown as clustering was performed on the extracted image features with PCA dimensionality reduction, where the number of classes is unknown. We tested different clustering algorithms: K-Means, Fuzzy K-Means and Gaussian Mixture Model using unsupervised clustering performance metrics such as Elbow Method [28], Silhouette Coefficient [35], Calinski-Harabaz Index [7], Davies-Bouldin Index [11] and amount of patients in each cluster. For both models Fuzzy K-Means with 4 clusters were found to give the most demonstrative results for all combinations.

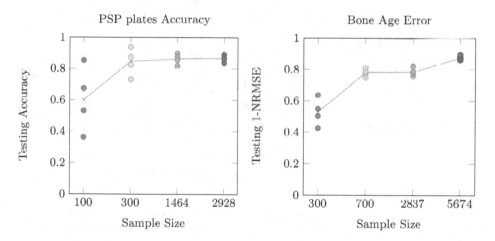

Fig. 2. PSP plates clusters testing accuracy over different sample sizes (left). Bone Age clusters testing error over different sample sizes (right). The blue line measure the whole dataset. (Color figure online)

Due to the stochastic nature of clustering, several trainings of the algorithm were made in order to average accurate clustering metrics. The way that a cluster algorithm assigns labels is arbitrarily, meaning that no criteria is used to label them making it random within each training. Thus, the algorithm was trained 10 times and cluster identifying and re-labeling was performed using the cluster patients and accuracy; in that way, each cluster had the same label across trainings. Every metric shown is the average of the several runs.

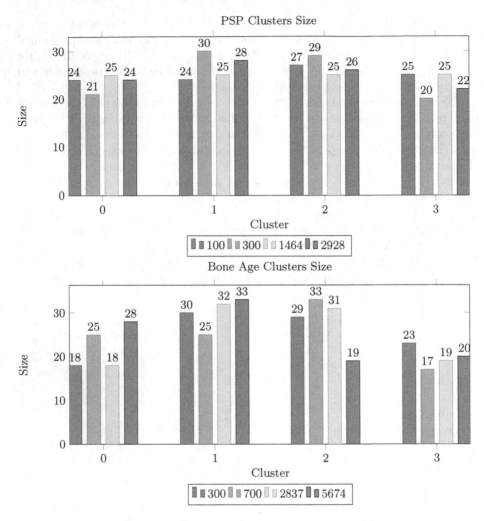

Fig. 3. PSP plates clusters' size over different sample sizes (top). Bone Age clusters' size over different sample sizes (bottom). The amount is shown as a percentage of the whole sample size. The clusters were made using Fuzzy K-Means.

In Fig. 2 is shown the evaluated clusters for each model using the selected sample sizes. In this figure is demonstrated that there was a relationship between sample size and heterogeneity that affected model test accuracy. The more data you have the better the model will generalize for every cluster of samples, reducing the negative effect of its heterogeneity.

Figure 3 displays clusters' sizes in percentage for each sample size, showing that Fuzzy K-Means is able to find significant clusters with characteristics in common and similar number of patients between each other. A bad clustering algorithm would give unrealistic clusters with few isolated patients that do not reflect real-world data samples.

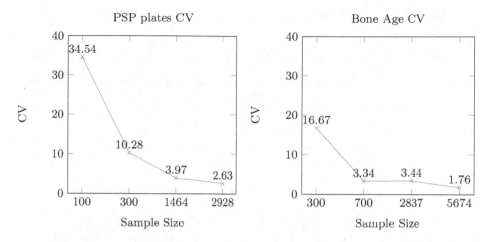

Fig. 4. The Coefficient of Variation for PSP plates clusters over different sample sizes (left). The Coefficient of Variation for Bone Age clusters over different sample sizes (right).

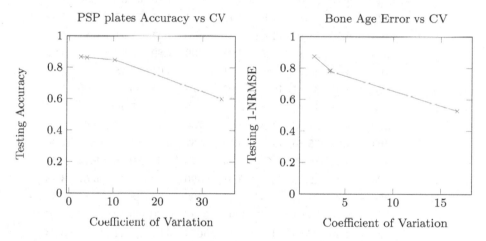

Fig. 5. The PSP plates Testing Accuracy over its Coefficient of Variation (left). The Bone Age Testing Error over its Coefficient of Variation (right).

Figure 4 shows the level of variation between clusters over the sample sizes. In clinical chemistry literature a CV < 10% is very good, 10%–20% is good, 20%–30% is acceptable, and CV > 30% is not acceptable [10]. The plots show that CV stability is achieved when more samples make relative small change to the dispersion of the clusters, that can translate into a model that performs almost the same for all clusters of samples.

Figure 5 shows the correlation between model accuracy and the CV for both models. In this figure is demonstrated how we are able to estimate the accuracy or error given a CV and viceversa. Both models show negative correlation with

Table 1. Centroid and closest-point euclidean distances between each cluster.

Model		PSP plates with Resnet18						Bone Age with VGG16					
Data Sizes/Clusters		0–1	0–2	0–3	1–2	1–3	2–3		0–1	0–2	0–3	1–2	1–3	2–3
Centroid distance	100	10.88	10.53	11.06	10.83	10.13	10.05	300	5.12	5.07	6.2	5.22	5.94	5.96
	300	10.91	10.30	10.16	10.57	10.79	10.74	700	13.06	11.92	9.27	9.42	11.26	9.76
	1464	11.26	10.29	9.82	10.59	10.98	10.21	2837	9.53	10.49	10.79	10.25	9.42	10.16
	2928	11.48	11.34	10.83	11.75	11.06	12.38	5674	11.5	10.72	10.52	11.21	11.67	11.65
Closes-point distance	100	6.63	6.74	6.7	6.79	6.18	6.98	300	1.44	1.48	1.49	1.13	1.26	1.29
	300	4.89	4.69	4.92	4.28	4.41	4.55	700	1.62	1.26	1.24	1.6	1.63	1.36
	1464	2.64	2.61	2.62	2.67	2.82	2.58	2837	1.47	1.22	1.79	1.20	1.31	1.57
	2928	2.01	1.96	2.02	1.91	2.14	2.14	5674	1.04	1.19	1.52	1.02	1.48	2.34

Table 2. Euclidean distance between the cluster centroids and their points.

Model		PSP with Resnet18					Bone Age with VGG16			
Clusters/distance		Min	Max	Mean	StDv		Min	Max	Mean	StDv
Cluster 0	100	5.65	18.38	11.52	3.02	300	2.49	21.40	6.10	3.80
	300	5.73	21.52	11.97	3.37	700	2.62	43.66	8.11	5.61
	1464	4.70	26.51	12.22	3.68	2837	4.10	56.36	11.36	6.45
	2928	4.42	29.84	11.67	3.48	5674	3.91	76.97	12.73	7.39
Cluster 1	100	6.55	18.85	11.92	3.3	300	2.44	27.51	6.81	4.35
	300	5.72	21.81	11.77	3.24	700	1.89	45.92	7.95	6.27
	1464	4.83	26.24	11.88	3.61	2837	3.01	78.48	9.69	6.08
	2928	4.41	31.11	12.11	4.03	5674	3.26	90.62	11.69	7.61
Cluster 2	100	6.68	21.95	13.38	3.65	300	2.38	27.46	7.08	4.38
	300	5.51	21.03	11.91	3.23	700	1.37	42.81	5.08	4.17
	1464	4.84	25.85	12.04	3.59	2837	3.72	80.60	12.83	7.30
	2928	4.14	30.49	11.49	3.94	5674	3.06	70.42	9.74	5.47
Cluster 3	100	7.55	22.75	13.82	3.58	300	2.44	23.73	6.57	3.93
	300	5.93	21.06	11.93	3.33	700	2.45	48.78	7.85	7.47
	1464	4.70	24.91	11.75	3.48	2837	3.70	53.70	11.47	6.19
	2928	4.40	27.94	11.60	3.78	5674	3.66	63.21	10.15	6.23

a Pearson Coefficient of -0.9871 for the PSP plates model and -0.9832 for the Bone Age model. A negative correlation means that the lower CV we have, the higher testing accuracy our model will get. Thus, if we want our model to perform over a certain accuracy, we have to achieve a generalization that gives a favorable CV. Although, 4 points are not enough for calculating a reliable coefficient, it shows an expectable negative trend. From the results in Fig. 5, we can infer that a CV lower than 5% is desirable in order to keep testing accuracy high.

We calculated the inter-cluster and intra-cluster Euclidean distances to analyze cluster quality and consistency. Table 1 shows how the distances between cluster change over sample sizes. On the other hand, Table 2 shows how clusters change when we increase the sample size. Both tables show the behavior of the clusters with increasing sample sizes. Within a specific sample size, the centroids appear to remain relatively fixed; however, as sample size increases, clusters grow in spread and get closer to each other until it becomes almost one big cluster. In a well-trained model every sample cluster should have almost the same accuracy as others; this is the result of how image-based extracted features improve its representation, and also the dataset increases its homogeneity when we more training samples are available.

4   Conclusions and Future Work

All figures showed that cluster analysis, using the right algorithm and number of clusters, is an effective way to identify and assess how affected the model testing accuracy is by dataset heterogeneity, in classification and regression problems. Moreover, CV can be used as a predictor of model testing accuracy and viceversa. We consider a dataset with a CV of less than 5%, homogeneous enough to allow the model generalize data properly and avoid overfitting.

Cluster analysis could be used as a tool to identify if the CNN model is affected by heterogeneity from the dataset fed; even if your model has a high accuracy it can still perform poorly for a cluster of samples and this method may serve to identify it. Furthermore, this approach could assist to calibrate a model to be able to perform well for every sample cluster, or discard under-performing data clusters.

As future work, we aim to experiment on more datasets and more models generalizing the application of using cluster analysis to identify heterogeneity affection on model training for a CNN transfer learning problem, obtaining more evidence of our claim.

Another approach proposed as future work is the tracking and identification of the image-based features belonging to a principal component, and identify which features define a good cluster of images. Understanding how features are related to patient samples can be useful to gain insight on how CNNs extract information from data. As well, knowing which features produce a better patient cluster can be useful to improve those samples that did not perform well.

References

1. Abdi, H.: Coefficient of variation. Encycl. Res. Des. **1**, 169–171 (2010)
2. Ahmadvand, P., Ebrahimpour, R., Ahmadvand, P.: How popular CNNs perform in real applications of face recognition. In: 2016 24th Telecommunications Forum (TELFOR), pp. 1–4. IEEE (2016)
3. Altman, D.G., Matthews, J.N.: Statistics notes: interaction 1: heterogeneity of effects. BMJ **313**(7055), 486 (1996)
4. Antoniou, A., Storkey, A., Edwards, H.: Data augmentation generative adversarial networks. stat **1050**, 8 (2018)

5. Bowden, J., Tierney, J.F., Copas, A.J., Burdett, S.: Quantifying, displaying and accounting for heterogeneity in the meta-analysis of RCTs using standard and generalised Qstatistics. BMC Med. Res. Methodol. **11**(1), 41 (2011)
6. Calderon, S., et al.: Assessing the impact of the deceived non local means filter as a preprocessing stage in a convolutional neural network based approach for age estimation using digital hand X-ray images. In: 2018 25th IEEE International Conference on Image Processing (ICIP), pp. 1752–1756. IEEE (2018)
7. Caliński, T., Harabasz, J.: A dendrite method for cluster analysis. Commun. Stat.-Theory Methods **3**(1), 1–27 (1974)
8. Chatfield, K., Simonyan, K., Vedaldi, A., Zisserman, A.: Return of the devil in the details: delving deep into convolutional nets. CoRR abs/1405.3531 (2014)
9. Collins, F.S., Varmus, H.: A new initiative on precision medicine. N. Engl. J. Med. **372**(9), 793–795 (2015)
10. Cui, Z.: Allowable limit of error in clinical chemistry quality control. Clin. Chem. **35**(4), 630–631 (1989)
11. Davies, D.L., Bouldin, D.W.: A cluster separation measure. IEEE Trans. Pattern Anal. Mach. Intell. **2**, 224–227 (1979)
12. Donahue, J., et al.: DeCAF: a deep convolutional activation feature for generic visual recognition. In: International Conference on Machine Learning, pp. 647–655 (2014)
13. Fitzpatrick, A.M., et al.: Heterogeneity of severe asthma in childhood: confirmation by cluster analysis of children in the national institutes of health/national heart, lung, and blood institute severe asthma research program. J. Allergy Clin. Immunol. **127**(2), 382–389 (2011)
14. Fletcher, J.: What is heterogeneity and is it important? BMJ **334**(7584), 94–96 (2007)
15. Frantziskonis, G.: Heterogeneity and implicated surface effects: statistical, fractal formulation and relevant analytical solution. Acta Mech. **108**(1–4), 157–178 (1995)
16. Frid-Adar, M., Klang, E., Amitai, M., Goldberger, J., Greenspan, H.: Synthetic data augmentation using GAN for improved liver lesion classification. In: 2018 IEEE 15th International Symposium on Biomedical Imaging (ISBI 2018), pp. 289–293. IEEE (2018)
17. Gertych, A., Zhang, A., Sayre, J., Pospiech-Kurkowska, S., Huang, H.: Bone age assessment of children using a digital hand atlas. Comput. Med. Imaging Graph. **31**(4–5), 322–331 (2007)
18. Girshick, R., Donahue, J., Darrell, T., Malik, J.: Rich feature hierarchies for accurate object detection and semantic segmentation. In: Proceedings of the IEEE Conference on Computer Vision and Pattern Recognition, pp. 580–587 (2014)
19. Goodfellow, I., Bengio, Y., Courville, A.: Deep Learning. MIT press (2016)
20. Guibas, J.T., Virdi, T.S., Li, P.S.: Synthetic medical images from dual generative adversarial networks. CoRR abs/1709.01872 (2017). http://arxiv.org/abs/1709.01872
21. Han, D., Liu, Q., Fan, W.: A new image classification method using CNN transfer learning and web data augmentation. Expert Syst. Appl. **95**, 43–56 (2018)
22. He, K., Zhang, X., Ren, S., Sun, J.: Deep residual learning for image recognition. In: Proceedings of the IEEE Conference on Computer Vision and Pattern Recognition, pp. 770–778 (2016)
23. Hervier, B., et al.: Hierarchical cluster and survival analyses of antisynthetase syndrome: phenotype and outcome are correlated with anti-tRNA synthetase antibody specificity. Autoimmun. Rev. **12**(2), 210–217 (2012)

24. Hosmer Jr., D.W., Lemeshow, S., Sturdivant, R.X.: Applied Logistic Regression, vol. 398. Wiley, Hoboken (2013)
25. Jain, A.K.: Data clustering: 50 years beyond k-means. Pattern Recogn. Lett. **31**(8), 651–666 (2010)
26. Jain, A.K., Murty, M.N., Flynn, P.J.: Data clustering: a review. ACM Comput. Surv. (CSUR) **31**(3), 264–323 (1999)
27. Jolliffe, I.: Principal Component Analysis. Springer, Heidelberg (2011)
28. Kodinariya, T.M., Makwana, P.R.: Review on determining number of cluster in k-means clustering. Int. J. **1**(6), 90–95 (2013)
29. Le Guennec, A., Malinowski, S., Tavenard, R.: Data augmentation for time series classification using convolutional neural networks. In: ECML/PKDD Workshop on Advanced Analytics and Learning on Temporal Data (2016)
30. Liang, Z., et al.: CNN-based image analysis for malaria diagnosis. In: 2016 IEEE International Conference on Bioinformatics and Biomedicine (BIBM), pp. 493–496. IEEE (2016)
31. Liu, Y., Hayes, D.N., Nobel, A., Marron, J.: Statistical significance of clustering for high-dimension, low-sample size data. J. Am. Stat. Assoc. **103**(483), 1281–1293 (2008)
32. Neff, T., Payer, C., Stern, D., Urschler, M.: Generative adversarial network based synthesis for supervised medical image segmentation. In: Proceedings of the OAGM and ARW Joint Workshop (2017)
33. Ng, H.W., Nguyen, V.D., Vonikakis, V., Winkler, S.: Deep learning for emotion recognition on small datasets using transfer learning. In: Proceedings of the 2015 ACM on International Conference on Multimodal Interaction, pp. 443–449. ACM (2015)
34. Parmar, C., et al.: Radiomic feature clusters and prognostic signatures specific for lung and head & neck cancer. Sci. Rep. **5**, 11044 (2015)
35. Rousseeuw, P.J.: Silhouettes: a graphical aid to the interpretation and validation of cluster analysis. J. Comput. Appl. Math. **20**, 53–65 (1987)
36. Sampaio, W.B., Diniz, E.M., Silva, A.C., De Paiva, A.C., Gattass, M.: Detection of masses in mammogram images using CNN, geostatistic functions and SVM. Comput. Biol. Med. **41**(8), 653–664 (2011)
37. Severyn, A., Moschitti, A.: Twitter sentiment analysis with deep convolutional neural networks. In: Proceedings of the 38th International ACM SIGIR Conference on Research and Development in Information Retrieval, pp. 959–962. ACM (2015)
38. Simonyan, K., Zisserman, A.: Very deep convolutional networks for large-scale image recognition. In: ICLR (2015)
39. Terrin, N., Schmid, C.H., Lau, J., Olkin, I.: Adjusting for publication bias in the presence of heterogeneity. Stat. Med. **22**(13), 2113–2126 (2003)
40. Wardenaar, K.J., de Jonge, P.: Diagnostic heterogeneity in psychiatry: towards an empirical solution. BMC Med. **11**(1), 201 (2013)
41. Wirapati, P., et al.: Meta-analysis of gene expression profiles in breast cancer: toward a unified understanding of breast cancer subtyping and prognosis signatures. Breast Cancer Res. **10**(4), R65 (2008)
42. Xu, J., et al.: Short text clustering via convolutional neural networks (2015)
43. Yamashita, R., Nishio, M., Do, R.K.G., Togashi, K.: Convolutional neural networks: an overview and application in radiology. Insights Imaging **9**(4), 611 (2018)
44. Yosinski, J., Clune, J., Bengio, Y., Lipson, H.: How transferable are features in deep neural networks? In: Advances in Neural Information Processing Systems, pp. 3320–3328 (2014)

Evolutionary Approach for Bus Synchronization

Sergio Nesmachnow[1(✉)], Jonathan Muraña[1(✉)], Gerardo Goñi[1],
Renzo Massobrio[1], and Andrei Tchernykh[2]

[1] Universidad de la República, Montevideo, Uruguay
{sergion,jmurana,gerardo.goni,renzom}@fing.edu.uy
[2] Centro de Investigación Científica y Educacion Superior de Ensenada,
Ensenada, BC, Mexico
chernykh@cicese.mx

Abstract. This article presents the application of evolutionary algorithms to solve the bus synchronization problem. The problem model includes extended synchronization points, accounting for every pair of bus stops in a city, and the transfer demands for each pair of lines on each pair of bus stops. A specific evolutionary algorithm is proposed to efficiently solve the problem and results are compared with intuitive algorithms and also with the current planning of the transportation system on real scenarios from the city of Montevideo, Uruguay. Experimental results indicate that the proposed evolutionary algorithm is able to improve in up to 13.33% the synchronizations with respect to the current planning and systematically outperforms other baseline methods.

1 Introduction

Transportation systems play a major role in nowadays society and are an important component of modern smart cities [7,14]. Public transportation accounts for the most travels in large cities and provides the most efficient and environmental-friendly mean for citizens' mobility. However, the efficacy of public transportation systems requires a proper planning of routes, timetabling, buses, drivers, and other relevant subproblems, in order to provide good quality of service [4].

Synchronization of bus frequencies is an important goal from the point of view of users. Traditional approaches for public transportation network design and planning considered that having many different lines with different destinations and few synchronization (or transfer) points in the network allows a better transportation system, but in turn, that approach significantly increases the operation costs, because a larger number of lines are needed. Good quality of service can also be provided having a reduced number of lines and allowing transfers between them. In this scenario, the synchronization problem tries to define frequencies and headways of each line in order to maximize the transfer of passengers without significant waiting times. This way, the resulting public transportation system is more attractive to passengers and provides a better

J. L. Crespo-Mariño and E. Meneses-Rojas (Eds.): CARLA 2019, CCIS 1087, pp. 320–336, 2020.
https://doi.org/10.1007/978-3-030-41005-6_22

quality of service [4]. Synchronization is one of the most difficult tasks in public transportation planning. It has been often addressed intuitively, assuming that experienced operators are able to take proper decisions [3].

Nowadays, some public transportation systems have no limitations on the number of transfers that a passenger can perform. All bus stops are possible synchronization points, providing a more freely scenario for passengers to commute. In this scenario, the bus synchronization problem is more complex, as updated information must be considered to take into account the more frequently used connections. This is the situation of the public transportation system in Montevideo, which is the case study addressed in this article. Since the implementation of the Urban Mobility Plan [10], all pairs of bus stops are possible synchronization points for passengers to transfer between buses of different lines, using an intelligent card for ticket sales and travels. Thus, the formulation and scenarios of the bus timetabling synchronization problem are different of the ones previously proposed in literature. Furthermore, synchronization has become more important for citizens, as transfers allow improved mobility and more tickets are sold as the system provides a better service.

This article proposes a specific Evolutionary Algorithm (EA) [13] for efficiently solve the bus synchronization problem. The experimental evaluation is performed over realistic instances built considering real data from the Metropolitan Transportation System in Montevideo, Uruguay. Results obtained by the proposed EA are compared with intuitive algorithms to optimize synchronizations and also with the current planning of the transportation system in Montevideo. Plannings computed by the proposed EA improve up to 13.33% the number of synchronized trips, with respect to the current planning.

The research reported in this article was developed within the project 'Public transportation planning in smart cities' [15], funded by Fondo Conjunto de Cooperación Uruguay–México (2018–2019). The article is organized as follows. Section 2 introduces the bus synchronization problem and Sect. 3 reviews related works. The proposed EA for bus synchronization is described in Sect. 4. The experimental evaluation of the proposed method over realistic instances in Montevideo is reported in Sect. 5. Finally, the conclusions and the main lines for future work are formulated in Sect. 6.

2   The Bus Synchronization Problem

This section presents an integer programming formulation for the bus synchronization problem, based on the previous model presented by Ibarra and Rios [9]. Specific features are included in order to model the reality and flexibility of nowadays Intelligent Transportation Systems.

2.1   Problem Model

The problem accounts for the main goals of a modern transportation system: providing a fast and reliable way for the movement of citizens, while maintaining reasonable fares. The problem model mainly focuses on the quality of service provided to the users, i.e., a better traveling experience with reduced waiting times when using more than one bus for consecutive trips.

In the proposed model, the events of favoring passenger transfers with limited waiting times are called *synchronization* events. The study is aimed at solving real scenarios, based on real data from urban transit systems that accounts for the number of passengers that perform transfers between lines on each bus stop.

The main idea of the problem model is to divide any day into several planning periods on the basis of demand and travel time behavior of passengers. This way, the analysis of historical data allows obtaining similar accurate and almost deterministic information to build the problem scenarios. The mathematical formulation of the bus synchronization problem addressed in this article is presented in the next subsection.

2.2   Problem Formulation

The mathematical formulation of the bus synchronization problem considers the following elements:

- A set of lines of the bus network $I = \{i_1, i_2, \ldots, i_n\}$. For each line $i \in I$, $J(i)$ is the set of lines that may synchronize with line i (in a synchronization node, see next item). Buses that operate each line have a maximum capacity C for passengers that board the bus in a second leg of a transfer trip.
- A set of synchronization nodes $B = \{b_1, b_2, \ldots, b_m\}$. Each node $b \in B$ is a triplet $<i, j, d_b^{ij}>$ indicating that lines i and j synchronize in b, and that the bus stops for lines i and j are separated by a distance d_b^{ij}.
- A planning period $[0, T]$, expressed in minutes, and the number of trips needed to fulfill the passengers' demand for each line, f_i.
- A *traveling time function* $TT : I \times B \rightarrow \mathbf{Z}$. $TT_b^i = TT(i, b)$ indicates the time to reach the synchronization node b for buses in line i (from the origin of the line). Generally, this value depends on several features, including the bus type, bus velocity, traffic in roads, passengers' demand, etc.
- A walking time function $WT : B \times I \times I \rightarrow \mathbf{N}$. $WT_b^{i,j} = WT(i, j, b)$ indicates the time needed for a pedestrian to walk the distance d_b^{ij}, according to a walking speed ws and specific features of synchronization node b (e.g, existence of pedestrian lines, crowding, traffic lights in intersections, etc.).
- A *demand function* $P : I \times I \times B \rightarrow \mathbf{Z}$. $P_b^{ij} = P(i, j, b)$ indicates the number of passengers that transfer from line i to line j in synchronization node b, in the planning period.
- A maximum waiting time W_b^{ij} for each synchronization node, indicating the maximum time that passengers are willing to wait for line j, after alighting from line i and walking to the stop of line j, in a synchronization node b.
- A headway time, defining the separation between consecutive trips of the same line i, defined in an interval $[h_i, H_i]$. Values of h_i and H_i are usually defined by the city administration.

The synchronization problem proposes finding appropriate values for the departure time for every trip of each line to guarantee the best synchronization for all lines with transfer demands in the planning period T.

The mathematical model is formulated in Eq. 1a–1g. Departure times of each trip are represented by integer variables X_r^i. Synchronizations are represented by binary variables Z_{rsb}^{ij} that define if trip r of line i and trip s of line j are synchronized in node b. The proposed objective function weights synchronizations according to the number of passengers that transfer in the planning period, thus giving priority to synchronization nodes with larger transfer demands.

$$\text{maximize} \quad \sum_{b \in B} \sum_{i \in I} \sum_{j \in J(i)} \sum_{r=1}^{f_i} \sum_{s=1}^{f_j} Z_{rsb}^{ij} \times \min\left(\frac{P_b^{ij}}{f_i}, C\right) \tag{1a}$$

$$\text{subject to} \quad X_1^i \leq H^i \tag{1b}$$

$$T - H^i \leq X_{f_i}^i \leq T \tag{1c}$$

$$h^i \leq X_{r+1}^i - X_r^i \leq H^i \tag{1d}$$

$$(X_s^j + TT_b^j) - (X_r^i + TT_b^i) > WT_b^{i,j} \text{ if } Z_{rsb}^{ij} = 1 \tag{1e}$$

$$(X_s^j + TT_b^j) - (X_r^i + TT_b^i) \leq W_b + WT_b^{i,j} \text{ if } Z_{rsb}^{ij} = 1 \tag{1f}$$

$$X_r^i \in \{1, \ldots, T\}, Z_{rsb}^{ij} \in \{0, 1\} \tag{1g}$$

The objective function of the problem (Eq. 1a) proposes maximizing the number of synchronized transfers, weighted by the corresponding transfer demand for each trip in each synchronization node. When computing the objective function, the demand is split uniformly among the f_j trips of line j. This is a realistic assumption for planning periods where demand does not vary significantly, such as in the case study presented in this article. The number of synchronized passengers on each synchronization node is bounded for the capacity for transfer passengers C. Equations 1a–1g specify the constraints of the problem.

3 Related Works

Daduna and Voß [5] studied the schedule synchronization problem on bus networks, to minimize the waiting time of passengers. Different objectives were studied, including a weighted sum considering transfers and the maximum waiting time at a transfer zone. Simulated Annealing and Tabu Search were analyzed for simple versions of the problem. Tabu Search computed better solutions than Simulated Annealing over randomly generated examples based on the Berlin Underground network. In addition, three real-world cases from different German cities were studied. The trade-off between operational costs and user efficiency suggested that multiobjective approaches should be considered.

Ceder et al. [2] studied the problem of maximizing the number of synchronization events between bus lines at shared stops, i.e., maximizing the number of simultaneous arrivals. An heuristic approach based on a greedy procedure to select nodes from the bus network was proposed, to efficiently solve the problem by defining custom timetables. Both articles were focused on simultaneous bus arrivals, and results reported consisted of examples is presented that illustrate synchronizations on small instances with few nodes and few lines.

Fleurent et al. [6] considered a synchronization metric including weights defined by experts and public transport authorities to minimize vehicle scheduling costs. An heuristic algorithm was proposed to solve network flow problems that accounts for the synchronization metric and other operation costs. Experiments performed on just two small scenarios from Montréal, Canada, computed different timetables when varying the weights used in the proposed metric.

Ibarra and Ríos [9] studied the bus synchronization problem in the bus network of Monterrey, Mexico. A flexible formulation of the problem was proposed, considering a time window between travel times to account for variations. A Multi-start Iterated Local Search (MILS) was evaluated over 8 instances modeling the bus network in Monterrey (15 to 200 lines, and 3 to 40 synchronization points). MILS was compared against a Branch & Bound method (which failed to compute optimal solutions in two hours) and a simple upper bound computed by adding the possible trips to synchronize. The method was able to compute efficient solutions for medium-size instances in less than one minute, but the gaps of MILS did not scale, as they were small for large instances.

Later, Ibarra et al. [8] solved the multiperiod bus synchronization problem, optimizing multiple trips of a given set of lines. MILS, Variable Neighborhood Search and a simple population-based approach were proposed to solve the problem. All methods computed solutions with similar quality to an exact approach over academic instances with few synchronization points. Multiperiod timetables were up to 20% better than merging single period timetables. Results for a sample case study using data for a single line showed that maximizing synchronizations for a specific node usually reduces synchronizations for other nodes.

The model considered in our article includes additional features to the one proposed by Ibarra and Ríos [9]: scenarios where every pair of bus stops are possible transfer zones to synchronize, and real transfer demand in each possible transfer zone. The proposed EA also captures the features of existing solutions and accounts for real operation constraints for the case study in Montevideo.

4   The Proposed EA for Bus Synchronization

This section describes the main features of the proposed EA for solving the bus synchronization problem.

4.1   Solution Encoding

Candidate solutions to the problem are represented using integer vectors, where each integer value represents the headway (in minutes) of a bus line, i.e., the time between consecutive trips of the same line. More formally, a candidate solution to the problem is represented by $X = x_1, x_2, \ldots x_n$, where n is the number of bus

12	8	9	10	...	...	...	...	...	...	7	15	8	12	10
line 1	line 2	line 3	line 4	...	...	...	...	...	...	...	...	...	line N-1	line N

Fig. 1. Example of a solution representation

lines in the problem instance, $x_i \in \mathbf{Z}^+$, and $h^i \le x_i \le H^i$. Figure 1 describes a solution representation for a problem instance with N bus lines. In the example shown, buses from line 1 are scheduled to depart every 12 min, buses from line 2 every 8 min, etc.

4.2   Evolution Model and Evolutionary Operators

Evolution Model. The $(\mu + \lambda)$ evolution model [1] is applied in the proposed EA: μ parents generate λ individuals, which compete between them and with their parents, to determine the individuals that form the new population on the next generation. Preliminary experiments demonstrated that $(\mu + \lambda)$ evolution was able to provide better solutions and more diversity than a traditional generational model.

Initialization Operator. A seeded initialization is applied in the proposed EA. Randomly generated solutions are included in the initial population, accounting for the constraints defined for the headways of each line. In addition, values for the headways from the currently real solution applied by the transportation administration in Montevideo are included in the initial population. Solutions generated by greedy approaches to maximize the number of synchronizations are also included. Some of the initial solutions are modified by applying a *shaking* procedure that randomly modifies some of the information for specific lines. This initialization procedure intends to capture the main features of existing solutions and accounts for real operation constraints for the case study in Montevideo, and also provide diversity to the evolutionary search.

Selection Operator. The traditional tournament selection is applied, with tournament size two individuals, and one individual survives. Tournament selection allowed to compute better results than proportional selection in preliminary calibration experiments, mainly due to the appropriate level of selection pressure for the evolution of solutions.

Recombination Operator. The recombination operator is a specific variant of two-point crossover. It defines two crossover points randomly and exchanges the information encoded in both parents between the crossover points. This operator was conceived to preserve specific features of lines already synchronized in parent solutions, trying to keep useful information in the offspring generation process. The recombination operator is applied to individuals returned by the selection operator, with a probability p_R.

Mutation Operator. The mutation operator applied is a specific variant of Gaussian mutation. Specific position(s) in a solution are modified according to a Gaussian distribution, and taking into account the thresholds defined by the minimum and maximum frequencies for each line. The mutation operator is applied to every gene with a probability p_M.

4.3 Fitness Function Description

The fitness function accounts for the number of synchronized trips and their corresponding demands, according to the formulation in Eq. 1a–1g. The fitness is computed by the procedure described in Algorithm 1. For each synchronization point (sp) of the scenario, the demand is accumulated for each pair of synchronized trips. Variables x, y are the frequencies assigned by the solution (sol) to the lines involved in the synchronization point sp, and the function get_trips generates two vectors with the departing time of each trip of these lines.

Algorithm 1. Fitness evaluation for solutions

INPUT: $sol, scenario$ **OUTPUT:** $fitness$

```
 1: fitness ← 0
 2: for sp in get_sync_points(scenario) do
 3:     line_i,line_j,TT_i,TT_j,dist,demand,W_b ← get_elements(sp)
 4:     t_dist ← ((dist/1000) /WALK_SPEED) × 60
 5:     x,y ← get_sol_freqs(sol,line_i,line_j)
 6:     trips_i,trips_j ← get_trips(x,y,T)
 7:     for i = 1 to len(trips_i) do
 8:         for j = 1 to len(trips_j) do
 9:             wait_time = (trips_j[j] + TT_j) − (trips_i[i] + TT_i) − t_dist
10:             if wait_time > y then
11:                 wait_time ← y
12:             end if
13:             if wait_time > 0 & wait_time ≤ W_b then
14:                 fitness ← fitness + min(demand × x, C × T)
15:                 break
16:             end if
17:         end for
18:     end for
19: end for
```

---

5 Experimental Evaluation

This section reports the experimental evaluation of the proposed EA for the bus synchronization problem.

5.1   Methodology for Generating Problem Instances: General Considerations

Real problem instances were built using real data from the Metropolitan Transportation System in Montevideo, Uruguay: bus lines description, routes, schedules, and bus stops location in the city. Transfers information corresponds to real data from 2015 [11].

The key elements of the scenario and problem instances and how they were built are described next:

– The *type of day* determines if the considered problem instance corresponds to a working day or a weekend.
– The *period* is the interval of hours considered for the schedule. A period is characterized by its duration, traffic level (rush hour, normal demand, or low demand) and overall bus demand.
– The *demand function* is computed from transfers information, registered by smart cards used to sell tickets.
– *Synchronization points* are chosen according to their demand. The pairs of bus stops with the largest number of registered transfers for the period in the corresponding type of day are selected.
– The *bus lines* are the ones passing by the synchronization points.
– The *time traveling function* $t(i,b)$ for line i in synchronization point b are computed by Eq. 2, where r are trips of line i in the period, at_{ro} is the arrival time of trip r to the first stop in the route, at_{rb} is the arrival time to the stop of the synchronization point b and f_i is the number of trips in the period.

$$t(i,b) = \frac{\sum_{r=1}^{f_i} at_{rb} - at_{ro}}{f_i} \tag{2}$$

– The *walking time function* is the estimated walking speed of a person multiplied by the distance between bus stops in each synchronization point, computed using geospatial information about stops.
– The *headway limits* for each line (h_i and H_i) are computed considering the real bus schedule in period.
– The *maximum waiting time* is equal to λH, with $\lambda \in [0.75, 0.9, 1.0]$. This formulation allows configuring instances with different levels of quality of service.

5.2   Problem Instances Using Data from Montevideo

Thirty problem instances were defined, accounting for three different dimensions (30, 70, and 110 synchronization points), using real information about bus operating in Montevideo, Uruguay. Synchronization points were chosen randomly from an universe of 170 points (the most demanded transfer zones for the considered period).

Each problem instance is named as BS.[hh].[HH].[NP].[NL].[T].[λ].[id]. hh is the start hour of the period, HH is the end hour of the period, NP is the number

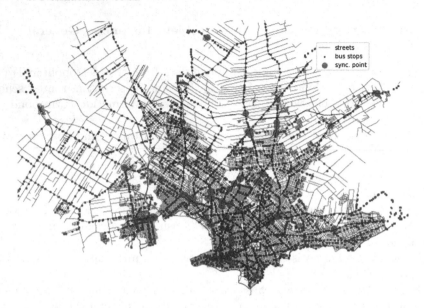

Fig. 2. Geographic distribution of synchronization points in Montevideo

of synchronization points in the instance, NL is the number of bus lines, T is the duration of the planning period, λ is the coefficient applied to W_b (percentage) and id is a relative identifier for instances with the same NL and λ.

In the instances solved in the experiments, hh is 12 (12:00 hs), HH is 14 (14:00 hs) NP in $[30, 70, 110]$, NL is determined by the selected synchronization points, the period T is 120 min, in line with related works, and λ in $[75, 90, 100]$. Figure 2 shows sample synchronization points chosen for building instances, distributed in the map of Montevideo.

5.3   Baseline Solutions and Metrics Description

A set of baseline solutions were considered for the comparison of the EA results. The main point for comparison is the current schedule in the transportation system of Montevideo (the *real timetable*), which provides the actual level of service regarding direct travels and transfers. In addition, solutions using the minimum headway (h_i) and the maximum headway for each line for each line (H_i) are used. These two solutions are included in the comparison, even though they are not useful to be implemented in practice, because configuring all lines to operate at minimum headway accounts for a very large (and expensive) number of trips, and configuring all lines to operate at maximum headway provides a very limited quality of service, regarding travel time.

The main metrics applied for the evaluation are the number of synchronized trips for passengers and the waiting time, computed as the average of the time difference between the arrivals of a trip of line i and the next trip of line j to the synchronization point, considering the walking time.

5.4   Parameter Setting

EAs are stochastic methods, thus parameter setting analysis are required to determine the configuration that allows computing the best results. The values of stopping criterion ($\#gen$), population size (ps), recombination probability (p_R), and mutation probability (p_M) were studied on three instances, different from the ones used in validation experiments, in order to avoid bias. Fifty independent executions of the proposed EA were performed for each problem instance. Candidate values for the studied parameters were $\#gen \in \{500, 1000, 2000\}$, $ps \in \{50, 100, 200\}$, $p_R \in \{0.6, 0.75, 0.9\}$, and $p_M \in \{0.01, 0.05, 0.1\}$.

Results allowed concluding that population size and stopping criterion did not affect solution quality, as the EA rapidly converges to high quality solutions in a few (i.e., hundred) generations, despite the population size, so $\#gen=1000$ and $ps=100$ were selected for validation experiments. Regarding operator probabilities, the best results according to a Student's t-test applied to analyze the results distributions were obtained with the configuration $p_R = 0.9$ and $p_M = 0.01$.

5.5   Development and Execution Platform

The proposed EA was implemented in Malva (github.com/themalvaproject). The experimental evaluation was performed on a Quad-core Xeon E5430 at 2.66 GHz, 8 GB RAM, from Cluster FING, Universidad de la República [12].

5.6   Numerical Results

Table 1 reports the numerical results of the proposed EA and the reference results for the baseline solutions. The number of synchronized trips (st) are also reported for both real timetable and EA solutions.

Results in Table 1 indicate that the proposed EA computed accurate solutions, systematically improving the number of synchronized trips over the current real solution according to the actual timetable defined for the transportation system in Montevideo. Best fitness and synchronized trips of the EA in each problem dimension, are marked in bold. Overall, the average number of synchronized trips for EA solutions was 37.62% greater than the one in the current timetable and the most notable difference was 51.92%. The percent improvements (GAP) of the solutions computed by the proposed EA over the considered baseline algorithms are reported in Table 2. The best GAPs of the EA regarding h_i, H_i, and current planning in each problem dimension are marked in bold.

Results confirm that the proposed EA is able to improve over both current planning and also over naive solutions that account for the minimum and maximum headway. The best improvement was 13.33% in (weighted) synchronizations with respect to the current planning in Montevideo. In average, the proposed EA improved 8.79% over the current planning.

Regarding robustness and scalability, results indicate that the EA scaled properly when solving problem instances with a larger number of synchronization points. GAPs improved from 7.77% (average) and 11.36% (best) in small problem instances with 30 synchronization points to 9.44% (average) and 13.33% (best) in medium problem instances with 70 synchronization points. The GAPs of the proposed EA over baseline solutions are graphically presented in Fig. 3.

Table 1. Numerical results for the bus synchronization problem.

Scenario	Real timetable		h_i	H_i	EA	
	fitness	*st*			*fitness*	*st*
BS.12-14.30.36.120.90.2	32194	244	33310	22990	34142	345
BS.12-14.30.37.120.100.2	27913	217	30148	22938	30868	301
BS.12-14.30.37.120.90.0	30005	235	32745	22644	33415	338
BS.12-14.30.38.120.100.3	30407	292	31082	27327	31843	346
BS.12-14.30.38.120.100.4	29222	288	30544	25409	31449	355
BS.12-14.30.38.120.90.3	30827	274	32181	23252	32725	305
BS.12-14.30.39.120.100.0	23380	210	24393	18707	25536	295
BS.12-14.30.39.120.75.3	31508	217	33147	22621	33710	386
BS.12-14.30.40.120.90.4	23199	235	24633	18006	25501	278
BS.12-14.30.41.120.100.1	33965	292	34896	29907	**35672**	**359**
BS.12-14.70.59.120.100.3	67065	607	69430	59005	71587	834
BS.12-14.70.62.120.100.0	57979	528	61179	47123	62988	786
BS.12-14.70.63.120.90.4	57665	522	62145	47087	63361	661
BS.12-14.70.64.120.90.2	64486	561	67972	49122	69912	776
BS.12-14.70.65.120.100.2	62293	510	66559	52874	68269	668
BS.12-14.70.65.120.90.0	65681	569	70446	48348	**71938**	808
BS.12-14.70.66.120.90.1	57007	551	60906	43406	62447	740
BS.12-14.70.66.120.90.3	66642	597	70380	50242	71696	**845**
BS.12-14.70.67.120.75.1	63145	525	67926	43789	70183	721
BS.12-14.70.68.120.75.0	61457	543	67678	40321	69648	783
BS.12-14.110.77.120.100.3	103929	935	108875	90401	111314	1335
BS.12-14.110.78.120.90.4	95902	845	101384	74668	103662	1262
BS.12-14.110.79.120.75.3	93480	855	101364	65490	103434	1291
BS.12-14.110.79.120.90.1	96438	838	101931	73964	104232	1111
BS.12-14.110.79.120.90.3	96064	912	101723	74398	103930	1325
BS.12-14.110.81.120.100.1	97745	908	102858	85600	105444	1273
BS.12-14.110.82.120.75.0	96298	886	105089	64377	**107311**	**1346**
BS.12-14.110.83.120.100.2	94269	834	100642	81916	102754	1191
BS.12-14.110.83.120.75.2	89073	799	96965	58840	99235	1113
BS.12-14.110.83.120.90.0	94522	829	101517	71081	103932	1163

Table 2. GAPs of the proposed EA over baseline algorithms.

Scenario	GAP real	GAP h_i	GAP H_i
BS.12-14.30.36.120.90.2	6.05%	2.50%	48.51%
BS.12-14.30.37.120.100.2	10.59%	2.39%	34.57%
BS.12-14.30.37.120.90.0	**11.36**%	2.05%	47.57%
BS.12-14.30.38.120.100.3	4.72%	2.45%	16.53%
BS.12-14.30.38.120.100.4	7.62%	2.96%	23.77%
BS.12-14.30.38.120.90.3	6.16%	1.69%	40.74%
BS.12-14.30.39.120.100.0	9.22%	**4.69**%	36.51%
BS.12-14.30.39.120.75.3	6.99%	1.70%	**49.02**%
BS.12-14.30.40.120.90.4	9.92%	3.52%	41.63%
BS.12-14.30.41.120.100.1	5.03%	2.22%	19.28%
Average $n = 30$	7.77%	2.62%	35.81%
BS.12-14.70.59.120.100.3	6.74%	3.11%	21.32%
BS.12-14.70.62.120.100.0	8.64%	2.96%	33.67%
BS.12-14.70.63.120.90.4	9.88%	1.96%	34.56%
BS.12-14.70.64.120.90.2	8.41%	2.85%	42.32%
BS.12-14.70.65.120.100.2	9.59%	2.57%	29.12%
BS.12-14.70.65.120.90.0	9.53%	2.12%	48.79%
BS.12-14.70.66.120.90.1	9.54%	2.53%	43.87%
BS.12-14.70.66.120.90.3	7.58%	1.87%	42.70%
BS.12-14.70.67.120.75.1	11.15%	**3.32**%	60.28%
BS.12-14.70.68.120.75.0	**13.33**%	2.91%	**72.73**%
Average $n = 70$	9.44%	2.62%	42.94%
BS.12-14.110.77.120.100.3	7.11%	2.24%	23.13%
BS.12-14.110.78.120.90.4	8.09%	2.25%	38.83%
BS.12-14.110.79.120.75.3	10.65%	2.04%	57.94%
BS.12-14.110.79.120.90.1	8.08%	2.26%	40.92%
BS.12-14.110.79.120.90.3	8.19%	2.17%	39.69%
BS.12-14.110.81.120.100.1	7.88%	**2.51**%	23.18%
BS.12-14.110.82.120.75.0	**11.44**%	2.11%	66.69%
BS.12-14.110.83.120.100.2	9.00%	2.10%	25.44%
BS.12-14.110.83.120.75.2	11.41%	2.34%	**68.65**%
BS.12-14.110.83.120.90.0	9.96%	2.38%	46.22%
Average $n = 110$	9.18%	2.24%	43.07%
Overall average	8.79%	2.49%	40.61%

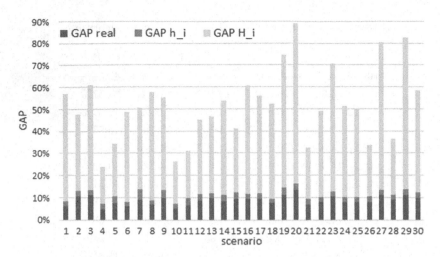

Fig. 3. Improvements (GAP) over baseline solutions

Regarding quality of service metrics, results of average waiting time per trip, reported in Tables 3 (values) and 4 (GAPs) indicates that the EA improves over the real timetable solutions for all scenarios. Furthermore, the EA also improves or equals h_i solutions in six scenarios (marked in bold). The best GAPs over h_i, H_i, and current planning in each problem dimension, are marked in bold.

Finally, regarding performance, the proposed EA had a remarkable computational efficiency. The average execution time required to perform 1000 generations was 78.2 s. The execution time did not increase significantly when solving the largest problem instances (in those instances, the average execution time was 122.7 s). These results confirm that the proposed EA is a useful tool for performing fast planning in Intelligent Transportation Systems, able to account for dynamic situations required in nowadays smart cities. Results demonstrated that the proposed EA can compute updated frequency plans (e.g., for the next hour) or even analyze different schedules accounting for different quality of service, a scenario that cannot be addressed with traditional exact methods (e.g. Branch and Bound), which fail to compute solutions in one hour for even small problem instances, as reported in related works [9].

Table 3. Average waiting time results.

Scenario	Real timetable	h_i	H_i	EA
BS.12-14.30.36.120.90.2	6.54	4.39	11.56	5.28
BS.12-14.30.37.120.100.2	8.14	5.34	14.11	6.08
BS.12-14.30.37.120.90.0	7.16	5.27	12.20	**5.14**
BS.12-14.30.38.120.100.3	7.53	5.25	12.65	6.36
BS.12-14.30.38.120.100.4	7.50	5.24	13.45	5.71
BS.12-14.30.38.120.90.3	6.78	4.59	12.60	6.19
BS.12-14.30.39.120.100.0	7.98	5.96	14.86	**5.86**
BS.12-14.30.39.120.75.3	8.31	5.93	15.17	**5.65**
BS.12-14.30.40.120.90.4	8.00	5.66	12.76	6.22
BS.12-14.30.41.120.100.1	7.50	5.67	14.62	6.42
BS.12-14.70.59.120.100.3	7.85	5.85	13.19	**5.85**
BS.12-14.70.62.120.100.0	7.68	5.46	13.50	5.60
BS.12-14.70.63.120.90.4	8.52	5.37	16.54	6.43
BS.12-14.70.64.120.90.2	7.88	5.40	13.84	5.59
BS.12-14.70.65.120.100.2	8.40	5.66	14.49	6.95
BS.12-14.70.65.120.90.0	7.34	5.05	12.75	**5.03**
BS.12-14.70.66.120.90.1	8.40	5.40	17.07	7.05
BS.12-14.70.66.120.90.3	8.08	5.61	14.76	5.82
BS.12-14.70.67.120.75.1	7.65	5.41	13.62	5.59
BS.12-14.70.68.120.75.0	7.81	5.75	13.48	6.55
BS.12-14.110.77.120.100.3	7.84	5.64	13.75	5.71
BS.12-14.110.78.120.90.4	8.02	5.39	15.42	5.73
BS.12-14.110.79.120.75.3	8.26	5.59	15.90	5.61
BS.12-14.110.79.120.90.1	7.83	5.28	15.06	6.62
BS.12-14.110.79.120.90.3	8.35	5.79	14.90	6.36
BS.12-14.110.81.120.100.1	8.20	5.50	14.47	6.08
BS.12-14.110.82.120.75.0	7.59	5.48	13.08	**5.42**
BS.12-14.110.83.120.100.2	8.27	5.57	15.86	5.81
BS.12-14.110.83.120.75.2	8.47	5.77	16.64	8.05
BS.12-14.110.83.120.90.0	7.88	5.36	13.88	6.27

Table 4. GAPs on waiting time of the proposed EA over baseline algorithms.

Scenario	GAP real	GAP h_i	GAP H_i
BS.12-14.110.77.120.100.3	27.17%	−1.24%	58.47%
BS.12-14.110.78.120.90.4	28.55%	−6.31%	62.84%
BS.12-14.110.79.120.75.3	**32.08**%	−0.36%	**64.72**%
BS.12-14.110.79.120.90.1	15.45%	−25.38%	56.04%
BS.12-14.110.79.120.90.3	23.83%	−9.84%	57.32%
BS.12-14.110.81.120.100.1	25.85%	−10.55%	57.98%
BS.12-14.110.82.120.75.0	28.59%	**1.09**%	58.56%
BS.12-14.110.83.120.100.2	29.75%	−4.31%	63.37%
BS.12-14.110.83.120.75.2	4.96%	−39.51%	51.62%
BS.12-14.110.83.120.90.0	20.43%	−16.98%	54.83%
Average $n = 30$	21.61%	−11.34%	55.79%
BS.12-14.70.59.120.100.3	25.48%	0.00%	55.65%
BS.12-14.70.62.120.100.0	27.08%	−2.56%	58.52%
BS.12-14.70.63.120.90.4	24.53%	−19.74%	**61.12**%
BS.12-14.70.64.120.90.2	29.06%	−3.52%	59.61%
BS.12-14.70.65.120.100.2	17.26%	−22.79%	52.04%
BS.12-14.70.65.120.90.0	**31.47**%	**0.40**%	60.55%
BS.12-14.70.66.120.90.1	16.07%	−30.56%	58.70%
BS.12-14.70.66.120.90.3	27.97%	−3.74%	60.57%
BS.12-14.70.67.120.75.1	26.93%	−3.33%	58.96%
BS.12-14.70.68.120.75.0	16.13%	−13.91%	51.41%
Average $n = 30$	24.20%	−9.98%	57.71%
BS.12-14.30.36.120.90.2	19.27%	−20.27%	54.33%
BS.12-14.30.37.120.100.2	25.31%	−13.86%	56.91%
BS.12-14.30.37.120.90.0	28.21%	2.47%	57.87%
BS.12-14.30.38.120.100.3	15.54%	−21.14%	49.72%
BS.12-14.30.38.120.100.4	23.87%	−8.97%	57.55%
BS.12-14.30.38.120.90.3	8.70%	−34.86%	50.87%
BS.12-14.30.39.120.100.0	26.57%	1.68%	60.57%
BS.12-14.30.39.120.75.3	**32.01**%	**4.72**%	**62.76**%
BS.12-14.30.40.120.90.4	22.25%	−9.89%	51.25%
BS.12-14.30.41.120.100.1	14.40%	−13.23%	56.09%
Average $n = 110$	23.67%	−11.34%	58.57%
Overall average	23.16%	−10.88%	57.36%

6   Conclusions and Future Work

This article presented a specific EA designed to efficiently solve a variant of the bus timetable synchronization problem.

A new problem formulation is presented, accounting for features of real scenarios modeled from data collected by nowadays Intelligent Transportation Systems. A specific EA was proposed to solve the problem, including simple and intuitive variation operators to provide both accuracy and diversity on solutions. The proposed fitness values takes into account the number of synchronized trips and the real demands of transfers on each bus stop. The proposed approach is generic and can be easily adapted to be applied and scale up to different scenarios.

The experimental evaluation of the proposed algorithm was performed over instances of significantly larger dimension than those previously addressed in the related literature. Problem instances based on real-data from the ITS in Montevideo, Uruguay were built, consisting of up to 83 lines and 110 synchronization points. Results show that the proposed evolutionary approach is able to compute accurate solutions, improving up to 13.33% in the fitness values and up to 24.20% in the waiting times, when compared to the current real timetable in Montevideo.

The main lines for future work are related to develop explicit multiobjective methods to solve the problem and improve the accuracy of the computed results. In this regard, historical GPS location data of buses can be used to obtain more accurate approximations of headways and travel times in the public transportation system. Furthermore, dynamic models should be explored to account for real-time location information to react to traffic congestion and demand spikes and deal with transfer synchronization at the operational level.

References

1. Bäck, T., Fogel, D., Michalewicz, Z. (eds.): Handbook of Evolutionary Computation. Oxford University Press, Oxford (1997)
2. Ceder, A., Golany, B., Tal, O.: Creating bus timetables with maximal synchronization. Transp. Res. Part A: Policy Pract. **35**(10), 913–928 (2001)
3. Ceder, A., Tal, O.: Timetable synchronization for buses. In: Wilson, N.H.M. (ed.) Computer-Aided Transit Scheduling. LNE, pp. 245–258. Springer, Heidelberg (1999). https://doi.org/10.1007/978-3-642-85970-0_12
4. Ceder, A., Wilson, N.: Bus network design. Transp. Res. Part B: Methodol. **20**(4), 331–344 (1986)
5. Daduna, J., Voß, S.: Practical experiences in schedule synchronization. In: Daduna, J.R., Branco, I., Paixão, J.M.P. (eds.) Computer-Aided Transit Scheduling. LNE, vol. 430, pp. 39–55. Springer, Heidelberg (1995). https://doi.org/10.1007/978-3-642-57762-8_4
6. Fleurent, C., Lessard, R., Séguin, L.: Transit timetable synchronization: evaluation and optimization. In: 9th International Conference on Computer-aided Scheduling of Public Transport (2004)

7. Grava, S.: Urban Transportation Systems: Choices for Communities. McGraw-Hill (2002)
8. Ibarra-Rojas, O., López-Irarragorri, F., Rios-Solis, Y.: Multiperiod bus timetabling. Transp. Sci. **50**(3), 805–822 (2016)
9. Ibarra-Rojas, O., Rios-Solis, Y.: Synchronization of bus timetabling. Transp. Res. Part B: Methodol. **46**(5), 599–614 (2012)
10. Intendencia de Montevideo: Plan de movilidad urbana: hacia un sistema de movilidad accesible, democrático y eficiente, April 2019. www.montevideo.gub.uy/aplicacion/plan-de-movilidad
11. Massobrio, R.: Urban mobility data analysis in Montevideo, Uruguay. Master's thesis, Universidad de la República, Uruguay (2018)
12. Nesmachnow, S.: Computación científica de alto desempeño en la Facultad de Ingeniería, Universidad de la República. Revista de la Asociación de Ingenieros del Uruguay **61**(1), 12–15 (2010)
13. Nesmachnow, S.: An overview of metaheuristics: accurate and efficient methods for optimisation. Int. J. Metaheuristics **3**(4), 320–347 (2014)
14. Nesmachnow, S., Baña, S., Massobrio, R.: A distributed platform for big data analysis in smart cities: combining intelligent transportation systems and socioeconomic data for Montevideo, Uruguay. EAI Endorsed Trans. Smart Cities **2**(5), 1–18 (2017)
15. Nesmachnow, S., Tchernykh, A., Cristóbal, A.: Planificación de transporte urbano en ciudades inteligentes. In: I Ibero-american Conference on Smart Cities, pp. 204–218 (2018)

Autonomous Flight of Unmanned Aerial Vehicles Using Evolutionary Algorithms

Américo Gaudín[1], Gabriel Madruga[1], Carlos Rodríguez[1],
Santiago Iturriaga[1(✉)], Sergio Nesmachnow[1], Claudio Paz[2],
Gregoire Danoy[3], and Pascal Bouvry[3]

[1] Universidad de la República, Montevideo, Uruguay
{siturria,sergion}@fing.edu.uy
[2] Universidad Tecnológica Nacional, Córdoba, Argentina
cpaz@frc.utn.edu.ar
[3] University of Luxembourg, Luxembourg City, Luxembourg
{gregoire.danoy,pascal.bouvry}@uni.lu

Abstract. This article explores the application of evolutionary algorithms and agent-oriented programming to solve the problem of searching and monitoring objectives through a fleet of unmanned aerial vehicles. The subproblem of static off-line planning is studied to find initial flight plans for each vehicle in the fleet, using evolutionary algorithms to achieve compromise values between the size of the explored area, the proximity of the vehicles, and the monitoring of points of interest defined in the area. The results obtained in the experimental analysis on representative instances of the surveillance problem indicate that the proposed techniques are capable of computing effective flight plans.

Keywords: Unmanned aerial vehicles · Autonomous flight · Evolutionary algorithms

1 Introduction

Unmanned Aerial Vehicles (UAVs) are aerial vehicles that do not have an onboard crew. They can be controlled remotely by a pilot on the ground or fly autonomously [18]. UAVs are often used in situations where manned flight is considered too dangerous. UAVs can remain in the sky over an area for a given period of time, sending information in real time to the pilot on the ground.

UAVs are very useful to perform various tasks in modern smart cities [3], including detection and management of risks, citizen safety, and traffic control, etc. Regarding disaster identification and management, UAVs can use their capabilities to observe the terrain from the air to carry out search and rescue operations, fight fires, inspect pipes, spray crops, make measurements, among others. In these cases, the ability to perform actions remotely through the use of UAVs results in an increase in the safety of people against traditional techniques. Regarding urban safety, UAVs provide an economical and safe alternative

© Springer Nature Switzerland AG 2020
J. L. Crespo-Mariño and E. Meneses-Rojas (Eds.): CARLA 2019, CCIS 1087, pp. 337–352, 2020.
https://doi.org/10.1007/978-3-030-41005-6_23

to perform surveillance tasks. UAVs provide an especially viable alternative for police departments and state agencies with limited economic resources that can not afford larger vehicles (helicopters or airplanes).

In order to carry out the activities described above it is of fundamental importance to have the possibility that the UAVs fly autonomously. An autonomous system is one that has the capacity to carry out actions and make decisions by itself [12]. Such systems try to achieve their objectives independently, without human intervention, even in situations of uncertainty or in the face of unforeseen situations. The UAVs have a control system that allows them to maintain a stable flight and perform movements according to orders sent by an operator or following a pre-established flight plan, providing a basic level of automated flight capacity. Transforming the specification of a task (provided by humans) into a low level description suitable for controlling a UAV is not an easy task, given the large number of variables involved. In this context, the application of computational intelligence techniques has been proposed in order to facilitate the generation of flight plans of UAVs that fulfill the objectives of a mission autonomously [4, 16].

Employing a fleet of UAVs allows the implementation of a cooperative approach to carry out the task that is to be carried out. This supposes a set of advantages, including: (i) granting a greater robustness, guaranteed by the existence of multiple agents that carry out the task; (ii) expanding the coverage area in which the mission is carried out; and (iii) specializing different UAVs to perform different tasks and improve flight time and the use of batteries, a fundamental requirement to offer a functional solution. To provide an effective and efficient cooperation scheme, it is necessary to apply flight planning techniques that allow the implementation of appropriate strategies to meet various objectives.

The flight route planning problem is NP-difficult, as it is a variant of the Orienteering Problem (OP) [15]. Heuristics and metaheuristics [9] are applied to find quality solutions at reasonable times, especially to compute solutions that can be implemented in real time.

In this line of work, this article presents an approach to solve the problem of searching and monitoring objectives through a fleet of unmanned aerial vehicles. The subproblem of static planning (off-line) is addressed by evolutionary algorithms to find a series of flight plans for each member of the fleet, with the aim of achieving good compromise values between the size of the area explored, the proximity of the UAVs and the monitoring of certain pre-established points of interest. The second proposed algorithm solves the subproblem of search and surveillance of objectives autonomously and cooperatively applying agent-oriented programming (POA), based on the offline planning found by the evolutionary algorithm. The combined approach proposed in this paper allows for efficient and versatile flight plans, taking offline planning as a solid starting point and including the flexibility to adapt to the changing situations of the environment provided by POA.

The document is structured as follows. Section 2 presents the formulation of the problems addressed in the work. The techniques applied in the study are described in Sect. 3. A review of the main related work is presented in Sect. 4. The proposed algorithms for solving the problem are described in Sect. 5. The experimental analysis is reported in Sect. 6. Finally, Sect. 7 presents the conclusions and the main lines of future work.

2 The Problem of Autonomous Flight Planning of a Fleet of UAVs

This section describes the problem of planning a fleet of UAVs and its mathematical fomulation.

2.1 Generic Description of the Planning Problem

Given a fleet of UAVs, the problem is to plan a set of routes or routes for each of the UAVs with the objectives of maximizing the surface explored, maintaining communication between agents and monitoring the objectives. The explored surface is defined as the union of the surfaces explored by each UAV in its route in the planned time. The area covered by a UAV at a given time is determined by a circumference of *coverage radius* that has it as its center. In order to ensure communication between the UAVs, a maximum distance to which the UAVs can be found is defined: two UAVs can communicate with each other when the distance between them is less than a *communication radio*.

There are two variants of the problem: (i) an *offline* version, where a static planning is sought, assuming perfect information about the elements of the problem; and (ii) an *online* version that considers partial information by the agents (i.e., UAVs), limited by their sensory capacity (camera images and messages received through the network). The static version corresponds to a simpler problem, whose solution is useful as a starting point for dynamic planning capable of interacting with the environment. The problem model assumes total autonomy of the UAVs, since it does not consider a central base that defines the movements to be performed by each UAV interactively.

2.2 Formulation of the Static Planning Problem

The mathematical formulation of the problem of static flight route planning for UAVs in surveillance missions considers the following elements:

- a set of UAVs, $U = \{u_1, \ldots u_{|U|}\}$
- a mission time period T, which is uniformly discretized in s time steps; $T = < t_1, t_2, \ldots t_s >$
- a maximum travel speed of UAVs, v_D
- a set of targets to surveil $O = \{o_1, \ldots, o_{|O|}\}$
- a maximum speed for the targets v_O

- a vector $P = (p_1, p_2, \ldots p_{|O|})$, where p_i is the benefit associated to surveil target o_i for all $i = 1 \ldots |O|$.
- an object position matrix OP (dimensions $|O| \times s$). OP_{ij} indicates the coordinates of the target o_i in timestep t_j.
- a coverage radius $\bar{r}_o$ and a circumscribed coverage square with side $r_o = \frac{2\bar{r}_o}{\sqrt{2}}$.
- a communication radius r_c.
- an area to explore of dimensions $H \times W$, discretized in squares of length r_o, defined by matrix A_j, as presented in Eq. 1. Matrix A_j determines the position of all UAVs at timestep t_j with $a^j_{x,y} \in Q$ with $Q = U \cup O \cup \{\emptyset\}$.

$$
A_j = \begin{bmatrix}
a^j_{11} & \cdots & a^j_{1(\lceil \frac{W}{r_o} \rceil)} \\
a^j_{21} & \cdots & a^j_{2(\lceil \frac{W}{r_o} \rceil)} \\
\vdots & & \vdots \\
a^j_{(\lceil \frac{H}{r_o} \rceil)1} & \cdots & a^j_{(\lceil \frac{H}{r_o} \rceil)(\lceil \frac{W}{r_o} \rceil)}
\end{bmatrix}
\tag{1}
$$

- a base B, defined by coordinates (x_B, y_B), which is the departing point for UAV missions. The base B is located within the area to explore, i.e., $1 \leq x_B \leq \lceil \frac{H}{r_o} \rceil)$ and $1 \leq y_B \leq \lceil \frac{W}{r_o} \rceil)$.

The problem proposes finding a planning for the fleet of UAVs, i.e., a function $p : U \times T \rightarrow Q^{\lceil \frac{H}{r_o} \rceil \times \lceil \frac{W}{r_o} \rceil}$, that maximizes three functions simultaneously: the benefit of having a vision of an objective ($\delta(p)$, Eq. 2), the benefit of forming an ad-hoc network ($\gamma(p)$, Eq. 3) and the benefit for exploring ($\phi(p)$, Eq. 4).

$$
\delta(p) = \sum_{i=1}^{|U|} \sum_{j=1}^{|T|} \sum_{z=1}^{|O|} found(pos(u_i, t_j), pos(o_z, t_j)) \times p_z
\tag{2}
$$

$$
\gamma(p) = \sum_{i=1}^{|U|} \sum_{h=i+1}^{|U|} \sum_{j=1}^{|T|} connected(pos(u_i, t_j), pos(u_h, t_j))
\tag{3}
$$

$$
\phi(p) = \sum_{x=1}^{\lceil \frac{H}{r_o} \rceil} \sum_{y=1}^{\lceil \frac{W}{r_o} \rceil} \sum_{j=1}^{|T|} explored(x, y, j) \times \frac{1}{r_o^2}
\tag{4}
$$

The auxiliary functions considered in the formulation correspond to the ones defined in Eqs. 6–8:

$$
pos(q_i \in Q, t_j \in T) = (x, y) \text{ such that } a^j_{x,y} = q_i
\tag{5}
$$

$$
found(c_1 \in \mathbb{N}^2, c_2 \in \mathbb{N}^2) = \begin{cases} 1 \text{ if } d(c_1, c_2) \leq \bar{r}_o \\ 0 \text{ otherwise} \end{cases}
\tag{6}
$$

$$
connected(c_1 \in \mathbb{N}^2, c_2 \in \mathbb{N}^2) = \begin{cases} 1 \text{ if } d(c_1, c_2) \leq r_c \\ 0 \text{ otherwise} \end{cases}
\tag{7}
$$

$$
explored(x \in \mathbb{N}, y \in \mathbb{N}, t_j \in T) = \begin{cases} 1 \text{ if } a^j_{x,y} \in U \\ 0 \text{ otherwise} \end{cases}
\tag{8}
$$

With d being the Euclidean distance. Given the definition of ϕ, the benefit obtained is inversely proportional to the size of the covered area. This performance indicator is called Spatial Exploration Ratio [17].

3 Evolutionary Algorithms

EAs are stochastic techniques that emulate the process of natural evolution to solve problems of optimization, search and learning [1]. They are especially useful for solving complex real-world problems in multiple application areas [9].

An EA is an iterative technique. In each iteration (called *generation*) probabilistic operators are applied on a set of individuals (the *population*). The initial population is generated by applying a random procedure or using a specific heuristic for the problem. Each individual codifies a tentative solution to the problem and has assigned a *fitness* value that determines its suitability to solve the problem. The goal of the EA is to improve the fitness of individuals in the population, applying *evolutionary operators*, such as the *recombination* of parts of two individuals and the random *mutation* of an individual's coding. These operators are applied to individuals selected according to their fitness, thus guiding the EA toward tentative solutions of higher quality. Algorithm 1 presents the generic schema of an EA with a population P.

Algorithm 1. Schema of an evolutionary algorithm.

1: **initialize**($P(0)$)
2: $t \leftarrow 0$ {generation counter}
3: **while** not stopping criterion **do**
4:    **evaluate**($P(t)$)
5:    parents←**selection**($P(t)$)
6:    children←**variation operators**(parents)
7:    newpop←**replacement**(children,$P(t)$)
8:    $t{+}{+}$
9:    $P(t)$←newpop
10: **end while**
11: **return** best individual found

The stop criterion usually involves a fixed number of generations, a quality level on the fitness of the best individual, or detecting convergence. An EA uses a policy of *selection* of individuals to participate in the recombination and a policy of *replacement* to determine which new individuals are inserted into the population in each new generation. Finally, the EA returns the best solution found in the iterative process, taking into account the fitness function considered. In this article, a traditional EA and a Mutation and Selection Only Evolutionary Strategy (MOSES) variant are proposed, the details of which are presented below.

MOSES [2] is an EA that uses only selection/mutation operators and an optimization scheme based on the Monte Carlo method. Working on a population P to optimize a function f, MOSES defines a Markov string X_n on E^k, where E is the problem state space and k the cardinality of P. The transitions of X_n are given by a mutation operator that defines a search graph specifying the adjacency between individuals of the population. Algorithm 2 presents the generic scheme of MOSES for solving a minimization problem.

Algorithm 2. Schema of the MOSES algorithm.

1: **initialize**($P(0)$)
2: $t \leftarrow 0$ {generation counter}
3: **while** not stopping criterion **do**
4:    **evaluate**($P(t)$)
5:    find the best individual $I^+ = \min f(I_h); 1 \leq h \leq k$
6:    sort an integer $Z \in (0, k]$ according to a Binomial law $(k, e^{-1/T})$
7:    **for** individuals $I_r, 1 \leq r \leq Z$ **do**
8:       change $I_r = (i_1, i_2, \ldots, i_s)$ by $I_q = (i'_1, \ldots, i'_s)$
9:    **end for**
10:   **for** individuals $I_r, Z + 1 \leq r \leq k$ **do**
11:      change $I_r = (i_1, \ldots, i_s)$ for I^+
12:   **end for**
13:   $t{+}{+}$
14: **end while**
15: **return** best individual found (I^+)

In each generation the best individual (I^+) is determined, according to the fitness values. For each individual in the population $I_r = (i_1, \ldots, i_s)$ it is decided, according to a mutation probability p_M, to transform it into another individual $I_q = (i'_1, \ldots, i'_s)$, following a stochastic walk defined over the search space by a motion operator or transforming it into the best individual I^+. This strategy introduces a mechanism of elitism implicit in the selection used by the MOSES algorithm.

Mutation probability p_M it is defined as a function of a parameter T that plays a role analogous to temperature in the metaheuristic Simulated Annealing [9]. In the canonical version of the MOSES algorithm (*ordered, with reinitialization*) $p_M = e^{-1/T}$ and a scaled decrementing scheme is applied for parameter T, defined by Eq. 9, where D is the diameter of the search space defined by the movement operator.

$$\forall q \in \mathbf{N}, \forall n \in \left(e^{(q-1) \cdot D}, e^{q \cdot D}\right) \qquad T(n) = {}^1\!/_q \tag{9}$$

In MOSES, the mutation probability is reinitialized when the decay scheme assigns a minimum value, given by a parameter p_{MIN}.

4   Related Works

The analysis of the related literature allows identifying several recent proposals on the application of computational strategies for the flight planning of a fleet of UAVs. The main related works are reviewed next.

Ponda et al. [11] studied methods to design trajectories to increase the amount of information provided by a set of measurements of an objective, made by sensors on board, to determine their position. Estimation algorithms for locating targets were explored, including Kalman extended filters, Fisher information matrix, and Cramér-Rao coordinates to evaluate the performance of the estimation of measurements. The experimental analysis considered two scenarios: (i) the identification of points to perform the measurements considering a maximum number of measurements, and (ii) the optimization of trajectories of a single UAV with movement restrictions. A gradient descent method was applied for optimization, which showed some drawbacks typical of a deterministic technique (e.g. it tended to group measurements). A case study was also proposed, simultaneously optimizing the trajectories and the estimation of objectives, for the cases of static and objective that follow a predetermined trajectory. The reported results show that the calculated trajectories improve the estimation, collecting the same amount of information as a non-optimized strategy with only half of the measures. The work did not propose the application to flight planning of UAV fleets, although the first scenario can be used to coordinate the measures provided by several UAVs to improve the movement estimates of the target. Mufalli et al. [7] studied the problem of sensor selection and route planning of UAVs in military reconnaissance missions, which is a generalization of the Team Orienteering Problem. The authors presented a mathematical programming model that they could only solve in an exact way (using CPLEX) for very simple missions. To address more realistic missions, the authors proposed two heuristics, augmented by the column generation technique. The results obtained on scenarios of up to 100×100 positions with up to 100 targets and fleets of up to eight UAVs indicated that the heuristics were able to find good solutions quickly. The generation of columns improved the solution in many instances, with a minimal impact on the execution time.

Schleich et al. [13] proposed a decentralized and localized approach to control mobility in fleets of UAVs flying from a base. The problem considered an area to be monitored and a fleet of UAVs in charge of patrolling it. The fleet is deployed from the base station and all UAVs are equipped with communication modules. A mobility model, called *connected coverage model* was proposed. It is responsible for physically moving the UAVs to fulfill the surveillance mission. The model consists of three sequential steps: selection of the neighborhood to stay connected, calculation of options for the future position of the UAV, and pheromone-based behavior to choose the best direction from the options. The mobility model was compared with a random strategy to select destinations according to quality metrics to evaluate coverage and connectivity. The numerical results show that the proposed mobility model has a reduced negative impact on coverage, but connectivity performance is significantly better than that of the other models. The work of Schleich et al. presents a very similar approach to the one proposed in this article, but without applying computational intelligence and without the reactive navigation component provided by agent-oriented programming.

Oh et al. [10] presented a framework to construct safe and feasible routes to visit a set of points in cooperative missions of multiple UAVs, maintaining communication with a ground control station that centrally controls the mission. Three methods were proposed: (i) an exact linear programming method to assign paths to UAVs by minimizing the total flight time; (ii) an heuristic to build routes by adding segments of transit routes considering their insertion cost; and (iii) a negotiation model to solve conflicts between areas visited by more than one UAV, to minimize the cost of flight plans. Two cases were studied: the planning of surveillance/search missions on a road network and the planning of routes to maintain communication with a command base. For missions planning, the insertion heuristic obtained paths 12% longer than the exact method, but it was effective for the online calculation of trajectories, finding paths in less than a second. For the cooperation problem, results considering only two UAVs indicated that the negotiation model was effective to generate flight plans to monitor the scenario and avoid prohibited zones. However, the communications were lost for a total time of 1200 s, suggesting that in order to successfully carry out the mission, it is necessary to have a larger fleet. The work presented a centralized approach due to the existence of the control base, for which reason the flight plans are not totally autonomous as those proposed in our research.

Shang et al. [14] proposed a hybrid EA with ant colony algorithm (ACO) to plan missions of a fleet of UAVs. The algorithm replaces bad individuals of the EA population with new individuals constructed using ACO and Path Relinking. Results suggested that the hybrid algorithm can solve test instances effectively in reasonable times. The hybrid was studied in selected test cases, and compared with several methods of the literature. Results indicate that the proposed algorithm can obtain better results in several of the instances and obtain optimal solutions in the majority, suggesting that it can be used in large-scale problems.

Han et al. [6] proposed a multi agent system integrating UAVs that collaborate to perform complex missions. Several mechanisms were proposed for coordination and cooperation: tracking to follow objectives, *artificial potential field* to maintain a formation and avoid obstacles, and auction to allocate and select missions. The developed system was tested using simulation, but the article did not present real experiments.

The analysis of the related works allows identifying several proposals of intelligent mobility models and algorithms to optimize the operation of UAV fleets for different missions. These proposals helped to model the problem and inspire the solutions developed in our research.

5   Evolutionary Algorithms for Flight Planning of UAVs for Surveillance

This section describes the proposed EAs to solve the problem of autonomous flight planning of a fleet of UAVs: a traditional EA and a MOSES algorithm in its ordered version with restart. Both methods use initialization and special operators to define a good scan pattern of the solution space of the problem.

5.1   Development and Execution Platform

The proposed EAs were developed on Watchmaker, a library for evolutionary object-oriented and extensible computing implemented in Java [5]. The classes provided by the library were extended to incorporate concepts related to the resolution method and the problem to be solved.

The experimental evaluation was performed on a Dell Power Edge server, Quad-core Xeon E5430 processor at 2.66 GHz, 8 GB RAM, from Cluster FING, Universidad de la República, Uruguay [8].

5.2   Solution Encoding

Individuals encode the position of each UAV at each instant of time. A matrix M (dimensions $u \times s$, number of UAVs $\times$ timesteps) is used, where each element M_{ij} is a pair (x_{ij}, y_{ij}) that represents the position of each UAV in a Cartesian coordinate system. A sample of solution encoding is presented Fig. 1 for an problem considering two UAVs and five time steps.

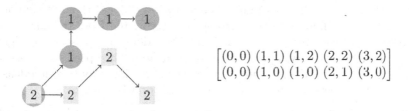

$$\begin{bmatrix} (0,0) & (1,1) & (1,2) & (2,2) & (3,2) \\ (0,0) & (1,0) & (1,0) & (2,1) & (3,0) \end{bmatrix}$$

Fig. 1. Sample solution encoding.

5.3   Fitness Function

The fitness function is defined as the linear aggregation of the benefit functions presented in the formulation: $fitness(p) = \delta(p) + \gamma(p) + \phi(p)$.

5.4 Evolutionary Operators

Population Initialization. The initial population is generated by the following procedure. The route of each UAV is established by generating a path that starts at the base position and moves away towards a certain direction at maximum speed. This direction is determined by the angle $i \times \frac{2\pi}{u} + j \times \frac{2\pi}{u \times Z}$, where $i \in [0, u - 1]$ is the UAV identification, $j \in [0, Z]$ is the number of the candidate solution, and Z is the population size. This way, each candidate solution is a rotation of another.

Selection. The *Stochastic Universal Sampling* (SUS) with *Sigma Escalation* (σ) is used as selection operator. There are mainly three advantages of using SUS+σ versus other selection techniques: i) SUS is not biased to highly fitted individuals; ii) in the initial stage of the algorithm, σ helps to avoid premature convergence caused by the dominance of a group of individuals with very high fitness, and ii) in the final stage, σ helps to amplify small differences in fitness when the rate of improvement has slowed down.

Recombination. The Single Point Crossover (SPX) operator is used for recombination. According to preliminary experiments, this operator provides an appropriate search pattern for the problem. Individuals resulting from the recombination may encode infeasible solutions. In this case, a correction procedure (described later on this section) is applied.

Mutation. A specific mutation operator was designed for the problem. First, the number of positions to be modified is selected uniformly in $[1, u \times \frac{t}{s}]$. Positions to mutate are randomly selected with uniform probability between the positions in the individual. Once the new direction has been defined, the sense of flight is chosen randomly in an equiprobable way and the speed of the UAV in this new direction is set as the maximum. The mutation changes the direction of the UAV to the perpendicular to the current one (computed from the current and next position). Once the new direction has been defined, the sense of flight is chosen randomly by applying a uniform distribution. The speed of the UAV is set to maximum. Individuals resulting from the mutation may encode infeasible solutions. In this case, a correction procedure is applied.

Correction of Unfeasible Solutions. There are two cases in which an individual may encode an unfeasible solution to the problem: (i) when the path of a UAV has two consecutive positions that are more distant than it can travel in a time interval, and (ii) when a UAV does not return to the base after completing a tour. To correct individuals that code solutions with infeasibility of type i, the position from which it is not possible to reach the nearest one when the UAV flies at maximum speed is changed. In order to correct infeasibility of type ii, the latest simulation step in which it is still possible to return to the base is determined, and the UAV trajectory is modified from that step towards the base.

Stopping Criterion. The proposed EA uses the *stagnation* technique: the execution of the algorithm stops when detecting a stagnation in the best fitness value of the population during a certain number of generations, assuming that the loss of diversity does not allow the EA to progress any further. On the other hand, the MOSES algorithm uses the predefined effort criterion, where the execution is interrupted after a certain number of generations. Stagnation is not useful in this case, as MOSES has a stronger selection pressure and diversity generation (MOSES relies on mutations to modify individuals), so the method usually is able to improve even after a stagnation situation is detected.

6 Experimental Analysis

This section presents the experimental analysis of the proposed EA.

6.1 Baseline Greedy Algorithm

A simple greedy algorithm was designed and implemented for baseline comparison. This strategy assigns a different objective to each UAV for surveillance and marks the assigned objectives as surveilled. Once a UAV finishes surveilling its assigned objective, a new objective is assigned to it until no more unsurveilled objectives are left or the UAV must return to the base.

6.2 Problem Instances

Four different problem instances were synthetically generated for the experimental evaluation: one small-sized instance, two medium-sized instances and a large-sized instance. The proposed instances are presented in Table 1, where all distances are expressed in m and all speeds in m/s.

Table 1. Proposed problem instances

#I	H	W	(x_B, y_B)	$\|U\|$	v_D	$\|T\|$	s	$\|O\|$	v_O	P	r_u	r_c
0	100	100	(50, 50)	5	2	100	10	2	1	<2,4>	3	2
1	1000	1000	(300, 300)	5	10	1000	10	4	5	<1,2,3,4>	5	5
2	1000	1000	(700, 700)	10	10	1000	10	4	5	<2,2,8,8>	5	10
3	10000	10000	(5000, 5000)	5	10	2000	20	5	0.1	<1,1,1,1,10>	2	1000

The starting location of each objective was generated randomly following a uniform distribution and its motion behavior was generated by applying Rapidly-exploring Random Tree, an efficient strategy for searching a multi-dimensional space using trees, biased towards unexplored sections of the search space.

6.3 Parametric Configuration Analysis

Configuration analysis was performed using instance #0 while the experimental evaluation is performed using instances #1 to #3 to avoid bias in the resulting configuration. The parameters p_C and p_M were studied for the EA while T and P_{min} were studied for MOSES. The studied candidate values for each parameter were the following: $p_C \in \{0.5, 0.8, 1.0\}$, $p_M \in \{0.001, 0.1, 0.15\}$, $T \in \{1, 5, 100\}$, $P_{min} \in \{0.1, 0.2, 0.3\}$. Population size and stopping condition are fixed and were configured to be 200 individuals and 2000 generations without improvement for both EA and MOSES. A total of 40 independent executions for each combination of candidate values was performed. Results are compared using the fitness function and a score function $score = mean(F) - 2 \times SD(F)$ that takes into account the mean ($mean$) and standard deviation (SD) of the set of computed fitness values (F).

Tables 2 and 3 report the score value and the minimum, median, maximum fitness along with the first and third quartile fitness results for each combination of parameter values. Best values are colored.

Table 2. Minimum (min), median (med), maximum (max), first (Q_1) and third (Q_3) quartile fitness and score values computed by the EA for instance 0.

p_M	p_C	Fitness					Score
		min	Q_1	med	Q_3	max	
0.01	0.5	537.22	624.88	725.83	946.44	1111.33	383.04
0.01	0.8	563.22	786.11	951.55	1043.50	1112.66	566.40
0.01	1.0	668.44	893.61	970.05	1058.61	1114.44	691.27
0.10	0.5	516.22	660.44	815.33	907.66	1097.33	405.56
0.10	0.8	671.77	838.72	928.33	982.72	1126.44	623.20
0.10	1.0	775.11	911.94	991.00	1047.22	1153.44	733.39
0.15	0.5	533.33	705.61	794.11	896.66	1480.33	381.58
0.15	0.8	730.11	851.44	937.61	965.22	1075.66	672.62
0.15	1.0	735.00	915.11	995.50	1064.16	1147.77	724.96

Results show that overall the best results are computed by the EA when configured with $p_M = 0.10$ and $p_C = 1.0$ and by MOSES when configured with $T = 1$ and $P_{min} = 0.2$. Henceforth, all experiments are performed using these configurations.

6.4 Experimental Results

A total of 40 independent executions where performed for both the EA and MOSES for each problem instance from #1 to #3. Table 4 presents efficacy and

Table 3. Minimum (min), median (med), maximum (max), first (Q_1) and third (Q_3) quartile fitness and score values computed by MOSES on instance #0.

T	P_{min}	fitness					score
		min	Q_1	med	Q_3	max	
1	0.1	361.55	397.83	434.83	464.44	592.66	296.03
1	0.2	363.33	408.05	427.94	459.00	558.55	299.18
1	0.3	353.88	394.72	416.00	459.61	539.77	293.65
5	0.1	247.66	290.88	342.00	413.00	585.88	158.45
5	0.2	292.66	316.11	362.44	422.44	502.11	213.59
5	0.3	223.11	273.77	323.11	376.38	517.22	147.28
100	0.1	243.77	261.77	278.55	296.22	336.11	205.69
100	0.2	293.66	309.66	333.83	353.33	433.00	243.23
100	0.3	192.33	197.50	205.33	213.83	234.33	151.18

Table 4. Efficacy and efficiency metrics for the EA, MOSES and greedy algorithm for problem instances #1 to #3.

	instance #1			instance #2			instance #3		
	EA	MOSES	Greedy	EA	MOSES	Greedy	EA	MOSES	Greedy
Fitness									
Best	5252.0	576.8	665.0	27222.5	2217.5	6608.0	22454.7	22461.5	3529.9
Mean	3167.1	495.5	–	12935.1	2059.8	–	22448.8	22452.6	–
σ	948.0	29.6	–	4404.2	54.1	–	3.58	3.3	–
Number of generations									
Mean	2335.9	1968.6	–	300.3	1976.1	–	343.0	1913.0	–
Execution time (s)									
Mean	307.1	179.8	0.1	437.2	457.6	0.1	429.1	388.3	0.1
σ	180.2	3.5	–	49.5	4.8	–	83.0	3.0	–

efficiency metrics for the EA, MOSES and the greedy algorithm for each problem instance.

Results show the EA is more accurate than MOSES and the greedy algorithm by one order of magnitude when solving problem instances #1 and #2. The greedy algorithm is the second most accurate when solving problem instances #1 and #2, outperforming MOSES in every execution. However, when solving problem instance #3, both the EA and MOSES outperform the greedy algorithm and present similar accuracy results with no significant difference between them.

Regarding efficiency, the greedy algorithm requires significantly less execution time than the EA and MOSES in every problem instance. In average, MOSES is the second most efficient algorithm, requiring less execution time than the EA for problem instances #1 and #3.

Figures 2 and 3 show the fitness computed by the EA, MOSES and greedy algorithm for problem instances #1 and #2. Fitness computed for problem #3 is not presented because there is no noticeable difference between the EA and MOSES.

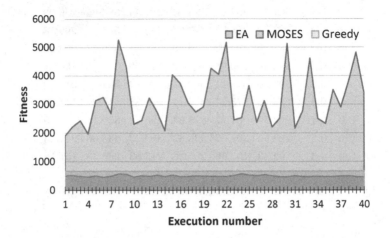

Fig. 2. Fitness computed by the EA, MOSES and the baseline greedy algorithm for problem instance #1.

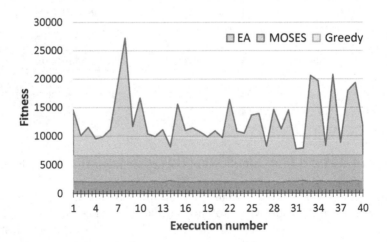

Fig. 3. Fitness computed by the EA, MOSES and the baseline greedy algorithm for problem instance #2.

7   Conclusions and Future Work

This article presented an approach to address the problem of searching and monitoring targets using a fleet of autonomous UAV. A mathematical formulation for the problem is proposed for maximizing the visual surveillance of the targets, the number of UAV connected to the ad-hoc communication network and the coverage of the area of interest.

A set of four realistic problem instances were synthetically generated with areas ranging from $300\,m \times 300\,m$ up to $20.000\,m \times 20.000\,m$ and with up to 5 moving targets for surveillance. Two different evolutionary algorithms were proposed for dealing with the off-line variant of the problem, one based on a EA and the other on MOSES. Furthermore, a baseline greedy algorithm was proposed for comparison. The smallest instance is used for calibrating the algorithm and the others for the experimental evaluation.

The experimental evaluation show that in average the proposed algorithm based on the EA is 2.2× more accurate than MOSES and the baseline greedy algorithm. The EA outperforms MOSES and the greedy algorithm in every execution when solving two of the three problem instances considered for the experimental analysis. However, the EA and MOSES compute equally accurate solutions for the remaining problem instance, both of them significantly outperforming the greedy baseline algorithm.

When considering the execution time, results show the EA and MOSES require around 6 min of execution time while the greedy algorithm requires just $0.1\,s$ of execution time. Hence, the greedy algorithm is suitable for addressing the on-line variant of the problem.

Overall, the proposed algorithm showed to be effective for addressing the optimization problem in a reasonable execution time. The main lines for future work are two. First, generating and studying a larger set of realistic problem instances, thus leveraging the efficacy of the proposed algorithm in a wide range of scenarios. Second, design additional planning algorithms for addressing both the offline and the online variant of the proposed problem.

References

1. Bäck, T., Fogel, D., Michalewicz, Z.: Handbook of Evolutionary Computation. Oxford University Press, Oxford (1997)
2. Cercueil, A., Francois, O.: Monte Carlo simulation and population-based optimization. In: Proceedings of the Congress on Evolutionary Computation, pp. 191–198 (2001)
3. Deakin, M., Waer, H.A.: From intelligent to smart cities. Intell. Build. Int. **3**, 133–139 (2011)
4. Díaz, S., Garate, B., Nesmachnow, S., Iturriaga, S.: Autonomous navigation of unmanned aerial vehicles using markers. In: II Ibero-American Congress on Smart Cities, pp. 1–15 (2019)
5. Dyer, D.: The watchmaker framework for evolutionary computation. http://watchmaker.uncommons.org/. Accessed May 2019
6. Han, J., Wang, C., Yi, G.: UAV robust strategy control based on MAS. Abstr. Appl. Anal. **2014**, 1–7 (2014)
7. Mufalli, F., Batta, R., Nagi, R.: Simultaneous sensor selection and routing of unmanned aerial vehicles for complex mission plans. Comput. Oper. Res. **39**(11), 2787–2799 (2012)

8. Nesmachnow, S.: Computación científica de alto desempeño en la Facultad de Ingeniería, Universidad de la República. Revista de la Asociación de Ingenieros del Uruguay **61**(1), 12–15 (2010)

9. Nesmachnow, S.: An overview of metaheuristics: accurate and efficient methods for optimisation. Int. J. Metaheuristics **3**(4), 320–347 (2014)

10. Oh, H., Shin, H., Kim, S., Tsourdos, A., White, B.: Cooperative mission and path planning for a team of UAVs. In: Valavanis, K., Vachtsevanos, G. (eds.) Handbook of Unmanned Aerial Vehicles, pp. 1509–1545. Springer, Dordrecht (2014). https://doi.org/10.1007/978-90-481-9707-1_14

11. Ponda, S., Kolacinski, R., Frazzoli, E.: Trajectory optimization for target localization using small unmanned aerial vehicles. In: American Institute of Aeronautics and Astronautics Guidance, Navigation, and Control Conference, pp. 1–25 (2009)

12. Raol, J., Gopal, A.: Mobile Intelligent Autonomous Systems. CRC Press (2012)

13. Schleich, J., Panchapakesan, A., Danoy, G., Bouvry, P.: UAV fleet area coverage with network connectivity constraint. In: 11th ACM International Symposium on Mobility Management and Wireless Access, pp. 131–138 (2013)

14. Shang, K., Karungaru, S., Feng, Z., Ke, L., Terada, K.: A GA-ACO hybrid algorithm for the multi-UAV mission planning problem. In: 14th International Symposium on Communications and Information Technologies (2014)

15. Shi, H., Sun, X., Sun, C., Chen, D., An, Y.: Research of the path planning complexity for autonomous mobile robot under dynamic environments. In: IEEE Sixth International Conference on Intelligent Systems Design and Applications, pp. 216–219 (2006)

16. Valavanis, K.: Advances in Unmanned Aerial Vehicles. Springer, Netherlands (2007). https://doi.org/10.1007/978-1-4020-6114-1

17. Wietfeld, C., Daniel, K.: Cognitive networking for UAV swarms. In: Valavanis, K., Vachtsevanos, G. (eds.) Handbook of Unmanned Aerial Vehicles, pp. 749–780. Springer, Netherlands (2015). https://doi.org/10.1007/978-90-481-9707-1_32

18. Zeng, Y., Zhang, R., Lim, T.: Wireless communications with unmanned aerial vehicles: opportunities and challenges. Commun. Mag. **54**(5), 36–42 (2016)

Special Track on Bioinspired Processing (BIP): Image and Signal Processing

An Experimental Study on Fundamental Frequency Detection in Reverberated Speech with Pre-trained Recurrent Neural Networks

Andrei Alfaro-Picado, Stacy Solís-Cerdas, and Marvin Coto-Jiménez(✉)

PRIS-Lab, Escuela de Ingeniería Eléctrica, Universidad de Costa Rica,
San Jose, Costa Rica
{andrei.alfaro,stacy.solis,marvin.coto}@ucr.ac.cr

Abstract. The detection of the fundamental frequency (f_0) in speech signals is relevant in areas such as automatic speech recognition and identification, with multiple potential applications. For example, in virtual assistants, assistive technology devices and biomedical applications. It has been acknowledged that the extraction of this parameter is affected in adverse conditions, for example, when reverberation or background noise is present. In this paper, we present a new method to improve the detection of the f_0 in speech signals with reverberation, based on initialized Long Short-term Memory (LSTM) neural networks. In previous works, LSTM has used weights initialized with random numbers. We propose an initialization in the form of an auto-associative memory, which learns the identity function from non-reverberated data. The advantages of our proposal are shown using different objective quality measures, in particular, in the detection of segments with and without f_0.

Keywords: Deep learning · Fundamental frequency · LSTM · Reverberation

1 Introduction

The analysis of noisy and reverberant speech signals has been a topic of interest over the past several decades. Moreover, it is well-known that speech signals are degraded in real-world environments. The quality of the communications systems or the recognition performance may affect their quality [3,30,40,41] with such background noise, reverberation or other distortions degrading the speech information.

The speech enhancement algorithms developed to enhance noisy or reverberated speech can be considered successful if they enhance the signal quality [20], according to objective or subjective measures. Also if the algorithms allow better detection of relevant parameters, such as fundamental frequency (f_0).

Supported by the University of Costa Rica.

J. L. Crespo-Mariño and E. Meneses-Rojas (Eds.): CARLA 2019, CCIS 1087, pp. 355–368, 2020.
https://doi.org/10.1007/978-3-030-41005-6_24

There are some signal processing-based methods for the problem of enhancing reverberated speech. But more recently, Deep Neural Networks (DNN) have been presented in [10,19,33] for this purpose. The main approach for DNN is the mapping of spectral features from degraded speech into the features of the corresponding clean speech.

The new types of recurrent neural networks (RNN) have been applied where there is a temporary dependence on the data. For example, in handwriting recognition or speech processing. One recent kind of RNN, the Long Short-Term Memory Network (LSTM) has succeeded over other the types of networks for noise reduction and reverberant distortions in speech signals.

Among the most important tasks in speech processing is the f_0 detection, because its accurately detection is very important in many applications. There are still many possibilities for improvement in the algorithms proposed so far [42].

In this paper, motivated by previous successful experiences using LSTM in enhancing speech signals, we present a new way to initialize LSTM neural networks to improve f_0 detection in signals degraded with reverberation. The initialization of the network is based on a supervised procedure. We show the benefits for the detection of f_0 in various conditions of reverberation, with the network initialized.

1.1   Related Work

Previous references on robust fundamental frequency detection with signal processing-based techniques have analyzed directly the information of the signals [19, 35], especially periodicity. In recent references, deep learning algorithms have been used to noise or reverberation reduction and parameter detection, especially using features derived from the spectrum. [1,7,24,34].

Some applications of deep learning have outperformed classical enhancing algorithms on speech signals [6,15,21,25,26].

Unsupervised initialization and then fine-tuning processes with other networks, such as Restricted Boltzmann Machines (RBM), have been presented to increase the effectiveness of the neural networks [9]. It is commonly considered the breakthrough of effective training for deep neural networks the algorithms for training deep belief networks (DBN), based on a combination of unsupervised pre-training and supervised fine-tuning [11].

The benefits of unsupervised pre-training stages before the training algorithms have been also verified in fields other than speech processing, such as music classification [38]. Semi-supervised techniques have been also applied in similar applications [39] combining at least one stage of unlabeled data to initialize the weights of the neural networks. In recurrent neural networks, supervised initialization has been previously applied for spectral parameters on noisy and artificial speech [5,6].

In fundamental frequency detection, deep LSTM networks have recently outperformed several other algorithms [28,29]. We use these previous works as references, and provide our work with a better initialization state of the network for the task of enhancing reverberated speech. The training process of neural networks is traditionally based on random initialization of weights, and then the process of adjustment of those weights is based on the data presented to the network.

The idea that a trained artificial neural network can be used as a guide to the training of other models was proposed by [22,27], assuming that the first model can transfer valuable information to other networks. This advantage has been known as transfer knowledge [36].

In our approach, the initialization is supervised, with an Auto-associative network trained to map the identity function between its inputs and its outputs, using clear speech parameters in this stage. In f_0 detection, this Auto-associative network provides better results in reverberated speech, due to the approximated state provided in the initialization.

1.2 Problem Statement

In real world environments, where a speech signal $x(t)$ is produced and registered using microphones, there are several conditions that degrade $x(t)$ to a $y_R(t)$ finally recorded or processed. For example, in reverberation, a multi-path propagation of $x(t)$ to the microphone register is what produces the distortion. In this case [31]:

$$y_R(t) = \mathbf{h}_R^T(n) * \mathbf{x}(t) \tag{1}$$

where $\mathbf{h}_R''$ is the impulse response of the transmission channel between the source of the speech and the microphone.

The reverberation enhancement of the signal, consist on the approximation of $x(t)$ from $y_R(t)$.

For deep learning-based algorithms for speech enhancement, $x(t)$ can be estimated directly from data, employing algorithms that can learn a mapping function $f(\cdot)$ between noisy and reverberated variables:

$$\hat{x}(t) = f(y(t)), \tag{2}$$

where $\hat{x}(t)$ is calculated from $x(t)$ at the output of the neural network.

The amount of training data, the architecture of neural network and the algorithm selected, are factors that modify the precision of the approximation $f(\cdot)$.

During the training process, the set of weights θ_i of the network, needed to start the process, are regularly established as random numbers. The process began and run until the stop criteria is reached, where a set of updated weights θ_i are stored and employed with the test sets.

For our proposal, θ_i is generated from a supervised process, in which is presented to the neural network the parameters of clean speech at the input and the output. This way $f(\cdot)$ is close to the identity function.

We pretend to demonstrate that the nonrandom set of weights is a better way to start the training process, in contrast with the random θ_i initialization, mainly in terms of detecting voiced and unvoiced sounds. Voiced sounds have values of $f_0 > 0$, and are present on vowels and some consonants, while unvoiced sounds are present in silence and most consonants.

The rest of this paper is organized as follows: Sect. 2 brings some information of the LSTM neural networks. Section 3 details the proposed system. Section 4 shows the experimental setup implemented to test the proposal. Section 5 expose and discuss the results, and at last, conclusions are stated in Sect. 6.

2　Autoencoders of Long Short-Term Memory Neural Networks

Over the last few decades, several kinds of neural networks have been implemented in speech recognition and speech enhancement of degraded signals. More recently, researchers have experimented with deep learning algorithms, consisting on several layers of abstraction (typically neural networks with over two hidden layers) when dealing with the problem of enhancing noisy or reverberated speech and detection of f_0 under degraded conditions. RNN [14], has helped to model the dependent nature of speech parameters, due to feedback connections within the neurons, to themselves but also other neurons on the same layer. LSTM is an extended kind of RNN, that has been presented in [23], with the capacity to learn long term relationships in data and store information for long or short intervals.

Automatic speech recognition systems, speech synthesis, and handwriting generation are only a few of successful implementations of LSTM, where the information of past values are crucial to classify of performing regression [17,18].

The structure of LSTM is the following: a set of units inputs the sequences $\mathbf{y} = (y_1, y_2, \ldots, y_T)$, then hidden vector sequences $\mathbf{h} = (h_1, h_2, \ldots, h_T)$ are calculated through the set of weights between inputs and hidden units, of between hidden and hidden units of the next layer. This structure is similar to those of basic RNN.

Every unit of the network has a series of gates that allow the passing or the storage of information through an arbitrary number of time steps. This characteristic enables to model time-dependent sequences in a better way. Figure 1 illustrates the basic cell of an LSTM.

The RNNs have been reported with some difficulties during training, specially for the vanishing gradient and exploding gradient problems described in [4]. The LSTM networks seems to address this problem [32]. Detailed mathematical description of the LSTM networks can be found on [14,16,23]. In this work we have followed the implementation described in [8].

2.1　f_0 Estimation with Autoencoders

The f_0 recognition in deep learning is performed by picking pairs of inputs and outputs (contemplating spectral information as part of the information), and training the neural networks with them. Subsequently, the f_0 might be inferred from this information.

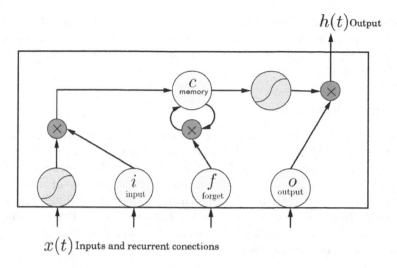

Fig. 1. Basic cell memory of a LSTM. $x(t)$ is the input and $h(t)$ the output of the unit. i, o, f represent the gates, and c the value of the memory.

The denoising autoencoder is part of the architectures of neural networks aimed to improve noisy or reverberant speech. The structure of an autoencoder is as follows: A first section is an encoder, which maps an input vector y into an internal representation h in the hidden layers. And a second section is the decoder, making a mapping from the hidden representation into a $\dot{x}$ vector.

The training process is performed presenting the corrupted reverberated features at the inputs of the decoders, while the equivalent clean attributes of the same dimensionality will be the outputs. The training algorithm adjusts the internal connections of the network to learn the complex relationships between input and output. After this process, an output with a better estimation of f_0 can be obtained.

3 Proposed System

To detect f_0 from reverberated speech, the mapping from corrupted f_0 can be learned directly from the data. For this purpose, we use sentences of reverberated utterances and the corresponding clean version to train the LSTM auto-encoder networks and divided the available set in training, validation, and test sets, as commonly defined in machine learning algorithms.

The weights of the recurrent LSTM networks are initialized in two ways:

- Randomly: All the weights have random numbers produced from a normal probability distribution (mean 0, standard deviation 1) at the first epoch of training.
- Initialized: An auto-associative network is a neural network whose input and target vectors are the same [2]. Here, the networks are trained a first time

presenting the same clean data at the input and at the output. After this first training, the weights of the Auto-associative networks became the initialized weights of the corresponding recurrent LSTM networks for the detection of the f_0 parameter.

3.1 Corpus Description

In our experiments, we use the Reverberant speech database [37]. The database was created at the University of Edinburg, and was designed to train and test speech dereverberation methods. Clean speech was made reverberant by convolving it with several room impulse responses. For the purpose of this work, we randomly chose five conditions from the whole data-set: ACE Building Lobby 1, ACE Lecture Room 1, ACE Lecture Room 2, ACE Meeting Room 1 and ACE Meeting Room 2. Those conditions contain utterances from the 28 speakers in the training set 1 of the database.

3.2 Feature Extraction

The audio files of the database were downsampled to 16 kHz, in order to extract the set of parameters from frames of speech using the Ahocoder system [12]. In this system, the fundamental frequency f_0^k (zero-valued if invoiced), 39 MFCC, plus an energy coefficient are extracted from each 10 ms frame. Details on the parameter extraction and waveform regeneration of the Ahocoder system can be found in [13].

3.3 Pre-trained Initialization

For each condition of reverberation, 400 utterances of clean speech (the approximate amount of files for each condition) were used in the initialization procedure. The 40-dimensional vectors (f_0 + 39MFCC) was presented at the input and output of the network simultaneously. The initial weights were established as random numbers. To update the weights, the back-propagation through time algorithm were applied. The stop criteria was twenty five epochs from the last best result, or a maximum of one thousand epochs.

4   Experimental Setup

The experimental setup followed in this work can be summarized in the following steps:

1. Feature extraction: A set of parameters was extracted from the reverberated and the corresponding clean audio files. Those from the reverberated files were used as inputs to the networks, while the corresponding clean features were the outputs.

2. Training and validation: During training, the weights of the networks were adjusted as the pairs of inputs and outputs were presented. A validation set of about 150 files for each case were also used.
3. Test: A subset of 50 randomly selected utterances (about 10% of the whole utterances of each condition) was chosen for the test set. These utterances were not part of the training process, to provide independence between the training and testing.

In order to determine the benefits of the proposal, the following objective measures were adopted [29], as previous references also applied:

- VDE (Voice Decision Error): This measure indicates the percentage of frames misclassified in terms of voicing (with $f_0 > 0$)/unvoicing (with $f_0 = 0$), according to the equation:

$$VDE = \frac{N_{V \to U} + N_{U \to V}}{N} \times 100\%, \qquad (3)$$

  where $N_{V \to U}$ and $N_{V \to U}$ represent classification errors of Voiced or Unvoiced frames into the other category.
- DR (Detection Rate): This objective measure is evaluated only on voiced frames. A correct value is considered correct if the deviation of the real clean value of f_0 is within 5%. This is performed following the equation:

$$DR = \frac{N_{0.05}}{N_p} \times 100\%, \qquad (4)$$

  where N represent number of frames, and p the total number of voiced frames of the clean speech.
- Sum of squared errors (sse): This is measure for the error in the validation and test sets during training of a neural network. It is defined as:

$$sse(\theta) = \sum_{n=1}^{T} (\mathbf{c_x} - \hat{\mathbf{c_x}})^2 \qquad (5)$$

$$= \sum_{n=1}^{T} (\mathbf{c_x} - f(\mathbf{c_x}))^2, \qquad (6)$$

where c_x is the known value of the outputs and $\hat{c}_x$ the its approximation from the network.

5 Results and Discussion

The following nomenclature is used to present the results:

1. Reverb: Refers to measures applied to the f_0 parameter detected directly from the reverberated speech.

2. LSTM: Refers to measures applied to f_0 detected with the recurrent LSTM networks initialized with random weights.
3. LSTM-AA: Represent the f_0 obtained from the networks initialized using the weights of the auto-associative network.

Table 1 shows the results of the VDE measure for the three systems (Reverb, LSTM and LSTM-AA), and the five cases contemplated from the dataset:

Table 1. Results for the VDE in the three systems. Lower values represent better results, and * is the best result.

Reverberating condition	None	Initialized	Random
ACE Building Lobby 1	15.59%	13.02% *	13.33%
ACE Lecture Room 1	16.00%	12.96%	12.69% *
ACE Lecture Room 2	19.11%	17.61% *	17.83%
ACE Meeting Room 1	17.76%	14.61% *	15.00%
ACE Meeting Room 2	21.83%	18.83% *	19.99%

Except for "ACE Lecture Room 1", the proposed initialization presents better values of VDE in all cases, compared to the random initialization. The exception can be explained in terms of the particular different parameters of the clean speech used at the initialization of the network, which differs greatly from those of the reverberated signal in each case and may affect differently the capacity of the network to enhance the result.

The exception of "ACE Lecture Room 1" can be considered a close value to the random initialization. The rest of results verified that the initialization allows the recurrent LSTM to provide better Voiced/Unvoiced decisions. This improvement in VDE could benefit automatic speech recognition systems and perceptual quality of the signals.

Table 2 shows the results of the VR measure, comparing only the results obtained with the recurrent LSTM in voiced frames. For these results, the initialization proposed presents better values on two of five cases. This few cases can be considered as a less satisfying result compared to the previous case. Nevertheless, it should be emphasized this measure is considering the precision of f_0 in voiced frames only. To have a meaningful improvement in this measurement, it is possible to foresee the application of new stages of enhancement applied exclusively to voiced frames.

One additional advantage of the initialized LSTM-AA is the lower sse error achieved. Table 3 shows the number of epochs required and the sse error for each of the five cases. It can be seen how the initialization achieved significant lower sse, and in one case even with fewer training epochs.

Figure 2 shows the evolution of sse in the validation set. It can be seen how a lower error is obtained with the proposed initialization in each epoch. The minimum value is achieved also in a less amount of epochs.

Table 2. Comparison of the results for the VR in the detection f_0. Higher values represent better results. * is the best result.

Reverberating condition	Random	Initialized
ACE Building Lobby 1	90.5%*	88.6%
ACE Lecture Room 1	77.5%	81.58% *
ACE Lecture Room 2	80.0% *	68.0%
ACE Meeting Room 1	83.5%	87.0% *
ACE Meeting Room 2	74.6% *	70.8%

Table 3. Comparison of the training epochs and sse error for the five cases of reverberated speech. * is the best result.

Reverberating condition	Initialized		Random	
	Epochs	sse	Epochs	sse
ACE Building Lobby 1	582	93.81*	526	127.42
ACE Lecture Room 1	736	101.76*	503	144.07
ACE Lecture Room 2	251	165.33*	160	201.13
ACE Meeting Room 1	374	167.87*	249	183.58
ACE Meeting Room 2	332	156.30*	355	193.95

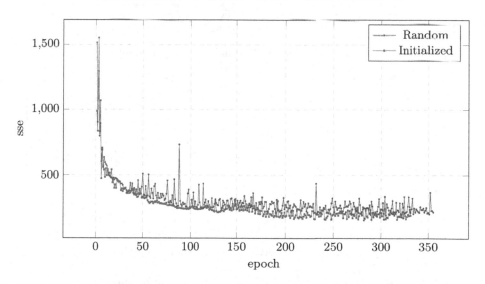

Fig. 2. Evolution of sse error for validation set of the ACE Meeting Room 2 case

Finally, in Fig. 3, three contours of f_0 are shown, for different conditions of reverberation. It can be seen how reverberated speech commonly presents some misclassification of voiced and unvoiced frames, especially with positive values of f_0. The initialized LSTM improve these errors in numerous cases.

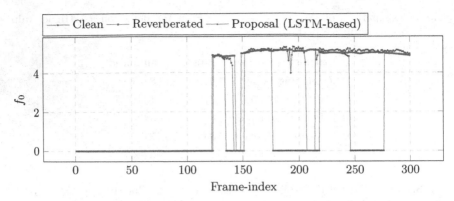

(a) f_0 contour of the ACE Lecture Room 1 condition

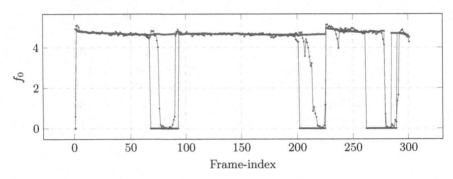

(b) f_0 contour of the ACE Building Lobby 1 condition

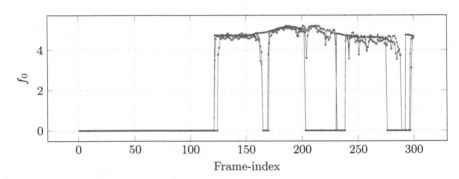

(c) f_0 contour of the ACE Meeting Room 2 condition

Fig. 3. Comparison of f_0 contour for several conditions

However, due to the nature of the neural networks, the values at the output cannot change the value instantly, as the natural speech signal does. As different phonemes occur in speech, the values of f_0 can go from 0 to a positive value immediately one frame after the other. Neural networks require some time steps to reach a stable value, and this is one reason the VR measure shown previously might be worse.

Further, from these results, we consider an improvement in fundamental frequency detection for the cases of reverberating speech, when the auto-associative initialization of the recurrent LSTM network is employed, especially with the VDE measure, and a more efficient way to train them.

6   Conclusions

In this paper, we implemented a new method of initialization LSTM neural networks, to improve the detection of the fundamental frequency in reverberated speech signals. The reverberation in speech considerably affects the detection of this parameter, as has been revealed with objective measures. As has been shown in previous references, recurrent LSTM networks, typically initialized with random numbers in their weights, can significantly enhance speech signals degraded with noise or reverberation.

The results of our supervised initialization presented in this work show even more significant improvements, given that pre-training the neural network affects the correct detection of frames with positive values of f_0, called voiced frames, or value frames with $f_0 = 0$, called unvoiced frames. The impact of this proposal has not yet been verified on the accuracy of the value of f_0 in the voiced frames, which represents a great opportunity to explore our method with more detail and with a wider variety of conditions. For example, new algorithms can be applied in subsequent stages of refinement.

The benefits of our results can represent improvements in voice recognition systems or analysis of speech signals registered in real-life environments, where reverberation is common.

For future work, we plan to verify the proposed initialization in the total set of conditions of reverberation presented in the database, and the refinement of the results with multiple stages.

Acknowledgments. This work was supported by the University of Costa Rica (UCR), Project No. 322-B9-105.

References

1. Abdel-Hamid, O., Mohamed, A.R., Jiang, H., Penn, G.: Applying convolutional neural networks concepts to hybrid NN-HMM model for speech recognition. In: 2012 IEEE International Conference on Acoustics, Speech and Signal Processing (ICASSP), pp. 4277–4280. IEEE (2012)
2. Baek, J., Cho, S.: Bankruptcy prediction for credit risk using an auto-associative neural network in Korean firms. In: 2003 Proceedings of the IEEE International Conference on Computational Intelligence for Financial Engineering, 2003. pp. 25–29. IEEE (2003)

3. Bagchi, D., Mandel, M.I., Wang, Z., He, Y., Plummer, A., Fosler-Lussier, E.: Combining spectral feature mapping and multi-channel model-based source separation for noise-robust automatic speech recognition. In: 2015 IEEE Workshop on Automatic Speech Recognition and Understanding (ASRU), pp. 496–503. IEEE (2015)
4. Bengio, Y., Frasconi, P., Simard, P.: The problem of learning long-term dependencies in recurrent networks. In: IEEE International Conference on Neural Networks, pp. 1183–1188. IEEE (1993)
5. Coto-Jiménez, M.: Pre-training long short-term memory neural networks for efficient regression in artificial speech postfiltering. In: 2018 IEEE International Work Conference on Bioinspired Intelligence (IWOBI), pp. 1–7. IEEE (2018)
6. Coto-Jiménez, M.: Improving post-filtering of artificial speech using pre-trained lstm neural networks. Biomimetics 4(2), 39 (2019)
7. Coto-Jiménez, M., Goddard-Close, J.: LSTM deep neural networks postfiltering for enhancing synthetic voices. Int. J. Pattern Recogn. Artif. Intell. **32**(01), 1860008 (2018)
8. Coto-Jiménez, M., Goddard-Close, J., Martínez-Licona, F.: Improving automatic speech recognition containing additive noise using deep denoising autoencoders of LSTM networks. In: Ronzhin, A., Potapova, R., Németh, G. (eds.) SPECOM 2016. LNCS (LNAI), vol. 9811, pp. 354–361. Springer, Cham (2016). https://doi.org/10.1007/978-3-319-43958-7_42
9. Dahl, G.E., Yu, D., Deng, L., Acero, A.: Context-dependent pre-trained deep neural networks for large-vocabulary speech recognition. IEEE Trans. Audio Speech Lang. Process. **20**(1), 30–42 (2011)
10. Du, J., Wang, Q., Gao, T., Xu, Y., Dai, L.R., Lee, C.H.: Robust speech recognition with speech enhanced deep neural networks. In: Fifteenth Annual Conference of the International Speech Communication Association (2014)
11. Erhan, D., Bengio, Y., Courville, A., Manzagol, P.A., Vincent, P., Bengio, S.: Why does unsupervised pre-training help deep learning? J. Mach. Learn. Res. **11**(Feb), 625–660 (2010)
12. Erro, D., Sainz, I., Navas, E., Hernáez, I.: Improved HNM-based vocoder for statistical synthesizers. In: Twelfth Annual Conference of the International Speech Communication Association (2011)
13. Erro, D., Sainz, I., Saratxaga, I., Navas, E., Hernáez, I.: MFCC+ F0 extraction and waveform reconstruction using HNM: preliminary results in an hmm-based synthesizer. In: Proceeding of the FALA, pp. 29–32 (2010)
14. Fan, Y., Qian, Y., Xie, F.L., Soong, F.K.: TTS synthesis with bidirectional LSTM based recurrent neural networks. In: Fifteenth Annual Conference of the International Speech Communication Association (2014)
15. Feng, X., Zhang, Y., Glass, J.: Speech feature denoising and dereverberation via deep autoencoders for noisy reverberant speech recognition. In: 2014 IEEE International Conference on Acoustics, Speech and Signal Processing (ICASSP), pp. 1759–1763. IEEE (2014)
16. Gers, F.A., Schraudolph, N.N., Schmidhuber, J.: Learning precise timing with LSTM recurrent networks. J. Mach. Learn. Res. **3**(Aug), 115–143 (2002)
17. Graves, A., Fernández, S., Schmidhuber, J.: Bidirectional LSTM networks for improved phoneme classification and recognition. In: Duch, W., Kacprzyk, J., Oja, E., Zadrożny, S. (eds.) ICANN 2005. LNCS, vol. 3697, pp. 799–804. Springer, Heidelberg (2005). https://doi.org/10.1007/11550907_126
18. Graves, A., Jaitly, N., Mohamed, A.R.: Hybrid speech recognition with deep bidirectional LSTM. In: 2013 IEEE Workshop on Automatic Speech Recognition and Understanding (ASRU), pp. 273–278. IEEE (2013)

19. Han, K., He, Y., Bagchi, D., Fosler-Lussier, E., Wang, D.: Deep neural network based spectral feature mapping for robust speech recognition. In: Sixteenth Annual Conference of the International Speech Communication Association (2015)

20. Hansen, J.H., Pellom, B.L.: An effective quality evaluation protocol for speech enhancement algorithms. In: Fifth International Conference on Spoken Language Processing (1998)

21. Hinton, G., et al.: Deep neural networks for acoustic modeling in speech recognition: the shared views of four research groups. IEEE Signal Process. Mag. **29**(6), 82–97 (2012)

22. Hinton, G., Vinyals, O., Dean, J.: Distilling the knowledge in a neural network. arXiv preprint arXiv:1503.02531 (2015)

23. Hochreiter, S., Schmidhuber, J.: Long short-term memory. Neural Comput. **9**(8), 1735–1780 (1997)

24. Huang, J., Kingsbury, B.: Audio-visual deep learning for noise robust speech recognition. In: 2013 IEEE International Conference on Acoustics, Speech and Signal Processing (ICASSP), pp. 7596–7599. IEEE (2013)

25. Ishii, T., Komiyama, H., Shinozaki, T., Horiuchi, Y., Kuroiwa, S.: Reverberant speech recognition based on denoising autoencoder. In: Interspeech, pp. 3512–3516 (2013)

26. Kumar, A., Florencio, D.: Speech enhancement in multiple-noise conditions using deep neural networks. arXiv preprint arXiv:1605.02427 (2016)

27. Li, J., Zhao, R., Huang, J.T., Gong, Y.: Learning small-size DNN with output-distribution-based criteria. In: Fifteenth Annual Conference of the International Speech Communication Association (2014)

28. Li, K., Mao, S., Li, X., Wu, Z., Meng, H.: Automatic lexical stress and pitch accent detection for L2 English speech using multi-distribution deep neural networks. Speech Commun. **96**, 28–36 (2018)

29. Liu, B., Tao, J., Zhang, D., Zheng, Y.: A novel pitch extraction based on jointly trained deep BLSTM recurrent neural networks with bottleneck features. In: 2017 IEEE International Conference on Acoustics, Speech and Signal Processing (ICASSP), pp. 336–340. IEEE (2017)

30. Narayanan, A., Wang, D.: Ideal ratio mask estimation using deep neural networks for robust speech recognition. In: 2013 IEEE International Conference on Acoustics, Speech and Signal Processing (ICASSP), pp. 7092–7096. IEEE (2013)

31. Naylor, P.A., Gaubitch, N.D.: Speech Dereverberation. Springer, London (2010). https://doi.org/10.1007/978-1-84996-056-4

32. Pascanu, R., Mikolov, T., Bengio, Y.: On the difficulty of training recurrent neural networks. In: International Conference on Machine Learning, pp. 1310–1318 (2013)

33. Ribas, D., Llombart, J., Miguel, A., Vicente, L.: Deep speech enhancement for reverberated and noisy signals using wide residual networks. arXiv preprint arXiv:1901.00660 (2019)

34. Seltzer, M.L., Yu, D., Wang, Y.: An investigation of deep neural networks for noise robust speech recognition. In: 2013 IEEE International Conference on Acoustics, Speech and Signal Processing (ICASSP), pp. 7398–7402. IEEE (2013)

35. Stahl, J., Mowlaee, P.: A pitch-synchronous simultaneous detection-estimation framework for speech enhancement. IEEE/ACM Trans. Audio Speech Langu. Process. (TASLP) **26**(2), 436–450 (2018)

36. Tang, Z., Wang, D., Zhang, Z.: Recurrent neural network training with dark knowledge transfer. In: 2016 IEEE International Conference on Acoustics, Speech and Signal Processing (ICASSP), pp. 5900–5904. IEEE (2016)

37. Valentini-Botinhao, C.: Noisy reverberant speech database for training speech enhancement algorithms and TTS models, 2016 [dataset] (2017). https://doi.org/10.7488/ds/2139

38. Van Den Oord, A., Dieleman, S., Schrauwen, B.: Transfer learning by supervised pre-training for audio-based music classification. In: Conference of the International Society for Music Information Retrieval (ISMIR 2014) (2014)

39. Veselý, K., Hannemann, M., Burget, L.: Semi-supervised training of deep neural networks. In: 2013 IEEE Workshop on Automatic Speech Recognition and Understanding, pp. 267–272. IEEE (2013)

40. Weninger, F., Geiger, J., Wöllmer, M., Schuller, B., Rigoll, G.: Feature enhancement by deep LSTM networks for ASR in reverberant multisource environments. Comput. Speech Lang. **28**(4), 888–902 (2014)

41. Weninger, F., Watanabe, S., Tachioka, Y., Schuller, B.: Deep recurrent de-noising auto-encoder and blind de-reverberation for reverberated speech recognition. In: 2014 IEEE International Conference on Acoustics, Speech and Signal Processing (ICASSP), pp. 4623–4627. IEEE (2014)

42. Wu, K., Zhang, D., Lu, G.: iPEEH: Improving pitch estimation by enhancing harmonics. Expert Syst. Appl. **64**, 317–329 (2016)

Measuring the Effect of Reverberation on Statistical Parametric Speech Synthesis

Marvin Coto-Jiménez$^{(\boxtimes)}$ iD

PRIS-Lab, Escuela de Ingeniería Eléctrica, Universidad de Costa Rica,
San Pedro, Costa Rica
marvin.coto@ucr.ac.cr

Abstract. Text-to-speech (TTS) synthesis is the technique of generating intelligible speech from a given text. The most recent techniques for TTS are based on machine learning, implementing systems which learn linguistic specifications and their corresponding parameters of the speech signal. Given the growing interest in implementing verbal communication systems in different devices, such as cell phones, car navigation system and personal assistants, it is important to use speech data from many sources. The speech recordings available for this purpose are not always generated with the best quality. For example, if an artificial voice is created from historical recordings, or a voice created from a person whom only a small set of recordings exists. In these cases, there is an additional challenge due to the adverse conditions in the data. Reverberation is one of the conditions that can be found in these cases, a product of the different trajectories that a speech signal can take in an environment before registering through a microphone. In the present work, we quantitatively explore the effect of different levels of reverberation on the quality of artificial voice generated with those references. The results show that the quality of the generated artificial speech is affected considerably with any level of reverberation. Thus, the application of algorithms for speech enhancement must be taken always into consideration before and after any process of TTS.

Keywords: Hidden Markov Models · PESQ · Reverberation · Speech synthesis

1 Introduction

Text-to-speech (TTS) synthesis is the technique created for the generation of artificial, intelligible speech from any given text [15], usually from computers or high technology devices. There are many implementations of TTS in commercial applications and many potential areas where it can be applied. For example,

Supported by the University of Costa Rica.

J. L. Crespo-Mariño and E. Meneses-Rojas (Eds.): CARLA 2019, CCIS 1087, pp. 369–382, 2020.
https://doi.org/10.1007/978-3-030-41005-6_25

any circumstance that requires the transfer of information between people and machines is a potential application. One of the main advantages of applying TTS for this purpose is the fact that speech is the most widely used communication method between humans. Additionally, verbal communication is natural and requires no special training [4].

TTS systems are divided into two main components [7]: A "front end", where the text is processed to produce a linguistic specification, so the units of speech (such as phonemes or syllables) can be described in terms of their surrounding components, and a "back end", that take the linguistic specification as input and generates a waveform.

The development of TTS has evolved from the creation of isolated words or phrases to general purpose voices in different languages, with different styles and emotions [1,3]. There is a significant effort in research to obtain improvements in the multiple challenges that TTS systems have today, as its extensive use in applications depends on obtaining more natural and close-to-human voices.

The most recent techniques to generate TTS have emerged from the idea of machine learning algorithms applied to store and reproduce parameters of the speech [19–21]. The first model that successfully applied those techniques was the Hidden Markov Models (HMM), learning parameters such as fundamental frequency (f_0) and Mel-Frequency Cepstral Coefficients (MFCC). This set of parameters and models were known as Statistical Parametric Speech Synthesis. More recently, Deep Learning-based algorithms have been applied to voice generation from text [9,12], or as post-filter to the results obtained with HMM [2,11].

Previous references have reported a significant quality drop in artificial speech when the training parameters of the speech data are noisy. This condition requires the compensation of the voice signals with several techniques [6,17,18]. For example, speech enhancement algorithms can be used to clean the available noisy data.

This problem has been addressed in several references, but only some of them have objectively measured the impact of specific conditions, particularly noise [10]. The interest in predicting the effects of different degrees of reverberation in the results of statistical parametric speech synthesis relies on the prior evaluation of usability for future experiences with speech synthesis.

For this purpose, in this work we want to address the impact of reverberation on objective quality measures in speech synthesis, in comparison to those produced with clean speech.

To answer this question, we made several experiments with different conditions of reverberation, and measure the impact between clean and reverberated speech, and between the artificial speech generated with both.

The rest of this paper is organized as follows: Sect. 2 gives the background and context of the problem. Section 3 describes the experimental setup, Sect. 4 presents the results with a discussion, and finally, in Sect. 5, we present the conclusions.

2 Background

2.1 Hidden Markov Models

Hidden Markov Models (HMM) can be described from a Markov process, in which state transitions are given by probability. There is a second process described with probability, which models the emission of symbols when it comes to each state, according to probabilistic rules. There are several kinds of HMM, applied to model many important areas.

In Fig. 1, a representation of a particular HMM, known as a left-to-right, is shown. This is the most common type of HMM applied in speech technologies. Here, the first state is at the left, from which transitions can occur. These transitions lead to the same state or to the next on the right, according to some probability p_{ij}. Transitions cannot occur in the reverse direction.

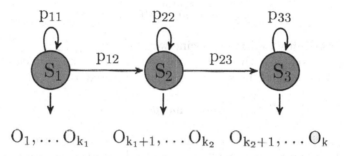

Fig. 1. Left to right example of an HMM with three states. O_k represents the observation emitted in state k.

An HMM can mathematically be described by a tuple:

$$\lambda = (S, \pi_i, a, b) \tag{1}$$

where S is the set of states, π a probability vector that establishes the probability of i to be the initial state. a is the transition probability matrix between states, and b the probabilistic rule of observations of specific symbols in each state.

2.2 Statistical Parametric Speech Synthesis

Statistical parametric speech synthesis based on HMM follows a procedure with a training part and a synthesis part. The training part requires recordings of speech and their corresponding text transcriptions. This data is presented to a set of HMM (or other machine learning algorithms) that learns the parameters corresponding to a certain sound of the speech.

In the synthesis part, any text can be applied to the models, which output the corresponding parameters to the specific sounds of the utterance, and then a filter produces the waveform. This scheme has been applied since the creation of the HMM-Based Speech Synthesis (HTS) System [16,24] for several languages, and allows specific definition for phonetic units, customizing training parameters according to needs and the amount of available data.

For applications of speech recognition and synthesis, the probabilistic rule at the output of each state of a HMM, named b in Eq. 1 is assumed as a multivariate Gaussian distribution defined as:

$$b_i(o_t) = \frac{1}{\sqrt{(2\pi)^d |\Sigma_i|}} \exp\left\{ \frac{-1}{2}(o_t - \mu_i)^\top \Sigma_i^{-1}(o_t) - \mu_i \right\} \tag{2}$$

where μ_i and Σ_i are mean vector and covariance matrix, respectively. d is the dimension of vector of acoustic parameters, and $o_t t$ is an observation vector of parameters at frame t.

The training process of a HMMs for a speech synthesis application can be described as finding the best parameters of λ given observed parameters of the speech (O). This process can be written as:

$$\lambda_{max} = \arg\max_\lambda p(O|\lambda, W), \tag{3}$$

where p is probability and W a specific word or sound.

In the synthesis part, the problem of getting the best parameters related to a given W which need to be synthesized can be stated as:

$$o_{max} = \arg\max_o p(o|\lambda_{max}, w) \tag{4}$$

In the following sections, we describe the application of these models to produce artificial speech and study the influence of reverberating conditions in training.

3 Experiments

In order to test the effects of reverberated speech to Statistical Parametric Speech Synthesis based on HMM, the experimental setup can be summarized in the following steps:

3.1 Database

For the experimentation, we used the SLT voice of the CMU Arctic databases, developed at the Language Technologies Institute at Carnegie Mellon University [8]. This database was specifically designed for research in speech synthesis. It consists of a number 1150 utterances selected from out-of-copyright texts from Project Gutenberg.

For degrade this data with reverberation, we use five impulse responses from the MARDY database [22] and the Center for Digital Music (C4DM) at Queen Mary, University of London [14].

The following nomenclature will be used for each condition:

– MARDY, from the corresponding database.
– GH (Great Hall), from the C4DM database.

- OC (Octagon), from the C4DM database.
- CR1 y CR2 (Classroom 1 y 2), from the C4DM database.

The speech files of the CMU database were convolved with the impulse responses of each condition. The output is the speech signal with the reverberation of the space where the impulse response was recorded.

3.2 Synthesis of Reverberated Speech

With the clean version of the SLT/CMU voice, an artificial voice where build using the HTS system [23]. To compare the influence of the different reverberating cases, the HMM-based synthetic voices were produced with each of the five conditions after the convolution: MARDY, GH, OC, CR1, CR2.

A set of comparisons between clear speech, artificial speech produced with the clear speech, artificial speech produced with reverberated speech and the reverberated speech were performed. This comparison was made to measure the effect of reverberation before and after the process to produce artificial speech.

Figure 2 illustrates the general procedure for each of the conditions of reverberation.

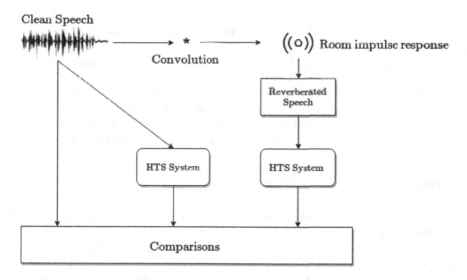

Fig. 2. Procedure to obtain and compare reverberated and artificial speech.

3.3 Evaluation

To evaluate the results given from our experiments, we use the PESQ (Perceptual Evaluation of Speech Quality), defined in the ITU-T recommendation

P.862.ITU. Results are given in interval $[0.5, 4.5]$, where 4.5 corresponds to a perfect reconstruction of the signal. PESQ is computed as [13]:

$$\text{PESQ} = a_0 + a_1 D_{ind} + a_2 A_{ind} \tag{5}$$

where the D_{ind} is the average disturbance and A_{ind} the asymmetrical disturbance. The a_k are chosen to optimize PESQ in measuring speech distortion, noise distortion, and overall quality.

We also use the MOS-LQO (Mean Opinion Score - Listening Quality Objective) measure, performing a mapping function from the PESQ, by the relation

$$\text{MOS-LQO} = 0.9999 + \frac{4.999 - 0.999}{1 + e^{-1.4945 \cdot \text{PESQ} + 4.6607}}, \tag{6}$$

according to the ITU-T P.862.1 [5].

We are interested in measuring the effects of reverberation in the speech signals before and after the process of generating artificial speech with the HTS System. To perform these measures, we applied the following comparisons between groups of utterances:

- Natural speech and HTS voice produced with natural speech.
- Natural speech and reverberated speech.
- Natural speech and HTS voice produced with reverberated speech.
- HTS voice produced with natural speech and HTS voice produced with reverberated speech.
- Reverberated speech and HTS voice produced with reverberated speech.

Besides those five comparisons, there are other possible combinations that do not give information about the effects on artificial voice generation. For each of the five cases of reverberation, we compare the PESQ measure. Additionally, we report spectrograms and pitch contours for direct visualization of the results.

4   Results and Discussion

In this section, we show the influence of the different reverberations on clean and artificial speech. The reverberation in speech signals greatly affects the estimation of the pitch, which is one of the most important parameters for speech recognition and generation.

For example, in Fig. 3 it is noticeable how the reverberation produces more voiced frames (those with positive values for pitch) in the MARDY condition. The GH, with a bigger degree of reverberation, almost produces only voiced frames, introducing great distortion and affecting the quality of the speech.

The spectrograms also show different levels of distortion when compared to the Clean voice and the correspondent artificial voice 4. For example, Fig. 5 show some recognizable characteristics of the spectrum in the MARDY condition, which seems to produce some light distortions in the artificial voice constructed from this data.

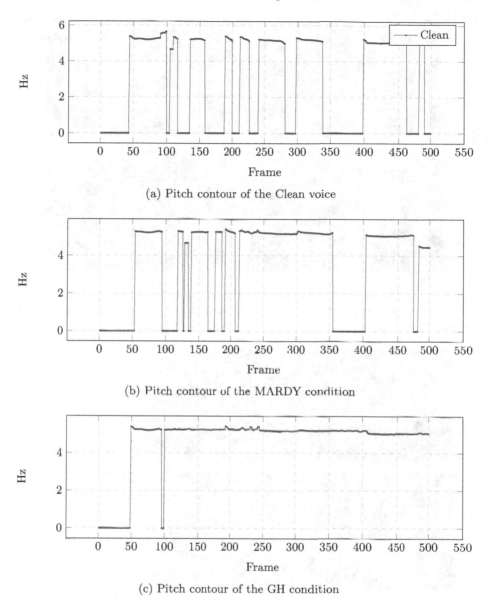

(a) Pitch contour of the Clean voice

(b) Pitch contour of the MARDY condition

(c) Pitch contour of the GH condition

Fig. 3. Comparison of pitch contours for clean voice and two reverberating conditions in the utterance: "Author of the danger trail, Philip Steels, etc."

On the other hand, Fig. 6 shows evident degradation of the signal with the OC condition and almost unrecognizable spectrum in the artificial speech. From this spectrograms, it is remarkable how different levels of reverberation can affect the quality of artificial speech.

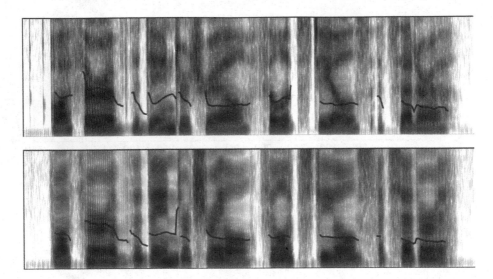

Fig. 4. Spectrograms of the utterance "Not at this particular case, Tom, apologized Wittmore", with the Clean Voice (at the top) and artificial voice (at the bottom). Pitch contour is also highlighted.

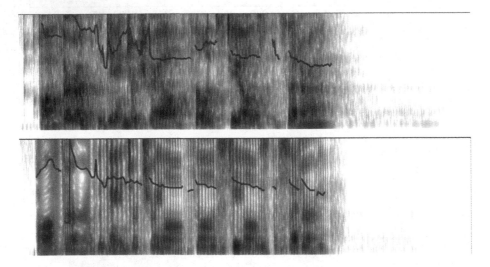

Fig. 5. Spectrograms of the utterance "Not at this particular case, Tom, apologized Wittmore", with reverberated voice with MARDY condition (at the top) and artificial voice produced with this reverberation (at the bottom). Pitch contour is also highlighted.

The results and comparisons for the PESQ measure are presented in form or radar plots. The radar plots allow the comparison between all the measures indicated in Sect. 3.3. The more contracted the radar plot, the lower perceptual quality in the reverberated and artificial voice. All the plots have the same scale.

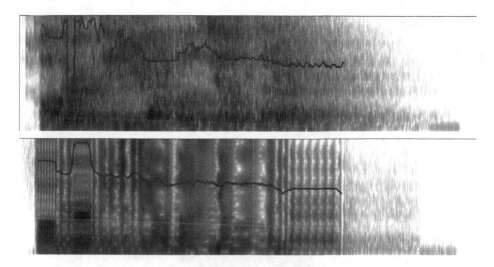

Fig. 6. Spectrograms of the utterance "Not at this particular case, Tom, apologized Wittmore", with reverberated voice with OC condition (at the top) and artificial voice produced with this reverberation (at the bottom). Pitch contour is also highlighted.

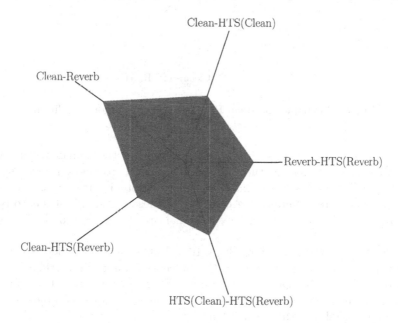

Fig. 7. Radar plot of Mean PSQ Values for MARDY Condition

Figure 7 shows the radar plot for the MARDY reverberation condition. As shown previously, this is the case where the reverberation produces lower distortion on the signal. When compared to the rest of the radar plots, this is the less contracted plot.

The radar plot for the Octagon condition (Fig. 8) shows a smaller value of PESQ for the reverberated voice. This lower quality also influences the lower perceptual quality for synthetic speech in relation to natural and artificial speech produced without reverberation.

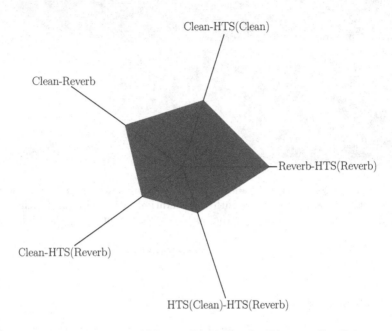

Fig. 8. Radar plot of Mean PSQ Values for Octagon Condition

The GH reverberation produces a degradation of the signal which heavily affects all the process, from the reverberated speech to the synthetic speech. As shown in Fig. 9, this is the most contracted plot in terms of all categories of speech without reverberation. According to these plots, this seems to be the condition that affects more the speech signal and the correspondent artificial voice.

Finally, the two CR conditions (Figs. 10 and 11) show similar degrees of reverberation and similar degradation on the perceptual quality of artificial speech. In comparison with GH, OC presents lower PESQ when compared the reverberated signal with the clean speech, and a better measure in the comparison of the reverberated signal and the artificial speech.

The results of the MOS-LQ measure, obtained from Eq. 6 are presented in Table 1. The greater effect on this measure before the generation of synthetic speech tend to produce bigger negative effects on the results. But the relationship does not seem to be linear.

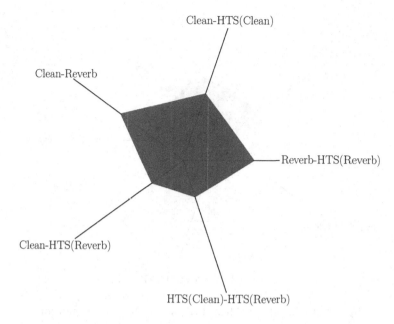

Fig. 9. Radar plot of Mean PSQ Values for GH Condition

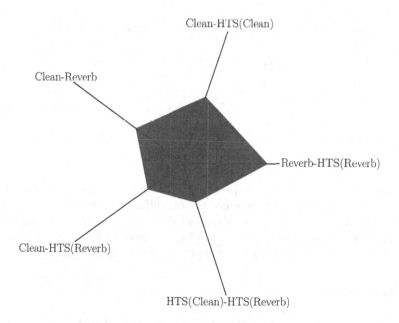

Fig. 10. Radar plot of Mean PSQ Values for CR1 Condition

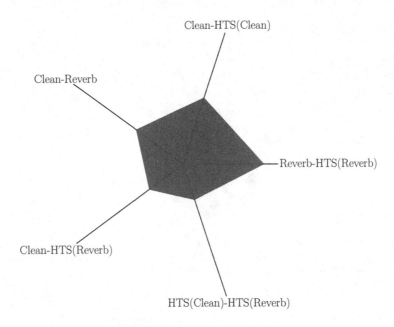

Fig. 11. Radar plot of Mean PSQ Values for CR2 Condition

Table 1. MOS-LQ values from the different cases of reverberation. The results are ordered from worst to best level of reverberation. Clean voice does not have MOS-LQ for being the reference.

Reverberation	MOS-LQ reverberated speech	MOS-LQ HTS
Clean	-	1.30
CR1	1.18	1.15
CR1	1.18	1.12
OC	1.26	1.13
GH	1.30	1.11
MARDY	1.56	1.16

All cases of reverberation produce artificial voice with lower MOS-LQ value than those produced with clean speech. But, different degrees of reverberation produces similar degradation, according to this measure. Being the reverberation a non-additive process, the results show also a complex relationship between the source speech and the result of the statistical parametric speech.

5   Conclusions

In this paper, it was explored the effects of reverberated speech on the creation of artificial voices obtained with statistical parametric techniques, based on Hidden Markov Models. The importance of this research relies on the application of objective measure to the quality of speech before and after the process of generating artificial voices.

For comparison purposes, we proposed the application of radar plots for the multiple visualizations of PESQ measures on all the relevant combinations of clean/artificial speech. These plots show how different levels of reverberation affects the signal before and after the generation of voices with the HTS system.

The results show that reverberation in all analyzed degree is an undesirable condition for the generation of artificial voices with statistical parametric techniques. Particularly for the effects on pitch detection.

This knowledge allows the discrimination of future sources of speech for generating synthetic voices. Having all degrees of reverberation significant negative effects on the quality of synthetic speech, it is critical for the speech synthesis the use of de-reverberation or enhancement procedures before the application of machine learning models.

For future work, new quality measures and more conditions of reverberation can be included. Additionally, statistical validation of results and extended graphical evidence of the degraded signals of natural and artificial speech.

Acknowledgements. This work was supported by the University of Costa Rica (UCR), Project No. 322-B9-105.

References

1. Black, A.W.: Unit selection and emotional speech. In: Eighth European Conference on Speech Communication and Technology (2003)
2. Coto-Jiménez, M.: Improving post-filtering of artificial speech using pre-trained LSTM neural networks. Biomimetics **4**(2), 39 (2019)
3. Coto-Jiménez, M., Goddard-Close, J.: LSTM deep neural networks postfiltering for enhancing synthetic voices. Int. J. Pattern Recognit Artif Intell. **32**(01), 1860008 (2018)
4. Holmes, W.: Speech Synthesis and Recognition. CRC Press, Boca Raton (2001)
5. ITU-T, R.P.: 862.1: Mapping function for transforming P. 862 raw result scores to MOS-LQO. International Telecommunication Union, Geneva, Switzerland, November 2003 (2003)
6. Karhila, R., Remes, U., Kurimo, M.: Noise in HMM-based speech synthesis adaptation: analysis, evaluation methods and experiments. IEEE J. Sel. Top. Signal Process. **8**(2), 285–295 (2013)
7. King, S.: Measuring a decade of progress in text-to-speech. Loquens **1**(1), e006 (2014)
8. Kominek, J., Black, A.W.: The CMU arctic speech databases. In: Fifth ISCA Workshop on Speech Synthesis (2004)
9. Lee, J., Song, K., Noh, K., Park, T.J., Chang, J.H.: DNN based multi-speaker speech synthesis with temporal auxiliary speaker id embedding. In: 2019 International Conference on Electronics, Information, and Communication (ICEIC), pp. 1–4. IEEE (2019)
10. Moreno Pimentel, J., et al.: Effects of noise on a speaker-adaptive statistical speech synthesis system (2014)

11. Öztürk, M.G., Ulusoy, O., Demiroglu, C.: DNN-based speaker-adaptive postfiltering with limited adaptation data for statistical speech synthesis systems. In: ICASSP 2019–2019 IEEE International Conference on Acoustics, Speech and Signal Processing (ICASSP), pp. 7030–7034. IEEE (2019)
12. Prenger, R., Valle, R., Catanzaro, B.: WaveGlow: a flow-based generative network for speech synthesis. In: ICASSP 2019–2019 IEEE International Conference on Acoustics, Speech and Signal Processing (ICASSP), pp. 3617–3621. IEEE (2019)
13. Rix, A.W., Hollier, M.P., Hekstra, A.P., Beerends, J.G.: Perceptual evaluation of speech quality (PESQ) the new itu standard for end-to-end speech quality assessment Part I-time-delay compensation. J. Audio Eng. Soc. **50**(10), 755–764 (2002)
14. Stewart, R., Sandler, M.: Database of omnidirectional and B-format room impulse responses. In: 2010 IEEE International Conference on Acoustics, Speech and Signal Processing, pp. 165–168. IEEE (2010)
15. Tokuda, K., Nankaku, Y., .Toda, T., Zen, H., Yamagishi, J., Oura, K.: Speech synthesis based on hidden Markov models. Proc. IEEE **101**(5), 1234–1252 (2013)
16. Tokuda, K., Zen, H., Black, A.W.: An HMM-based speech synthesis system applied to English. In: IEEE Speech Synthesis Workshop, pp. 227–230 (2002)
17. Valentini-Botinhao, C., Wang, X., Takaki, S., Yamagishi, J.: Speech enhancement for a noise-robust text-to-speech synthesis system using deep recurrent neural networks. In: Interspeech, pp. 352–356 (2016)
18. Valentini-Botinhao, C., Yamagishi, J.: Speech enhancement of noisy and reverberant speech for text-to-speech. IEEE/ACM Trans. Audio Speech Lang. Process. **26**(8), 1420–1433 (2018)
19. Valin, J.M., Skoglund, J.: LPCNet: improving neural speech synthesis through linear prediction. In: ICASSP 2019–2019 IEEE International Conference on Acoustics, Speech and Signal Processing (ICASSP), pp. 5891–5895. IEEE (2019)
20. Wang, X., Lorenzo-Trueba, J., Takaki, S., Juvela, L., Yamagishi, J.: A comparison of recent waveform generation and acoustic modeling methods for neural-network-based speech synthesis. In: 2018 IEEE International Conference on Acoustics, Speech and Signal Processing (ICASSP), pp. 4804–4808. IEEE (2018)
21. Wang, X., Takaki, S., Yamagishi, J.: Investigating very deep highway networks for parametric speech synthesis. Speech Commun. **96**, 1–9 (2018)
22. Wen, J.Y., Gaubitch, N.D., Habets, E.A., Myatt, T., Naylor, P.A.: Evaluation of speech dereverberation algorithms using the MARDY database. In: Proceedings of the International Workshop Acoustic Echo Noise Control (IWAENC). Citeseer (2006)
23. Zen, H., et al.: The HMM-based speech synthesis system (HTS) version 2.0. In: SSW, pp. 294–299. Citeseer (2007)
24. Zen, H., et al.: Recent development of the HMM-based speech synthesis system (HTS) (2009)

Enhancing Speech Recorded from a Wearable Sensor Using a Collection of Autoencoders

Astryd González-Salazar(ID), Michelle Gutiérrez-Muñoz(ID),
and Marvin Coto-Jiménez(✉)(ID)

PRIS-Lab, Escuela de Ingeniería Eléctrica, Universidad de Costa Rica,
San Pedro, Costa Rica
{astryd.gonzalez,michelle.gutierrezmunoz,marvin.coto}@ucr.ac.cr

Abstract. Assistive Technology (AT) is a concept which includes the use of technological devices to improve the learning process or the general capabilities of people with disabilities. One of the major tasks of the AT is the development of devices that offer alternative or augmentative communication capabilities.

In this work, we implemented a simple AT device with a low-cost sensor for registering speech signals, in which the sound is perceived as low quality and corrupted. Thus, it is not suitable to integrate into speech recognition systems, automatic transcription or general recognition of vocal-tract sounds for people with disabilities.

We propose the use of a group of artificial neural networks that improve different aspects of the signal. In the study of the speech enhancement, it is normal to focus on how to make improvements in specific conditions of the signal, such as background noise, reverberation, natural noises, among others. In this case, the conditions that degrade the sound are unknown. This uncertainty represents a bigger challenge for the enhancement of the speech, in a real-life application.

The results show the capacity of the artificial neural networks to enhance the quality of the sound, under several objective evaluation measurements. Therefore, this proposal can become a way of treating these kinds of signals to improve robust speech recognition systems and increase the real possibilities for implementing low-cost AT devices.

Keywords: Artificial neural networks · Assistive Technology · LSTM · Speech enhancement

1 Introduction

Assistive Technology (AT) devices are important for many applications, as they represent potential aids for people with physical and sensory disabilities which might lead to improvements in the quality of life [34]. The wearable devices

Supported by the University of Costa Rica.

© Springer Nature Switzerland AG 2020
J. L. Crespo-Mariño and E. Meneses-Rojas (Eds.): CARLA 2019, CCIS 1087, pp. 383–397, 2020.
https://doi.org/10.1007/978-3-030-41005-6_26

provides hands-free interaction, and are among the most valuable in the research of AT, for purposes such as augmentative or alternative communication. The development of these devices has been considered a rapidly evolving field, and is expected to grow even more in the next ten years [27].

The speech signals used in AT, general-purpose communication devices or any speech technologies are affected by distortions and became degraded in several ways. For example additive noises, reverberations or others, produced by the environment, or by the transmission, coding or reconstruction of the speech signal. Applications that use these signals may be affected in their performance because of these signal degradation.

In the past few decades, speech enhancement algorithms with many approaches have been presented to suppress or reduce such distortions and preserve or enhance the perceived signal quality. Several recent algorithms for enhancing speech signals are based on deep neural networks (DNN) [8,17]. The most common approach is learning mapping functions from degraded speech into the features of the corresponding clean speech, using autoencoders or similar architectures of networks [6,7].

Among the new types of artificial neural networks, the Recurrent Neural Networks (RNN), and specially the Long Short-Term Memory Network (LSTM) has succeeded in mapping features derived from the spectrum, usually Mel-Frequency Cepstrum Coefficients (MFCC) and also fundamental frequency (f_0) [3]. The LSTM networks have overcome classical algorithms for enhancing based on digital signal processing. These spectral and f_0 features have been used widely in speech-related tasks since the beginning of developing automatic speech recognition systems.

In this work, we apply and extend previous experiences of speech enhancement with LSTM networks for these parameters in real-world conditions of an AT device, and applying several networks simultaneously. Benefits from this proposal can be applied to realistic tasks of registering, recognizing and enhance voice or any vocal-tract sounds produced in AT devices [18].

1.1   Related Work

Wearable assistive devices have been developed as task-specific solutions for the blind, and hearing impaired, among other conditions, for activities such as reading and travel [34]. Existing devices are very diverse, depending on the necessity, the technology used and the location of the device on the body.

For example, in [37] a system for wearable audio navigation (called SWAN) has been developed to serve as a navigation and orientation aid for persons visually impaired. In this case, the device is audio-only output and tactile input via a handheld interface. The automatic speech recognition for the input of this device has not been implemented in the reference. Moreover, other devices with tactile inputs have been also presented in [22,28], which are specifically designed for visually impaired individuals.

Necklace-like devices, with sensors that use piezoelectric technology, have been used to nutrition intake studies [1,2], analyzing features such as the spectrum of the output of the sensor. Also, with a sonar function for assisting people with visually impaired [35].

According to [23] a necklace is among the favorite placement of sensors for elderly people and health professionals for this population (just behind watch and bracelet). It is also the preferred option for relatives of the users. For speech recognition and related technologies applied in AT devices, a necklace is a natural option for its simplicity and little notoriety.

One of the main problems with the simplest sensors available for necklace and registering speech signals is the low quality at the output of the sensor. For the wearable use of personal assistants or augmentative communication systems with a classification of audible vocalizations, is essential to provide a signal with a high quality of sound. Several attempts in specific conditions for enhancing signals from piezoelectric sensors have been conducted [26,38].

For the general case of enhancing speech signals, a great amount of research has been conducted over several decades, more recently based on Deep Learning. Typically, these techniques rely on the enhancement of spectral features of the speech, such as MFCC [31].

The deep learning approaches, especially those based on DNN have succeeded in outperforming the classical signal processing-based methods when the speech signals contain known noise of different types [5–7,19,36], or reverberant speech [11,21,24,30].

The principal method for enhancing the signals using deep learning is to apply the networks as regression models, mapping the corrupted parameters of the speech into the corresponding of the clean speech.

One of the recent DNN models has included Recurrent Neural Networks and specifically the LSTM units. Although the LSTM networks outperform other deep networks in this task of speech enhancement [4,5], the training process for its successful implementation requires single specific noise conditions and prior knowledge of the SNR during the test procedure.

In the present paper, we consider the more realistic and challenging scenarios of speech being registered with a piezoelectric sensor in a wearable necklace device designed for AT. None of the previous references address this issue with DNN. This study under uncertain corrupted signals is of importance for future implementation of AT devices.

The rest of this paper is organized: Sect. 2 provides the background and context of the problem of denoising speech signals registered using piezoelectric sensors and the LSTM, Sect. 3 describes the experimental setup, Sect. 4 presents the results with a discussion. Finally, in Sect. 5, we present the conclusions.

2   Background

2.1   Piezoelectric Sensors

A piezoelectric sensor, also known as a vibration sensor, produces an electrical potential when subjected to physical strain [1], for example, pressure or acceleration. It has been used in many devices and applications. For the purpose of this paper, it was used to register speech signals, which was possible by placing the sensor against the throat. This way, the muscle contractions while speaking is represented in the output voltage of the sensor.

The simplicity and availability of piezoelectric sensors make their use in wearable devices ideal. The vibration produced in the throat when speaking can also capture the signal with little influence of surrounding sounds, which constitute an undesirable effect on the applications for the sensor. Further details of these sensors and related explanations of its physical behavior can be found in [12,32,33].

2.2   Problem Statement

In the field of enhancing speech signals, it can be assumed that a signal with background noise $y_R(t)$ (such as environmental noise or artificial noise caused by the transmission or register of the signal), can be modeled as the sum of the speech signal $x(t)$, and a noise d, given by:

$$y(t) = x(t) + d(t). \tag{1}$$

In the spectral domain, the formulation of the modeling of noisy signals becomes:

$$Y_k(n) = X_k(n) + D_k(n), \tag{2}$$

where k is the frequency index and n the time-segment index.

In the case of reverberated speech, it can be assumed that the signal with reverberation y_R, is a degraded version of x, as a result of the multiple directions from which the microphone receives the signal after the reflections produced by the propagation of the sound in a particular environment. The relation between them can be expressed as [29]

$$x(n) = \mathbf{h}^T(n)\mathbf{s}(n), \tag{3}$$

where $\mathbf{h} = [h_1, h_2, \ldots, h_L]^T$ is the impulse response of the acoustic channel from the source to microphone. The effects of the reverberation usually increase as the distance from the speaker to the microphone increases.

The effect of the reverberation combined with background noise can be modeled as

$$y(n) = \mathbf{h}^T(n)\mathbf{x}(n) + d(n). \tag{4}$$

However, when the speech signal is degraded in an unknown way, it can not be assumed the model of additive or convolutive degradation. In this case, it must be assumed that $y(t)$ is related to $x(t)$ through a function f, which can have elements of noise or reverberation, but also other specific perturbations in particular segments of the spectrum.

Signal improvement methods based on Deep Learning have made estimations of f for conditions of noise and reverberation without assuming a priori the characteristic of the distortion. This is why these methods constitute a viable option to improve the degraded signal from the piezoelectric sensor y_p.

Having parallel registers of speech produced by a piezoelectric sensor and a traditional microphone, makes it possible to estimate the function f with algorithms based on DNN, due to the alignment between the registers from both signals. The basic scheme is shown in the Fig. 1.

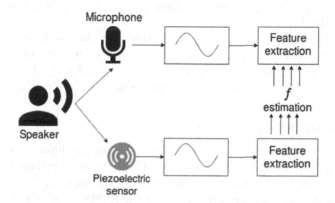

Fig. 1. Scheme of parallel register of a voice with a microphone and a wearable piezo-electric sensor. The estimation of f is made with algorithms based on Deep Learning.

In DNN methods, an enhanced version of $y_p(t)$ can be estimated using algorithms that learn an approximated function $f(\cdot)$ between $y_p(t)$ and the clean data of the microphone $x(t)$ of the form

$$\hat{y}_p(t) = f\left(x(t)\right). \tag{5}$$

The precision of the approximation $f(\cdot)$ usually depends on the amount of training data, the type of artificial neural network or algorithm selected.

Previous attempts has estimated $f(\cdot)$ for specific conditions or noise levels. In our approach, we apply a set of LSTM neural networks trained and then applied separately to estimate a set of functions $f_1(\cdot)$, $f_2(\cdot)$ for $f_0|MFCC$ (fundamental frequency as a reconstruction of the MFCC coefficients) and 39 MFCC.

The description of LSTM network is presented in the following section.

2.3   Long Short-Term Memory Neural Networks

Over the past decades, several kinds of artificial neural networks have been tested for classification and regression purposes in many areas. In the recent past DNNs, which are organized in many layers, have achieved good results in problems that cover a wide range of applications. A new branch of possibilities for modeling problems that naturally depend on sequential information has been opened since the arising of RNNs, which allow storing information through feedback connections between units to themselves or other neurons in the same layer [10, 39].

A special kinf of RNN, the LSTM presented in [20], have introduced a set of gates within the units, which control the access, storing and propagation of information over the network, with the objective of enlarging the capabilities of RNN by storing information in the short and the long term. These networks presented promising results in different tasks, where information strongly depend on previous states, such as speech recognition, handwriting synthesis, and music composition [14,15,20].

The LSTM has four gates that control the operations of input, output, and erasing the memory in order to achieve the goal of preserving values in the long-term and the short-term. A more detailed exposition on the mathematical modeling of the LSTM and the training procedure can be found in [13].

2.4   Denoising with Autoencoders

Denoising autoencoder is considered as one of recent architectures of artificial neural networks that have achieved success. This innovative find consisting of two steps: the first one, is the encoder, which performs a mapping f that transforms an input vector y into a representation h in the hidden layers. The next step is the decoder, which mapped back the hidden representation into a vector $\hat{x}$ in input space.

In the course of the training stage, the inputs of the denoising autoencoders are the noise corrupted features, while the corresponding clean features became the outputs. The training algorithm adjusts the parameters of the network in order to learn the complex relationships between them. Current computers allow the training of many hidden layers and larger sets of data.

3   Experimental Setup

In order to test the benefits of our approach for this low quality/corrupted speech, the experimental setup, from data generation to evaluation, can be summarized in the following steps:

1. Database generation: Two volunteer speakers recorded the database with the wearable sensor in a necklace and with a microphone, as shown in Fig. 2. The corresponding files were edited and represent parallel corrupted and clean data.
2. Feature extraction and input-output correspondence: A set of parameters was extracted from the speech of the wearable piezoelectric sensor, and the clean audio files. Those from the piezoelectric sensor were used as inputs to the networks, while the corresponding clean features were the outputs. The low-latency that could exist between the inputs and outputs are compensated with the RNNs.
3. Training: During training, using forward pass and back-propagation through time algorithm, the weights of the networks were adjusted as the corrupted and clean parameters were presented at the inputs and at the outputs. Details of the training algorithm followed can be found in [16].

Fig. 2. Recording with the wearable device and the microphone

4. Validation: After each training step, the sum of squared errors were computed within the validation set of 40 utterances (about 20% of the total database), and the weights of the network updated in each improvement.
5. Test: A subset of 30 randomly selected utterances (about 15% of the total amount of utterances of the database) was chosen for the test set, for each speaker. To provide independence between the training and testing, these utterances were not part of the training process.

In the following subsections, further details of the main experimental setup are given.

3.1 Database

Two Costa Rican speakers, recorded a set of 184 Spanish speech utterances each. The 184 utterances included isolated words as well as sentences which could be in the affirmative or interrogative forms. The distribution is shown in Table 1.

Table 1. Costa Rican wearable/clean corpus contents.

Identifier	Corpus contents
1–100	Affirmative
101–134	Interrogative
135–150	Paragraphs
151–160	Digits
161–184	Isolated words

The recording were performed using the necklace wearable device and a professional microphone, to achieve parallel register of the signals. The selection of the words, sentences and paragraphs were the same as that of [25], originally developed by the Center for Language and Speech Technologies and Applications of the Polytechnic University of Catalonia for the purpose of emotional speech research. The recordings were performed in a quiet studio.

3.2 Feature Extraction

The audio files of the necklace piezoelectric sensor and the clean recordings with the microphone were downsampled to 16 kHz, 16 bits, to extract parameters using the Ahocoder system [9]. A frame size of 160 samples and frame shift of 80 samples were used to extract 39 MFCC, f_0 and energy of each sentence. The energy parameter were not part of the experiments, as we considered the fundamental frequency and the spectrum the most important parameters for speech perception.

3.3 Evaluation

To evaluate the results given by the enhancement method, we use the following well-known measures:

– Mean Absolute Distance between spectrum coefficients: This measure is computed as

$$MAD(\mathbf{x_j}, \hat{\mathbf{x}_j}) = \frac{1}{39} \sum_{j=1}^{39} \frac{1}{n} \sum_{i=1}^{n} |x_{j_i} - \hat{x_{j_i}}|, \tag{6}$$

where $\mathbf{x_j}, \hat{\mathbf{x}_j}$ are the MFCC coefficients of the natural and the wearable device or enhanced speech.

– Frequency Domain Segmental SNR (SegSNR$_f$): This is a frame-based measure, calculated by averaging the frame level Signal-to-Noise Ratio (SNR) estimates, following the equation:

$$\text{SegSNR}_f = \frac{10}{N} \sum_{i=1}^{N} \log \left[\frac{\sum_{j=0}^{L-1} S^2(i,j)}{\sum_{j=0}^{L-1} (S(i,j) - X(i,j))^2} \right], \tag{7}$$

where $X(i,j)$ is Fourier transform coefficient of frame i at frequency bin j, and $S(i,j)$ is the corresponding coefficient for the processed speech. N is the number of frames and L the number of frequency bins. The values are limited to the interval $[-20, 35]$ dB.

The following two measures correspond to the fundamental frequency parameter:

– VDE (Voice Decision Error): Indicates the percentage of frames misclassified in terms of voicing (with $f_0 > 0$)/unvoicing (with $f_0 = 0$), according to the equation:

$$VDE = \frac{N_{V \to U} + N_{U \to V}}{N} \times 100\%, \tag{8}$$

where $N_{V \to U}$ and $N_{V \to U}$ represent misclassification of Voiced or Unvoiced frames.

– DR (Detection Rate): This objective measure is evaluated only on voiced frames, where a f_0 estimate is considered correct if the deviation of its value is within 5% of the clean value of f_0. This is performed following the equation:

$$DR = \frac{N_{0.05}}{N_p} \times 100\%, \qquad (9)$$

where N represent number of frames, and p the total number of voiced frames of the clean speech.

Additionally, we show spectrograms to illustrate the result for the different experiments.

3.4 Experiments

For the purpose of testing the proposal, for each speaker we train a sets of two LSTM Autoencoder Networks to directly map the corrupted features to clean features.

The LSTM architecture for the networks was defined by trial and error. The final selection consisted of a network with three layers containing 100, 100 and 100 units in each one. This network gave the best results in the trial experiments, and also had a manageable training time. This procedure was accelerated by a NVIDIA GPU system, taking about 7 h to train each LSTM.

4   Results and Discussion

As mentioned, the approximation function between the speech of a wearable device and clean speech is an unknown function. Moreover, it does not have accurate modeling, as opposed to the degradation by additive or convolutional noises. Figure 3 shows an example of the trajectory of an MFCC coefficient of the signal recorded with the microphone and the recording with the wearable device. It is noticeable how the trajectory differs significantly and randomly, which represents a complex problem for an estimate the best function f between both.

Since noise is one components which is perceived the most in this wearable device, the Segmental SNR measurement is necessary to quantify the noise reduction, as shown in Table 2. It is important to note that noise reduction is only one of the tasks required by the set of LSTM networks, given that the signal is also degraded by unknown conditions.

LSTM autoencoders significantly improve the objective measure of the present noise, which indicates benefits in the proposed system for this application. The spectrum improvement can also be verified with a MAD smaller distance between the MFCC coefficients for both speakers, as it is present in Figs. 4 and 5.

All MFCC coefficients are at a lower mean absolute distance after the LSTM autoencoders compared to the wearable device. It is notorious how the distortion

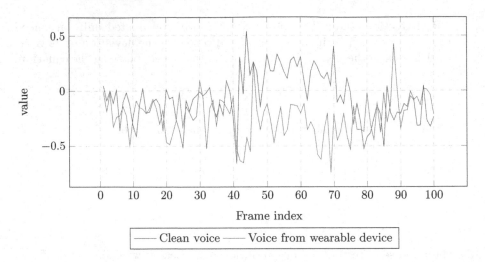

Fig. 3. Comparison of the trajectory of the first MFCC

Table 2. Comparison of the results for the Segmental SNR measure. Higher values represent better results.

Speaker	Wearable device	Enhanced voice
Speaker 1	0.41	0.54
Speaker 2	0.47	0.58

presented in both speakers differs significantly, but the improved result has a similar benefit.

The spectrograms of Fig. 6 show the comparison of the clean speech signal, wearable device and the improved signal with the LSTM autoencoders. It is remarkable how the speech of the wearable device is considerably noisy, while the enhanced version resembles more to natural speech.

Finally, the case of improving the fundamental frequency parameter is presented in Table 3. The VDE measurement improved considerably with the LSTM, which indicated to have more precision for the detection of the voiced/unvoiced segments for two speakers. Despite this, VR measurement did not improve with the proposal.

Although the f_0 detection improves in the decision of voiced/unvoiced, the known nature in the prediction of the LSTM networks (the abrupt changes are made gradually) maybe affects the precision of the value f_0 in first frames of the voiced segments are presented.

Although the results of the proposal related to the spectrum are significant, in the case of the fundamental frequency, there is a considerable margin of improvement, especially for the specific values of parameters in the voiced segments. The results can be considered the first of several stages in the process of reconstructing the speech signal coming from the piezoelectric sensor and the

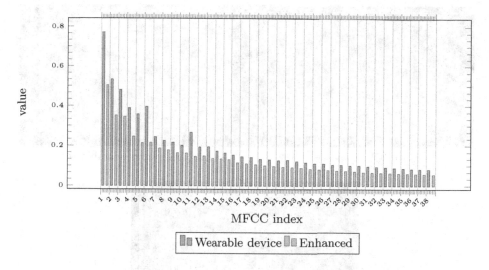

Fig. 4. Mean absolute distance between MFCC (Speaker 1)

Table 3. Comparison of the results for the VDE and VR in the detection f_0. Lower values of VDE represent better results, and higher values of VR represent better values.

Speaker	Wearable device		Enhanced	
	VR	VDE	VR	VDE
Speaker 1	52.3%	24.3%	41.8%	12.9%
Speaker 2	65.7%	23%	51.6%	9.9%

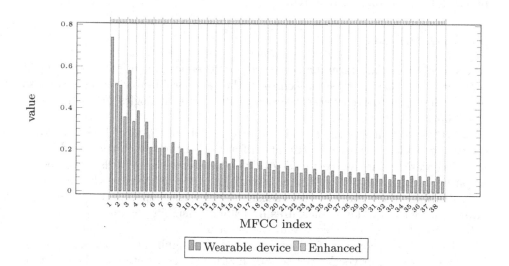

Fig. 5. Mean absolute distance between MFCC (Speaker 2)

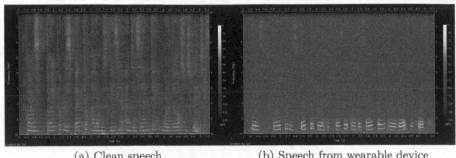

(a) Clean speech   (b) Speech from wearable device

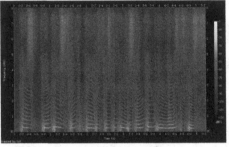

(c) Enhanced speech

Fig. 6. Example of spectrograms (Speaker 1)

wearable device. The search for greater precision in the detection of f_0 and incorporating new algorithms that provide the results closer to clean speech should be considered for further research.

5   Conclusions

In the present work, we conducted a study of the enhancement of a speech signal registered with a piezoelectric sensor within a wearable device. The purpose of this device is to incorporate it into assistance technologies for people with disabilities.

Further, to enhance the signal, we proposed a collection of LSTM autoencoders, which learned an approximation function of the speech registered in the wearable device, with noisy and degraded characteristics, towards clean speech registered with a professional microphone. In order to measure the results, it was established several objective measurements on the spectrum and the fundamental frequency. These measures indicate that significant improvements are achieved on the signal, especially in the spectral part.

Although the proposal of enhancing represents significant progress to utilize the device as voice or vocal-tract sounds interface to recognition or classification systems in real contexts where the user performs, the present work can be considered as the first stage of trial for the real device with own data. Moreover, through the processed signal using LSTM autoencoders, other algorithms that provide further enhancement of the signal can be used, in more specific aspects such as the fundamental frequency in the voiced frames, or in the spectrum in particular sub-bands.

For future work, it can be considered the extension of the present work with new quality measurements and new environmental conditions, also with several stages of algorithms for the reconstruction of the signal, combining diverse models of artificial neural networks or other machine learning algorithms.

Acknowledgements. This work was supported by the University of Costa Rica (UCR), Project No. 322-B9-105 and ED-3416.

References

1. Alshurafa, N., et al.: Recognition of nutrition intake using time-frequency decomposition in a wearable necklace using a piezoelectric sensor. IEEE Sens. J. **15**(7), 3909–3916 (2015)
2. Alshurafa, N., Kalantarian, H., Pourhomayoun, M., Sarin, S., Liu, J.J., Sarrafzadeh, M.: Non-invasive monitoring of eating behavior using spectrogram analysis in a wearable necklace. In: 2014 IEEE Healthcare Innovation Conference (HIC), pp. 71–74. IEEE (2014)
3. Coto-Jiménez, M.: Pre-training long short-term memory neural networks for efficient regression in artificial speech postfiltering. In: 2018 IEEE International Work Conference on Bioinspired Intelligence (IWOBI), pp. 1–7. IEEE (2018)
4. Coto-Jiménez, M., Goddard-Close, J.: LSTM deep neural networks postfiltering for improving the quality of synthetic voices. In: Martínez-Trinidad, J.F., Carrasco-Ochoa, J.A., Ayala-Ramírez, V., Olvera-López, J.A., Jiang, X. (eds.) MCPR 2016. LNCS, vol. 9703, pp. 280–289. Springer, Cham (2016). https://doi.org/10.1007/978-3-319-39393-3_28
5. Coto-Jiménez, M., Goddard-Close, J.: LSTM deep neural networks postfiltering for enhancing synthetic voices. Int. J. Pattern Recogn. Artif. Intell. **32**(01), 1860008 (2018)
6. Coto-Jimenez, M., Goddard-Close, J., Di Persia, L., Rufiner, H.L.: Hybrid speech enhancement with wiener filters and deep LSTM denoising autoencoders. In: 2018 IEEE International Work Conference on Bioinspired Intelligence (IWOBI), pp. 1–8. IEEE (2018)
7. Coto-Jiménez, M., Goddard-Close, J., Martínez-Licona, F.: Improving automatic speech recognition containing additive noise using deep denoising autoencoders of LSTM networks. In: Ronzhin, A., Potapova, R., Németh, G. (eds.) SPECOM 2016. LNCS (LNAI), vol. 9811, pp. 354–361. Springer, Cham (2016). https://doi.org/10.1007/978-3-319-43958-7_42
8. Du, J., Wang, Q., Gao, T., Xu, Y., Dai, L.R., Lee, C.H.: Robust speech recognition with speech enhanced deep neural networks. In: Fifteenth Annual Conference of the International Speech Communication Association (2014)
9. Erro, D., Sainz, I., Navas, E., Hernáez, I.: Improved HNM-based vocoder for statistical synthesizers. In: Twelfth Annual Conference of the International Speech Communication Association (2011)

10. Fan, Y., Qian, Y., Xie, F.L., Soong, F.K.: TTS synthesis with bidirectional LSTM based recurrent neural networks. In: Fifteenth Annual Conference of the International Speech Communication Association (2014)

11. Feng, X., Zhang, Y., Glass, J.: Speech feature denoising and dereverberation via deep autoencoders for noisy reverberant speech recognition. In: 2014 IEEE International Conference on Acoustics, Speech and Signal Processing (ICASSP), pp. 1759–1763. IEEE (2014)

12. Gautschi, G.: Piezoelectric sensors. In: Gautschi, G. (ed.) Piezoelectric Sensorics, pp. 73–91. Springer, Heidelberg (2002). https://doi.org/10.1007/978-3-662-04732-3_5

13. Gers, F.A., Schraudolph, N.N., Schmidhuber, J.: Learning precise timing with LSTM recurrent networks. J. Mach. Learn. Res. **3**(Aug), 115–143 (2002)

14. Graves, A., Fernández, S., Schmidhuber, J.: Bidirectional LSTM networks for improved phoneme classification and recognition. In: Duch, W., Kacprzyk, J., Oja, E., Zadrożny, S. (eds.) ICANN 2005. LNCS, vol. 3697, pp. 799–804. Springer, Heidelberg (2005). https://doi.org/10.1007/11550907_126

15. Graves, A., Jaitly, N., Mohamed, A.R.: Hybrid speech recognition with deep bidirectional LSTM. In: 2013 IEEE Workshop on Automatic Speech Recognition and Understanding (ASRU), pp. 273–278. IEEE (2013)

16. Greff, K., Srivastava, R.K., Koutník, J., Steunebrink, B.R., Schmidhuber, J.: LSTM: a search space odyssey. IEEE Trans. Neural Netw. Learn. Syst. **28**(10), 2222–2232 (2017)

17. Han, K., He, Y., Bagchi, D., Fosler-Lussier, E., Wang, D.: Deep neural network based spectral feature mapping for robust speech recognition. In: Sixteenth Annual Conference of the International Speech Communication Association (2015)

18. Healy, E.W., Yoho, S.E., Wang, Y., Wang, D.: An algorithm to improve speech recognition in noise for hearing-impaired listeners. J. Acoust. Soc. Am. **134**(4), 3029–3038 (2013)

19. Hinton, G., et al.: Deep neural networks for acoustic modeling in speech recognition: the shared views of four research groups. IEEE Sig. Process. Mag. **29**(6), 82–97 (2012)

20. Hochreiter, S., Schmidhuber, J.: Long short-term memory. Neural Comput. **9**(8), 1735–1780 (1997)

21. Ishii, T., Komiyama, H., Shinozaki, T., Horiuchi, Y., Kuroiwa, S.: Reverberant speech recognition based on denoising autoencoder. In: INTERSPEECH, pp. 3512–3516 (2013)

22. Kim, D., et al.: Digits: freehand 3D interactions anywhere using a wrist-worn gloveless sensor. In: Proceedings of the 25th Annual ACM Symposium on User Interface Software and Technology, pp. 167–176. ACM (2012)

23. Kolasinska, A., Quadrio, G., Gaggi, O., Palazzi, C.E.: Technology and aging: users' preferences in wearable sensor networks. In: Proceedings of the 4th EAI International Conference on Smart Objects and Technologies for Social Good, pp. 77–81. ACM (2018)

24. Llombart, J., Ribas, D., Miguel, A., Vicente, L., Ortega, A., Lleida, E.: Speech enhancement with wide residual networks in reverberant environments. arXiv preprint arXiv:1904.05167 (2019)

25. Maegaard, B., Choukri, K., Calzolari, N., Odijk, J.: ELRA-European Language Resources Association-background, recent developments and future perspectives. Lang. Resour. Eval. **39**(1), 9–23 (2005)

26. Manganiello, L., Vega, C., Ríos, A., Valcárcel, M.: Use of wavelet transform to enhance piezoelectric signals for analytical purposes. Anal. Chim. Acta **456**(1), 93–103 (2002)
27. Morabito, V.: Wearable technologies. The Future of Digital Business Innovation, pp. 23–42. Springer, Cham (2016). https://doi.org/10.1007/978-3-319-26874-3_2
28. Nanayakkara, S., Shilkrot, R., Yeo, K.P., Maes, P.: EyeRing: a finger-worn input device for seamless interactions with our surroundings. In: Proceedings of the 4th Augmented Human International Conference, pp. 13–20. ACM (2013)
29. Naylor, P.A., Gaubitch, N.D.: Speech Dereverberation. Springer, Heidelberg (2010). https://doi.org/10.1007/978-1-84996-056-4
30. Ribas, D., Llombart, J., Miguel, A., Vicente, L.: Deep speech enhancement for reverberated and noisy signals using wide residual networks. arXiv preprint arXiv:1901.00660 (2019)
31. Seltzer, M.L., Yu, D., Wang, Y.: An investigation of deep neural networks for noise robust speech recognition. In: 2013 IEEE International Conference on Acoustics, Speech and Signal Processing (ICASSP), pp. 7398–7402. IEEE (2013)
32. Sirohi, J., Chopra, I.: Fundamental understanding of piezoelectric strain sensors. J. Intell. Mater. Syst. Struct. **11**(4), 246–257 (2000)
33. Tressler, J.F., Alkoy, S., Newnham, R.E.: Piezoelectric sensors and sensor materials. J. Electroceram. **2**(4), 257–272 (1998)
34. Velázquez, R.: Wearable assistive devices for the blind. In: Lay-Ekuakille, A., Mukhopadhyay, S.C. (eds.) Wearable and Autonomous Biomedical Devices and Systems for Smart Environment. LNEE, vol. 75, pp. 331–349. Springer, Heidelberg (2010). https://doi.org/10.1007/978-3-642-15687-8_17
35. Villamizar, L.H., Cualdron, M., Gonzalez, F., Aceros, J., Rizzo-Sierra, C.V.: A necklace sonar with adjustable scope range for assisting the visually impaired. In: 2013 35th Annual International Conference of the IEEE Engineering in Medicine and Biology Society (EMBC), pp. 1450–1453. IEEE (2013)
36. Vincent, E., Watanabe, S., Nugraha, A.A., Barker, J., Marxer, R.: An analysis of environment, microphone and data simulation mismatches in robust speech recognition. Comput. Speech Lang. **46**, 535–557 (2017)
37. Wilson, J., Walker, B.N., Lindsay, J., Cambias, C., Dellaert, F.: Swan: system for wearable audio navigation. In: 2007 11th IEEE International Symposium on Wearable Computers, pp. 91–98. IEEE (2007)
38. Yu, L., Bao, J., Giurgiutiu, V.: Signal processing techniques for damage detection with piezoelectric wafer active sensors and embedded ultrasonic structural radar. In: Smart Structures and Materials 2004: Sensors and Smart Structures Technologies for Civil, Mechanical, and Aerospace Systems, vol. 5391, pp. 492–504. International Society for Optics and Photonics (2004)
39. Zen, H., Sak, H.: Unidirectional long short-term memory recurrent neural network with recurrent output layer for low-latency speech synthesis. In: 2015 IEEE International Conference on Acoustics, Speech and Signal Processing (ICASSP), pp. 4470–4474. IEEE (2015)

Insight GT: A Public, Fast, Web Image Ground Truth Authoring Tool

Barrantes-Garro Joel[1]([✉]), Rodríguez-Morales Hellen[2],
Garnier-Artiñano Adrián[1], Calderón-Ramírez Saúl[1], Porras-Jiménez Fabian[2],
Corrales-Arley Luís Carlos[3], and Brenes-Camacho Ricardo[3]

[1] PAttern Recognition and MAchine Learning Group (PARMA-Group),
Computing Engineering School, Instituto Tecnológico de Costa Rica,
Cartago, Costa Rica
{ibarrantes,agarnier}@ic-itcr.ac.cr, sacalderon@itcr.ac.cr
[2] Industrial Design School, Instituto Tecnológico de Costa Rica, Cartago, Costa Rica
herodriguez@estudiantec.cr, fporras@tec.ac.cr
[3] Huli, Curridabat, Costa Rica
{luis.corrales,ricardo.brenes}@huli.io
https://www.tec.ac.cr/en/grupo-investigacion/parma

Abstract. This paper proposes the community the development of a
public web tool for fast image Ground Truth Authoring Tool (GTAT).
Image ground truth authoring tools are key to generate training and
validation data for image segmentation and classification systems. The
paper does a short review of similar publicly available GTAT's, its features and short-comings, in order to spot the key features missing for a
public GTAT to the community. Based in the concluded wished features,
we aim to develop a free and open GTAT in the future.

Keywords: Ground truth authoring tools · Machine learning ·
Labeling · Deep learning

1 Introduction

Over the last few years, image analysis has taken an important role in multiple
applications and fields, such as robotics, medical imaging, botany and microbiology. The sheer amount of images and videos produced for further analysis
demands instruments and tools that ease the work that has to be done to obtain
results. The generation and analysis of such data is increasingly assisted by several techniques associated to computer vision, pattern recognition, machine and
deep learning, for instance image segmentation and classification tasks. Image
segmentation refers to the pixel wise classification in an image or frame into
different categories [1], which is also referred as semantic segmentation. If the
classification aims to distinguish different instances of the same object category,
the task is known as instance segmentation. Images and videos can be segmented
to track objects like cells or distinguish relevant items from the background, as
in [2–5].

© Springer Nature Switzerland AG 2020
J. L. Crespo-Mariño and E. Meneses-Rojas (Eds.): CARLA 2019, CCIS 1087, pp. 398–405, 2020.
https://doi.org/10.1007/978-3-030-41005-6_27

Image segmentation is a common problem in computer vision, well addressed in literature. To measure metrics for an image segmentation algorithm, proper ground truth data is needed, which means that a human must assist the segmentation of a set of images. Generally, it is required that the generated ground truth has few to no flaws, and ideally must be statistically relevant, thus several subjects must build ground truth data. Nonetheless, ground truth generation can make use of machine learning models and segmentation techniques to speed up or semi-automate the process, an useful feature increasingly available in modern ground truth authoring tools. For instance, sophisticated ground truth authoring tools implement automatic region initialization to speed the ground truth authoring process. An example of a technique which could be used to initialize ground truth masks is superpixels. In [6], pancreas computerized tomography (CT) scans are sliced into 2D images. These images are segmented using a superpixels based technique, which are later forwarded into a deep convolutional neural network to aid image classification in computer assisted diagnosis. The result is a faster and more reliable method to achieve pancreas image segmentation.

Superpixels typically over-segment the image, with groups of pixels clustered into regions or segments. The segments generated contain enough information to produce a valid initial segmentation and also, a segmentation easier to optimize compared to an initial segmentation based on a grid of pixels [7]. For example, a superpixels based web tool was also used by [5] to generate input for the training of a convolutional neural network model.

In this paper, we propose a public available ground truth authoring tool (GTAT) to validate image segmentation and object tracking algorithms. In Sect. 2 we address previous similar GTAT tools, to identify missing and useful GTA functionalities. Later we address our proposed GTAT, Insight GT, and perform a set of experiments to compare existing GTATs with the proposed prototype in Sect. 4, to finally reach the conclusions and future work in Sect. 5.

2   State of the Art

In this section, we review several tools and available software that addresses ground-truth generation for image/video segmentation and object tracking.

FAST-GT (FAst Semi-automatic Tool for Ground Truth generation) [8] is a generic framework for semiautomatic generation of ground truth, which allows different implementations of building blocks. FAST-GT implements a detection layer, which applies multiple object detectors to a frame or image, and takes into account previous annotations (called trackers). Manual intervention is then applied to the output of the previous layer. Finally, the trackers of the detection layer are updated according to the resulting annotation of the manual step. This tool is available to the general public. Its most important drawback is the need of installing and compiling the source code, which depends on the OpenCV and Eigen libraries.

LabelMe [9] is a GTAT which consists of a database of labeled images and a web tool to manually annotate images. The LabelMe web tool provides an unsophisticated canvas that allows the user to annotate an image using a tool-box consisting of a polygon tool and a paintbrush to generate a mask. LabelMe presents the disadvantage that only accepts images in JPG format and the tool-box available to annotate images is quite restricted.

In [10], VATIC is proposed as a tool that helps video annotation tasks by providing a web based platform for crowd-sourced video labeling. VATIC allows the user to annotate and delimit objects by surrounding them with a rectangular shape. The user only needs to manually annotate a subset of the frames of a given video, called the key frames. Then, VATIC performs an annotation for the remaining frames, using interpolation methods. VATIC is web based, however there is no free server running it, and it does not allow pixel wise tagging.

Sensarea, a public video editing tool, provides users with interactive tools to perform video editing and effect generation, as also object tracking in videos and ground-truth authoring. Before the object tracking process, the user can anno-tate the first frame of the video, using basic tools such as paintbrush, polygon and ellipse tools, for example. Then, the user can start the object tracking process to readjust the mask automatically, enabling the user to correct it afterwards. We experienced major performance shortcomings when drawing many masks, while using Sensarea. Another drawback of Sensarea is its low portability given the need of a Windows based installation.

In [11], it is presented interactive Video Annotation Tool (iVAT) as a tool that aid and ease annotation tasks. iVAT provides manual, semi-automatic and automatic annotation for videos. In the manual mode, the user must generate a ground-truth mask for each frame on the video. The semi-automatic approach requires ground-truth annotation for a given frame, to later calculate an annota-tion mask for the next frames automatically. The automatic annotation involves supervised detectors where a learning step has taken place, making the automatic approach domain dependent. The tool does not allow image GT authoring, and is not web based.

Ilastik [12] is a GTAT proposed as an easy-to-use tool to perform image segmentation and classification. Ilastik makes use of user manual annotation to begin a learning phase, which usually consists on mouse strokes across a canvas to label regions of pixels. The tool implements the following steps: first, ilastik calculates a generic basis to represent general image features. Later, a random forest classifier is trained using user-labeled data to initialize pixel labels. Ilastik is not web based, and its GUI usability is limited.

In addition, the tool Supervisely [13] allows to mark both images and videos in a semi-automatic way, selecting the desired area to create the marking and automatically generating the required shape. Supervisely also has tools to draw the masks in a completely manual way. It has quick access commands to make the marking process more efficient. Another important function is the ability to make brightness and contrast adjustments to improve the marking process.

Another tool analyzed is LabelBox [14], it is a platform that allows to mark and classify images and video manually. Labelbox enables collaborative work, making possible to see and review the markings made by other people. A deficiency found is that to mark video it must be converted into a sequence of images before uploading it. Also it requires the user to define the objects before they start labeling the images and if there is a new or different object, the user must go to the project menu, settings and add the new object.

Table 1 summarizes a feature comparison of the analyzed GTATs.

3   Proposed Tool

Given the presented state of the art, we propose Insight GT, a public web tool consisting in a canvas that allows manual image annotation and a semi-automatic segmentation approach to generate ground truth data from 2d images and videos.

The following the proposed functionalities implemented so far in our prototype available at https://insight-gt.hulilabs.xyz/canvas/. For region initialization, SLIC superpixels are computed [15]. A javascript implementation of the algorithm can be found at [16].

- A canvas that allows manual image annotation with different brushes and tools, as seen in [9,17,18], aided by region initialization, using super pixels or a similar algorithm.
- Web tool: The GT authoring tool must be web based, to increment the tool portability, and open to the community.
- Flexible storing format: The format must allow its usage with GT compromising several (thousands) of GT masks, avoiding performance degradation.
- A semi-automatic algorithm for mask initialization: The tool must implement a technique for initializing the foreground masks, and allow user to make adjustments to the masks.
- A semi-automatic algorithm for mask readjustment: For video segmentation, the masks drawn for the first frame can be readjusted for next frames. An algorithm which automatically estimates such readjustment is useful for a GTAT, as implemented in Sensarea.
- Collaborative support and crowd-sourcing support: The tool must allow several concurrent users working on the same project.
- Evaluation module: The tool must provide means to evaluate metrics for the segmentation algorithms, including but not limited to: sensitivity, specificity, accuracy, F-score, among others.
- Change history: the changes made by other users in the markings of the images are shown in the tool.

4   Experiments and Results

We selected Supervisely and LableBox in order to compare it to Insight GT. This applications where selected because they are all web applications. Additionally, they allow to label different objects in order to track them.

Table 1. Comparison of GTATs

	Proposed tool	FAST-GT	ITK-SNAP	ROXAS	LabelME	Sensarea	iVAT	TWS	Ilastik
Platform	Web based	Desktop	Desktop	Desktop	Web based	Desktop	Desktop	Desktop	Desktop
Cross-platform	●	○	●	○	●	○	●	●	●
Image batch segmentation	●	○	●	●	○	●	○	●	●
Video segmentation	●	●	○	●	○	●	●	○	○
Manual segmentation	●	○	●	○	●	●	●	○	●
Available toolbox	Brush, polygon	Rectangle	Brush, polygon	?	Brush	Brush, polygon	?	Scribble	Scribble
Semi-automatic segmentation	●	●	●	●	○	●	●	●	●
Automatic segmentation	○	○	○	●	○	●	●	●	●
Mask correction	●	●	?	●	○	●	●	○	●
Region initialization	●	○	○	○	○	○	○	○	○
Metric Evaluation	●	○	○	●	○	○	●	○	○
Restricted Domain	○	○	●	●	○	○	○	○	○

4.1   Quantitative Experiments and Results

To quantify user experience for each selected tool, we defined the following tests:

1. Open an image and with the rectangle tool mark the same sample image with car that is in it. The input image is stored in a known location.
2. Mark with the brush tool one of the figures in the image. For this second task, the user will modify an image that is already open.
3. With the eraser tool, correct the edge that is left of the image. The user must open a mask that has been previously marked with a flaw easy to detect.
4. Save a previously created mask. The file containing the mask representation must be in a previously known route by the user.
5. Open a previously created mask again. The file containing the mask representation must be in a previously known route by the user.

The following are key aspects taken into account during the execution of the proposed tests.

- Only initial and simple instructions were given to the user. We wrote down the users' mistakes.
- We performed simple questions to understand the user's thought process.
- If the subject performs a faulty action several times, the test is finished. We aim to understand how the person performs a task without knowledge of the application, if the user tries many times to perform an action, it is likely that the user will learn to do it by trial and error, and not by intuition.
- We collected a set of observations and suggestions per user for each tool.

Table 2. Mean and Std. time in seconds for each test in each tool

Tool		Test 1	Test 2	Test 3	Test 4	Test 5
Insight GT	Mean	45.653	19.503	18.023	10.188	38.418
	Std.	25.698	15.413	7.703	5.959	36.495
LabelBox	Mean	83.995	19.069	11.185	103.97	20.454
	Std.	13.654	6.838	7.055	24.636	12.531
Supervisely	Mean	25.33	26.805	29.740	13.905	13.905
	Std.	7.835	35.094	78.022	17.748	5.353

We tested 30 university engineering students, between the age of 18 and 25 that had no previous experience with any of the tools presented to them. Then they were split into 3 groups of 10 for each tool. This was made in order to prevent the user to learn from the similarities from the other tools (Table 2).

The first test measured the speed of opening an image for a project. Here is the first difference between the platforms. In Insight GT user performed this action in an average of 46 s, but it only loads one image, for LabelBox and Supervisely the is able to select a folder or a group of images for the labeling project.

The process in Supervisely was very straightforward and simple for loading a group of photos. Labelbox was also simple to load images, but it required a couple extra steps like defining the objects and color for labels, the tools to use, and there a couple of screens that let you pick the objects that you will mark on the images before you get to the marking screen.

The second and third tests the results were similar, with Insight GT yielding the lowest times by a low margin. The resulting similar times for these tests are likely to be explained by the simplicity of the tests. In the case of LabelBox, the process to enable the necessary functionalities for tests 2 and 3 required to manipulate a JSON file, however we did not include the time to perform this task.

In the fourth test, LabelBox was the slowest, since it required the user an extensive search for the functionality interface. Additionally, Labelbox only allows to download the whole data set. As for Supervisely, the process was rather simple, however it downloads a JSON file, not the mask in an image format. Insight GT yielded the lowest average time for the fourth test.

For the last test, corresponding to opening a previously saved mask, it was faster in average for Supervisely and LableBox, since both tools implemented a cloud based recently saved mask option access.

5   Conclusions

The test showed that in the core functionalities of the tools, they are similar, but upon further inspection of the work flow, it can be seen that the Supervisely and LabelBox need some extra effort in learning the tool for some parts of the process that require editing JSON files. Insight GT keeps the core functionalities simple and easier to learn.

We aim to make available Insight GT publicly available with its core functionalities, along its source code. We think its important to build an user friendly and web based GTAT with a powerful set of customizable mask initialization algorithms to speed up image and pixel labeling.

As future work, we think it is possible to improve the accuracy of the usability tests, with more accurate and modern tools like eye tracking, which would allow us to validate and compare more accurately the implemented functions of the proposed Insight GT tool with existing tools.

Thus, as future work, an user experience research should be develop to find the requirements of the users with the objective of enhance the learning curve and add features that improve the user experience and learning curve of the web tool Insight GT.

References

1. Shapiro, L.G., Stockman, G.C.: Computer Vision. Prentice Hall, Upper Saddle River (2001)
2. Liu, J., Tong, X., Li, W., Wang, T., Zhang, Y., Wang, H.: Automatic player detection, labeling and tracking in broadcast soccer video. Pattern Recogn. Lett. **30**, 103–113 (2009)
3. Grady, L., Funka-Lea, G.: Multi-label image segmentation for medical applications based on graph-theoretic electrical potentials. In: Sonka, M., Kakadiaris, I.A., Kybic, J. (eds.) CVAMIA/MMBIA -2004. LNCS, vol. 3117, pp. 230–245. Springer, Heidelberg (2004). https://doi.org/10.1007/978-3-540-27816-0_20
4. Suri, J.S., Setarehdan, S.K., Singh, S.: Advanced Algorithmic Approaches to Medical Image Segmentation: State-of-the-Art Applications in Cardiology, Neurology, Mammography and Pathology. Springer, London (2002). https://doi.org/10.1007/978-0-85729-333-6
5. Aydin, A.S., Dubey, A., Dovrat, D., Aharoni, A., Shilkrot, R.: CNN based yeast cell segmentation in multi-modal fluorescent microscopy data
6. Farag, A., Lu, L., Roth, H.R., Liu, J., Turkbey, E., Summers, R.M.: A bottom-up approach for pancreas segmentation using cascaded superpixels and (deep) image patch labeling. IEEE Trans. Image Process. **26**, 386–399 (2017)
7. Ren, X., Malik, J.: Learning a classification model for segmentation
8. Comaschi, F., Stuijk, S., Basten, T., Corporaal, H.: A tool for fast ground truth generation for object detection and tracking from video. In: 2014 IEEE International Conference on Image Processing, ICIP 2014 (2014)
9. Russell, B.C., Torralba, A., Murphy, K.P., Freeman, W.T.: LabelMe: a database and web-based tool for image annotation. Int. J. Comput. Vis. **77**(1–3), 157–173 (2008)
10. Vondrick, C., Patterson, D., Ramanan, D.: Efficiently scaling up crowdsourced video annotation a set of best practices for high quality, economical video labeling. Int. J. Comput. Vis. **101**, 184–204 (2012)
11. Bianco, S., Ciocca, G., Napoletano, P., Schettini, R.: An interactive tool for manual, semi-automatic and automatic video annotation. Comput. Vis. Image Underst. **131**, 88–99 (2015)

12. Sommer, C., Straehle, C., Koethe, U., Hamprecht, F.A.: Ilastik: interactive learning and segmentation toolkit. In: 2011 IEEE International Symposium on Biomedical Imaging: From Nano to Macro, pp. 230–233. IEEE (March 2011)
13. Supervisely: Overview (2019). https://docs.supervise.ly/cluster/overview/. Accessed 05 May 2019
14. LabelBox: Overview (2019). https://support.labelbox.com/docs. Accessed 11 May 2019
15. Achanta, R., Shaji, A., Smith, K., Lucchi, A., Fua, P., Süsstrunk, S.: Slic superpixels (2010)
16. Tangseng, P., Wu, Z., Yamaguchi, K.: Looking at outfit to parse clothing (March 2017)
17. Bertolino, P.: Sensarea: an authoring tool to create accurate clickable videos
18. Yushkevich, P.A., Gerig, G.: ITK-SNAP: an intractive medical image segmentation tool to meet the need for expert-guided segmentation of complex medical images. IEEE Pulse 8, 54–57 (2017)

Comparison of Four Automatic Classifiers for Cancer Cell Phenotypes Using M-Phase Features Extracted from Brightfield Microscopy Images

Francisco Siles[1]([✉]), Andrés Mora-Zúñiga[1], and Steve Quiros[2]

[1] PRIS-Lab: Pattern Recognition and Intelligent Systems Laboratory,
Department of Electrical Engineering, School of Engineering,
Universidad de Costa Rica (UCR), San José, Costa Rica
{francisco.siles,andres.morazuniga}@ucr.ac.cr
[2] LabQT: Tumoral Chemosensitivity Laboratory,
Research Center on Tropical Diseases (CIET), School of Microbiology,
Universidad de Costa Rica (UCR), San José, Costa Rica
steve.quiros@ucr.ac.cr

Abstract. In our in vitro study to model and understand the regulation
networks that control the live and death of the cells, it is fundamental to
quantify the contribution of each of the cancer cell' phenotypes: apoptosis, cell cycle arrest, DNA damage repair, and DNA damage proliferation.
For that, an automatic microscope is used to generate several images of
cell populations using brightfield microscopy. In the scientific literature,
several methods to extract features from microscopy images are available, but mostly for fluorescence or contrast phase microscopy, which
have the disadvantage of being phototoxic to the cells, and therefore
unsuitable for our study. In this paper a successful method to automatically extract and classify the phenotypes of cancer cells is presented. The
method uses features extracted automatically from the M-phase (mitosis)
of cells from images obtained by brightfield microscopy. The classification results are validated by comparing them with the correct manually
annotated classes for each instance. Four different classifiers: Support
Vector Machine (SVM), Linear Discriminant Analysis (LDA), k-Nearest
Neighbours (kNN), and Random Forests (RF) are compared using standard comparison metrics, such as precision, recall and F1-score. It is
finally shown that the LDA classifier provided the best results, reaching
an overall f1-score of 0.78 and an overall weighted f1-score of 0.88.

Keywords: In vitro cell research · Cancer phenotype classification ·
Brightfield microscopy · Mitosis features · Pattern recognition classifiers

1 Introduction

One of the most common mechanisms to treat cancer is Chemotherapy, which
aims to try to stop the growth of cancer cells [17]. The Chemotherapy uses

© Springer Nature Switzerland AG 2020
J. L. Crespo-Mariño and E. Meneses-Rojas (Eds.): CARLA 2019, CCIS 1087, pp. 406–419, 2020.
https://doi.org/10.1007/978-3-030-41005-6_28

genotoxic drugs, that might damage the DNA in the cells, in order to force the cancer cells to enter (1) *cell cycle arrest*, defined as the interruption of the normal cell cycle, that is, cells are unable to replicate as usual; or (2) *apoptosis*, which consists of a programmed cell death, present in multicellular organisms.

Previous results of our research group have shown that some cancer cells with enough DNA damage to force apoptosis, as a result of their treatment with genotoxic drugs, are still proliferating [26]. The proliferation of cells with DNA damage contributes to the propagation of cells that are genetically unstable, which in fact may cause malign transformations on normal cells or propitiate the evolution to multiresistance species or more aggressive cancer types [8, 12, 16, 27]. This phenomenon of DNA damage proliferation has raised the interest of the international scientific community to model and understand the regulation networks, responsible to define the survival or death of the cells [10, 32, 34].

In order to obtain information about those regulatory networks, we have been performing experiments, where different levels of chemotherapy are being applied to different living cell samples. For each cell sample, a microscopy image is obtained every 10 min for about 92 h, using an automatic microscope. This process is repeated for different cell samples. Four phenotypes are to be expected in any such cell sample: (1) *cell cycle arrest*, (2) *apoptosis*, (3) *DNA repaired cells*, and (4) *DNA damage proliferation*. Where DNA repaired cell phenotype corresponds to those cells that have fixed the DNA damages caused by the genotoxicity of the drugs, and therefore can continue their normal cell cycle, and DNA damage proliferation phenotype consisting of those cells that, even though present enough damage that should have been forcing them into cell cycle arrest or apoptosis, continue to proliferate and propagate their DNA damage to their offspring. The phenotypes present in the cell samples are to be quantified based on the microscopy images in order to understand their contribution to the regulatory networks.

Most of the available microscopy techniques use fluorescence staining to make the cells glow, increasing their visibility and their contrast with respect to the background [2, 7, 9, 22, 29, 36]. The fluorescence staining is phototoxic to the cells, an effect that would negatively affect the quantification of the phenotypes, producing biased results. Therefore, brightfield microscopy is the only technique available for our purposes.

In brightfield microscopy, there is no high contrast between each cell and its surroundings, making the direct observation and counting of the cells a challenging task. Besides, the density of the live cells is increasing over time (to the hundreds or even thousands), making almost impossible for a human being (even for an experienced cell biologist) to be able to reliably annotate the required information about the cell phenotypes in several samples. The characteristics of our brightfield microscopy images (from now on referred to as 3J images) are: (1) low contrast, (2) high cell density, and (3) high levels of brightness.

Due to the above-mentioned limitations, this paper presents the results of the classification of the four cell phenotypes using features extracted from M-phase in brightfield microscopy images. The different cell phenotypes can be distinguished by their visual clues and behaviour over time, for example, some of the phenotypes change their intensity and shape, or take longer periods to perform the cell division (M-phase).

2   Related Work

In order to classify the different dendritic cells' phenotypes, in [35] they have used gene expression. In that study, the phenotypes are not of interest for the current study, and the type of input data does not correspond to microscopy images. In [15] they have extracted features from the microscopy images, such as the location of the chromosomes and organelles inside the cell, of the early or late start of the stages of the cell cycles, and the time spent in each stage of the cell cycle. But most of the used features cannot be extracted from the 3J images.

On the other hand, characteristics of the mitosis have been used in order to determine the phenotype of a cell. Mitosis is the process by which an animal cell divides into two genetically identical daughter cells, and the cell cycle phase in which this division occurs is called mitotic phase or simply M-phase [24]. Some of the characteristics of normal mitosis are: (1) rounded cell before cell division, (2) two daughter cells emerge quickly, (3) reduction in the migration rate of the parent and offspring cells, (4) similar size and shape of the offspring with respect to the parent [7]. Therefore, the duration of the M-phase can be an indicator of DNA damage in case it extends longer periods. Also the number of daughter cells (if different that two) can be another particular phenotype indicator.

Several methods have been presented for mitosis detection, for example: symmetry analysis [13], hidden-state-conditional neural fields [33], 3D convolutional networks [23], support vector machine classifiers [18], and the Hough Circular Transform (HCT) [14]. Some of these methods are not suitable for detection of mitosis in 3J images. For example, in [13] the symmetry of the mitosis in fluorescence images is used to detect it, but in 3J images of cancer cells, the cancer cell mitosis is not always symmetrical. In the case of [18], the required features are: area, area of the convex hull, eccentricity, major axis length, minor axis length, orientation, maximum intensity, mean intensity, and minimum intensity, but a good segmentation is required in order to extract such features from the images, which is not possible with 3J images. Also, in [23,33], more annotated images than what it is available for our 3J images is required for the neural networks' method proposed.

Also, since the (animal) cells during the M-Phase turn into a sphere [19, 20,28], approaches such as Hough Circular Transform (HCT) have proven to be useful [14]. But the results were reported for phase-contrast microscopy, and uses an active contour method to detect rounded cells. Active contours do not work correctly in 3J images due to the lack of contrast, producing a weak external energy component. Also, a local tracking (forward and backward) was used to detect the start and end of the M-phase, and if cell division has occurred. In [25] they have used as indicator of cell division, a level-set method to identify if a region of single intensity transforms into two.

In [11] the features were extracted using deep convolutional neural networks, so not much information about the meaning of the features is available. In [1] supervised learning using features extracted from the images by using the software CellProfiler [6] is presented. Also, in [1] the best classification results were obtained by using support vector machines (SVM), random forests (RF), and linear discriminant analysis (LDA).

In general, as far as we know, not many sources are available that tackle the problem of phenotype classification based solely on microscopy images, and none of them face the problem for 3J images.

3   Methodology

For this study, the images used were generated with a Cytation 3 from BioTek, which is a cell imaging multi-mode microplate reader, combining automated digital microscopy and conventional microplate detection. All the experiments were performed on in vitro cell lines acquired from the American Type Culture Collection and from the NCI-60 from the National Cancer Institute repositories, United States. Those cell lines were designed for research purposes.

All the images used are brightfield images, even though the majority of studies reported in the literature make use of fluorescence imaging, and being one of the most important capabilities of the Cytation 3. The reason for choosing brightfield, instead of fluorescence responds to the fact that fluorescence staining of the cells is phototoxic to them, and this will is unacceptable in our live-cell assay to study the cell proliferation under chemotherapy dose testing. The brightfield images present a highly reduced contrast in comparison with the fluorescence images reported in the literature, and therefore it is a harder problem to solve.

The dataset is comprised of 360 brightfield images, in which a number of 261 M-phase cells occurred, and their corresponding phenotypes are described in Table 1. The phenotypes in this dataset were manually annotated by expert cell biologists.

Table 1. Number of M-phase cells per phenotype in the dataset

Id	Phenotype	Number of M-phase instances
P	DNA damage proliferation	43
C	Cell cycle arrest	13
A	Apoptosis	29
R	DNA repair	176
Total		**261**

The feature extraction algorithm has four parts: (1) Preprocessing, (2) M-phase detection, (3) Find M-start, and (4) Find M-end. The preprocessing is mostly performed to remove an undesired spotlight effect in the images, caused

by the microscope's light source, but it also serves to the increase in the contrast
between the cells and the background. By removing such effect, the contrast
of the image can be normalized, since before the correction the contrast in the
center of the image is different with respect to that in the corners. The correction
consists basically in the subtraction of an illumination model to each of the
images in the dataset.

The M-phase detection was performed with an HCT, as suggested in [14]. A
local spatial variance filter (LSVF) [30,31] was computed in a predefined window,
around the centers found. The LSVF is used as an alternative to edge detection
for a latter morphology transformation that is used to detect the cells and if cell
division occurred (see Fig. 1).

Fig. 1. M-phase detection. Left: HCT circle hit. Center: LSVF applied. Right: Morphology filtering (reproduced from [21]).

In the third part, the aim is to find the start frame of each detected cell in
M-phase. For that, a backward tracking from the detection frame is performed,
and is kept until a circularity measure is below an empirically defined threshold.
That frame is selected as the start frame (M-start).

The final part searches for the end frame of each detected cell in M-phase
(see Fig. 2). A forward tracking from the detection frame is performed, and is
being kept until a circularity measure is below the predefined threshold and
no cell division was detected. In the case a cell division is detected, then the
frame before that is assumed as the frame end of that cell M-phase (M-end).
The cell division is detected by counting the objects after a simple thresholding
technique.

Finally, the required features can be extracted: o number of offspring cells,
i average pixel intensity inside the cell, r radius, a area and c circularity, e
euclidean distance traveled during M-phase, d amount of frames that the cell
spent in M-Phase. The feature vector can be represented as $\overline{F} = (o, i, r, a, c, e, d)$.

Once the features are obtained from the samples, the aim of the current
paper is to evaluate and compare the results of four different classifiers using the
automatically extracted features with respect to the groundtruth. The classifier
that obtained the best results reported by Abbas et al. in [1] is the Support

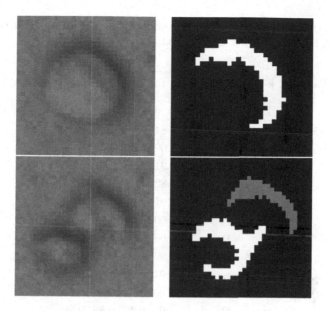

Fig. 2. M-end search. Left: mother cell (top) and two offspring cells (bottom). Right: Blob count, one blob (top), two blobs (bottom) (reproduced from [21]).

Vector Machine (SVM), with small different performances between the linear and radial versions, this is why we have considered the linear SVM in the alternatives to test. Also, the Linear Discriminant Analysis (LDA) is considered as a good benchmark classifier. Finally, the other two: the k-Nearest Neighbours (kNN), and the Random Forests (RF) are added to the list of classifiers in order to test for other simpler algorithms. The hyperparameters of the classifiers are described in our git repository available on request.

A k-fold approach was used in order to test for different subsets of the available dataset. Finally, the comparison was carried out using the three common classification metrics: precision (P), recall (R) and F1-Score ($F1$).

With regards to the hyperparameters of the classifiers, for the kNN we have selected 3 as the number of neighbors. The LDA is followed by a Naive Bayes. For the Random Classifier the number of estimators was 100, the max depth of 2 and the random state of 0. Finally, for the SVM the gamma values selected was 1/N, where N was the number of features, with Radial basis function kernel.

4 Results and Analysis

The results of the evaluation of the classifiers are shown in Table 2 for the LDA, in Table 3 for the kNN, in Table 4 for the SVM, in Table 5 for the RF. Each of the tables shows the results for the k-folds for each of the metrics, and for each of the classes. An average F1-score (avg F1) including the average for all the classes is shown at the end of each table, as well as an averaged weighted

F1-score (avg wF1), which took into consideration the number of cells in each class. Finally, the accuracy a is obtained for each of the folds.

Table 2. k-fold classification results for the LDA classifier.

k-fold	Metric	R	C	P	A
0	p	0.84	0.50	1.00	0.71
	r	1.00	0.50	0.55	0.62
	f1	0.91	0.50	0.71	0.67
	a	0.82			
1	p	0.91	0.67	1.00	0.86
	r	1.00	0.67	0.70	0.86
	f1	0.96	0.67	0.82	0.86
	a	0.90			
2	p	0.94	0.50	1.00	0.75
	r	1.00	0.33	0.80	0.86
	f1	0.97	0.40	0.89	0.80
	a	0.90			
3	p	0.89	0.67	1.00	0.86
	r	1.00	0.67	0.60	0.86
	f1	0.94	0.67	0.75	0.86
	a	0.71			
	Avg a	**0.83**			
	Avg f1	**0.77**			
	Avg wf1	**0.87**			

Since the k-fold method generates different results for each run, the averages for the metrics obtained for each class for every classifier is shown in Table 6. Also, a summary of the overall average F1 and weighted average F1 scores is shown in Table 7.

The first thing to notice about the results is that for example, the precision p for the LDA classifier was 1.00 in all the folds in Table 2. That means that the likelihood of being of class P for any P-labelled phenotype is 100%. This is quite important, since P (the DNA damage proliferation phenotype) is the most relevant class for the current study. The classifier that obtained the second best result for p is the RF classifier, which averaged a 92% (see Table 6). The other 2 classifiers did not obtain good values for p in the P class. It is also interesting, that the SVM classifier obtained a 0.0 for precision in all the folds. The SVM obtained precision and recall values for classes C, P and A of 0.0 in all the folds, reaching an average F1 score of only 0.19 (see Table 4).

Table 3. k-fold classification results for the kNN classifier.

k-fold	Metric	R	C	P	A
0	p	0.79	0.33	0.29	0.43
	r	0.94	0.25	0.18	0.38
	f1	0.86	0.29	0.22	0.40
	a	0.65			
1	p	0.81	0.33	0.29	0.80
	r	0.94	0.33	0.20	0.57
	f1	0.87	0.33	0.24	0.67
	a	0.71			
2	p	0.84	0.00	0.33	0.60
	r	0.84	0.00	0.30	0.43
	f1	0.84	0.00	0.32	0.50
	a	0.63			
3	p	0.86	0.00	0.33	0.60
	r	0.97	0.00	0.30	0.43
	f1	0.91	0.00	0.32	0.50
	a	0.71			
	Avg a	**0.68**			
	Avg f1	**0.45**			
	Avg wf1	**0.70**			

Even though, the precision values were high for class P for the LDA and RF classifiers, the recall values correspond to 0.66 and 0.71 respectively, as shown in the averages table. The raw values for recall in the folds for the two classifiers ranges from 0.50 to 0.80, and with such variability, is seems that the algorithm is still not capable of detecting all the relevant instances of the P class. The average F1 score for the P class for both classifiers corresponds to 0.79 (see Table 6).

Another thing to notice from the results is that since R (repaired DNA damage) is the most common class in the dataset, the corresponding precision and recall for the LDA classifier are 0.90 and 1.00 respectively; and 0.89 and 0.98 for the RF classifier, as shown in the averages table. The average F1 score was 0.95 and 0.93 for the two best classifiers. This means that a good classification was obtained with any of those classifiers.

Since C (cell cycle arrest) is the least represented class in the dataset, the corresponding average results of precision and recall for the LDA, and RF classifiers are correspondingly 0.59, 0.54, and 0.00, 0.00. The RF classifier obtained 0.00 for precision and recall for all folds in Table 5. The ranges for the average F1 scores for each classifier went from 0.40 to 0.67, and from 0.00 to 0.00 respectively. For this class, the LDA was again the best classifier compared to the other 3.

Table 4. k-fold classification results for the SVM classifier.

k-fold	Metric	R	C	P	A
0	p	0.58	0.00	0.00	0.00
	r	1.00	0.00	0.00	0.00
	f1	0.74	0.00	0.00	0.00
	a	0.58			
1	p	0.62	0.00	0.00	0.00
	r	1.00	0.00	0.00	0.00
	f1	0.76	0.00	0.00	0.00
	a	0.62			
2	p	0.61	0.00	0.00	0.00
	r	1.00	0.00	0.00	0.00
	f1	0.76	0.00	0.00	0.00
	a	0.61			
3	p	0.61	0.00	0.00	0.00
	r	1.00	0.00	0.00	0.00
	f1	0.76	0.00	0.00	0.00
	a	0.61			
	Avg a	**0.61**			
	Avg f1	**0.19**			
	Avg wf1	**0.51**			

With respect to the class A (apoptosis), the best two classifiers are again LDA and RF. The average precision, and recall for that classifiers are 0.80, 0.80, and 0.69, 0.90 respectively. Again, the LDA classifier was the best.

In order to compensate the results for those classes that were not evenly represented, an average weighted f1 (wf1) score was obtained for each of the classifiers. These scores include the results for all the classes. The results are summarized in the Table 7. From that values, it is clear that the LDA classifier outperformed the other selected classifiers for this task. The LDA wf1 obtained was of 0.88, and the average accuracy obtained was of 0.83 and part of our future work will be to extract better features to increase the overall results. With regard to accuracy, the best result corresponds to the RF classifier with a value of 0.85, but the LDA accuracy was 0.83.

In the Fig. 3, a plot from two different perspectives of the LDA classifier data can be seen. The green triangles correspond to the P class, and it can be seen that most of them are separated from the remaining points, making them suitable for a good classification using the LDA classifier. The purple circles correspond to the R class, the repaired DNA damage, which has some instances where the mitosis takes longer time, and somehow can be confused by the classifier as DNA

Table 5. k-fold classification results for the RF classifier.

k-fold	Metric	R	C	P	A
0	p	0.83	0.00	0.78	0.60
	r	0.94	0.00	0.64	0.75
	f1	0.88	0.00	0.70	0.67
	a	0.78			
1	p	0.84	0.00	1.00	0.78
	r	1.00	0.00	0.50	1.00
	f1	0.91	0.00	0.67	0.88
	a	0.85			
2	p	0.94	0.00	1.00	0.67
	r	1.00	0.00	0.90	0.86
	f1	0.97	0.00	0.95	0.75
	a	0.90			
3	P	0.94	0.00	0.89	0.70
	R	0.97	0.00	0.80	1.00
	F1	0.95	0.00	0.84	0.82
	a	0.88			
	Avg a	**0.85**			
	Avg f1	**0.62**			
	Avg wf1	**0.84**			

Table 6. Averages of the metrics per class for the classifiers (in bold the higher results per metric per class).

Metric	R				1				P				A			
	LDA	kNN	SVM	RF	LDA	kNN	SVM	RF	LDA	kNN	SVM	RF	LDA	kNN	SVM	RF
p	**0,90**	0,83	0,61	0,89	**0,59**	0,17	0,00	0,00	**1,00**	0,31	0,00	0,92	**0,80**	0,61	0,00	0,69
r	**1,00**	0,92	**1,00**	0,98	**0,54**	0,15	0,00	0,00	0,66	0,25	0,00	**0,71**	0,80	0,45	0,00	**0,90**
f1	**0,95**	0,87	0,75	0,93	**0,56**	0,16	0,00	0,00	**0,79**	0,28	0,00	**0,79**	0,80	0,52	0,00	0,78

damage proliferation behaviour. This is the reason for some of the green triangles to be mixed with the purple circles in the center of the feature space.

As can be seen in Fig. 3, the red stars and blue squares that correspond to the cell cycle arrest class (C) and the apoptosis class (A) respectively, share similarities and therefore are not linearly separable. In particular, both phenotypes cause the cell to remain in mitosis for longer (than "normal") periods of time, produce no offspring, and have darker values for the pixel intensities. Their differences mainly occurred in their radiuses and circularities.

Table 7. Summary of F1-Scores (**avg F1**) and weighted F1-Scores (**avg wF1**) and accuracies (**avg a**).

Metric	Classifier			
	LDA	kNN	SVM	RF
f1	**0.77**	0.45	0.19	0.62
wf1	**0.87**	0.70	0.51	0.84
a	0.83	0.68	0.61	**0.85**

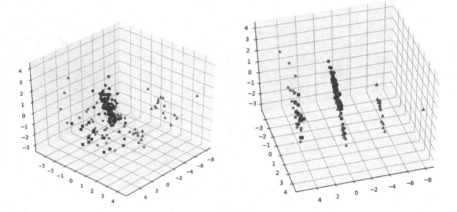

Fig. 3. Plot of the tree-dimensional space obtained after the LDA transformation (two different perspectives). Purple circles: R, blue squares: C, green triangles: P, red stars: A (reproduced from [21]) (Color figure online)

5   Conclusions and Future Work

A relatively successful method to automatically extract and classify the cancer cells' phenotypes based on M-phase features obtained from bright-field microscopy was developed and validated against manually annotated groundtruth.

Four different classifiers were compared in order to find the best one that produces the best classification metrics given the dataset and the groundtruth. That classifier was the LDA classifier, that reached the best average $f1$ scores (0.95, 0.56, 0.79, and 0.80 respectively) for the R, C, P and A classes. The LDA classifier also obtained the best overall average $f1$ and weighted $wf1$ scores of 0.77 and 0.88 compared to the other classifiers. Those values are comparable to previous results in the literature, but using fluorescence or contrast phase microscopy images, and not the more difficult 3J images.

The RF and LDA classifiers have had similar performance for the correct classification of the DNA damage proliferation class (P), reaching similar metrics.

With respect to future work, several courses of action might be taken, for example, for the local tracking used in the detection of the M-start and M-end, a bipartite graph matching (as described in [31]), or a multipartite graph matching (as described in [37]) can be used to increase the accuracy.

Also, a more robust preprocessing stage might prove to be useful in order to increase the contrast and reduce noise in the images, and therefore producing better features, for example by applying a Deceived Bilateral Filter as described in [3–5]. Finally, an optimization of the preprocessing for the removal of the spotlight effect might provide better feature extraction results, and therefore better classification results.

Finally, the addition of more features to the feature vector to be able to increase the distance of the data point in the LDA plot (see Fig. 3) might increase the overall performance of the classifier.

Acknowledgments. The present paper is a partial result of a research project funded by CONARE with a FEES grant entitled *Genomic Functional Analysis of Cancer Cells by Interference RNA for the Identification of Regulation Networks Associated to Proliferation and Death in Response to Genotoxic Chemotherapy* with id 803-B8-653, registered at the Research Center for Tropical Diseases (CIET) and the Department of Electrical Engineering (EIE), both from UCR.

And a special thanks to the PRIS-Lab and LQT members for their help and support during the present work.

References

1. Abbas, S.S., Dijkstra, T., Heskes, T.: A comparative study of cell classifiers for image-based high-throughput screening. BMC Bioinform. **15**(1), 342 (2014). https://doi.org/10.1186/1471-2105-15-342
2. Buggenthin, F., et al.: An automatic method for robust and fast cell detection in bright field images from high-throughput microscopy. BMC Bioinform. **14**, 297 (2013). https://doi.org/10.1186/1471-2105-14-297
3. Calderón, S., Castro, J., Sáenz, A., Siles, F., Mora, R.: Automatic cell segmentation and tracking in the NF-kB pathway using time-lapse fluorescence microscopy videos without nuclear staining. In: VI Latin American Conference on Biomedical Engineering CLAIB 2014, Paraná, Argentina (2014)
4. Calderón, S., Siles, F.: Deceived bilateral filter for improving the classification of football players from TV broadcast. In: 3rd IEEE International Work-Conference on Bioinspired Intelligence, pp. 98–105 (2014). https://doi.org/10.1109/IWOBI. 2014.6913946
5. Calderón, S., Sáenz, A., Mora, R., Siles, F., Orozco, I., Buemi, M.E.: A novel image abstraction approach to improve the performance of a cell tracking system. In: 2015 4th International Work Conference on Bioinspired Intelligence (IWOBI), pp. 81–88 (2015). https://doi.org/10.1109/IWOBI.2015.7160148
6. Carpenter, A., et al.: CellProfiler: image analysis software for identifying and quantifying cell phenotypes. Genome Biol. **7**(10), r100 (2006)
7. Chalfoun, J., Majurski, M., Dima, A., Halter, M., Bhadriraju, K., Brady, M.: Lineage mapper: a versatile cell and particle tracker. Nat. Sci. Rep. **6** (2016). https://doi.org/10.1038/srep36984, Article number: 36984
8. Chen, G., et al.: Targeting the adaptability of heterogeneous aneuploids. Cell **160**(4), 771–784 (2015). https://doi.org/10.1016/j.cell.2015.01.026

9. Chenouard, N., et al.: Objective comparison of particle tracking methods. Nat. Methods **11**, 281 (2014). https://doi.org/10.1038/nmeth.2808

10. Choi, M., Shi, J., Jung, S.H., Chen, X., Cho, K.H.: Attractor landscape analysis reveals feedback loops in the p53 network that control the cellular response to DNA damage. Sci. Sig. **5**(251), 83 (2012). https://doi.org/10.1126/scisignal. 2003363. http://stke.sciencemag.org/content/5/251/ra83.full.pdf

11. Dürr, O., Sick, B.: Single-cell phenotype classification using deep convolutional neural networks. J. Biomol. Screen. **21**(9), 998–1003 (2016). https://doi.org/10. 1177/1087057116631284

12. Giam, M., Rancati, G.: Aneuploidy and chromosomal instability in cancer: a jackpot to chaos. Cell Div. **10**(1) (2015). https://doi.org/10.1186/s13008-015-0009-7

13. Gilad, T., Bray, M.A., Carpenter, A.E., Raviv, T.R.: Symmetry-based mitosis detection in time-lapse microscopy. In: IEEE 12th International Symposium on Biomedical Imaging (ISBI), pp. 164–167 (2015). https://doi.org/10.1109/ISBI. 2015.7163841

14. Grah, J.S., et al.: Mathematical imaging methods for mitosis analysis in live-cell phase contrast microscopy. Image Process. Biol. **115**, 91–99 (2017). https://doi. org/10.1016/j.ymeth.2017.02.001

15. Harder, N., et al.: Automatic analysis of dividing cells in live cell movies to detect mitotic delays and correlate phenotypes in time. Genome Res. **19**(11), 2113–2124 (2009). https://doi.org/10.1101/gr.092494.109. http://genome.cshlp.org/content/19/11/2113.full.pdf+html

16. Hayashi, M.T., Karlseder, J.: DNA damage associated with mitosis and cytokinesis failure. Oncogene **32**(39), 4593–4601 (2013). https://doi.org/10.1038/onc.2012.615

17. National Cancer Institute: NCI dictionary of cancer terms: chemotherapy (2017). https://www.cancer.gov/publications/dictionaries/cancer-terms?cdrid=45214

18. Liu, A., Li, K., Kanade, T.: Spatiotemporal mitosis event detection in time-lapse phase contrast microscopy image sequences. In: 2010 IEEE International Conference on Multimedia and Expo (2010). https://doi.org/10.1109/icme.2010.5583299

19. Luxenburg, C., Pasolli, H.A., Williams, S.E., Fuchs, E.: Developmental roles for Srf, cortical cytoskeleton and cell shape in epidermal spindle orientation. Nat. Cell Biol. **13**(3), 203–214 (2011). https://doi.org/10.1038/Ncb2163

20. Meyer, E.J., Ikmi, A., Gibson, M.C.: Interkinetic nuclear migration is a broadly conserved feature of cell division in pseudostratified epithelia. Curr. Biol. **21**(6), 485–491 (2011). https://doi.org/10.1016/j.cub.2011.02.002

21. Mora-Zúñiga, A.: Cell phenotype classification using M-phase features in live-cell bright field time-lapse microscopy. Master's thesis, PRIS-Lab, Programa de Posgrado en Ingeniería Eléctrica, Universidad de Costa Rica, Costa Rica (2019)

22. Mualla, F., Scholl, S., Sommerfeldt, B., Maier, A., Hornegger, J.: Automatic cell detection in bright-field microscope images using SIFT, random forests, and hierarchical clustering. IEEE Trans. Med. Imaging **32**(12), 2274–2286 (2013). https:// doi.org/10.1109/tmi.2013.2280380

23. Nie, W.Z., Li, W.H., Liu, A.A., Hao, T., Su, Y.T.: 3D convolutional networks-based mitotic event detection in time-lapse phase contrast microscopy image sequences of stem cell populations. In: 2016 IEEE Conference on Computer Vision and Pattern Recognition Workshops (CVPRW), pp. 1359–1366 (2016). https://doi.org/10. 1109/CVPRW.2016.171

24. O'Connor, C.: Cell division: stages of mitosis. Nat. Educ. **1**(1), 188 (2008)

25. Padfield, D., Rittscher, J., Thomas, N., Roysam, B.: Spatio-temporal cell cycle phase analysis using level sets and fast marching methods. Med. Image Anal. **13**(1), 143–155 (2009). https://doi.org/10.1016/j.media.2008.06.018. Includes Special Section on Medical Image Analysis on the 2006 Workshop Microscopic Image Analysis with Applications in Biology

26. Quiros, S., Roos, W., Kaina, B.: Processing of o^6-methylguanine into DNA double-strand breaks requires two rounds of replication whereas apoptosis is also induced in subsequent cell cycles. Cell Cycle **9**(1), 168–178 (2010)

27. Santaguida, S., Amon, A.: Short-and long-term effects of chromosome mis-segregation and aneuploidy. Nat. Rev. Mol. Cell Biol. **16**(8), 473–485 (2015). https://doi.org/10.1038/nrm4025

28. Sauer, F.C.: Mitosis in the neural tube. J. Comp. Neurol. **62**(2), 377–405 (1935). https://doi.org/10.1002/cne.900620207

29. Selinummi, J., et al.: Bright field microscopy as an alternative to whole cell fluorescence in automated analysis of macrophage images. PLoS ONE **4**(10), e7497 (2009). https://doi.org/10.1371/journal.pone.0007497

30. Siles, F.: Estimación de la Forma y Textura Celular para Microscopía In-Situ. Master's thesis, Tesis de Licenciatura, Universidad de Costa Rica (2004)

31. Siles, F.: Automated semantic annotation of football games from TV broadcast. Ph.D. thesis, Dissertation, Technische Universität München (2014)

32. von Stechow, L., van de Water, B., Danen, E.H.J.: Unraveling DNA damage response-signaling networks through systems approaches. Arch. Toxicol. **87**(9), 1635–1648 (2013). https://doi.org/10.1007/s00204-013-1106-5

33. Su, Y., Yu, J., Liu, A., Gao, Z., Hao, T., Yang, Z.: Cell type-independent mitosis event detection via hidden-state conditional neural fields. In: 2014 IEEE 11th International Symposium on Biomedical Imaging (ISBI), pp. 222–225 (2014). https://doi.org/10.1109/isbi.2014.6867849

34. Tkach, J.M., et al.: Dissecting DNA damage response pathways by analysing protein localization and abundance changes during DNA replication stress. Nat. Cell Biol. **14**(9), 966–976 (2012). https://doi.org/10.1038/ncb2549

35. Tuana, G., Volpato, V., Ricciardi-Castagnoli, P., Zolezzi, F., Stella, F., Foti, M.: Classification of dendritic cell phenotypes from gene expression data. BMC Immunol. **12**(1), 50 (2011). https://doi.org/10.1186/1471-2172-12-50

36. Versari, C., et al.: Long-term tracking of budding yeast cells in brightfield microscopy: CellStar and the evaluation platform. J. Roy. Soc. Interface **14**(127) (2017). https://doi.org/10.1098/rsif.2016.0705, http://rsif.royalsocietypublishing.org/content/14/127/20160705.full.pdf

37. Villalta, M., Siles, F.: Parallelization of a multipartite graph matching algorithm for tracking multiple football players. In: 5th IEEE International Conference on Parallel, Distributed and Grid Computing, PDGC 2018, Himachal Pradesh, India (2018)

Special Track on Bioinspired Processing (BIP): Biodiversity Informatics and Computational Biology

Diaforá: A Visualization Tool for the Comparison of Biological Taxonomies

Lilliana Sancho-Chavarría[1]([✉]), Carlos Gómez-Soza[1], Fabian Beck[2], and Erick Mata-Montero[1]

[1] Escuela de Computación, Instituto Tecnológico de Costa Rica, Cartago, Costa Rica
{lsancho,emata}@tec.ac.cr, carlos.gomezsoza@gmail.com
[2] paluno, University of Duisburg-Essen, Duisburg, Germany
fabian.beck@paluno.uni-due.de

Abstract. We address the problem of visualizing differences between two versions of a biological taxonomy. Given the dynamics of the taxonomic work, taxonomists are often faced with alternative versions of a taxonomy that need to be reconciled. Nevertheless, visual comparison of hierarchies is an open problem that involves several difficult challenges in Visual Analytics. First, how to display not one but two possibly large taxonomies on a fixed-size screen. Second, how to highlight all differences between the two taxonomies. We present *Diaforá*, an interactive tool that infers and visualizes the differences. Automatic inference is achieved by incorporating taxonomy rules to identify operations such as merging, splitting, and renaming of taxa, among others. Highlighting of differences is accomplished by using the *edge drawing* technique, which has been enhanced with a number of features suggested by users of a prototype version. *Diaforá* has been implemented and tested with real world taxonomies such as Bryozoa and Annelida as well as with artificial taxonomies.

Keywords: Biological taxonomies · Information visualization · Hierarchy comparison

1 Introduction

Herbaria, museums, and biodiversity conservation initiatives maintain local, regional or global records of species, which are constantly updated due to taxonomic revisions, the discovery of new species, and the need to complete or correct the recorded information. Biological taxonomies are structures in which species are classified hierarchically according to the system proposed by Linnaeus in the 18th century [15, 24], where living organisms are classified into a hierarchical structure that includes the following taxonomic ranks: *domain, kingdom, phylum, class, order, family, genus,* and *species*. Living organisms are classified into groups, for example, birds. From a computing perspective, each group is represented by a node in the hierarchy, which in turn corresponds to a taxon (taxa

© Springer Nature Switzerland AG 2020
J. L. Crespo-Mariño and E. Meneses-Rojas (Eds.): CARLA 2019, CCIS 1087, pp. 423–437, 2020.
https://doi.org/10.1007/978-3-030-41005-6_29

in plural). For instance, the human being has been classified as species *Homo sapiens*, which belongs to the genus *Homo*, to the family *Hominidae*, and to the order *Primates*. In this example, each group designated as *Homo sapiens*, *Homo*, *Hominidae*, and *Primates* correspond to a taxon. Taxonomists analyze the phenotypic characteristics of species given a set of criteria that they consider valid, they classify the species and describe them through scientific peer-reviewed publications. For more than two centuries, taxonomic information was only printed and scattered around the world. Consequently, before the digital revolution, integrating taxonomies developed world wide was not even feasible.

Given the dynamic nature of the biological taxonomies, it is common for taxonomists to come across different versions, which they can correct by applying comparisons. Since taxonomies can be large, the comparison becomes challenging. International initiatives such as Catalogue of Life have recorded approximately 1.8 million species of macro organisms, although many taxonomists believe that the planet's biodiversity is approximately six times that amount.[1]

It is important to mention that in this work we focus on biological taxonomies and not on phylogenetic trees. The latter are also hierarchical classifications of living organisms, but show the evolutionary relationships between species that have a common ancestry, and provide information regarding the evolution of species.

Visualization and comparison between hierarchies has been a prominent research topic in information visualization [8,21]. However, despite these efforts, taxonomists do not yet have visual comparison tools readily available to facilitate the curation of taxonomies. The visualization of large individual hierarchies on a screen is in itself a complex problem because of the amount of taxa involved and limited screen space available. Consequently, comparing two hierarchies is an even more complex problem due to information overload and cluttering. When comparing two versions of a taxonomy, T_1 and T_2, taxonomists must perform several domain specific tasks [23] such as identification of taxa that in T_1 are shown as a single group and in T_2 appear divided (splits), or conversely, taxa that in T_1 appear separately and in T_2 are grouped under the same taxonomic concept (merges), identification of taxa that are located in a different place within the hierarchy (moved taxa), or that appear with a different name (renamed taxa), or that are not in a version of the taxonomy (excluded), or that have been added (added). In our research, we have worked with expert taxonomists from several countries and realized that some taxonomists work with very large groups of species whereas others with small groups. Also, when comparing two versions of a taxonomy, taxonomists might need a global view of the differences before focusing on a smaller group of species, or they might prefer to inspect directly a target group. They also value to have statistical information of the changes.

We present *Diaforá*[2], an interactive tool that automatically computes the differences between two versions of a taxonomy (see Fig. 1). *Diaforá* shows changes

---

[1] The exact number of species of macro organisms is unknown because it is estimated that only about 20% of them have been identified [3].

[2] The word *diaforá* stands for *difference* in Greek.

through explicit representations that make the visual recognition more efficient. It uses the *edge drawing* method for hierarchy comparison and color codes to explicitly represent the changes between the two versions of a taxonomy. It introduces the concept of *visual target synchronization* through which, if a taxon is the focus of interest of the user, the corresponding taxon in the other version of the taxonomy will be moved into the user's visual space so that both taxa can be visually compared side-by-side. It also allows the reorganization of data by users' demand in order to avoid cluttering, and provides visual summaries of the comparison to quickly get an overall sense of the magnitude of the differences. *Diaforá* also supports data cleaning tasks by highlighting, for example, undefined names and other naming errors. It also provides numerical summaries of the taxonomies and of the comparison. The code and sample data are publicly available at https://github.com/lsanchoc/Diafora.

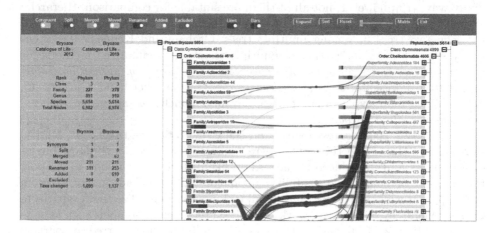

Fig. 1. An overview of *Diaforá*.

For testing, we first used artificial taxonomies in which we introduced representative cases of all types of changes in order to analyze alternative design features. We also tested with real public data from Catalogue of Life with taxonomies of up to approximately 15,000 species, which were displayed without noticeable lags.

This paper is structured as follows. Section 2 presents related work on hierarchy comparison and its application in the comparison of biological taxonomies. Section 3 introduces characteristics of the data. In Sect. 4 we describe the design requirements based on insights from previous research. Section 5 presents the interface design. Section 6 explains some considerations of implementation and testing. In Sect. 7 we discuss results and lessons learned, and finally in Sect. 8 we present conclusions and future work.

2   Related Work

The visual comparison of complex entities, whose complexity is due to multi-dimensionality and large number of components, is a common need in Visual Analytics [5]. It involves finding –visually– differences and similarities between objects of some domain and providing information for analysis. A comparison evidently involves a set of elements to be compared, which have specific characteristics that impose challenges; for example, the challenge of scalability. It also considers tasks of interest to the user, the strategies and methods to facilitate the comparison, and the selected visual design that allows an adequate visualization of the comparison.

Comparisons between hierarchies seek to find differences and similarities between information sets structured as trees. Differences can occur in the topologies and in the data associated with each node. Hierarchies can be represented in many ways [12]; however, not all of them are suitable for comparison. Hierarchy visualization can also consider multiple views [25]. Comparisons can take place between two trees or among multiple trees. Graham and Kennedy [8] extensively studied the visualization of multiple trees and summarized methods for comparing two hierarchies into five categories: *edge drawing, animation, coloring, matrix representation*, and *agglomeration*. On the other hand, Gleicher [6], defines three main types of comparison layouts, namely, *juxtaposition, superposition*, and *explicit encoding*.

The InfoVis 2003 contest focused on the visualization and pairwise comparison of trees [18]. From this contest TreeJuxtaposer [17] compares large phylogenetic trees and introduced an accordion-like distortion technique to support the concept of guaranteed visibility. Zoomology [27] took advantage of zoom techniques as well as overview and detail techniques to visualize the comparison. Further hierarchy comparison works have been reported in domains such as software evolution [2,11,20] and budget comparison [9]. In Biology, tree comparison has been directed to both phylogenetic trees [16,17,19] and biological taxonomies [4,7,14,27]. Tasks for the comparison of biological taxonomies have been characterized [22] and show that taxonomists are interested in the identification of cases where taxa have been involved in splits, merges, moves or renames, or has either been added or removed from a version of a taxonomy. A study on methods for visualizing comparison and performing tasks for biological taxonomies comparison [21] indicates that taxonomists prefer the *edge drawing* representation method over the other techniques defined by Graham and Kennedy [8].

Edge drawing has been an issue in graph visualization because of cluttering when graphs are large [1]. Since trees are a special case of the graphs, they share similar concerns. Hierarchical Edge Bundles (HEB) [10] is a technique that nicely lays out edges while trying to reduce cluttering; however, it shows limitations [11] when it is required to distinguish individual relations among nodes.

3   Data

In simple terms, biological taxonomies are lists of taxa organized hierarchically where each inner taxon represents a category and each lower level taxon in the hierarchy represents a species. Global initiatives such as the Biodiversity Information Standards (TDWG)[3] and the Global Biodiversity Information Facility (GBIF)[4] make great efforts to standardize information in the databases and to promote sharing biodiversity knowledge. However, standardization remains an ongoing issue, because of the dispersion of information throughout databases in the world. Catalogue of Life (COL)[5] holds a comprehensive list of taxonomic information. It gathers about 1.8 million of species from about 168 databases, generates monthly and yearly versions of the lists, and provides open access to the information through JSON/XML/PHP-based web services.

The JSON format is lightweight and facilitates data exchange; however, since it uses textual labels, files could end up being heavy, and this can bring up to memory issues when working with large taxonomies. We reduced the label names to a one-character label (for instance, *n* stands for *name* and *s* for *synonyms*) and the labels are still easy to understand.

We downloaded taxonomies from COL of various sizes and of different years, so that we could compare different year versions. For each taxon, we obtained taxon name, taxonomic rank, source or author(s), date of publication, access date, the list of synonyms, and the list of descendants. Descendants correspond to a lower-level taxonomic rank; for instance, for the genus *Homo*, descendants would be all species that are grouped within that genus (i.e., *Homo rudolfensis*, *Homo helmei*, and *Homo sapiens*, among others). These data fields are fundamental to run the inference algorithms and automatically recognize the differences between the two versions T_1 and T_2 of the taxonomy. It is not just enough to compare the taxa names when looking for differences. We can infer that two taxa refer to the same concept when the name of a taxon, the authors, and the year of publication are the same in both versions of the taxonomy. Synonyms play an indispensable role in the identification of changes because they link a taxon to its previous version. For example, we can recognize that a species x in the version T_1 of the taxonomy was split into three species p, q, and r, if x appears in T_2 as synonym of those three species. The more complete and accurate are the databases, the more precise would be the automatic inference of changes.

4   Design Requirements

The problem to be solved is the visualization of differences between two versions of a biological taxonomy. It is necessary not only to recognize general-type changes (e.g., difference in size between the two hierarchies) but also what are

---

[3] https://www.tdwg.org/.
[4] https://www.gbif.org/.
[5] http://www.catalogueoflife.org/.

the types of changes that occurred (e.g., if there were splits) as well as the specific changes (e.g., taxon x was split into p, q, and r). We consider insights obtained from previous research [21] as a framework of reference for the design of the tool. We synthesize the design requirements in terms of six aspects: the representation of the hierarchies, the comparison layout, the explicit representation of changes, multiple views, visual and numerical summaries, and efficiency.

- **Hierarchy representation.** Taxa names legibility is mandatory for taxonomists to analyze the taxonomies and to understand their differences. Thus, taxa names should be readable and visible at all times and the hierarchical representation should be such as to facilitate the reading of names. Compact representations of hierarchies, such as matrices, treemaps and icicle plots make an efficient use of space because nodes can be represented through a few pixels, so that large hierarchies can be displayed in a small area. They provide overview information as well as the possibility to identify patterns in changes. However, the space left to display the labels (that is, the taxa names) is so small that they are difficult to read or cannot be shown at all. The requirement of legibility of names lead us to consider indented lists as a design alternative.

- **Comparison layout.** Our framework of reference indicates that taxonomists preferred the *edge drawing* method over *matrix representation, animation* and *agglomeration*. Therefore, we consider a juxtaposed design that uses *edge drawing* as the central method to visualize the comparison. Taxonomies should be placed separately, side by side, to ease the comparison.

  In addition to representation, the role of interaction is key in information visualization. Interaction is also key in visual comparison [13] and it encompasses techniques such as: select, explore, encode, filter, connect and abstract/elaborate [26]. Given the potential number of relationships that could be visualized between the two taxonomies, selecting is necessary for users to study a type of change or a taxon of interest. By exploring, users should be able to examine a subset of the data (e.g., a family or a genus). Coding visual information into numerical information can allow users to quantify changes. Filtering is required to search for information that meets certain conditions (for instance, to know which species have been published by the same author). In the case of taxonomy comparison through the *edge drawing method*, connecting can be naturally implemented by the relationships among taxa, i.e., edges, which highlight changes between the two versions of the taxonomy.

- **Explicit representation of differences.** It is important for taxonomists to be able to recognize differences quickly and to clearly spot the *origin* and *destination* of changes. The *edge drawing* method fulfills this requirement, where edges take the leading role in the explicit representation of changes. In the main view, changes can be represented explicitly by colored lines that go from taxa in T_1 to taxa in T_2. The use of color for the explicit representation of changes is also very useful. All types of changes and all changes should be visualized by means of distinctive colors. In our design color is used as following: pink for splits, orange for merges, brown for moves, blue for renames, red for exclusions, and green for added taxa.

In spite that edges make relations easy to understand, cluttering might be a problem. The hierarchical edge bundling technique was introduced to represent hierarchical graphs and reduce clutter [10], and then applied to the visual comparison of hierarchies [11]. Hierarchical edge bundling nicely packs together edges and, at the same time, the resulting visualizations provide overview information on changes. However, individual edges are hard to distinguish and, since the visual comparison of biological taxonomies requires clear recognition of origin and destination, the bundles should be such that this relationship does not get lost. The solution should reduce edge congestion and crossings but edges should clearly communicate individual relations, showing origin and destination.

- **Multiple views.** While the main method we propose for comparing taxonomies is edge drawing, in a previous work we found that expert taxonomists consider that comparison using matrices works better than edge drawing when it comes to globally overviewing changes and, that by combining several methods, the disadvantages of one method could be outweighed by the advantages of another. We propose a design in which global comparison is accomplished through a matrix representation and, by selecting an area of interest in the matrix, users can navigate to the edge drawing view where changes are visualized in more detail.

- **Visual and numerical summaries.** Visually identifying differences between higher level corresponding taxonomic groups is more complex than identifying differences at the species level because it requires more mental effort for users to summarize what happens at lower levels. Through summaries (visual and numerical) users could obtain information on the magnitude of changes at each taxonomic level.

- **Efficiency.** This involves effective and quick identification of differences as well as good performance in the visualization of large taxonomies. The first one is transversely addressed by the other five design criteria discussed here; for example, the more legible are the taxonomies and the more explicit the changes, the more efficient will be the identification of changes. The second one refers to how quickly taxonomies area loaded and to the response time during navigation.

5   Interface Design

Figure 2 illustrates the visual design of *Diaforá*. The window is divided into three panes. Pane 1 contains the main menu, pane 2 displays the numerical summaries of the comparison, and pane 3 is reserved for visualizing the comparison of the taxonomies.

The main menu (pane 1) is divided into five parts. Part A contains seven toggle buttons to perform the domain specific tasks for the identification of similarities and differences; that is, for the identification of congruent taxa, splits,

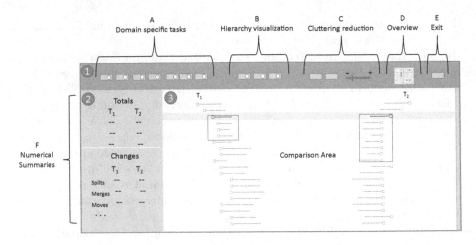

Fig. 2. The interface layout of *Diaforá*.

merges, moves, renames, added taxa, and excluded taxa. The toggle buttons allow users to visualize either one specific type of change or all changes. Part B contains buttons to control the hierarchy look; that is, a button to add or remove the hierarchy lines, a button to expand all sub-trees of a selected node down to the leaf level, and a button that would display the visual summary of changes next to each high-level taxon. Part C of the main menu includes functions to manage edge cluttering. It contains functions designed to reorganize the taxa within T_2, as close as possible to their related taxa in order to reduce edge cluttering. The menu also considers a reset button to return to the initial state of the taxonomies when they were first loaded. Another edge-managing function in this part of the menu is a slider control used to separate the edges when they appear too close together, making it easier to distinguish individual relations. Part D of the menu is reserved to navigate to an alternative overview, implemented through a matrix representation, that will be added to the tool in future work. Finally, part E for the menu is for exiting the system.

Pane 2 presents numerical summaries. The top part of the pane provides a summary on the structure of the taxonomies for each taxonomic rank; that is, it shows the amount of species, genera, families, orders, etc. of the two taxonomies being compared. The bottom part of the pane provides statistics on the amount of changes of the selected taxon; that is, it indicates the amount of splits, merges, renames, etc. that the comparison found.

Visual comparison takes place in pane 3, where hierarchies are placed juxtaposed, in a mirrored arrangement. Hierarchies are represented by indented lists where hierarchical relations are highlighted through edges. The edges are optional to keep the comparison area as clear as possible. The mirrored arrangement is also a strategy to avoid crossings between the lines of the hierarchy and the edges. A drawback of node-link representations is the limitation on the number of nodes that can be displayed on the screen. To counteract, we make use of collapse/expand and zoom in/out mechanisms, which make it possible to enlarge and reduce the number of nodes in the visual space through interaction.

We synchronize the user selected taxon with the corresponding taxon in the alternative taxonomy; the alternative taxonomy moves either up or down, so that the two compared taxa are placed next to each other, highlighted by a horizontal grey line, in order to ease comparison (see Fig. 2). Taxonomists might want to understand what happened to either a specific species or to a group of species and might require to do visual searches, so navigation throughout the different levels in the taxonomy should be fluid. *Diaforá* lets users fully expand a branch of their interest. As users expand a selected branch, the corresponding changes of its descendants are refreshed.

The *edge drawing* method can clearly communicate the changes between the two versions of the taxonomy. The distinctive colors make it easy to recognize the different types of changes. Users can interact with the visualization and inspect changes that call their attention. Changes at the species level can be noticed by individual links between the involved taxa. Changes between higher-level groups (for example, between two versions of a genus or between two versions of a family) are displayed in two ways. One, for a higher level collapsed taxon, the amount of displayed links depicts the amount of differences detected between the two groups. The resulting thickness of the accumulated edges between the two compared taxa provides a cue on the magnitude of the changes for that group; although it has been limited to the height of the text. Second, changes between higher-level groups are summarized by bars that indicate the amount of changes proportional to the size of the group. This satisfies the design requirements on visual summaries (see Fig. 3). Visual summaries of changes are shown encoded as colored bars next to each higher level taxon. The assigned colors correspond to the previously discussed color coding for each type of change. The example illustrates the summary view when performing a comparison at *class*-level for the class *Clitellanata*. The pink color in the bar on the left refers to the amount of splitted taxa found in the *Clitellanata* group in T_1, and the green color in the bar on the right provides the amount of added taxa to the *Clitellanata* group in T_2. Additionally, the amount of species of each group is displayed next to each taxon name.

Fig. 3. Visual summary of the comparison between higher-level groups.

Cluttering of the edges is reduced in *Diaforá* in two ways: by grouping the edges and also by ordering the taxa. Edges are grouped by using a density-based spatial clustering algorithm (DBScan). We calculate a common central point where nearby edges are grouped. They are not bundled as in hierarchical edge bundling [10,11] because in taxonomy comparison we always need to have the notion of origin and destination. The bundling we use can be controlled through the slider on the main menu. Users can also order the taxa through a commutation function (i.e, *Sort* function on the top panel). Commutation does not alter the hierarchical relationships but makes edges that go to the same neighborhood to be grouped together in order to provide a cleaner visual space.

Computational efficiency when dealing with large taxonomies is approached by implementing a paging mechanism that loads into memory only the visible area of the screen, which contributes to the efficient management of pairs of large taxonomies.

6   Implementation and Testing

Figure 4 presents the implementation of *Diaforá*'s main window. It shows the comparison of versions 2012 and 2018 of the phylum *Cnidaria*. Notice how the thickness of edges provides a cue on magnitude of changes. In this case, the visualization indicates that many taxa were renamed (blue edges), also that new taxa was added (green names), some taxa were excluded (red names) and few taxa were merged (orange edge). The tool was implemented in Processing 3.4, HTML, database MongoDB, server Node.js and data files in JSON format.

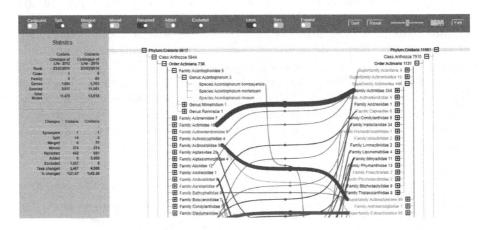

Fig. 4. Example containing *Diaforá*'s main window. (Color figure online)

We tested *Diaforá* with three pairs of taxonomies: Lycopodiopsida 2012 (158 species) VS Lycopodiopsida 2018 (1,415 species) for a total of 1,573 loaded, Marchantiophyta 2012 (773 species) VS Marchantiophyta 2018 (7,433 species) for a total of 8,206 species, and Annelida 2012 (12,635 species) VS Annelida 2019 (15,016 species) for a total of 27,651 species. All sets of taxonomies were loaded easily, smoothly visualized, and navigation and interaction were fluid. Further, we did profiling tests to know *Diaforá*'s usage of memory and CPU, and rendering times as taxonomies size increased. Our goal was to find out and extrapolate the impact of size on the tool's performance. We used the Google Chrome profiler tool. Testing results are presented in Fig. 5. Results indicate low increase on CPU and rendering times as taxonomy size increases. The displaying time is almost constant in all three cases; this is explained by the paging strategy where only the expanded taxa located within the boundaries of the screen are displayed. RAM presented the highest variation. Notice that, when comparing the Lycopodiopsida versions (1,573 species total), memory usage was 59.1 MB, for Marchantiophyta (8,206 species total) memory usage was 59.7 MB, and for Annelida (27,651 species total) memory usage increased to 140 MB. If we assume that the tool uses a constant amount of RAM for the browser and code, we can estimate that the increase from Lycopodiopsida to Annelida was 26.078 species and 81 MB, which represents a memory increase of 3.18 KB per specie approximately. We can use this number to extrapolate to any taxonomy size; for instance, a pair of taxonomies that sum up 100,000 species would require approximately 370 MB of RAM (that is, 59 MB + 3.1 KB * 100,000), which is a reasonable number. In other words, testing indicates that *Diaforá* tool is expected to perform well as taxonomies size increases.

7 Discussion

Diaforá contributes to taxonomists work in identifying differences and similarities between two versions of a taxonomy. Our work concentrates on the comparison of two taxonomies given that it is more likely that taxonomists perform pairwise comparison when looking for differences between a version that is familiar to them and a reference version. *Diaforá* was tested with pairs of taxonomies that together summed up to 27,651 species. It provides visual information for users to quickly recognize changes and it also provides numerical summaries on changes, which give information about the magnitude of the differences.

The availability of data is fundamental for testing the tool. We chose COL data because they provide access to taxonomic lists from several years, which makes it easier to have data in order to compare two versions of the same taxonomy. Through COL web services, we are able to download a complete version of the taxonomy or parts of it by selecting a specific taxon. The COL database is constantly being updated and improved, and it is likely that some detected changes between two different year versions are due to database cleaning instead of taxonomic reasons. Changes due to taxonomic reasons would be such as the discovery of a new species or the redefinition of the taxonomic concept; for instance, a species of trees that had been considered part of a genus and recently taxonomists considered that it should be classified under another genus. Database cleaning usually involves completing missing information, for example, authors name or synonyms, and correcting misspelling. As a species is identified by the triplet (name, authors, year) a change in any of these data

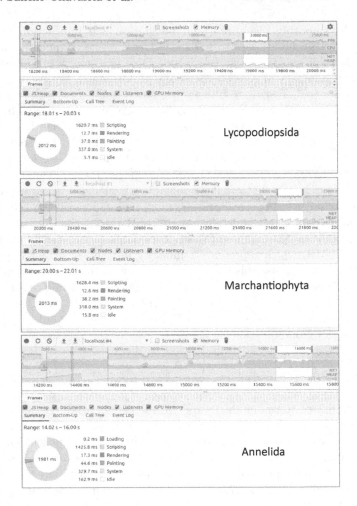

Fig. 5. Profiling tests.

could be interpreted as a *rename*, despite what happened was an update of the data. We notice that the visual comparison is useful not only to identify the differences and similarities between two versions of a taxonomy but also to discover inconsistencies and assist with data cleansing. It is also important to highlight that the precision of the inference algorithms for the identification of differences relies on the completeness and accuracy of the data.

Previous works on the comparison of biological taxonomies differ from *Diaforá* specially on the types of differences that the tool is capable of visualizing. We base our work on a set of required tasks for the curation of the taxonomies (i.e., identify splits, identify merges, etc.) whereas other works focus on the visualization of structural differences between the taxonomies [17], ancestor or descendants differences [14] or genus-corresponding species within other taxonomies [7]. The design requirements and features of *Diaforá* come from a research work where 12 experts provided feedback to a preceding version (functional prototype) of the tool [21] and so our contribution lies on the visual identification of changes that would support the curation tasks. Besides the specific identification of *splits, merges*, taxa *moved, renamed, added*, or *excluded, Diaforá* presents visual cues on the magnitude of changes at higher-level taxa, as well as numerical summaries of the comparison, which aid in the identification of changes at an overview level. Additionally, the strategies implemented to reduce edge cluttering within the comparison area (i.e, the reorganization of taxa without losing the hierarchical structure, and the way edges are bundled) make the visualization cleaner for comparison.

8 Conclusions and Future Work

In this work we described a set of design requirements and proposed a visualization tool to solve the problem of visualizing and identifying differences between two versions of a biological taxonomy. We presented a tool that automatically infers the differences and highlights them through direct and explicit representation of changes. Both the visual representation of changes and the numerical summaries provide quick and valuable information to users.

Future work will be directed to perform several user studies and usability tests. We would like to test *Diaforá* with taxonomies that come from different organizations (different origins) and experiment with the data in order to get insights for further work. We also expect to add edit functionality to the tool, so that taxonomists would not only be able to quickly visualize the differences but also would decide which changes keep and which not, in order to support the curation process of a taxonomy.

Acknowledgments. This research is funded in part by Instituto Tecnológico de Costa Rica. We also want to thank Computer Science student Bryan Hernández for his support on data acquisition and formatting.

References

1. Bach, B., Henry-Riche, N., Hurter, C., Marriott, K., Dwyer, T.: Towards unambiguous edge bundling: investigating confluent drawings for network visualization. IEEE Trans. Vis. Comput. Graph. **23**(1), 541–550 (2017)
2. Beck, F., Wiszniewsky, F.J., Burch, M., Diehl, S., Weiskopf, D.: Asymmetric visual hierarchy comparison with nested icicle plots. In: Joint Proceedings of the Fourth International Workshop on Euler Diagrams and the First International Workshop on Graph Visualization in Practice, pp. 53–62. GraphVIP (2014)
3. Census of Marine Life: How many species on Earth? About 8.7 million, new estimate says (2011). https://www.sciencedaily.com/releases/2011/08/110823180459. htm

4. Dang, T., Franz, N., Ludäscher, B., Forbes, A.G.: ProvenanceMatrix: a visualization tool for multi-taxonomy alignments. In: Proceedings of the International Workshop on Visualizations and User Interfaces for Ontologies and Linked Data. CEUR Workshop Proceedings, vol. 1456, p. 13. CEUR-WS.org (2015)
5. Gleicher, M.: Considerations for visualizing comparison. IEEE Trans. Vis. Comput. Graph. **24**(1), 413–423 (2018)
6. Gleicher, M., Albers, D., Walker, R., Jusufi, I., Hansen, C.D., Roberts, J.C.: Visual comparison for information visualization. Inf. Vis. **10**(4), 289–309 (2011)
7. Graham, M., Craig, P., Kennedy, J.: Visualisation to aid biodiversity studies through accurate taxonomic reconciliation. In: Gray, A., Jeffery, K., Shao, J. (eds.) BNCOD 2008. LNCS, vol. 5071, pp. 280–291. Springer, Heidelberg (2008). https://doi.org/10.1007/978-3-540-70504-8_29
8. Graham, M., Kennedy, J.: A survey of multiple tree visualisation. Inf. Vis. **9**(4), 235–252 (2010)
9. Guerra-Gómez, J.A., Buck-Coleman, A., Plaisant, C., Shneiderman, B.: TreeVersity: interactive visualizations for comparing two trees with structure and node value changes. In: Proceedings Conference of the Design Research Society, vol. 1, p. 10 (2012)
10. Holten, D.: Hierarchical edge bundles: visualization of adjacency relations in hierarchical data. IEEE Trans. Vis. Comput. Graph. **12**, 741–748 (2006)
11. Holten, D., van Wijk, J.J.: Visual comparison of hierarchically organized data. Comput. Graph. Forum **27**(3), 759–766 (2008)
12. Jürgensmann, S., Schulz, H.J.: A visual survey of tree visualization. Poster at Proceedings of IEEE Information Visualization. IEEE (2010)
13. von Landesberger, T.: Insights by visual comparison: the state and challenges. IEEE Comput. Graph. Appl. **38**(3), 140–148 (2018)
14. Lin, C., Qiao, H., Wang, J., Ji, L.: The taxonomic tree tool. http://ttt.biodinfo.org/TF/
15. Linn, C., Gmelin, J.F.: Systema naturae per regna tria naturae: secundum classes, ordines, genera, species, cum characteribus, differentiis, synonymis, locis., vol. Tomus 1. Impensis Georg Emanuel Beer, Lipsiae (1767)
16. Liu, Z., Zhan, S.H., Munzner, T.: Aggregated dendrograms for visual comparison between many phylogenetic trees. IEEE Trans. Vis. Comput. Graph. **PP**(99), 1 (2019). https://doi.org/10.1109/TVCG.2019.2898186
17. Munzner, T., Guimbretière, F., Tasiran, S., Zhang, L., Zhou, Y.: TreeJuxtaposer: scalable tree comparison using Focus+Context with guaranteed visibility. ACM Trans. Graph. **22**(3), 453–462 (2003)
18. Plaisant, C., Fekete, J.D., Grinstein, G.: Promoting insight-based evaluation of visualizations: from contest to benchmark repository. IEEE Trans. Vis. Comput. Graph. **14**(1), 120–134 (2008)
19. Robinson, O., Dylus, D., Dessimoz, C.: Phylo.io: interactive viewing and comparison of large phylogenetic trees on the web. Mol. Biol. Evol. **33**(8), 2163–2166 (2016)
20. Rufiange, S., Melançon, G.: AniMatrix: a matrix-based visualization of software evolution. In: Proceedings of the 2nd IEEE Working Conference on Software Visualization, VISSOFT 2014, pp. 137–146 (2014)
21. Sancho-Chavarria, L., Beck, F., Mata-Montero, E.: An expert study on hierarchy comparison methods applied to biological taxonomies curation. PeerJ Preprints **7**, e27903v1 (2019). https://doi.org/10.7287/peerj.preprints.27903v1

22. Sancho-Chavarria, L., Beck, F., Mata-Montero, E., Weiskopf, D.: Visual comparison of biological taxonomies: a task characterization. In: Poster Submitted and Presented at EuroVis2016 (2016)
23. Sancho-Chavarria, L., Beck, F., Weiskopf, D., Mata-Montero, E.: Task-based assessment of visualization tools for the comparison of biological taxonomies. Res. Ideas Outcomes **4** (2018). https://doi.org/10.3897/rio.4.e25742
24. Schuh, R.T.: Biological Systematics: Principles and Applications. Cornell University Press, Ithaca (2000)
25. Teoh, S.T.: A study on multiple views for tree visualization, vol. 6495, p. 64950B. International Society for Optics and Photonics (2007)
26. Yi, J.S., ah Kang, Y., Stasko, J.: Toward a deeper understanding of the role of interaction in information visualization. IEEE Trans. Vis. Comput. Graph. **13**(6), 1224–1231 (2007)
27. Hong, J.Y., D'Andries, J., Richman, M., Westfall, M.: Zoomology: comparing two large hierarchical trees. In: Proceedings IEEE InfoVis Poster Compendium, pp. 120–121. IEEE Computer Society Press, Seattle (2003)

A First Glance into Reversing Senescence on Herbarium Sample Images Through Conditional Generative Adversarial Networks

Juan Villacis-Llobet$^{(\boxtimes)}$, Marco Lucio-Troya, Marvin Calvo-Navarro,
Saul Calderon-Ramirez, and Erick Mata-Montero

Instituto Tecnológico de Costa Rica, Cartago, Costa Rica
{jvillacis,mlucio,mcalvo}@ic-itcr.ac.cr,
{sacalderon,emata}@itcr.ac.cr

Abstract. In this paper we describe a novel approach to perform senescense reversal on photos of leaves based on Conditional Generative Adversarial Networks, which have been used succesfully to perform similar tasks on faces of humans and other picture to picture translations. We show that their use can lead to a valid solution to this problem, as long as the task of creating a large and comprehensive dataset is surpassed. Additionally, we present a new dataset that consists of 120 paired photos of leaves manually collected for this work, in their fresh and senescenced states. We used the structure similarity index to compare the ground truth with the generated images and yielded an average of 0.9.

Keywords: Senescence · Herbaria · Conditional-GANs · Bioinformatics

1 Introduction

Herbaria around the world have accumulated valuable collections of plant samples over the course of several centuries. The process of cataloguing and systematically storing specimen samples that has been carried out by specialists now provides a large pool of data that can be used for research purposes. Collected samples undergo a curation process that involves adding geospatial and taxonomic metadata, drying and carefully placing each dried sample on a separate sheet of paper, and then placing this *herbarium sheet* inside a large manila folder to keep the specimens from getting accidentally harmed in any way [4]. This process that dries up plant sample – known in the natural world as *senescence* – primarily causes changes in the color, texture and shape of the specimens that can be significant and lead to problems when relating fresh samples with those stored in herbaria [17].

Because the majority of professionally tagged images of plants are in datasets of digitized herbarium sheets, reversing this senescense process can be very useful

© Springer Nature Switzerland AG 2020
J. L. Crespo-Mariño and E. Meneses-Rojas (Eds.): CARLA 2019, CCIS 1087, pp. 438–447, 2020.
https://doi.org/10.1007/978-3-030-41005-6_30

in the field of biodiversity informatics, specially for plant species identification with machine learning models, where researchers need large datasets of images of plants to train their models [7,15]. Reversing senescense is further supported by the work of Carranza-Rojas et al. [4], which shows that the accuracy of deep learning algorithms that use herbarium sheets to identify fresh samples of plants is too low. So, a digital process of "aging" the fresh sample to be identified or "rejuvenating" the dataset of dried herbarium sheets are worth exploring. In our work we investigate the latter.

Other areas in which these methods can have useful applications are in the entertainment industry, specially in the film and video games industry, where it can be applied to generate realistic renderings of non-static scenes, where the leaves of trees can change over time [6,17]. Most papers discussing the subject of rendering realistic trees and leaves on videogames discuss the topics of lighting, wind, shadows, detail and movement, but leave out the topic of senescense [3].

We approach the challenge of reversing senescence on herbarium sheet images by focusing on leaves only. To our knowledge no previous publication has tackled the problem of reversing senescence on images of leaves. The opposite problem of simulating senescence has been studied more deeply. Previous work has proposed the use of triangulation and Voronoi Diagramas [13], geometry and color maps [17], models based on physics and geometry [6], and correlating the amount of chlorophyll on leaves with their color [16]. Although these approaches have had some level of success, they have important constraints, such as their fixture on leaf or shape only [17] and their dependence on data that is difficult and expensive to obtain, such as chlorophyll level in leaves [16] and venation maps [17]. Novel approaches used to simulate aging use Generative Adversarial Networks (GANs), such as in [2] and [19], where they use this kind of networks to simulate aging while preserving the identity on faces of people. These approaches have taken advantage of the ability of GANs to generate images of extraordinary visual fidelity [2]. Other papers that have proposed the use of GANs to apply transformations on images include [11], where they propose a model that can apply image-to-image translations, such as in day-to-night, cats-to-dogs and borders-to-images.

In addition to the results presented in this paper we also worked on the development of a small benchmark dataset that comprises 60 images of leaves from three different species. For each image we provide a photo of the leaf in its fresh state and a photo of the leaf after it has been dried in a herbarium setting. In total, the dataset comprises 120 images. Figure 1 presents one example of a pair of leaves from the dataset, where the left leaf is fresh and the right one has been dried.

In this paper we propose the use of the pi2pix model presented in [11] to reverse senescence on images of leaves. Our use of GANs is based on the success had by [11] when this approach is applied to other types of translations between images.

This paper is structured as follows, Sect. 2 explores the state of the art concerning simulation of senescence on images of leaves and other objects of interest.

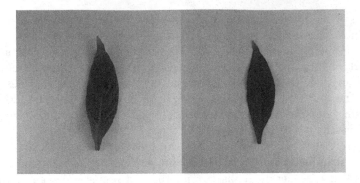

Fig. 1. An example of the leaves in the dataset created for the experiments. The left side image is the young one and the right side one is the senescent one

Section 3 describes the methodology followed to carry out this research, Sect. 4 describes the results obtained in the experiments and in Sect. 5 we present the conclusions obtained and further work which could be carry on this domain.

2   State of the Art

In this section we describe the approaches employed by other researchers when they tackle the problem of simulating aging/senescense on images of leaves or other objects of interest. We also describe approaches used by other researchers when they address the problem of applying a transformation to an image. Their works are categorized in the following paragraphs according to the techniques they employ in their experiments.

One example of approaches to simulate senescence is the work by Silva et al. [17]. They present a method to simulate the color evolution in leaves or petals during their growth and senescent phases. They consider each leaf and petal represented as a geometry color map, which will change the color from its initial value to a value that would be very similar by natural aging. For the input flow it uses a venation map, that represents the fluidity at each point in the leaf. Each pixel in this map represents how easily the fluid flows in that region. White values represent more flow capacity, and as the pixels get darker it represents less flow capacity. Then, it uses a diffusion process to simulate the flow in the venation. For the outward flow it uses a stomata map. It considers the evaporation as a form of extracting the fluid out of the leaf. Each pixel in this map represents how easily the fluid flows out of that region. White means more transpiration and it goes down as the color gets darker. To create the senescent color image, they use a sample image of a senescent leaf as reference and perform histogram matching [12]. To mimic the color of a senescent leaf, it helps if the reference image content is an example of the desired color.

Generative adversarial networks are increasingly used for image-to-image translation. Many problems in image processing, graphics, and computer vision involve translating an input image into a corresponding output image. These problems are often treated with application-specific algorithms, even though the setting is always the same: map pixels to pixels. In [2,19] GANs are used to produce the most plausible and realistic images of aged faces.

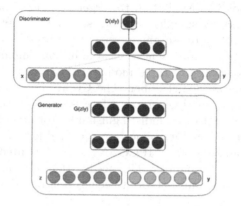

Fig. 2. Applications of CGANs taken from [11]

In [11], Isola et al. present conditional generative adversarial networks as a general-purpose solution that performed adequately on a variety of image-to-image translations. Their framework generalizes the pixel to pixel mapping, in spite to prior work. Figure 2 shows some examples of problems tackled with the proposed framework. It is important to mention that for each case, the same architecture and objective were used, only training data differs. As seen, there are diverse tasks represented in Fig. 2; from label to scene generation, to coloring black and white pictures, generating a map representation from a given aerial photo, and day to night conversion [11]. Isola et al. conclude that conditional adversarial networks are a promising approach for many image-to-image translation tasks. These networks learn a loss adapted to the task and data at hand, which makes them applicable in a wide variety of settings.

Cycle generative adversarial networks, commonly known as CycleGANs, work without paired examples of transformations from source to target domain. The CycleGAN is able to learn such transformations without one-to-one mappings between training data in the source and target domains. By making a two-step transformation of the source domain image, the need for a paired image in the target domain is eliminated. This two-step transformation consists of, first trying to map it to the target domain and then back to the original image. A generator network is used to map the image to the target domain. The generated image quality is improved by launching the generator against a discriminator. In the work by Zhu et al. [14], they present an approach for learning to translate an image from a source domain X to a target domain Y, in the absence of paired examples by using cycle-Consistent Adversarial Networks. The model includes two mappings $G : X \rightarrow Y$ and $F : Y \rightarrow X$. They use an adversarial loss [9] to learn the mapping $G : X \rightarrow Y$ such that the translated image $G(X)$ cannot be distinguished from images in the target domain Y. Because this mapping is highly under-constrained, they couple it with an inverse mapping $F : Y \rightarrow X$. To regularize the model, the authors introduce the constraint of cycle-consistency, to prevent the learned mappings G and F from contradicting each other. If we transform from source distribution to target and then back again to source distribution, we should get samples from our source distribution.

In [19], Wang et al. propose an approach to avoid losing specific subject identity traits when performing synthethical aging on human faces. To achieve that, the model is composed of three modules: a CGANs module, an identity-preserved module and an age classifier. The CGAN takes an input image and a target age as its input, and generates a face resembling the target age. This generated face is expected to be indistinguishable from real faces. To maintain the identity information, they introduce a preceptual loss [1] in the objective of the CGAN. As the authors state, IPCGANs are not limited to the face aging problem, it is a general framework. This means that without any modification it can be applied to other multi-attribute generation tasks.

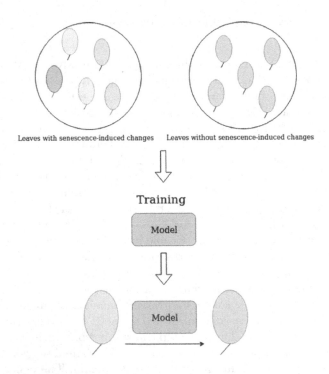

Leaves with senescence-induced changes   Leaves without senescence-induced changes

Training

Model

Model

Fig. 3. Methodology used in the experiments

3 Proposed Method

The main objective of this paper is to develop a method that can reverse senescence on images of leaves. As a result, it creates new samples that can be used to train models for plant species identification for a given image of a fresh leaf. In this section we describe the methodology employed to tackle this problem. The pipeline of tasks performed can be observed in Fig. 3.

3.1 Dataset

Due to the lack of data in the domain of this problem we created a new dataset in order to perform the experiments. This dataset is composed of 20 images of each of the following species: *Pachystachys lutea*, *Lantana camara* and *Catharanthus roseus*, collected in the wild. For each specie the leaves where taken from 5 different specimens. While the leaves where still fresh their front sides where photographed with a white background. Following this, they where dried using a special oven from the School of Forestry of the Costa Rica Institute of Technology. Finally, the dataset was completed by taking pictures of the front side of each of the dried leaves. In total we collected 120 images, 40 per species, and each specie has 20 photos of dry leaves and another 20 photos of fresh leaves. Each photo of a fresh leaf has its counterpart in the photos of dry leaves. The dataset can be found in the following repository https://www.github.com/4a75616e/leavesdryfresh.

Fig. 4. Generated image for *Pachystachys lutea*

3.2 Senescence Reversion

For the process of reversing senescence we trained a pix2pix model [11] with a dataset that contains images that belong to two classes. Pix2pix is based in a conditional generative adversarial network, which is simple to train and receives the pair of images (fresh and dried leaf).

The first class corresponds to images of leaves that have gone trough senescence, the other class consists of the fresh leaves counterpart.

Figure 1 shows an example of a leaf in class A and its counterpart in class B. The pix2pix model is trained to transform senescenced images into images of fresh leaves. Figure 3 shows the pipeline followed to perform this training. The model was trained on the dataset described previously, with 80% of the images used for training and 20% for validation.

Fig. 5. Generated image for *Lantana camara*

4   Experiments and Results

The model was trained 10 times (replicas) using the same hyper-parameters to give it statistical validity. For each run the weights in the generator and the discriminator where initialized using a normal distribution with mean 0 and standard deviation 0.2 For each of the 10 runs the results are described in Table 1. After the translation has been performed, an important step is to measure the quality of the results generated by the model. To quantitatively compare the output of the model to the ground truth we propose the use of the structural similarity index [20], a measure of the similarity between two images. This technique is used due to its advantages over other methods like mean squared error [18], which are not good indicators of human perception of image fidelity and quality.

In Figs. 4, 5 and 6 it is possible to observe the generated image for each specie.

Table 1. Results for 10 executions of the model

Run	Overall SSIM	SSIM for *Catharanthus roseus b*	SSIM for *Lantana camara p*	SSIM for *Pachystachys lutea i*
1	0.897916	0.901575	0.91325	0.878925
2	0.897141	0.901825	0.9116	0.878
3	0.898225	0.903175	0.913225	0.878275
4	0.897283	0.902274	0.911825	0.87775
5	0.896241	0.900375	0.910525	0.877825
6	0,904283	0,9134	0,915075	0,884375
7	0,9035	0,913475	0,91275	0,884275
8	0,903925	0,912625	0,91365	0,885225
9	0,90383	0,912625	0,91365	0,885225
10	0,903683	0,91175	0,913925	0,885375
Averages for all runs	0.903845	0.912775	0.91381	0.884895

Input Image   Ground Truth   Predicted Image

Fig. 6. Generated image for *Catharanthus roseus*

5 Conclusions and Future Work

From the results shown in Table 1, we can conclude that the model yielded stable and moderately high structure similarity indices in the ten executions. These results, although preliminary, suggest that the use of conditional-GANs could be a valid solution for reversing leaf senescence, even with a relatively small dataset.

The source and destination domains are very similar given that both are photos of the same leaves with several modifications due to the drying process, primarily in color, shape and size. By observing the resulting images it can be seen that the most significant changes made by the generative network to the input correspond to a size increase and a lightening in color. These could indicate that the model learned the significant features that differentiate dried leaves from fresh leaves. The SSIM measurement values obtained indicate that the model had a similar behaviour for leaves of different species, although the average for *Pachystachys lutea* is slightly lower than the other two. This might be caused by a higher variance between the size of the leaves of this specie in the dataset; several of the leaves in the dataset are small while the others are large; there is no such variance for the other species.

The dataset we built can be considered as moderately challenging, as the species of the dried leafs did not suffer of significant changes, as seen in Fig. 4. In the near future we plan to make the dataset larger and include more species. Also, both the front and back side of each leaf should be used, as for different species it has been shown [5] that one could be more significant the other. Existing herbarium datasets are not useful for training, Conditional GANs as only images of the dried specimens are preserved, however if Cycle GANs are used the dataset built on for the experiments could be used for validation purposes.

Also, in the immediate future we plan to compare other generative adversarial network architectures (like CycleGANS [14]), and explore preprocessing techniques for image enhancement prior to training the model, as the one presented in [10]. It is also interesting to explore more specific senescence metrics, as we used the widely popular structure similarity index. Considering the experts opinion on the quality of the automatically estimated senescence we could assess a more proper and specific metric. Another technique for evaluating the model could be to train the model using only a subset of the species and evaluating with the unused species.

Finally, it is important to measure the impact of using artificially rejuvenated images for training plant recognition models as the one developed in [8].

References

1. Dosovitskiy, A., Brox, T.: Generating images with perceptual similarity metrics based on deep networks. In: Advances in Neural Information Processing Systems, pp. 658–666 (2016)
2. Antipov, G., Baccouche, M., Dugelay, J.L.: Face aging with conditional generative adversarial networks. In: 2017 IEEE International Conference on Image Processing (ICIP), pp. 2089–2093. IEEE (2017)
3. Candussi, A., Candussi, N., Höllerer, T.: Rendering realistic trees and forests in real time. In: Eurographics (Short Presentations), pp. 73–76. Citeseer (2005)
4. Carranza-Rojas, J., Goeau, H., Bonnet, P., Mata-Montero, E., Joly, A.: Going deeper in the automated identification of Herbarium specimens. BMC Evol. Biol. **17**(1), 181 (2017)
5. Carranza-Rojas, J., Mata-Montero, E.: On the significance of leaf sides in automatic leaf-based plant species identification. In: 2016 IEEE 36th Central American and Panama Convention (CONCAPAN XXXVI), pp. 1–6, November 2016. https://doi.org/10.1109/CONCAPAN.2016.7942341
6. Chi, X., Sheng, B., Chen, Y., Wu, E.H.: Physically based simulation of weathering plant leaves. Chin. J. Comput. **32**, 221–230 (2009)
7. Gaston, K.J., O'Neill, M.A.: Automated species identification: why not? Philos. Trans. R. Soc. Lond. Ser. B: Biol. Sci. **359**(1444), 655–667 (2004)
8. Goëau, H., et al.: PlantNet participation at lifeclef2014 plant identification task. In: CLEF2014 Working Notes. Working Notes for CLEF 2014 Conference, Sheffield, UK, 15–18 September 2014, pp. 724–737. CEUR-WS (2013)

9. Goodfellow, I., et al.: Generative adversarial nets. In: Advances in Neural Information Processing Systems, pp. 2672–2680 (2014)
10. Guan, R., Wan, Y.: An improved unsharp masking sharpening algorithm for image enhancement. In: Eighth International Conference on Digital Image Processing (ICDIP 2016), vol. 10033, p. 100332A. International Society for Optics and Photonics (2016)
11. Isola, P., Zhu, J.Y., Zhou, T., Efros, A.A.: Image-to-image translation with conditional adversarial networks. In: Proceedings of the IEEE Conference on Computer Vision and Pattern Recognition, pp. 1125–1134 (2017)
12. Rolland, J.P., Vo, V., Bloss, B., Abbey, C.K.: Fast algorithms for histogram matching: application to texture synthesis. J. Electron. Imaging $9(1)$, 39–45 (2000)
13. Jeong, S., Park, S.H., Kim, C.H.: Simulation of morphology changes in drying leaves. In: Computer Graphics Forum, vol. 32, pp. 204–215. Wiley Online Library (2013)
14. Zhu, J.-Y., Park, T., Isola, P., Efros, A.A.: Unpaired image-to-image translation using cycle-consistent adversarial networks (2017)
15. Mata-Montero, E., Carranza-Rojas, J.: Automated plant species identification: challenges and opportunities. In: Mata, F.J., Pont, A. (eds.) WITFOR 2016. IAICT, vol. 481, pp. 26–36. Springer, Cham (2016). https://doi.org/10.1007/978-3-319-44447-5_3
16. Miao, T., Zhao, C., Guo, X., Lu, S., Wen, W., et al.: Simulation of plant leaf color based on relative content of chlorophyll. Nongye Jixie Xuebao = Trans. Chin. Soc. Agric. Mach. $45(8)$, 282–287 (2014)
17. Silva, P., Yue, Y., Chen, B.Y., Nishita, T.: Simulating plant color aging taking into account the sap flow in the venation (2012)
18. Wang, Z., Bovik, A.C.: Mean squared error: Love it or leave it? A new look at signal fidelity measures. IEEE Signal Process. Mag. $26(1)$, 98–117 (2009)
19. Wang, Z., Tang, X., Luo, W., Gao, S.: Face aging with identity-preserved conditional generative adversarial networks. In: Proceedings of the IEEE Conference on Computer Vision and Pattern Recognition, pp. 7939–7947 (2018)
20. Wang, Z., Bovik, A.C., Sheikh, H.R., Simoncelli, E.P.: Image quality assessment: from error visibility to structural similarity. IEEE Trans. Image Process. $13(4)$, 600–612 (2004). https://doi.org/10.1109/TIP.2003.819861

Performance Evaluation of Parallel Inference of Large Phylogenetic Trees in Santos Dumont Supercomputer: A Practical Approach

Kary Ocaña[1](✉), Carla Osthoff[1](✉), Micaella Coelho[1](✉),
Marcelo Galheigo[1](✉), Isabela Canuto[1](✉), Douglas de Oliveira[1](✉),
and Daniel de Oliveira[2](✉) (iD)

[1] National Laboratory of Scientific Computing, Petrópolis, Brazil
{osthoff,karyann,micaela,galheigo,iramos,ericson}@lncc.br
[2] Fluminense Federal University (UFF), Niterói, RJ, Brazil
danielcmo@ic.uff.br

Abstract. The modern high-throughput techniques of analytical chemistry and molecular biology produce a massive amount of data. Omics sciences cover complex areas as next-generation sequencing for genomics, systems biology studies of biochemical pathways, or novel bioactive compounds discovery and they can be fostered by the use of high-performance computing. Nowadays, the effective use of supercomputers plays an important role in phyloinformatics since most of these applications are considered as memory or compute-bound and have large number of simple and regular computations which exhibit potentially massive parallelism. Phyloinformatics analyses cover phylogenomic and computational evolutionary studies of the life of genomes of organisms. RAxML is a popular phylogenomic software based on maximum likelihood algorithms used for the analyses of phylogenetic trees, which require high computational computing to process large amounts of data. RAxML implements several phylogenetic likelihood function kernel variants (SSE3, AVX, AVX2) and offers coarse-grain/fine-grain parallelism via Hybrid and MPI/PThread versions. The present paper aims at exploring the performance and scalability of RAxML in the Santos Dumont supercomputer. Machine learning analyses were applied to support the choice of features which lead to the efficient allocation of resources in Santos Dumont. Recommending features such as type of clusters, number of cores, input data size, or RAxML historical performance results were used for generating the predictive models used for allocating computational resources. In the experiments, the hybrid version of RAxML improves the speedup significantly while maintaining efficiency over 75%.

Supported by FAPERJ, CNPq and CAPES.

J. L. Crespo-Mariño and E. Meneses-Rojas (Eds.): CARLA 2019, CCIS 1087, pp. 448–463, 2020.
https://doi.org/10.1007/978-3-030-41005-6_31

1   Introduction

During the last decade, phylogenetic experiments [12] have been evolving rapidly with new-generation high-throughput DNA-sequencing (NGS) techniques and novel scientific apparatus. Consequently, databases such as Uniprot[1] and NCBI[2] now contain millions of protein sequences, which must be analyzed to understand the biological behavior of genes and genomes better. Analyzing this volume of data is far from trivial. The integration of the novel approaches in biomedical technology, High Performance Computing (HPC), High Throughput Computing (HTC), and Database Management Systems (DBMS) can foster the advances in the fields of healthcare, drug discovery, genome research, computational biology, system biology, *etc.*

Molecular phylogeny typically involves not only the retrieval of homologous sequences but also the generation of sequence alignments and construction of phylogenetic trees. Several phylogenetics algorithms have been developed to calculate the tree to which the similarity/inheritance relationships among the sequences are best-reflected [12]. However, there are many potential biological problems or incongruence when attempting to infer phylogeny *i.e.,* violations of the orthology, stochastic, and systematic errors [13]. Recent advances in parallel techniques and HPC infrastructures have opened room for new solutions to manage phylogenetics analyses. Therefore, the progress in the field has been attained through algorithmic innovations rather than by brute force allocation of all phylogenetic executions in available computational resources, *e.g.* large supercomputers, grids, and clouds [3,16]. In fact, due to significant algorithmic advances over the last years, HPC-oriented implementation aspects of phylogenetic applications are fundamental for scientists' daily duties [7].

Many state-of-the-art sequential algorithms, which in principle can reconstruct huge trees of 5,000 taxa and more, face significant technical problems concerning lack of available memory and CPU. Parallel versions of these applications that can infer large trees and align sequences such as RAxML, MrBayes, PHYML, BEAST, BEAST2, GARLI, MAFFT, ExaBayes, DPPDIV, FastTree, PAUP, ParallelStructure, PartitionFinder, IQ Tree, and Migrate N can benefit from HPC infrastructure. The open source software RAxML (Randomized Axelerated Maximum Likelihood) [14] aims at providing Maximum Likelihood (ML) based on the inference of large phylogenetics trees. There are sequential and parallel versions of RAxML. RAxML can also be used for post-analyses of phylogenetics trees, to analyze alignments and, for inferring evolutionary life and phylogenetics relationships between genomes. RAxML is particularly useful for performing large-scale tree searches on supercomputers. Phylogenetics experiments require an adequate computational infrastructure that supports the needs in terms of memory, I/O and CPU. However, for researchers in the biological field, some difficulties remain to efficiently use such programs in supercomputers

---

[1] https://www.uniprot.org.
[2] https://www.ncbi.nlm.nih.gov.

mainly due to the lack of information on the software execution and management of large amounts of data, especially for non-computer science experts.

This way, studies that recommend scientists to choose the suitable environment and features for running their applications are attractive. Provenance data [4] can play an important role in this recommendation. Provenance refers to the process of tracing and recording the origin of data. Provenance contains the derivation process of a specific portion of data and other metrics such as memory and CPU consuming. It provides valuable documentation required to preserve the data, to determine their quality and authorship, as well as, to reproduce, interpret, and validate the results generated by large-scale scientific executions. It is particularly important in phylogenetics experiments where thousands of intermediate data files are produced. Without provenance, scientists have to analyze each one of the data files, manually associating their content to performance metrics, for instance.

The Brazilian Bioinformatics Network (RNBio) aims at strengthening the bioinformatics research projects in Brazil in a multi-institutional format with the training of scientists in thematic studies involving bioinformatics and computational biology. RNBio has scientific collaborations with the Brazilian National System for High Performance Computing (SINAPAD[3]), which offers users several heterogeneous and geographically distributed resources with high performance/throughput computing (HPC/HTC) capabilities and customized security models, such as the supercomputer Santos Dumont[4]. In a previous work [9] the science gateway BioinfoPortal[5] was introduced, which brings out the possibility of reproducible science as this portal integrates programs, data, pipelines, and HPC resources. BioinfoPortal integrates a suite of bioinformatics applications which are executed/managed in HPC resources of SINAPAD. However as researches in science gateways are continually evolving, there are open, yet essential, problems in designing a multiuser computational platform that efficiently allocates scientists' workloads in HPC environments and optimizes the use of HPC resources depending on the past and current performance of large-scale bioinformatics executions.

This paper presents a study of performance and scalability of the RAxML in the supercomputer Santos Dumont. This way, our work aims to provide basis for the efficient resource allocation to execute software in HPC environments. BioinfoPortal offers the required provenance data information for analyses based on prior parallel performance executions, according to input and data file parameters. Besides the analysis of past executions performance, we presented prediction models supported by machine learning algorithms for the efficient allocation/usage of RAxML in Santos Dumont. Results offer important information required to decide about the amount of cores/nodes that must be allocated to optimise the rationale use of executions of applications in BioinfoPortal. RAxML was evaluated using computational speedup, execution time, and efficiency as

---

[3] https://www.lncc.br/sinapad/.
[4] https://sdumont.lncc.br/.
[5] https://bioinfo.lncc.br/.

parallel processing metrics that lead to the better configuration that optimise the use of the supercomputer. Data mining and machine learning algorithms were executed for constructing model predictions based on provenance data and using Orange and Scikit-learn tools [4, 15].

This paper is organized as follows. Section 2 presents related work. Section 3 shows the methodology, experimental results and discussion and Sect. 4 concludes the paper and points out future work.

2 Related Work

Multiprocessor clusters are the most currently used architecture for large scale applications. Combining MPI and OpenMP models is regarded as a suitable programming model for such architectures. However, writing efficient MPI+OpenMP programs requires expertise and performance analysis to determine the best number of processes and threads for the optimal execution for a given application on a given platform. Hamidouche et al. [6] propose a framework for the development of Hybrid MPI+OpenMP programs based on compiler analyses that estimate the computing time of a sequential function and a simple analytical parallel performance prediction model to estimate execution time of the hybrid systems. Our work aims to provide the efficient resource allocation to execute software from a portal. Analyses are based on the prior parallel performance information (e.g. input data, software parameters) related to an existing hybrid MPI+OpenMP application and supported by machine learning for recommending features on a predicted model.

In a previous work [9], we introduced the science gateway BioinfoPortal, which was designed as a multiuser computational platform that integrates bioinformatics applications (programs, data, pipelines) in HPC resources. BioinfoPortal is managed by the middleware CSGrid at the HPC infrastructure of SINAPAD. Machine learning analyses were performed based on result executions and provenance data information provided by BioinfoPortal that lead to optimize the use of BioinfoPortal (clusters and computational resources), in particular when large-scale bioinformatics executions are performed. The present paper aims at exploring the performance and scalability of the software RAxML coupled to the supercomputer Santos Dumont and executed via BioinfoPortal to recommend models for an efficient resource allocation, based on the execution using a set of features (input data and parameters). Machine learning was applied for recommending features that lead to the efficient resource allocation for software execution in Santos Dumont based on the previous executions.

Rodrigo et al. [11] present a methodology to characterise workloads and assess their heterogeneity, at particular time period and evolution over time. They apply this methodology to the workloads systems at the National Energy Research Scientific Computing Center (NERSC) in order to understand main features belonging to the HPC workloads and to enable the efficient scheduling in HPC systems. The present work explore the behaviour of the performance and scalability features of the bioinformatics HPC software RAxML in the supercomputer Santos Dumont. Machine learning analyses are utilised for building the predictive models in order to reach an efficient job allocation for BioinfoPortal Science Gateway. Features as the type of clusters, quantity of cores, input data size, and RAxML performance results were used as input data information in the machine learning analyses.

Pfeiffer and Stamatakis [10] present a performance analysis of the parallel versions implemented in RAxML, supporting the Hybrid version as the most efficient. Zhou *et al.* [17] present a comparative analysis between the PhyML, IQ-TREE and RAxML/ExaML programs, concluding that RAxML, in addition to being more scalable, generates better-quality tree topologies. This paper explores the performance of RAxML in the Santos Dumont supercomputer, exploring environment configurations and RAxML settings (as bootstrap values and data size features, and the evolutionary models) that influence executions. They are complementary work since exploring HPC software as RAxML presents several challenges as coupling to HPC infrastructures to demonstrate performance behaviour and scalability for processing parallel and distributed executions.

3   Methodology and Experimental Results

This section presents two main results. The former, experimental performance analyses of RAxML in the Santos Dumont supercomputer. These analyses consider size of input data and the RAxML parameters (bootstrap replication values, the evolutionary model). The latter, we present machine learning models to predict the efficient allocation/usage of the Santos Dumont supercomputer based on features as the type of clusters, amount of cores, software parameters, and efficiency.

In Bioinformatics, the evolutionary phylogenomics analysis of genomes is a traditional problem that demands high memory and CPU time. The software RAxML (Randomized Axelerated Maximum Likelihood) is an open source based on Maximum Likelihood (ML) algorithms for statistical calculations that generates phylogenetics trees for supporting evolutionary inferences and phylogenetics relationships between genomes. RAxML is executed in the Santos Dumont infrastructure and it is scheduled using the middleware CSGrid[6] of SINAPAD. Santos Dumont consists of 16 TB RAM, storage totalling 1,7 PetaBytes (Seagate 1.5 Buster), 10.692 cores, 1.1 PetaFlops, Intel Xeon E5-2695v2, 30 MB cache, 12 cores – 3.2 GHz.

3.1   Data Input and Experiments Setup

The input files of four amino acid alignments (D1, D2, D3, D4) in format PHYLIP were used in the performance experiments. Detailed information is presented in Fig. 1. The simple gene alignment is D1 and the superalignments (D2, D3, D4) were formed of 31 concatenated universal orthologous (UO) genes of protozoan genomes. The parameters used for setting RAxML are the evolutionary model (WAG), the rate of model heterogeneity (GAMMA), and the

---

[6] https://jira.tecgraf.puc-rio.br/confluence/display/CN/CSGrid+Home.

bootstrap values of replications (100; 1,000; 2,000; 4,000; 6,000). The experiment was performed, as presented in Fig. 1, fixing the evolutionary model WAG and varying the bootstrap values. (Those model and bootstrap values are aforementioned).

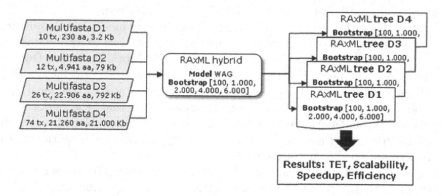

Fig. 1. Experiment configuration for the execution of RAxML in Santos Dumont.

3.2 The Software RAxML

RAxML was compiled to be compatible to the Santos Dumont infrastructure. Depending on the processor features, RAxML supports three instructions which accelerate the likelihood and parsimony computations: Streaming SIMD Extensions 3 (SSE3), Advanced Vector Extensions (AVX), and AVX2 vector [8]. Since the architecture of Santos Dumont (CPU Intel Xeon E5-2695v2 Ivy Bridge) supports AVX, our experiments perform the parallel executions of RAxML with Hybrid version and the streaming SIMD extension's AVX. RAxML presents four options of execution using multi-core shared memory systems, one sequential (for small datasets) and three parallel versions using MPI, PThreads, or Hybrid (MPI + PThreads) [5]. The efficiency of the parallel versions depends on the alignment length and the choice of RAxML parameter values. However parallel versions work well for long alignments, the performance is extremely hardware-dependent. The efficiency depends on the number of states of the data; the more states the data have (4 for DNA, 20 amino acid), the fewer site patterns are needed for an efficient parallel execution per thread/core. The parallel efficiency also depends on the rate of heterogeneity of the model; the GAMMA model entails more computations than the CAT model, which needs approximately 1/4 of the computations than the GAMMA model requires. RAxML Hybrid version 8.2.12 was used for experiments [14].

3.3 Performance and Scalability of RAxML in Santos Dumont

To evaluate the performance gain according to the number of processing units, we used the speedup and efficiency metrics. An ideal speedup reduces the sequential time dividing this time by the number of processing units used, and it was defined to evaluate performance gains of parallel computers.

The ideal (linear) efficiency curve is obtained by dividing the parallel speedup by the number of processors. These metrics were used to evaluate even though there are gains by adding more nodes from 2 up to 64 for execution may (or not) bring the expected benefit, mainly if CPU costs are involved.

RAxML Hybrid was executed fixing the evolutionary model WAG and varying the bootstrap replication values. This experiment aims at evaluating the performance and scalability (in minutes) of RAxML Hybrid in Santos Dumont according to the number of nodes. The performance of RAxML was measured on a single processor node (24 cores per processor node) to analyze the local optimization before scaling up the number of nodes. After that, the performance and scalability of RAxML were measured using from 2 node (48 cores) to 64 nodes (1,536 cores). Each experimental result presented in this section is the mean value obtained from 3 executions.

Figure 2 presents the total execution time curve from D1 dataset varying bootstrap from 100 to 6,000. Figure 3(a) presents the speedup and Fig. 3(b) presents the efficiency of the execution from D1 dataset experiment. We can observe that for all bootstrap values, 4 nodes are the minimum number of nodes that presents an efficiency above 75% and also presents total execution time belonging to the smallest "quartile" from Fig. 2. For instance, as it can be observed in Fig. 2 the total execution time (TET) of D1: (1) the best TET case was obtained with bootstrap 100, where the TET on 1 node is 1.6 min, TET on 4 nodes is 0.5 min and up to the TET stabilises on 0.1 min and (2) the worst TET case was obtained with bootstrap 6,000, where the TET on 1 node is 1,429 min, TET on 4 nodes is 385 min and up to the TET stabilises on 22.3 min.

Our results demonstrated that efficiency values reaching over 75% can be considered in order to determine "the optimal" CPU configuration (*i.e.* type of cluster, quantity of node/cores) to execute datasets (in this study: D1, D2, D3, D4). Thus, an efficiency value of 75% can be fixed as a parameter for taking decision about the number of nodes for the automatic allocation of tasks executed at Santos Dumont. For instance, this information was assumed by the science gateway BionfoPortal and included as a decision parameter in the configuration script at the resource management layer responsible by the node allocations. This fact allows that for smaller files (as D1) be allocated just 2 nodes, for medium-to-large files (as D2, D3) be allocated up to 32 nodes, and for the largest files (as D4) be allocated up to 64 nodes. Before those results, executions were submitted by the BionfoPortal users using, in most cases, 1 node (24 cores). However, our performance and machine learning analyses determined that the configuration must be adapted depending on features of data and parameters, for reach the best efficiency, as possible.

RAxML Hybrid Performance Using Small Alignment of Genes (D1).
Figure 3(a) presents the speedup and Fig. 3(b) presents the efficiency of the execution of RAxML Hybrid in Santos Dumont using the alignment D1. Results

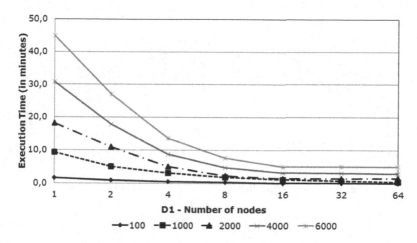

Fig. 2. D1 - RAxML total execution time

demonstrate that small alignments of single genes do not benefit from the parallelism and distribution of tasks of the Santos Dumont clusters. The execution of RAxML with D1 using 4 nodes led to a speedup of 3.5, 2.98, 3.61, 3.49, 3.30 (for bootstrap values of 100; 1,000; 2,000; 4,000; 6,000, respectively). Even though there was always a gain by adding more nodes, from 4 up to 64 nodes, the speedup presented some degradation. The efficiency is less than 0.7 since the size of the input dataset of small alignments is very low and the CPU time required is so fast in comparison to the available CPU machine processors.

RAxML Hybrid Performance Using Superalignments (D2, D3, D4).
Figures 4, 5, and 6 present results of speedup (a) and efficiency (b) of the execution of RAxML Hybrid in Santos Dumont using the superalignments D2, D3, and D4 (information detailed in Fig. 1). For setting RAxML parameters were used the evolutionary model WAG and the bootstrap replication values 100; 1,000; 2,000; 4,000; and 6,000. Results demonstrated that superalignments better benefit from the Santos Dumont HPC infrastructure. Since more complex are the features of data (size) and RAxML (bootstrap, models), the parallelism/distribution of RAxML task executions are better performed using more amount of CPU machine processors (in this experiment up to 64 nodes *i.e.* 1,536 cores).

The speedup is near linear for all the superalignments using all bootstrap values. Superalignments D2 and D3 (size medium) presented a linear speedup but with also a small degradation between 4 nodes to 64 nodes (also supported by the efficiency of 75% to 100%). The superalignment D4 (size large) also presented a linear speedup up to 64 nodes with efficiency values of 100%.

The efficiency for the files D2, D3, and D4 ranged from 80 to 100 (only D1 presented the smallest values). The larger file D4 is the most scalable and benefits from the environment and parallel configurations. According to the bench-

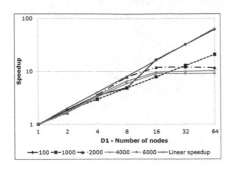
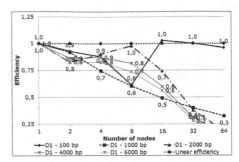

Fig. 3. (a) D1 - `RAxML` speedup; (b) D1 - `RAxML` efficiency

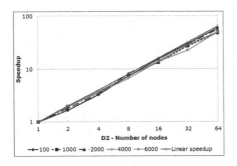
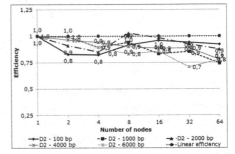

Fig. 4. (a) D2 - `RAxML` speedup; (b) D2 - `RAxML` efficiency

mark tests [10], it is expected that as the bootstrap increases with supermatrix (larger) files, executions become more scalable. It can be concluded from Fig. 3, that D1 becomes more efficient with 2 nodes and superalignments D2, D3, and D4 (Figs. 4(b), 5(b), 6(b)), respectively by using 4 nodes (or more). Reinforcing results, if we extrapolate these execution values to the actual usage in Santos Dumont, this would allocate files and settings of these types directly to up to 4 nodes. Also for the largest files as D4, based on the performance (efficiency) obtained from executions, for bootstrap values less than 4,000 the best configuration for executions is presented with 2 to 4 nodes.

3.4 Machine Learning Analyses

An exploratory data analysis using classification trees was performed with the available data of executions using RAxML Hybrid in Santos Dumont. Machine learning techniques were used to generate predictive models to set the parameters values that optimize the RAxML executions. For inferring knowledge about the most adequate computational resource configurations for performing executions, we applied regression models with decision trees [1] using the Orange and scikit-learn data mining tools which apply statistical analyses to discover patterns. The Orange Data Mining Tool [2] implements the core algorithm ID3 and

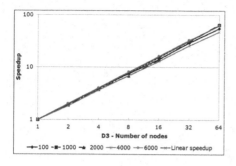 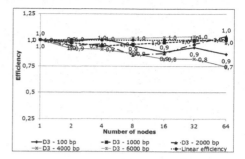

Fig. 5. (a) D3 - `RAxML` speedup; (b) D3 - `RAxML` efficiency

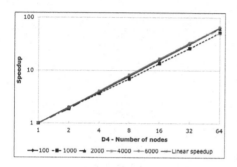 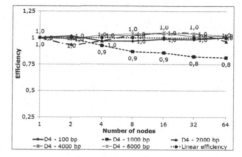

Fig. 6. (a) D4 - `RAxML` speedup; (b) D4 - `RAxML` efficiency

employs a top-down, greedy search through the space of possible branches with no backtracking. scikit-learn is a Python module for machine learning built on top of SciPy and distributed under the 3-Clause BSD license, scikit-learn also uses CBLAS, the C interface to the Basic Linear Algebra Subprograms library. Nevertheless, before generating the decision tree, we had to evaluate the statistics obtained form each attribute used in the model (*i.e.* threads, data size, node attributes). The main idea of the attribute analyses is to identify potential problems with the chosen attributes and decide if an action needs to be taken, *i.e.* to fix a type of machine processors or to choose the amount of nodes that may be required from a particular size of data or bootstrap values of RAxML.

First, we can state that there is no one dominant attribute value and the distribution is not even, as presented in Fig. 7(a), (b) and (c). Then, these results indicate that attributes can be used in the predictions. Figure 7(a) presents the attributes of threads, we can observe that 75% of the number of threads used was 24, from an interval of 24 (1 node) to 240 (10 nodes). Figure 7(b) shows that 75% of data input presented size of 204 KB, from an interval of 3.2 to 610,000. Moreover, evaluating the node attribute in Fig. 7(c), we observed that 75% of the number of nodes used was 1, from an interval of 1 to 10. This information can assist users to distinguish outlier points to find anomalies or specific biological

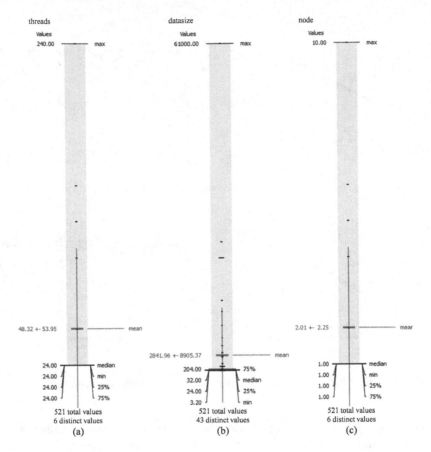

Fig. 7. *The attributes of the statistics (value distribution)*: `AtributeStatistics`. (a) Threads (number of threads). (b) Datasize (size of alignments in KB). (c) Node (number of nodes).

characteristics. By using these attributes to build estimation models, we can discover, using classification or regression algorithms, the relation of biological input data size (in KB) and the number of threads which can be determined for generating maximum values of efficiency.

Inhere, we presented results of machine learning analyses. We considered four main stages: training, discretization, classification and validation.

Training: Several parameters combinations were evaluated, following the order of the parameters used to execute RAxML, as presented in Fig. 1. For each parameter combination set evaluated, 3 executions were performed. In the experiments described in this subsection we evaluated 6 combinations of parameters thus generating a total of 141 RAxML executions.

Discretization: The data obtained with the processing of the 141 executions were submitted to the discretization method and three groups were obtained, as presented in Fig. 8: *Low* executions whose efficiency is less than 85, *i.e.*, [0, 85[, *Mid* executions whose efficiency is between 85 and 95, *i.e.*, [85, 95[, and *High* executions whose efficiency is above 95, *i.e.*, [95, 100].

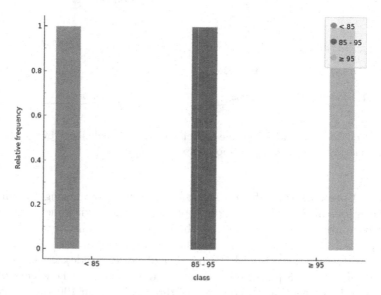

Fig. 8. *The attributes of the statistics:* `Distribution`. (a) Threads (number of threads). (b) Data size (data size of the alignment in KB). (c) Node (number of nodes).

Classification: Figure 9 shows the decision tree with three levels obtained with Orange. It is observed that the group in which an execution is based on the efficiency metric will be classified as *medium*, and is defined by the parameters data size of alignments (in KB) and bootstrap. This highlights that the execution of RAxML on Santos Dumont is mainly impacted by the way input dataset is organized. Therefore, the decision tree evaluates the importance of using a data partitioning method and knowledge of the criterion adopted to obtain an execution classified as medium. For example, the data size medium (D2, D3) with a bootstrap value of 100 present an efficiency of 58,3%.

Evaluation: The evaluation results of the predictive model using the 5-fold Cross Validation method showed that the prediction was correct in 97.8% of the cases, according to F1 metric, considered satisfactory because it is greater than 70%. Besides, it is a compact predictive model, with rules of good coverage and produce consistent knowledge of the problem. Precision and Recall also presented high values.

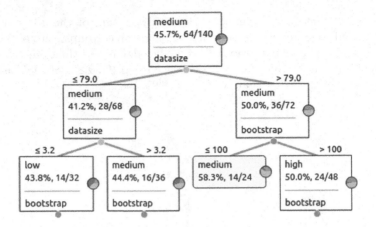

Fig. 9. The decision tree with Orange associated with the efficiency of the executions of RAxML based on data size and bootstrap.

Figure 10 presents the inferred rules for analyzing/predicting the efficiency of the executions of RAxML based on applications and environment characteristics. In this analysis, we can state that the efficiency of computational resources is determined by 3 parameters: the number of threads (threads), the size of the alignment in KB (datasize), and the number of nodes (node) *i.e.* the combination of values of these 3 parameters defines the efficiency of the executions. For example, Fig. 10 shows that the number of threads between 100 and 81 with less than 36,000 KB of data size will obtain, on average, an efficiency value near to 100%. The machine-learning strategies appoint, for the actual scenario, that the best machine setup in a heterogeneous environment for executing applications presented at least 75% of efficiency.

Figure 11 presents the inferred rules for exploring the efficiency of the executions of RAxML using scikit-learn. In this analysis, we can state that the efficiency of computational resources is determined by 2 parameters: the alignment size in KB (datasize) and the number of nodes (node) *i.e.* the combination of values of these 2 parameters defines the efficiency of the executions.

For example, Fig. 11 at the third level (datasize $\leq$ 1,0896.0, samples = 48, value = [24, 2, 22]) presents a class *low* of efficiency (1%–89%) when RAxML is executed using 2 nodes. The machine-learning strategies appoint, for the actual scenario, that the best machine setup in a heterogeneous environment for executing applications presented at least 75% of efficiency.

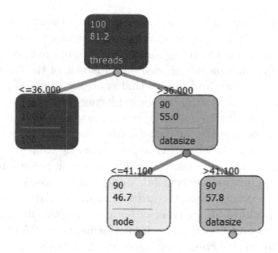

Fig. 10. The decision tree with Orange associated with the efficiency of the executions of RAxML based on datasize and nodes.

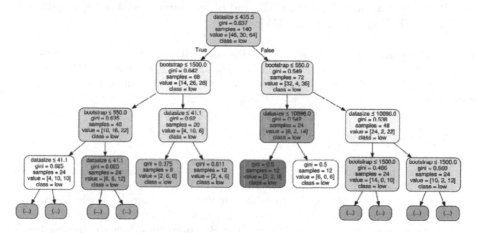

Fig. 11. The decision tree with scikit-learn associated with the efficiency of the executions of RAxML based on datasize and bootstrap.

4   Conclusions

The results of RAxML executed in Santos Dumont were analyzed based on performance and efficiency metrics and supported by machine learning algorithms. The provenance data information were obtained from RAxML executions provided by CSGrid/SINAPAD, by submitting high level database analytical queries. These results show that RAxML in Santos Dumont using multithreads and MPI improved the performance, as more nodes are added as it processed larger data size and high bootstrap values. First, we analysed the general features related to RAxML (input size, setting RAxML by bootstrap, efficiency of machines capacity) in order to provide information about the better efficiency for the allocation of HPC resources. We further explore that features and the obtained performance results using machine learning analyses. Decision trees generated with regression models, based on a historic of the dataset, provided a promissory learning module and proved that choosing the platform configuration for performing executions is valuable for exploring the better usage of the HPC infrastructure. Data analytic is essential to support the exploratory nature of science. Large-scale experiments can benefit from data analytics facilities to ease the results, reduce the incidence of errors, decrease the total execution time, and sometimes reduce the financial cost. The data analytic process needs to explore statistics of the applications execution, performance issues, and attributes of data files. RAxML executions may consist of hours or days of processing, thus, it is unfeasible to perform an analysis without automatic and analytic computational support. This paper evaluates the performance of RAxML in the Santos Dumont supercomputer to choose the best configurations for future executions. We are also concerned of coupling to BioinfoPortal with the best configurations for the efficient use of the computational resources, especially for the MPI and multithreading applications RAxML, and other similar as SPAdes, FragGeneScan, MAFFT, Ray, Bowtie, and HMMER.

Acknowledgements. The funding for this research was provided by the Brazilian sponsors projects CNPq/Universal (Grant no. 429328/2016-8) and FAPERJ/JCNE (Grant no. 232985/2017-03). We are also grateful to the comments made by the anonymous referees.

References

1. Breiman, L., Friedman, J., Olshen, R., Stone, C.: Classification and Regression Trees. Wadsworth and Brooks, Monterey (1984)
2. Demšar, J., et al.: Orange: data mining toolbox in python. J. Mach. Learn. Res. **14**, 2349–2353 (2013). http://jmlr.org/papers/v14/demsar13a.html
3. Foster, I., Kesselman, C. (eds.): The Grid: Blueprint for a New Computing Infrastructure. Morgan Kaufmann Publishers Inc., San Francisco (2004)
4. Freire, J., Koop, D., Santos, E., Silva, C.: Provenance for computational tasks: a survey. Comput. Sci. Eng. **10**, 11–21 (2008). https://doi.org/10.1109/MCSE.2008.79
5. Hager, G., Jost, G., Rabenseifner, R.: Communication characteristics and hybrid MPI/OpenMP parallel programming on clusters of multi-core SMP nodes. In: Proceedings of Cray User Group Conference, vol. 4, no. 500, p. 5455 (2009)
6. Hamidouche, K., Falcou, J., Etiemble, D.: A framework for an automatic hybrid MPI+OpenMP code generation (2011)
7. Hey, T., Tansley, S., Tolle, K. (eds.): The Fourth Paradigm: Data-Intensive Scientific Discovery. Microsoft Research, Redmond (2009)
8. Lomont, C.: Introduction to Intel Advanced Vector Extensions. Intel White Paper (2011)

9. Ocaña, K., et al.: Towards a science gateway for bioinformatics: experiences in the Brazilian system of high performance computing. In: 2019 Proceedings of the Workshop on Clusters, Clouds and Grids for Life Sciences (In Conjunction with CCGrid 2019 - 19th IEEE/ACM International Symposium on Cluster, Cloud and Grid Computing) (2019)

10. Pfeiffer, W., Stamatakis, A.: Hybrid MPI/Pthreads parallelization of the RAxML phylogenetics code. In: 2010 IEEE International Symposium on Parallel Distributed Processing, Workshops and Phd Forum (IPDPSW), pp. 1–8, April 2010. https://doi.org/10.1109/IPDPSW.2010.5470900

11. Rodrigo, G.P., Östberg, P.O., Elmroth, E., Antypas, K., Gerber, R., Ramakrishnan, L.: Towards understanding HPC users and systems: a NERSC case study. J. Parallel Distrib. Comput. **111**, 206–221 (2018). https://doi.org/10.1016/j.jpdc.2017.09.002. http://www.sciencedirect.com/science/article/pii/S0743731517302563

12. Rohlf, F.: J. Felsenstein, Inferring phylogenies, Sinauer Assoc., 2004, pp. xx + 664. J. Classif. **22**, 139–142 (2005). https://doi.org/10.1007/s00357-005-0009-4

13. Som, A.: Causes, consequences and solutions of phylogenetic incongruence. Brief. Bioinform. **16** (2014). https://doi.org/10.1093/bib/bbu015

14. Stamatakis, A.: RAxML version 8: a tool for phylogenetic analysis and post-analysis of large phylogenies. Bioinformatics **30**(9), 1312–1313 (2014). https://doi.org/10.1093/bioinformatics/btu033

15. Weiss, S., Kulikowski, C.: Computer Systems That Learn: Classification and Prediction Methods from Statistics, Neural Nets, Machine Learning, and Expert Systems. Morgan Kaufmann Publishers Inc., San Francisco (1991)

16. Younge, A.J., Pedretti, K., Grant, R.E., Brightwell, R.: A tale of two systems: using containers to deploy HPC applications on supercomputers and clouds. In: 2017 IEEE International Conference on Cloud Computing Technology and Science (CloudCom), pp. 74–81. IEEE (2017)

17. Zhou, X., Shen, X.X., Todd Hittinger, C., Rokas, A.: Evaluating fast maximum likelihood-based phylogenetic programs using empirical phylogenomic data sets. Mol. Biol. Evol. **35** (2017). https://doi.org/10.1093/molbev/msx302

Matching of EM Map Segments to Structurally-Relevant Bio-molecular Regions

Manuel Zumbado-Corrales[1,2], Luis Castillo-Valverde[1], José Salas-Bonilla[1],
Julio Víquez-Murillo[1], Daisuke Kihara[3], and Juan Esquivel-Rodríguez[1(✉)]

[1] Instituto Tecnológico de Costa Rica, Escuela de Computación, Campus Cartago,
Cartago, Costa Rica
manzumbado@ic-itcr.ac.cr, jesquivel@tec.ac.cr
[2] Advanced Computing Laboratory, National High Technology Center,
San José, Costa Rica
[3] Department of Biological Sciences/Department of Computer Science,
Purdue University, West Lafayette, IN, USA
dkihara@purdue.edu

Abstract. Electron microscopy is a technique used to determine the
structure of bio-molecular machines via three-dimensional images (called
maps). The state-of-the-art is able to determine structures at resolutions
that allow us to identify up to secondary structural features, in some
cases, but it is not widespread. Furthermore, because molecular interactions often require atomic-level details to be understood, it is still necessary to complement current maps with techniques that provide finer-
grain structural details. We applied segmentation techniques to maps in
the Electron Microscopy Data Bank (EMDB), the standard community
repository for these data. We assessed the potential of these algorithms
to match functionally relevant regions in their atomic-resolution image
counterparts by comparing against three protein systems, each with multiple atomic-detailed domains. We found that at least 80% of amino acid
residues in 7 out of 12 domains were assigned to single segments, suggesting there is potential to match the lower resolution segmented regions
to the atomic counterparts. We also qualitatively analyzed the potential
on other EMDB structures, as well as generating the raw segmentation
information for the complete EMDB, for interested researchers to use.
Results can be accessed online and the library developed is provided as
part of an open-source project.

Keywords: Computational biology · Computational protein
structures · Electron microscopy · 3DEM · Segmentation

1 Introduction

Structural biology has seen enormous progress in the 21st century, particularly
with the rise of open databases that host three-dimensional models of bio-
molecular structures. On one hand, we have the Protein Data Bank (PDB)

© Springer Nature Switzerland AG 2020
J. L. Crespo-Mariño and E. Meneses-Rojas (Eds.): CARLA 2019, CCIS 1087, pp. 464–478, 2020.
https://doi.org/10.1007/978-3-030-41005-6_32

[7] that hosts over 150,000 atomic-detailed structures of proteins, DNA and RNA. Most of the structures deposited in PDB correspond to relatively small bio-molecular complexes. A second database, the Electron Microscopy Data Bank (EMDB) [16], focuses on three-dimensional models created from electron microscopy (3DEM), which can power the imaging of larger macro-molecular complexes that have been historically deposited in the PDB. Very significant structures have been identified thanks to 3DEM [19,20,32].

Because protein interactions actually happen at the atomic level, ideally we want EM maps to give us atomic details so that we can do functional analysis by just using this type of image. In [24] the authors were able to generate a reconstruction with a resolution of 3.5 Å that allowed them to create an all-atom model. Even when there have been steady improvements on attainable resolutions over the years, this level of detail is not widespread. A gamut of computational techniques are often applied to be able to obtain details that go beyond the density envelope that EM maps provide. Hybrid approaches have been used to extract finer-grain details out of EM maps up to 10 Å [18]. Techniques like these have been applied to shed light into the organization of proteomes, for instance [6]. The field of Electron Microscopy fitting deals with finding atomic-level details based on existing high-resolution structures that match EM maps [8,10,28].

Even if we are not able to identify all atoms in a map, other structural elements and annotations can also be useful, for functional analysis purposes. For example, the architecture and helical regions of 26S proteasome were determined this way in [5]. Annotations directly on density maps have shown previously unknown interactions in complexes [11]. A significant number of algorithms and tools have been developed to identify secondary structure elements [2,3,12–14]. More recently, de novo modeling of proteins has also been applied to EM maps [26].

Segmentation is another technique used to identify structural features in maps. The basic notion here is to divide EM maps into density regions that should match individual protein structures, or functionally relevant sections, like domains. Some automated techniques that assume the knowledge of the components, or the symmetry of the complexes have been previously developed [4,27,33]. Atomic models are not always available for the maps under study and we also need to deal with the added complexity of images in more complex, environments, that can lead to lower resolution images [21].

In this work, we study the potential to identify functionally-relevant regions in 3D Electron Microscopy maps by applying automated segmentation. Our goal is not only to approximate near-atomic features but, more in general, to identify structural hot-spots within maps that can later be mapped to larger images. Through the open-source library we have developed for this work, we aim to provide a way to both visually and analytically study EM maps. We apply these techniques to all the structures currently in the EMDB and show sample cases that highlight the potential of this type of method. As noted in [21], trying to bridge the gap between cellular and molecular structural data is key for the field to advance.

2   Methods

2.1   Watershed Segmentation

Our segmentation method uses the immersive watershed transform to generate region labels as a first step, then we perform region grouping with scale-space filtering as proposed in [22]. This approach is useful to reduce over-segmentation as reported by authors.

The watershed algorithm can be understood following the same analogy presented in [31]. Consider EM map densities as a topographic surface as seen in Fig. 1, where holes are pierced at surface local minima to let water flood basins. If each voxel located in a catchment basin would merge with water coming from different local minima, a dam is built to separate water from different regions. At the end, each resulting flooded region is separated by built dams, also called watershed lines, which coincide with surface local maxima.

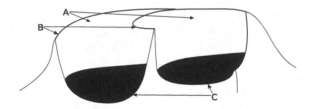

Fig. 1. Representation of watershed process with A as catchment basins, B as watershed lines and C as local minima (conceptual illustration inspired by [31]).

We take the additive inverse of an EM map as the topographic surface, regarding higher densities as surface local minima. Thus we get watershed regions surrounding higher density locations, separated by lowest surface densities. A fixed connectivity of 26 voxels is used in each dimension to connect neighbors in the process of assign adjoin voxels to the same region.

2.2   Scale-Space Grouping

Region grouping is performed by progressively smoothing the EM map using a Gaussian filter. This concept was introduced in [35] and is called scale-space filtering. Scale-space representation $L(x, y, z; \sigma) \in \mathbb{R}^3 \times \mathbb{R}^+$ of an EM map $f(x, y, z) \in \mathbb{R}^3$ is defined scale-space representation $L(x, y, z; \sigma) \in \mathbb{R}^3 \times$ scale-space representation $L(x, y, z; \sigma) \in \mathbb{R}^3 \times \mathbb{R}^+$ of an EM map $f(x, y, z) \in \mathbb{R}^3$

is defined as and is called scale-space filtering. The scale-space representation $L(x, y, z; \sigma) \in \mathbb{R}^3 \times \mathbb{R}^+$ of an EM maa$f(x, y, z) \in \mathbb{R}^3$ is defined as

$$L(x, y, z; \sigma) = (f * g)(x, y, z; \sigma), \tag{1}$$

where $\sigma \in \mathbb{R}^+$ controls the variance of the Gaussian kernel $g(x, y, z; \sigma) \in \mathbb{R}^3 \times \mathbb{R}^+$, defined as

$$g(x, y, z; \sigma) = \frac{1}{\sigma^3 (2\pi)^{\frac{3}{2}}} \exp\left(-\frac{x^2 + y^2 + z^2}{2\sigma^2} \right). \tag{2}$$

In order to group regions, an initial local maxima point set is computed from original EM map. Then, each initial local maxima point is successively moved up to the local maxima of a subsequent smoothed scale corresponding to the steepest ascent in terms of density intensity, as shown in Algorithm 1.

The process of Scale-Space filtering produces an EM map for each step with progressive attenuation of energy on higher density locations. Thus, computed local maxima of a succeeding step in the Scale-Space representation would replace several local maxima of a current step. After N number of smoothing steps, resulting local maxima points having the same coordinates in space would merge into a new region.

Parameters used for segmentation and grouping follow the same approach presented in [22]. The number of steps N controls how many steps of Scale-Space grouping are performed. Smoothing step size S regulates how much smoothing is achieved at each step. A density threshold level defines the structure contour to be segmented and also affects the isosurface generated by the Marching Cubes algorithm.

Algorithm 1. Space-scale grouping of watershed regions of segmented EM map

Input	: Watershed segmented map
Input	: Collection of successively smoothed maps
Input	: Steps
Output:	Grouped regions

1 $N \leftarrow$ Steps;
2 $M \leftarrow$ Watershed segmented EM map;
3 $S \leftarrow$ Collection of successively smoothed maps;
4 $L \leftarrow$ Collection of local maxima of M;
5 **for** i **in** N :
6 $\quad$ **for** p **in** L :
7 $\quad\quad$ $B \leftarrow$ Collection of local maxima of S for corresponding i;
8 $\quad\quad$ Replace p with the steepest local maxima in B respect to p;
9 Find duplicates in L and merge corresponding regions into new one;

2.3   Marching Cubes and Isosurface Generation

Marching cubes is a reference algorithm for isosurface reconstruction from sampling data. Several optimizations have been proposed to extend the basic approach, improve its performance and solve ambiguities. Our method relies on an efficient implementation of Marching Cubes algorithm proposed in [17]. Isosurface visualization of protein structures is essential to later identify segments enclosed in the three dimensional space of an EM map.

2.4   Library Design

The created library is composed of the following Python modules: `processing`, `visualizer`, `reader` and `molecule`. The `processing` module object contains watershed and space-scale implementations. Later, the `visualizer` module object implements main methods exposed to the user, namely, `segmentation`, `show` and `show_atom_matching`. The `reader` module object implements `read` function to read map files from disk and returns created `map` object.

Our library supports GPU accelerated visualization by using Glumpy [25] which is a fast and scalable open source library that takes advantage of the computational power of GPU through OpenGL.

In this work we show the effectiveness of open source scientific Python libraries such as Scikit-image, Biopandas and Numpy [23,30,34]. At the same time, we identify potential areas of improvement that will allow us, in the future, to augment them with custom features to scale up our system.

2.5   Validation Data Set

In order to determine the potential to identify structurally relevant regions through segmentation, we used three protein systems from a data set previously identified as suitable for the analysis of algorithms related Electron Microscopy map fitting [1]. The data set focuses on proteins for which we have both low-resolution EM maps but also there is an atomic level Protein Data Bank structure that matches the map. While we are not directly tackling the EM-fitting problem in this study, the data set is still very much valid for our purposes. In particular, the fact that the authors have divided each of the protein systems into regions, using PDB structures, allows us to compare the segments that our library generates with the annotated domains. Intuitively, if each of the segments that we generate has a high overlap with the domains identified in that study, then the structural correspondence that we propose is valid. Table 1 summarizes the characteristics of the data set.

In addition to testing against these controlled protein systems we have also run the segmentation over two larger macro molecular structures to illustrate how promising the methods are at identifying not only structural regions within isolated proteins, but also in large complexes. For this purpose we have analyzed **EMDB ID: 1048** and **EMDB ID:2596**.

Table 1. Validation data set metadata

EMDB ID	PDB ID	Units	Residues	Description
1010	1GQE	4	362	Release Factor (RF2)
1364	1FNM	5	655	Elongation Factor G (EFG)
5017	1N0U	3	654	Elongation Factor 2 (EF2)

3   Results

Our method validation is based on the comparison between computational and biological segments. While the computational ones are obtained applying the methods described in Sect. 2, the biological segments are more difficult to come by. As we have described in Sect. 2.5, we have used a previously derived definition of domains in a protein. In general, domains are regions within a protein that have been conserved through evolution *for a good reason*, be that structural, functional, etc. Our premise is that segmentation algorithms that are able to closely predict the matching between computational and biological segments can allow us to better understand the different sections in a macro-molecule.

3.1   Atomic-Detailed Validation

Figure 2 shows the structural baseline for our detailed analysis. The wireframe representation shows the density envelope identified using the author-recommended contour level to create isosurfaces that resemble the true volume of the protein. In bright green we can see the ribbon representation of the protein backbone, which is important to determine the rough high density regions that should be expected to be identified. However, the knowledge of the backbone does not tell us on its own what biological sections we are supposed to target. For that, we fitted each of the domains (as found in [1]) using a method developed by the authors that uses Markov Random Fields to generate candidate alignments[1].

The fitted structures, shown in separate colors for each domain become our validation targets. We assessed what fraction of the residues were assigned to different segments, per domain. The theoretical ideal result is for every residue to be assigned to a single segment. We tackled this problem from both quantitative and qualitative angles.

Quantitative Results. Table 2 shows our way of quantitatively determining how well the segments generated for **EMDB ID: 1010** matched the domains. In this particular case, the results mostly meet our expectations. Two of the four

---

[1] This method is based on the combination of physico-chemical, shape and cross correlation features between each of the domains and the EM map. This work is not part of a stand-alone article as of this writing.

1010   1364   5017

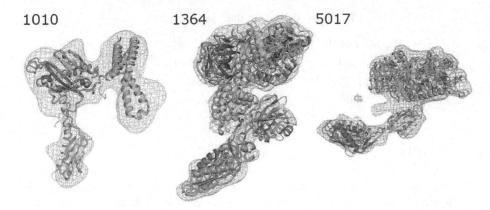

Fig. 2. EM maps in the data set aligned to the C-α trace (bright green) and a candidate fitting of the domains in each protein system (individually colored). Each label corresponds to the EMDB ID for each map. (Color figure online)

domains, **B** and **D**, are matched to a single segment, as well as 94.12% of residues in **A**. **C** has a slightly worse result since 16.48% of residues are not assigned to a single segment, but it can still be considered promising[2]. The drawback with **EMDB ID: 1010**'s results is that we should have identified 4 segments, as opposed to 3. That suggests that there is some density noise that we cannot overcome that yields two regions that should be separate to become a single one.

Table 2. Segment matches for EMDB ID 1010. The **All** row summarizes the overall assignment. The remaining rows show the per-domain assignment

Domain	Segment	Percentage (within domain)	Residues Assigned
All	1	31.22%	113/362
	3	46.96%	170/362
	2	21.82%	79/362
A	1	94.12%	112/119
	3	5.88%	7/119
	3	100.00%	99/99
C	3	16.48%	15/91
	2	83.52%	76/91
D	3	100.00%	45/45

---

[2] Note that for 1010 there are 8 missing residues, observed in the C-α trace but not the PDB with all atomic details. They are ommitted for analysis purposes.

Similarly, Table 3 summarizes the matches found for **EMDB ID: 1364**. In this case we can claim successful results for domains **A**, **D** and **E**, since they were mostly assigned to a single segment (82.87%, 95.52% and 98.61%, respectively). However, domains **B** and **C** are more evenly distributed across multiple segments, which is not the desirable outcome. As we will see in our qualitative analysis, there is a region where densities are more difficult to differentiate. We can also observe that we are identifying one less segment than we should. There are 5 domains in this protein but we are only generating 4. This can also explain the difficulty in assigning clear-cut segments.

Table 3. Segment matches for EMDB ID 1364. The **All** row summarizes the overall assignment. The remaining rows show the per-domain assignment

Domain	Segment	Percentage (within domain)	Residues Assigned
All	4	11.45%	75/655
	3	16.95%	111/655
	1	49.92%	327/655
	2	21.68%	142/655
A	4	1.20%	3/251
	3	15.94%	40/251
	1	82.87%	208/251
B	4	60.50%	72/119
	3	39.50%	47/119
C	3	30.38%	24/79
	1	53.16%	42/79
	2	16.46%	13/79
D	1	4.48%	6/134
	2	95.52%	128/134
E	1	98.61%	71/72
	2	1.39%	1/72

The last case analyzed was **EMDB ID: 5017**. As Table 4 reflects, this was the most challenging case from a quantitative point of view. The best match obtained corresponded to domain **C** with 64.79%, but **A** and **B** are generally split between two segments. On the flip side, this case correctly identified that 3 segments were needed to have a correct matching of domains. We will discuss in the qualitative analysis why this protein structure could have behaved this way.

Qualitative Results. The previous section had the purpose of providing a non-subjective metric that would shed light in terms of whether or not a large portion of residues were assigned to expected segments. We can argue that just looking at proportions is not enough to determine how good the assignment was.

Table 4. Segment matches for EMDB ID 5017. The **All** row summarizes the overall assignment. The remaining rows show the per-domain assignment

Domain	Segment	Percentage (within domain)	Residues Assigned
All	2	46.48%	304/654
	1	32.42%	212/654
	3	21.10%	138/654
A	2	44.35%	204/460
	1	40.65%	187/460
	3	15.00%	69/460
B	2	43.90%	54/123
	3	56.10%	69/123
C	2	64.79%	46/71
	1	35.21%	25/71

As we have stated in this work, the actual 3D structure of proteins is crucial to determine how well they function. Thus, a presumably good match of 80%+ that misses the key 20% of a protein is not necessarily the best result.

To complement the quantitative arguments made before, Fig. 3 shows the colored assignment of EM map regions to segments, made by our library. We contrast this against the fitted structures shown in Fig. 2. Based on the results obtained in the quantitative analysis, we assessed three elements. First, are the domains with majority single-segment assignments consistent with the expected structure? Second, are there clues as to why the algorithm identified one fewer segment for **EMDB ID: 1010** and **EMDB ID: 1364**? Finally, for the domains with unclear assignments, is there any structural reason that may explain them?

The general 3D structure of **EMDB ID: 1010** from Fig. 2 can be summarized as two separate domains on the left (yellow) and right (cyan) and two others that are tightly coupled between them (purple and orange). From that point of view, it is not unexpected that the algorithm identified only 3 segments, assuming that the main difficulty was separating the link domains. If we look at the segmentation from Fig. 3 we see that the overall left and right domains are captured by the blue and yellow segments. It appears as if the orange domain (in Fig. 2) corresponds roughly to the red segment in Fig. 3, which is encouraging. We do see that all segments over extend, which could be an artifact of the space scale filtering applied. We need to remember that the surfaces here are based on contour values that are suitable to convey the actual shape of the proteins, but the EM maps contain density in surrounding voxels too and there is no guarantee that at the contour level we used there is no noise. The two parts in the red segment are particularly interesting when compared to the fitted structure. The EM map, at the recommended contour, shows a gap not filled by the C-α trace in Fig. 2 which could back the idea that we're dealing with a noisy region.

1010   1364   5017

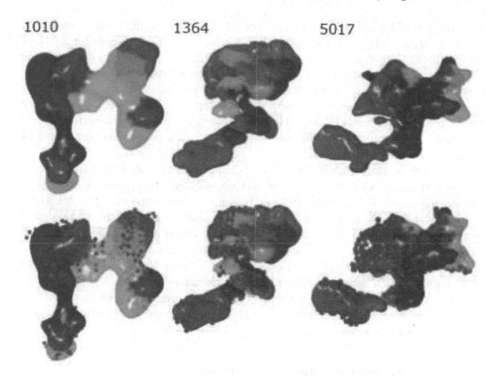

Fig. 3. Segmentation applied to EMDB ID 1010, 1364 and 5017 as detailed in Sect. 2. Every color represents an individual segment identified. The top row shows only the segments, for clarity, while the bottom row adds spheres to highlight the C-α atoms. Those atoms are expected to be slightly shifted due to small adjustments done to contour thresholds in the segmentation (Color figure online)

For **EMDB ID: 1364**, Fig. 2 shows a big domain on the top right corner of the structure that is segmented into multiple ones (as opposed to just a single one). This particular problem is less troublesome than some of the aspects found for **EMDB ID: 1010**. Refinement of segment assignments that are *supposed to be one* can be performed as a post-processing step. On a more critical note, there are 2 red segments in Fig. 3, but it is possible that the top one should have been colored yellow. Making that change should have mostly captured the structure, starting from the bottom of a red domain, followed by blue and then yellow (with some over extension of the red segment, though). Even though this case shows better metrics than **EMDB ID: 5017**, discussed below, it is arguably the most challenging structurally.

Finally, in the case of **EMDB ID: 5017** the overall coloring of the lower segments is not incompatible with the purple and yellow domains, in the fitted structure. We can argue that the lower left section should indeed have been colored red, and the lower center section should have been all blue, albeit with higher precision required to differentiate where the red section finished and the blue started. The main issue in this complex though comes from domain **A**, which is significantly larger than the other two. As it was the case for **EMDB ID: 1364**, the problem here is that a single domain was broken up into multiple segments. Post-processing could solve this in a later iteration of our algorithm. For the purposes of this study, we tried multiple thresholds for the parameters that could be tuned and the results were similar, in every case. Note that, as it was the case for **EMDB ID: 1010**, there is a region in the wire frame that does not correspond to our reference C-α trace, which could also be a factor in the less accurate segmentation.

There are two key takeaways from our qualitative analysis. First, even though we applied space scale filtering, that did not solve all the problems related to integrating multiple segments into one, when that was expected. Second, there is clear over extension of some segments into small areas that they should not, and it could be due to noise spreading from one region to the other. Even with these two areas to improve that we identified, the results are generally good. The segmentation of these types of density maps could generate a very large number of segments, which makes it very difficult to then map domains of the size that we are testing in this study. Furthermore, there are regions in each map where there is clear correspondence between both fitted structures and segments, which shows the promise of the approach.

3.2 Large Macro-molecule Segmentation

The three protein systems studied are useful for detailed analysis because there is atomic-level information throughout the structure. The more complex macro-molecules do not necessarily have that type of information available in databases, to serve as a larger scale evaluation target.

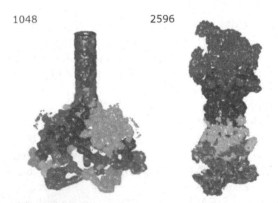

Fig. 4. Segmentation applied to EMDB ID 1048, 2596 as detailed in Sect. 2. Every color represents an individual segment identified. EMDB ID 1048 is an image of bacteriophage T4 baseplate while EMDB ID 2596 is a 26S proteasome structure (Color figure online)

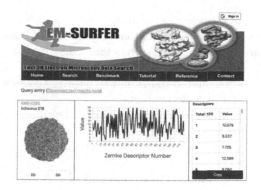

Fig. 5. Sample segmentation result from alpha release of EM-SURFER (http://emsurfer.tecdatalab.org/result/0185). The 3D section shows images generated by our library.

Even though we cannot provide rigorous analysis about the quality of the segmentation applied to large-scale macro-molecules, we applied the algorithm to two sample systems that are both interesting biologically but also have much larger scale. Figure 4 shows the segmentation results for **EMDB ID: 1048** and **EMDB ID: 2596**. The former is the structure of bateriophage T4 baseplate, which is a virus that infects *Escherichia coli* [15]. This structure is in the range of hundreds of nanometers. The latter structure, a 26S proteasome, is in charge of breaking down proteins [29].

The results obtained are sensible and resemble some fitted results referenced in the EM Data Bank. This path towards the validation of segmentation for larger structures is one that we want to explore further in the future.

3.3   Online Results

We have generated segmentation results for maps in the Electron Microscopy Data Bank, which can be accessed as part of an alpha release of the latest version of EM-SURFER [9], an EM map search engine that relies on the fast comparison of structural features. Figure 5 shows a screen shot of a sample result generated for **EMDB ID: 0185**[3].

4   Conclusions

In this work we have shown the potential to match biological domains to computationally derived segments using watershed segmentation with space-scale

---

[3] The production version of EM-SURFER is hosted at http://kiharalab.org/em-surfer. An example result from our alpha release of the latest version, that includes segmentation results, can be accessed at is available at http://emsurfer.tecdatalab.org/result/0185.

grouping. Our methods represent a valid approach to elucidate what regions in an EM map correspond to relevant regions in proteins. We have first evaluated this by analyzing three protein systems in detail, where we have both the atomic-details and the EM maps, which allowed us to do a thorough validation. We have also evaluated much larger macro-molecular structures to assess the potential to apply our methods to large scale problems.

As discussed in the Results section, we have identified areas where results can be refined. Those revolve mainly around the decision to integrate or break apart density clusters, but not to an extent that diminishes the positive results obtained.

As part of our work, we offer the community a library that is accessible as an open source project, which contains both the algorithms and visualization features to reproduce our results (github.com/tecdatalab/biostructure). Furthermore, we publish our segmentation results online through a new version of EM-SURFER.

Acknowledgements. Funded by the *Vicerrectoría de Investigación y Extensión* at *Instituto Tecnológico de Costa Rica*.

References

1. Ahmed, A., Whitford, P.C., Sanbonmatsu, K.Y., Tama, F.: Consensus among flexible fitting approaches improves the interpretation of cryo-EM data. J. Struct. Biol. **177**(2), 561–570 (2012). https://doi.org/10.1016/j.jsb.2011.10.002
2. Baker, M.L., Baker, M.R., Hryc, C.F., Ju, T., Chiu, W.: Gorgon and pathwalking: macromolecular modeling tools for subnanometer resolution density maps. Biopolymers **97**(9), 655–668 (2012). https://doi.org/10.1002/bip.22065
3. Baker, M.L., Ju, T., Chiu, W.: Identification of secondary structure elements in intermediate-resolution density maps. Structure **15**(1), 7–19 (2007). https://doi.org/10.1016/j.str.2006.11.008
4. Baker, M.L., Yu, Z., Chiu, W., Bajaj, C.: Automated segmentation of molecular subunits in electron cryomicroscopy density maps. J. Struct. Biol. **156**(3), 432–441 (2006). https://doi.org/10.1016/j.jsb.2006.05.013
5. Beck, F., et al.: Near-atomic resolution structural model of the yeast 26S proteasome. Proc. Natl. Acad. Sci. U.S.A. **109**(37), 14870–14875 (2012). https://doi.org/10.1073/pnas.1213333109
6. Beck, M., et al.: Exploring the spatial and temporal organization of a cell's proteome. J. Struct. Biol. **173**(3), 483–496 (2011). https://doi.org/10.1016/j.jsb.2010.11.011
7. Burley, S.K., et al.: Protein data bank: the single global archive for 3D macromolecular structure data. Nucleic Acids Res. **47**(D1), D520–D528 (2019). https://doi.org/10.1093/nar/gky949
8. Dou, H., Burrows, D.W., Baker, M.L., Ju, T.: Flexible fitting of atomic models into cryo-EM density maps guided by helix correspondences. Biophys. J. **112**(12), 2479–2493 (2017). https://doi.org/10.1016/j.bpj.2017.04.054
9. Esquivel-Rodríguez, J., Xiong, Y., Han, X., Guang, S., Christoffer, C., Kihara, D.: Navigating 3D electron microscopy maps with EM-SURFER. BMC Bioinform. **16**, 181 (2015). https://doi.org/10.1186/s12859-015-0580-6

10. Fabiola, F., Chapman, M.S.: Fitting of high-resolution structures into electron microscopy reconstruction images. Structure **13**(3), 389–400 (2005). https://doi.org/10.1016/j.str.2005.01.007

11. Hryc, C.F., et al.: Accurate model annotation of a near-atomic resolution cryo-EM map. Proc. Natl. Acad. Sci. **114**(12), 3103–3108 (2017). https://doi.org/10.1073/PNAS.1621152114

12. Jiang, W., Baker, M.L., Ludtke, S.J., Chiu, W.: Bridging the information gap: computational tools for intermediate resolution structure interpretation. J. Mol. Biol. **308**(5), 1033–1044 (2001). https://doi.org/10.1006/jmbi.2001.4633

13. Kong, Y., Ma, J.: A structural-informatics approach for mining beta-sheets: locating sheets in intermediate-resolution density maps. J. Mol. Biol. **332**(2), 399–413 (2003)

14. Kong, Y., Zhang, X., Baker, T.S., Ma, J.: A structural-informatics approach for tracing beta-sheets: building pseudo-C(alpha) traces for beta-strands in intermediate-resolution density maps. J. Mol. Biol. **339**(1), 117–130 (2004). https://doi.org/10.1016/j.jmb.2004.03.038

15. Kostyuchenko, V.A., et al.: Three-dimensional structure of bacteriophage T4 baseplate. Nat. Struct. Biol. **10**(9), 688–693 (2003). https://doi.org/10.1038/nsb970

16. Lawson, C.L., et al.: EMDataBank unified data resource for 3DEM. Nucleic Acids Res. **44**(D1), D396–D403 (2016). https://doi.org/10.1093/nar/gkv1126

17. Lewiner, T., Lopes, H., Vieira, A.W., Tavares, G.: Efficient implementation of marching cubes' cases with topological guarantees. J. Graph.Tools **8**(2), 1–15 (2003). https://doi.org/10.1080/10867651.2003.10487582

18. Lindert, S., Stewart, P.L., Meiler, J.: Hybrid approaches: applying computational methods in cryo-electron microscopy. Curr. Opin. Struct. Biol. **19**(2), 218–225 (2009). https://doi.org/10.1016/j.sbi.2009.02.010

19. Ludtke, S.J., Chen, D.H., Song, J.L., Chuang, D.T., Chiu, W.: Seeing GroEL at 6 A resolution by single particle electron cryomicroscopy. Structure **12**(7), 1129–1136 (2004). https://doi.org/10.1016/j.str.2004.05.006

20. Mitra, K., et al.: Structure of the E. Coli protein-conducting channel bound to a translating ribosome. Nature **438**(7066), 318–324 (2005). https://doi.org/10.1038/nature04133

21. Patwardhan, A., et al.: Building bridges between cellular and molecular structural biology. eLife **6** (2017). https://doi.org/10.7554/eLife.25835

22. Pintilie, G.D., Zhang, J., Goddard, T.D., Chiu, W., Gossard, D.C.: Quantitative analysis of cryo-EM density map segmentation by watershed and scale-space filtering, and fitting of structures by alignment to regions. J. Struct. Biol. **170**(3), 427–438 (2010). https://doi.org/10.1016/j.jsb.2010.03.007

23. Raschka, S.: BioPandas: working with molecular structures in pandas dataframes. J. Open Source Softw. **2**(14) (2017). https://doi.org/10.21105/joss.00279

24. Roh, S.H., et al.: The 3.5-Å CryoEM structure of nanodisc-reconstituted yeast vacuolar ATPase Vo proton channel. Mol. Cell **69**(6), 993.e3–1004.e3 (2018). https://doi.org/10.1016/j.molcel.2018.02.006

25. Rougier, N.P.: Glumpy. In: EuroScipy (2015)

26. Terashi, G., Kihara, D.: De novo main-chain modeling with MAINMAST in 2015/2016 EM model challenge. J. Struct. Biol. **204**(2), 351–359 (2018). https://doi.org/10.1016/J.JSB.2018.07.013

27. Terwilliger, T.C., Adams, P.D., Afonine, P.V., Sobolev, O.V.: A fully automatic method yielding initial models from high-resolution cryo-electron microscopy maps. Nat. Methods **15**(11), 905–908 (2018). https://doi.org/10.1038/s41592-018-0173-1

28. Topf, M., Baker, M.L., John, B., Chiu, W., Sali, A.: Structural characterization of components of protein assemblies by comparative modeling and electron cryo-microscopy. J. Struct. Biol. **149**(2), 191–203 (2005). https://doi.org/10.1016/j.jsb. 2004.11.004

29. Unverdorben, P., et al.: Deep classification of a large cryo-EM dataset defines the conformational landscape of the 26S proteasome. Proc. Natl. Acad. Sci. U.S.A. **111**(15), 5544–5549 (2014). https://doi.org/10.1073/pnas.1403409111

30. van der Walt, S., Colbert, S.C., Varoquaux, G.: The numpy array: a structure for efficient numerical computation. Comput. Sci. Eng. **13**(2), 22–30 (2011). https://doi.org/10.1109/MCSE.2011.37

31. Vincent, L., Soille, P.: Watersheds in digital spaces: an efficient algorithm based on immersion simulations. IEEE Trans. Pattern Anal. Mach. Intell. **13**(6), 583–598 (1991). https://doi.org/10.1109/34.87344

32. Volkmann, N., Hanein, D., Ouyang, G., Trybus, K.M., DeRosier, D.J., Lowey, S.: Evidence for cleft closure in actomyosin upon ADP release. Nat. Struct. Biol. **7**(12), 1147–1155 (2000). https://doi.org/10.1038/82008

33. Volkmann, N.: A novel three-dimensional variant of the watershed transform for segmentation of electron density maps. J. Struct. Biol. **138**(1–2), 123–129 (2002). https://doi.org/10.1016/S1047-8477(02)00009-6

34. Van der Walt, S., et al.: Scikit-image: image processing in python. PeerJ **2**, e453 (2014)

35. Witkin, A.P.: Scale-space filtering. In: Readings in Computer Vision, pp. 329–332. Elsevier (1987). https://doi.org/10.1016/B978-0-08-051581-6.50036-2. https://linkinghub.elsevier.com/retrieve/pii/B9780080515816500362

Author Index

Printed in the United States
By Bookmasters